W9-BFQ-286

PREFACE

In preparing this index to the History of The Church of Jesus Christ of Latter-day Saints, it is felt that a source of knowledge and heritage of unequaled importance is given to the members of the Church and to the world. The History consists of seven volumes which were compiled by the Church historians, with introduction and notes written by B. H. Roberts. It offers to the student of religious history, and particularly to the Church member, an exciting reference into the foundations of the Church of Jesus Christ in the last days.

Each of these volumes contains a small index. However, in the great and voluminous work of compiling the main body of the manuscript, the index placed in each volume becomes merely a touchstone to some important people and events in Church history. Each index is chronological in nature, which adds to the difficulty in use, making the researcher view all of each index in order to discover any particular point of interest or research. Further, it has been necessary to go to each of the seven volumes individually if the researcher was to discover information concerning the entire Joseph Smith period of the Church.

Because of the importance of the Documentary History and the valuable materials found therein, including not only doctrinal items discoursed by Joseph Smith and other leading members of the Church, but also the details of the persecutions which befell the people of early Church history and the miracles and stories which have been unparalleled since the time of Christ, the author decided some years ago to do a complete and comprehensive index of the Joseph Smith period of Church history. Therefore, the index which follows was developed and offers to the individual some unique and valuable materials for the study of Church history.

The following is a simple explanation of the index and its use: first, the index is totally alphabetical. The index includes the introductions, main body, and all footnotes within each volume, and each item includes all references within all seven volumes. No attempt has been made to reference every time a name or occurrence takes place, but all important events are indexed.

Since all but two of the sections of the Doctrine and Covenants are found in the Documentary History of the Church, it should be noted that the body of the Doctrine and Covenants is not here indexed. For references therein, refer to the complete index in the Doctrine and Covenants itself. Sections and revelations in the Doctrine and Covenants are, however, included in this index.

Second, the index is complete as to proper names. It offers a genealogy of activities in Church history and, although some names are listed as a last name only, or are indexed as merely "mentioned" in the pages of the manuscript, they were indexed to give a complete and full account of all persons who played a part in the pages of history.

Third, there are cross-references within titles; and, in some important events, the title may be listed several places and under several different titles. However, the user is directed to go to the other obvious cross-references or individual listings in order to fully discover the materials available.

Fourth, there are several unique sources available in the index. As an example, the title "STORIES." Under this heading the attempt was made to compile in one place the most important and most interesting sagas of Church history. Other such titles exist, and the user need only use his imagination to be directed to them.

Fifth, in different titles, the author has annotated suggested cross-references. No attempt has been made to be exhaustive, and the user should again proceed with his imagination and common sense to fully research any given topic.

It is hoped that the compilation and publication of this index will be of value to the student of Church history and allow more people to acquaint themselves with episodes and circumstances of a heritage second to none.

The author gratefully acknowledges the valuable assistance which was rendered to him by his wife, who aided in the proofreading of the manuscript and who gave encouragement to proceed in the work; and his secretary, Joan Moon, whose tireless efforts in typing and correcting the manuscript are appreciated.

E. Keith Howick

PREFACE TO THE STUDY EDITION
OF HISTORY OF THE CHURCH

One of the basic reference works of The Church of Jesus Christ of Latter-day Saints is the seven-volume set known as *History of the Church* (and sometimes referred to as *Documentary History of the Church*), by Joseph Smith.

In the earliest days of the Church in this dispensation, the Prophet and the Saints were admonished to keep a history "of all things that transpire in Zion, . . . And also their manner of life, their faith, and works. . . ." (D&C 85:1-2.) Setting the example for his followers, the Prophet faithfully kept a journal, or manuscript history, of the heavenly instructions and revelations he received from the Lord, the day-to-day activities of the Church, and important letters, statements, and interpretations of doctrine as given in meetings, funerals, and other public and private occasions.

After the Prophet's martyrdom, the Saints continued to keep records as they prepared for the exodus to the Rocky Mountains as well as after their arrival in the valley of the Great Salt Lake, where they established their new Zion. At the direction of President Brigham Young, the Prophet's writings and the records of other Church leaders and historians were gathered together, resulting in this seven-volume set. The index was prepared in recent years by E. Keith Howick and included in a matching binding, making eight volumes in all.

With publication of this new paperbound study edition, *History of the Church* is now available more economically for student, teacher, and scholar alike.

The Publishers

HISTORY

of

THE CHURCH OF JESUS CHRIST

of

LATTER-DAY SAINTS

INDEX

Compiled and edited by
E. Keith Howick

Published by
Deseret Book Company,
Salt Lake City, Utah
1978

© 1978 by Deseret Book Company
All rights reserved
Printed in the United States of America
ISBN 0-87747-697-7

INDEX TO THE HISTORY OF THE CHURCH OF JESUS CHRIST OF LATTER-DAY SAINTS

—A—

Aaron, John the Baptist descendant of, V5:257.

Aaronic Priesthood, see Priesthood, Aaronic.

Abbott, Brother and Sister mentioned, V3:172.

Abbott, Hiram, killed at Haun's Mills by mob, V3:186; 326, ftnt only.

Abbott, Lewis, sustained member of Salt Lake High Council, V7:629.

Abbott, Stephen, Joseph, on relief expedition for, V5:486
    mission to Wisconsin, V5:413.

Abel, Atonement, offering of accepted because of faith in, V2:15
    Paul appeared to, V4:208-9
    sacrifice of, accepted and explained, V2:16
    sacrifice of, accepted by faith, V4:208.

Abernethy, William D., anti-Mormon committee chairman, V6:8
    anti-Mormon, at meeting of, V5:537
    martyrdom mob, member of, V7:144.

Abimelech, false claim of ancient mummies as, V2:348.

Able, Elijah, Joseph leaves to rescue, V4:365.

abolition, Church stand on, V3:29
    Joseph, views on, V2:436
    lies concerning refuted, V2:453, 457-8.

abominations, saints commanded to put out of mind, V7:350.

Abraham, gospel preached to, V2:17.

Abraham, Book of, alphabet to, V2:238
    astronomy in, V2:286
    described, V2:349, 350, ftnt only
    facsimile, published, V5:11
    facsimiles, shown, V4:543
    mummies, found with, V2:236
    published, V4:520, et seq
    records, first cut of prepared, V4:519.
    See also Egyptian.

accountability, children who die before age of, saved, V2:381.

Acker, William, counselor to bishop in New York branch, V4:344.

Acre, Nelson, excommunicated for abstinence from meetings, V1:469.

Acts, Book of, Christ is prophet in, V3:22-3, V1:13
    Moroni quotes, V1:13.

Adam, Adam-ondi-Ahman place where dwelt, V3:35 and ftnt
    Ancient of Days, V3:386 and ftnt, V4:207
    Christ revealed to, V4:207
    devil, detects as angel of light, V1:40, ftnt only
    dispensations, holds presidency of all, V4:209
    father of all, V3:387
    fruit, partook of knowingly, V7:344
    fullness of times, holds keys of, V4:207
    God, received commands and revelations from, V4:208
    gospel, keys of, must be given thru, V3:386
    gospel, revealed to, IntroV1:XXIV
    human family, head of, V3:387
    Joseph sees, V3:388
    Kingdom of God, had, V5:256
    man, first, V4:207
    Michel the Archangel, is, V3:386
    Olney, Oliver, claims to have been visited by, V5:269
    priesthood, commenced with, V4:207
    priesthood, had, and First Presidency key, V3:385
    prophecy, first by, V4:207.
    See also dispensation.

"Adam-ondi-Ahman," song sung at temple dedication, V2:416 and ftnt;
    V3:35, ftnt only.

Adam-ondi-Ahman, Adam blesses posterity at, V3:388
    Adam, place where shall come, V3:35 and ftnt
    Canadian brethren settlement at, V3:48
    description of, V3:39 and ftnt
    location of, V3:39 and ftnt
    saints, arms of, taken, V3:199
    saints ordered to leave, V3:207
    site of, V3:35 and ftnt
    song of and historical note, V2:364 and ftnt
    stake organization, V3:38
    trial of prisoners at, V3:205-7
    Wilson, General, to arrest members at, V3:204-5.
    See also Missouri persecutions, mob, saints.

Adams, Mr., mentioned, V6:553, 559.

Adams, Arza, (also spelled Azra), martyrdom, receives note of, for
    Nauvoo, V6:622

ADAMS, ARZA (continued)

    mission, assigned to go on, V4:429

    Missouri, covenanted to assist saints in removing from, V3:252

    Nauvoo, policeman in, V6:150.

Adams, C., letter to Joseph concerning cause of saints before Illinois legislature, V4:53.

Adams, Charles A., mission appointment and field of labor, V6:335.

Adams, Chole, mother of James, V4:20, ftnt only.

Adams, George J., adultery, accused of, V5:271

    disfellowshipped, to be, V7:395

    high priest, ordained, V4:333

    Jerusalem, sails for, with Orson Hyde, V4:298

    mission, call in Illinois to disabuse public mind over Joseph's arrest, V5:485

    mission, fails to perform, of carrying message of martyrdom to Apostles, V7:158

    mission to Russia, V5:417

    prayer to stop mad career of, V7:425

    witness for Joseph at Carthage martyrdom, V6:576.

    See also literature.

Adams, Henry, gives money for lands in Zion, V2:174.

Adams, James, arrest, warns Prophet of impending, V5:433

    death and obituary of, V5:527

    demise, Joseph gives discourse on life and death at, V6:50-2

    endowments, present at introduction of, at Nauvoo, V5:1-2

    endowments, receives, V5:409

    genealogy of, V4:20, ftnt only

    just man made perfect, now is, V6:51

    letter to Joseph advising to appear before court, V5:206

    mentioned, V5:380

    Prophet, friend of, V4:20.

Adams, John, appointed elder, V4:13.

Adams, John Quincy, House of Representatives, chairman, V4:41, 44

    slavery, petition to eliminate, V5:283 and ftnt.

Adams, Lucien B., mentioned, V7:545.

Adams, Parmenio, father of James, V4:20, ftnt only.

Adams, Samuel, mentioned, V7:504.

Adams, Zebulon, gives money for lands in Zion, V2:174.

adulterer, curse upon, V4:587.

adultery, celestial kingdom, cannot receive, if commit, V6:81

ADULTERY (continued)

Joseph condemns, V4:587-8.

adversary, aware of Joseph's call, V1:6.

affidavit, Bennett, John C., city council concerning, V5:67-8

Bennett, John C., William Law anent, V5:75-7

Bennett, John C., Hyrum Smith anent, V5:71-5

Black, Adam, states saints are mob, V3:64-5

Boggs, Lilburn W., on attempted assassination, V5:67

Chase, Amos, on mob to retake arrested John Elliott, V6:121

Dryden, William, states that law and order cannot be had in Caldwell County, V3:77

Foutz, Jacob, on Missouri persecutions, V4:68

Garner, William, of mob attempting to draft into service, V6:511

Gates, Gibson, Missouri persecutions, V4:71

Greene and Bernhisel, threatened invasion from Missouri, V6:516

Hawk, William, on Missouri persecutions, V4:58

Higbee, Elias, on character of John Bennett and Joseph, V5:77-8

Higbee, Chauncey, Margaret J. Nyman et al, against, V6:407

Hyde, Orson, against saints in Missouri, V3:167-8, ftnt only

immorality, John C. Bennett exonerating Prophet from accusation on teaching, V5:11, V5:38

immorality, Wilson Law et al exonerating Prophet from accusation of teaching, V5:38-9

Joseph, attorneys in Dixon, arrest case, V5:476

Joseph, Luman H. Calkins on conspiracy in Nauvoo against, V6:531-2

Joseph, conspiracy against life of, V6:523

Joseph, correcting public statements concerning second arrest in Illinois, V6:67-8

Joseph, M. G. Eaton on conspiracy against, V6:279-80 and ftnt

Joseph, John P. Greene on threats against life of, V6:522-3

Joseph, Joseph Jackson on threats to kill and mob movement, V6:524

Joseph, Aaron Johnson on accusations against, V6:350

Joseph, Alfred Randall on threats of life of while in Carthage jail, V6:586

Joseph, A. B. Williams on conspiracy against, V6:278

Joseph, J. C. Wright on conspiracy against while in Carthage jail, V6:587-8

kidnapping, Philander Avery on Missouri, V6:122

kidnapping, D. Chapman on, of D. Avery, V6:100

kidnapping, S. A. Chase on Brother Avery proceedings, V6:109

kidnapping, Andrew and James Hamilton on, of D. Avery, V6:123

kidnapping, requesting prevention of further, V6:103

Law, William, T. Gillett on treachery of, V6:500-1

AFFIDAVIT (continued)

Law, William, Jesse Price on murderous intentions of, V7:227

Marsh, Thomas B., against saints in Missouri, V3:166-7 and ftnt

martyrdom, W. M. Daniels on murderers, V7:162-3 and ftnt

Missouri, Daniel Avery, on treatment in, V6:145-8

Missouri, G. Belknap concerning threats of invasion from, V6:502

Missouri, Cyrus Canfield concerning threats of invasion from, V6:502

Missouri, on suffering of saints in, V4:49-53, 56-73 and ftnts

Missouri, threats of invasion from, V6:511, 516

Missouri persecutions, Caleb Baldwin on, V5:495-7

Missouri persecutions, Joseph to Governor Ford on, V5:493-5

Missouri persecutions, Abigail Leonard on husband's beatings, V1:480

Missouri persecutions, Alanson Ripley on, V5:495

mob, on attempts to draft into, V6:508-12

mob, John Cunningham on attempt to draft into service, V6:508

mob, Enos Curtis on house burning by, V7:488

mob, Gideon Gibbs on LaHarpe road, V6:530

mob, Carlos W. Lyon on arms to, V6:507

mob, Hiram B. Mount on attempt to draft into service, V6:508

mob, James Olive on movements on Carthage road, V6:529

mob, Willard Richards, that Nauvoo was in danger from, V6:119

mob, T. G. Wilson on movement of, V6:480-1

Morrison, Thomas, against Nauvoo City Council, V7:66

murder, Joseph Swymler on Durfee, V7:530

murder, J. H. Woodland on Durfee, V7:529

Nauvoo, Anson Call on treatment of committee by Levi Williams, V6:505-6

Nauvoo, David Evans on treatment of committee by Levi Williams, V6:505-6

Nauvoo, William E. Horner on treatment of committee by Levi Williams, V6:505-6

Nauvoo, H. T. Hugins on threat to bring dragoons against, V6:423

Nauvoo, George G. Johnstone, militia to move on, V6:530

Nauvoo, Stephen Markham that is to be attacked, V6:492

Nauvoo, Edward Robinson on threats against, V6:528

Nauvoo, O. P. Rockwell on Governor Ford in, V6:588

Nauvoo, William G. Stewart on conduct of Governor Ford and posse while in, V6:589-90

Nauvoo Expositor, J. R. Wakefield on destruction of, V7:130

Pratt, Orson, against Higbee, V6:177-8

Root, Henry, on mob in DeWitt, V3:149

saints, Orson Hyde on mob threats to drive out, V6:145

AFFIDAVIT (continued)

theft, Hyrum Smith denouncing, V4:460-1

Tippetts, A., of violence upon, V6:514

Wells, Daniel H., concerning character of J. C. Bennett and extolling innocence of Joseph, V5:80

Wells, Daniel H., concerning kidnapping by Missourians, V4:154. See also Latter-day Saints, Church of Jesus Christ of; letters; Missouri correspondence; persecutions; persecutions, Illinois; persecutions, Missouri.

age of accountability, see accountability, age of.

Agnew, Joseph, mobber in Illinois, V7:530

Nauvoo Temple, arson of, V7:618, ftnt only.

Agriculture Companies, organized by saints as community groups, V3:64.

Aikin, James, Joseph, on relief expedition for, V5:482.

Ainscough, Richard, on first sailing of saints from England, V4:134.

Aitkin, Robert, attacks Church in England, V4:318.

Albertson, John, patriarch, ordained second in England, V4:333

patriarchal blessing of, V4:334.

Albison, John, (also spelled Albiston), British Mission, mission in, V4:150

elder, ordained, V4:148

Aldrich, Andrew Hazen, apostate, helps form group, V5:215, ftnt only

Kirtland Temple, blessing for work on, V2:206

mentioned, V2:244

Missouri High Council, member, V2:164

seventies, named president of, V2:203

Zions Camp, member of, V2:183.

Aldrich, Jaman, blessing for work on Kirtland Temple, V2:205.

Aldrich, James, mentioned, V2:326.

Aldrich, Mark, anti-Mormon committee chairman, V6:8

Joseph, acquitted of murder of, V7:420

Joseph, indicted for murder of, V7:314

martyrdom mob, no business, member of, V7:143

Warsaw militia leader, V7:143.

Aldridge, Bro., Joseph rebukes for evil spirit, V2:274.

"Alesto," saints' emigrant ship, V4:310.

Alexander, H. M., Joseph on relief expedition for, V5:482.

Alexander, Horace, ordained elder, V3:155.

Alexander, Randolph, mission call given, V4:589

Nauvoo, delegate to political convention at, V6:390.

Alger, Samuel, mob, makes conciliation offer to, V7:441-2.

Ali, Mehemet, mentioned, V2:348.

Allen, Mr., threatened by court as testifies for saints, V3:211.

Allen, Abram, Missouri, covenanted to assist saints in removing from, V3:254.

Allen, Charles, Missouri mob tars and feathers, V1:391 and ftnt.

Allen, Colonel, saints desire arms returned through, V2:75.

Allen, Daniel, Church removal, utility committee member to aid, V7:474
mission and field of labor, V6:340
mission to disabuse public mind over arrest of Joseph, V5:485.

Allen, Daniel, Jr., Kirtland Camp, subscribed to constitution of, V3:92.

Allen, Ethan, mentioned, V6:92.

Allen, Felatiah, encouraged mob, V1:264.

Allen, George, given care of Church at Woferwood Common, V4:139.

Allen, Isaac Van, mentioned, V3:298.

Allen, Israel, Kirtland Camp, mentioned in, V3:104.

Allen, James, ordained elder, V4:298.

Allen, James, Mormon Battalion, appointed to raise, V7:612
Mormon Battalion, in contact with President Young on raising, V7:612
Mormon Battalion, leads, V7:614.

Allen, John, bishop, appointed counselor to, V4:233
elder, ordained, V4:148
mentioned, V4:215.

Allen, Jonathan, mission and field of labor, V5:348.

Allen, Joseph S., Church district, appointed to preside over new, V7:306
high priests quorum, counselor of, at Yelrome, V6:346
Lima, named to high council at, V5:428
Zions Camp member, V2:183.

Allen, O. M., mission and field of labor, V6:340.

Allen, Rufas, petitions Governor Boggs on mob violence in DeWitt, V3:83.

Allen, William, mentioned, V5:372
public, delegate to present truth to, V6:483.

Allensworth, William, kidnaps members of Church and takes to Missouri, V4:155.

Alley, Sarah, baptized, V5:385.

Allred, Isaac, Zions Camp member, V2:183.

Allred, James, constable, sworn as, V4:308

ALLRED, JAMES (continued)
   high council, sustained to, V4:341
   Joseph, bodyguard to, on return to Nauvoo, V7:135
   kidnapped by Missourians, V4:156-7
   kidnapping, statement on, V4:156-7
   Nauvoo, supervisor of streets in, V4:308, V5:270
   Nauvoo High Council, sustained to, after death of Joseph, V7:296
   Taylor, John, aids, on return to Nauvoo, V7:117-8.

Allred, James, Sr., Zions Camp, joins with party, V2:88, ftnt only
   Zions Camp member, V2:183.

Allred, Martin C., Missouri, arraigned for treason, murder, burglary,
      arson, robbery and larceny at Richmond, V3:209
   Missouri, covenanted to assist saints in removing from, V3:253
   Missouri, discharged as innocent at trials, V3:211
   Zions Camp member, V2:183.

Allred, Reddick N., appointed elder, V4:13.

Allred, Reddin A., elder, appointed, V4:12
   Joseph, on relief expedition for, V5:482
   MIA, aids in movement toward, V5:322.

Allred, William, elder, appointed, V4:13
   Missouri, arraigned for treason, murder, burglary, arson, robbery and
      larceny at Richmond, V3:209
   Missouri, covenanted to assist saints in removing from, V3:252
   Missouri, discharged as innocent from trials, V3:211
   mob, captures military supplies of, V3:74
   mob, prisoners tried, V3:76
   revelation on duties, V4:311.

Alvord, Charlotte, Zions Camp member, V2:185.

Alvord, T., Missouri outrages, affidavit on, V4:57.

"Amaranth," saints' emigrant ship, V4:594.

America, see United States of America.

Ames, Ira, Doctrine & Covenants, testifies to, V2:246
   Kirtland Camp, mentioned in, V3:144
   Kirtland Temple, blessing for work on, V2:206
   priest, acts as president of, V2:244
   Zions Camp, exonerates Joseph in, V2:149.

Ames, Justus, mentioned, V7:310.

Amherst, Loraine County, Ohio, conference held at, on January 25, 1832,
      V1:242
   Joseph sustained President of High Priesthood at, V1:267

AMHERST (continued)

Pratt, Parley P., from, V1:121.

amusements, have baneful influence in religious society, V7:282-3.

Ancient of Days, is Adam, V3:386.

See also Adam.

ancients, order of councils in, V2:25.

Anderson, Brother, mentioned, V5:406.

Anderson, Chief, visited and preached to by missionaries, V1:183, ftnt only.

Anderson, George C., anti-Mormons, fire at boat of, V7:95

martyrdom, witness for Joseph at Carthage, V6:576

Nauvoo, certificate on retention of people in, V6:553.

Anderson, J. R., mentioned, V5:395.

Anderson, John, mentioned, V2:523-4.

Anderson, Miles, mission and field of labor, V6:337

Nauvoo, delegate to political convention at, V6:390.

Anderson, S. H., mentioned, V4:245.

Andrews, Benjamin, petitions Maine to aid in redress for Missouri persecutions, V6:178.

Andrews, J. A. W., recorder for baptisms for dead, V5:522.

Andrus, Milo, mission and field of labor, V6:339

refellowshipment of, V4:12

seventies, named to first quorum of, V2:204.

angel, apostles, minister to, V2:383

appear, how, V3:392

bodily shape, light and glory tabernacled in, V6:51

brethren, speak with, V2:383

characters revealed by, V1:20

dress, have particular, V5:267

Melchizedek Priesthood, promised by, V1:60

minister to Joseph and brethren, V2:381

minister to some, V2:382

ministering of, generally how, V5:31

ministering spirit, difference of, from, explained, V4:425

plates, final return of, to, V1:2, ftnt only

sacrament, appears to instruct on, V1:106

wings, never has, V3:392

witnesses, appears to, V1:54-5.

See also parables.

Angel, Solomon, seventies, named to first quorum of, V2:204

Zions Camp member, V2:64, 183.

Angell, Truman O., (also spelled Angel), Joseph, pays money to, in hour
      of need, V2:327
   Kirtland Camp, subscribed to constitution of, V3:92
   Nauvoo Temple, appointed carpenter on, V7:326.

Angus, John O., mission and field of labor, V6:338.

Annis, Brother, mentioned, V4:46.

Annis, John C., mentioned, V5:272
   Nauvoo Legion, in, V4:295.

Anthon, Charles, certificate, gives, V1:20
   Harris, Martin, letter describing, V1:20, ftnt only
   translation, taken to, V1:20.

anti-Mormons, agitation by, V6:516, V7:66
   character of, V7:60
   Circuit Court, proposed action against in mockery of, V7:493-4
   martyrdom, activities of, after, V7:42
   mob, drafts members to, V6:508-14
   mobocracy by, V7:68.
   See also mob, persecutions.

Apocrypha, revelation of, (D&C § 91), V1:331.

apoplexy, Rigdon, Sidney, experiences, V3:445.

apostasy, Bennett, John C., impressions of John Taylor after, V7:57
   Bennett, John C., position of reviewed, IntroV5:XVII, et seq
   Booth, Ezra, at Kirtland, V1:215-6 and ftnt
   Boynton, John F., of, V2:528
   Christianity,. testimony of prophecy as to, from early, IntroV1:XCI
   Coe, Joseph, of, V2:528
   Cowdery, Oliver, begins, V1:104-5
   Cowles, A. W., excommunicated for, V6:398
   excommunication, J. Blakesley for, V6:398
   Higbee, Francis M., excommunicated for, V6:398
   Hurlburt, Dr. P., actions of, in, V1:475
   Hyde, Orson, of, V3:167-8 and ftnt
   Ivins, Charles, excommunicated for, V6:398
   Johnson, Edward, in, V1:260
   Johnson, Eli, in, V1:260
   Johnson, John Jr., in, V1:260
   Johnson, Luke S., of, V2:528
   Marsh, Thomas B., of, V3:166-7 and ftnt
   mysteries, high road to, explained as key of, V3:385
   Parrish, Warren, of, V2:528

APOSTASY (continued)

Russell, Isaac, in England, V3:342

Ryder, Simonds, of, because name misspelled, V1:260 and ftnt

universal, announcement of, IntroV1:XL.

apostates, adulterous actions of, V6:407

Booth, Ezra, V1:215-6 and ftnt

burned, end of to be, V2:23

church, plans for organization of new, V6:346-7

darkness, after becoming, fall into great, V2:23

excommunication in Nauvoo of, V6:341

falsehoods, spread, V2:22

first, V1:216 and ftnt

Hiram, Ohio, at, V1:260

Joseph, actions and threats of, upon arrival in Carthage, V6:560

Joseph, reported swore to kill, V6:566

Kirtland Temple, take control of, V7:484

martyrdom, at Nauvoo preceding the, V7:56

Nauvoo, conspirators in, IntroV6:XXXVI

Nauvoo, issue newspaper prospectus in, V6:363

persecutions, saints receive severe, from, V2:23

plunder, reported intent to, V6:564

Taylor, John, impressions of, V7:58

unrepented, will have many because must exclude if remain, V2:22.

See also Foster, Robert D.; Higbee, Chauncey; Higbee, Francis; Christ, Church of.

Apostles, adversary will seek lives of, V2:196

America, resolved to leave England for, V4:326

authorities, accountable only to general council of, not to High Council, V2:285

baptism for dead, epistle to saints on, V4:472-5

baptism for dead, expounded to by epistle, V4:231

Bennett, John C., leaves Nauvoo to confound, V5:160

Benson, Ezra T., chosen member of, V7:628

blessings, on awaiting spiritual, V7:281

bogus money, charged with making, V7:491

Book of Mormon, on, V6:24

California, instructed to send delegation to, V6:222-4

calling of, expounded, V2:200

calling, when first made known, V2:186, ftnt only

calm sea, V4:360

charge, general, given to, V2:194-8

charge, to see Christ and bear testimony, V2:193

APOSTLES (continued)

chosen and comprised of, V2:187

chosen, meeting at which, V2:181, et seq

Church, epistle to, on exhortations of organization of, V7:250

Church, investigate within the boundaries of conference, V2:223

Church, letter to, from retirement, V7:412, et seq

Church, sustained as authorities of, at October 1844 conference, V7:294

Church, sustained as leaders of, V7:392

churches, instructions to, V7:347

Cleveland, meeting at, V4:19-20

common, movement west on plan of all things in, V7:442

conterence at Black River, V2:225

conference at Freedom, V2:224

conference, importance of, on gathering and donations, September 9, 1843, V6:11

conference at Maine, Farmington, V2:253

conference at Maine, Saco, V2:252

conference at Massachusetts, V2:241

conference to receive mission charge, V2:218

conference, request revelation, V2:209

conference at Vermont, V2:238

conference at Westfield, V2:222

conferences, appointed in United States, V6:334-5

contribute, call on members to, V4:517

council of, at Boston, V7:159

counsel, fall by rejecting, V6:30

covetousness and lack of humility, revelation condemning for, V2:300

Cowdery, Oliver, calling to be, (D&C § 18:9), V1:62

Cowdery, Oliver, exhorted to be rebaptized, V7:619

credential, form of, V5:416

debt, on, V7:526

devil, attacks and causes disunity, V2:352

devil, will seek lives of, V2:196

doctrine, on consciousness of sound, V7:281

doctrines, epistle to saints on various, V7:280, et seq

Doctrine and Covenants, testimony as to, V2:245

duty, failure of, results, V2:195

elders, on duty of, V3:395-6

endowment, too dark to understand at present, V2:309

endowment, on getting, V6:13

endowment, more of, given by, V6:98

APOSTLES (continued)

endowment, to receive, V2:287

England, council of April 2, 1841, V4:324

England, council on hymn book and Star, V4:118

England, council in, ordination of Willard Richards, V4:114

England, departure from, V4:352

England, granted permission to publish certain books in, V4:161-2

England, letter to Wilford Woodruff on, V7:407

England, meeting of April 7, 1841, V4:332-5

England, trials of en route for, V4:15

epistle to brethren of, October 12, 1841, V4:433-8

epistle to British Mission, V4:344-8

epistle to Church, V3:393-8

epistle to elders and churches abroad, V6:63-4

epistle of Joseph to, on sundry instructions, V4:226, et seq

epistle to saints in America, V4:590, et seq

epistle to saints in Europe of November 15, 1841, V4:448-53

epistle to saints of March 1842, V4:558, et seq

faith, cannot heal those without, V2:309

false doctrines, development of after death of early, IntroV1:LII

false doctrines, warning against, V7:199

Far West, arrive at, V3:336

Far West, minutes of meeting, V3:47

Far West, minutes of meeting of April 26, 1839, V3:336

Far West, proceedings at, V3:337

fellowship withdrawn from two, while on first mission, V2:240

first, record of faithfulness of, V5:412

First Presidency, subject to no other but, V2:373-4

First Presidency, tried by, V2:283

forgive one another, meeting to, V2:219

gathering, on, V6:11, V7:280

gathering, epistle to Saints abroad on, V4:409-10

God, see face of, V2:195

God, on serving, V6:14

gospel, to spread, V6:27

High Council, sanctioned by, V2:240

history and debt, epistle to Church on collection of, V7:526

Holy Ghost, as witness to prophet, V6:13

home, called, V6:519

hymns, engage in selecting, V4:3

Illinois, to labor in, V5:160

Joseph, council at home of, V5:268

APOSTLES (continued)

Joseph, council at office of, V5:369

Joseph, instruction by, V2:287

Joseph, instructions by on December 19, 1841, V4:478-9

Joseph, letter of, calling for assistance for, V5:279

Joseph, letter on affairs of June 19, 1844, V7:136

Joseph, letter of, to Ramus on assistance for, V5:293

Joseph, meeting organized in Nauvoo for successor of, V7:231

Joseph, only two of original had not fought, V5:412

Joseph, proclamation of, to raise funds for, V5:248

Joseph, whereabouts at death of, V7:132

key of first mission call, V3:384

Kimball, Hiram, gift to, V4:484

Lyman, Amasa M., ordained to, V5:120

martyrdom, arrival in Nauvoo, V7:228

martyrdom, reactions upon first news of, V7:175

material help, letter to Morley settlement requesting for, V6:176

members, on selfish, V6:21

ministry, place first, V2:195

minutes, instructed to keep, prophecy of failing if do not, V2:199

minutes of, on replacement of fallen members, V3:47

mission to England expounded upon, IntroV4:XXX

mission, first of, commenced May 4, 1835, V2:222

mission, Joseph gives instructions on, V5:366

mission, Joseph gives instructions to proceed on, V3:383-5, et seq

mission, Joseph recounts of, to England, V4:390

mission, return to Kirtland from first, V2:283

mission, sent on first, V2:209

missionaries, families of, to be provided for by Church while, V4:5

missionaries, publish list of and field of labor, V6:335, et seq

missions, assign, V4:429-30

missions and Church property, council meeting on, V4:412-3

mob, appeal to Governor Ford concerning, V7:489

money, on giving, V6:14

municipal positions, members decline accepting any, V7:350

mysteries, on, V6:18

names given to, V7:435

Nauvoo, called home in face of persecution in, V6:486

Nauvoo, commence return to, V7:209

Nauvoo, council in, V5:194

Nauvoo, on economies of, V7:281

Nauvoo, epistle requesting brethren to return to, V7:198

APOSTLES (continued)

Nauvoo, instructs members at Philadelphia to move to, V5:413

Nauvoo, to leave as early as possible, V7:578

Nauvoo, return to, V4:390, V6:60

Nauvoo Temple, on, V7:280

Nauvoo Temple, on building, V6:13

Nauvoo Temple, epistle to saints on, V4:517

Nauvoo Temple, meeting emphasizing need for completing, V6:230

New York, arrival at, V4:360-1

New York, minutes of meeting in, 1843, V5:550

obedience, on, V6:12

ordained, V2:187, ftnt only

ordinance on thieves, V4:463, et seq and ftnts

ordination, Oliver Cowdery assists in, V2:187, et seq

ordination full when, V2:196

organization, answers questions on, V5:551

organization, placed in proper place in, V4:403

organization, struggle to find place in, V2:372

Page, John E., commanded to go to Washington to labor, V6:81

people, duty to warn, V2:197

Philadelphia, meeting in August 1843, V5:527

phrenological charts, some receive, V6:37

Pratt, Parley P., chosen president of conference over Brigham Young, explanation, V4:146 and ftnt

prejudice against for failure to mingle, V7:213

proceedings of, approved by conference, V3:345

prophecy, fulfillment of, V3:339

prophecy, leave for Far West to fulfill, V3:335

prophet, on heeding, V6:23

Prophet meeting with in Masonic lodge, V4:589

Prophet, remarks to, V2:308-9

Prophet, to share in labors of, V4:400, 403-4

Prophets, Seers and Revelators, sustained as, V2:417

publications, action on, V6:66

reaping, on, V6:20

reorganization, on, V7:283

revelation, ask for instruction and comfort, V2:209

revelation, giving instructions to and replacing fallen, (D&C § 118), V3:46

Rigdon, Sidney, demand license of, V7:267

righteousness, resolutions to proceed in all, V7:249

saints, farewell to, V4:1, et seq

APOSTLES (continued)

saints, letter to, on continuing on, V7:189
Savior, all who are pure will see, V2:310
seniority, organized into, V2:219 and ftnt
seventies, forbidden to ordain, V4:162
seventies, report proceedings of, V3:363
signature used, V7:213
Smith, William, against, V7:420
Smith, William, consider case of, V2:347
Smith, William, rejected at general conference, V7:458-9
Snyder, John, call on mission or damned, V4:503
spirit of darkness in, V2:488 and ftnt
spirits, on discerning, V6:29
succession on, V3:261 and ftnt
support, ministry and Church to, V2:221
sustained at Far West, V2:524
sustained as prophets at temple dedication, V2:417
sustained, some rejected at Kirtland, V2:509
teachings, leave to confound, V5:160
temple and proposed tabernacle, letter to saints on, V7:427
temple and tithing, epistle to Church on, V7:356, et seq
testimony, need to receive from heaven, V2:195
thieves, warning against, V4:463-6
three witnesses to choose, (D&C § 48:37), V2:186 and ftnt
twelve, arrangements made to choose, V2:180
vice, against in all forms, V7:282
vice, instructions on, V7:280
visions and experiences as of old, V1:85
western country, assign brethren to go investigate, V6:223
westward movement, captain of first company in, V7:481
westward movement, epistle to Church on, V7:478
whereabouts of, January 1, 1841, V4:256
whereabouts of, January 1842, V4:490
Whitmer, David, called to be, (D&C § 18:9), V1:62
Wight, Lyman, letter to, pleading for union, V7:400
Wight, Lyman, sustained to be, V4:341
Woodruff, Wilford, extracts from journal of, V7:149
Winchester, Benjamin, case of before, V4:443
writs, not to be served on, V7:492
Young, Brigham, chosen president of, and how, V4:115 and ftnt
Young, Brigham, council at home of, V5:265
See also British Mission; conference; devil; disfellowship; epistle;

APOSTLES (continued)

excommunication; gathering; Latter-day Saints, Church of Jesus Christ of; letters; Nauvoo; prophecy; temples; westward movement.

apostleship, oath and covenant of, V2:198 and ftnt
Smith, Joseph, restored to, V7:287, ftnt only.

Apostolic Interregnum, explanation of, V7:246
period covered from, V7:245.

"Appeal," of saints to the world concerning their freedom and rights, V2:126 and ftnt.

Appelby, William I., mentioned, V7:266, 588, 620, 623.

Arago, M., mentioned, V5:308.

"Ariel," saints' emigrant ship, V4:569.

Arkansas, governor of, cannot protect Church, suggests westward settlement, V7:419 and ftnt.

Arlick, John, given care of Church at Norton, V4:135.

arms, public, for Legion, V6:31.

Armstrong, S., writes letter for O. P. Rockwell, V5:198.

Armstrong, Sybella, mentioned, V5:409.

Arne, Dusten, delegate to political convention in Nauvoo, V6:389.

Arnold, Josiah, Joseph saves, V7:57
Nauvoo, policeman in, V6:149.

arsenal, ground dedicated, V7:271
Nauvoo, ordered built at, V5:422, 430.

Arthur, Mr., goods of attacked by mob, V2:61 and ftnt.

Arthur, M., letter to legislature noting depredations against saints, V3:213.

Arthur, Michael, committee member to talk to saints on removal, V2:452.

Arthurs, Colonel, mentioned, V2:122.

Articles of Faith, composed in the Wentworth letter, V4:535, et seq and ftnt.

Ashby, Mr., mentioned, V3:186.

Ashby, Daniel, Haun's Mills, mob member at. and state legislator, V3:186
Haun's Mills massacre, admits being in, V3:212
mob, member of legislature heads, V3:158
speech of, against saints, V3:239.

Ashby, Nathaniel, mission appointment and field of labor, V6:335.

Ashkenazi, Aaron Selig, mentioned, V4:176.

Ashley, Mr., officer, Missouri mobber, V3:158, 412; V4:84.

Ashley, Benjamin, member of mob at Haun's Mills massacre, V3:325.

Ashworth, Nancy, on first sailing of saints from England, V4:134.

assassination, Carthage, article on, V7:422
 Joseph and Hyrum, press opinions on, V7:177.

assault and battery, T. S. Edwards expelled from Church for, V4:454.

assembly, Doctrine and Covenants, general of Church to accept, V2:243,
  et seq
 solemn, notice of at Kirtland, V2:475
 solemn, preparations for, V2:364.

assembly, general, Carter's settlement at, V3:5
 case, action of on John Whitmer and W. W. Phelps, V3:5
 Church, of, at Far West, V3:3-8
 Far West Presidency, action on, V3:5-6
 Far West Presidency, at Nahum Curtis' dwelling house, action on,
  V3:6
 Far West Presidency, at Durfee's settlement, action on, V3:6
 Far West Presidency, at Haun's Mills, action on, V3:6.

assembly, solemn, held, V2:475, et seq
 preparations for, V2:364
 priesthood quorums placed in order for, V2:386, et seq.

astronomy, in Book of Abraham, V2:286.

Atchison, David R., Boggs, Governor, communication to, V3:65
 military movements, report of to Governor, V3:80-1
 militia, notifies Governor of calling out, V3:76
 Missouri, drafts resolution of public meeting in, V2:449
 mob militia, withdraws from, V3:187
 Mormons, comments on change of heart against, V3:176 and ftnt
 Mormons, requests Governor Boggs to come to seat of war with,
  V3:176
 Prophet, in conference with on Daviess County troubles, V3:69
 saints, attorney for in Missouri, V1:425
 saints, reports favorable of, V3:85
 Zion, appointed to assist saints in removal from, V2:455
 Zions Camp, meets near Liberty, V2:112.
 See also letters; persecutions, Missouri.

Atherton, John R., anti-Mormon committee chairman, V6:8.

Athey, J. W., no business, member of martyrdom mob, V7:144.

Atkins, Thomas, delegate to political convention in Nauvoo, V6:390.

atonement, Abel's offering accepted because of faith in, V2:15
 Cain's offering rejected because of lack of faith in, V2:15
 doctrine of, V1:72 and ftnt, et seq
 sacrifice, fulfillment by, V2:16-7.

Ausdall, William Van, covenanted to assist saints in removing from Missouri, V3:253.

Austin, Mr., loafer, member of martyrdom mob, V7:144.

Austin, Dr., mentioned in mob action in Missouri, V3:156.

Austin, Erastus, constable, member of martyrdom mob, V7:144.

Austin, James, mobber who prevents group from traveling to Missouri, V3:324.

Austin, William W., Sr., heads mob, V4:63.

Australia, report of missionary work in, V4:343.

authorities, Carter, Jared, convicted for not heeding, V2:280.
 See also counsel, sustain.

Avard, Sampson, buffetings of Satan, turned over to and condemned as openly sinning against Jesus, V3:232
 character witness, as a, V3:209-10
 Church, excommunicated from, V3:181, 284
 Church, tells mob that Danites are of, V3:192-3
 Danites, instructions to, V3:180
 license taken from, V2:519
 Missouri trials, first witness called against heads of Church in, V3:209
 Satan possesses, raised secret band Danites, V3:178-82
 treachery of, V3:192-3
 witness before grand jury, V3:310.
 See also Danites.

Averett, Mr., delegate to present truth to public, V6:483.

Averett, Elijah, Joseph, on relief expedition for, V5:482
 teachers quorum, counselor in, at Nauvoo, V5:169.

Averett, Elisha (also spelled Everett), doorkeeper, V7:554
 Legion, martial band member, V7:135
 Missouri, covenanted to assist saints in removing from, V3:253
 Nauvoo Temple, to administer in, V7:555
 teachers quorum, president of, in Nauvoo, V4:312, 354; V5:169; V7:298.

Avery, Allen, priesthood, restored to, by high council, V2:286
 Zions Camp member, V2:183.

Avery, Daniel, affidavit of D. Chapman on kidnapping of, V6:100

AVERY, DANIEL (continued)

    affidavit of Sessions Chase on proceedings in kidnapping of, V6:109

    elders, ordained president of, at Montrose, V4:54

    elders quorum, to organize, V4:42

    exploring, volunteers for, V6:224

    kidnapped by Missourians and carried off, V6:99

    kidnapped, released from imprisonment, V6:142

    mission to disabuse public mind over arrest of Joseph, V5:485

    Missouri, affidavit on treatment in, V6:145

    Missouri, escape from, V6:143

    Missouri, held as prisoner in, V6:108

    Missouri persecutions, affidavit concerning, V4:60-1

    Nauvoo Temple, appointed carpenter on, V7:326.

Avery, Philander, affidavit of D. Chapman on kidnapping of, V6:100

    kidnappers, escapes from, V6:113

    Missouri, covenanted to assist saints in removing from, V3:254

    Missouri kidnappings, affidavit on, V6:122.

Avigdor, Mordecai, mentioned, V4:175.

Avory, Daniel, Joseph, on relief expedition for, V5:482.

Aylmer, Lord, governor-general of Canada, V3:155, ftnt only.

—B—

Babbitt, Almon W., biographical note on, V2:76, ftnt only

    Church removal, utility committee member to aid,V7:474

    disfellowshipped from Church, V4:424

    errors, correct at Springfield branch, V3:346

    fellowship, restored to, V5:350

    high council, tried before for breaking Word of Wisdom and stating that Book of Mormon not essential to salvation, reproved, V2:252

    Indiana, preaches in, V4:17

    Joseph, charges against for traducing character of, V2:346

    Joseph, prefers charges against and withdraws them, V4:187

    Kirtland, permitted to build up, V4:476

    libelous reports, appointed to gather, V3:346

    mission to France, V6:356

    Missouri, arrival with Canadian company, V3:48

    Nauvoo, preaches at, V6:34

    Nauvoo Charter, reports on repeal of, V7:363

    orders, refuses to obey, V6:514-5

    Prophet, engaged as counsel against, V6:600

    Prophet, visits in prison, V6:612-3

BABBITT, ALMON W. (continued)

    Ramus, presiding elder at, V5:302-3

    seventies, named to first quorum of, V2:204

    stake, appointed head of, at Kirtland, V4:204

    stake, president of, at Kirtland, V4:361

    traitorous acts of, V4:165-7

    trial, confesses and forgiven, V2:354

    Zions Camp member, V2:183

    Zions Camp, various responsibilities in, V2:76, 77, 87, ftnt only, 88 ftnt only.

Babbitt, Brother, charges against and dismissed, V1:470.

Babbitt, Erastus, Doctrine and Covenants, testifies to truthfulness of, V2:246

    high council, testifies in, V2:33

    Hodges, Brother, testifies at trial of, V2:33

    Kirtland Temple, blessing for work on, V2:206

    teachers president, acts as, V2:244.

Babbitt, Ira, father of Almon W., V2:76, ftnt only.

Babbitt, Loren, Green, H., testifies at trial of, V2:274

    Kirtland Temple, blessing for work on, V2:206

    mission and field of labor, V6:339.

Babbitt, Nancy, mother of Almon W., V2:76, ftnt only.

Babcock, Mr., Joseph, on relief expedition for, V5:486.

Babcock, Amos, president of elders at Kirtland, V4:362.

Backenstos, Jacob B., Deming, Miner R., reports death of, V7:439

    martyrdom, letter on members of mob at, V7:142-5

    mob, cannot control, V7:445

    mob, letter on trial by, V7:483

    mobs, threats against, V7:390

    murder, acquitted for, V7:541

    Nauvoo Charter, defends, V7:349

    sheriff of Hancock County, member of state legislature, against repeal of Nauvoo Charter, V7:368

    Twelve, note to on Durfee murder, V7:525

    Warsaw, mobbed and driven from. V7:446.

Backenstos, William, marriage to Clara M. Wesson, V6:43

    mentioned, V6:359-60.

Backman, Mr., attorney for Joseph, V5:473; V6:173-4.

Backman, George, arrested for Durfee murder, V7:527

    martyrdom mob, member of, V7:145.

Backman, Hiram, Zions Camp member, V2:183.

Bacon, Samuel P., mission and field of labor, V6:336.

Badger, John, appointed to high council at Far West, V3:225
  Missouri, covenanted to assist saints in removing from, V3:253
  Missouri persecutions, expresses faith in work after, V3:225.

Badham, Richard, assaulted by mob, V6:110, 409-10.

Badham, Samuel, Church, given care of at Dunsclose, V4:139
  priest, ordained, V4:138.

Badlam, Alexander, Joseph, pays money in hour of need, V2:327
  Missouri, covenanted to assist saints in removal from, V3:253
  seventies, named to first quorum of, V2:204
  Zions Camp member, V2:183.

Badlock, A., delegate to political convention in Nauvoo, V6:389.

Bagby, Walter, Carthage Greys, member of, V7:143
  meeting, at anti-Mormon, V5:537; V6:41
  Nauvoo, unjust tax collector in, V6:4
  Prophet, injustice to the, V6:4.

Bagley, Eli, covenanted to assist saints in removing from Missouri, V3:252.

Bailey, Alice, to receive Church aid in emigrating from England, V5:412.

Bailey, Brother, mentioned, V3:27.

Bailey, Mary, mentioned, V7:219.

Bailey, Moses, blessing for work on Kirtland Temple, V2:206.

Bailey, Thomas, blessing given to, V2:207.

Bain, John, kidnaps members and takes to Missouri, V4:155.

Bainbridge, South Chenango County, New York, Joseph arraigned in court at, V1:89
  Joseph married at, V1:17.

Bair, John, Joseph, on relief expedition for, V5:482.

Baker, Benjamin, subscribed to constitution of Kirtland Camp, V3:92.

Baker, Elizabeth, marriage to Thomas Carrico, V2:369.

Baker, George, mob, requests members to join, V6:511
  mobber, makes threats, V6:481.

Baker, Henry, blessing for work on Kirtland Temple, V2:206.

Baker, Jesse, elders quorum, sustained counselor in, V7:297
  Kirtland Camp, subscribed to constitution of, V3:92
  troops, commands anti-Mormon, V7:46-7.

Baker, Samuel, Zions Camp member, V2:183.

Baker, William, blessing of, V2:208.

Baldwin, Amos, subscribed to constitution of Kirtland Camp, V3:92.

Baldwin, Blake, blessing for work on Kirtland Temple, V2:206.

Baldwin, Caleb, extradition demanded by Governor Boggs, V4:198
    grand jury, brings in bill against for treason, murder, etc., V3:315
    Missouri, arraigned for treason, murder, burglary, arson, robbery,
        and larceny at Richmond, V3:209
    trial for murder and treason at Liberty, V3:212.

Baldwin, Charles N., Kirtland Camp, subscribed to constitution of, V3:93
    Missouri, covenanted to assist saints in removing from, V3:252.

Baldwin, Edwin, Carthage Greys, member of, V7:142.

Baldwin, James, Church, given care of at Wind Point, V4:139
    ordained priest, V4:138.

Baldwin, Joseph B., blessing of, V2:208.

Baldwin, Nathan B., Kirtland Camp, mentioned in, V3:105
    Kirtland Camp, subscribed to constitution of, V3:92
    Missouri, covenanted to assist saints in removing from, V3:254
    murmuring, complains of Abram Bond for, V3:107
    seventies, named to first quorum of, V2:203
    Zions Camp member, V2:183.

Baldwin, Wheeler, mentioned, V4:94.

Baldwin, William, martyrdom, guard on jail at, V7:142.

Bale, David, witnesses celestial phenomenon, V6:121.

Ball, Elder, mentioned, V4:6.

Ball, Joseph, mission, assigned to go on, V4:429
    South America, to go on mission to, V4:413.

Ballance, Charles C., mentioned, V5:486.

Ballantyne, Richard, visits Brother Taylor in Carthage after martyrdom,
    V7:116.

Ballard, Philip, covenanted to assist saints in removing from Missouri,
    V3:253.

bank, Joseph proposes national, V6:206-7.

bankruptcy, Hyrum, of, V5:200-5
    Joseph, of, V4:594-5, 600
    Joseph, letter on taking same, V5:6.

Banks, John, English conference, represents branches at, V6:327.

Banks, John, mob, requests members to join, V6:510
    mobber, makes threats, V6:481.

Banks, William L., mob member writes lies concerning DeWitt, V3:156.

baptism, celestial ordinance, V1:283

> children, of little, V4:554
> Church, desire of some to join without, (D&C § 22), V1:79
> Church, members previous to organization of, V1:76-7, ftnt only
> Church organization, rebaptism necessary after, (D&C § 22), V1:79
> churches, Joseph's comment on other, V3:29
> Cowdery, Oliver, of, V1:39
> dead, for the, V4:568-9
> dead, for the, editorial in *Times and Seasons* on, V4:595, et seq
> dead, for the, first mentioned, V4:231
> discourse on, V6:316
> dispensation, first in new, V1:42
> England, where person drowned, V6:160
> God, sign to obey, V4:555
> Harris, Martin, of, V1:79
> Holy Ghost, channel and key to, V3:379
> Joseph, of, V1:39
> Lord, Joseph and Oliver Cowdery inquire of, with regards to, V1:39
> Matthews, Timothy R., self, and attacks Church, V2:506-7
> meeting, after first public, V1:81
> Mississippi River, in, V4:557
> mob, dam broken by, repaired, V1:87
> mob, scheduled but breaks dam, V1:86
> organization, after, V1:79
> principle of, explained, ordained sign, V4:554
> Prophet, parents of, V1:79
> Rockwell, Orrin Porter, of, V1:79
> sectarian, reason for not accepting, V4:426
> Seneca Lake, in, V1:86
> sickness, of Emma in river for, V5:167-8
> sins, refused for not repenting and confessing, V2:235
> Smith, Hyrum, of, V1:51
> Smith, Joseph, Church did not in name of, V3:29
> temple, in font of, V4:558
> translation, question about in, V1:39
> Whitmer, David, of, V1:51
> Whitmer, Peter, Jr., of, V1:51
> women, not right to persuade, contrary to husband, V2:247.
> See also dead, baptism for; doctrine.

baptism, sectarian, reasons for not accepting, V4:426.

baptismal font, description of Nauvoo Temple, V4:446.

Baptist Church, contending for, V1:3
    member, excommunication for joining Church, V5:166
    minister of, requests duty in Church, V1:143
    Missouri mobs, participated in, V1:392
    Mormons, differences from, V4:348
    Presbyterians, against, V1:4
    saints, differs from former-day, V4:350-1
    tenants, try to establish own, V1:4.

Baptist, John the, see John the Baptist.

Barber, Andrew, first martyr killed by mob, V1:431 and ftnt.

Barber, Benjamin, ordained elder, V5:349.

Barber, Elam, Zions Camp member, V2:183.

Barber, Joseph, mob, requests members to join, V6:510
    mobber, makes threats, V6:481.

Bardsley, Mr., prayer to soften heart of, V2:24.

Barkdall, Mr., mentioned, V2:227.

Barker, Benjamin, Kirtland Camp, mentioned in, V3:139.

Barker, Jonathan, mentioned, V7:436.

Barker, John, Nauvoo, elected constable and coroner of, V5:270.

Barker, William, blessing for work on Kirtland Temple, V2:206.

Barkman, Anthony, martyrdom, guard on jail at, V7:142.

Barlow, Israel, Galland, Isaac, meeting with, V3:265
    mission and field of labor, V6:335
    Nauvoo, reports threat to, V6:565
    seventies, named to first quorum of, V2:204
    Young, Brigham, assists on journey, V4:9
    Zions Camp member, V2:63, 183.

Barlow, Jonathan W., witness for defense of saints in Missouri, intimidated, V3:211.

Barlow, Truman R., Joseph, on relief expedition for, V5:486
    Nauvoo, policeman in, V6:150.

Barlow, Watson, mentioned, V3:312.

Barnard, Brother, mentioned, V3:8.

Barnes, Asa W., petitions Governor Boggs on mob violence in DeWitt, V3:83.

Barnes, Dr., serves writ for arrest of members, V7:124.

Barnes, D. H., petitions Governor Boggs on mob violence in DeWitt, V3:83.

Barnes, Ezekiel, petitions Governor Boggs on mob violence in DeWitt, V3:83.

Barnes, H. W., mission appointment and field of labor, V6:340.

Barnes, James D., Carthage Greys, member of, V7:142.

Barnes, John, mobber gives martyrdom note for Nauvoo, V6:622.

Barnes, Lorenzo Dow, British Mission, assigned to, V4:413
    death of, in England, V5:207
    England, appointed to go to, with Twelve, V3:347
    eulogy of, by Joseph, V5:360-3
    eulogy of, by Parley P. Pratt, V5:319-20
    funds, appointed to raise to purchase mob's lands, V4:84
    genealogy, V5:320, ftnt only
    high council, chosen to Adam-ondi-Ahman, V3:38
    labors, letter of, reporting, V4:569-70
    seventies, named to first quorum of, V2:203
    seventy, ordained, V2:221
    Zions Camp member, V2:183.

Barnes, Michael, Jr., Carthage Greys, member of, V7:142
    mentioned, V7:442, 444, 493.

Barnes, Thomas, ordained priest, V4:298.

Barnes, Thomas L., quack doctor, member of martyrdom mob, V7:144.

Barnes, William, mobber, gives martyrdom note for Nauvoo, V6:622.

Barnet, Mr., aids driven saints, V1:436.

Barnet, Samuel, disfellowshipped for following false revelation, V2:525
    Kirtland Camp, subscribed to constitution of, V3:392.

Barnett, A. L., mentioned, V4:176.

Barnett, John T., delegate to present truth to public, V6:483
    mentioned, V5:365
    Nauvoo, first elected councilor of, V4:287
    Nauvoo Legion, in, V4:295.

Barney, Edson, mission and field of labor, V6:339
    seventies, named to first quorum of, V2:203
    Zions Camp member, V2:183.

Barney, Hiram, mentioned, V4:543.

Barney, Royal, seventies, named to first quorum of, V2:203
    seventy, ordained, V2:221
    Zions Camp member, V2:183.

Barnum, Job V., mentioned, V5:172.

Barnum, Samuel, cannot exercise gift of being healed, V2:332.

Barradale, Elder, mentioned, V5:419.

Barratt, W. J., reports that work in Australia slow, V4:343.

Barrett, William, elder, ordained, V4:154
    mission, letter pertaining to, V4:161
    mission, to South Australia, V4:154.

Barroes, Mr., mentioned, V4:215.

Barrows, Maria, to receive Church aid in emigrating from England, V5:412.

Barrus, Ethan, mission appointment and field of labor, V6:338.

Bartee, P. Y. G., appointed by public to assist saints in removal from Zion, V2:455.

Bartholemew, Noah Willis, Indian trouble, in, V7:627
    mentioned, V7:133.

Bartlet, T. J., at anti-Mormon meeting at Carthage, V6:4.

Bartlett, Mr., mentioned, V6:172; V7:531.

Bartlett, F. J., martyrdom mob, member of, miller, V7:144
    meeting, at anti-Mormon, V5:537.

Bartlett, Milton F., mission call in Illinois to disabuse public mind over arrest of Joseph, V5:485
    mission and field of labor, V6:335.

Bartlett, Sylvester M., martyrdom mob, editor of *Quincy Whig*, member of, V7:144
    mentioned, V4:267.

Bartley, B. B., petitions Governor Boggs on mob violence in DeWitt, V3:83.

Bartolph, John L., utility committee member to aid Church removal, V7:474.

Barton, Michael H., refused baptism because would not repent and confess, V2:235.

Barton, Reuben, approved for ordination, V2:400.

Barton, William, covenanted to assist saints in removing from Missouri, V3:253.

Barton, William P. C., mentioned, V2:350, ftnt only.

Bassett, Mr., mentioned, V5:273.

Bates, Archibald, mission and field of labor, V6:336.

Bates, Brother, apostasy of, V1:380-1.

Bates, Marcellus L., MIA, aids in movement toward, V5:321
mission and field of labor, V5:348; V6:336.

Bates, Richard, ordained priest, V4:298.

Bathrick, Almon, mission and field of labor, V6:340.

Batson, Mr., testifies in Hulet Branch trial, V2:140.

Batson, William, mission and field of labor, V6:338
priesthood taken for failure to have discretion and understanding to
act wisely, V2:141.

Batten, John, mentioned, V4:180.

Baum, Jacob, mentioned, V5:525.

Baxter, John, committee member to talk to saints on removal, V2:452.

Baxter, Zimri H., Nauvoo Temple, appointed carpenter on, V7:326
priest, ordained, V6:400.

Bayliss, William, assistant at care of Church at Apperley, V4:135.

Beach, Rufus, Church, to aid in removal of, V7:474
exploring expedition, volunteers for, V6:227.

Beaman, Alva, (also spelled Alvah), Book of Mormon, helped conceal
plates, V2:43, ftnt only
conference at home of, in Avon, V2:44
doubts of, V2:384
elders, to be president of, at Kirtland, V2:370
Prophet, an early friend of, V2:43, ftnt only
Prophet, entertains, V2:43
seventies, recommends elders for, V2:391
Zion, appointed to high council at, V2:367
Zion, consults Prophet regarding journey to, V2:316.

Beaman, Henry, ordained seventy, V2:208.

Beaman, Mother, mentioned, V3:11.

Bear, John, mentioned, V5:269.

Beard, J. R., mentioned, V4:421, ftnt only.

beast, apostate church, when used in scripture, represents, V5:324
Book of Revelation, beasts in, V5:324, 339-45
differences between Revelation and Daniel expressed, V5:325
heaven, in, and understood, V5:343
Joseph, explains some of, V1:253.

Beaver, Daniel, anti-Mormon committee chairman, V6:8
Carthage, at anti-Mormon meeting at, V6:4.

Bebee, George, beating of, V3:437.

Beck, Charles, mentioned, V5:523, 525.

Beck, Jacob, one of the Durfee murderers, member of martyrdom mob, V7:145.

Beck, John, Baptist deacon mentioned, V5:166.

Beck, Thomas, arraigned for treason, murder, burglary, arson, robbery and larceny at Richmond, Missouri, V3:209.

Beckelshimer, Jonathan, covenanted to assist saints in removing from Missouri, V3:252.

Bedell, Mrs., mentioned, V7:112.

Bedell, E. A., mentioned, V7:449, 492-3, 502.

Beebe, Calvin, high council, sustained member of Far West, V2:523
high council, sustained member of Missouri, V2:124
mission appointment, V2:164
Missouri, appointed branch president in, V1:409, ftnt only.

Beebe, Isaac, mission and field of labor, V6:337.

Beebe, J. A., at anti-Mormon meeting, V5:537.

Beebe, Joseph, mentioned, V4:429.

Beeman, Louisa, baptized, V5:385.

Belknap, Gilbert, affidavit concerning threats of invasion from Missouri, V6:502-3.

Bell, Alfred, mission and field of labor, V6:338
Taylor. John, supplies aid to, V7:79-80.

Beloved Son, see Jesus Christ.

Beman, Mr., mentioned, V1:422.

Benbow, John, baptized, V4:151
Church, to aid removal of, V7:474
Churches, given charge of, at Froome's Hill, V4:139
clerk of conference, V4:138
hymns, aids publication of, V4:131
liberality of, V4:188
mentioned, V5:12
testimony, receives, V4:150.

Bend, Samuel, mentioned, V3:144-5.

Benedict, Elder, mentioned, V4:22.

Benner, Elias, Haun's Mills, killed by mob at, V3:326, ftnt only
Zions Camp, joins, V2:65.

Benner, Henry, seventies, named to first quorum of, V2:203

BENNER, HENRY (continued)

seventy, ordained, V2:221.

Bennett, Caleb, conference at home of, V4:6.

Bennett, David, beaten by mob, V1:429.

Bennett, Hiram, mission and field of labor, V6:336.

Bennett, James Arlington, anti-Mormon, letter to Joseph advising of, book by John C. Bennett, V5:112-4

anti-Mormon, letter to Joseph on, book by John C. Bennett, V5:162-4

baptism of, V5:556

Church, seeks personal aggrandizement as military commander-in-chief of, V7:528

confirmation of, V5:556

honored, V4:600-1

Joseph, dreams of death of, V7:261

Legion, inspector-general of, V4:593

Legion, resignation from, V6:71

Legion, writes for personal aggrandizement in, V7:429

Mormon in sympathy, V5:163

Mormons, publishes article on, defending, V5:170

Nauvoo, opposed to saints removing from, V7:483-4

Prophet, letter from, V5:156, et seq

Prophet, letter to, V5:112

Rocky Mountains, declaration to go to, V7:488

saints, evil influence of his letters on the purported movements of, V7:577

vice president, ineligible to be, V6:244

vice president, Joseph nominates for, V6:230

vice president, letter to, on candidacy for, V6:231-3.

Bennett, James Gordon, editor of *New York Herald*, course of approved, V4:477-8.

Bennett, John Cook, agitation, continued of, V5:307

anti-Mormon book of, to be published, V5:112-3 and ftnt

apostasy, impressions of John Taylor after, V7:57

apostasy, position of reviewed, IntroV5:XVII, et seq

attitude, letters of, and, V4:544, et seq and ftnts

biography, V4:169, ftnt only

character, affidavit of William Law concerning and extolling innocence of Joseph, V5:75-7

character, affidavit of Hyrum Smith concerning, V5:71-3

character, affidavit of Daniel H. Wells concerning and extolling innocence of Joseph, V5:80-2

BENNETT, JOHN COOK (continued)

character, certificate of Elias Higbee concerning and extolling
    innocence of Joseph, V5:77

character, certificate of Francis M. Higbee concerning and extolling
    innocence of Joseph, V5:80

character, *Times & Seasons* article concerning and extolling innocence
    of Joseph, V5:78-9 and ftnt

Church, letter to Joseph declaring intent to join, V4:168

Church, letter tendering services to, V4:169-70

Church, reasons for joining and character, V5:79-81, ftnt only

destroying angels, accused Joseph of having, V5:364

elders, Joseph sends forth to defend against, V5:131-2

excommunication of reported, V5:75-6

exposed, begs not to be, V5:18

fellowship withdrawn, V5:18

females, confesses sins against, in Nauvoo, V5:18

Joseph, affidavit of, on character and teachings of, V5:11

Joseph, letter to, announcing arrival soon, V4:179

Joseph, letter to, expressing anxiety to be with, V4:172

Joseph, letter to Illinois governor concerning, V5:42-4

Joseph, letter on new attempts to arrest, V5:250

Joseph, political trick to arrest, V5:513-15

Joseph, receives whisperings concerning, V5:4-5

Joseph, sins and character of, published by, V5:35-8

letter to Sidney Rigdon and Orson Pratt, V5:251

Masonic lodge, expulsion from, V5:22

Missouri, letter to Joseph on, V4:547

Missouri persecutions, letter to Dyer on slavery and, V4:544-5

Nauvoo, first elected mayor of, V4:287; V7:56

Nauvoo, inaugural address of, as mayor of, V4:288-92 and ftnt

Nauvoo, letter of Joseph welcoming to, V4:177-8

Nauvoo, mass meeting at, against, V5:70

Nauvoo, resigns as mayor of, V5:12

Nauvoo Charter, letter announcing passage of, V4:248-9

Nauvoo City Council, on, V5:67-8

Nauvoo City Council, petition to Governor Carlin on, V5:68-70

Nauvoo Legion, cashiered from, V5:49

Nauvoo Legion, elected major-general of, V4:296

Nauvoo masonic lodge, expelled from, V5:32

president, sustained assistant, V4:341

Twelve Apostles, leave to confound, V5:160

University of Nauvoo, discharged as chancellor of, V5:120

BENNETT, JOHN COOK (continued)

  wickedness, confesses to, V5:18-19

  wickedness of, disclosed, V5:12

  wickedness, statement of concerning his, V5:13.

  See also affidavit; Latter-day Saints, Church of Jesus Christ of; Nauvoo; Nauvoo Legion; Smith, Joseph.

Bennett, Samuel, arrest for destruction of *Expositor*, trial of, V6:487, et seq

  branch, appointed head of Cincinnati, V4:204

  Carthage, accompanies Sister Taylor to, V7:111

  Joseph, on relief expedition for, V5:486

  Nauvoo, elected market inspector in, V5:271.

Benson, Mr., mentioned, V3:334.

Benson, A. G. & Company, contract with, attempt to take Nauvoo property, V7:589.

Benson, Ezra T., appointed to preside over new district of Church, V7:306

  high priest, ordained, V4:233

  mission and field of labor, V6:337

  Nauvoo High Council, sustained member of, after death of Joseph, V7:296

  Nauvoo Temple, to administer in, V7:555

  stake, appointed counselor of, V4:233

  Twelve, sustained member of, V7:628.

Benson, Richard, Church, represents branch of, at English conference, V4:116, 148; V5:10

  elder, ordained, V4:333

  volunteers for service in vineyard, V4:217.

Benson, William, Baptist Church clerk, mentioned, V5:166.

Bent, Samuel, Church, credentials to raise funds for, V4:164

  exploring, volunteers for, V6:224

  mission, sent on, V4:161

  Missouri persecutions, expresses faith in work after, V3:225

  money, letter to Presidency reporting labors of collecting, V4:199-200

  Nauvoo High Council, appointed to, V4:12

  Nauvoo High Council, sustained member after death of Joseph, V7:296

  redress, witness suggested to appear before Congress on, V4:97

  westward movement, captain of second company in, V7:481

  Zion High Council, appointed to, V3:155

  Zions Camp member, V2:183.

Bentley, Adamson, Baptist minister, V1:121, ftnt only

BENTLEY, ADAMSON (continued)

  Rigdon, Sidney, injures character of, V2:270

  Rigdon, Sidney, stays at home of, V1:121, ftnt only.

Bentley, Gregory, mission and field of labor, V6:336.

Bently, Jeremiah, mobber, requests members to join mob, V6:511.

Benton, Mr., swore out first warrant against Joseph, V1:97.

Benton, Thomas H., mentioned, V3:351

  Phelps, W. W., letter to, V1:487-8.

Bernhisel, John M., bishop, appointed traveling, V7:374

  bishop of New York branch, V4:344

  bond, to Joseph, V5:414

  Ford, Governor, appointed with John Taylor as committee to wait on, V7:71

  Ford, Governor, letter confirming Joseph's letter on Expositor affair, V6:467-8

  history, approves martyrdom, V7:55

  Joseph, on relief expedition for, V5:482

  martyrdom, witness for Joseph at Carthage, V6:576

  Missouri, affidavit on threats of invasion from, V6:516

  Nauvoo, delegate to political convention in, V6:389.

Berry, William, ordained elder and blessed, V2:207.

Berry, William, Church, represents branches at British conference, V4:148

  elder, ordained, V4:148.

Bethers, Zadok, ordained elder, V4:13.

Bettisworth, David, Carthage, constable of, V7:66

  Carthage, illegal actions of, at V7:98

  Joseph, arrests, on Expositor affair, V6:453

  treason, arrests Prophet for, V6:561-2.

Betts, Brother, counselor in priests quorum, V7:463.

Betts, John F., mission and field of labor, V6:337.

Betts, Thadeus, death of, V4:112.

"Beware of False Prophets," tract against Mormonism written by Reverend Pixley in Missouri, V1:373 and ftnt.

Bible, books, lost of, V1:132 and ftnt

  Church believes and this is difference from other churches, V3:28

  full, defective if claimed to be, V3:30

  German translation of, most correct, V6:364

  important points lost from, V1:245

  incomplete and lacking, V2:18

BIBLE (continued)

    Malachi 4:5, Joseph retranslates, V6:184

    Matthew 24:2, retranslated, V6:184

    mistranslation, Joseph on, V6:307

    New Testament, translation of completed, V1:324 and ftnt

    religious questions, cannot be settled from, V1:4

    revelations, authorizes modern, V3:30

    revision of, V1:215, ftnt only

    translating of, by Joseph, V1:170

    translation commenced, V1:132

    translation, Emma won't give up when sought, V7:260

    translation finished, V1:368-9

    translation, Joseph prepares to recommence, V1:215 and ftnt

    translation, Joseph prepares to renew, V1:211

    translation renewed, V1:219.

    See also doctrine, scripture, translation.

Bidamon, Lewis A., Nauvoo Temple, reports arsons of, V7:618, ftnt
    only.

Bigelow, Nathan, house burning threatened, V7:485-6.

Bigler, Bathsheba W., marries George A. Smith, V4:389.

Bigler, Jacob G., mission call and field of labor, V5:349

    Missouri, covenanted to assist saints in removing from, V3:252.

Bigler, Mark, letter to, V3:366.

Biles, Brother, mission and field of labor, V7:260.

Billings, Mrs., mentioned, V1:417.

Billings, Samuel, policeman in Nauvoo, V6:149.

Billings, Titus, bishop, counselor to, at Far West, V2:504

    bishop, sustained counselor to, at Far West, V2:524

    Church, appointed to preside over new district of, V7:306

    genealogy, V1:266, ftnt only

    high priest, to be ordained, V1:363

    Legion, officer in, V4:295

    presidency, opposed to, at Far West, V3:5.

Bills, John, mentioned, V6:95, 492.

Binby, John, Joseph, on relief expedition for, V5:482.

Bingham, Erastus, Missouri, on committee for removal from, V3:255

    Missouri, covenanted to assist saints in removing from, V3:253.

Bingham, L. A., utility committee member to aid Church removal, V7:474.

Birch, Judge, drunken judge in Missouri persecutions, V3:321, ftnt only,
    423, 449.

Birch, Thomas C., (also spelled Burch), mentioned, V3:81, 414, 463; V5:495; V6:108
  saints, misrepresents, V3:166
  state, attorney for, before court at Richmond, V3:209.

Birch, Weston F., editor of *Western Monitor,* V1:395.

Birchard, M., mentioned, V2:49, ftnt only.

Bird, Benjamin F., covenanted to assist saints in removing from Missouri, V3:254.

Bird, Charles, Kirtland Camp, subscribed to constitution of, V3:92
  Missouri, covenanted to assist saints in removing from, V3:252
  poor, solicits means to help, V3:254.

Bird, John, presides at public meeting in Missouri, V2:448, et seq
  saints, committee member to talk on removal of, V2:452
  Zion, appointed by public to assist saints in removing from, V2:455.

Bird, Phinehas R., (also spelled Phineas), deacons quorum, president of, in Nauvoo, V4:312
  mentioned, V6:257
  Missouri, covenanted to assist saints in removing from, V3:252.

Bird, William, called on mission and field of labor, V5:349.

Birge, Brother, mentioned, V4:22.

Birney, John, mentioned, V6:447.

bishop, duty and calling, V2:477
  iniquity, taught to expose, V5:18
  Nauvoo, appointment of, to wards, V5:119-20
  poor, responsibility of, to, V1:365.

Bishop, Francis Gladden, Church, president of, at Westfield, New York, V1:335
  convicted, public confession required, V2:285
  disfellowshipped for lack of proper spirit, V2:241
  disfellowshipped for receiving false revelations, V4:550
  elder, reordained, V2:285
  seventies, placed back into, V4:105
  trial of for advancing heretical doctrines, V2:284
  trial, suspended from Church and referred to, V2:241.

Bishop, Isaac G., blessing for work on Kirtland Temple, V2:206.

Bishop, Isaac H., high council, commanded to make public confession for speaking evil of, V2:236
  stake presidency, appointed counselor to, V4:236
  trial of, V2:236-7.

bishop's court, Church, disposition of property by, V3:47-8
excommunicates Wesley Hurlburt for denying the faith, V2:2.

bishop's storehouse, first established, (D&C § 41:13-14), V1:174.

Black, Adam, communications, sends more inflammatory to Boggs, V3:166
Hyrum, incident reported by, V3:405
Joseph, affidavit on incident with, V3:70-2
judge, sits as, against saints, V3:205
mob, affidavit of, concerning covenant, states saints are, V3:64-5
mob, covenant not to join, V3:59-60
mob, with, V3:59
saints, agrees to expulsion of, V3:216
saints, judge at trial of, V3:207.

Black River conference, of apostles to examine Church, V2:225.

Black, William, British Mission, mission in, V4:150
volunteers for service in vineyard, V4:217.

Black, William, elder, ordained, V4:333
priest, ordained, V4:148.

Blackburn, Abner, mentioned, V7:596.

Blackburn, Anthony, mentioned, V7:596.

Blackhawk, brother of, visits Joseph, V6:401.

Blackman, Hiram, named to first quorum of seventies, V2:204.

Blair, John, mission and field of labor, V5:347.

Blakely, Mr., mentioned, V3:314-5.

Blakesley, James, apostasy, excommunicated for, V6:398
apostate, joins group of, V6:347
appointed counselor in apostate church, V6:354
mission assignment, V4:430.

Blakesly, Brother, mentioned, V4:48.

Blakey, Mr., British conference, represents branches at, V6:328.

Blanchard, Asaph, Kirtland Camp, leaves, V3:141
Kirtland Camp, subscribed to constitution of, V3:93.

Blanchard, James, excommunicated for repeated sins and failure to repent, V1:469.

Blanchard, John R., mission and field of labor, V6:335.

Blanchard, Richard D., Kirtland Camp, joins near Dayton, Ohio, V3:126
Kirtland Camp, mentioned in, V3:146.

blasphemy, Curtis, Theodore, imprisoned in England for, V4:380.

Blazard, John, ordained priest, V4:118.

Bleckley, Charles, saints, witness for state in Missouri trials of, V3:210

Bledsor (family), V7:143.

Blennarhassett, R. S., (also spelled Blanerhasset), mentioned, V5:307; V6:136.

blessings, Kirtland Temple, given in, V2:379-80
law, predicated on, V5:325
Lord's Anointed, of the, V2:383
patriarchal, V2:346-7
quorums, arrangement to receive, V2:391.

Bleven, Jane, mentioned, V3:257.

Blezzard, John, British Mission, mission in, V4:150
elder, ordained, V4:148
ministry, devote all time to labors of, V4:148.

Bliss, Daniel, Kirtland Camp, leaves, V3:129-30
Kirtland Camp, subscribed to constitution of, V3:93.

Blodgett, Mr., Unitarian minister speaks in Nauvoo, V6:34.

Blodgett, N. G., mentioned, V5:371.

blood, showers of, recorded, V4:415
trail indicates path of expelled saints in Missouri, V3:439.

blood atonement, discussed before Nauvoo City Council, V5:296
espoused, V1:435, ftnt only.

Blood, Justin, subscribed to constitution of Kirtland Camp, V3:92.

Blue, Big, battle of, V1:429-31 and ftnts
river in Jackson County, meeting of saints on banks of, V1:336-7.

Bogard, Reverend, against saints in Missouri, V1:372, ftnt only; V3:407.

Bogart, Samuel, Methodist minister heads mob, V3:158
Missouri, named one of chief mobbers in, V3:327
Missouri trials, witness for state in, V3:210
mob leader accuses saints of burning and murder, V3:165
saints, captures witnesses of and imprisons them, V3:210-11
threats of, V3:169.

Boggs, Lilburn W., assassination attempt explained, IntroV5:XXI
assassination, implicating O. P. Rockwell in attempt at, V5:67
assassination of, reported, V5:14
Atchison, General. letter explaining uprising, V3:81-2
Church, refuses aid to, V3:157
extermination, order of, V3:175

BOGGS, LILBURN W. (continued)

extermination, order to General Lucas to complete job of, V3:192

Joseph, comments on attitude of, V3:178

Joseph, demands extradition of, V4:198

Joseph, treachery of, exposed and opinion of, V1:434-5

militia, orders to call out to assist peace officers, V3:77-8

militia, orders raised, V3:65

militia, raising of, to protect citizens, V3:173

militia movements, report of, V3:195, et seq

Missouri, governor of, V3:65

Missouri Legislature, reports information to, V3:217

Missouri persecutions, part in, expounded, V3:328

mob, calls up militia composed of, V1:433

mob, head of, V1:437

mobbing, Missouri Lieutenant-Governor participates in, V1:391-2

Monmouth trials, Joseph demands expenses of, from, V4:420

Mormons, remarks on leaving of the state, V3:234

Mormons, requested to be at seat of war with, V3:176 and ftnt

saints, hears petition from and promises help, V3:234

saints, instructs General Clark to expel and punish leaders, V3:204

saints, orders arms returned to, V3:262

saints, orders more militia to area of, V3:81

saints, petition to, from, V3:82

saints, report of General Clark on crimes of, and legal problems, V3:206-7

shot, report of being, V5:9

Springfield trial, affidavit in, V5:234-5

troops, orders discharge of, V3:83.

See also affidavit; Latter-day Saints, Church of Jesus Christ of; letters; Missouri correspondence; mob; persecution; persecution, Missouri; Smith, Joseph.

bogus, makers of, activity at Nauvoo, V7:574

saints, commanded to put out of mind, V7:350

west, presence of en route to the, V7:609

See also Apostles; Latter-day Saints, Church of Jesus Christ of.

"bogus Brigham" incident, report of and laughter over, V7:549-51.

Boles, William, affiant to public proclamation on mob lies, V6:495.

Boley, Henry, shot accidentally, V6:121.

Bolton, Curtis E., mentioned, V7:593.

Bolton, Emma, excommunicated from Church for disorderly conduct, V4:216.

Bolton, Lewis, major-general in Missouri militia, V3:65.

Bond, Abram, disfellowshipped for murmuring, V3:117
Kirtland Camp, subscribed to constitution of, V3:93
murmuring and unchristianlike conduct, tried for, V3:107, 110, 111.

Bond, Ira, deacons, presides over, V2:371
Kirtland Temple, blessing for work on, V2:206.

Bond, John, represents Church branch at English conference, V4:147.

Bonney, Eaton, mentioned, V6:450, 488, 490.

Bonney, Edward, witness for Joseph at Carthage martyrdom, V6:576.

Book of Esdras, claimed inspired translation, V5:215, ftnt only.

Book of, see title, example, Mormon, Book of.

books, list of, for and against Church, V4:253-6.

Booth, Mr., editor of *Quincy Herald*, V7:484.

Booth, Ezra, apostatizes at Kirtland, V1:215-6 and ftnt
converted at miraculous healing, V1:215, ftnt only
Joseph, letters confounded by, V1:241
mission, appointed to go to Missouri, V1:178
Missouri, arrives in, V1:191.

Booth, Lorenzo, seventies, named to first quorum of, V2:204
theft, testimony concerning, V2:157
Zions Camp member, V2:64, 183.

Borkdull, Michel, covenanted to assist saints in removing from Missouri, V3:253.

born again, comes through ordinances, V3:292.

Boscow, Nicholas, delegate to present truth to public, V6:483.

Bosier, Brother, mentioned, V3:382.

Bosley, Edmund, excommunicated for breaking covenant of consecration, V2:236
Kirtland Temple, blessing for work on, V2:205
Lord, covenant to assist printing word of, V2:161
priests, to teach sectarian, V2:207.

Bosley, Edward, called on mission and field of labor, V5:349.

Bosley, Father, entertains the Prophet, V2:43, 44.

Bosley, Joshua, approved for ordination, V2:407.

Bosley, William, elder, ordained, V2:207
Kirtland Camp, subscribed to constitution of, V3:92
Kirtland Temple, blessing for work on, V2:205
mission, assigned to go on, V4:429

BOSLEY, WILLIAM (continued)

stake president, appointed, V4:236.

Bosman, Mr., mentioned in Kirtland Camp, V3:112.

Boss, Mrs., mentioned, V7:488.

Bossinger, George, ordained high priest, V2:429.

Boston Bee, Joseph, publishes character sketch of, V5:406-8
  Mormonism, article on enlargement of, "Missouri Rapped," V5:518-28
  Mormonism, article printed on, V5:322.

Boston Daily Ledger, publishes Book of Abraham facsimile, V5:11.

Bosworth, Mr., reports conference proceedings, V2:25.

Bosworth, Joseph B., authority, refuses to accept and consequences, V2:162-4
  clerk at council meeting, V2:317
  Kirtland Temple, blessing for work on, V2:206
  mission and field of labor, V6:338
  Prophet, entertains, V2:50
  Zion, on deliverance of, V2:53
  Zions Camp, exonerates Joseph's actions in, V2:149.

Botswick, Orsimus F., trial for slander, V6:225.

Bough, Henry Our, appointed elder, V4:12.

Bourne, John, mentioned, V4:360.

Bowen, Daniel, Kirtland Camp, subscribed to constitution of, V3:92
  Young, J., baptized, V1:295, ftnt only.

Bowen, Obadiah, affidavit on mob attempting to draft into services, V6:512.

Bowen, P., delegate to political convention in Nauvoo, V6:389.

Bowers, William, anti-Mormon committee member, V1:399.

Bowman, William, guard for prisoners in Missouri, V3:309
  Joseph, swears not to eat or drink until kill, V3:306
  mentioned, V3:321, ftnt only
  mob, oath of that saints have acted as, V3:61.

Box, William, chosen counselor of priests quorum, V6:175.

Boyce, Benjamin, kidnapped by Missourians, V4:154-6
  kidnapping, testimony of, V4:180
  Nauvoo, policeman in, V6:150.

Boyington, Doctor, Presbyterian persecutor, V1:97.

Boyle, Hiram, at anti-Mormon meeting, V5:537.

Boynton, A. D., mission and field of labor, V6:335.

Boynton, Abram, subscribed to construction of Kirtland Camp, V3:93

Boynton, John F., apostasy of, V2:528

BOYNTON, JOHN F. (continued)

Apostles, blessing as member of, V2:191
Apostles, chosen one of, V2:187
confesses and retains membership and apostleship, V2:512
disfellowshipped and rejected as apostle, V2:509
Joseph, visits, V5:144-5
marriage to Susan Lowell, V2:377
mission in Maine, letter on, V2:40-1
ordinations, withdraws objections to, V2:408
sins, confession of, rejected unanimously, V2:510.

Bozarth, Squire, covenanted to assist saints in removing from Missouri, V3:253.

Bozier, Brother, mentioned, V4:46.

Brace, Truman, covenanted to assist saints in removing from Missouri, V3:254.

Brackenbury, Benjamin B., witness against murderers of Joseph, harassed by mob, V7:380-4
witness at murder trial, V7:50, ftnt only.

Bradbury, William, America, to be brought over to, V5:406.

Braddock, Ann, baptized and lodges elders, V2:506.

Braden, James, ordination illegal and rejected, V1:343.

Braden, Solomon, Kirtland Camp, mentioned in, V3:107.

Bradin, James, covenanted to assist saints in removing from Missouri, V3:252.

Bradley, Mr., mentioned, V2:290.

Bradshaw, Mr., represents branch of Church at British conference, V4:148.

Brady, Mr., threatens Joseph's life, V4:72.

Bragg, David, gives money for lands in Zion, V2:174.

Brailey, Jesse, mentioned, V7:514.

Brakenbury, Joseph B., poisoned by mob, V7:524.

Braman, Mr., agent of Governor Ford, V5:493.

Brandon, George W., mission and field of labor, V5:348; V6:338.

Brandon, T. J., mission and field of labor, V6:338.

Brannan, Samuel S., California, company to go to, V7:516-22, 445, 567, 588
disfellowshipped, to be, V7:395
fellowship restored to, V7:418
Kirtland Temple, blessing for work on, V2:206
Nauvoo, letter of, on A. G. Benson & Company attempt to take property in, V7:587.

Brasier, Richard, (also spelled Brasher), Kirtland Camp, leaves, V3:140

BRASIER, RICHARD (continued)

   Kirtland Camp, subscribed to construction of, V3:92.

Brassfield, John, guard for prisoners in Missouri, V3:309.

Brattle, James W., land shark, member of martyrdom mob, V7:144.

Brayman, M., mentioned, V7:493, 527, 532.

Brazeale, Hugh L., (also spelled Brazile), anti-Mormon committee member, V1:399

   boast of, V1:430

   mentioned, V1:412

   mob member killed by saints, V1:430.

Braziel, Hugh, mobber, V4:72.

Brazier, Edward, death of, V5:390.

Brazier, Richard, mentioned, V6:532.

breastplate, Joseph, beheld by, V1:16

   received, V1:18

   show, cannot, V1:13

   Urim and Thummim, part of, V1:12.

Breneman, A., Kirtland Camp, mentioned in, V3:115.

Brewer, J., witness for Joseph at Carthage martyrdom, V6:576.

Brewster, James Collins, disfellowshiped for following false revelations, V2:525

   Moroni, claims to have seen, V2:520

   revelations, Joseph declares to be false, V5:214-5 and ftnt.

Brewster, Jane, disfellowshiped for following false revelations, V2:525.

Brewster, Zenos H., disfellowshiped for following false revelations, V2:525.

   Kirtland Camp, in, V3:132

   Kirtland Temple, blessing for work on, V2:206.

Brewster, Zephaniah W., subscribed to construction of Kirtland Camp, V3:93.

Brewyer, Mr., mentioned, V7:496.

bribe, Joseph offers to pay double for any offered to police, V6:153.

Bridges, James, charged with disorderly conduct, V6:155.

Brien, Jefferson, mobber who prevents group from traveling to Missouri, V3:324.

Briggs, S. H., mission and field of labor, V6:340.

Brigham, Fitch, cousin to Brigham Young, V4:46.

Brigham, Phinehas, cousin to Brigham Young, V4:46.

Brigham, Salmon, cousin to Brigham Young, V4:46.

Briley, Thomas, Joseph, on relief expedition for, V5:482.

Brink, William B., elder, ordained, V5:349

mentioned, V5:293

mission call and field of labor, V5:349

mission in Illinois to disabuse public mind over arrest of Joseph, V5:485.

Britannia, emigrant ship, V4:134.

Bristoe, Richard, mentioned, V1:411.

British Mission, America, saints leave for, V4:134

Apostles arrive in, V4:76

Apostles, expounded upon, IntroV4:XXX

Apostles, report work after departure, V5:505, et seq

appointed, V2:489 and ftnts, 490 and ftnt

baptism, George D. Watt, first in, V2:504

Barnes, L., dies in, V5:207

bickerings in, V3:276

clothing, agitation in, over Sister Richards', V3:276-7

conference of June 14, 1840, V4:134

conference of July 6, 1840, V4:146

conference, membership enumerated, V7:56

confirmation, Jenetta Richards first in, V2:504

departure for, V2:493

elders, arrival in Liverpool, V2:498

elders, arrival in New York, V2:494-5

elders, labors in, V4:76

elders quorums organized in, V4:136, 140

emigration, agency in, V4:484

emigration, counsel on, V4:346-7

evil spirits, attacked by, V2:503

false doctrine, spread in, by I. Russell, V3:343-4

gathering, not to be taught in, V2:492

general conference of October 6, 1840, V4:214

general conference of April 1844, V6:326, et seq

healings, elders exhorted to keep journals of, V6:186

history of, written, 1837-1841, V4:313, et seq

Kimball, Heber C., letter on affairs in, V4:114

members of, enumerated, V4:147, et seq

minutes of Manchester, England, conference of June 4, 1843, V5:418

missionary assignments given in, V4:149, et seq

mob violence in, V4:361

BRITISH MISSION (continued)

progress in, V2:502-4
Prophet's instruction to, V2:492; V4:226-32
pruning, receives general, V3:155, 162
publications of, V5:308
publications to cease in, V5:194
vision taught contrary to instructions, V2:505
Woodruff, Wilford, account of success in, V4:122
work, progress of, V5:6
work, summary of, V4:390; V5:308
Young, Brigham, letter on affairs of, V4:125.
See also Apostles; Fielding, James; Fielding, Joseph; Hedlock, Reuben;
    Kimball, Heber C.; Latter-day Saints, Church of Jesus Christ of;
    Pratt, Orson; Pratt, Parley P.; Woodruff, Wilford.

Brittle, Captain, mentioned, V1:266.

Bronder, J., encourages Joseph to remain political candidate, V6:416.

Brook, Phebe, marries Sidney Rigdon, V1:121 ftnt only.

Brook, Richard, brother-in-law to Sidney Rigdon, V1:121, ftnt only.

Brooklyn, ship for California pioneers, V7:599.

Brooks, C., delegate to political convention in Nauvoo, V6:389.

Brooks, George, ordained teacher, V4:138.

Brooks, George W., Kirtland Camp, expelled from for failure to keep house
    in order, V3:128, 129
Kirtland Camp, subscribed to constitution of, V3:92
seventies, named to first quorum of, V2:203
tried for wife's use of tea and profane language, V3:127
Zions Camp member, V2:183.

Brooks, Lester, Church, appointed to preside over new district of, V7:305
Kirtland stake, councilor of, V4:361
mission and field of labor, V6:388.

Brooks, Thomas, given care of Church at Ryton, V4:135.

brothels, actions of Nauvoo City Council against, V7:248 and ftnt.

Brothers, W., mission and field of labor, V6:339.

Brotherton, Edward, publishes anti-Mormon literature, V6:154.

Brotherton, John, mentioned, V4:508.

Brotherton, Joseph, ordained elder, V4:333.

Brotherton, Theophilus, ordained elder, V4:333.

Brower, Brother, mentioned, V7:79.

Browett, Daniel, Church, given care of at south side of river Severn, V4:135

BROWETT, DANIEL (continued)

clerk of conference in England, V4:134
England, head of company sailing from, V4:297
mentioned, V4:147.

Brown, Abraham, baptized, V4:110, ftnt only.

Brown, Alanson, extradition of demanded by Governor Boggs, V4:198
high council, chosen to Adam-ondi- Ahman, V3:38
kidnapped by Missourians, V4:154-6, 180
larceny, expelled from Church for, V4:454.

Brown, Albert, Black, A., falsely accused of threatening, V3:64
Church, appointed to preside over new district of, V7:306
Joseph, pays money to, in hour of need, V2:327
meeting house, appointed to collect money to pay rent of, V1:342
Zions Camp member, V2:183.

Brown, Alfred, Joseph, on relief expedition for, V5:486
Kirtland Camp, subscribed to constitution of, V3:91
mission call and field of labor, V5:349; V6:338
mission in Illinois to disabuse public mind over arrest of Joseph, V5:485.

Brown, Benjamin, healed, Joseph commands to be, V4:4, ftnt only
mission in Illinois to disabuse public mind over arrest of Joseph, V5:485
Nova Scotia, missionary call to, V5:413.

Brown, E. L., chosen clerk of New Orleans branch, V6:176.

Brown, Ebenezer, discharged as innocent at Missouri trials, V3:211.

Brown, Eleazer, utility committee member to aid Church removal, V7:474.

Brown, Eliza, marriage of, V2:292.

Brown, Francis, petitions Governor Boggs on mob violence in DeWitt, V3:83.

Brown, Hannah, trial of for unchristianlike conduct, V2:442.

Brown, Harry, seventies, named to first quorum of, V2:204
Zions Camp member, V2:183.

Brown, Henry, appointed seventy, V2:208.

Brown, I., mentioned, V4:215.

Brown, Isaac, mentioned, V4:216.

Brown, James, Augusta, appointed presiding elder at, V5:318
Church, appointed to preside over new district of, V7:306
elder, appointed, V4:13
Kirtland Camp, subscribed to constitution of, V3:93
Legion, officer in, V4:582
mission call and field of labor, V5:370.

Brown, Jay, mentioned, V5:378, ftnt only.

Brown, John, Alabama, president of conference in, V6:210
mission call and field of labor, V5:349
mission, reports, V7:253
Nauvoo Temple, appointed to officiate in, V7:548
southern states, work of, in Kentucky, Tennessee and Alabama, V7:253.

Brown, Judge, mentioned, V5:449.

Brown, Pelatiah, beasts in heaven, ideas of, V5:340-1
Church, appointed to preside over district of, V7:305
mission appointment, V5:337.

Brown, Samuel, confession of, V2:138
mission call and field of labor, V5:348
mission in Illinois to disabuse public mind over arrest of Joseph,
V5:485
Nauvoo, delegate to political convention in, V6:389
priesthood taken, V2:137
seventies, named to first quorum of, V2:203
voting, attacked by Richard Welding while, V3:57
Zions Camp member, V2:183.

Brown, Samuel C., Joseph, gives gold watch, V5:288
mission and field of labor, V5:349.

Brown, Sheriff, mentioned, V3:360-1.

Brown, Thomas, mentioned, V6:72.

Brown, Uriah, mentioned, V5:210
Nauvoo, chairman of state convention at, V6:386.

Brown, William, elder, ordained, V5:349
mission call and field of labor, V5:348.

Brown, William, constable, signed mob manifesto, V1:376.

Brownell, John, Zions Camp member, V2:183.

Browning, J., delegate to political convention in Nauvoo, V6:389.

Browning, O. H., lawyer for the Prophet at Monmouth trial, V4:367, et seq
murderers, attorney for defense of, of Joseph, V7:50.

Bruce, Mr., testifies before high council, V2:137.

Bruce, Major, mentioned, V2:67, ftnt only.

Bruce, Vernon H., mentioned, V6:274
policeman in Nauvoo, V6:150.

Brunel, J. M., mentioned, V4:402.

Brunett, Jason, subscribed to constitution of Kirtland Camp, V3:92.

Brunson, Seymour, Cowdery, Oliver, charges against, V3:16
    death of, V4:179
    marriage, performs, V2:292
    mentioned, V2:481; V4:39
    Nauvoo High Council, appointed to, V4:12
    witness, suggested to appear before Congress on redress, V4:97.

Bryant, Mr., mentioned, V3:172; V6:236.

Bryon, Thomas O., member of Haun's Mills mob and clerk of Livingston
    County, V3:186.

Buchanan, John, Missouri, arraigned for treason, murder, burglary, arson,
    robbery and larceny at Richmond, V3:209
    trials, discharged as innocent from Missouri, V3:211.

Buchannan, Peter, seventies, named to first quorum of, V2:203
    Zions Camp member, V2:183.

Buckmaster, Colonel, mentioned, V7:22.

buffetings of Satan, eternal life, once sealed to and sin turned over to, V1:323
    members and others turned over to, V3:232
    Peterson, Ziba, turned over to, V1:367
    sacrament, Brother Draper turned over to for leaving meetings before,
    V2:326.
    See also devil.

Bull, Norman, Mrs., letter to Joseph, concern for saints shown, V3:285.

Bullock, Thomas, Church, statement as to original members of, V1:76, ftnt
    only.
    Joseph, clerk to, V6:88
    mentioned, V5:299.

Bulware, John, mentioned, V3:78.

Bump, Jacob, Kirtland Temple, blessing for work on, V2:205
    mob, leads in Kirtland against Church, V7:484
    Zions Camp, exonerates Joseph's actions in, V2:149.

Bunnel, Sister, mentioned, V2:146.

Burbanks, Daniel M., account of *Maid of Iowa* expedition to relieve Joseph,
    V5:482.

Burch, Thomas C., Joseph, persecution at trial of, V1:92
    saints, prosecutor of, in Missouri trials, V3:209.

Burdick, Alden, seventies, named to first quorum of, V2:203
    Zions Camp member, V2:183.

Burdick, Thomas, affliction, Joseph rebukes, V2:301-2
    bishop at Kirtland, V4:362

BURDICK, THOMAS (continued)

    clerk, chosen, V2:243, 400
    high council, appointment, V2:522
    Kirtland Temple, blessing for work on, V2:205.

Burge, Richard, counselor to bishop at New York branch, V4:344.

Burgess, Harrison, seventies, named to first quorum of, V2:204
    Zions Camp member, V2:183.

Burgess, Horace, elder, ordained, V2:207
    Kirtland Temple, blessing for work on, V2:206.

Burgess, James, mentioned, V6:404.

Burgess, William, deacons, acts as president of, V2:244
    Doctrine and Covenants, testifies to truthfulness of, V2:246
    Joseph, exonerates actions of, in Zions Camp, V2:149
    Kirtland Temple, blessing for work on, V2:206.

Burghard, John H., assaulted, V5:317.

Burk, John M., Iowa Territory High Council, appointed to, V4:12
    Missouri persecutions, affidavit concerning, V4:56
    saints, signs Memorial of, in Missouri, V3:224
    witness, suggested to appear before Congress on redress, V4:97.

Burke, Brother, mentioned, V1:370.

Burke, Edmond, mentioned, V6:94, ftnt only.

Burkdall, Mr., settle differences or will be excommunicated, V2:228.

Burket, Mr., (also spelled Burghart), Zions Camp stops in field of, V2:112
    and ftnt.

Burkett, Brother, mentioned, V1:362-3.

Burnes, John, volunteers for service in vineyard, V4:217.

Burnett, Francis, mentioned, V4:140.

Burnett, Irenas, conference of October 25, 1831, held at, V1:219.

Burnett, Stephen, mission appointment, V1:245.

Burnham, Jacob L., mission and field of labor, V6:340.

Burnham, James, death of, V5:309
    England, letter on gospel in and opposition, V4:297
    Missouri, covenanted to assist saints in removing from, V3:252.

burnings, everlasting, V6:366
    righteous to dwell in everlasting, V6:306.

Burns, James, given care of Church at Ridgway Cross, V4:138.

Burns, John, mentioned, V4:217.

Burroughs, Philip, mentioned, V1:116.

Burton, Brother, mentioned, V3:319.

Burton, George, ordained teacher, V4:135.

Burton, Isaac, mission and field of labor, V6:335.

Burton, William, prophecy, present in Missouri at Apostles' departure to fulfill, V3:339
 Twelve, appointed to go to England with, V3:347.

Busard, Phillip Hammond, ordained high priest, V7:312.

Bush, C., publishes anti-Mormon literature, V4:255.

Bushaw, James, mentioned, V4:324.

Bushnell, Mr., mentioned, V3:270-1.

Bushnell, Esquire, mentioned, V4:468.

Bushnell, Henry N., mentioned, V4:267.

Butler, Mr., mentioned, V7:540.

Butler, Mr., disfellowshipped for following false revelation, V2:525.

Butler, Charles, covenanted to assist saints in moving from Missouri, V3:253.

Butler, Jemima, disfellowshipped for following false revelations, V2:525.

Butler, John L., Black, A., falsely accused of threatening, V3:65
 fireman, V7:554
 Joseph, on mission to rescue, V5:451
 mission and field of labor, V5:348
 mission in Illinois to disabuse public mind over arrest of Joseph, V5:485
 mob, resists, V3:58
 Nauvoo, policeman in, V6:150
 Nauvoo Temple, to administer in, December 27, 1845, V7:555
 Nauvoo Temple, appointed to officiate in, V7:548
 protects members from mob at voting incident, V3:57-8.

Butler, John S., bodyguard to Joseph's body on return to Nauvoo, V7:135
 rebaptized, V7:495.

Butler, L. D., mission and field of labor, V6:338

Butterfield, Abel, mission call in Illinois to disabuse public mind over arrest of Joseph, V5:485.

Butterfield, Benjamin, Kirtland Camp, deserts, V3:103, 108
 Kirtland Camp, returns to, V3:108
 Kirtland Camp, subscribed to constitution of, V3:92.

Butterfield, Jacob H., mission call in Illinois to disabuse public mind over arrest of Joseph, V5:485.

Butterfield, Joseph, mentioned, V4:501.

Butterfield, Josiah, arrested for Joseph Young, V3:108
    excommunicated for getting money and lifted up, V7:297
    Kirtland Camp, of first council of seventy, presides over meeting, V3:93
    Kirtland Camp, subscribed to constitution of, V3:91
    Kirtland Temple, blessing for work on, V2:205
    mission and field of labor, V6:335
    Missouri, covenanted to assist saints in removing from, V3:252.
    Prophet, insults and results, V5:316
    seventies, sustained president of, V2:510.

Butterfield, Justin, extradition, legal opinion of, on proceedings against
        Joseph, V5:173, et seq
    extradition, summary of argument for Joseph before court during trial
        of Joseph, V5:221
    Joseph, letter to, discharged from Missouri warrants if pursue court
        remedy, V5:206
    Prophet, counsel for at Springfield trial, V5:215-23.

Butterfield, Thomas, Kirtland Camp, subscribed to constitution of, V3:92
    Missouri, covenants to assist saints in removing from, V3:252.

Buys, H. D., mission and field of labor, V6:338.

Buzzard, P. H., mission and field of labor, V6:340.

Byers, John, killed at Haun's Mills massacre, V3:186.

Byington, Hirum H., child dies, V3:124
    Kirtland Camp, leaves, V3:140
    Kirtland Camp, subscribed to constitution of, V3:91.

Byrrs (family), mentioned, V7:143.

Byur, David, Zions Camp member, V2:183.

—C—

Cahoon, Andrew, MIA, aids in movement toward, V5:321.

Cahoon, Daniel F., Joseph, on mission to rescue, V5:451.

Cahoon, Larona, marriage to Harvey Stanley, V2:376.

Cahoon, Pulaski S., grog shop of removed, V4:442.

Cahoon, Reynolds, children, sanctioned before high council for failure to
        correct and properly instruct, V2:242
    elders, appointed to obtain money to build school house for, V1:343
    endowment, receives in Nauvoo Temple, V7:543
    Joseph, accompanies in arrest, V4:365
    Joseph, accuses of cowardice for leaving, V6:549, 552

CAHOON, REYNOLDS (continued)

Kirtland, sustained as counselor to bishop at, V2:509
Kirtland Temple, blessing for work on, V2:205
M'Lellin, William, converts, V1:220, ftnt only
meetings, appointed to instruct on how to conduct, V1:219
Montrose High Council, member of, V4:16
Nauvoo, bodyguard to Joseph's body on return to, V7:135
revelation, chastisement by, V2:299
stake of Zion, first counselor of, V3:28
westward movement, captain of sixth company in, V7:482
westward movement, counselor in, V7:626.

Cahoon, Thirza, receives endowment in Nauvoo Temple, V7:543.

Cahoon, William F., abuses child, V1:219
Joseph, pays money to in hour of need, V2:327
marriage to Maranda Gibbs, V2:376
mission call, V1:332
Missouri, affidavit concerning sufferings in, V4:52
Nauvoo Temple, appointed carpenter, V7:326
seventies, named to first quorum of, V2:204
Zions Camp member, V2:183.

Cain, atonement, offering of rejected for lack of faith in, V2:15
cursed, sacrifice rejected and, V4:208-9
Negro, son of, V4:501
sacrifice, offered wrong and therefore no faith, V2:15.

Cain, Joseph, mentioned, V7:79-80.

Cairnes, John, (also spelled Cairns), Church, represents branches of, V6:327
high priest, ordained, V5:405
mission call to England, V5:386
mission call and field of labor, V5:370.

calamities, recorded up to June of 1843, V5:433.

Calbert, Mr., stabs another man, V2:98.

Caldwell, Mr., messenger to Governor Boggs, no assistance for saints, V3:157.

Caldwell, A. L., petitions Governor Boggs on mob violence in DeWitt, V3:83.

Caldwell County, Missouri, Far West, meeting of citizens at, V3:55
saints, formed by, V2:468.

Calhoun, John C., Prophet, interview with, V4:80
saints, letter of Joseph on feelings toward, V6:64
saints, letter to Joseph on feelings toward if elected, V6:155.

California, Church, movement to, considered, V7:350
    ship, company to go by, V7:588.

Calkins, Israel, bishop, appointed, V5:119
    bishop, sustained, of Nauvoo ward, V7:298.

Calkins, Luman H., mission call and field of labor, V5:349
    mission in Illinois to disabuse public mind over arrest of Joseph,
    V5:485
    Nauvoo, affidavit on conspiracy in, against Joseph, V6:531.

Call, Anson, Kirtland Camp, suscribed to constitution of, V3:91
    Missouri, covenanted to assist saints in removing from, V3:252
    mob, attempts to regain property, beaten by, V3:242, 245
    Nauvoo committee, affidavit on treatment by Levi Williams, V6:505
    Rocky Mountain prophecy, statement on, V5:85-6, ftnt only
    truth, delegate to present, to public, V6:483.

calling, of apostles expounded, V2:200.

calling and election, doctrine explained with Spirit of Elijah, V6:252
    explained, V5:402
    make sure, V5:388
    received by sure word of prophecy, V5:388.

Cameron, Elisha, appointed by public to assist saints in removal from
    Zion, V2:455.

Cameron, John, at anti-Mormon meeting, V5:537.

Cameron, Judge, persecutes saints, V3:243.

Campbell, Mr., mentioned, V5:444; V6:75.

Campbell, Alexander, Haun's Mill, killed by mob at, V3:326, ftnt only
    Kirtland Camp, subscribed to constitution of, V3:93.

Campbell, Alexander, debate, Joseph challenges to public, V2:269
    The Disciples, founder of, V1:121, ftnt only
    Joseph, assaults as wicked sorcerer, V2:268-9 and ftnt
    Rigdon, Sidney, relations with, V1:120, ftnt only.

Campbell, James, drowned in crossing Missouri, V2:100
    mob, carries proposals to saints from, V1:398
    prophesies destruction of Joseph and seals own fate, V2:99.

Campbell, Maria L., mentioned, V6:176.

Campbell, Robert, reporter, V6:497.

Campbell, Robert L., statement on original members of Church, V1:76,
    ftnt only.

Campbell, Thomas, signs proposition to buy lands of saints, V2:96-7.

Campbell, William M., offers resolutions to Missouri Senate, V3:246, ftnt only.

Campbellite Church, bitter spirit of, V1:188
founders, Reverend Walter Scott one of, V1:188
Hyde, Orson, member of, V1:218, ftnt only
Pratt, Parley P., member of, V1:119, ftnt only
Rigdon, Sidney, member of, V1:121, ftnt only.

Camron, Elisha, witness for state in Missouri trials of saints, V3:210.

Canada, British provinces, report of missionary work in, V7:317
Joseph on annexation of, V6:244
Joseph, journey of through upper, V1:421
mission opened to, V1:416-22
rumors of war in, V3:117 and ftnt
Wesleyan Methodist, opposed at Colburn by, V1:421.

Canadian Camp, proceedings of, to Zion, V3:27, 48, 85.

Candland, David, clerk, V7:554
mission appointment to England, V7:562
mission and field of labor, V6:340.

Canfield, Cyrus, mission in Illinois to disabuse public mind over arrest of Joseph, V5:485
Missouri, affidavit concerning threats of invasion from, V6:502
witness in *Expositor* trial of Joseph, V6:457-8.

Canfield, Samuel, elder, ordained, V2:208
Kirtland Temple, blessing for work on, V2:206.

Cannon, Agnus M., mentioned, V4:556, ftnt only.

Cannon, Dr., mentioned, V7:399.

Cannon, George, father-in-law to John Taylor, grandfather to George Q. Cannon, V3:155, ftnt only.

Cannon, George Q., mentioned, V1:324, ftnt only; V3:155, ftnt only.

Cannon, Leonora, wife of John Taylor, V3:155, ftnt only.

Cantrell, Mr., mob member in Missouri, V1:480.

Cantwell, J. S., English conference, clerk of, V6:327.

Capron, Henry, visits Joseph, V2:322.

Carey, William, Kirtland Camp, subscribed to constitution of, V3:93
mob, wounded and taken prisoner by, V3:182
wounds, dies of, V3:190.

Carigan, James, represents British conference, V5:419.

Carl, John, mentioned, V6:163.

Carlin, Edward, mission and field of labor, V6:339.

Carlin, Thomas, governor of Illinois, issues order for arrest of Joseph, V4:198-9

    illegal, acknowledges proceedings against Joseph, V5:91

    letter to Joseph on Bennett affairs, V5:49

    letter to Joseph on Bennett problems, V5:82

    letter to Emma Smith on Joseph's difficulties in Missouri, V5:130

    letter to Emma Smith on Nauvoo's powers, V5:153

    opinion of, on Mormon situation, designs of, V5:118-9

    proclamation of, in Joseph's Springfield trial, V5:236

    Relief Society, petitions for protection, V5:146-7

    saints, aids, V3:310-1; V4:108.

Carlin, Thomas, recommends Brother Green to collect for poor, V3:348.

Carmichael, William, Nauvoo Temple, appointed carpenter on, V7:326

    priests quorum, chosen counselor of, V6:175.

Carn, Daniel, mentioned, V6:165.

Carnes, Daniel, Joseph, on relief expedition for, V5:486.

Carns, John, anti-Mormon committee member of Warsaw meeting, V6:464.

Carns, John, mission and field of labor, V5:349.

Carpenter, Brother, mentioned, V2:52, 162.

Carpenter, Mr., mentioned, V2:291.

Carpenter, Sister, death, prophecy concerning false, V3:163.

Carpenter, John, Zions Camp member, V2:183.

Carpenter, S. E., mission and field of labor, V6:337.

Carpenter, William, Kirtland Camp, subscribed to constitution of, V3:92.

Carpenters' Hall, England, leased by the saints in, V4:141.

Carr, Nathaniel, witness for state in Missouri trials of saints, V3:210.

Carrico, Thomas, (also spelled Carico), child of dies, V3:125

    House of Lord, appointed doorkeeper to, V2:367

    Joseph, on relief expedition for, V5:482

    Kirtland Camp, mentioned in, V3:142

    marriage to Elizabeth Baker, V2:369.

Carrier, Daniel, mentioned, V4:505.

Carrington, Albert, mentioned, V7:581

    Seventies Library and Institute Association, elected trustee of, V7:328.

Carroll, James, (also spelled Carrol, Caroll), Church, expelled from, V7:376
    mission amidst mob action in Missouri, V3:153
    mission and field of labor, V5:349; V6:339
    mission in Illinois to disabuse public mind over arrest of Joseph, V5:485
    Missouri, covenanted to assist saints in removing from, V3:252.

Carter, Brother, letter to, from Joseph, V1:338-40.

Carter, Angeline, receives partiarchial blessing, V2:387.

Carter, Daniel, Adam-ondi-Ahman High Council, chosen to, V3:38
    Church, to preside over new district of, V7:306.

Carter, Dominicus, daughter of dies, V3:125
    Kirtland Camp, accompanies leaders of, to prison, V3:109
    Kirtland Camp, subscribed to constitution of, V3:92
    Legion, martial band member of, V7:135
    mission and field of labor, V5:347; V6:336.

Carter, Elder, mentioned, V7:260.

Carter, Gideon H., killed at Crooked River by mob, V3:170
    Kirtland, in council at, V1:388
    presidency, on council to try, V2:484.

Carter, Jared, Church, confesses and asks to return to, V7:271
    confession, sentenced to public, V2:280
    elders, appointed to obtain money to build a school house for, V1:342
    high council, appointed to, at Far West, V3:14
    high council, ordained to, at Kirtland, V2:511
    high council, sustained to Kirtland, V2:281, 510
    high council, trial before erring in speech and not adhering to council of authorities, V2:277
    Kirtland Temple, blessing for work on, V2:205
    mission appointment to Canada, V2:35
    mission in Illinois to disabuse public mind over arrest of Joseph, V5:485
    Missouri persecutions, expresses faith in work after, V3:225
    presidency, on council to try, V2:484.

Carter, Joanna, witness to apostate vandalizing of saints' homes, V3:288.

Carter, Johanna, receives patriarchal blessing, V2:387.

Carter, John, Kirtland Camp, subscribed to constitution of, V3:93
    Zions Camp, preaches at meeting of, V2:78 and ftnt.

Carter, John S., (also C.), cholera, died attempting to rebuke judgment of, V2:115
  mission appointment to East, V2:35
  Zions Camp member, V2:183

Carter, Luman, Kirtland Temple, blessing for work on, 2:206
  teaches music, V2:474.

Carter, Marietta, receives patriarchal blessing, V2:387.

Carter, Nancy, receives patriarchal blessing, V2:388.

Carter, Phebe W., wife of Wilford Woodruff, V3:337, ftnt only.

Carter, S., mission and field of labor, V6:339.

Carter, Samuel P., ordained elder, V5:349.

Carter, Sarah Emily, Kirtland Camp, dies in, V3:125.

Carter, Simeon, Church, appointed to preside over new district of, V7:306
  committee, on meeting conducting, V1:219
  endowments, called to go to Kirtland to receive, V2:113
  general assembly, regards action at Far West as hasty, V3:5
  high council, sustained member of Far West, V2:523
  high council, sustained member of Missouri, V2:124
  Hulet Branch, mission to, V2:139, et seq
  Missouri, affidavit on sufferings in, V4:49
  Missouri, appointed branch president in, V1:409, ftnt only
  Missouri persecutions, expresses faith in work after, V3:225.

Carter, William, Kirtland Temple, blessing for work on, V2:206
  Legion, martial band member of, V7:135
  sight, bless with, if faithful, V2:207.

Carter's Settlement, assembly of saints, V3:5.

Carthage, Hancock County, affair, disgraceful at, V6:171-3; V7:83
  anti-Mormon convention at, V6:221
  anti-Mormon meeting at, V6:4 and ftnt, 43
  assassins at, V7:422
  Joseph, reaction of citizens at death of, V7:108, et seq
  mob, list of names from, V7:143
  mob, threats of violence at, V5:528
  murderers, trial of, and nature of court proceedings, V7:420 and ftnt
  Nauvoo ordinances, complaints of citizens against, V6:173-4
  press opinions on assassination of Joseph and Hyrum at, V7:177
  Taylor and Bernhisel, agitation of, at, V7:72
  "wolf hunt," citizens call for, V6:222.

Carthage Greys, arrest of, ordered, V7:84

CARTHAGE GREYS (continued)

Carthage jail, appointed to guard, V7:17
Carthage jail, to guard Joseph and, V6:606-7; V7:100
Carthage jail, selection to guard, V7:18
conduct of, at arrival of Joseph in Carthage, V6:559-60; V7:83-4 and ftnts
Joseph, party in massacre of, V7:143
Joseph, revolt upon seeing, V6:564
martyrdom, communication with conspirators in, V7:31
martyrdom, roll in, V7:142.

Carthage jail, assault upon, V7:30, 102
attack, Governor Ford disclaims fears of, on, V7:13
Carthage Greys, left to guard Joseph and, V6:606-7
Carthage Greys, reasons for using to guard, V7:17, et seq
Joseph, testimony of, while in, V6:610
prisoners' defense within, V7:102
wine, obtained for inmates in, V7:101.

Cartwright, Mrs., dies by drowning at baptism, V6:160-2.

Cartwright, Thomas, baptized and story of wife's drowning at her baptism, V6:160, et seq.

Case, Nathaniel, petitions to hear Joseph speak, V6:533.

Casper, J. A., mission and field of labor, V6:339.

Casper, Thomas D., affidavit of, concerning Missouri persecutions, V4:63.

Cass, Lewis, mentioned, V6:144
saints, letter on feelings toward, V6:65
United States, reply to saints' petition to, V1:493.

Cassel, Frederick, Kirtland Camp, mentioned in, V3:108.

Castell, J. J., mission and field of labor, V6:338.

Casto, Abel, confirmed member, V4:13.

Cathcart, Daniel, mission and field of labor, V5:348
Missouri, covenanted to assist saints in removing from, V3:254
Zions Camp member, V2:183.

Catherwood, Mr., mentioned, V5:44.

Catholic Apostolic Church, formal name of Irvingites, V2:233, ftnt only.

Catholic Church, Jews, proscription against, V5:434
Nauvoo, interest in purchasing lands in, V7:537, 565
Nauvoo, representatives of, visit and inquire on property sale, V7:539
Nauvoo Temple, inspects, V7:539.

Catlin, Mr., mentioned, V3:382.

Catlin, Joel, anti-Mormon committee member of Warsaw meeting, V6:464
 martyrdom mob, farmer, member of, V7:144.

Caton, John D., mentioned, V5:444, 447.

Cavanaugh, Sister, excommunicated from Church, V3:336.

Celestial Kingdom, adultery, cannot receive if commit, V6:81
 all will receive who have died if they would have received it, V2:380
 Joseph sees, V2:380
 Joseph sees presidency in, V2:382
 Smith, Alvin, seen in, V2:380
 three degrees in, V5:392, 402, 426.

certificate, of George C. Anderson on retention of people in Nauvoo, V6:553.

Chamberlain, Brother, V6:196; V7:522.

Chamberlain, Mr., V5:443.

Chamberlain, Joseph, justice of the peace, Joseph arraigned before, V1:95, ftnt only.

Chamberlin, George, (also spelled Chamberlain), mission and field of labor, V6:337
 mission in Illinois to disabuse public mind over arrest of Joseph, V5:485.

Chambers, Mr., Governor of Iowa, mentioned, V6:421.

Champlin, Alonzo, Zions Camp member, V2:183.

Chandler, Michael H., Egyptian mummies, displays, V2:235
 Joseph brings Book of Abraham to, for translation, V2:236
 Joseph, certificate to, V2:235
 mummies, gets story of, V2:349, et seq.

Chaos, emigrant ship, V4:441.

Chapin, Brother, mentioned, V1:363

Chapin, Catherine, mother of D. H. Wells, V4:154, ftnt only.

Chapin, David, grandfather of D. H. Wells, V4:155, ftnt only.

Chapman, Abigail Chase, mother-in-law of Freeman Nickerson, V1:416, ftnt only.

Chapman, Delmore, affidavit on kidnapping of Daniel Avery, V6:100.

Chapman, Eliphalet, father-in-law of Freeman Nickerson, V1:416, ftnt only.

Chapman, Huldah, marries F. Nickerson, V1:416, ftnt only.

Chapman, Isaac B., covenanted to assist saints in removing from Missouri, V3:252.

Chapman, Jacob, Kirtland Camp, mentioned in, V3:122
    seventies, named to first quorum of, V2:203
    Zions Camp member, V2:183.

Chapman, John, mentioned, V7:547.

Chapman, Welcome, Joseph, on relief expedition for, V5:482
    Missouri, covenanted to assist saints in removing from, V3:252.

Chapplin, William, witness suggested to appear before Congress on redress, V4:97.

characters, Book of Mormon, in Egyptian, Chaldaic, Assyric, Arabic, V1:20
    copies, plates from, V1:19.

Chardon, Geauga County, Ohio, Rigdon, Sidney, moves to, V1:265.

charges, false against saints refuted, V1:376-7, ftnt only.

Chariton County, committee of, inquiry from, V3:73-4
    committee report concerning DeWitt problem, V3:151.

Charles, James, constable of Hancock County, V6:504.

Charles, John F., mentioned, V4:477; V6:133.

Chartists, religion of, explained, V4:508, ftnt only.

charts, Richards, Willard, phrenological chart of, V5:58-60
    Smith, Joseph, phrenological chart of, V5:52-5.

Chase, Brother, mentioned, V4:510; V5:317.

Chase, Mr., priesthood taken because of gambling for money, V2:241.

Chase, Amos, affidavit on attempted retaking of John Elliott, V6:121.

Chase, Darwin, delegate to present truth to public, V6:483
    jail, charges against, dismissed, V3:334
    jail, placed in, at Richmond to stand trial for murder and treason, V3:212
    Joseph, accompanies in arrest, V4:366
    mission and field of labor, V6:338
    Missouri, arraigned for treason, murder, burglary, arson, robbery and larceny at Richmond, V3:209
    prophecy, present in Missouri at Apostles' departure to fulfill, V3:339
    seventy, ordained, V3:338.

Chase, Eli, refuses aid to Church, V6:54.

Chase, Ezra, mission call in Illinois to disabuse public mind over arrest of Joseph, V5:485.

Chase, Francis, covenanted to assist saints in removing from Missouri, V3:253.

Chase, George M., mission and field of labor, V5:349.

Chase, Isaac, mission and field of labor, V6:336
  missionary call to Eastern states, V5:413.

Chase, Jesse, mission call in Illinois to disabuse public mind over arrest of Joseph, V5:485.

Chase, John D., Church, appointed to preside over new district of, V7:306
  mission and field of labor, V5:348; V6:336.

Chase, Levi R., prepares harvest feast in Nauvoo, V7:437.

Chase, Sission A., affidavit on D. Avery kidnapping, V6:109.

Chase, Stephen, elders quorum, ordained president of, in Far West, V3:155
  high council, appointed to Iowa Territory, V4:12.

Cheese, John, Churches, given charge of, at Stokes Lane, Woferwood Common, Bishop Froome, V4:139
  counselor on sailing from England, V4:297
  mentioned, V4:138.

Cheney, Brother, mentioned, V5:431.

Cheney, Aaron, Kirtland Camp, dissents against, V3:138
  Kirtland Camp, subscribed to constitution of, V3:93.

Cheney, Amasa, subscribed to constitution of Kirtland Camp, V3:92.

Cheney, Echoed, asks assistance from Church, V3:261.

Cheney, Elijah, Kirtland Camp, overtakes near Dayton, Ohio, V3:127
  Kirtland Camp, subscribed to constitution of, V3:92.

Cheney, Nathan, Kirtland Camp, dissents against, V3:138
  Kirtland Camp, subscribed to constitution of, V3:93
  Missouri, covenanted to assist saints in removing from, V3:254.

Cheney, Orin, subscribed to constitution of Kirtland Camp, V3:92.

Cherry, E., Kirtland Camp, mentioned in, V3:136.

Cherry, William, false report corrected, V2:161
  Zions Camp, drills, V2:88, ftnt only
  Zions Camp member, V2:183.

Chicago Democrat, arrest, account of Joseph's in, V5:448-9
  Wentworth letter, written for, V4:535, et seq.

Chidester, Eunice, daughter of John M. Chidester, Zions Camp member, V2:185.

Chidester, John M., Zions Camp member, V2:183.

Chidester, John P., son of John M. Chidester, Zions Camp member, V2:185.

Chidester, Mary, Zions Camp member, V2:185.

children, age of accountability, die before saved, V2:381
    baptism of, not scriptural, V4:554
    death of, V6:316
    good, to be taught, V1:276
    gospel, duty of those who embrace, V2:262
    parents, should not persuade them contrary to, V2:247
    parents, stay with and obey, V2:247
    parents, to be taught after, V2:262
    parents, unruly reported to, V2:520
    properly instruct, failure to, brings charges before high council, V2:242
    resurrection of, V4:556 and ftnt
    resurrection and salvation of, V4:553, et seq
    training properly, David Elliott reproved for not, V2:295.

Childs, Captain, mentioned, V3:81.

Childs, Mr., member of Missouri Legislature, speech of against the saints, V3:238-9.

Childs, Alden, Zions Camp member, V2:183.

Childs, Alford P., covenanted to assist saints in removing from Missouri, V3:253.

Childs, Mark, kidnapper of saints, V6:122.

Childs, Nathaniel, mission and field of labor, V6:339
    Zions Camp member, V2:183.

Childs, Stephen, Zions Camp member, V2:183.

Chiles, Henry, anti-Mormon committee member, V1:399
    mentioned, V2:93, ftnt only
    mob manifesto, attorney at law, signed, V1:376
    saints, committee to rid Missouri of, V1:395
    saints, mobber in militia, appointed to receive arms of, V1:434.

Chiles, Joel F., mob, carries proposals to saints from, V1:398
    saints, on committee to rid Missouri of, V1:395.

China earthquake, convert, brings, V1:158 and ftnt
    floods, reports of, V7:379.

Chipley, William B., doctor, member of martyrdom mob, V7:144.

Chipman, Ezra, witness for defense of saints in Missouri, intimidated, V3:211.

Chipman, H. T., petitions Governor Boggs on mob violence in DeWitt, V3:83.

Chism, Mr., Negro, case of whipping, V6:281, 284.

Chittendens, Brothers, Joseph, plot to kill, V7:163
 martyrdom mob, different occupations, members of, V7:144.

cholera, dies attempting to rebuke judgment of, John S. Carter, V2:115
 effects, remedy for, discovered, V2:119
 Joseph, rejected by household and disease attacks, and kills, V2:115
 Joseph, stayed at command of, V2:120
 pestilence which God rules, V1:282
 prediction concerning, V2:80
 ravages of, V1:301
 results summarized, V2:120
 victims, names of those who nursed, V2:120
 Zions Camp, God uses as judgment upon for evil, V2:114.

Christ, Church of, organized by apostate group of Church, V2:528.

Christ, Church of Jesus, see Latter-day Saints, Church of Jesus Christ of.

Christ, Jesus, Acts 3:22-23, prophet in, V1:13
 Adam, revealed to, V4:207
 advents of, V2:52
 birthday of (D&C § 20:1), V1:64
 Church, early of, displaced by churches of men, IntroV1:LXXXVII
 Church, establishment of ancient by, IntroV1:XXVI
 Coltrin, Zebedee, sees, V2:387
 created all things, V4:257
 devil, rebuked in name of, V1:83
 died, date of, V1:337
 false teachings, rise of, in early Church, IntroV1:XLVII, et seq
 Father, did as, had done, V5:426
 foreseen by some, V2:382
 gospel, antiquity of, IntroV1:XXIII
 gospel, delivered to ancient people by, V1:12
 Jewish leaders' comments on, V3:357-9, ftnts only
 John, greater than, because, V5:258
 Joseph, announced to, V1:5
 Joseph sees and speaks to, V1:5
 kingdom, instructions on, V1:16
 Matthias, Robert, claims to be possessed of soul of, V2:307
 meekness and lowliness of explained, V5:218
 millennium, reign of, during described, V5:212

CHRIST, JESUS (continued)

Pilate, Pontius, statement of, condemning found, V4:420-1 and ftnt
priesthood, received ordination to, V4:257
resurrection overcomes temporal death, V2:19
retranslated words of, on cross to thief, V5:424
revelation concerns advents of, V2:52
righteousness, takes some because of, V4:553
saints, ancient to reign with, during millennium, V2:53
Second Comforter, V3:381
second coming, false prediction of, exposed, V5:326
second coming, Joseph on, V5:336
seen by Newel Knight, V1:85
seen by many, March 18, 1833, V1:335
sign of, Joseph on, V5:290-1
sin, committed no, V2:23
virtue, leaves, explained, V5:303
Wight, Lyman, sees, V1:176, ftnt only.
See also doctrine; Latter-day Saints, Church of Jesus Christ of;
    Second Comforter; Smith, Joseph.

Christianity, apostasy, testimony of prophecy to from early, IntroV1:XCI
Church of Christ, displaced by churches of men, IntroV1:LXXXVII
conclusion of, IntroV1:XCIII
Constantine, before and after, IntroV1:LXVIII
Constantine, revolution of fourth century, IntroV1:LIV
corrupted early, becomes persecuting religion, IntroV1:LXI
Deity, departure of early from true doctrine of, IntroV1:LXXXIX
devil is hope of salvation of, V5:218
false doctrines, development of, after death of early apostles, Intro-
    V1:LII
false teachers, rise of, in early, IntroV1:XLVII
God, early doctrine of, IntroV1:LXXIX
God, paganization of early doctrine of, IntroV1:LXXXII
heretics, persecution by early, IntroV1:LXV
moral and spiritual living, decline in early, IntroV1:LXIX
spiritual gifts, loss in early, IntroV1:LXXVI.
See also doctrine; God; Smith, Joseph.

Christians, character of early discussed, IntroV1:XLI; V2:13.

Church, see Latter-day Saints, Church of Jesus Christ of.

Church court, council of high priests to try cases, V1:354.

Church, Haden W., mission of, V7:253.

Church publications, proceeds of devoted to the priesthood, V7:273

CHURCH PUBLICATIONS (continued)

for 1844, V7:345-6
for 1845, V7:558-9.

churches, official opinion of, not the gospel, V2:6
sectarian, all wrong, V1:6.

circular, for subscriptions to Kirtland Temple, V1:349.

Civil War, acts against Missouri in, vs. Retribution, IntroV3:LXII, et seq
prophecy of, (D&C § 87), V1:301.

Clapp, Benjamin L., genealogy of, V3:153 and ftnt
Joseph, on relief expedition for, V5:482
mission and field of labor, V5:347; V6:338
mission reports of the South, Kentucky, V3:153; V7:316
Nauvoo Temple, to administer in, V7:555
Nauvoo Temple, appointed to officiate in, V7:548
seventies, ordained president of, V7:538
seventies, sustained president of, to Church at Salt Lake City, V7:629.

Clapp, Matthew, mentioned, V2:270.

Clare, Moses, (also spelled Claire), appointed bishop's counselor, V4:236
delegate to present truth to public, V6:483.

Clark, Elder, mentioned, V3:325-6; V6:351.

Clark, Andrew, Baptist minister, V1:121, ftnt only.

Clark, Caroline, witness to apostate vandalizing of saints' homes, V3:288.

Clark, Daniel, petitions Governor Boggs on mob violence in DeWitt, V3:83.

Clark, Delecta, mother-in-law to Samuel Smith, V7:221.

Clark, Francis, represents branch of Church at English conference, V4:117, 147.

Clark, Gardner, bishop, appointed, V4:236
Nauvoo, prepares harvest feast in, V7:437
Smith, Samuel, father-in-law to, V7:221.

Clark, H., sails for British Mission, V7:324.

Clark, Hiram, (also spelled Hyrum), British Mission, mission in, V4:76, 149
emigration, appointed to take charge of, from England, V5:26
England, arrives in Preston, V4:45
England, ordained counselor in, V4:118
Joseph, petitions to hear, speak, V6:533
ministry, devote all time to labors of, V4:148
mission, assigned to go on, V4:429
mission, starts on, to England, V4:7

CLARK, HIRAM (continued)

 prophecy, present in Missouri at Apostles' departure to fulfill, V3:339
 Twelve, appointed to go to England with, V3:347
 volunteers for service in vineyard, V4:216.

Clark, Hugh, letter to V6:403-4.

Clark, Isaac, bishop's counselor, appointed, V4:233
 Church, appointed to preside over new district of, V7:305
 Church, utility committee member to aid removal of, V7:474.

Clark, James A., child of, dies, V3:136
 Kirtland Camp, expelled from, V3:130
 Kirtland Camp, mentioned in, V3:111.

Clark, Jesse, mobber in Missouri, V4:61.

Clark, John, Church, utility committee member to aid removal of, V7:474
 DeWitt, petitions Governor Boggs on mob violence in, V3:83.

Clark, John, mobber, requests members to join mob, V6:511.

Clark, John B., Boggs, Governor, receives instructions from, to
  expel people and punish leaders, V3:204, 426
 Boggs, Governor, report of crimes and proposed trial problems to,
  V3:206-7
 God, asks unknown to liberalize saints' beliefs, IntroV3:XLIX
 harangue of saints at Far West, invokes unknown God to help saints,
  V3:201-4
 major-general in Missouri militia, V3:65
 militia, ordered to raise to protect citizens, V3:173
 Missouri, false certificate on conduct of, in, V3:359, ftnt only
 Missouri, named as one of chief mobbers in, V3:327
 mob, endorses at DeWitt, V3:157
 prisoners, orders General Wilson to go to Adam-ondi-Ahman and
  arrest, V3:204
 Prophet, seeks to try by court-martial, V3:206.

Clark, John W., elder, ordained, V2:525
 prophecy, present in Missouri at Apostles' departure to fulfill, V3:339.

Clark, Joseph, affidavit concerning Missouri persecutions, V4:63.

Clark, Joseph C., Kirtland Camp, mentioned in, V3:106
 Kirtland Camp, subscribed to constitution of, V3:93.

Clark, Josiah, sickness rebuked, V2:321.

Clark, Leonard, covenanted to assist saints in removal from Missouri,
 V3:254.

Clark, Levira, second wife of Samuel Smith, V7:221.

Clark, Lorenzo, Missouri, covenanted to assist saints in removal from,
    V3:252
  Nauvoo, policeman in, V6:150.
Clark, Moses F., affiant to public proclamation on mob lies, V6:495.
Clark, Rodman, called on mission and field of labor, V5:349.
Clark, Thomas, Churches, given charge of, at Dunsclose, Old Starridge,
    Ashfield, Crowcut, V4:139
  elder, ordained, V4:138.
Clark, Timothy B., affidavit concerning Missouri persecutions, V4:58.
Clark, William, kidnaps Daniel Avery, V6:146.
Clark, William O., Joseph, gives to assist, V5:300
  mission and field of labor, V5:347; V6:340
  prophecy, present in Missouri at Apostles' departure to fulfill, V3:339
  Prophet, reproved by, V4:445.
Clark, Moses, Church, appointed to preside over new district of, V7:
    305
  high council, named to, at Lima, V5:427
  Missouri, arraigned for treason, murder, burglary, arson, robbery and
    larceny at Richmond, V3:209.
Clay, Cassius M., mentioned, V6:227.
Clay County, elections in, V2:137
  exiles flee to, V1:438
  high council, organized in, V2:122-3
  Mormons, petition of citizens to move out, V2:448
  saints, move from, V2:452-4
  saints, petition of citizens to accept move of, V2:454.
Clay, Henry, letter to Joseph, V6:376
  letter, Joseph's answer to, V6:376-7
  letter, requesting feelings toward saints, V6:65
  letters, use against, V7:116
  saints, receives history of persecutions of, V6:94.
Clayton, David, mentioned, V7:275.
Clayton, Elizabeth, to receive aid in emigrating from England, V5:412.
Clayton, Ruth, receives endowment in Nauvoo Temple, V7:544.
Clayton, William, Carlin, Governor, visit to, V5:118
  Carthage jail, letter on conditions in Nauvoo while Joseph in, V6:598
  Church, English conference, represents branch at, V4:117, 147, 148
  Church ministry, enters, V3:164
  clerk, appointed, V4:382; V6:263, 483

CLAYTON, WILLIAM (continued)

clerk, becomes Joseph's, V5:49

Dixon, attends court at, V6:350

endowment, receives, in Nauvoo Temple, V7:544

eternal life, sealed to, V5:391

Ford, Governor, letter of, comments on, V7:168

genealogy, V3:20 and ftnt

high council, appointed to, V4:352

Illinois, letter to *Times & Seasons* on Joseph's second trial in, V6:380-4

Joseph, accompanies for trial on Missouri warrants, V5:210

Joseph, declares gratefulness for aid rendered while in seclusion, V5:108

Joseph, secretly goes to inform of sheriff's movements, V5:97

Joseph, witness at *Expositor* trial of, V6:457

ministry, devote all time to labors of, V3:164; V4:148

mission in British Mission, V3:164; V4:7, 76, 149

musician, performs, V7:561

president, counselor to, in England, V3:20

Prophet, messenger to warn of impending arrest, V5:436, 438-9.

Clegg, Edward, ordained elder, V5:349.

Clegg, Edwin, called on mission and field of labor, V5:349.

Clements, Ada, Zions Camp member, V2:185.

Clements, Albert, Zions Camp member, V2:183.

Cleminson, John, clerk of general conference, V3:5

Far West, offered life if leave, V3:410

Missouri trials, witness for state in, V3:210

satan, turned over to buffetings of, and condemned as openly sinning against Jesus, V3:232

signs attempted whitewash of General Clark's activity, V3:360, ftnt only.

clergy, promote early religious zeal, V1:3

stand of, in Missouri, V1:372, ftnt only; 392; V2:3-4.

clerk, duty of, V1:298.

Cleveland, Isaac, blessing for work on Kirtland Temple, V2:206.

Cleveland, Rufas, mentioned, V3:362-3.

Cleveland, Sarah M., counselor in Relief Society, V4:552.

Clift, Robert, Church, given care of at Dymark, V4:135

Joseph, witness in *Expositor* trial of, V6:457.

Clothier, A. J., martial band member of Legion, V7:135.

Clough, David, blessing for work on Kirtland Temple, V2:206.

Clough, David, Sr., mission and field of labor, V6:335.

Cluff, David, approved for ordination, V2:400.

Clyde, George W., Joseph, leaves to rescue, V4:365
    policeman in Nauvoo, V6:150.

coal, discovered near Nauvoo, V4:493-4.

Coates, Jesse, petitions for militia to be called out against saints, V3:76.

Coates, Thomas, fined for beatings, V6:190.

Coats, R. J., clerk of New York conference, V5:352.

Cobb, Colonel, Indian speech of, V5:358-9.

Cobb, Mrs., sister-in-law to Martin Harris, to see translation, V1:21.

Cobb, James, witness for state in Missouri trials of saints, V3:210.

Cobridge, James, ordained priest, V4:118.

Coburn, Emily, baptized and confirmed, V1:87
    Church, efforts to prevent from joining, V1:87
    Knight, Newel, sister-in-law of, V1:87.

Cochran, William, mobber in Missouri, V4:66.

Cock Pit, Preston, England, preaching of Twelve in, V4:114.

Cocknu, F. G., issues permit for travel to saints, V3:210.

Coe, Joseph, apostasy of, V2:528
    high council, rejected as member of Kirtland, V2:510
    high council, speaks in, V2:34
    Kirtland Temple, blessing for work on, V2:206
    mission, leaves for, with Joseph, V1:188
    presidency, on high council to try, V2:484
    stake of Zion, ordained to purchase land for, V1:335
    Zion Temple, at dedication, V1:199.

Colburn, Thomas, ordained elder, V2:139.

Colburn Village, Canada, Prophet preaches in, V1:421.

Colby, Alanson, Zions Camp member, V2:183.

Cole, Brother, mentioned, V5:512.

Cole, Mr., school teacher, V6:65-6.

Cole, Barnet, Missouri, covenanted to assist saints in removing from,
    V3:254
    mob, severely beaten by, V1:483.

Cole, Calvin, tavern keeper, member of martyrdom mob, V7:144.

Cole, Elvira, treasurer of Relief Society, V4:567.

Cole, Joseph M., baptisms for dead, recorder for, V5:522.

COLE, JOSEPH M. (continued)

    letter informing of election returns threatened, V7:227

    mission and field of labor, V6:337.

Cole, Owen, affidavit concerning Missouri persecutions, V4:64.

Cole, Squire, attempts to publish false Book of Mormon, V1:76, ftnt only.

Cole, William, witnesses celestial phenomenon, V6:121.

Cole, Zera S., seventies, named to first quorum of, V2:204

    Zions Camp member, V2:183.

Coleman, William, ordained priest and given care of Church at Bran Green, V4:135.

Colesville Branch, conference at, first in Missouri, V1:199

    Missouri, arrives in, V1:191

    Missouri, removed to, V1:181, ftnt only

    Ohio, removed to, V1:173

    Thompson, settled at, V1:180 and ftnt

    Zion, Joseph helps establishment in, V1:196 and ftnt.

Colesville, Broome County, New York, baptism, efforts to prevent at, V1:87, 88

    Joseph, dream of visiting, V1:101

    Joseph returns to, unrecognized, V1:109

    Joseph, trial of, at, V1:92

    Joseph, visits in April, 1830, V1:81

    Knight, Joseph, Sr., from, V1:47

    mob, threatens branch at, V1:109

    work, opposition to, at, V1:86-7, 97.

Colfax, Schuyler, vice-president of United States mentioned, V3:168.

collections, Joseph on, V5:329.

Collins, James, proposition of Mormons addressed to, V2:122.

Colson, George, appointed to preside over new Church district, V7:306.

Colton, Andrew, mentioned, V6:333.

Colton, Philander, delegate to present truth to public, V6:483

    Joseph, on mission to rescue, V5:451.

Coltrin, Mr., mentioned, V6:172.

Coltrin, Graham, Church, appointed to preside over new district of, V7:305

    Church courts, accuses Anson Matthews before, of unfair dealings, V5:371

    elder, ordained, V4:13

    Joseph, on mission to rescue, V5:451

    mission and field of labor, V5:347; V6:339

COLTRIN, GRAHAM (continued)

    mission in Illinois to disabuse public mind over arrest of Joseph, V5:485.

Coltrin, John, father of Zebedee, V1:322, ftnt only.

Coltrin, M. J., delegate to political convention in Nauvoo, V6:389.

Coltrin, Sarah, mother of Zebedee, V1:322, ftnt only.

Coltrin, Zebedee, genealogy, V1:322 and ftnt
    high council, member of, V2:164
    Joseph, on mission to rescue, V5:451
    Kirtland stake, counselor of, V4:361
    mission, appointment to Canada, V2:35
    mission and field of labor, V5:347; V6:339
    mission in Illinois to disabuse public mind over arrest of Joseph, V5:485
    partiality, reprimanded for, V2:75
    Prophet, accompanies to New Portage, V2:50
    Prophet, blessed by, V2:51
    Savior, sees, V2:387
    seventies, named president of, V2:203
    tongues, speaks in, V1:323
    vision of Lord's host, V2:392
    Zions Camp member, V2:183.

Combs, Leslie, mentioned, V7:499.

"Come to Me," hymn by W. W. Phelps sung at dedication of Seventies Hall, V7:331.

Comer, John B., arrested for supplying mob and trial, V3:75-6.

Comfort, Simeon J., bishop's clerk, appointed, V4:233
    elder, appointed, V4:13.

commandment, Church, if knew all they would condemn one-half, V2:477
    write, attempt to, V1:226.

Commandments, Book of, first edition, number of copies made of, V1:222, ftnt only
    first edition, ordered printed, V1:270
    Joseph, appointed steward of, V1:236, ftnt only
    Joseph, dedicated by, V1:234
    testimony of the witnesses of, V1:226 and ftnt
    value and importance of, V1:235.
    See also Doctrine and Covenants.

committee, Senate Judiciary, Missouri saints, case of before, V4:81-8
    Nauvoo, citizens' resolutions before, V4:157-9

COMMITTEE (continued)

saints vs Missouri, report adverse of, on, V4:90-2.

common stock, plan of by false spirits, abandoned, V1:146, ftnt only.

compromise, several suggested by Governor Dunklin, V2:86.

Comstock brothers, two brothers, members of mob at Haun's Mills massacre, V3:325.

Comstock, Charles, anti-Mormon committee chairman, V6:8.

Comstock, Hiram, (also spelled Cumstock), mobber in Missouri, V4:68.

Comstock, Nehemiah, Haun's Mills massacre leader, V3:184, 412.

Condit, A. W., mission and field of labor, V6:339.

conference, accounts, general settlement of, proposed at, V7:475

Apostles, of Church in New York, sustain, V7:520-2

Apostles, give out appointments for, within United States, V6:334-5

Apostles, special of Church to place in proper place, V4:402-4

authorities, at Far West, sustaining and rejecting of, V2:522, et seq.

authorities, general, sustained at, V7:624

authorities, general, sustained at October 6, 1845, V7:458-63

Black River, V2:225

Boston, V5:268

Boston, Ralston Hall, of the Twelve, V6:11-30

British Mission, V4:114, et seq, 134

Burnett, I., held at home of, October 25, 1831, V1:219

Canada, Loborough, of Twelve at, V2:235

cases, no individual to be brought before, V4:109

Church, first of, V1:84

Church, of September 26, 1830, V1:115, et seq

Church, of January 2, 1831, V1:140

Church, of June 3, 1831, V1:175

Church, of October 1839 in Commerce, V4:12-4

Church, of October 1840, V4:204

Church, of April 1844, V6:287, et seq

Church, of October 6, 1844, V7:284, et seq

Church, of April 6, 1845, V7:391, et seq

Church, general of April 6, 1840, V4:105, et seq

Church, general of April 7, 1841, V4:336, et seq

Church, general of October 2, 1841, in Nauvoo, V4:423-9

Church, general of April 6, 1842, in Nauvoo, V4:583, et seq

Church, general, minutes of April 6, 1843, V5:327, et seq

Church, general of April 6, 1848, V7:624

Church, name of adopted at, V2:62 and ftnt

Church, officers of, sustained at October 6, 1844, V7:294, et seq

CONFERENCE (continued)

Church, special at Nauvoo, August 29, 1842, to defend, V5:136
Commerce, minutes of, at, V4:12, et seq
disputes of elders held September 8, 1834, to hear, V2:162-3
England, of Church in, October 6, 1840, V4:214, et seq
England, first in, V2:529
England, Gadfield Elm, V4:131, 134, et seq
England, Liverpool, general at, V6:326-30
England, London, of February 14, 1841, V4:298
England, London, minutes of, V4:360
England, Manchester, V5:21
England, Manchester, of Church at, V4:146, et seq
England, Manchester, minutes of, V6:2
England, Manchester, minutes of June 4, 1843, V5:418-9
England, Preston, V3:20
England, reports members, V5:9-10
England, Stanley Hall, minutes, V4:138, et seq
Far West, of April 1838, V3:13-4
Far West, first quarterly at, V3:14-5
Far West, quarterly at, V3:152, 155
first, gifts of Holy Ghost manifest at, V1:85
first, Holy Ghost witnessed at, V1:85
first, many prophesied at, V1:85
first, powers of priesthood manifest at, V1:85
first, proceedings at, V1:84
First Presidency, of Church of October 1848 in Salt Lake City, sustains new, V7:628
First Presidency, of Great Britain and Pacific Islands, three sustained by, V7:629-30
Freedom, V2:224
Freedom Branch, minutes of April 3, 1835, V2:218
heavens opened at, V1:85
high priests in Kirtland, V1:342, 352, 354
high priests and elders in Kirtland, V1:322, 323
high priests and elders at New Portage, Ohio, V2:24
Hiram, V1:219, 221, 222 and ftnts
Illinois, Walnut Grove, V4:287
Iowa, Augusta, minutes of April 1, 1843, V5:318
Kanesville, general at, sustaining of new Church authorities and new First Presidency, V7:623-4
Kaw Township, first in Missouri, V1:199
Kirtland, V4:361-2

CONFERENCE (continued)

Kirtland, minutes of, V2:468-9, 509-10

Kirtland, special at, V1:219 and ftnt

Lima, of October 23, 1841, V4:439-40

Maine, Saco, V2:252-3

Maine, Vinalhaven, Fox Island, V5:360

Massachusetts, of high council at, V2:239-41

Massachusetts, minutes of, V2:241, 242

Michigan, Brownstown, V6:175

missions, of elders for, V5:347-52

missions, of Twelve Apostles and seventies to receive charge to leave for, V2:218

Missouri, Clay County, V2:1

Nauvoo, printed word to be discontinued at, V7:473

Nauvoo, special at, V6:47-52

Nauvoo, special held on building public building, V5:369

Nauvoo Temple, general of October 1845 in, V7:457, et seq

New Portage, V2:273

New Portage, minutes of, V2:227, 228

New York, V6:286

New York, Alexander, V6:98

New York, Attica, V4:412

New York, Avon, Livingston County, V2:44

New York, Batavia, V5:352

New York, Lyonstown, of Twelve at, V2:225

New York City, V4:344

occurrences at, V1:115

Ohio, Amherst, Lorain County, V1:242, 243 and ftnt

Ohio, Norton, Medina County, minutes of, V2:52, et seq

Philadelphia, V4:331

poor and gathering, at Kirtland concerning, V2:468-9

priesthood, article on, given at, V4:207-12

resolutions passed at, November 12, 1845, V7:520-2

sacred shout at, V7:624 and ftnt

school books, provisions made for publication of, in wilderness, V7:474

seventies hall, of Church at dedication of, V7:330, et seq

trial of Sidney Rigdon, of Church of October 1843, V6:47-9

United States, list of, appointed in, V6:334-5

Vermont, minutes of, V2:238

Westfield, of Twelve at, V2:222-4

Young, Brigham, Kanesville, sustained as President of the Church, V7:623-4 and ftnts

CONFERENCE (conference)

    Zion, first of April 6, V1:336-7.

    See also Apostles; British Mission; Latter-day Saints, Church of Jesus
       Christ of.

confirmation, England, Jenetta Richards first in, V2:504

    Knight, Lydia, and Emma Smith, of, V1:106, 108

    members, first, V1:78

    spirit, as directed by, V1:61.

    See also Latter-day Saints, Church of Jesus Christ of.

congress, Church feelings on actions of, V4:107.

Connor, Henry, baptism of, V4:184.

Conover, Peter W., Joseph, on mission to rescue, V5:451

    Joseph, reveals plot against, V5:452-3

    relief expedition, his account of, V5:450-1.

consecration and stewardship, law of, Church, of all in, V7:464

    Church, commanded to cease living, V4:93 and ftnt

    deed forms, V1:365, ftnt only

    doctrine of explained, V7:412

    Joseph on, V1:219-20, ftnt only

    property, instructions on, V1:364

    saints, broken by at Thompson, Ohio, (D&C § 51), V1:180 and ftnt

    taken, (D&C § 54), V1:181

    Zion, how used in, V1:381.

conspiracy, in Nauvoo, V6:272, et seq and ftnts.

constable, Joseph, aids in evading mob, V1:96

    Joseph, apologizes to, V1:95

    Joseph, arrests, V1:88

    second, serves warrant on Joseph, V1:91

    second, treatment by, V1:91.

Constantine, Christianity before and after, IntroV1:LXVIII

    Christianity, his revolution in early, IntroV1:LIV.

Constitution, Joseph, on powers of, V5:289

    Kirtland Camp, of, V3:90-1

    Kirtland Camp, violations of, V3:128-9

    Missouri, Articles on religious freedom, V1:374 and ftnt

    Mob Manifesto, secret V1:374 and ftnt

    persecuted even though protected by, V1:97.

contentions, be careful as to while preaching, V1:468.

contributions, Joseph requests in meeting for redemption of Zion, V2:50.

convention, Carthage, anti-Mormon at, V6:221

CONVENTION (continued)

Nauvoo, presidential at, V6:386-97.

Conyers, Mr., mentioned, V7:142, 148, 152, 195.

Cook, Mr., mentioned, V3:419.

Cook, Ahaz, called on mission amidst mob action in Missouri, V3:154.

Cook, Edward, clerk to Nova Scotia conference, V6:79.

Cook, Frederick, volunteers for service in vineyard, V4:217.

Cook, Giles, Jr., elder, ordained, V2:207
Kirtland Temple, blessing for work on, V2:206.

Cook, Henry L., mission and field of labor, V6:336.

Cook, Lieutenant, Missouri mobber, V3:419, 433; V6:108.

Cook, Milton, refuses arrest by a Mormon, V6:171.

Cook, Sarah, aided and abetted martyrdom mob, V7:146.

Cook, William, aided and abetted martyrdom mob, V7:146.

Coolbirth, Agnes, (also spelled Coolbrith), wife of Don Carlos Smith, V3:43, ftnt only; V4:393.

Cooley, Adonijah, subscribed to constitution of Kirtland Camp, V3:92.

Cooley, Alvin, mission and field of labor, V6:335.

Coolidge, Brother, mentioned, V6:226.

Coolidge, Charles, kidnapper of Daniel Avery, V6:146.

Coolidge, Joseph W., *Expositor,* arrest for destruction of, and trial on, V6:487, et seq
mentioned, V5:6, 420
Missouri, covenanted to assist saints in removal from, V3:252.

Coolie, Mr., mentioned, V7:83.

Coon, Joseph, Kirtland Camp, mentioned in, V3:138.
Kirtland Camp, subscribed to constitution of, V3:93.

Coons, Libbeus T., (also spelled Lebbeus, Libeus Coon), Church, appointed to preside over new district of, V7:305
mentioned, V5:309
mission and field of labor, V6:338
seventies, named to first quorum of, V2:203
seventy, ordained, V2:221
Zions Camp member, V2:183.

Cooper, Jeremiah, mentioned, V5:521.

Cooper, John, mission and field of labor, V6:339.

co-operative, plans for store, V6:263.

Copeland, Solomon, considered as vice president nominee, V6:248.

Copeland, W., clerk of English conference, V4:298.

Copley, Daniel, excommunicated for failure to fulfill mission, V1:354.

Copley, Leman, Church, Shaking Quaker joins, V1:167
consecration and stewardship, breaks law of, V1:180, ftnt only
Joseph, confesses to and is rebaptized, V2:433
Quakers, called on mission to, (D&C § 49), V1:167, 169, ftnt only.

Coray, George, mentioned, V6:230.

Coray, Howard, Church, appointed to preside over new district of, V7:305
mentioned, V7:519
mission and field of labor, V6:340.

Coray, M. J., compiles Lucy Smith's history, V7:519, ftnt only.

Coray, William, mission and field of labor, V6:340.

Corbitt, Thomas, prepares harvest feast in Nauvoo, V7:437.

Corbridge, James, ordained priest, V4:118.

Cordon, Alfred, British conference, represents branch at, V4:147; V5:10
England, letter on affairs in, V4:515
high priest, ordained, V4:148
mission and field of labor, V6:336
mob, prevented from speaking by, in England, V4:361
volunteers for service in vineyard, V4:216.

Corey, Lyman, utility committee member to aid Church removal, V7:474.

Corinthians, Book of First, Chapter 7:14 explained, (D&C § 74), V1:242
Chapter 14:27 explained, V4:486 and ftnt

Cornet, John, mobber in Missouri, V4:72.

Cornish, Denman, mission and field of labor, V6:336.

Corrill, John, bishop, to be, in Zion, V1:363
buffetings of Satan, turned over to, and condemned as openly sinning against Jesus, V3:232
Doctrine and Covenants, testifies to truthfulness of, V2:246
endowments, called to go to Kirtland to receive, V2:112
excommunicated from Church, V3:284
general assembly, opposed proceedings of, at Far West, V3:4-5
Joseph, exhorts but relies on own judgment, V3:65-6
Joseph, letter from, V2:508-9
Joseph, pays money to, in time of need, V2:327
Liberty, letter to lawyer at, concerning compromise offers, V2:135
Lord's storehouse, appointed keeper of, at Far West, V2:524
Missouri, appointed branch president in, V1:409, ftnt only

CORRILL, JOHN (continued)

Missouri Legislature, presents saints' petition to, V3:238-9 and ftnt

Missouri trials, witness for state in, of saints, V3:210

mob activities, letter to *Star* reporting to prevent saints' return to Jackson County, V2:92, ftnt only

mob, arrested by and freed, V1:431-2

sacrament, labored with for not taking, V2:304

saints, offers himself a ransom for, in Jackson County, V1:394, ftnt only

saints' arms, letter to Colonel Pitcher requesting, V2:135

signs attempted whitewash of General Clark's activities, V3:360, ftnt only

Wight, Lyman, prefers charges against, V2:147.

Corvin, Horace, mission call, V1:332

ordained, V1:333.

Corwin, Mr., hears saints' petition in Congressional Committee, V4:83, et seq.

Coulson, George, captain of 18th company in westward movement, V7:482.

council, doings of, reviewed, V1:343

Kirtland, appoints committee to purchase land in, V1:335

Kirtland, Zion to effect reconciliation with brethren in, V1:335

Kirtland Camp, action of, in, V3:131

Kirtland Camp, assistant for, organized with three members, V3:121-2

procedures in, not to be uneasy or leave, V2:25

Twelve Apostles, sanctioned by, V2:240

Welton, Baldwin, to consider standing of, et al, V1:343

Zion, of high priests in, V1:407.

council, common, V3:5, ftnt only.

council, special, ancient order in, V2:25

endowments, meets to choose who will receive in Kirtland, V2:112

First Presidency, to try, V2:150 and ftnt, et seq

First Presidency and Twelve, of, V2:283

Liverpool, England, V4:296-7

minutes of, V2:39

Missouri High Council at Kirtland to fill vacancies in, V2:356-7; V3:5, ftnt only

Nauvoo, at, V6:39

New Portage, minutes at, V2:317

priesthood, general minutes of, V2:219

Prophet, of high priests and elders to consider difficulty between Sylvester Smith and, V2:150, et seq

COUNCIL, SPECIAL (continued)

    Prophet, of high priests and elders at home of, in Kirtland, V2:25

    Prophet, of high priests at home of in Kirtland, minutes of, V2:47

    Prophet, at Kirtland to consider resolutions vindicating the, V2:147, et seq

    Prophet, of Twelve and, V2:307, et seq.

Council of Fifty, see Fifty, Council of.

counsel, dissatisfied and murmured because of failure to follow, V5:181

    Haun's Mills massacre death caused because would not heed, V5:137

    obey, necessary to, V6:30.

Courier des Etats Unis, publishes proposed statement of Pilate condemning Jesus, V4:420-1.

Court, Mayor's evidence, approve copies before, V5:497

    Nauvoo, proceedings in, V5:365-8.

covenant, debt, with God to be relieved from, V2:175

    Zion, to redeem, V2:282.

Covenants, Book of Doctrine and, see Doctrine and Covenants, Book of.

Covert, William S., elder, ordained, V5:349

    mission call in Illinois to disabuse public mind over arrest of Joseph, V5:485.

covetousness, Joseph left Church uninformed because of, V7:545.

Covey, Benjamin, bishop in Nauvoo, V3:257

    Missouri, arraigned for treason, murder, burglary, arson, robbery, larceny at Richmond, V3:209

    Missouri, covenanted to assist saints in removal from, V3:253

    Missouri trials, discharged as innocent from, V3:211.

Covill, James, Baptist minister, requests duty, V1:143

    calling of, (D&C § 39), V1:144

    calling of, rejects, V1:145

    revelation to, V1:143, et seq

    revelation on reasons for breaking covenant (D&C § 40), V1:145.

Cowan, Mr., delegate to political convention in Nauvoo, V6:390.

Cowan, Horace, Zions Camp member, V2:183.

Cowan, John B., mentioned, V5:268, 277-9, 287, 299.

Cowan, John F., appointed aide-de-camp, V5:364.

Cowan, R., ordained elder, V5:419.

cowardice, Cahoon, R., accuses Joseph of, for leaving, V6:549-52.

Cowdery, F. W., mentioned, V2:486.

Cowdery, Marcellus F., holds high council at Far West an illegal body and disfellowshipped, V3:8.

Cowdery, Oliver, Aaronic Priesthood given to, V1:39
    Aaronic Priesthood, gives to Joseph, V1:39
    apostasy of, starts, V1:105
    Apostle, assists at the ordination of, V2:187, et seq and ftnts
    Apostle, called to be, (D&C § 18:9), V1:62
    Apostles, gives general charge to, V2:194, et seq
    Apostolic charge, gives, V2:192, et seq
    baptism of, V1:41
    baptism, description of, V1:42, ftnt only
    baptism, prophesied after, V1:42
    baptizes after first public discourse, V1:81
    Book of Commandments, appointed to carry manuscript of, to Zion, V1:221, 222, 229, 234 and ftnt
    buffetings of Satan, turned over to and openly condemned as sinning against Jesus, V3:232
    Catteraugus tribe, visits, V1:120 and ftnt
    charges, letter to high council concerning some of, against, V3:17, ftnt only
    charges, preferred against to high council at Far West, V3:16
    Church, appointed recorder for, V2:273
    Church, ordained assistant president of, V2:176 and ftnt
    Church, ordained Joseph first elder in, V1:78
    Church, second elder in, V1:41, 61
    Church doctrine, outlines basis of, October 1834, V2:167, ftnt only
    Church historian, released as, V1:166 and ftnt
    Colesville, baptizes at, V1:88
    Cumorah, described by, V1:15, ftnt only
    Delaware chief, reply of, V1:184-5, ftnts only
    Delawares, speech to, V1:183, ftnt only
    discussion on the steamer "Monroe," V2:168-9 and ftnt
    editor, appointed of *Messenger and Advocate* at Kirtland, also editor of reprinted *Star,* V1:409
    elder, ordained by Joseph, V1:77
    elder, to be ordained, V1:60-1
    excommunication, V3:17-8 and ftnts
    First Presidency, sustained assistant counselor to, V2:509
    genealogy, V1:32, ftnt only
    high council, refuses to be tried by, V3:17-8 and ftnts

COWDERY, OLIVER (continued)

high council, speaks in, V2:33
Joseph, baptized, V1:39
Joseph, becomes scribe to, V1:33
Joseph, blessed and chastened by, V1:465
Joseph, first visit to, V1:32
Joseph, visits Joseph Knight with, V1:86
Joseph's death, confronts one named Ellmer who reports of, V2:168-9
    and ftnt
Kirtland, arrives at, V1:120
Kirtland, public ministry at, V1:124-5
Kirtland Temple, blessing for work on, V2:205
Kirtland Temple, subscribes to, and pays within one hour, V2:234
licenses rejected as authorized to sign, V3:6 and ftnt
Messenger & Advocate, replaced by John Whitmer in conducting,
    V2:227
mission, appointed to Lamanites, (D&C § 32), V1:118 and ftnt
mission, call to Lamanites, (D&C § 28:8-10), V1:111
mission, departs on, V1:120 and ftnt
mission, reports Lamanite by letter, V1:182-5 and ftnts
Missouri, arrives at Kirtland from, V1:206
Palmyra, meets David Whitmer at, V1:32, ftnt only
plates, hears of, V1:32
plates, obtains view of, V1:54
Pratt, Parley P., charge of, to, V2:192, et seq
preaches at meeting at Joseph Knight's, V1:86
preaches at Sidney Rigdon's chapel, V1:124
priestcraft, letter to Joseph accusing of, V1:104-5
Prophet, blessed by, V2:51
Prophet, falls into error in commanding, V1:105
public discourse, preaches first, V1:81
rebaptized, exhorted to be, V7:619
repent, letter sent to, to see if wants to, V5:368
revelation to, (D&C § 23:1-2), V1:80
revelation, accepts of Hiram Page, V1:109-10
revelation to, instructing to be obedient, (D&C § 28:1-7), V1:110
revelations, to review and prepare for printing, V1:270 and ftnts
revelations, to take to Missouri for printing, V1:229
Rigdon, Sidney, confirmed to assist in Joseph's absence, V2:51
Satan, believed revelations of, V1:109-10
scribe, called to be, V1:33
sin, announce to be in, and in First Presidency, V2:511

COWDERY, OLIVER (continued)

translate, desires to, V1:36

translate, fails to, reason, (D&C § 9), V1:37-8

translating power taken from, V1:37

truth, previous manifestation of, V1:35

westward movement, tenders aid and service for, V7:482

witness, commanded to be, V1:55

witness, prays for, of plates, V1:54

witness, requests to be, V1:53

Zion, at temple dedication, V1:199

Zions Camp, remains at Kirtland during, V2:64.

See also Apostles; Latter-day Saints, Church of Jesus Christ of; letters; Smith, Joseph.

Cowdery, Oliver and Company, dissolved, V2:475.

Cowdery, Warren A., apology of, V2:374, ftnt only

Church, called to lead Freedom Branch of, (D&C § 106), V2:170

clerk, appointed, V2:218, 228

Kirtland Temple, letter on subscriptions to, V2:239

Prophet, entertains, V2:42

reconciles self with Apostles, V2:374, ftnt only.

Cowdery, William, mentioned, V2:244

priests, president of, V2:371.

Cowin, Horace, mission appointment, V1:332

mob, jailed for debt by, V3:289.

Cowles, Austin W., (also A.), apostates, appointed counselor of new church by, V6:347

apostasy, excommunicated for, V6:398

Kirtland Camp, subscribed to constitution of, V3:92

Nauvoo, elected supervisor of streets in, V4:292

Nauvoo stake, counselor of, V4:323.

Cowles, Richard B., mentioned, V3:337, ftnt only.

Cox, Simon, killed at Haun's Mills by mob, V3:326, ftnt only.

Cox, Walter, appointed counselor of stake at Lima, V4:233; V5:427.

Coxe, John Redman, mentioned, V2:350, ftnt only.

Crandall, Sally, deceived by devil through interpretation of tongues and visions of hearts, V2:140.

Crane, Mr., mentioned, V5:278; V6:604.

Crane, A., publishes phrenological chart of Joseph, V5:52, et seq.

Crane, John M., reports arms shipment to Warsaw, V6:471.

Crane, Joseph Smith, Joseph blesses, V5:219.

Crane, Michael, mentioned, V5:454.

Crane, Samuel, ordained elder, V5:349.

Cravens, Wyatt, witness for state in Missouri trials of saints, V3:210.

Crawford, General, mentioned, V2:65.

Crawford, Harrison P., mentioned, V6:506
  mobber, breathes threats against Mormons, V6:509.

Crawford, S., appointed by public to assist saints in removal from Zion,
  V2:455.

Crawther, Henry W. (also spelled Crowther), major-general in Missouri
  militia, V3:65, 83.

create, Christ, all things, by, V4:257
  eternal, anything, cannot be, V3:387
  meaning of, V6:308-9 and ftnt
  nature of, V2:14; V6:307-11.

Cree, Mr., mentioned, V1:287, ftnt only.

creed, Church has none, V5:215.

Crichfield, Absalom, testifies at Hulet Branch trial, V2:140.

Crigler, George, mob member writes lies concerning DeWitt, V3:156.

crime, excommunication proposed for committing of, V7:259, 365.

Crismon, Charles, appointed to preside over new Church district, V7:305.

Crittenden, Mr., mentioned, V4:85.

Crockett, S. B., mentioned, V3:13.

Crook, Mr., English conference, represents branches at, V6:327.

Crook, Mr., mentioned, V7:597.

Crook, Robert, English conference, represents branches at, V6:328.

Crooked River, battle of, V3:170-1, et seq
  Patten, David W., killed in battle of, V3:171.

Crooks, Robert, volunteers for service in vineyard, V4:217.

Crosby, Jesse W., Canadian Provinces, reports mission to, V7:317
  mission call in Illinois to disabuse public mind over arrest of Joseph,
    V5:485
  Nova Scotia, missionary call to, V5:413.

Crosby, Jonathan, subscribed to constitution of Kirtland Camp, V3:92.

Crosby, Jonathan, Jr., teaches music, V2:474.

Crosby, William, Nauvoo Temple, to administer in, V7:555
  Nauvoo Temple, appointed to officiate in, V7:547.

Crosier, Harlow, pays Joseph money in hour of need, V2:327.

Crosier, Munro, (also spelled Monro), Kirtland Camp, leaves, V3:140
  Kirtland Camp, subscribed to constitution of, V3:93.

cross, Joseph retranslates words of Christ to thief on, V5:424-5.

Cross, William, mentioned, V4:600.

Crouse, George W., bishop, appointed, V4:233
  mentioned, V6:168
  mission and field of labor, V6:337.

Crow, J. T., mission call, V7:260.

Cuerden, Henry, represents area in British conference, V5:10.

Culberston, James G., ordained elder, V5:349.

Culver, Aaron, and wife baptized, V1:88.

Cummins, James, mentioned, V4:477.

Cummins, R. W., Indian agent signed Mob Manifesto, V1:376.

Cummings, Horace, writes account of threats on Joseph's life, V6:281,
  ftnt only.

Cummings, James W., Joseph, on relief expedition for, V5:486
  Legion, martial band member of, V7:135
  mission call in Illinois to disabuse public mind over arrest of Joseph,
  V5:485.

Cumorah, described by Oliver Cowdery, V1:15, ftnt only
  Joseph to return to yearly, V1:16
  location of, V2:79-80
  mentioned, V1:184, ftnt only.

Cunningham, John, affidavit of mob attempting to draft into service,
  V6:508.

Curd, Willis, mentioned, V6:148.

Curling Mr., mentioned, V5:523.

Curran, Mr., mentioned, V4:254.

currency, ordinance on, at Nauvoo, V5:297.

curse, adulterers, fornicators and unvirtuous persons, upon, V4:587
  Cain received, V4:209
  Missouri, remain on until saints redressed, V5:211
  money, on, as result of wrongful taking of, V2:292
  unrepentant, upon, V2:237
  water, on, V5:56 and ftnt.

Curtis, Dorr P., ordained elder, V5:349.

Curtis, Enos, affidavit on mob house burning, V7:488
  baptized, V4:110, ftnt only.

Curtis, Ira, S., testify to finding Kinderhook plates, V5:377.

Curtis, Jacob, covenanted to assist saints in removing from Missouri, V3:254.

Curtis, Jeremiah, mission and field of labor, V6:339
   mission in Illinois to disabuse public mind over arrest of Joseph, V5:485.

Curtis, Joseph, mission and field of labor, V6:339.

Curtis, Lyman, Missouri, covenanted to assist saints in removal from, V3:253
   Zions Camp member, V2:183.

Curtis, Mecham, Zions Camp member, V2:183.

Curtis, Mitchell, mentioned, V6:222.

Curtis, Nahum, covenanted to assist saints in removing from Missouri, V3:253.

Curtis, Noah, called on mission and field of labor, V5:349.

Curtis, Simons P., affidavit of, concerning Missouri persecutions, V4:67.

Curtis, Sophronia, Zions Camp member, V2:185.

Curtis, Stephen, mentioned, V6:222.

Curtis, Theodore, blasphemy, imprisoned in England for, V4:380
   British conference, represents area in, V5:10
   mission call in Illinois to disabuse public mind over arrest of Joseph, V5:485
   volunteers for service in vineyard, V4:217.

Curtis, William, mission call, V5:429.

Curtis, Zenas, covenanted to assist saints in removing from Missouri, V3:252.

Cushman, Mr., mentioned, V2:300.

Cutler, A., mentioned, V7:322.

Cutler, Alpheus, Kirtland Temple, blessing for work on, V2:205
   mentioned, V2:151-2; V4:18; V6:49
   Nauvoo, bodyguard to Joseph's body on return to, V7:135
   Nauvoo High Council, appointed to, V4:12
   Nauvoo High Council, sustained member of, after death of Joseph, V7:296
   Nauvoo Temple, receives endowment in, V7:543
   prophecy, present in Missouri at Apostles' departure to fulfill, V3:339
   westward movement, captain of third company in, V7:481.

Cutler, Lois, receives endowment in Nauvoo Temple, V7:543.

Cutler, Louisa, marriage to Tunis Rapley, V2:376.

Cutler, William L., Joseph, on mission to rescue, V5:451
mentioned, V5:449
MIA, aids in movement toward, V5:321, 322.

—D—

Dale, D., appointed by public to assist saints in removing from Zion, V2:455.

Dale, Richard, Carthage Greys, member of, V7:143.

Dale, Thomas J., Carthage Greys, member of, V7:143.

Daley, Brother, mentioned, V7:620.

Daley, James, covenanted to assist saints in removing from Missouri, V3:253.

Daley, John, mentioned, V4:12.

Daley, Moses (also spelled Daily, Dailey), Joseph, stays at home of, V3:38
Kirtland, appointed to purchase lands in, V1:335
Missouri, covenanted to assist saints in removal from, V3:253
ordination, approved for, V2:400.

Dalrymple, L. S., mentioned, V7:158.

"Dalston," song sung at Kirtland Temple dedication, V2:419 and ftnt.

Dalton, Joseph, witness in Expositor trial of Joseph, V6:457, 458.

damnation, of hell, explained, V4:555.
See also devil, hell.

damned, everyone but Mormons, V3:28
Gilmour, C., would rather be, than believe, V4:110, ftnt only.
See also devil, hell.

Dana, Charles R., mentioned, V5:293.

Dana, James, called on mission amidst mob action in Missouri, V3:154.

Dana, Lewis, sent on mission to Lamanites, V7:401.

dancing, disfellowshipped for joining world in, V2:519.

Daniel, beasts, prophet saw only images of, V5:343
prophecy of, on rise of the Kingdom of God in last days, Intro-V1:XXXIV
treason, saints' belief in prophecy of condemned as, IntroV3:L.

Daniels, Abigail, mentioned, V2:482.

Daniels, Chillion, called on mission and field of labor, V5:348.

Daniels, Cyrus, mentioned, V3:257, 281; V6:258.

Daniels, Reuben, high council, named to, at Lima, V5:482
Kirtland Camp, leaves, V3:138
Kirtland Camp, subscribed to constitution of, V3:92
son born to, V3:138.

Daniels, Sheffield, elder, ordained, V4:13
mentioned, V2:482
Missouri, arraigned for treason, murder, arson, burglary, robbery
and larceny at Richmond, V3:209
Missouri trials, discharged as innocent from, V3:211.

Daniels, William M., Carthage trial, witness at Prophet's murder,
V7:49-50 and ftnt
martyrdom murderers, affidavit on, V7:162-3
testimony, goes to Governor Ford with, V7:168.

Danites, Avard, Sampson, organized as secret band of, V3:178-80
Church, Sampson Avard lies concerning, V3:192
Church, distinguished from, V3:182
Marsh affidavit first mentioned in, V3:167, ftnt only
Nauvoo, accused of being in, V6:345
Nauvoo, none in, V5:68
protection, reported as formed for mutual, V3:453-4.
See also Avard, Sampson; Latter-day Saints, Church of Jesus Christ of;
Nauvoo.

Darby, John, mentioned, V5:214.

Darnell, William, anti-Mormon committee chairman, V6:8.

Davidson, George W., covenanted to assist saints in removing from
Missouri, V3:252.

Davidson, James, counsel for Joseph at Colesville, New York, V1:93
counsel for Joseph at South Bainbridge, V1:89.

Davies, Mr., mentioned, V6:414.

Daviess, Rolla M., mob member writes lies concerning DeWitt, V3:156.

Daviess County, Missouri, Saints expelled from, V2:496; V3:73.
See also persecutions, Missouri.

Davis, Brother, mentioned, V1:439.

Davis, Mr., representative in Illinois House of Representatives, introduces resolution calling for repeal of Nauvoo Charter, V5:201.
See also Nauvoo, Nauvoo Charter.

Davis, Mr., mentioned, V7:432.

Davis, Amos, Joseph, tried and convicted of abusive language against,
V4:549

DAVIS, AMOS (continued)

mission and field of labor, V6:338.

Davis, Charles A., mentioned, V7:369.

Davis, Daniel C., Keokuk, called to move to, to build city, V5:164
mentioned, V4:16
westward movement, captain of twentieth company in, V7:482.

Davis, E. H., mission and field of labor, V6:336.

Davis, George T. M., mentioned, V6:587; V7:180.

Davis, Jacob C., lawyer, member of martyrdom mob, V7:143.
murder, acquitted of Joseph's, V7:420
murder, indicted for, of Joseph, V7:314
Warsaw militia leader, V7:143.

Davis, James, mentioned, V6:554.

Davis, Joe, mission call in Illinois to disabuse public mind over arrest of Joseph, V5:485.

Davis, John, signs proposition to buy land of saints, V2:96-7.

Davis, John, given assistant care of Church at Leigh, V4:135.

Davis, Lawyer, mentioned, V5:473.

Davis, Malcham C., baptized during intermission of Sunday meetings, V2:355.

Davis, Maleum C., elder, ordained, V2:207
Kirtland Temple, blessing for work on, V2:205
mentioned, V2:412.

Davis, Mathew S., description of Joseph and report of Washington discourse, V4:78, et seq.

Davis, William Rees, baptism of, in Wales, V5:282
priest, ordained, V5:312.

Dawson, Ann, America, to be brought to, V5:406
English members confirmed in home of, V2:506.

Dawson, William, Jr., excommunicated from Church, and wife, V3:336.

Dawson, William, Sr., excommunicated from Church, and wife, V3:336.

Day, Abram, martial band member of Legion, V7:135.

Dayton, Hiram, (also spelled Hyrum), elder, to be, V2:354
Kirtland Camp, subscribed to constitution of, V3:92
Mayor's Court, before, V6:155
mentioned, V5:282; V7:379
mission and field of labor, V6:339.

Dayton, Lysander, mission and field of labor, V6:339.

deacons, duties of, in Zion expounded, V2:330, ftnt only

DEACONS (continued)

Nauvoo, duties of, in, V7:388
police, watch over Nauvoo as, V7:399.
See also Nauvoo.

dead, gospel, dead must hear before being judged, V3:29
ordinances for, V6:319
raising from, V5:121; V6:186-7
work for, V6:366.
See also dead, baptism for; doctrine; Latter-day Saints, Church of Jesus Christ of.

dead, baptism for, Apostles baptized for, V7:261, ftnt only
editorial on, V4:595, et seq
epistle, expounded to Twelve by, V4:231
first performed in font, V4:454
font for dedicated and described, V4:446
Iowa, practiced in, 1841, V4:383
Iowa, recorded in, V4:382
Joseph on, V4:568-9
Joseph, directions on, (D&C § 127), V5:142
Joseph, directions on, (D&C § 128), V5:148
Joseph, resumed after death of, IntroV7:XXVII
necessity of, expounded, V4:426
New Testament, clearly shown in, V5:425
recorder, when performed must have, present, V5:141
recorders, appointed for, V5:522
river, to be done in, while font not in use, V5:350
saints, epistle of Apostles to, concerning, V4:472-5
Taylor, John, on, V7:292
Young, Brigham, on, V7:254
Zion, only means to become saviors on Mount, V4:424.
See also Apostles; doctrine; Elijah; Latter-day Saints, Church of Jesus Christ of.

Dead Sea, must be healed before second coming, V5:337.

Dean, Henry, bishop's counselor, V4:233
bishop's counselor at Lima, V5:427
mission and field of labor, V6:337.

death, the second, V6:317.

debate, Joseph challenges Alexander Campbell to public, V2:269 and ftnt
Joseph, opinion of, on, V2:318
miracles, principle of, by elders V2:317
Nauvoo, held regularly in, V4:514

DEBATE (continued)

revelation, question of necessity of, V2:330.
See also Nauvoo; Smith, Joseph.

debt, Apostles on, V7:526
Church, of, expounded, V2:480
Nauvoo, Church members not to leave, in, V7:475
pay, all should, V1:339
prayer, by Joseph to be free from, V2:291
sisters counseled not to pay while husband on mission, V5:351.

Deckenson, George, testify to finding Kinderhook plates, V5:377.

Decker, Brother, assist elders Young and Kimball en route to England, V4:11.

Decker, Isaac, called on mission amidst mob action in Missouri, V3:154.

dedication, see Temple, Kirtland; Temple, Nauvoo; Temple, Zion.

deeds, of consecration and stewardship, forms of, V1:365 and ftnt, et seq.

DeHart, Thos., petitions Governor Boggs on mob violence in DeWitt, V3:83.

Deming, Miner R., Carthage, left in command at, by Governor Ford, V7:22, 27, 31
Carthage, satisfied with Dr. Willard Richards, proceedings at, V7:168
Carthage Greys, arrested by, V7:84
death of, V7:439
jail, letter on admissions to see Joseph in, V6:593
Marshal, Sam, shoots, V7:428
martyrdom, letter to saints to keep quiet concerning, V6:625
mentioned, V7:45, 111, 146
proclamation of, V7:133
Richards, W., receives letter from, anent R. D. Foster, V7:169
wealthy Nauvoo brethren become bondsmen for, V7:432.

Deming, D. C., Kirtland Camp, leaves, V3:140.

Demming, David D., subscribed to constitution of Kirtland Camp, V3:91.

democrat, Church members generally are, V3:31 and ftnt.

Dennison, Doctor, member of Hiram mob, V1:264, ftnt only.

denominations, priests of all, unite to prevent saints from returning to Jackson County, V2:3.

Dent, Samuel, mentioned, V4:18.

Denton, Solomon W., seventy, ordained, V2:204
Zions Camp member, V2:183.

Denton, Wilbur, mentioned, V4:393.
preaches at meeting, V2:363.

Derby, Erastus H., Joseph, blessing on, for rendering aid, V5:106-7
 mission call in Illinois to disabuse public mind over arrest of Joseph, V5:485
 priesthood, gives up, V5:556
 Prophet, assists, in retirement, V5:90.

destroyer, Kirtland Camp, afflicts with sickness, V3:124
 Zions Camp, sent among as punishment, V2:116 and ftnt.

devil, angel of light, can appear as, V3:392
 Apostles, will seek lives of, V2:196
 attacks made by, to kill Prophet and clerk, V5:22-3
 attacks William Smith, Twelve Apostles and seventies, V2:352-3
 Book of Revelation, dragon in, should be translated, V5:345
 Christianity is the base of hope in salvation for professor of, V5:218
 Church, bitterness of, to, IntroV3:LXI
 Church of Joseph, fails to destroy, V2:355
 Cowdery, Oliver, believes in revelations of, V1:110
 deceives by giving visions of hearts, V2:140
 doctrine on, V4:358
 fate of, V7:413
 gift of seeing from, V2:141
 gift of tongues, can use, V3:392
 gift of tongues, deceives saints through, V2:141
 Joseph, tempted with riches of plates, V1:14
 Knight, Newel, cast out of, V1:83
 Knight, Newel, possessed of, V1:82
 Missouri, stirs mischief within the Mormon camp in, V3:178-9
 Missouri mission, against, V1:182
 Missouri persecutions, major factor in, IntroV3:LIX
 mob, father of, V3:68
 polygamy, projects sinful prototype of, in Nauvoo, V5:36-7
 revealed at conference, V1:175, ftnt only
 revelations, gives to Hiram Page, V1:109
 revelations, Whitmer family believes in, V1:110
 saints, use greatest efforts to trap in place of refuge, V3:391
 self-righteousness, doctrine of, V5:24
 seventies, attacks, V2:352
 sickness, teaching that all is of, rebuked, V2:147
 Son of Man, does not know sign of, V4:608
 stone of, renounced, V1:115
 tongues, uses to deceive, V2:140-1
 united order, establishes order similar to, V1:146 and ftnt

DEVIL (continued)

waters, seen riding upon, V1:203

wickedness, cannot compel men to do, V4:358

Zion, deceives Hulet branch in, V2:139-41

See also Apostles; curse; destroyer; doctrine; persecutions, Missouri; Smith, Joseph.

Devolue, Peter, abuses Whitney child, V1:219

Dewellin, John W., mentioned, V6:148.

DeWitt, Carroll County, attack upon, begun, V3:149-50

Boggs, Governor, petition of saints in, to, V3:82

Chariton County committee, problem reported on, by, V3:151

mob, account of settlement and siege of, by, V3:450, et seq

mob, saints leave, as a result of, V3:159

mob, saints warned to leave by, V3:64, 77

mob, surrounding, call on citizens of Howard County for help, V3:156

mob presses, V3:85

mob, writes lies concerning, V3:156

saints at, hard pressed, V3:157-8

situation, letter of General Parks to General Atchison concerning, V3:155.

DeWitt, Isaac, subscribed to constitution of Kirtland Camp, V3:93.

DeWolfe, Mr., Nauvoo, Episcopal minister, preaches at, V5:427

Nauvoo, lectures at, V6:223.

Diahman, saints expelled from, V3:207.

Dibble, Lydia, wife of Oliver Granger, V4:408.

Dibble, Philo, wounded by mob but miraculously healed, V1:431, ftnt only.

Dicken, Whitfield, mob member writes lies concerning DeWitt, V3:156.

Dickey, Judge, sons of mobbers, V3:242.

Dickson, Joseph, reports Mormons massacred citizens, V3:168.

Dickson, Robert, mentioned, V6:222.

diety, departure of early Christianity from true doctrine of, IntroV1: LXXIX.

See also Christ, Jesus; Christianity; doctrine; God; Latter-day Saints, Church of Jesus Christ of; Smith, Joseph.

disciples, Joseph tries for lodging in name of, but unsuccessful, V2:45.

Disciples, The, Campbell, Alexander, founder of, V1:120, ftnt only

Pratt, Parley P., relation to, V1:119, ftnt only

Rigdon, Sidney, aids in organization of, V1:121, ftnt only.

discourse, Elias, Elijah, Messiah, V6:249

DISCOURSE (continued)

first public in new dispensation, V1:81

Godhead, plurality of Gods, V6:473-9

Nauvoo, on conspiracies in, V6:272-4

Nauvoo, dissenters at, V6:408-12

Nauvoo, the Prophet's in, V4:358-60

prophetic calling and fullness of ordinances for living and dead, V6: 363-7

sealing powers, on, V6:183-4.

See also Apostles; doctrine; Latter-day Saints, Church of Jesus Christ of; Smith, Joseph.

disease, devil not sole cause of, V2:147.

disfellowship, Adams, George J., to be, V7:395

Babbitt, Almon W., for teaching contrary to doctrine, V4:424

Bennett, J. C., withdrawn from, V5:18

Bishop, Gladden, for lack of proper spirit, V2:241

Bishop, Gladden, for receiving false revelations, V4:550

Bond, Abram, for murmuring, V3:117

Boynton, J. F., and rejected as Apostle, V2:509

Brannan, Sam, to be, V7:395

Cowdery, Marcellus F., for insult to high council, V3:8

dance, of twenty-two brethren and sisters for uniting with the world in, V2:519

Emmett, James, for unwise conduct, V2:482; V7:618

examples and reasons for, adopted by resolution, V4:16

Harris, Preserved, for want of benevolence to the poor and charity to the Church, V2:445

Hawkins, Uriah and Lydia Ann, for unlawful marriage and deceiving, V2:511

Hyde, Orson, for insulting School of Prophets, V2:240

Johnson, Luke, and rejected as Apostle, V2:509

Johnson, Lyman E., and rejected as Apostle, V2:509

Kelly, Charles, of, V2:442

Kirtland, for moving to, V4:39

law, voted at Montrose to, if brethren sued at, V4:54

M'Lellin, William E., for insulting School of Prophets, V2:240

members would be who move to Nauvoo without holding recommend, V4:205

Miller, George, of, V7:618

Missouri debts, all to be who call for, V4:42

Olney, Oliver, for setting self up as prophet, V4:552

Patten, John, for not keeping contracts, V2:482

DISFELLOWSHIP (continued)

revelations, for heeding false, V2:525

Soby, Leonard, for following Sidney Rigdon, V7:268

"tippling shops," high council at Montrose voted to, all who keep, V4:80

Winchester, Benjamin, for disobedience, V4:494; V5:409

Word of Wisdom, will not fellowship any for breaking, V2:482.

See also excommunication; Latter-day Saints, Church of Jesus Christ of.

dispensation, Adam holds presidency of all, V4:209

definition of, IntroV1:XXIII

Enoch, a president of, V4:209

fulness of times, of, IntroV1:XXX

fulness of times, to be conducted as all previous, V4:208

Joel's prophecy of the last days, IntroV1:XXXI

Joseph, at head of this, V7:250

meridian of time, of the, IntroV1:XXIX

meridian of time, as to fulness of times considered, IntroV1:XXX

priesthood, nature of, explained, V4:209

talents, parable of, applied to last, V2:24.

See also doctrine; epistle; Latter-day Saints, Church of Jesus Christ of; Smith, Joseph.

Divine, J. G., appointed to preside over new Church district, V7:305.

Dixon, Brother, mentioned, V5:273, 288, 290.

Dixon, David, mentioned, V7:593

petitions Governor Boggs on mob violence in DeWitt, V3:83.

Dixon, Father, mentioned, V3:273; V6:381.

Dixon, John, testifies on Joseph's second arrest in Illinois, V6:67.

Dixon, Robert, president of Nova Scotia conference, V6:35.

Dobson, Thomas, mission and field of labor, V6:340

mission call in Illinois to disabuse public mind over arrest of Joseph, V5:485.

doctrine, all points, would have been explained and recorded if minutes had been recorded of every meeting, V2:198-9

Apostles, development of false after death of early, IntroV1:LII, et seq

atonement, of, and eternal punishment, V1:72 and ftnt

baptism, V6:316-7

baptism for dead, V6:365

Bible, mistranslation of, V6:307-8

body, state of, when quickened, V6:366

DOCTRINE (continued)

buffetings of Satan, once sealed to eternal life and sin, turned over to, V1:323-4

burnings, righteous to dwell in, V6:306-8

calling and election, of, V5:388, 402-3; V6:252

children at death, V6:316 and ftnt

Church, development of, during Illinois period of, IntroV4:XXXIII, et seq

consecration explained, V7:412

create, meaning of, V6:308-9 and ftnt

dove, sign of, explained, V5:261

earth described in sanctified state, V5:279 and ftnt

election, V4:359-60

election and reprobation, Brigham Young and W. Richards on, V4:256, et seq

elements, eternal existence of, V6:308-9 and ftnts

Elias, gave keys to Peter, James and John on Mount, V3:387

errs in, V5:340

exaltation, keys of, V5:403

false development of, after death of early apostles, IntroV1:LII, et seq

fast, of the, V7:413

gathering, purpose of, expounded, V5:423

God, character of, V6:303-4

God, early of, IntroV1:LXXIX

God, an exalted man, V6:305

God, man to, relation to, V6:312-3

God, paganization of early of, IntroV1:LXXXII, et seq

God and Jesus, must know, V6:305-6

Godhead, Christian and plurality of, V6:473, et seq

Gods, council of, V6:308

Gods, men must learn to be, V6:306

grand keys, three to exaltation, V5:403

instructions on, V5:323-4

intelligence, immortal, V6:310-12 and ftnts

Joseph, always teaches stronger in public than private, V6:474

knowledge, as saving power, V6:314

life and death, Joseph on, V6:50-2

murder, V4:359

obedience, man must have absolute in all things to be saved, V6:223

144,000 selections already commenced, V6:196

predestination, V4:258-9

priesthood, all revealed through, V4:207

DOCTRINE (continued)

prophecy, more sure word of, defined, V5:392
religious freedom, V6:304-5
responsibility, man's greatest, V6:313
resurrection of dead, V6:363, et seq
retranslating of John 14, V6:365
revelation, how Lord proceeds in, V7:372
Satan, V4:358
second death, V6:317
sin, V4:358
sin, unpardonable, V6:313-4
sins, forgiveness of, V6:314-5
Son of Man, sign of the, V5:290-1, 336-7
sons of perdition, fate of, V7:413-4
summary outlined, October 1834 in *Messenger & Advocate*, V2:167-8, ftnts only
thinking, free on, V5:340
Twelve, instructions of, to Church on, V7:280, et seq
Twelve, warned by, against false, V7:199
veil, learn gospel after passing through, V6:307
washing of feet, V1:323; V2:430, 476
wickedness, discourse of Brigham Young against, V7:350
Zion, whole of America is, V6:318-9.
See also Apostles; discourse; dispensation; doctrinal development; dream; election; Elias; Elias, spirit of; Elijah; Elijah, spirit of; epistle; *Evening & Morning Star;* faith; gathering; God; gospel; Holy Ghost; Latter-day Saints, Church of Jesus Christ of; Mormons; mysteries; Smith, Joseph; spirit.

Doctrine & Covenants, Book of, Section 1, V1:222-4 and ftnt
Section 2, V1:12
Section 3, V1:22
Section 4, V1:28
Section 5, V1:28-31
Section 6, V1:33-5
Section 7, V1:36
Section 8, V1:36-7
Section 9, V1:37-8
Section 10, V1:23 and ftnt
Section 11, V1:45-6
Section 12, V1:48
Section 13, V1:39
Section 14, V1:49-50

DOCTRINE & COVENANTS, BOOK OF (continued)

Section 15, V1:50
Section 16, V1:51
Section 17, V1:53
Section 18, V1:62, et seq
Section 19, V1:72 and ftnt, et seq
Section 20, V1:64, et seq
Section 21, V1:78-9
Section 22, V1:79-80
Section 23, V1:80
Section 24, V1:101, et seq
Section 25, V1:103-4
Section 26, V1:104
Section 27, V1:106, et seq
Section 28, V1:110-1
Section 29, V1:111, et seq
Section 30, V1:116
Section 31, V1:116-7
Section 32, V1:118-20
Section 33, V1:126-7
Section 34, V1:128
Section 35, V1:129, et seq
Section 36, V1:131
Section 37, V1:139
Section 38, V1:140, et seq
Section 39, V1:143, et seq
Section 40, V1:145
Section 41, V1:147
Section 42, V1:148, et seq
Section 43, V1:154-6
Section 44, V1:157
Section 45, V1:159, et seq
Section 46, V1:163-5 and ftnts
Section 47, V1:166
Section 48, V1:166-7
Section 49, V1:167, et seq
Section 50, V1:170-3 and ftnts
Section 51, V1:173-4
Section 52, V1:177-9
Section 53, V1:179-80
Section 54, V1:181
Section 55, V1:185-6

DOCTRINE & COVENANTS, BOOK OF (continued)

Section 56, V1:186-8 and ftnt
Section 57, V1:189-90
Section 58, V1:191, et seq
Section 59, V1:200-1
Section 60, V1:201-2
Section 61, V1:203-5
Section 62, V1:206
Section 63, V1:207, et seq
Section 64, V1:211, et seq
Section 65, V1:218
Section 66, V1:220-1
Section 67, V1:225
Section 68, V1:227, et seq
Section 69, V1:234-5 and ftnt
Section 70, V1:236-7
Section 71, V1:238-9
Section 72, V1:239, et seq
Section 73, V1:241-2
Section 74, V1:242
Section 75, V1:243, et seq
Section 76, V1:245, et seq
Section 77, V1:253, et seq
section 78, V1:255 and ftnt, et seq
Section 79, V1:257
Section 80, V1:257
Section 81, V1:257-8 and ftnt
Section 82, V1:267-9
Section 83, V1:269-70
Section 84, V1:287, et seq
Section 85, V1:298-9 and ftnts
Section 86, V1:300
Section 87, V1:301-2
Section 88, V1:302 and ftnt, et seq
Section 89, V1:327, et seq
Section 90, V1:329, et seq
Section 91, V1:331-2
Section 92, V1:333
Section 93, V1:343, et seq
Section 94, V1:346-7
Section 95, V1:350-2
Section 96, V1:352-3

DOCTRINE & COVENANTS, BOOK OF (continued)

Section 97, V1:400-2 and ftnts
Section 98, V1:403, et seq
Section 99, not recorded in the Documentary History of the Church
Section 100, V1:420-1
Section 101, V1:458 and ftnt, et seq
Section 102, V2:28, et seq
Section 103, V2:38, et seq
Section 104, V2:54, et seq
Section 105, V2:108, et seq
Section 106, V2:170-1
Section 107, V2:210 and ftnt, et seq
Section 108, V2:345
Section 109, V2:420, et seq
Section 110, V2:435-6
Section 111, V2:465-6
Section 112, V2:499, et seq
Section 113, V3:9-10
Section 114, V3:23
Section 115, V3:23, et seq and ftnts
Section 116, V3:35
Section 117, V3:45-6
Section 118, V3:46-7 and ftnt
Section 119, V3:44
Section 120, V3:44
Section 121, V3:289 and ftnt, et seq
Section 122, V3:289 and ftnt, et seq
Section 123, V3:289 and ftnt, et seq
Section 124, V4:274, et seq
Section 125, V4:311
Section 126, V4:382
Section 127, V5:142, et seq
Section 128, V5:148, et seq
Section 129, V5:267
Section 130, V5:323-4, 325
Section 131, V5:392-3 and ftnts
Section 132, V5:501 and ftnt, et seq
Section 133, V1:229, et seq
Section 134, V2:247, et seq
Section 135, V6:612, et seq
Section 136, not recorded in the Documentary History of the Church
British Mission, not to be taught in, V2:492

DOCTRINE & COVENANTS, BOOK OF (continued)

   Church, presented to, for acceptance, V2:243

   congregation, presented before, V1:236, ftnt only

   mentioned, first time, V1:105

   Norwegian, to be translated into, V7:425

   preface to, V2:250-1, ftnts only

   printing, first ordered, V1:270 and ftnt

   read for publication, V5:264

   title page to, V2:250, ftnt only

   Twelve, testimony of, to, V2:245 and ftnt.

   See also Commandments, Book of; epistles; prophecy; revelation; Smith, Joseph.

doctrine, erroneous, trial of Lyman Wight for teaching, V2:481.

doctrine, false, Hayes, Ezra, license taken from for teaching, V4:14.

   See also disfellowship; excommunication; Smith, Joseph.

doctrinal development, outline of churches belief in *Messenger & Advocate,* October 1834, V2:167, ftnt only.

   See also Apostles; doctrine; Latter-Day Saints, Church of Jesus Christ of; Smith, Joseph.

Dodge, A., mentioned, V6:2.

Dodge, Colonel, mentioned, V1:452.

Dodge, Reverend, mentioned, V6:557.

Dodge, S., mentioned, V6:2.

Doff, Peter, Zions Camp member, V2:183.

Dogberry Paper on Winter Hill, periodical, attempt to publish Book of Mormon in, V1:76, ftnt only.

Doherty, John F., secretary at public meeting in Missouri, V2:448, et seq.

Dollar Week Bostonian, publishes Book of Abraham facsimile, V5:11.

Dolph, Aaron, Kirtland Camp, expelled from, V3:128.

Domville, Thomas, ordained high priest, V4:333.

Donaldson, William, receives vision of going to Egypt, V4:168.

Doniphan, Alexander W., King, Judge, remarks on, V3:212-3

   Lucas, General, rebels against, V 3:190-1, ftnt only

   mentioned, V2:97, 98, 114-5

   military report of militia movements to David R. Atchison, V3:78-9

   Missouri, drafts resolution of public meeting in, V2:449

   Missouri saints, attorney for, V1:425

   Prophet, informs of mob movements in Daviess County, V3:161-2

   saints, lawyer and general in Missouri militia engaged as counsel for the, V3:69.

Doolittle, Leyrand, Carthage Greys, member of, V7:142.

Dopp, Peter, covenanted to assist saints in removing from Missouri, V3: 252.

Dorlan, Mr., delegate to political convention in Nauvoo, V6:389.

Dorman, Joseph, mentioned, V1:287, ftnt only.

Dort, David D., high council, appointed to Far West, V3:225
  Kirtland High Council, ordained to, V2:511
  Kirtland High Council, sustained to, V2:510
  Missouri, covenanted to assist saints in removal from, V3:253
  Missouri persecutions, expresses faith in work after, V3:225
  Nauvoo High Council, appointed to, V4:12
  Zions Camp member, V2:183

Doty, John, vice president of Warsaw anti-Mormon meeting, V6:462.

Doty, Vernon, mentioned, V6:123.

Dougherty, Edward, mentioned, V6:404
  Nauvoo, delegate to political convention in, V6:390.

Dougherty, John, petitions Governor Boggs on mob violence in DeWitt, V3:83.

Douglas, Stephen A., Nauvoo, visits, V4:356
  prophecy, explanation of fulfillment of, concerning, V6:395, ftnt only, et seq
  prophecy, on head of, V5:393
  Quincy committee on saints removal, member of, V7:450.
  See also persecutions, Illinois; prophecy; Smith, Joseph.

Douglas, Stephen L., renders decision on Joseph's trial at Monmouth, Illinois, V4:370.

Douglass, Mr., schoolmaster, member of martyrdom mob, V7:145.

dove, sign of, explanation of, V5:261.

Downe, Samuel, (also spelled Downes), British conference, represents, V5:420
  elder, ordained, V5:419.

Downey, Harvey, covenanted to assist saints in removing from Missouri, V3:252.

Downing, James, mission and field of labor, V6:337.

Doyle, John, father-in-law to John Lee, V3:56, ftnt only.

Drake, Diana, Zions Camp member, V2:185.

drama, in Nauvoo, V6:349-50.

Draper, Brother, turned over to buffetings of Satan for leaving meetings before sacrament, V2:326.

Draper, Alfred, Kirtland Camp, dissents against, V3:138.

Draper, Father, assists Elders Young and Kimball, et al, en route to England, V4:14.

Draper, Themira, Kirtland Camp, dissents against, V3:138.

Draper, Thomas, Kirtland Camp, dissents against, V3:138
    Kirtland Camp, subscribed to constitution of, V3:93.

Draper, William, Sr., Kirtland Camp, dissents against, V3:138
    Kirtland Camp, subscribed to constitution of, V3:93.
    Kirtland Temple, blessing for work on, V2:206
    patriarch, called to be, V7:624.

Draper, Zemira, Kirtland Camp, subscribed to constitution of, V3:93
    pays Joseph money in hour of need, V2:327.

dream, Carthage prison, of Joseph while in, V6:609
    Church, of Heber C Kimball on continuance and organization of, V7:228
    counsel, of Brigham Young, being given by Joseph, V7:435
    endowments, of Heber C. Kimball concerning receiving, V7:561
    flying and swimming, of, interpreted, V5:255
    God, from, only to and about calling at hand, V5:350
    gospel, of Heber C. Kimball on preaching, in London, V4:203
    Joseph, of fish and, V5:306
    Joseph interprets, V4:501
    Joseph, on plea to call out Nauvoo Legion, V5:301
    Kimball, Heber C., of, in Cincinnatti, V5:515-6
    Knight, Sister, fulfilled, V1:101
    mob, of Brigham Young to use Thomas Ford to knock down, V7:439
    Nauvoo, of Joseph concerning enemies at, V6:461
    troubled waters, of Joseph on, overcome, V6:194

Drew, Governor, of Arkansas, states cannot protect and suggests settle out west, V7:419.

drinking, members expelled from membership for, V3:341
    See also disfellowship; excommunication; liquor; Word of Wisdom.

Drovetti, Chevalier, mentioned, V2:348.

Drown, Charles, mentioned, V6:56.

Drummond, Henry, quoted, V6:306, ftnt only.

Drury, Joel, subscribed to constitution of Kirtland Camp, V3:92.

Dryden, Jonathan J., accuses saints of murder and burning, V3:165.

Dryden, William, arrest, issues writ for, of George A. Smith and Alanson Ripley, V3:77
  Governor, communication of, to the, V3:77
  Missouri, justice of the peace in, V3:64
  Mormons, states affidavit that law and order cannot be had in Caldwell County because of, V3:77.

Dryer, William W., mission and field of labor, V6:336
  Nauvoo, delegate to political convention in, V6:389.

Dudley, General, mentioned, V4:542.

Duel, Osman M., disfellowship, for following false revelation, V2:525
  Joseph, on relief expedition for, V5:486
  mission, assists Elders Young and Kimball on, V4:9-10
  mission and field of labor, V6:336
  ordination, approved for, V2:407.

Duel, Sister O. M., cares for Elders Young and Kimball, V4:10.

Duke, Jonathan O., mission and field of labor, V6:337.

Dunavan, Brother, mentioned, V7:311.

Duncan, Chapman, mission and field of labor, V6:337
  ordination, approved for, V2:407
  witness, suggested to appear before Congress on redress, V4:97.

Duncan, Father, mentioned, V2:242.

Duncan, James, utility committee member to aid Church removal, V7:474.

Duncan, Joe, Smith, Joseph, horse of, V5:60.

Duncan, John, mission and field of labor, V6:337
  Zions Camp member, V2:183.

Duncan, Joseph, anti-Mormon, governor of Illinois, V7:58
  saints, candidate for Illinois governor, against, V4:480, ftnt only, 490.
  See also persecutions, Illinois.

Duncan, Robert Kennedy, quoted, V6:310, ftnt only.

Duncan, William A., Church removal, utility committee member to aid, V7:474
  mission and field of labor, V6:340.

Dunham, Elder, mentioned, V4:6.

Dunham, Jonathan, arsenal, appointed superintendent to build, V5:430
  death of, V7:437
  Expositor, arrest of, for destruction of, trial on, V6:487, et seq
  Ford, Governor, on mission to, V6:61

DUNHAM, JOHATHAN (continued)

Joseph declares gratefulness to, V5:109

Joseph, on relief expedition for, V5:482

Kirtland Camp, subscribed to constitution of, V3:92

martyrdom, witness for Joseph at Carthage, V6:576

mission call and field of labor, V5:348

mission to Lamanites, V7:401

mob, letter to Ford for more militia to check, V7:159

Nauvoo, policeman in, V6:149

Nauvoo guard, orders to, V7:129

Nauvoo Legion, orders to, V7:134

shooting, threatened with, V3:116

west, returns from expedition from, V5:541

western country, to go to investigate for settlement, V6:223

western country, report on exploration of, V5:542, et seq

western country, starts on excursion to, V5:509

wharfmaster, made, V6:229

Young, Joseph, arrested for, V3:108.

Dunklin, Daniel, compromises suggested, V2:86

Kirtland, message of, arrives in, V2:177

Missouri governor, petition to, V1:410

mob, asserts that he is uncommitted to either, or Mormons, V2:85

Mormons, message to Missouri legislature concerning, V2:171-2

Mormons, states cause of unrest is beliefs and practices of, V2:85

negotiation, letter of, ordering arms back, V2:89

protection, letter rejecting, V1:476-8 and ftnts

saints, informs that arms were wrongfully taken and will be restored, V1:491

saints, letter to Clay County, questioning their conduct, V2:461

saints, letter describing status of, June 26, 1834, V2:117

saints, letter to, stating only redress in courts, V2:383-4 and ftnts

saints, refuses to reinstate in Jackson County, V2:94 and ftnt

saints, refusing to write President in behalf of, V1:488-9

saints, reply to petition of, V1:423-4

saints' arms, letter to Colonel Pitcher ordering him to return, V2:89.
See also letters; persecutions, Missouri; Smith, Joseph.

Dunlap, John S., mentioned, V6:422.

Dunlop, Dr., mentioned, V6:494, 502.

Dunn, Captain, Legion, sent to demand state arms from, V6:554-5

Nauvoo, comes to, for state arms, V7:83.

Dunn, Crandall, mentioned, V7:133

Michigan conference, presides at, V7:324

DUNN, CRANDALL (continued)

    mission and field of labor, V5:348.

Dunn, James, mentioned, V5:333
    Missouri, covenanted to assist saints in removing from, V3:253
    Zions Camp member, V2:183.

Dunn, James E., tavern keeper, member of martyrdom mob, V7:144.

Dunn, Simeon A., mission and field of labor, V6:336
    mission call in Illinois to disabuse public mind over arrest of Joseph,
        V5:485
    Nauvoo, policeman in, V6:150.

Dunn, Thomas, mission and field of labor, V6:339.

Dunn, William A., mentioned, V3:78.

Durfee, Amos, in high council, V2:151.

Durfee C., mentioned, V3:152.

Durfee, Edmund, Jr., elder, ordained, V2:207
    Kirtland Temple, blessing for work on, V2:206.

Durfee, Edmund, Sr., (also spelled Edmond), Backman, George, one of
        murderers of, V7:145
    bibliographical note of, V7:523-4
    high council, named to, at Lima, V5:427
    Kirtland Temple, blessing for work on, V2:206
    Missouri, covenanted to assist saints in removal from, V3:254
    mob, affiant to threats of, V6:481-2
    mob, attempting to draft into service, V6:510
    mob, shot by, and death of, V7:523 and ftnt
    murder, case of, V7:527, et seq
    murder of, discharged by magistrate, V7:532
    murder, witnesses in, discharged without hearing, V7:532
    Nauvoo Neighbor reports murder of, V7:528-30.
    See also persecutions, Illinois.

Durfee, James, Kirtland Temple, blessing for work on, V2:206
    mission appointment to East, V2:35.

Durphy, Francisco, prepares harvest feast in Nauvoo, V7:437.

Durphy, Jabez, mentioned, V4:18
    Nauvoo Temple, appointed carpenter on, V7:326.

Durphy, Perry, attacked by mob at voting incident, V3:57.

Durphy, Sister, mentioned, V5:294.

Dustin, Azariah, appointed counselor to bishop, V4:233.

Dustin, D. H., disfellowshipped for following false revelations, V2:525.

Dustin, David K., subscribed to constitution of Kirtland Camp, V3:92.

Dustin, Peter, appointed branch president in Missouri, V1:409, ftnt only
high council, on, V2:164.

Dutcher, Frederick R., justice of the peace, V6:68.

Duzette, Edward P., Legion, martial band member of, V4:300; V7:135
mission call and field of labor, V5:349.

Duzette, Philemon, Zions Camp member, V2:183.

Duzette, Sylvester, martial band member of Legion, V7:135.

Dyer, Charles V., letter to Brother Bennett on slavery, V4:544 and ftnt.

Dyer, John, Church, given care of, at Marden, V4:139
priest, ordained, V4:138.

Dykes, George P., Church, appointed to preside over new district of,
V7:306
letter on work among Illinois Scandinavians, V5:395
mission and field of labor, V5:348; V6:339
mission call in Illinois to disabuse public mind over arrest of Joseph,
V5:485
westward movement, captain of twenty-second company in, V7:482.

—E—

Eager, Lewis, subscribed to constitution of Kirtland Camp, V3:92.

Eagle, (Indian Chief), mentioned, V7:496-7.

Eagle, John, martyrdom, member of mob at, V7:146
mentioned, V5:290.

Eames, Ellis, mission and field of labor, V6:336
witness suggested to appear before Congress on redress, V4:97.

Earl, Jesse, martial band member of Legion, V7:135.

Earl, John T., Missouri, arraigned for treason, murder, burglary, arson,
robbery and larceny at Richmond, V3:209
Missouri trials, discharged as innocent from, V3:211.

Earl, Sylvester H., ordained elder, V2:525.

Earl, Wilbur J., duel, challenged to, V7:609.

Earl, William, Kirtland Camp, subscribed to constitution of, V3:93
Missouri, covenanted to assist saints in removal from, V3:252
Missouri, permit to travel in, V3:210.

earth, Joseph described in sanctified state, V5:279 and ftnt
See also doctrine; Smith, Joseph.

Easton, J., accessory to whipping, V6:284.

Eaton, E., publisher of *North Star,* V2:40.

Eaton, Francis, mentioned, V2:331.

Eaton, M. G., Joseph, affidavit on conspiracy against, V6:279
    witness for Joseph at Carthage martyrdom, V6:576.

Eaton, William, called on mission and field of labor, V5:347.

Eaves, Richard, on first sailing of saints from England, V4:134.

Echo, emigration ship, V4:297.

Eddy, Brother, mentioned, V7:80.

Eden, Garden of, marriage instituted in, V2:320.

editorials, ancient records, *Times & Seasons* on, V5:372-4
    happiness, on, V5:134-6, ftnt only
    Jews, on proscription of the, V5:434
    Joseph, the "Lions of the Press," V5:274-7
    Nauvoo Charter, *Wasp,* on, V5:306
    Nauvoo Neighbor, introductory editorial, V5:380-2
    persecution, *Times & Seasons* on, V5:98-103
    presidential election, *Times & Season,* V6:214-7
    Prophet, on recent arrest of, V5:507.

Edmiston, John, affidavit of mob attempting to draft into service, V6:510.

Edmonds, Esquire, mentioned, V7:550.

Edmunds, Brother, mentioned, V4:46.

education, Nauvoo, in, IntroV6:XXIV
    Nauvoo, outlined in, V4:290.
    See also Latter-day Saints, Church of Jesus Christ of.

Edwards, B. S., counsel for the Prophet, V5:221.

Edwards, Elisha, mission call and field of labor, V5:349
    Missouri, arraigned for treason, murder, burglary, arson, robbery and
        larceny at Richmond, V3:209
    Missouri trials, discharged as innocent from, V3:211.

Edwards, Esaias, appointed elder, V4:13.

Edwards, Francis M., mission and field of labor, V5:349; V6:339
    Nauvoo, policeman in, V6:150.

Edwards, John C., supreme court justice of Missouri, V3:289.

Edwards, Lieutenant, shot by member by mistake, V7:486.

Edwards, Thomas S., Church, expelled from, for assault and battery,
    V4:454
    elder, appointed, V4:13

EDWARDS, THOMAS S. (continued)

    elder, rejects appointment of, V4:13

    exploring expedition, volunteers for, V6:227.

Edwards, William, Joseph, on relief expedition for, V5:486.

Edwards, William H., Jr., elder, appointed, V4:13

    policeman in Nauvoo, V6:150.

Edwards, William W., Sr., Church, expelled from, for larceny, V4:454

    elder, appointed, V4:13

    Expositor, arrested for destruction of, V6:460.

Egan, Howard, Indian trouble, in, V7:627

    mission and field of labor, V6:335

    Nauvoo, policeman in, V6:150.

Egbert, Robert C., Joseph, on relief expedition for, V5:482.

Eggleston, Samuel, scribe in teachers quorum in Nauvoo, V5:169.

Egyptian, Book of Mormon, characters in, V1:20

    Joseph arranges grammar of, V2:238

    Joseph studies alphabet of, V2:286

    mummies displayed, V2:235

    mummies, story of how Joseph acquired, V2:348-51 and ftnt.

    See also Abraham, Book of.

elder, Apostles, on duty of, V3:395-6

    British Mission, quorums organized in, V4:136, 140

    calling, commanded to magnify, V7:307

    children, to preach first to parents before, V2:262

    Church, address of, to, V1:277, et seq, 280, 379, et seq

    Cowdery, Oliver, to be ordained, V1:60

    duties, in Zion expounded, V2:229, ftnt only

    eternal life, some sealed to, V1:323

    head of household, duty of, to preach to, V2:263

    head of household, preach only with consent of, V2:263

    high priests, no ordinations without conference of, V1:407

    high priests, relation to, V1:338-9

    iniquity, duty of, toward, V1:371

    Joseph, ordained, V1:78

    journals, importance of keeping, V6:186

    Missouri, mob, sign treaty with, V1:394 and ftnt

    ordination, defer to, V1:61

    president of, may ordain own counselors, V2:504

    quorum of, refuse order and spirit withdraws, V2:392

    Smith, Joseph, to be ordained, V1:61

    transgressor, rebuked for not punishing, V1:371.

Elder's Journal, epistle of David W. Patten in, V3:49, et seq
    Far West, published in, V3:28-30
    Kirtland, last number of, printed in, attacked and burned, V2:528
    prospectus of, V2:505
    questions, answers to, in, V3:28-30
    third number of, V3:49.

elder's school, commenced November 2, 1835, V2:299
    object of, V2:301
    organized, V2:169, 176
    organized and blessed, V2:301.

Eldredge, Horace S., mission and field of labor, V6:336
    mission call in Illinois to disabuse public mind over arrest of Joseph,
        V5:485
    westward movement, marshal in, V7:626.

Eldredge, Ira, sustained member of Salt Lake High Council, V7:629.

election, doctrine of, explained, V4:359
    expounded and explained, V3:379, et seq
    expounded upon, V4:256, et seq
    predestination, compared to, V4:258.
    See also doctrine; election and reprobation; Smith, Joseph.

election, presidential, candidate, 1844, who shall be, V6:187-8
    Times & Seasons, editorial on, V6:214-7.

election, state and national, 1844, V7:44
    relation of Mormons to, V7:44.

election and reprobation, Elders Brigham Young and Willard Richards
        on, V4:256.
    See also doctrine; doctrine of election; Smith, Joseph.

elements, eternal existence of, V6·308-9 and ftnts.

Elias, gave keys of priesthood to Peter, James and John on Mount,
        V3:387.

Elias, spirit of, Elijah, difference from spirit of, V6:252
    meaning and doctrine of, V6:249, et seq; 354.

Elijah, discourse on, V6:249, et seq
    mission of, reviewed, IntroV2:XXIX; V6:183-4
    priesthood, last to hold prior to Christ, V4:211.
    See also doctrine.

Elijah, spirit of, calling and election, makes sure, V6:252
    dead, is redemption of, V6:252
    Elias, spirit of, difference from, V6:252

ELIJAH, SPIRIT OF (continued)

meaning and doctrine of, V6:251.

Elkin, William F., mentioned, V5:238.

Ell, Doctor, mentioned, V4:94.

Eller, John, mobber at Haun's Mills, V6:503.

Elliot, Brother, charges against and dismissed, V1:470.

Elliot, Bradford W., Zions Camp member, V2:183.

Elliot, David, seventies, named to first quorum of, V2:203
    trial of, for whipping daughter unreasonably, V2:293, 295
    Zions Camp member, V2:183
    Zions Camp, shod horses of, V2:88, ftnt only.

Elliot, John C., Joseph, arrest for murder of, V7:372
    martyrdom mob, no business, member of, V7:144.

Elliot, L., trial of, for unchristianlike conduct, V2:442.

Elliot, Sister, mentioned, V2:295.

Elliott, Bradford W., mission and field of labor, V6:336.

Elliott, Henry, mission and field of labor, V6:339.

Elliott, John, arrested for kidnapping Daniel Avery, V6:117
    kidnaps Daniel Avery, V6:146
    recapture, attempted, V6:121
    trial of, for kidnapping, V6:117-8.

Elliott, John C., murderer of Joseph, V7:372.

Ellis, Philomen, mobber in Missouri, V4:61.

Ellison, John, beaten, V6:190
    Church, represents branches of, at English conference, V4:117, 147
    England, counselor on sailing from, V4:297.

Ellmer, Mr., Joseph reports death of, to Oliver Cowdery in the presence
    of Joseph, V2:169 and ftnt
    Prophet, mistreats, V2:168-9.

Ells, Dr., mentioned, V7:117-8.

Ells, Hannah, mentioned, V5:248.

Ells, Josiah, Joseph, on relief expedition for, V5:486.

Ellsworth, Edmund, mission and field of labor, V6:336.

Elmer, John, excommunicated for false teachings, V2:225.

Elsworth, B. C., mission and field of labor, V6:336.

Emell, John M., mission and field of labor, V6:337.

Emerald, emigrant ship, V5:180.

emigrants, letter reporting arrival of, V5:184

EMIGRANTS (continued)

    members, tried for fellowship if influence improperly, V4:403-4

    mentioned, V4:134, 412

    Nauvoo, arrival in, and remarks to, V5:354

    Nauvoo, recommend needed for acceptance in, V7:388, 405.

emigration, of saints from England, article on, and opposition, V4:510-13.

Emmett, J. M., mission and field of labor, V6:339.

Emmett, James, (also spelled Emmet, Emmitt), company, condition of, V7:383-5

    company, letter to, counseling, V7:377

    disfellowship for unwise conduct, V2:482

    exploring, volunteers for, V6:224

    fellowship restored to, V2:482; V7:434

    fellowship withdrawn from, V7:618

    genealogy, tries to lead away saints and, V7:269-70 and ftnt

    high council, appointed to, V4:352

    Joseph, pays money to, in time of need, V2:327

    mission, account of J. S. Fullmer to camp of, V7:495

    Nauvoo, bodyguard to Joseph's body on return to, V7:135

    Nauvoo, policeman in, V6:149

    son of, dies, V5:513

    status of, V7:383-4

    western country, to go investigate for settlement, V6:223.

Emmons, Sylvester, member of mob at martyrdom, V7:146

    mentioned, V5:415; V6:596

    publisher of *Nauvoo Expositor,* V6:430.

Empy, William, elder, ordained, V5:349

    mentioned, V5:454.

Endor, witch of, raised Prophet Samuel from grave, V4:571.

endowment, Apostles, of, foretold, V2:287

    Apostles, on getting, V6:13

    dream of Heber C. Kimball concerning receiving of, V7:561

    Kirtland, in, shortly to be fulfilled, V2:431

    Kirtland, some called to go to, to receive, V2:113

    mentioned, V2:197, 385; V4:277; V5:409; V6:319

    Nauvoo Temple, performed day and night in, V7:570

    Nauvoo Temple, received by members in, V7:543

    Prophet introduces, V5:2 and ftnt

    received, 1,000 had, V7:556

    Twelve, too dark to understand at present, V2:309

    Twelve, more of given, V6:98.

ENDOWMENT (continued)

See also Apostles; Smith, Joseph.

enemies, eyes of, blinded, V1:109.

England, see British Mission.

England, Allen, mobber wounded at Hauns' Mills massacre, V3:326, ftnt only.

English, Charles, testifies before high council, V2:137.

Enoch, dispensation, a president of, V4:209
Jude, appeared to, V4:209
Paul, appeared to, V4:209
prophecy of, V1:133
salvation, ministers to heirs of, V4:209
translated by God to be terrestial, V4:209.

Episcopal, clergyman of, preaches at Nauvoo, V5:427.

epistle, baptism for dead, expounded to Apostles by, V4:231
baptism for dead, Twelve Apostles to saints on, V4:472
Church, from Joseph in Liberty prison, V3:289 and ftnt, et seq
Church, Twelve to, on organization of, V7:250-2
Church papers, Twelve Apostles to Church instructing to subscribe to, V6:63
dispensations, David W. Patten on, V3:49
doctrines, Twelve to saints on various, V7:280, et seq
elders, instruct missionaries, V1:467-9
Europe, Apostles to saints in, V4:558, et seq
First Presidency to saints at Thompson, Ohio, V1:324
gathering, on, V1:379-87
gathering, Twelve Apostles to saints on, V4:409
gospel, Nauvoo High Council to saints on living, V5:15
Hancock County, Governor Ford warning people of, V6:189
history, Twelve to Church on collection of, and debt, V7:526
instructions, to Twelve on, V4:226, et seq
Kirtland, Nauvoo High Council counseling brethren not to return to, V4:45, ftnt only
Nauvoo, Twelve requesting brethren to return to, V7:198-9
Nauvoo Temple, Twelve Apostles on, V4:590
tithing, Twelve to Church on Temple and, V7:356, et seq
Twelve Apostles, V4:344, et seq
Twelve Apostles, to brethren, V4:433
Twelve Apostles, to Church, V3:393, et seq
Twelve Apostles, Joseph to, on instructions, V4:226, et seq
Twelve Apostles to saints, V4:558

EPISTLE (continued)

    Twelve Apostles to saints in Europe, V4:448

    westward movement, general to Church on, V7:478-80

    See also Apostles; doctrine; Latter-day Saints, Church of Jesus Christ of.

equipment, for family crossing the plains, V7:454-5.

Erickson, Judge, citizens committee to aid saints leaving DeWitt, V3:159.

Erving, W. L. D., letter of, on state payment for service in Nauvoo Legion, V6:95.

Ervingites, religious body sends representative to investigate Church, V2:233 and ftnt.

eternal judgment, necessary to gospel, V3:379.

    See also doctrine; judgment; Smith, Joseph.

eternal life, buffetings of Satan, once sealed to and sin, turned over to, V1:323

    children, can have in, V5:391

    Clayton, William, sealed to, V5:391

    elders, sealed to, by Joseph, V1:323

    God and Jesus Christ, to know, is, V6:305

    marriage, necessity of, to obtain, V5:391.

    See also doctrine; Latter-day Saints, Church of Jesus Christ of; Smith, Joseph.

eternal punishment, doctrine of, V1:72 and ftnt, et seq.

    See also doctrine; Latter-day Saints, Church of Jesus Christ of; Smith, Joseph.

Ettleman, Henry, named to high council at Lima, V5:428.

Ettleman, Philip, Zions Camp member, V2:183.

eulogy, of Lorenzo D. Barnes written by Parley P. Pratt, V5:319.

evangelical order, Joseph preaches on, V2:234 and ftnt.

    See also evangelist.

Evans, David, bishop, V5:311

    bishop, appointed, V5:119

    bishop, of a Nauvoo ward, V7:298

    Church, appointed to preside over new district of, V7:305

    delegate to present truth to public, V6:483

    Haun's Mills, cries for peace at, V3:184

    mission, assigned to go on, V4:429

    mission and field of labor, V6:337

    Nauvoo committee, affidavit on treatment of, by Levi Williams, V6:505

EVANS, DAVID (continued)

seventies, named to first quorum of, V2:203

westward movement, captain of 19th company in, V7:482

Zions Camp member, V2:183.

Evans, Doctor, mentioned, V7:124.

Evans, George H., (also spelled Geore), solicits Joseph's views on politics and views, V6:387-8.

Evans, Horace, covenanted to assist saints in removing from Missouri, V3:253.

Evans, Lewis F., vice-president of Warsaw anti-Mormon meeting, V6:462.

Evans, Roswell, covenanted to assist saints in removal from Missouri, V3:254

Zions Camp, exonerates Joseph's actions in, V2:149.

Evans, William, given care of Church at Stokes Lane, V4:139.

evangelist, is patriarch, V3:381.

See also doctrine; evangelical order; Smith, Joseph.

Evening & Morning Star, articles from, V1:273, 275, 276, 277, 280, 282, 283, 377 and ftnt

discontinued, V2:167 and ftnt

doctrinal instruction, December issue, 1833, to elders in Kirtland on ordination, stirring up contentions, boys to preach gospel, V1:467-8

Extra, V1:378-9 and ftnt

false prophets, answers Reverend Pixley's tract on, V1:373 and ftnt

"Free People of Color," article in, on, V1:377 and ftnt

Missouri, to be commenced in, V1:217

Missouri Enquirer, started from ruins of, V1:470

mob, concerning, V1:394, 398-9

Negro problem, V1:378 and ftnt

office location, V1:277

press of, demolished, V1:390

press purchased for, V1:217

prospectus, V1:259 and ftnt

prospectus sent to Joseph, V1:259

public opinion of, V2:40

published first number, V1:273

published second number, V1:277

published third number, V1:282

purpose devoted to, V1:275

republish, resolution to, at Kirtland, V1:409

saints' "Appeal," comments by Oliver Cowdery on, V2:126 and ftnt

world, state of, reported in, V1:388.

EVENING & MORNING STAR (continued)

   See also Latter-day Saints, Church of Jesus Christ of; newspapers.

Everett, Addison, Church, appointed to preside over new district of, V7:305

   counselor of New York branch, V4:344

   mob, affiant to public proclamation on lies of, V6:495

   Nauvoo Temple, appointed carpenter on, V7:326

   witness at *Expositor* affair trial, V6:491.

evil, exposed, not to be, at that time, V5:20

   good becomes, when used improperly, V5:209

   little does most injury to Church, V5:140.

   See also devil; doctrine; Latter-day Saints, Church of Jesus Christ of; Smith, Joseph.

evil spirits, attack brethren in England, V2:503

   nature of, V4:576.

   See also devil; evil.

Evord, Moses, covenanted to assist saints in removal from Missouri, V3:253.

Ewell, Pleasant, elder, ordained, V4:13

   mission and field of labor, V6:337.

Ewell, William, mobber who prevents group from traveling to Missouri, V3:324.

Ewing, Finis, Church, opposes, V1:372 and ftnt, 392

   Missouri mob, participated in, V1:392

   Missouri mob, prominence in, noted, V1:372, ftnt only.

Ewing, William L. D., mentioned, V4:245, 302, 305; V6:95-6.

exaltation, three keys to, V5:403.

   See also doctrine; God.

excommunication, acquired, to be more easily, V7:307

   adultery, of Lorenzo L. Lewis for, V2:285

   apostasy, James Blacksley for, V6:398

   apostasy, Austin Cowles for, V6:398

   apostasy, Francis M. Higbee for, V6:398

   apostasy, Charles Ivins for, V6:398

   Apostles, Benjamin Winchester for failure to follow, V7:275

   assault and battery, of Thomas S. Edwards for, V4:454

   Avard, Sampson, V3:284

   Carrol, James, V7:376

   Cavanaugh, Sister, V3:336

   Church, Job L. Lewis for treating with contempt, V2:444

   Church, R. Orton for showing contempt for authorities of, V2:527

EXCOMMUNICATION (continued)

Church, if shoot cattle and have unruly cattle, V7:476

Church counsel, those who produce lands without, V5:272-3

consecration, Edmund Bosley for breaking covenant of, V2:236

conversation, John A. Hicks for falsehood and schismatical, V4:428

Corrill, John, V3:284

Cowdery, Oliver, for various charges, V3:16-7 and ftnts

Dawson, William, Jr., and wife, V3:336

Dawson, William, Sr., and wife, V3:336

differences, Elders Barkdall and Keeler commanded to settle or will be, V2:228

disorderly conduct, Emma Bolton for, V4:216

faith, Wesley Hurlburt for denying, V2:2

false and slanderous reports, James Higby for, V1:355

false teachings, John Elmer for, V2:225

Foster, James, V7:297

Gardner, Freeborn, V3:336

Gardner, Simeon, V3:336

Gates, Hiram, V7:376

Gibbs, Luman, V3:336

Goodson, John, and wife, V3:336

Grigg, John, and wife, V3:336

high council, Joseph Henry Green for questioning and offending, V2:274-6

Hinkle, George M., V3:284

Hurlburt, "Doctor" Philastus, V1:352

Hurlburt, Philastus, second of, for deceiving Joseph, V1:355

improper conduct, James Patten for, V2:241

imprudent conduct, T. Tripp for, V2:54

Johnson, Lyman E., V3:20

larceny, Alanson Brown for, V4:454

larceny, William H. Edwards for, V4:454

larceny, James B. T. Page for, V4:454

Marsh, Thomas B., V3:284

Maynard, Jonathan, V3:336

Maynard, Nelson, V3:336

meetings, Nelson Acre for abstinance from, V1:469

Methodist Church, Erastus Holmes for receiving missionaries, V2:312

Miller, George, V3:336

mission, Daniel Copley for failure to fulfill, V1:354

money, Josiah Butterfield for getting and lifted up, V7:297

Nauvoo High Council, letter of, on saints that have been, V6:228-9

EXCOMMUNICATION (continued)

Nelson, George, V3:336
Nelson, Joseph, and wife, and mother, V3:336
Page, John E., V7:582-3
Peck, Reed, V3:284
Phelps, W. W., V3:8, 284
repent, must to every member who will not, V2:22
revelation, Sidney Roberts for false, V4:237
Rigdon, Sidney, V7:268-9
Rigdon, Sidney, Mr. Small for believing, V7:299
Riggs, Burr, V3:284
Riggs, Burr, for neglect of duty, V1:327
Russell, Mary, V3:336
Scott, Ann, V3:336
Scott, Isaac, V3:336
Scott, Jacob, Jr., V3:336
Scott, Jacob, Sr., V3:336
secret society, Sampson Avard for forming, V3:181
sins, Alonzo Rider and James Blanchard for failure to repent and,
    V1:469
Smith, William, V7:483
unchristianlike conduct, Robert D. Foster for, V6:341
unchristianlike conduct, Curtis Hodges for, V5:350
unchristianlike conduct, Charles Kelly for, V2:444
unchristianlike conduct, Jane Law for, V6:341
unchristianlike conduct, William Law for, V6:341
unchristianlike conduct, Wilson Law for, V6:341
unchristianlike conduct, Asael Perry for, V2:444
unchristianlike conduct, Wilkins J. Salisbury for, V2:442
unchristianlike conduct, Howard Smith for, V6:341
unvirtuous conduct, Chauncey L. Higbee for, V5:18
Walton, Robert, and wife, V3:336
Wanless, Ann, V3:336
Warnock, William, and wife, V3:336
Whitmer, David, for various charges, V3:18-9 and ftnts
Whitmer, John, V3:8
Williams, F. G., V3:284
Word of Wisdom, Milo Hays for breaking, V2:228
Word of Wisdom, Chester L. Heath for breaking, and covenants
    V2:218.
See also disfellowship; Latter-day Saints, Church of Jesus Christ of.
exploring, expedition formed, V6:227.

extermination order, of Governor Boggs against Mormons, V3:175, 426.
See also affidavits; Boggs, Lilburn W.; letters; mob; persecution; persecutions, Missouri; Smith, Joseph.

extradition, of Joseph, etc., by Governor Boggs requested, V4:198
legal opinion of attempt of Governor Boggs, of Joseph, V5:173
trial, argument at, of Joseph's, V5:221.

Eyres, George, devotes time to ministry, V5:419-20.

Ezekiel, Chapter 32 and 33, actions of world compared to, V5:22.

Ezra, Chapter 2:61-62 quoted, V1:299 and ftnt
fate of members, priesthood if cut off, V1:299.

—F—

facsimile, of Book of Abraham published, V5:11
of Book of Abraham shown, V4:543.
See also Abraham, Book of.

Fairchild, Joshua, mentioned, V2:482.

faith, atonement, shedding of blood in, cannot be exercised without, V2:15
comes by hearing word through servants, V3:379
explained, as wanting, V5:218
gifts, where lack of, no, V5:218
sin, without, is, V2:16
See also Abel; Apostles; Cain; doctrine; Latter-day Saints, Church of Jesus Christ of.

Faith, Articles of, see Articles of Faith.

faith, lectures on, taught to School of Prophets, V2:176, ftnt only.

falsehoods, published against Church, V1:158.

family, the, a church at Kirtland, existed in common stock prior to Church, V1:146 and ftnt.

Fanny, Barque, arrives in New Orleans, V6:244.

Far West, affairs of, V2:504-5
Caldwell, petition to locate county seat at, V3:56
Clark, General, arrival at, V3:201
fortification of, V3:188
Gallatin troubles, Ray County committee visits to inquire into, V3:62
Gallatin troubles, report of, reaches, V3:58
Kirtland Camp, arrival of, at, V3:85
land companies, organization of, at V3:64

FAR WEST (continued)

    liquor, use influence to stop selling of, in, V3:48

    mob commences action near, V3:166

    mob loots, V3:322-3

    Prophet, departure of, from, V3:193-4

    public meetings at, V3:249-50

    Twelve, meeting at, V3:336-9.

    See also Latter-day Saints, Church of Jesus Christ of; persecutions,
      Missouri.

Farlin, Orrin D., mission and field of labor, V6:337.

Farnham, Brother, mentioned, V6:248.

Farnham, Agustus A., mission and field of labor, V6:336

    witness in *Expositor* trial of Joseph, V6:457.

Farnhaus, Thomas J., recommends California for movement, V7:510.

Farnsworth, Philo, mentioned, V7:594.

Farnsworth, Stephen M., priests quorum, chosen president of, V6:175

    priests quorum, sustained president of, V7:298.

Farr, A. F., mission and field of labor, V6:339.

Farr, Lorin, mission and field of labor, V5:348.

Farr, Winslow, Church, appointed to preside over new district of, V7:305

    Church removal, utility committee member to aid, V7:474

    presides at New York conference, V7:405

    Twelve, appointed to go to England with, V3:347.

Farrar, Ann, to receive Church aid in emigrating from England, V5:412.

fasting, anti-Mormons call for, to bring Joseph to repentance, V6:221

    doctrine of, explained, V7:413

    Nauvoo, for Senator, V4:389.

    See also doctrine; Smith, Joseph.

father, head of house, duty to preach to, V2:263

    head of household, preach only with consent of, V2:263

    police in Nauvoo to act as, V6:124.

fault finding, key to apostasy, V3:385.

Fayette, New York, Church organized at, V1:76-7

    conference of Church in, V1:140

    first public meeting held at, V1:81

    Joseph moves to, V1:109

    Joseph returns after Newel Knight miracle, V1:84

    Prophet moves to, V1:49

    Whitmer, Peter, Sr., from, V1:48

    Whitmers, residence of, V1:49.

Fellows, Albert G., mentioned, V6:554.

Fellows, Hart, mentioned, V7:83
    Nauvoo, Ford's messenger to, V7:149
    Nauvoo City Council, communication to, V7:150.

Felshaw, William, Church, appointed to preside over new district of, V7:305
    mission and field of labor, V6:336
    Missouri, covenanted to assist saints in removal from, V3:254
    Nauvoo Temple, appointed carpenter on, V7:326
    pays Joseph money in hour of need, V2:327.

Felt, N. H., mentioned, V7:620.

Ferrin, Samuel, ordained elder, V5:349.

Ferris, John M., anti-Mormon committee member of Warsaw meeting, V6:464.

Ferry, L. H., appointed to preside over new Church district, V7:305.

Fidoe, John, (also spelled Fido), Church, given care of, at Bishop Froome, V4:139
    Joseph, on relief expedition for, V5:482.

Field, Mr., editor of Reveille, V7:152.

Field, Asa, Zions Camp member, V2:183.

Field, William, subscribed to constitution of Kirtland Camp, V3:92.

Fielding, Amos, British Mission, mission in, V4:149
    Church, to return to England as agent of, V6:263
    English conference, represents branch of Church at, V4:116, 148
    exploring, volunteers for, V6:224
    high priest, ordained, V4:333
    ministry, devote all time to labors of, V4:148
    Nauvoo, arrives in, V5:8; V6:171
    Nauvoo, commanded to return to, V5:386
    volunteers for service in vineyard, V4:217.

Fielding, James, Church, closes doors and fights, V2:502
    elders, accuses of stealing flock, V2:506
    English minister offers pulpit to brethren, V2:499.

Fielding, John, father to Joseph, V2:492, ftnt only.

Fielding, Joseph, British Mission, departs for, V2:493
    British Mission, mission in, V4:149
    Church, chosen president of, in England, V3:20
    Church, represents branch at English conference, V4:116, 147
    elder, ordained, V2:529

FIELDING, JOSEPH (continued)

    England, preaches in, V4:7

    genealogy, missionary to England and, V2:492 and ftnt

    Greenwood, Hannah, marries, V3:38

    ministry, devotes all time to labors of, V4:148

    Warsaw, arrives in, V4:471

    westward movement, captain of ninth company in, V7:481.

Fielding, Mary, sister to Joseph, V2:492, ftnt only.

Fielding, Mercy Rachel, wife of Robert B. Thompson, V4:411.

Fielding, Rachel, mother to Joseph, V2:492, ftnt only.

Fielding, Rachel, sister to Joseph, V2:492, ftnt only.

Fields, A., arrested, V5:311.

Fife, Peter, mission and field of labor, V6:337.

Fifty, Council of, meeting of, V7:379 and ftnt

    note on, V7:381-2

    purpose of, explained, V7:213.

    See also Apostles; Latter-day Saints, Church of Jesus Christ of;
        Smith, Joseph.

Filcher, Thomas J., ordained elder, V4:322.

Finch, John M., Illinois, mobber in, V7:530

    martyrdom mob, member of, V7:144, 146

    socialist, lectures in Nauvoo, V6:32.

Findley T., appointed by public to assist saints in removal from Zion,
    V2:455.

Firkins, Joseph, ordained priest, V4:135.

firms, Cowdery and Co., dissolved, V2:475

    Gilbert & Whitney, mob wrecks store, V1:427-8

    United Zion and Kirtland, V1:270 and ftnt.

    See also Latter-day Saints, Church of Jesus Christ of.

First Presidency, see Presidency, First.

Fisher, Cyrus B., Kirtland Camp, leaves, V3:140

    Kirtland Camp, subscribed to constitution of, V3:92.

Fisher, Daniel, mission and field of labor, V6:336.

Fisher, Edmund, seventies, named to first quorum of, V2:203

    Zions Camp member, V2:183.

Fisher, Edward, Church, appointed to preside over new district of,
    V7:306

    Iowa Territory High Council, appointed to, V4:12.

Fisher, Jonathan, Kirtland Camp, leaves, V3:140

FISHER, JONATHAN (continued)

Kirtland Camp, subscribed to constitution of, V3:92.

Fisher, Rufas, appointed to preside over new Church district, V7:305.

Fisher, Thomas, blessing for work on Kirtland Temple, V2:206.

Fisher, Thomas G., subscribed to constitution of Kirtland Camp, V3:91.

Fisher, Thomas J., covenanted to assist saints in removal from Missouri, V3:253.

fisher's net, parable of, explained, V2:272.

Fisk, Alfred, dies of cholera in Missouri, V2:120
Zions Camp member, V2:183.

Fisk, Hezekiah, Zions Camp member, V2:183.

Fisk, Starry, blessing for work on Kirtland Temple, V2:206.

Fisk, William, blessing for work on Kirtland Temple, V2:206.

Fiske, Mr., quoted, V6:310, ftnt only.

Fitzhugh, Reverend, participated in Missouri mobs, V1:372, ftnt only, 392.

Flack, James, mentioned, V5:454; V6:414.

flag, blood red, seen in heavens, V4:252.

Flagg, Brother, mentioned, V6:62.

Flanigan, James H., mission and field of labor, V5:347
mission to Great Britain, V7:625
mission, report of, V7:522.

Fleming, Samuel, constable, member of martyrdom mob, V7:144.

flesh, Mormon prisoners fed, in Missouri, V3:420, 448.

flesh and blood, shower of, reported, V4:383, 414.

Flint, J., ordained priest, V5:419.

Flood, William G., mentioned, V6:561.

Florey, Major, citizens committee to aid saints leaving DeWitt, V3:159.

Flournoy, James H., postmaster, signed mob manifesto, V1:376
secretary to anti-Mormon meeting in Missouri, V1:395.

Folger, John R., subscribed to constitution of Kirtland Camp, V3:91.

Follet, John, mentioned, V2:46.

Follett, King, biography, V6:249
Columbia prison, escape, recapture and release from, V3:401-2 and ftnt
death of, V6:248
funeral, V6:249
Joseph, funeral sermon delivered by, V6:302, et seq

FOLLETT, KING (continued)

    just, gone to home of, V6:315

    Missouri prison, set free from, V4:17

    Richmond, imprisoned at, V3:335

    robbery, indictment for, V3:360

    witness, suggested to appear before Congress on redress, V4:97

    Zion, arrives in, V2:301.

Folsom, William H., clerk of New York conference, V6:1 and ftnt

    genealogy of, Church architect, V6:1, ftnt only

    mission and field of labor, V6:339.

font, baptismal, of Nauvoo Temple described, V4:446.

Foot, Reuben, ordained elder, V4:13.

Foot, Stephen V., covenanted to assist saints in removal from Missouri, V3:252.

Foote, David, (also spelled Foot), buried, genealogy of, V7:436-7

    Missouri, covenanted to assist saints in removal from, V3:253.

Foote, Timothy B., mission and field of labor, V6:336.

Forboin, R., appointed by public to assist saints in removing from Zion, V2:455.

Forbush, Mr., asks assistance from Church, V3:261.

Ford, Mr., mentioned, V2:63.

Ford, Jonathan, mentioned, V7:371.

Ford, Thomas, Carthage, address of, to troops in, V7:5

    Carthage, arrival at, accepts mob as militia, V6:542

    Carthage, course at, V6:625

    Carthage jail, admits that did suspect some attack would be made, V7:22 and ftnt

    Carthage jail, again disclaims knowledge of assault on, V7:20

    Carthage jail, defense of, use of Carthage Greys as guard on, V7:17, et seq and ftnts

    Carthage jail, directs justice R. F. Smith to use Carthage Greys, V6:594-5

    Carthage jail, disclaims all fears of assault on, V7:13

    Carthage jail, interview with Joseph in, V7:88, et seq

    Carthage jail, mob action, attack on, V7:30-1

    Carthage jail, orders Captain R. F. Smith of Carthage Greys to guard, reasons, V7:17, et seq

    character, of men surrounding, V7:75

    Church, on the reorganization of, V7:37, et seq

    Church, suggests western movement of, V7:398

FORD, THOMAS (continued)

Church, on teachings and spread of the, V7:39, et seq

court, letters to General Deming on defense in murder case, V7:409

daily reports to, V7:69

epistle of, to citizens of Hancock County, warning, V6:189-90

extermination or expulsion, appeals made to, for clean sweep from state, V7:20

forces at his command, V7:14

forces, threats of rebellion within own, V7:15

Ford's History of Illinois, excerpt from Part I, V7:1; Part II, V7:33

fury, on blowing up in Hancock County, V7:65

Illinois, article of, to people of, V7:140-1

Illinois, governor of, speaks again of powers of Nauvoo, V5:200

interruptions by, V7:76

interview of, with Taylor and Bernhisel, V6:543-5

jailor, suggestions to, for comfort of prisoners, V6:598

Joseph, account of interview with, by John Taylor, V6:579, et seq

Joseph, admits pledging safety of, V7:48-9

Joseph, answer of, to Warsaw mob, review of murder of, V7:160, et seq

Joseph, attitude when informed of death of, V7:24

Joseph, believes that assassination meant for him as well as, V7:26

Joseph, consents to interview with, in Carthage jail, V6:576

Joseph, defense for permitting commitment of, to prison, V7:13

Joseph, documents, proving no militia call to arrest, prior to elections, V5:533, et seq

Joseph, hears threats of killing, V6:603

Joseph, hears threats on life of, V6:594

Joseph, informed of illegal arrest for treason of, V7:85

Joseph, interview of, with, at Carthage jail, V6:77, et seq

Joseph, letter to, dispelling ideas of invasion by Missourians, V6:35

Joseph, letter to, guaranteeing safety in Carthage, V6:533, et seq

Joseph, letter to, on Missouri writs and kidnapping, V6:113, et seq

Joseph, letter to, refusing to recind arrest orders, V5:205-6

Joseph, letter to, requesting he come to Carthage, V6:521

Joseph, openly subjects Hyrum and, to imprisonment, V6:570

Joseph, opinion and description of, V7:35, et seq

Joseph, opinion of followers of, V7:36-7

Joseph, order of arrest of, in Springfield trial, V5:235-6

Joseph, order of release of, in Springfield trial, V5:244

Joseph, pledge of, to, V7:77

Joseph, pledge of, as governor to protect, V6:561

Joseph, pledge of, to go to Nauvoo, V6:585

FORD, THOMAS (continued)

Joseph, presents to militia, V6:564

Joseph, refuses escort to Carthage, for safety, V6:552

Joseph, replies to petition for military to arrest, V5:492

Joseph, report of speech of, before militia at Carthage against, V6:563

Joseph, responsibility in martyrdom of, V7:113, et seq

Joseph, sent transcripts of second trial of, V5:478-9

Joseph, John Taylor on responsibility for murder of, V7:113, et seq

Joseph, John Taylor sent to, from, on problems, V7:71, et seq

Joseph, threatens writ against, V5:433

Joseph, trial of the murderers of, V7:49, et seq

Joseph, warned of conspiracy to take life of, V6:611

Joseph, was Governor Ford responsible for the murder of—summary of
    evidence, V7:113, et seq

Joseph, writ on, V5:465

law enforcement, on status of, in Hancock County, V7:51

martyrdom, account of, V7:30-1

martyrdom, apparent zeal for the law in connection with, V7:5

martyrdom, control of local authorities of, V7:12-3

martyrdom, expected civil war to follow, V7:26-7

martyrdom, flees the zone of, V6:625

martyrdom, governor and party thrown into confusion by the news of,
    V7:25

martyrdom, hears signal of, V7:110

martyrdom, intercepts messenger carrying news of, to Nauvoo, V7:24

martyrdom, letter of, desiring brethren to come converse with, on,
    V7:200

martyrdom, letter to General Deming on threatened outbreaks after,
    V7:146

martyrdom, prevents news of, from reaching Nauvoo, V6:624

martyrdom, report of message of, to legislature, V7:328

martyrdom, review of performances of, pertaining to, V7:2

martyrdom, visit to Nauvoo after, V7:276

militia, general orders of, to, in Western Illinois, V7:141-2

militia, interview of Bishop Miller with, on, and mob in Hancock,
    V7:492-3

Missouri extradition, hears petition for repeal of, V5:205

mob, Joseph accuses of being part of, V6:542

mob, pacifies, V6:560

Mormon period, supplies history of, V7:1, et seq

Mormonism, in perspective, a possible development, V7:40-1

Mormons, declares government at an end for, in Hancock County,
    V7:51

FORD, THOMAS (continued)

Mormons, had plan to rid state of, V7:14

Mormons, promise of protection to, in case they surrender, V7:5

Mormons, threatens to call full force of state unless submit, V7:6

murderers, letter to Almon Babbitt, vacillation on trial of, V7:409-11

Nauvoo, advice on status of, sought, V7:389

Nauvoo, denies menacing citizens of, as election bribe, V5:532

Nauvoo, determines on conciliation visit to, V7:17

Nauvoo, dissuaded from militia march by militia officers, V7:6-7

Nauvoo, fears of consequences in destroying, V7:15-6

Nauvoo, holds militia council on visit to, V6:599-600

Nauvoo, infamous speech at, V6:623

Nauvoo, instructions to, V7:150

Nauvoo, leaves for, V6:612

Nauvoo, letter on organization of town government within, V7:396, et seq

Nauvoo, proposal to march state militia into, V7:6

Nauvoo, speech at, V7:23

Nauvoo, visit to, V6:623

Nauvoo Legion, demands state arms of, V6:555

Nauvoo Legion, letter authorizing use of, to protect courts, V7:309

Nauvoo Mansion, arrives at, V7:132

peace, article to people of Hancock on, V7:214-5

peace, false attempt of, at procuring United States troops for, V7:28-9 and ftnts

perplexity of, V6:552

political considerations, on the, after Joseph's death, V7:44, et seq

political voting, comments on, of saints as unit, V7:2-3

Rigdon, Sidney, estimate of, V7:38

saints, demands on to expel from Illinois, V7:28

saints, letter to Sheriff Backenstos informing that United States government after, V7:562-4 and ftnts

saints, letter to Phelps on official position and feelings toward, V7:203, et seq

saints, opinion on understanding of the, on law, V7:24

saints, states he will not intervene with expulsion of, from state, V7:94 and ftnt

saints, turned against, V7:577

sermons, on the, delivered, V7:41-2 and ftnt

Smiths, believed his own death part of the scheme against, V7:26

Smiths, charges that anti-Mormons stimulated followers to murder, V7:13

Spencer, O., letter to George Miller repudiating letter of, V7:505

FORD, THOMAS (continued)

Spencer, O., letter to, repudiating former's letter, V7:505

Spencer, O., reported interview with, V7:423-4

state arms, the amount of, surrendered, V7:10

state arms, demands, V7:9

thefts, misled by false reports of, V7:4.

See also Carthage, Illinois; Carthage jail; letters; martyrdom; mob; Nauvoo; persecutions, Illinois; Smith, Joseph.

Ford, William, mentioned, V5:299.

Fordham, Elijah, Church, appointed to preside over new district of, V7:305

elder, to be, V2:354

healed by the Prophet, V4:4, ftnt only

Iowa Territory High Council, appointed to, V4:12

Joseph commands to be healed, V4:4

mission call in Illinois to disabuse public mind over arrest of Joseph, V5:485

Nauvoo, before high council at, V4:180

Nauvoo Temple, worked on, V4:446; V7:394

New York, only member in, assists British Mission on way, V2:494

pays Joseph money in time of need, V2:327

Zions Camp member, V2:183.

Fordham, George, Zions Camp member, V2:183.

foreign affairs, Glasgow, of Church in, V7:536.

See also Latter-day Saints, Church of Jesus Christ of.

Forgeus, John A., mission in Illinois to disabuse public mind over arrest of Joseph, V5:485.

forgiveness, charity and, V4:445

give on first intimations of repentance, V3:383.

See also doctrine; repentance; Smith, Joseph.

Forney, Frederick, Zions Camp member, V2:183.

fornicator, curse upon, V4:587.

Fosdick, Sister, mentioned, V3:319.

Fossett, John, Zions Camp member, V2:183.

Fossett, William M., covenanted to assist saints in removing from Missouri, V3:252.

Foster, Charles A., Joseph, accuses of being meanest man in world, V6:451

Joseph, draws gun on, arrested, V6:344

mob, member of, at martyrdom, V7:146.

Foster, Elder, mentioned, V4:22.

Foster, J. H., mission and field of labor, V6:339.

Foster, James, blessing given to, V2:244
excommunication of, V7:297
Kirtland Camp, addresses meeting of, V3:97
Kirtland Camp, leaves to go to DeWitt, V3:145-6
Kirtland Camp, mentioned in, V3:125
Kirtland Camp, proposes disbandment of, V3:144
Kirtland Camp, subscribed to constitution of, V3:91
rejected by vote and resustained by confession, V4:342
seventies, reports movements of, V3:93
seventies, sustained president of, V2:510; V4:285
seventy, member of first council of, favors organization of Kirtland Camp, V3:88-9
Zions Camp member, V2:88, ftnt only; 183.

Foster, Lucien R., clerk, V7:554
Joseph, visits, V6:347
Nauvoo, delegate to convention in, V6:389
president of New York branch, V4:344.

Foster, Mrs., mentioned, V6:271.

Foster, Robert D., abusive language, charges preferred against for, V5:14
apostle, appointed of new church by apostates, V6:347
charges, acquitted of, V4:250
committee, on Church, V4:107
court martial of, V6:362
elder, appointed, V4:13
excommunicated for unchristianlike conduct, V6:341
Joseph, account of accosting, V6:348
Joseph, accusations against, V6:345
Joseph, fear of meeting at bar of God, V7:513
Joseph, shakes garments against, V6:345
lying, slandering and profane language, tried for, V4:239, 250
martyrdom, feelings of, on, and position, V7:513
martyrdom, member of mob at, V7:146
mentioned, V5:252, 287; V7:66-7, 75, 176
mission and field of labor, V5:348
mob movements, letter on, V6:520
Nauvoo, ordered from by Mrs. Hyrum Smith, et al., V7:176
Nauvoo, prominent in life of, V7:57
Nauvoo court, case of, before, V6:345

FOSTER, ROBERT D. (continued)

Nauvoo Legion, court-martial called on, in, V6:355

positions, requests return to former, V6:429

Prophet, fails to keep journal of, V4:89

Prophet, misunderstanding of, with, V6:332-3, 344-5

Prophet, seeks private interview with, V6:430

Prophet and Patriarch, thought to be accessory to the murder of, V7:169

Redden, Jackson, attempts to kidnap, V7:486-7

Rigdon, Sidney, attends, V4:19-21

Taylor, John, impressions of, after apostasy, V7:57.

Foster, Sister, interview of Joseph with concerning accusations on Joseph's virtue, V6:271.

Foster, Solon, elder, ordained, V2:321

mission and field of labor, V6:336

Zions Camp member, V2:183.

Fouts, Noal, mentioned in Kirtland Camp, V3:136.

Foutz, Jacob, bishop, appointed, V5:119

bishop, sustained of a Nauvoo ward, V7:298

bishop's counselor, appointed, V4:233

Church, appointed to preside over new district of, V7:306

Haun's Mills, wounded by mob at, V3:326, ftnt only

Joseph, on relief expedition for, V5:482

Missouri persecutions, affidavit of, concerning, V4:68-9.

Fowler, George W., mission and field of labor, V6:336.

Fowler, O. S., gives phrenological charts of Apostles, V6:37.

Fowler, Samuel, Kirtland Camp, subscribed to constitution of, V3:92

stake president, counselor to, V4:236.

Fox, Jesse, witnesses celestial phenomenon, V6:121.

Fox, John, kidnapper of D. Avery, V6:123.

Fox, Lorenzo, witnesses celestial phenomenon, V6:121.

Fox, S., captain of steamship, V2:463.

Fox, William, witnesses celestial phenomenon, V6:121.

Fox Island, mission to, V2:507 and ftnt

work of Church on, V4:418.

Foy, Matthew, blessing for work on Kirtland Temple, V2:205.

Frampton, David, Missouri, arraigned for treason, murder, burglary, arson, robbery and larceny at Richmond, V3:209

Missouri, covenanted to assist saints in removal from, V3:254

Missouri trials, discharged as innocent from, V3:211.

Frampton, Nathaniel, mentioned, V4:144.

France, mission to, opened, V6:356.

Franklin, L., mentioned, V2:93, ftnt only.

Franklin, Lewis, jailor, signed mob manifesto, V1:376
 mob, carries proposals to saints from, V1:398
 mobber, in militia appointed to receive arms of saints, V1:434.

"Free People of Color," published in *Evening & Morning Star*, as answer
 to mob manifesto Negro accusation, V1:377 and ftnt.

Freedom, Adams County, Illinois, stake organized at, V4:233.

freedom, religious, Joseph on, V6:304
 Missouri Constitution on, V1:374.

Freedom conference, of Apostles to examine Church, V2:224.

Freeman, Brother, mentioned, V2:526.

Freeman, Elam L., messenger from Governor Ford, V6:520.

Freeman, E. S., blacksmith, member of martyrdom mob, V7:144.

Freeman, Schrench, mentioned, V6:109.

Freeman, William S., messenger to governor from anti-Mormon meeting,
 V6:466.

Fremont, J. C., mentioned, V6:375.

French, Peter, mentioned, V4:77
 saints to purchase farm of, V1:335-6.

friendship, Joseph on, V5:517
 oaths weaken, V3:303.

Frierson, John, Calhoun, John C., represents, V6:81 and ftnt
 Missouri persecutions, writes memorial to Congress for redress on,
  V6:83, et seq and ftnt.

Frink, J. M., martial band member of Legion, V7:135.

Fristoe, Richard, mob, carries proposals to saints from, V1:398
 saints, signs proposition to buy land of, V2:96-7.

Frodsham, John, charged with disorderly conduct, V6:155.

Frost, Olive, mentioned, V7:315.

Frost, Samuel B., mission and field of labor, V6:338.

Frye, William, mentioned, V2:350, ftnt only.

Fugate, W., testifies to finding Kinderhook plates, V5:377.

Fulkerson, John, chains Joseph and prisoners, V3:206.

Fullars, Mr., member of mob, V1:265, ftnt only.

Fuller, Amos B., Kirtland Camp, subscribed to constitution of, V3:91

FULLER, AMOS B. (continued)

    mentioned, V4:416

    mission and field of labor, V5:348

    revelation to, V4:483.

Fuller, Elijah, mentioned, V2:398.

Fuller, Josiah, Haun's Mills, killed by mob, V3:326, ftnt only

    Kirtland Temple, blessing for work on, V2:206.

Fuller, Samuel, mentioned, V5:399.

Fuller, Thomas, mission and field of labor, V6:336.

Fullmer, Almon L., Joseph, on relief expedition for, V5:486

    volunteers for exploring expedition, V6:226.

Fullmer, B., mentioned, V6:425.

Fullmer, David, Church, appointed to preside over new district of, V7:306

    exploring, volunteers for, V6:224

    Nauvoo High Council, appointed to, V4:12

    Nauvoo High Council, sustained member of, after death of Joseph, V7:296

    western country, to go to investigate for settlement, V6:233

    westward movement, captain of eleventh company in, V7:482.

Fullmer, John L., mission and field of labor, V6:338.

Fullmer, John S., baptized for sickness, V7:495

    Carthage prison, with Prophet in, V6:600-1

    Church, appointed to preside over new district of, V7:305

    elder, appointed, V4:12

    exploring, volunteers for, V6:224

    mission, account of, to Emmett's Camp, V7:495-8

    Nauvoo, goes to, after witnesses, V7:101.

fulness of times, dispensation of, Adam holds keys of, V4:207

    epistle of David W. Patten on, V3:49, et seq

    to be exactly like all previous ones, V4:208.

    See also dispensation; doctrine.

—G—

Gabriel, is Noah, V3:386.

Gaines, General, mentioned, V6:373-4.

Gallaher, Byrant, (also spelled Gallacher), grandfather to Sidney Rigdon, V1:120, ftnt only.

Gallaher, Elizabeth Reed, grandmother to Sidney Rigdon, V1:120, ftnt only.

Gallaher (family), mentioned, V7:143.

Galland, Isaac, baptized and ordained elder, V3:393
Church, introduces to Commerce, Illinois, V3:265
Church, letter of, concerning welfare of members, V3:265-7
letter, power of attorney for the Prophet cancelled, V4:495, 500
letter, Prophet's to V4:8-9
letter to *Quincy Argus* on saints' reception in Iowa, V3:317
witness, suggested to appear before Congress, V4:97.

"The Gallant Ship is Under Weigh," sung at departure for British Mission, V4:103 and ftnt.

Gallatin, county seat of Daviess County, election trouble at, V3:56, et seq.

Galley, Mr., English conference, represents branches at, V6:327.

Galley, James, British conference, represents area in, V5:9, 419
high priest, ordained, V4:333.

Galley, John, given care of Church at Hope Rough, V4:139.

Galliher, James, (also spelled Gallaher), mission call amidst mob action in Missouri, V3:153
Missouri, covenanted to assist saints in removal from, V3:253.

gambling, priesthood taken because of, V2:241
saints, commanded to put out of minds, V7:350.

Gannet, Henry, receives patriarchal blessing, V2:387.

Garden of Eden, see Eden, Garden of.

Gardner, A., mentioned, V4:489.

Gardner, Daniel W., mission and field of labor, V6:335.

Gardner, Freeborn, excommunicated from Church, V3:336.

Gardner, Freeburn H., witness for state in Missouri trials of saints, V3:210.

Gardner, John, mobber in Missouri, V4:61.

Gardner, Morgan L., Church, wife of, asks assistance from, V3:261
mission and field of labor, V6:337.

Gardner, Philip, selected counselor of high priests quorum at Yelrome, V6:346.

Gardner, Simeon, excommunicated from Church, V3:336.

Gardner, William, affidavit on attempt to draft into mob, V6:510-11.

Garn, Daniel, (also spelled Garns), bishop, appointed, V5:119
bishop, sustained of a Nauvoo ward, V7:298

GARN, DANIEL (continued)

Carthage, threatened with arrest at, V7:71

Church, appointed to preside over new district of, V7:305

elders quorum, president of, V4:430

Joseph, false writ against for aiding, V7:444

Joseph, guard at home of, V7:57

Missouri, arraigned for murder, treason, burglary, arson, robbery and larceny at Richmond, V3:209

Nauvoo, policeman in, V6:149

Nauvoo Temple, appointed to officiate in, V7:548

westward movement, in organization of, V7:626.

Garner, Philip, named to high council at Lima, V5:428.

Garner, William, affidavit of mob attempting to draft into service, V6:511.

Garnett, Henry, farmer, member of martyrdom mob, V7:144.

Garrick, preaching on board of, V2:498

vessel, carried first missionaries to England, V2:494.

Gates, Benjamin B., anti-Mormon committee chairman, V6:8.

Gates, Gibson, affidavit of, concerning Missouri persecutions, V4:71.

Gates, Henry, reports mob movements, V6:519.

Gates, Hiram, expelled from Church, V7:376.

Gates, Jacob, mission and field of labor, V5:348

Missouri, arraigned for treason, murder, burglary, arson, robbery and larceny at Richmond, V3:209

Zions Camp member, V2:183.

Gates, Mary Snow, Zions Camp member, V2:185.

Gates, Thomas, Church, appointed to preside over new district of, V7:306

Doctrine & Covenants, testifies to truthfulness of, V2:246

Kirtland Temple, blessing for work on, V2:206

mentioned, V2:244

Missouri, covenanted to assist saints in removing from, V3:253.

gathering, anti-scriptural, example of argument as, V4:250

British Mission, not to be taught in, V2:492

Church, keys of restored to, IntroV2:XXVI

Christ's rejection prevents, V1:313

comments on, V2:357-8

explanation of, V1:277, et seq

Israel of old, as to, V1:381-3

Israel, John E. Page on, of, V3:125-6 and ftnt

Jews, spirit of, on, IntroV2:XXVII

GATHERING (continued)

Joseph expounds, V2:260, et seq

Joseph expounds upon, V2:264, et seq

limited to Hancock County, Illinois, and Lee County, Iowa, V4:410

Missouri, discussion of correctness after, V3:260

motives of, V2:254

Nauvoo, called for at, V4:362

Nauvoo, to be continued at, V7:250

pure language, to have at time of, V2:357

purpose, V5:423

several stakes for, V3:390

spirit of Lord is, V6:12

Twelve, instructions to Church, V7:280

Twelve on, V6:11

Zion, dedicated for, V1:196, ftnt only

Zion, state of, in, reported, V1:379.

See also Hyde, Orson; Jerusalem; Jews.

Gause, Jesse, mentioned, V1:265.

Gay, A., mentioned, V5:380.

Gaylord, Elijah B., (also spelled Gayland), Kirtland Camp, mentioned in, V3:125, 142

Kirtland Camp, subscribed to constitution of, V3:92

Missouri, covenanted to assist saints in removal from, V3:253

Missouri, permit to travel in, V3:210.

Gaylord, John, sustained president of seventies, V2:510.

Gaylord, Leicester, covenanted to assist saints in removal from Missouri, V3:252.

Geddes, Thomas, (also spelled Geddis), anti-Mormon committee chairman, V6:8

Carthage prison, report of Governor Ford's statement on leaving, V6:585 and ftnt

Carthage prison, with governor at interview in, V6:576

mentioned, V7:94, ftnt only.

Gee, Elias S., son of George W. Gee, V4:500, ftnt only.

Gee, George Washington, Church recorder, appointed in Zarahemla, V4:400

death and genealogy of, V4:500 and ftnt

elder, appointed, V4:12

Kirtland Temple, blessing for work on, V2:206

mission, assigned to go on, V4:430.

Gee, George W., son of George W. Gee, V4:500, ftnt only.

Gee, Salmon, elder, ordained, to preside over Thompson, Ohio, branch, V1:324
    Joseph, pays money in hour of need, V2:327
    Kirtland Temple, blessing for work on, V2:206
    mentioned, V1:355
    seventies, sustained president of, V2:510.

Gee, Sarah W., mother to George W., V4:500, ftnt only.

Gee, Solomon, father to George W., V4:500, ftnt only.

Geneva, Morgan County, Illinois, stake organized at, V4:236.

gentiles, fulness of, to come soon, V1:13.

Germany, Church pamphlet published in, V5:142
    missionaries sent to, V5:368.

Gettis, Mr., farmer, member of martyrdom mob, V7:144.

Gheen, William A., (also M.), mentioned, V4:416; V5:58; V7:158.

Gibbs, Mr., mentioned, V6:285.

Gibbs, Gideon, affidavit on mob on LaHarpe road, V6:530
    Nauvoo Temple, appointed carpenter on, V7:326.

Gibbs, Luman, Church, excommunicated from, V3:336
    denied faith to save life, V3:335
    escape, refused and apostasy of, V3:335, 402
    Missouri, arraigned for treason, murder, burglary, arson, robbery and
        larceny at Richmond, V3:209
    murder, indicted for, V3:360
    Richmond jail, placed in, to stand trial for murder and treason, V3:212.

Gibbs, Nancy Maranda, marriage to Wm. F. Cahoon, V2:376, 377.

Gibbs, Norton, mentioned, V6:520.

Gibson, Jacob, ordained priest, V4:311.

Gifford, Alpheus, death of, V4:484
    genealogy of, V4:109-10 and ftnt
    mission call amidst mob action in Missouri, V3:154
    Young, Brigham, brought gospel to, V1:296.

Gifford, Benjamin, blessing given to, V2:244
    Zions Camp member, V2:183.

Gifford, James, mentioned, V4:49.

Gifford, Levi, Church, appointed to preside over new district of, V7:306
    Missouri, covenanted to assist saints in removal from, V3:254
    seventies, named to first quorum of, V2:203
    Zions Camp member, V2:184.

gift of healing, see healing, gift of.

Gilbert, Algernon Sidney, assaulted by Thomas Wilson, V1:432
 character of, V2:118 and ftnt
 civil trial difficulties, V1:478
 Dunklin, Governor, letter to, on restoring saints' possessions and regarding Missouri persecution and guarding witnesses, V1:472
 duty, inquires of the Lord concerning (D&C § 53), V1:179
 endowments, called to go to Kirtland to receive, rejects, V2:113
 Gilbert and Whitney, senior member of, V1:145, ftnt only
 mission, declines appointment to, V2:113, 118 and ftnt
 mission, leaves Kirtland for, V1:188
 Missouri, arrives in, V1:191
 Missouri, arrives in Kirtland from, V1:206
 Missouri, dies of cholera in, V2:118 and ftnt
 mob, forces store closing, V1:391
 petition for assistance to president of the United States accompanying saints, V1:485
 prison, committed to Jackson County, V1:432
 saints, offers himself as ransom for, in Jackson County, V1:394, ftnt only
 Zion, accompanies Prophet to, V1:188.

Gilbert, Eli, gospel preached to, V2:119, ftnt only.

Gilbert, J. H., principal compositor on Book of Mormon, V1:75, ftnt only.

Gilbert, Sherman A., (also spelled Shearman), elder, ordained, V2:244
 Kirtland Camp, subscribed to constitution of, V3:92
 Missouri, covenanted to assist saints in removing from, V3:252
 stake president, appointed counselor to, V4:233
 Zions Camp member, V2:184.

Gilbert & Company, A. S., V3:218, 438.

Gilbert & Whitney, Messrs., mentioned, V1:217, 270, ftnt only; 390, ftnt only
 merchants, store wrecked, V1:427-8
 principles in, V1:145, ftnt only.

Gillet, John, mentioned, V4:435.

Gillett, Truman, Sr., (also spelled Gillet), affidavit on treachery of William Law, V6:500
 delegate to present truth to public, V6:483
 mission and field of labor, V5:347; V6:336

GILLETT, TRUMAN, SR. (continued)

    mission call in Illinois to disabuse public mind over arrest of Joseph, V5:485.

Gillhams, (family), mentioned, V7:143.

Gillium, Cornelius, (also spelled Gilliam), *Enquirer,* publishes correspondence between Joseph and, in Zions Camp, V2:121

    Missouri, named as one of chief mobbers in, V3:327; V4:411, 434

    Missouri, raises mob in, V3:161

    sheriff, Joseph discloses identity to, V2:108

    Zions Camp, visits, V2:108.

Gilman, Mr., mentioned, V6:271.

Gilmer, Jesse, anti-Mormon committee chairman, V6:8.

Gilmour, Calvin, would rather be damned than believe, V4:110, ftnt only.

Glaefke, A. J., mission and field of labor, V6:337.

Glaze, Mr., mentioned, V3:185.

Gleason, John S., mission and field of labor, V5:348

    witness in *Expositor* trial of Joseph, V6:457.

Glidden, True, seventies, named to first quorum of, V2:204

    Zions Camp member, V2:184.

Glines, James H., ordained elder, V7:149.

Glover, Henry, mission report of, V4:252.

God, Adam, had kingdom of, V5:256

    Adam, received commandments and revelation from, V4:208

    baptism, sign to obey, V4:555

    called, will only acknowledge that which He has, V4:208

    character of, Joseph on, V6:303

    cholera, pestilence which rules, V1:282

    Christ, has body and laid down life as, V5:426

    Christian and plurality of, discourse of, V6:473, et seq

    Christianity, departure of early from true doctrine of, IntroV1:LXXXIX

    Christianity, early doctrine of, IntroV1:LXXIX

    Church of, differs from Kingdom of, V7:382

    commandment, never will give unless good for people, V5:135

    council of, V6:308

    Father was a Son, V6:476

    government of, explained, V5:61

    Jesus, eternal life to know, and, V6:305

    Joseph sees, V1:5

    judgments of, people receive when, V1:278

    man, as exalted, V6:305

GOD (continued)

man, relation of, to, V6:312

men must learn to be, V6:306

ordained, systems and administrations of no use unless, V5:259

paganization of early doctrine of, IntroV1:LXXXII

pestilence, rules, V1:282

plates, get only to glorify, V1:14

plates, wisdom of, preserves, V1:18

right, whatever requires is, V5:135

saints considered themselves favored of, IntroV3:XXXIII

sign in heaven, word, spelled out in, V5:309

unknown, called upon to liberalize saints' beliefs, IntroV3:XLIX

unknown, General Clark invokes, to help saints, V3:201-4

witnesses, voice heard by, V1:54-5 and ftnt

Zions Camp, judgment of, upon, in form of cholera epidemic, V2:114.
See also burnings; Christ, Jesus; doctrine; dream; God, kingdom of;
Latter-day Saints, Church of Jesus Christ of; Smith, Joseph.

God, government of, dissertation on, V5:61-6.

God, kingdom of, Adam, set up from time of, V5:256-9

apostles on, V7:337

beasts, never represented by, V5:341

Church of God, different from, V7:382

Daniel's prophecy of rise of, in last days considered, IntroV1:XXXIV

John the Baptist had, V5:258

Joseph has whole plan and only one who has, V5:139

reject, judgment of those who, V5:257

what constitutes, V5:257.

Gods, council of, V6:308

plurality of, V6:473-9.
See also doctrine; God.

Goddard, Joel, covenanted to assist saints in removing from Missouri,
V3:252.

Goddard, Stephen H., policeman in Nauvoo, V6:149.

Godkin, Elizabeth, wife of Thomas Marsh, V1:117, ftnt only.

Goff, James, witness in *Expositor* trial of Joseph, V6:457.

Goff, John H., covenanted to assist saints in removal from Missouri,
V3:252.

Goff, Mary, covenanted to assist saints in removal from Missouri, V3:253.

Goforth, W. G., (also spelled G. W.), high priest, baptized and ordained, V7:394
  Nauvoo, delegate to political convention in, V6:389.

Gog and Magog, when battle of, to take place, V5:298.

Golden, Aaron H., elected officer of Nauvoo Legion, V4:353.

Goldsmith, Gilbert D., mission and field of labor, V6:336.

Goldthwaite, Lydia, marriage to Newel Knight, V2:320.

good, becomes evil when used improperly, V5:209.

Goodale, J., mission and field of labor, V5:347.

Goodfellow, John, ordained elder, V4:333.

Goodman, Brother, mentioned, V7:312.

Goodrich, Mr., mentioned, V2:291.

Goodson, John, British Mission, call to, V2:490, ftnt only
  British Mission, joins at New York and genealogy, V2:494 and ftnt
  British Mission, leaves, V2:528
  Church, he and wife excommunicated from, V3:336.
  vision, teaches in England contrary to instruction, results, V2:505.

Goodwin, Mr., nonmember, petitions governor to not persecute the saints, V6:101.

Gool, John, mentioned, V7:599.

Gordon, Thomas C., Adam-ondi-Ahman High Council, chosen to, V3:38
  tongues, improperly used, V2:162-3
  Zion, appointed to assist saints in removal from, V2:455.

gospel, Abel, taught to, V2:16
  Abraham and ancients, preached to, V2:17
  Adam, revealed to, IntroV1:XXIV
  ancients cannot claim promises of, V2:21
  antiquity of, IntroV1:XXIII
  apostates of, spreading falsehoods, V2:22
  children to be taught only by consent of parents, V2:262
  churches of today not enlightened by, V2:6
  commandment, cannot live parts of, without, V5:135
  first principles, condemned by mob, V1:374-6
  first principles of enumerated, V2:255
  fullness of, on plates, V1:12
  John the Baptist, from Moses to, IntroV1:XXVIII

GOSPEL (continued)

judgment, necessary to, V3:379

keys, when are given, it is through Adam, V3:386

law versus, IntroV1:XXVII

living and dead, all to hear, V4:598

man, position of, in, V2:8

master of house, consent of, necessary before teaching, V2:263

miracles, not to be established by, V2:317

obedience brings, V2:7-8, 14-5, 19

preach just to head of household, V2:263

priesthood, where ordinances are, there is, V3:387

promises of, to, how obtained, V2:21

resurrection, relation to laws of, V2:18

sins, must exclude from membership all who have unrepented, V2:22

teaching, arrangements for, V2:514

wife taught alone only when husband consents, V2:263.

See also doctrine; Latter-day Saints, Church of Jesus Christ of; man; missionaries; Smith, Joseph.

Gotthell, Gustav, rabbi's comment on Christ, V3:359, ftnt only.

Gough, Hugh, mentioned, V4:363.

Gould, Dean C., baptized, V2:95

blessing given to, V2:244

trial of, for speaking unadvisedly against Sidney Rigdon, V2:286

Zions Camp, non-Mormon member of, V2:72, 184.

Gould, E. W., merchant, member of martyrdom mob, V7:144.

Gould, John, Doctrine and Covenants, testifies to truthfulness of, V2:246

mission, accompanies Prophet on, V2:41

mission and field of labor, V6:340

seventy, rejected as president of, V2:510

trial of, for injurious expressions and dissatisfaction of teachings of Presidency, V2:286

Zion, accompanies Orson Hyde as special messenger to, V1:407 and ftnt

Zion, dispatched from, with petition to governor of Missouri, V1:410

Zion, left by Prophet in Cattaraugus County, New York, to gather up volunteers for, V2:42.

Gould, William, covenanted to assist saints in removal from Missouri, V3:253.

Gourze, Dr., falsly accused of threatening A. Black, V3:65.

government, overthrown when corrupted, V2:11
selfishness brings downfall of, V5:61.

Graham, General, mentioned, V3:196, 413.

Graham, James, anti-Mormon committee chairman, V6:8.

Graham, James, mission and field of labor, V6:340.

Graham, Miss, mentioned, V7:164, ftnt only.

Grainger, Artimesa, prophecy, present in Missouri at Apostles' departure to fulfill, V3:339.

Grainger, Sarah, prophecy, present in Missouri at Apostles' departure to fulfill, V3:339.

grand jury, drunken brawl before in trial of saints in Missouri, V3:422-3.

Grandin, Egbert B., published Book of Mormon, V1:58, ftnt only; 71.

Granger, Carlos, Joseph hides at home of, V5:118.

Granger, Gilbert, difficulty in settlement of father's estate, V4:542.

Granger, Lydia, baptism of, V5:256.

Granger, Oliver, biography of, V4:408
death of, V4:408
Dibble, Lydia, wife of, V4:408
First Presidency, letter of recommendation from, V3:350
Kirtland, Joseph appointed agent to settle his affairs in, V3:164-5
Kirtland, letter of Joseph to, on affairs at, V4:164
Kirtland Camp, views on, V3:96
Kirtland High Council, ordained to, V2:511
Kirtland High Council, sustained to, V2:510
Kirtland Temple, blessing for work on, V2:206
mentioned, V3:174
mission appointment to the East, V2:35
presidency, on high council to try, V2:484
publication, to provide funds for, V4:18.

Grant, Austin, mentioned, V7:310.

Grant, Caroline, wife of Wm. Smith, death of, V7:417.

Grant, George D., Missouri, arraigned for treason, murder, arson, burglary, robbery and larceny at Richmond, V3:209
Nauvoo, messenger of martyrdom to, V7:110.

Grant, Jedediah M., Mansion, preaches at, V6:356
martyrdom, carries message of, V7:159
Nauvoo Temple, to administer in, V7:555

GRANT, JEDEDIAH M. (continued)

Nauvoo Temple, appointed to officiate in, V7:547
questions the Prophet, V5:503
seventies, named to first quorum of, V2:204, 297
seventies, ordained president of, V7:538
seventies, sustained as one of the presidents of, V7:297, 392, 461
seventies, sustained president of, to Church at Salt Lake City, V7:629
westward movement, captain of 14th company in, V7:482
Zions Camp member, V2:184.

Grant, Josuah, blessing for work on Kirtland Temple, V2:206.

Grant, Thalia, mother of Caroline, V7:418.

Grant, Thomas D., major-general in Missouri militia, V3:65.

Graves, Reuben, at anti-Mormon meeting, V5:537
farmer, member of martyrdom mob, V7:144.

Gray, David, subscribed to constitution of Kirtland Camp, V3:91.

Grays, Silver, company of, part of Prophet's camp mess, V2:91.

Greabble, John, subscribed to constitution of Kirtland Camp, V3:92.

Great Salt Lake Valley, viewed as prospective move of Church, V7:439.

Green, Addison, Missouri persecutions, affidavit concerning, V4:65
Missouri trials, witness for state in, V3:210
mob, taken prisoner by, V3:169
Zions Camp member, V2:184.

Green, Dr., counselor in bishopric, V6:354.

Green, Evan M., labors of, in Maine, V2:40-1.

Green, Harvey, Church, appointed to preside over new district of, V7:305
Joseph's home, accused of stealing and looting from, V3:287
mission call in Illinois to disabuse public mind over arrest of Joseph,
    V5:485
mission and field of labor, V5:348; V6:339
president, elders quorum, V3:15.

Green, Henry, elders, ordained president of, in Caldwell County, V2:507
evil spirit, accused by Joseph of falsely accusing him of possessing,
    V2:274
excommunication for offending and questioning Joseph, V2:276
high council, trial of, before, V2:274, et seq.

Green, Mrs., mentioned, V7:217.

Green, Philip, given charge of churches at Schucknall Hill, Lugwardine,
    Marden, V4:139.

Green, T., suspended from office for false spirit and abuses, V4:147.

Green, W., delegate to political convention in Nauvoo, V6:389.

Green, William, ordained elder, V4:333.

Green Plain, house burning at, V7:444.

Greene, Evan M., Kirtland Temple, blessing for work on, V2:206
mission of, reported, V2:40-1.

Greene, John P., (also spelled Green), affiant to public proclamation on
mob lies, V6:495

Church, appointed to take charge of, in Parkham County, V1:342

death of, V7:270

Expositor, arrest for destruction of, trial on, V6:487, et seq

Expositor, ordered to destroy, V7:63

high council, on, V2:151, 165

high council, appointed to, at Far West, V3:14

high council, confesses and retains membership and position on,
V2:512

high council, elected to, at Kirtland, V2:366

Joseph, accompanies in arrest, V4:366

Joseph's life, affidavit on threats against, V6:522

Kirtland High Council, ordained to, V2:511

Kirtland Temple, blessing for work on,V2:205

mentioned, V2:510; V3:260; V7:93

mission, appointed to, V2:222, 224-5

mission, returns from, V6:60

mission to Strongville, V2:35

Missouri, affidavit of, on threats of invasion from, V6:516

Missouri persecutions, affidavit of, concerning, V4:65

Nauvoo, account of refusing writ to public officer in, V6:348-9

Nauvoo, first elected councilor of, V4:287

Nauvoo, letter of, informing General Deming that R. D. Foster was in,
V7:169

Nauvoo, marshal of, V6:124

New York branch, letter of appointment over, V3:347

Presidency, on high council to try, V2:484

tongues, speaks in, V1:296.

Greenhalgh, Mary, to receive aid in emigrating from England, V5:412.

Greenhill, George, mentioned, V4:324.

Greenhow, John, anti-Mormon article on horse thieves, V6:43-4
represents area in British conference, V5:9.

Greenleaf, David, probate judge, V6:35, 576

Greenwood, Brother, mentioned, V6:341.

Greenwood, Hannah, marries Joseph Fielding, V3:38.

Gregg, Harmon, anti-Mormon committee member, V1:399.

Gregg, Jas., member of martyrdom mob, no business, V7:144.

Gregg, Thomas, Book of Mormon, records statement on publishing, V1:75, ftnt only
    Carthage jail, interview with Governor Ford in, reports incident of Joseph's, V6:585, ftnt only.

Gregory, Mr., mentioned, V3:146.

Gregory, William, covenanted to assist saints in removal from Missouri. V3:252.

Gribble, William, Kirtland Camp, leaves, V3:140
    Kirtland Camp, subscribed to constitution of, V3:93
    mission and field of labor, V6:339.

Griffith, John, mentioned, V4:298.

Griffith, Michael, Kirtland Camp, subscribed to constitution of, V3:92
    seventies, named to first quorum of, V2:203
    seventy, ordained, V2:221
    Zions Camp member, V2:184.

Griffith, Thomas, attests to honesty of saints in Kirtland, V3:165.

Griffith, Thomas, Carthage Greys, member of, V7:143.

Griffiths, Hiram, subscribed to constitution of Kirtland Camp, V3:93.

Griffiths, Sara, marriage of, to Levi Richards, V6:134.

Grigg, John, excommunicated from Church, and wife, V3:336.

Grinold, Mother, mentioned, V3:273.

Griswold, Everett, Zions Camp member, V2:184.

Grouard, Benjamin F., mission call to Pacific Isles, V5:386.
    seventy, ordained, V5:405.

Grovenor, Captain, martyrdom murderer, V7:163.

Grover, Brother, mentioned, V7:432.

Grover, Thomas, Church, appointed to preside over new district of, V7:306
    Cowdery, Oliver, speaks against, V3:4
    elder, to be, V2:354
    Far West High Council, sustained member of, V2:523
    high council, elected to, at Far West, V2:504
    high council, elected to, at Kirtland, V2:366
    Joseph, on mission to rescue, V5:451
    Mississippi River, accident on, V7:582

GROVER, THOMAS (continued)

    Missouri, covenanted to assist saints in removal from, V3:253
    Missouri persecutions, expresses faith in work after, V3:225
    Nauvoo, bodyguard to Joseph's body on return to, V7:135
    Nauvoo High Council, appointed to, V4:12
    Nauvoo High Council, sustained to, after death of Joseph,
      V7:296
    witness, suggested to appear before Congress on redress, V4:97.

Grover, William N., lawyer, member of martyrdom mob, V7:143
    martyrdom, acquitted of Joseph's murder, V7:420
    Warsaw militia leader, V7:143.

Groves, Elder, opposes action of general assembly at Far West, V3:5.

Groves, Elisha H., blessing given to, V2:244
    Church, appointed to preside over new district of, V7:305
    Far West High Council, sustained member of, V2:524
    high priest, ordained, V2:164
    mentioned, V1:387; V2:164
    mission, assigned to go on, V4:429
    mission call in Illinois to disabuse public mind over arrest of Joseph,
      V5:485
    mission and field of labor, V5:348; V6:339
    Missouri persecutions, affidavit of, concerning, V4:68
    Zion High Council, appointed to, V2:357
    Zions Camp member, V2:184.

Groves, Reuben, mentioned, V6:4, ftnt only.

Grubb, Fayette, testifies to finding Kinderhook plates, V5:377.

Guard, David, mentioned, V7:137.

Gudgel, Jacob, sends more inflammatory communication to Boggs,
    V3:166.

Gully, S., delegate to political convention in Nauvoo, V6:390.

Gulley, Samuel, Joseph, on relief expedition for, V5:486.

Gurley, Zenos H., mentioned, V4:342
    mission and field of labor, V6:340
    Missouri, covenanted to assist saints in removal from, V3:252.

Guyman, James, affidavit on threats of invasion from Missouri, V6:511.

Guyman, Noah T., covenanted to assist saints in removal from Missouri,
    V3:253.

Guyman, Thomas, mission and field of labor, V6:337
    Missouri, covenanted to assist saints in removing from, V3:253.

Gyer, Mr., on exterminating order, V3:239-40.

—H—

habeas corpus, city council, bill on, V5:84
    Joseph, issued for in second arrest in Illinois, V5:463
    Nauvoo, ordinance on, V5:57
    Nauvoo, ordinance on procedure for, V5:87-8
    Nauvoo, ordinance on return of, V5:161
    ordinance on proceedings on writs of, V5:185, et seq.
Hadley, Samuel, jailer in Missouri, V3:215.
Hagerman, Alanson, mentioned, V5:454.
Haggart, Brother, charges against and dismissed, V1:470.
Haight, Isaac C., policeman in Nauvoo, V6:150.
Haight, Isaac G., elders, entertains, V4:39
    mission call and field of labor, V5:347
    Young, Brigham, assists on journey, V4:44.
Haight, Silas, marshal from Iowa, V7:491.
Haight, William, mission and field of labor, V6:336.
Haining, Samuel, publishes anti-Mormon literature, V4:254.
Hale, Aroet, martial band member of Legion, V7:135.
Hale, Emma, see Smith, Emma.
Hale, Isaac, father of Emma, V1:17
    Harmony, Pennsylvania, of, Prophet boards with, V1:17
    Prophet, embittered against, V1:108 and ftnt.
Hale, James, mission in Illinois to disabuse public mind over Joseph's arrest, V5:485.
Hale, Jonathan H., assessor and collector for Nauvoo first Ward, V6:71

    baptisms for dead, recorder for, V5:522
    bishop, appointed, V5:119
    bishop, sustained of Nauvoo ward, V7:298
    Church, appointed to preside over new district of, V7:305
    Kirtland Camp, appointed treasurer of, V3:97
    Kirtland Camp, subscribed to constitution of, V3:92
    mentioned, V7:375
    mission and field of labor, V6:335
    mission to Fox Island, V2:507 and ftnt
    Missouri, covenanted to assist saints in removing from, V3:252

HALE, JONATHAN H. (continued)

Missouri, permit to travel in, V3:210

westward movement, captain of 21st company in, V7:482

Young, Joseph, arrested for, V3:108.

Hale, Levi, baptized, V1:88.

Hale, Samuel, Kirtland Camp, leaves, V3:140

Kirtland Camp, subscribed to constitution of, V3:92.

Hall, B. K., mentioned, V3:141.

Hall, J., letter on arrest and trial of Prophet, V5:538-9.

Hall, Lyman, mission and field of labor, V6:336.

Hallet, Clark, counselor to bishop at Lima, V5:427.

Halsey, Thankful, wife of Parley P. Pratt, V1:119, ftnt only.

Ham, Negroes descendants of, V1:191

plates, descendant of, discovered with ancient, V5:372.

Hamblin, Jacob, mission and field of labor, V6:337.

Hambright, James, committee to rid Missouri of saints, V1:395.

Hamilton, Brother, mentioned, V6:173.

Hamilton, Mr., deputy sheriff in Missouri, V3:365.

Hamilton, Mr., proprietor of Hamilton Hotel at Carthage, V7:71.

Hamilton, Mr., rejoiced at martyrdom, V7:112.

Hamilton, Andrew M., affidavit on Missouri kidnapping, V6:123.

Hamilton, James, petitions to hear Joseph speak, V6:533.

Hamilton, James B., affidavit on Missouri kidnapping, V6:123.

Hamilton, Marvin, Carthage Greys, member of, V7:143.

Hamilton, Milton, mentioned, V6:529.

Hamilton, Robert, mentioned, V7:260

mission and field of labor, V6:337.

Hamilton, Thomas, opposes Elder Taylor and vanquished, V4:235, ftnt only.

Hammond, John, Kirtland Camp, excluded from, for not standing at head of family, V3:130

Kirtland Camp, mentioned in, V3:104, 124

Kirtland Camp, subscribed to constitution of, V3:93

mission and field of labor, V6:340.

Hampton, James, mission and field of labor, V6:338

Missouri, covenanted to assist saints in removal from, V3:252

petitions Governor Boggs on mob violence in DeWitt, V3:83.

Hampton, Jonathan, Kirtland Camp, subscribed to constitution of, V3:92

HAMPTON, JONATHAN (continued)

Missouri, covenanted to assist saints in removal from, V3:252

petitions Governor Boggs on mob violence in DeWitt, V3:83.

Hampton, Robert, petitions Governor Boggs on mob violence in DeWitt, V3:83.

Hanchet, Martin, subscribed to constitution of Kirtland Camp, V3:92.

Hancock, Amy Ward, mother of Levi, V1:322, ftnt only.

Hancock, Joseph, cholera, seized with, V2:106

seventies, named to first quorum of, V2:203

Zions Camp, chased by riders on horseback while on, V2:91

Zions Camp member, V2:184.

Hancock, Levi Ward, genealogy, V1:322 and ftnt

high council, member of, V3:89

Joseph, on relief expedition for, V5:482

Legion, martial band member of, V7:135

mission and field of labor, V6:336

Missouri, covenanted to assist saints in removal from, V3:253

Nauvoo, policeman in, V6:149

seventies, named president of, V2:203

seventies, sustained one of presidents of, V7:297

seventies, sustained president of, V2:510; V4:285

seventies, sustained president of, in Salt Lake City, V7:629

Seventies Library and Institute Association, elected trustee of, V7:328

song by, V3:42

Zions Camp member, V2:184.

Hancock, Solomon, Church, appointed to preside over new district of, V7:305

endowments, called to go to Kirtland to receive, V2:113

Far West, sustained local presidency at, V3:4

high council, elected to, at Zion, V2:523

high council, named to, at Lima, V5:427

high council, sustained member of Missouri, V2:124

mentioned, V2:164, 367; V3:42

Missouri, covenanted to assist saints in removal from, V3:252

Missouri persecutions, expresses faith in work after, V3:225

mob, affidavit on attempting to draft into, V6:511

murder, letter to, on Durfee's, V7:528

petitions to hear Joseph speak, V6:533

utility committee to aid Church removal, V7:474

wife of, dies, V2:406.

Hancock, Thomas, blessing for work on Kirtland Temple, V2:206

HANCOCK, THOMAS (continued)

father of Levi, V1:322, ftnt only.

Hancock Eagle, prospectus of, published in Nauvoo, V7:596.

Hanks, Knowlton F., island mission, set apart for, V5:405
mission call to Pacific Isles, V5:386
mission, death while on, V6:64.

Hanson, Brother, V7:552, 557, 564.

Hanson, Hans C., doorkeeper of Temple, V7:535.

Hanson, Peter O., Book of Mormon, translating into Danish language, V7:554
Danish, to translate standard works into, V7:425
doorkeeper of Temple, V7:535.

happiness, essay on, V5:134 and ftnt, et seq.

Hardin, Mr., mentioned, V6:369-70.

Hardin, Dwight, (also spelled Harding), covenanted to assist saints in removing from Missouri, V3:252
policeman in Nauvoo, V6:150.

Hardin, John J., militia commander, V7:46
Nauvoo, in commmand of governor's troops in, V7:447-8
Rockwell, Orrin P., threatens to arrest, V7:481
saints removal, member of Quincy committee on, V7:450.

Hardin, Napoleon, mentioned, V6:530.

Harding, A. M., mission call and field of labor, V5:348; V6:336.

Harding, Stephen S., statement respecting translation of Book of Mormon, V1:75 and ftnt.

Hardman, William, ordained elder, V4:333.

Hardy, Leonard W., British Mission, sails for, V7:324
Legion, martial band member of, V7:135.

Hardy, Lewis, martial band member of Legion, V7:135.

Hardy, Zachariah, mission and field of labor, V6:340.

"Hark, Listen to the Trumpeters," hymn sung at meeting to choose Apostles, V2:186 and ftnt.

Harlan, Richard, mentioned, V2:350, ftnt only.

Harman, J., delegate to political convention in Nauvoo, V6:390.

Harman, Nehemiah, blessing for work on Kirtland Temple, V2:206.

Harmar, Elias, called on mission and field of labor, V5:348.

Harmer, Brother, mentioned, V5:21.

Harmon, Alpheus, blessing for work on Kirtland Temple, V2:206

HARMON, ALPHEUS (continued)

freezes to death, V5:193.

Harmon, Appleton M., mentioned, V7:484
policeman in Nauvoo, V6:150.

Harmon, Jesse D., Nauvoo Temple, appointed to officiate in, V7:547
seventies, named to first quorum of, V2:203.

Harmon, Jesse P., *Expositor,* arrest for destruction of, trial on, V6:487, et seq
Joseph, on relief expedition for, V5:483, 486
Kirtland Camp, subscribed to constitution of, V3:93
Nauvoo, arrested in, V7:428
Nauvoo, policeman in, V6:149.

Harmon, Joseph, Zions Camp member, V2:184.

Harmon, Nehemiah, covenanted to assist saints in removal from Missouri, V3:254.

Harner, Augustine, (also spelled Harmer), killed at Haun's Mills by mob, V3:186, 326, ftnt only.

Harper, William, covenanted to assist saints in removal from Missouri, V3:253.

Harriman, Henry, Kirtland Camp, mentioned in, V3:105
Kirtland Camp, subscribed to constitution of, V3:91
Kirtland Camp, one of the first council of seventy and presidents of, V3:93
Kirtland Camp, presides at, V3:97
Nauvoo Temple, to administer in, V7:555
seventies, sustained one of presidents, V7:297
seventies, sustained president of, at Salt Lake City, V7:629.

Harris, Brother, mentioned, V3:376.

Harris, Mr., spies for mob and attacks Parley P. Pratt, V1:427.

Harris, Dennison L., reveals conspiracy against Prophet, V6:280-1, ftnt only.

Harris, E. W., Joseph's letter to, on land purchase, V3:362.

Harris, Eleazer, covenanted to assist saints in removal from Missouri, V3:253.

Harris, Elmer, baptized John Page, V3:240, ftnt only.

Harris, Emer, on meeting conducting committee, V1:219 and ftnt
pays Joseph money in hour of need, V2:327

Harris, George W., Church, credentials to raise funds for, V4:164
Expositor, signs bill for removal of, V7:63

HARRIS, GEORGE W. (continued)

Far West, receives the Prophet and family at, V3:9

high council, appointed to, at Far West, V3:14

high priest, appointed, V3:15

lies, affiant to public proclamation on mob, V6:495

mentioned, V3:283, 404

mission, sent on special, V4:161

Missouri, covenanted to assist saints in removal from, V3:252

Missouri persecutions, expresses faith in work after, V3:225

Nauvoo, elected to alderman, V4:442

Nauvoo High Council, appointed to, V4:12

presidency, letter reporting labors of collecting money, V4:199

resolutions, V7:150

saints, signs memorial of, in Missouri, V3:224

westward movement, appointed commissary of first encampment in, V7:586.

Harris, John, anti-Mormon committee member, V1:399.

Harris, Jonathan, petitions Governor Boggs on mob violence in DeWitt, V3:83.

Harris, Martin, baptized, V1:79

Book of Mormon, desires witness that the Prophet has plates of, V1:28

Book of Mormon, receives witness of, V1:55 and ftnt

buffetings of Satan, turned over to, and condemned as openly sinning against Jesus, V3:232

error, confession of, V2:26

genealogy, V1:19 and ftnt

high council, rejected as member of, at Kirtland, V2:510

Joseph, gives $50.00 to, V1:19

manuscript, loses, V1:21-2

mission, leaves Kirtland with Joseph on, V1:188

New York, occurrences in, with translation, V1:20 and ftnt

plates, prays for witness of, V1:54

presidency, on high council to try, V2:484

Prophet, reproved by, V2:95-6 and ftnt

scribe, becomes Joseph's, V1:20

snakes, boasts of handling and is bitten, V2:95

transcript, presents, of Nephite characters to Dr. Mitchell and Professor Anthon, V1:20

translation, asks for 116 pages of, V1:21

translation, takes to New York, V1:19

travel alone whenever he travels, V2:35

HARRIS, MARTIN (continued)

tried before council for accusing Joseph of drinking and other, forgiven, V2:26

witness, requests to be, V1:53

witnesses, withdraws from prayer of, V1:54

Zion, at temple dedication in, V1:199

Zions Camp member, V2:184.

Harris, Morris, covenanted to assist saints in removal from Missouri, V3:254.

Harris, Moses, petitions Governor Boggs on mob violence in DeWitt, V3:83.

Harris, Ophelia, covenanted to assist saints in removal from Missouri, V3:253.

Harris, Preserved, brother to Martin, to see translation, V1:21

disfellowship for want of benevolence to the poor and charity to the Church, V2:445

father's funeral, Joseph preaches at, V2:317.

Harris, Robert, counselor on sailing from England, V4:297

elder, ordained, V4:297

priest, ordained, V4:135.

Harris, S., appointed to assist saints in removing from Zion by public, V2:455.

Harris, Thomas, anti-Mormon committee chairman, V6:8.

Harris, W. P., comment on Kinderhook plates, V5:377.

Harrison, Nathan, petitions Governor Boggs on mob violence in DeWitt, V3:83.

Harrison, Richard, mentioned, V4:296.

Harrison, Ruth, wife of Peter Maughan, V4:493, ftnt only.

Harrison, William Henry, death of, V4:326

mentioned, V6:116, ftnt only

United States, inaugurated president of, V4:308.

Harshman, Mr., mentioned, in Kirtland Camp, V3:129.

Hart, Mr., mobber wounded at Haun's Mills massacre, V3:326, ftnt only.

Hartshorn, Joseph, blessing given to, V2:244

Zions Camp member, V2:184.

Hartshorn, Orin, covenanted to assist saints in removal from Missouri, V3:253.

Hartwell, Reuben P., covenanted to assist saints in removal from Missouri, V3:252.

harvest feast, near Nauvoo, V7:437-8.

Harvey, Joel, Kirtland Camp, leaves, V3:138
    Kirtland Camp, mentioned in, V3:125
    Kirtland Camp, subscribed to constitution of, V3:92.

Harvey, John, in westward movement organization, V7:626.

Haskins, Nathan, complains against Far West presidency, V2:484-5.

Hastings, Mr., mentioned, V7:500.

Hastings, Samuel J., mentioned, V7:566
    western pathfinder, interview with Church leaders, V7:598.

Hatch, Jeremiah, elder, ordained, V5:349
    mission and field of labor, V6:336
    Nauvoo, delegate to political convention in, V6:390
    public, delegate to present truth to, V6:483.

Hatfield, Andy, mobber in Missouri, V4:66.

Hatfield, Calvin, mobber in Missouri, V4:66.

Hatfield, John, mentioned, V6:412.

Hatfield, Stanley, mobber in Missouri, V4:66.

Hatfield, Wm. J., petitions Governor Boggs on mob violence in DeWitt, V3:83.

Hathaway, Mr., delegate to political convention in Nauvoo, V6:390.

Haugaas, Gudmund, mentioned, V5:395.

Haun, Jacob, founder of Haun's Mills and wounded at, by mob, V3:326, ftnt only.

Haun's Mills, Comstock brothers members of mob at, V3:325
    killed at, enumerated, V3:186
    killed and wounded, list of, V3:326, ftnt only
    massacre at, V3:182-6
    McBride, Mr., cut to pieces with corn cutter by Rogers of Daviess County, V3:185
    mob, treaty extended by for peace, V3:183
    mob attack, Nehemiah Comstock leads, V3:184
    Smith, Amanda, massacre at, recorded, V5:323, et seq
    Smith, Sardius, killed at, nine years of age by Mr. Stanley of Carroll County, V3:185.
    See also massacre, Haun's Mills; mob; persecutions, Missouri.

Haun's Mills massacre, see massacre, Haun's Mills.

Haven, John, mentioned, V7:350.

Hawden, John W., letter attesting to Joseph's integrity, V3:174.

Hawes, H. M., teacher of high school, Kirtland, V2:474.

Hawes, Peter, cautioned to curtail his boy's wickedness, V5:305.

Hawk, William, affidavit concerning Missouri persecutions, V4:58.

Hawk Eye, publishes article on Mormon improvements, V6:195.

Hawke, Nathan, covenanted to assist saints in removal from Missouri, V3:253.

hawkers, ordinance on, in Nauvoo, V4:461.

Hawkes, Mr., mentioned, V2:291.

Hawkes, William, mentioned, V7:593.

Hawkins, Lydia Ann, disfellowshipped for unlawful matrimony and deceiving, V2:511.

Hawkins, Uriah, disfellowshipped for unlawful matrimony and deceiving, V2:511.

Hawley, Mr., mentioned, V5:542.

Hawley, Joseph, martyrdom, guard on jail at, V7:142.

Hawley, Pierce, covenanted to assist saints in removal from Missouri, V3:253
mentioned, V6:257.

Haws, J., delegate to political convention in Nauvoo, V6:390.

Haws, Elder, mentioned, V6:230.

Haws, Peter, Church, appointed to preside over new district of, V7:306
Joseph, accompanies for trial on Missouri warrants, V5:210
mission and field of labor, V5:370
Nauvoo, in, V4:301, 303, 311; V5:283, 369.
westward movement, captain of eighth company in, V7:482.

Haws, William, mentioned, V5:486.

Hay, John, mentioned, V6:606, ftnt only
Secretary of State (McKinley-Roosevelt administration), comment on court of Carthage trial, V7:420, ftnt only.

Hayes, Charles, given care of Church at Deer Hurst, V4:135.

Hayes, Ezra, license taken from for teaching false doctrine, V4:14.

Hayes, Robert, mentioned, V4:238.

Hayes, Thomas, Zions Camp member, V2:184.

Hays, Mr., doctor, member of martyrdom mob, V7:144.

Hays, Mr., ordination illegal and rejected, V1:343.

Hays, Milo, excommunicated for breaking Word of Wisdom and covenant breaking, V2:228.

Hays, Robert, Wesleyan minister opposes Church on Isle of Man, V4:238.

Hayden, Mr., quoted from, V1:158, ftnt only.

Hayton, Thomas, Sr., signs proposition to buy land of saints, V2:96-7.

Head, Doctor, mentioned, V4:61.

Head, Anthony, Missouri, arraigned for treason, murder, burglary, arson, robbery and larceny at Richmond, V3:209
    Missouri, covenanted to assist saints in removal from, V3:252
    Missouri trials, discharged from, as innocent, V3:211.

Head, D. E., (also E. D.), mentioned, V6:360; V7:493.

Head, Norvil M., covenanted to assist saints in removal from Missouri, V3:252.

Head, William Y., secretary of Warsaw anti-Mormon meeting, V6:462.

Headlock, Stephen, Kirtland Camp, leaves, V3:141
    Kirtland Camp, subscribed to constitution of, V3:91
    reproved, complains of Camp murmuring, V3:119.

Healey, Arnold, subscribed to constitution of Kirtland Camp, V3:92.

healing, gift of, Barnum, Samuel, cannot exercise, V2:332
    Carter, W., of sight if faithful, V2:207
    deaf, exercised on, V4:361
    Dibble, Philo, wounded by mob but miraculously healed, V1:431, ftnt only
    England, exercised on ship from, V5:309
    exercised to heal rheumatic fever, V2:354
    exhortation to record instances of, V6:186
    girl raised from death, V6:186-7
    Joseph gives handkerchief which is used to heal two children, V4:5, ftnt only
    lame made to walk, V5:518
    Lyman, Amasa M., of, V7:271
    medicine, Joseph on, as compared with use of, V4:414
    Nauvoo, greatly manifest at, V4:3 and ftnt
    Peck, M. H., son of, run over and, V3:113
    promise of, no claim on if trifle with, V2:95-6
    Rigdon, Sidney, affliction rebuked of, V2:367
    Rigdon, Sister, exercised in behalf of, V2:400
    Smith, Don Carlos, account of his, V4:398-9
    women and, V4:604.
    See also gifts of the Spirit.

Heath, Chester L., clerk of council of elders, V1:355
excommunication for breaking Word of Wisdom and covenants, V2:218.

Heath, Samuel, British Mission, mission in, V4:150
Church, represents branches of, in English conference, V4:148
devote all time to labors of ministry, V4:148
volunteers for service in vineyard, V4:217.

heathens, nations of, will be destroyed, V5:212.

heaven, kingdoms, includes more than one, V1:245
laws of, explained, V2:8
opened to many at first conference, V1:85.

Hebrew, Book of Mormon, title page written in, V1:71
Kirtland, school at, V2:318, 355, 356, 376-7, 391
teacher, difficulty with, V2:355
translating, school begins, V2:396.

Hedlock, Reuben, (also spelled Headlock), Book of Abraham, prepares cut for and aids, V4:519, 543
Brigham, accompanies on preaching tour, V4:88
British Mission, leaves Nauvoo for, sick, V4:10
British Mission, mission to, V5:405
British Mission, presides in, V5:386, 405
British Mission, work in, V6:65-6
condition of, during trip and arrival, V4:104
elders quorum, chosen president of, at Kirtland, V2:526
England, arrival in, V4:102
England, mission call to, V5:385
England, presides at conference in, V6:327-30
England, sails for, V4:94
Kirtland Camp, subscribed to constitution of, V3:93
mentioned, V3:323; V4:89, 218
ministry, devote all time to labors of, V4:148
mission, letter to Church on, V6:44
Missouri, covenanted to assist saints in removal from, V3:252.

Helfenstein, J. Albert, testifies on Joseph's second arrest in Illinois, V6:67.

hell, damnation of, explained, V4:555,
nature of, V5:425-6.

Helm, William, ordained elder, V4:13.

Helme, Mr., mentioned, V5:22.

Hemmic, James M., discharged from camp for dueling, V7:609.

Henderson, James M., mission call in Illinois to disabuse public mind over Joseph's arrest, V5:485
  Missouri, arraigned for treason, murder, burglary, arson, robbery and larceny at Richmond, V3:209.

Henderson, Brother, mentioned, V3:272.

Henderson, William, ordained elder, V7:149.

Hendricks, Daniel, assessor and collector for Nauvoo First Ward, V6:71.

Hendricks, James, (also spelled Hendrix), Nauvoo, lot and house donated by high council at, V4:76
  teachers quorum, counselor to, in Nauvoo, V4:312
  teachers quorum, counselor in Nauvoo, V4:354.

Henry, emigration ship, V5:165.

Henry, Andrew, appointed elder, V4:13.

Henshaw, William, mission call to South Wales, V5:281
  presides at Wales conference, V7:425.

Hensley, Benjamin, petitions Governor Boggs on mob violence in DeWitt, V3:83.

heretics, persecuted by early Christianity, IntroV1:LXV.

Herinshaw, Hugh, delegate to political convention in Nauvoo, V6:389.

Herrick, Amos F., blessing for work on Kirtland Temple, V2:206

Herrick, Lester, mentioned, V7:528.

Herrick, Nelson, mentioned, V7:528.

Herriman, Henry, mission appointment to Canada, V2:35
  mission and field of labor, V6:335
  Missouri, permit to travel in, V3:210
  seventies, named to first quorum of, V2:204
  seventy, ordained, V2:221
  Zions Camp member, V2:184.

Herring, Brother, mentioned, V7:434.

Herrot, John, to be elder, V2:354.

Herschel, John, mentioned, V5:308.

Hess, Peter, mission and field of labor, V5:349.

Hess, Thomas, mission and field of labor, V6:337.

Hewitt, George, ordained teacher, V5:419.

Hewitt, Father, mentioned, V5:510.

Hewitt, John, Church, sent from Europe to investigate, V2:230
  Irvingite Church, elder of, V2:233 and ftnt

HEWITT, JOHN (continued)

    letter of introduction from council of pastors, V2:230
    visits the Prophet, V2:230-4 and ftnts.

Hewitt, Mrs., mentioned, V2:233

Hewitt, Wilkinson, mission and field of labor, V5:347.

Hewitt, William, publishes anti-Mormon literature, V4:255.

Heyes, Thomas, cholera strikes, V2:106.

Heywood, Joseph L., bishop, ordained, V7:307
    Church, utility committee member to aid removal of, V7:474
    Missouri persecutions, letter to Joseph suggesting a memoralizing of Congress on, V6:62-3.

Hibbard, Mr., confirmed along with wife and children, V4:7.

Hibbard, Davison, (also spelled Davidson), mentioned, V4:18; V5:263; V6:117.

Hibbert, Elder, mission appointment, V5:420.

Hickerson, G. W., mission and field of labor, V6:340.

Hickman, William A., Joseph, leaves to rescue, V4:365.

Hickock, Luther W., (also spelled Hickok, Hicock), Joseph, letter on probability of indictment of, at Springville, V6:450
    mentioned, V6:416, 420-2, 494.

Hicks, Mr., favors state arms taken from Mormons, V5:201; V6:526.

Hicks, Burrell, mentioned, V3:461.

Hicks, John, mentioned, V4:144.

Hicks, John A., elders president, rejected as, V4:341
    excommunicated for falsehood and schismatical conversation, V4:428
    Joseph, determined to shed blood of, V6:560.

Hicks, Lawyer, mentioned, V2:93, ftnt only.

Hicks, Russel, anti-Mormon committee, member of, V1:399
    mob, carries proposals to saints from, V1:398
    mob manifesto, deputy county clerk, signed, V1:376
    saints, committee to rid Missouri of, V1:395.

Hicks, Samuel, mob treatment of, V7:530.

Hicks, Sylvanus, covenanted to assist saints in removal from Missouri, V3:253.

Higbee, A. J., mentioned, V6:537.

Higbee, Chauncey L., anti-Mormon committee member of Warsaw meeting, V6:464
    apostate, testimony of adulterous actions of, V6:407
    character of, V7:57

HIGBEE, CHAUNCEY L. (continued)

Church, expelled from, at Nauvoo, V7:57

excommunicated for unvirtuous conduct, V5:18

Joseph, determined to kill, V6:604

martyrdom, member of mob at, V7:146

mentioned, V4:295; V7:67, 72-3

Nauvoo, vexatious actions of, against authorities of, V6:285.

Higbee, Elias, Church, letter to, confirming actions and listing possible witnesses, V4:96-8

Congress, letter to Joseph telling him papers before, have been withdrawn, V4:98

Congress, writes petition to, V4:237

death and genealogy of, V5:420-21 and ftnt

Far West, accompanies First Presidency to found city north of, V3:67

Far West, orders out militia at, V3:169

Far West, speaks against conduct of local presidency at, V3:4

Far West High Council, sustained member of, V2:523

funeral, Joseph preaches at, V5:529

genealogy, V1:410 and ftnt

high priest, ordained, V1:410; V2:141

honorable man, V7:57

Joseph, accompanies in arrest, V4:365

Joseph, affidavit concerning character of John C. Bennett and, V5:77

Joseph, appointed to go to Washington with, V4:13

Joseph, fifth letter to, affairs of saints in Washington, V4:94

Joseph, first letter on cause, V4:81

Joseph, fourth letter to, announcing the senate committee report will be unfavorable, V4:88

Joseph, letter to exhorting him in suffering, V3:319

Joseph, letter to, on cause, V4:83

Joseph, pays money to, in hour of need, V2:327

Joseph, third letter to, on cause, V4:85

Nauvoo, presides at mass meeting in, V4:157-60

Prophet, reproved by, V4:503

United States, letters of, concerning case of saints before, V4:81, et seq

Washington, course of, approved at, V4:96, et seq

Washington, leaves Nauvoo for, V4:19

Washington, letter to high council at Nauvoo concerning preliminary hearing of grievances in, V4:43

Young, Richard, letter to, V4:111

Zion High Council, appointed to, V2:357.

Higbee, Francis M., affidavit concerning character of John C. Bennett and Joseph, V5:77-8
    anti-Mormon, messenger to governor from meeting, V6:466
    Carthage jail, conceals threat of mob on Joseph's life, V7:130
    character of, V7:57
    Court, before Municipal, V6:357-61
    excommunicated for apostasy, V6:398
    Joseph, exposed by, and called to repentance, V5:49
    Joseph, threats against, V6:457-8, 524
    Joseph, trial of, before city council for slandering, V6:178
    Legion, elected colonel of, V4:353
    martyrdom, member of mob at, V7:144, 146
    mentioned, V7:66, 75, 124
    Missouri, arraigned for treason, murder, burglary, arson, robbery and larceny at Richmond, V3:209
    Nauvoo, expelled from Church at, V7:57
    Nauvoo, vexatious actions against authorities in, V6:285
    Prophet, charges with slander, V6:174
    Prophet, threatens with bonds, V6:176
    witness, suggested to appear before Congress on redress, V4:97.

Higbee, Heziah String, wife of Isaac, V1:410, ftnt only.

Higbee, Isaac, Jr., bishop, sustained, of a Nauvoo ward, V7:298
    Church, appointed to preside over new district of, V7:305
    genealogy, V1:410 and ftnt
    high priest, ordained, V1:410; V2:141
    Joseph, on relief expedition for, V5:482
    Zion High Council, appointed to, V2:164; V3:155.

Higbee, Isaac, Sr., father of Elias and Isaac Higbee, Jr., V1:410, ftnt only; V5:420, ftnt only.

Higbee, John S., Joseph, leaves to rescue, V4:365
    Joseph, on relief expedition for, V5:482
    Missouri, arraigned for murder, treason, robbery, arson, burglary, and larceny at Richmond, V3:209.

Higbee, Keziah, delivers child amidst persecution in Missouri, V3:439-40.

Higbee, N. J., aided and abetted martyrdom mob, V7:146.

Higbee, Oliver, mentioned, V2:207.

Higbee, Sarah Ann, persecution of, in Missouri, V3:439-40.

Higbee, Sophia, mother of Elias and Isaac Higbee, Jr., V1:410, ftnt only; V5:420, ftnt only.

Higby, James, excommunicated for false and slanderous reports, V1:356
    Kirtland, trial of, in, V1:355
    Kirtland Camp, in, V3:132.

Higby, Martha, child of, dies, V3:129.

Higginbottom, W. E., mission and field of labor, V6:337.

Higgins, Nelson, ordained J. Page, V3:240, ftnt only
    seventies, named to first quorum of, V2:204
    utility committee member to aid Church removal, V7:474
    Zions Camp member, V2:184.

High Council, Adam-ondi-Ahman, appoints committee to purchase mob
    lands, V3:84
    organized, V3:38.

High Council, Commerce, see High Council, Nauvoo.

High Council, Far West, Missouri, Zion, accepts ordination resolutions,
    V2:397
    Brown, Samuel, charges heard against for teaching contrary to council
        and illegally ordaining a high priest, V2:137
    Brown, Samuel, found guilty and allowed to repent, V2:138
    cases, sundry, before, V2:125
    compensation, question of, before, V2:527
    composed of, V3:225
    excommunication of W. W. Phelps and John Whitmer by, V3:8
    Far West, meets at, to reorganize, V3:224
    Lord, resolve to build house of, at, V2:481
    members elected in, V2:367
    members, meeting of, on military duty of, V3:6 and ftnt
    members replaced, V2:357
    members of sustained, V2:523
    minutes of, V2:481
    minutes of appointing new Apostles, V3:240-1
    minutes of meeting of, V3:6-8
    minutes of meeting of on business of members, V2:491
    Missouri, considers affairs in, V3:224-5
    organization of, V2:122, 124
    Phelps, W. W., and John Whitmer, proceedings of, against, V2:483,
        ftnt only
    Presidency and members of, V2:124
    presidents, rejection of, V2:522, et seq
    Prophet, instructed by, V2:124
    saints, appoints elders to visit scattered, V2:136

HIGH COUNCIL, FAR WEST (continued)

saints, authorizes draft of a petition to the general government in behalf of, V3:241

services, committee to study propriety of paying for, V2:527

services, to receive pay for, V2:528

tongues and visions, hears Hulet Branch case on improper use of, V2:139

trial of Aaron Lyon before, V3:25-6

trial of W. W. Phelps and John Whitmer before, V3:6

Zion, Clay County, minutes of, V2:164

Zion, decides against holding public meetings, V2:136.

High Council, Iowa, changes in, V4:352

disfellowship, resolves to any who call for Missouri debts, V4:42-54

minutes of, V4:93-4

organization of, completed, V4:21

speaking order of, V4:16 and ftnt

stake in Iowa, appointed for, V4:16.

High Council, Kirtland, Apostles, sanctions, V2:239-41

Brewsters, case of, before, V2:525-6

case, first before, V2:33

children, convicts R. Cahoon for failure to correct and instruct, V2:242

disfellowships members, V2:519

Elliot case before, V2:295

evils, to commence pruning vineyard and reforming, V2:519

Gould, John, case of, before, V2:286

instructions, special to, V2:31-2

Joseph, rejects Twelve's amendments to ordinations and accepts resolutions of, V2:396

Joseph, resolution adopted exonerating on charges of criminal conduct, published, V2:147

members, new ordained into, V2:366

members, rearrangement of, V2:511

minutes of, V2:34-5, 165, 172, 242, 252, 274, et seq, 277, et seq, 284, 519, 520

minutes of, on trials for fellowship, V2:525-6

Missouri, gives audience to delegation from, V2:39

patriarch, provides remuneration for, V2:273

presidency, attempts to try members of, but procedure problems confuse them, V2:485

presidency, question of, V2:521-2

president, cannot decide who presides when gone, V2:522

revelation organizing, V2:28, et seq

HIGH COUNCIL, KIRTLAND (continued)

sundry action of, V2:253, 520

sustained, some rejected, V2:510

Zion, considers redemption of, V2:281-2

Zions Camp, Joseph charged before, for criminal conduct in, acquitted, V2:142.

High Council, Montrose, voted to disfellowship all those who keep "tippling shops," V4:80.

High Council, Nauvoo, Bennett, John C., investigates charges against, V5:21

Bishop, Gladden, trial of, before, V4:550

consecrations, votes to return to the people, V4:88

councilors, names of, V4:12

courts, appoints committee to collect testimony on case before, V4:49

epistle of, to saints on living gospel, V5:15

Fordham, Elijah, before, V4:180

Hoyt, decision on, V5:311

hymn book, authorizes publication of, V4:49

Joseph, relieves of secular duties and provides for necessities, V4:136-8, 141, 144

Joseph, sustained after death of, V7:296

members, report on strife between, V4:504-5

minutes, V4:187-8, 219-20

minutes of October 20, 1839, V4:16

minutes of trial of A. W. Babbitt, V4:187-8

minutes of trial of Gladden Bishop, V4:550

Nickerson and Wilson Law, case of, before, V5:280

poor, votes money for, V4:75, 76

saints, letter on excommunicated, V6:228

temporal business, resolves to transfer all, V4:144

trials, instructions on, V4:154

unfair dealings, trial of Anson Matthews for, V5:371-2

unvirtuous conduct, sits day to day on, V5:21

wards, divides Nauvoo into, V5:199

wards, meeting of dividing city into, V5:119

westward movement, circular to Church informing of, V7:570

witchcraft, commands Benjamin Hoyt to cease certain actions of, V5:311.

High Council, Ohio, organized, V4:12.

High Council, Salt Lake, organized, V7:629.

high priest, building proposed for, V7:364

. HIGH PRIEST (continued)

Church, selected to govern over districts of, V7:305
Church court, council of, to try cases, V1:354
duty of, explained, V1:338-9
first conferred, V1:176, ftnt only
ordinations, none without conference of, V1:407
organized, V1:334
president of may ordain own counselors, V2:504
priesthood of, explained, V2:477
publicly required to disclose whether they lived Word of Wisdom and
    had family prayer, V5:84.

Higley, Oliver, Joseph, exonerates actions of, in Zions Camp, V2:149
Kirtland Temple, blessing for work on, V2:206
mentioned, V2:244.

Hill, Isaac, Church case settled, retained in, after public confession, V2:
    312
Joseph, exonerates actions of, in Zions Camp, V2:149
Kirtland Temple, blessing for work on, V2:205
rebaptized, publicly confesses sins, Church votes to, V2:303.

Hill, James, churches, given charge of, at Hope Rough, Stanley Hill,
    V4:139
elder, ordained, V4:138.

Hill, John, given care of Church at Twigworth, V4:135.

Hill, Robert, ordained teacher, V4:138.

Hillman, Mayhew, (also spelled Matthew), Adam-ondi-Ahman, High
    Council, chosen to, V3:38
Kirtland Camp, upholds movement, V3:97
Kirtland High Council, ordained to, V2:511
Kirtland High Council, sustained to, V2:510
Kirtland Temple, blessing for work on, V2:206
mentioned, V2:207
Missouri, permit to travel in, V3:210.

Hills, Cyrus, mentioned, V6:439.

Hills, Gustavus, clerk of conference, V4:423, 429
mentioned, V3:404, 421; V5:365, 473; V6:286, 357
Times & Seasons, on staff of, V4:454.

Hilmer, Brother, mentioned, V7:385.

Hinckley, Ira M., mentioned, V2:507, ftnt only.

Hinkle, George M., (also spelled Hinckle), Boggs, Governor, petitions on
    mob violence in DeWitt, V3:83

HINKLE, GEORGE M. (continued)

buffetings of Satan, turned over to and condemned as openly sinning
   against Jesus, V3:232

Church, accuses Elders Phelps and Whitmer in the general assembly
   of, at Far West, V3:4

DeWitt, removes to, V3:155

Diahman, leads company of militia from Far West to, V3:162

excommunication from Church, V3:284

high council, sustained member of, at Far West, V2:524

Joseph sues for robbing house, V4:423

Missouri trials, witness for state in, of saints, V3:210

mob, actions against, V3:169-70

mob, agreements with, V3:196-8

mob, makes secret arrangements with, to turn over Joseph, V3:188-9
   and ftnt

signs attempted whitewash of General Clark's activity, V3:360, ftnt
   only

traitorous acts of, V3:228-9, 278

Zion High Council, appointed to, V2:357.

Hinkle, John M., Far West High Council, sustained member of, V2:523

preaching without authority, V3:398.

Hinkle, Sally, witness to apostate vandalizing of saints' homes, V3:288.

Hirsch, Emil G., quoted, V3:358-9, ftnt only.

Hirschell, Solomon, Jewish Rabbi, letter to, V4:374-8.

History, *Comprehensive,* Century I, (six volumes) referred to, V7:614-5

contains story of march from Missouri to Salt Lake Valley, also return
   of Brigham Young and some other pioneers to Winter Quarters,
   V7:616

Hayden's, of disciples, V1:158, ftnt only, 215, ftnt only, 261, ftnt only

Manuscript of Brigham Young, Part V, V7:245, et seq.

See also Latter-day Saints, Church of Jesus Christ of.

History of Church, see Latter-day Saints, Church of Jesus Christ of.

Hitchcock, Isaac, mentioned, V2:452.

Hitchcock, Jesse, (also spelled Hithcock), high council, cut off from at
   Far West, V2:482

high priest, ordained, V1:410; V2:141

mission call in Illinois to disabuse public mind over arrest of Joseph,
   V5:485

Missouri, arrival from, V2:320.

Hitchcock, John, appointed to Zion High Council, V2:357.

Hitchcock, Seth, dies of cholera in Missouri, V2:115

HITCHCOCK, SETH (continued)

Zions Camp member, V2:184.

hitchhiker, spirit prompts to leave, a mobber, V2:50.

Hobert, William, mentioned, V1:368

Zion, to take sister to, V1:342.

Hodge, Abraham C., (also spelled Abram), Carthage, sent on special mission to, V6:557

Foster, Dr. R. D., reports conversation with, V7:513

Indians, militia to fight, V7:627

Nauvoo, policeman in, V6:149

west, reports Prophet's determination to go, V6:545.

Hodge, Amos C., bodyguard to Joseph's body on return to Nauvoo, V7:135.

Hodges, Amos, mission and field of labor, V6:336.

Hodges, Brother, mentioned, V1:355.

Hodges, Curtis, Sr., charged with loud speaking and error in spirit, V2:33

excommunicated for unchristianlike conduct, V5:350

found guilty, confessed and forgiven, V2:34

high council, first case tried before, V2:32-3.

Hodgin, Alice, death of, in England, V3:149.

Hoge, J. B., mentioned, V7:406.

Hoge, Joseph P., candidate for Congress, conversation with Prophet, V5:518, 521

mentioned, V7:547

Nauvoo Charter, acknowledges power of habeas corpus, V5:524.

Hogers, Amos, Zions Camp member, V2:184

Hoier, Ole, called to preside over branch, V5:395.

Hoit, Timothy S., mission and field of labor, V6:340.

Holbrook, Mr., mentioned, V4:483.

Holbrook, Chandler, mission and field of labor, V6:336

Missouri, arraigned for treason, murder, burglary, arson, robbery and larceny at Richmond, V3:209

Missouri, covenanted to assist saints in removal from, V3:251

Missouri trials, discharged as innocent from, V3:211

Zions Camp member, V2:184.

Holbrook, Charlotte, daughter of Joseph Holbrook, Zions Camp member, V2:185.

Holbrook, Diana, daughter of Chandler Holbrook, Zions Camp member, V2:185.

Holbrook, Eunice, Zions Camp member, V2:185.

Holbrook, Joseph, Church, appointed to preside over new district of, V7:305
mission and field of labor, V6:338
mob, appointed to watch movements of, V3:169
Prophet, entertains the, V2:45
Zions Camp member, V2:184.

Holbrook, Nancy Lambson, Zions Camp member, V2:185.

Holbrook, Sarah Lucretia, daughter of Joseph Holbrook, Zions Camp member, V2:185.

Holebrook, Joseph, mentioned, V4:144.

"Holiness to the Lord," millennium, written on bells of horses in, V2:358
temples, inscription on, V1:359.

Holliday, Benjamin, mentioned, V3:79.

Hollingshead, Thos., petitions Governor Boggs on mob violence in De-Witt, V3:83.

Hollister, Brother, mentioned, V5:103, 145, 511.

Hollister, David S., letter on election matters, V6:416, et seq
mentioned, V6:56.

Hollister, John, gospel, declares belief in, V2:326
religious information, asks Joseph for, V2:325.

Holloway, Joseph, mentioned, V4:322.

Holman, David, mentioned, V5:333
Missouri, covenanted to assist saints in removal from, V3:252
mob, house burned in Illinois by, V6:133
permit, issued to live in Caldwell County or leave state, V3:206.

Holman, James S., Kirtland Camp, mentioned in, V3:125
mentioned, V7:306
Missouri, covenanted to assit saints in removal from, V3:252.

Holman, Joshua S., (also H.), Church, appointed to preside over new district of, V7:305
Kirtland Camp, mentioned in, V3:147
Kirtland Camp, subscribed to constitution of, V3:91
mentioned, V7:609
mission and field of labor, V5:347.

Holmer, Jonathan H., subscribed to constitution of Kirtland Camp, V3:92.

Holmes, Bro., mentioned, V7:485.

Holmes, Charles A., mentioned, V2:49, ftnt only.

Holmes, Elder, priesthood taken because could not rule own home, V2:241.

Holmes, Erastus, Church, inquires of and intends joining, V2:312
Kirtland, counseled not to be baptized at, V2:316
Methodist Church, excommunicated from, for receiving missionaries, V2:312.

Holmes, George, counselor of New York branch, V4:344.

Holmes, J. T., mentioned, V3:271; V4:267
recommends Brother Green to collect for poor, V3:348.

Holmes, Jonathan H., *Expositor*, arrest of, for destruction of, trial on, V6:487, et seq
Joseph, on relief expedition for, V5:482
Kirtland Camp, mentioned in, V3:146.

Holmes, Mary Ann, mentioned, V5:515.

Holmes, Milton, appointed to go to England with Twelve, V3:347
British Mission, sails for, V7:324
mentioned, V7:159
mission to Canada, V2:35
Zions Camp member, V2:184.

Holmes, Samuel, mentioned, V4:267
recommends Brother Green to collect for poor, V3:348.

Holmes and Co., mentioned, V4:51-2.

Holmon, James S., subscribed to constitution of Kirtland Camp, V3:92.

Holt, James, mission and field of labor, V6:338.

Holt, John, mission and field of labor, V6:337.

Holton, John H., mentioned, V4:65.

Holy Ghost, Christianity, loss of gifts of, in early, IntroV1:LXXVI
Church, evidenced at organization of, V1:78
Church, witnessed powers at organization of, V1:79
conference, manifestations at, V1:323
conference, poured out at first, V1:85
confirmations, to direct, V1:61
discourse, V5:26, et seq
gift of, difference from, V4:555
gifts and blessings manifest, V1:85
gifts of, believed in, V5:27
manifestation of, seldom public, V5:31
manifestation, usually none of, V5:28
missionaries must preach with, V4:13

HOLY GHOST(continued)

    office, none called to, without, V5:27

    priesthood, necessary to organize, V5:27

    Prophet, as a witness to, V6:13

    pure intelligence, effect of, is, V3:380

    repentance follows, V2:256

    revelations, cannot receive without having, V6:58

    seventies, attests to, that they should move to Zion as a quorum, V3:89

    sign of the dove as, V5:261

    unrighteous, withdraws if, V3:379

    Word of Wisdom, will not dwell in those who break, V5:428.

    See also doctrine; Smith, Joseph.

Holy Ghost, gift of, Aaronic Priesthood, cannot give, V1:39

    Church, given to members at organization of, V1:78

    editorial on, V5:26, et seq

    Holy Ghost, difference from, V4:555

    laying of hands, given by, V3:379

    manifestation of seldom public, V5:31

    manifestation, usually none of, V5:28

    Melchizedek Priesthood holds power, V1:60

    office, none called to without, V5:27

    sees, multitude seldom, V5:29

    priesthood, necessary, to organize, V5:27.

    See also doctrine; Holy Ghost; Smith, Joseph.

Holy Ghost, sin against, murderers commit, V6:253.

Holy Land, Jews, time of, to return to, arrived, V4:113.

    See also Hyde, Orson; Jerusalem; Jews; Palestine.

Holy Spirit, see Holy Ghost.

home, priesthood taken for failure to rule, V2:241.

honesty, excommunicated for not having, V4:454, 463-6

    spirit discerns, V6:28-9.

Hoopes, Jonathan, mentioned, V5:326.

Hoopes, Lewis, mentioned, V5:326.

Hoops, Warner, mission and field of labor, V5:348.

Hope, emigrant ship, V4:514.

Hopkins, Charles, Joseph, accompanies in arrest, V4:365

    mission and field of labor, V6:339.

Horace, Mr., letter threatening invasion of Nauvoo, V6:426.

horn, consecrated, left in Illinois by Joseph, V2:146.

Horn, Joseph, mentioned, V7:369.

Horn, Moses, death of, at Temple Quarry, V7:381.

Horne, Joseph, testimony of Joseph's remarks on children, V4:556, ftnt only.

Horne, M. Isabella, testimony of Joseph's remarks on children, V4:556, ftnt only.

Horner, E., delegate to present truth to public, V6:483.

Horner, J., delegate to political convention in Nauvoo, V6:390.

Horner, William E., mentioned, V2:350, ftnt only
Nauvoo committee, affidavit on treatment of, by Levi Williams, V6:505.

horns, saints thought to have, V5:214.

Horrocks, Edward, mentioned, V4:216.

Horrocks, John, mentioned, V4:216.

"Hossana," song sung at Kirtland Temple dedication, V2:416 and ftnt, 426-7 and ftnt.

Hosford, Trueman, farmer, member of martyrdom mob, V7:144.

Hotchkiss, Horace R., letter to Joseph on anti-Mormon sentiments in Carthage and reply, V6:55
letter to Joseph on bankruptcy, V5:51
letter to Joseph offering land for sale, V4:100
letter to Joseph on property title, V5:382
letter of Joseph to, on purchase of lands, V4:170
letter to Joseph and Sidney concerning progress before Congress, V4:98
letter of Joseph to, on taking out bankruptcy, V5:6
letter on land affairs in Nauvoo, V4:405
letter of Prophet, V4:406-8.
See also letters.

Houck, Mr., tailor, member of martyrdom mob, V7:163.

Houghman, Mr., Kirtland Camp, mentioned in, V3:116.

Houghton, Mr., Zions Camp member, V2:185.

Houghton, Mrs., Zions Camp member, V2:185.

Houghton, Osmon, Zions Camp member, V2:184.

Houston, Mr., mentioned, V5:415.

Houston, Captain, mentioned, V3:149.

Houston, Isaac, mission and field of labor, V6:336
Nauvoo, prepares harvest feast in, V7:437.

Houston, James, British conference, represents branches of Church at, V6:328.

Houston, John, mission and field of labor, V6:337
  Nauvoo, delegate to political convention in, V6:390.

Hovey, Mr., mentioned, V6:38.

Hovey, Joseph G., appointed elder, V4:13
  reporter, V6:497.

Hovey, Orlando D., elder, ordained, V4:13
  mission and field of labor, V5:349; V6:335.

Howard, Richard, Iowa Territory High Council, appointed to, V4:12
  prophecy, present in Missouri at Apostles' departure to fulfill, V3:339.

Howe, Daniel, covenanted to assist saints in removing from Missouri, V3:252.

Howe, Edward D., author, *Mormonism Unveiled,* V1:217, ftnt only
  Harris, Martin, admits visit of, to Professor Anthon, V1:20, ftnt only
  mentioned, V2:268, 270; V4:489.

Howe, Harriet, Joseph stays at home of, V2:324
  witness against "Doctor" Hurlbut, V2:2.

Howe, Nabby, wife of John Young, V1:295, ftnt only.

Hoyt, Benjamin, commanded to cease certain actions, V5:311.

Hoyt, Henry, Joseph, on mission to rescue, V5:451.

Hoyt, Homer C., mission and field of labor, V6:336.

Hoyt, Samuel P., mission and field of labor, V6:335.

Hubbard, Charles, appointed to go to England with Twelve, V3:347
  mentioned, V1:9-10, ftnt only.

Hubbard, Charles W., Joseph, on relief expedition for, V5:486
  mission and field of labor, V6:339.

Hubbard, Isaac, blessing for work on Kirtland Temple, V2:206.

Hubbard, Marshal, Zions Camp member, V2:184.

Hubble, Mrs., woman pretends revelation, V1:154, ftnt only.

Hudgins, Mr., sends more inflammatory communication to Boggs, V3:166.

Hudson, John, ordained priest, V4:311.

Hudspeth, Thomas, committee to rid Missouri of saints, V1:395.

Huffaker, S. D., ordained priest, V6:400.

Hughes, James H., drafts resolution of public meeting in Missouri, V2:449.

Hughes, James M., committee member to talk to saints on removal, V2:452
  Joseph, receives petition from, V3:248.

Hughes, John, witness in *Expositor* trial of Joseph, V6:457.

Hughes, Judge, judge of Clay County, remarks concerning brethren, V3:264-5.

Hughs, Major, mentioned, V7:138.

Hugins, Mr., mentioned, V3:360.

Hugins, Horace T., Joseph, letter on probable indictment of, V6:494
Joseph, letter warning of probable indictment, V6:451
lawyer in case of Jeremiah Smith, V6:421
Nauvoo, affidavit on threat to bring dragoons against, V6:423.

Hulet, Brother, teaches false doctrine, V1:366.

Hulet, Clark, bishop's counselor, V4:233.

Hulet, Sylvester, (also spelled Hulett), devil, deceived by, through gift of tongues, V2:139
high priest, improperly ordained, V2:137
Missouri trials, discharged as innocent from, V3:211
ordination illegal, V2:138.

Hulet Branch, devil deceives through gift of tongues, called before high council in Zion, V2:139, et seq.

Hull, Benjamin K., (also spelled Hall), Kirtland Camp, leaves, V3:141
Kirtland Camp, subscribed to constitution of, V3:92.

human family, Adam head of, V3:387
world, to be harvested at end of, V2:271.

Humphrey, Henry, Missouri, permit to travel in, V3:210.

Humphrey, Smith, DeWitt, petitions Governor Boggs on mob violence in, V3:83
Missouri persecutions, affidavit concerning, V4:62
mob, goods stolen and house burned by, V3:157; V4:58
witness, suggested to appear before Congress on redress, V4:97

Humphrey, Solomon, confirms George A. Smith, V1:285.

Humphreys, Solomon, protects rattlesnakes, V2:73-4
Zions Camp member, V2:184.

Humstead, Harvey, falsely accused of threatening A. Black, V3:64.

Hunt, Mr., delegate to political convention in Nauvoo, V6:390.

Hunt, D. D., mission and field of labor, V6:338.

Hunt, Jefferson, Church, appointed to preside over new district of, V7:305
mission and field of labor, V6:340.

Hunter, Mr., mentioned, V6:543.

Hunter, Edward, bishop, ordained, V7:317
Ford, Governor, sent as special messenger to, V6:492
genealogy, V4:416-7 and ftnt

HUNTER, EDWARD (continued)

Joseph goes into hiding at home of, V5:160
mentioned, V4:481-2; V5:97; V7:70
Missouri warrants, accompanies Joseph for trial on, V5:210
mob lies, affiant to public proclamation on, V6:495
Nauvoo, bodyguard to Joseph's body on return to, V7:135
Nauvoo, delegate to political convention in, V6:389
Nauvoo, visits, V4:416
utility committee member to aid Church removal, V7:474.

Hunter, Edward, father of Edward Hunter, V4:416, ftnt only.

Hunter, Hannah, wife of Edward Hunter, V4:416, ftnt only.

Hunter, Henry, at anti-Mormon meeting, V5:537.

Hunter, James M., mob, carries proposals to saints from, V1:398
saints, committee to rid Missouri of, V1:395.

Hunter, Jesse D., mission, returns from, V7:390
Missouri, arraigned for treason, murder, burglary, arson, robbery and lar-
ceny at Richmond, V3:209
Nauvoo Legion, major in, V5:443

Hunter, John, great-grandfather of Edward H., Sr., V4:416, ftnt only.

Hunter, Reverend, participated in Missouri mobs, V1:372, ftnt only; 392
and ftnt.

Huntington, Dimick B., Church, appointed to preside over new district of,
V7:305
constable, sworn as, V4:308
Expositor, arrest of, for destruction of, trial on, V6:487, et seq
Joseph, declares gratefulness for aid rendered while in seclusion, V5:108
Joseph, on relief expedition for, V5:482
Legion, martial band member, V7:135
mentioned, V4:17; V6:627-8
Nauvoo, elected coroner of, V5:18
Nauvoo, elected coroner and constable of, V5:270.

Huntington, Oliver B., ordained elder, V5:349.

Huntington, William D., Legion, martial band member of, V7:135
Missouri, covenanted to assist saints in removing from, V3:251
Missouri, permit to travel in, V3:210
Nauvoo, elected constable and coroner of, V5:270
Nauvoo High Council, appointed to, V4:12
westward movement, captain of 25th company in, V7:482.

Huntsman, James W., counselor to teachers quorum in Nauvoo, V4:312, 354;
V5:169.

Huntsman, Jesse, named to first quorum of seventies, V2:204.

Huntsman, Joseph, Zions Camp member, V2:184.

Hurlburt, Philastus, apostasy, against the Church and attempts to discredit Joseph, V1:475
 character of, V1:355 and ftnt
 council, presents appeal to, V1:354
 criminal trial of, V2:46-7
 criminal trial, convicted in, V2:49 and ftnt
 elder, ordained, V1:334
 excommunicated, V1:352
 excommunicated again from Church, V1:355
 membership, liberal confession of unchristianlike conduct with women restores him to, V1:354
 "Mormonism Unveiled," author of, V2:269-70
 peace, bound over to keep, V2:49 and ftnt
 prayer against, V2:3
 trial of, V1:352.

Hurlburt, Wesley, excommunicated for denying faith, V2:2.

husbands, curse on, if refuse family to hear gospel, V2:263
 wives and children, to obey, V2:247.

Hushman, Mr., mentioned, V3:119, 125.

Hustin, John, Zions Camp member, V2:184.

Hutchings, Elias, seventies, named to first quorum of, V2:203
 Zions Camp member, V2:184.

Hutchins, James, mission and field of labor, V5:349.

Hutchins, S. P., mission and field of labor, V6:339.

Hutchinson, J. F., musician performs, V7:561.

Hyam, Uriah S., mentioned, V4:175.

Hyatt, Elder, mentioned, V7:260.

Hyde, Heman T., approved for ordination, V2:407
 baptism of, V2:43 and ftnt
 seventies, named to first quorum of, V2:203
 Zions Camp member, V2:184.

Hyde, Nancy Marinda, circumstances, revelation to, on, V4:467
 mentioned, V4:125; V6:82
 Nauvoo Temple, receives endowment in, V7:543.

Hyde, Nathan, father of Orson, V1:217, ftnt only.

Hyde, Orson, America, departs for, V3:22

HYDE, ORSON (continued)

apostasy of, and affidavit against saints, V3:167-8 and ftnt
Apostle, sustained as, V2:509
Apostle, sustained as, by Church after death of Joseph, V7:294
Apostles, as witnesses for God, V7:336
baptized, V1:217 and ftnt
British Mission, departs for, V2:493
Church, remarks of, on death of Joseph and continuation of, V7:197-8
clerk for Gilbert & Whitney, V1:217
committee, on meeting conducting, V1:219
complaints, letter of, to Joseph on, V2:335, et seq
conference, attends, at Avon, V2:44
Congress, credentials of, to present Joseph's memorial to, V6:283
Congress, letter on labors in Washington and Joseph's memorial to,
     V6:369, et seq
doctrine, corrected by Joseph on, V5:323, et seq
Dunklin, Governor, sent with dispatch to, V2:88
endowment, receives, V6:98
endowment, receives in Nauvoo Temple, V7:543
England, arrives in, V2:498
England, arrives at Kirtland from, V3:36
England, farewell visit to churches in, V3:21
England, set apart to go to, V2:490
fall, his allusion to his, V4:2
Far West, arrival of, at, V3:48
Far West, departure from, V3:165
fellowship withdrawn from for insulting School of Prophets, V2:240
high priests, appointed clerk of, V1:353
Holy Land, letter of, on mission to, V4:496, et seq
house, collection taken to build for, V5:491
Jerusalem, appointed on mission to, V4:106
Jerusalem, leaves for, V4:114
Jerusalem, letter of July 17, 1841, detailing events en route to, V4:384,
     et seq
Jerusalem, letter of, recounting incidents on, V4:372, et seq
Jerusalem, sails on way to, V4:298
Jerusalem mission, return of, from, V5:200
Jews, commences mission to, V4:106
Joseph, accompanies on trial on Missouri warrants, V5:210
Joseph, gives bond for collection of funds to, V5:414
Judah, letter to Rabbi Hirschell calling to repentance, V4:374, et seq
land speculators, letter to saints warning against, V7:348

HYDE, ORSON (continued)

mission call in Illinois to disabuse public mind over arrest of Joseph, V5:485

mission, letter of, requesting to proceed to, V4:123-4

Missouri, epistle to, January 14, 1833, V1:317, et seq

Mount of Olives, prayer of dedication on, V4:454, et seq

murder, letter to Major Warren reporting Durfee, V7:525

Nauvoo Temple, appointed to officiate in, V7:547-8

New York, at conference in, V4:237

New York ministers, posts "Timely Warnings" to, V2:495

Olive Branch of Israel, designated as, V7:435

Palestine, credentials of, as missionary to, V4:112-3

Palestine, letter to, from Joseph on mission, V4:128-9

Palestine, mission to, IntroV4:XXXI, et seq

Palestine, reproved for delaying mission to, V4:274

petition to Missouri governor for saints carried by, V1:410

Phelps, Brother, letter of, pleading for, V4:142-3

Philadelphia, at conference in, V4:224

preach, appointed to, in regions about, V2:44

Presidency, reproved by, V2:48-9

priesthood, restored to, V3:379

prophecy of, concerning apostasy of Thomas Webster, V3:21

restored as Apostle, V4:12

revelation to, V1:218

Russia, appointed missionary to, V5:488

Russia, to go on mission to, V5:417

saints, affidavit of, on mob threats to drive out, V6:145

saints, discourse of, at Seventies Hall dedication, on unity of, V7:335, et seq

signs in heavens, letter of, noting, V4:202-3

signs of times, letter of, on remarkable, V4:439

suspended from office and asked to account, V3:345

tent tabernacle, appointed to purchase canvas for, in the wilderness, V7:426-7

Twelve, blessing of, as member of, V2:189-90

Twelve, dissatisfaction of, with temple committee and questions of, concerning revelation to, V2:333 and ftnt

Twelve, sustained member of, at Salt Lake City, V7:628

Twelve Apostles, chosen a member of, V2:187

Washington, sent to aid in presentation of memorial, V6:286 and ftnt

western movement, letter on, of the Church, route, V6:373, et seq

witness, suggested to appear before Congress on redress, V4:97

HYDE ORSON (continued)

 Zion, sent from Kirtland to, as special messenger, V1:407
 Zions Camp member, V2:184.
 See also Apostles; Jerusalem; Jews; letters; Palestine.

Hyde, Sally, mother to Orson, V1:217, ftnt only.

Hyde, William, elder, appointed, V4:13
 mission and field of labor, V6:336.

hymns, "Adam-ondi-Ahman," V2:365, ftnt only, 417
 book of, authorized to be published, V4:49
 "Come Let Us Rejoice," V2:366
 "Ere Long the Veil Will Rend in Twain," V2:412-3
 first selection of, to be printed, V1:270
 "The Gallant Ship Is Under Weigh," V4:103, 4, ftnt only
 "Glorious Things of Thee Are Spoken," V2:189
 "Hark, Listen to the Trumpeters," V2:186, ftnt only
 "How Pleased and Blessed Was I," V2:419
 "Now Let Us Rejoice," V2:416
 "O Happy Souls Who Pray," V2:413
 published in England, V4:118, 131, 132, 143, 148, 228, 253, 326, 447.
 Smith, Emma, to select, V4:17-8
 "The Spirit of God Like a Fire Is Burning," V2:426-7.

—I—

Ide, Brother, mentioned, V3:126, 127.

Idle, W. B., delegate to political convention in Nauvoo, V6:389.

Illinois, Church, situation of entry into, IntroV4:XIX, et seq
 counterfeiters in, V7:59
 lawlessness of northern part of, Ford, V7:59
 Nauvoo, founding of, by Church, IntroV4:XXII
 people in, IntroV6:XXVI; IntroV6:XXVIII.
 See also Latter-day Saints, Church of Jesus Christ of; persecutions,
  Illinois.

Illinois, Commerce, boundary lines to be changed, V4:39
 description of, V3:375
 lands, purchase of, at, V3:342
 Nauvoo, changed to, V4:121
 Nauvoo, merged into, V4:322
 Nauvoo, post office changed to, V4:121
 stake of Zion, appointed a, V4:12.
 See also Nauvoo.

Illinois, Monmouth, Warren County, Joseph's trial at, V4:365, et seq letter on Joseph's trial at, V4:380.

Illinois persecutions, see persecutions, Illinois.

Illinois Springfield Register, publishes article of Joseph's condidacy for president, V6:268.

Illinois State Register, Dixon arrest of the Prophet, was it a political trick?, V5:513-5
martyrdom, account of, in, V7:178.

Independence, Declaration of, anniversary of, celebrated at Far West, V3:41
of saints, from mob, V3:41.
See also Nauvoo.

Indian agent, Cummins, R. W., signed mob manifesto, V1:376.

Indians, Appenoose chief visits Joseph, V4:401
Church, communicated with, IntroV3:XXX
Church, never stirred up, V3:29
Church position on, in Missouri, IntroV3:XXXI
conditions, speech on, April 1843, V5:358
Congress, report to, on, V2:361
gathering, part of, V2:357
Jackson, Andrew, views on, of, V2:358
Joseph, chiefs of Pottawattamie interview, V5:479-80
Joseph, Pottawattamie chiefs visit for advice, V5:365
Missouri, problem concerning, made possible expulsion of saints in, IntroV3:XXXII
Missouri vs retribution, used against, IntroV3:LXXI
Missouri, saints and, in, IntroV3:XXIX, et seq
mob militia painted as, V3:411
Nauvoo, Sacs and Foxes visit, V6:401-2
trouble of, V7:627.
See also doctrine; Lamanites; Latter-day Saints, Church of Jesus Christ of; Mormon, Book of; Smith, Joseph.

Indians, Appenoose, Indian chief meets Joseph, V4:401.

infancy, many taken in, because too pure to stay, V4:553.

Ingalls, Warren S., dies of cholera in Missouri, V2:120
Zions Camp member, V2:184.

Ingersoll, J. R., mentioned, V6:282, ftnt only.

iniquity, as grows, easy to discern righteousness, V2:268.

inspiration, Joseph's doctrine on, V5:406, et seq.

intelligence, attainment of, V5:325

INTELLIGENCE (continued)

immortality of, V6:310 and ftnt.

intemperance, Joseph on the monster of, V2:406.

See also alcohol, liquor, temperance, Word of Wisdom.

Iowa, communication to governor of, on passage through territory of, V7:599-601

conditions in, V5:334, et seq.

See also persecutions, Iowa.

Iowa, Montrose, opposite Nauvoo, gathering of brethren at, to go West, V7:81.

Iowa Democrat, publishes article of Joseph's candidacy for president, V6:268.

Iowa persecutions, see persecutions, Iowa.

Ireland, introduction of gospel to, V4:170 and ftnt.

Irving, Edward, founder of Irvingite Church, V2:233, ftnt only.

Irvingites, Church, sends representative to investigate, V2:233 and ftnt

false beliefs of, expounded, V4:577, et seq.

Irwin, William L., (also M.L.), anti-Mormon committee member, V1:399, 412.

Isaiah, Moroni quotes, V1:12

prophecy fulfilled of Book of Mormon, V1:84.

Isherwood, William, ordained elder, V5:349.

Israel, twelve tribes of, honored at establishment of Zion, V1:196.

Israel, Camp of, employment offered to, V7:597

encampment, prominent places of en marche, V7:606

en marche, irregularities in, V7:607-10

mail service improvised for, V7:610

organization developments of, V7:605

westward camp, name given to, V7:606.

See also Latter-day Saints, Church of Jesus Christ of; westward movement.

Israel, James, named to high council at Lima, V5:427.

Ivans, Garret, MIA, aids in movement toward, V5:322.

Ives, Edward, dies of cholera in Missouri, V2:120.

Ives, Sebe, blessing for work on Kirtland Temple, V2:206.

Ivie, Edward, Zions Camp member, V2:184.

Ivie, James R., Zions Camp member, V2:184.

Ivie, John A., Zions Camp member, V2:184.

Ivie, Warren, Zions Camp member, V2:184.

Ivie, William S., Zions Camp member, V2:183.

Ivins, Mr., mentioned, V6:38

Ivins, Charles, anti-Mormon activities of, V7:61, et seq
    apostasy, excommunicated for, V6:398.
    bishop, chosen of apostate church, V6:347, 354
    martyrdom mob, aided and abetted, V7:146.

Ivins, James, mentioned, V4:503, 608.

—J—

Jaap, Thomas, mentioned, V7:323.

Jacaway, Fields B., elder, appointed, V4:13
    mission and field of labor, V5:349.

Jack Mormon, nonmember, anti-Mob called, V7:3
    nonmember, friendly, V7:390.

Jackaway, T. G., chosen president of New Orleans branch, V6:176.

Jackman, Henry, ordained elder, V2:525.

Jackman, Levi, Doctrine & Covenants, testifies to truthfulness of, V2:244
    high council, sustained member of Far West, V2:524
    high council, sustained member of Missouri, V2:124
    high council, sustained member of Salt Lake, V7:629
    mentioned, V2:164, 275
    mission and field of labor, V6:340
    Missouri, covenanted to assist saints in removing from, V3:253
    Missouri persecutions, expresses faith in work after, V3:225
    pays Joseph money in hour of need, V2:327.

Jackson, Mr., mentioned, V3:157.

Jackson, Amos, mentioned in Zions Camp, V3:128.

Jackson, Andrew, President, views on Indians, V2:358, et seq.

Jackson, Col., mentioned, V6:190.

Jackson, Congrave, mob member, writes lies concerning DeWitt, V3:156.

Jackson, James, witness in *Expositor* trial of Joseph, V6:457.

Jackson, James, Jr., mob member, writes lies concerning DeWitt, V3:156.

Jackson, John, represents branch of Church at English conference, V4:116.

Jackson, Johnson, mob member, writes lies concerning DeWitt, V3:156.

Jackson, Joseph, affidavits on threat to kill Joseph and mob movements, V6:524.

Jackson, Joseph H., adventurer and fraud, interview with Joseph, V6:149 and ftnt

JACKSON, JOSEPH H. (continued)

    arrest, attempt to, V6:521
    Catholic priest visits Joseph, V5:394
    criminal activities of, V6:435-6
    martyrdom, member of mob at, V7:146
    Prophet, threats against, V6:569.

Jackson, Robert, covenanted to assist saints in removing from Missouri,
    V3:253.

Jackson, Thomas, ordained priest, V5:419.

Jackson, Thomas, mob member writes lies concerning DeWitt, V3:156.

Jackson, Truman, Joseph, pays money to, in hour of need, V2:327
    ordination, approved for, V2:400.

Jackson, W. H., mobber mentioned, V7:148.

Jackson, County, Missouri, see Missouri, Independence, Zion.

Jacobs, Henry B., (also C.), martial band member of Legion, V7:135
    mission and field of labor, V5:348; V6:338
    Missouri, covenanted to assist saints in removing from, V3:252.

Jacobs, Norton, mentioned, V6:401.

Jacobs, Vance, ordained priest, V6:400.

Jacobsen, Oder, ordained priest, V6:400.

James, Mr., mentioned, V6:543, 578; V7:226.

James, Epistle of, Joseph reads concerning answer to prayer, V1:4.

James, George F., letter to, on actions, V2:170
    mission, to go on, V1:369
    trial of, before council for failure to go on mission and attend meetings,
    V2:47.

James, John, given care of Church at Froomes Hill, V4:138
    ordained priest, V4:138.

James, Samuel, elder, to be, V2:354
    high council, elected to, at Kirtland, V2:366
    mentioned, V7:70
    mission appointment, V4:403
    mission, to go on, to England, V5:367, 386
    mission, in Illinois to disabuse public mind over arrest of Joseph, V5:485.

Jamieson, Mr., hears saints' petition in Congressional Committee, V4:83,
    et seq.

Japheth, descendants of, at meeting in Missouri, V1:191.

Jaques, Vienna, Kirtland, in, V1:342
    letter from Joseph on personal counsel, V1:407-8
    mentioned, V1:331, 368

JAQUES, VIENNA (continued)

    Zion, counseled to wait to go to, V1:342
    Zion, in, V1:407.

Jarman, Sister, mentioned, V5:409.

Jasher, Book of, lost book of Bible not found, V1:363.

Jasper, Thomas, constable of Quincy, V4:364.

jayhawkers, destruction of Missouri vs retribution, IntroV3:LXVI.

Jeffreys, Mr., mentioned, V6:41.

Jeffreys, Thomas, signs proposition to buy land of saints, V2:96-7.

Jenkins, Thomas, mentioned, V4:140.

Jenkins, William, Church, given care of, on north side of river Severn, V4:135
    counselor on sailing from England, V4:297
    elder, ordained, V4:135.

Jenks, Elder, mentioned, V4:22.

Jennings, Mr., member of Haun's Mills mob and colonel of militia, V3:186.

Jennings, Ebenezar, blessing for work on Kirtland Temple, V2:206.

Jennings, Messr., attorney, against Joseph, influences public mind in Illinois, V4:367.

Jennings, Thomas, ordained teacher, V5:419.

Jensen, Mr., dies as result of mob violence in DeWitt, V3:159.

Jeremiah, parable of potters clay explained, V4:478.

Jermen, J., clerk of Nova Scotia conference, V6:35.

Jermon, William G., mentioned, V6:44.

Jerusalem, Adams, George J., sails for, with Orson Hyde, V4:298
    Hyde, Orson, leaves for, V4:114
    Hyde, Orson, prayer of dedication on Mount of Olives, V4:454
    report from, on Orson Hyde's mission, V4:495.
    See also Hyde, Orson; Jews.

Jessop, William, Zions Camp member, V2:183.

Jews, Catholic Church, proscription against, by, V5:434
    Christianity, opinion of several as to, V3:357, ftnt only
    gathering, spirit of, on, IntroV2:XXVII
    Holy Land, time of return to, arrived, V4:113
    Hyde, Orson, credentials to, as missionary, V4:112
    Jerusalem, circular to, from, V4:173-5
    memorial to, in *Millennial Star,* V4:167, ftnt only
    mission, Orson Hyde commences, to, V4:106
    Page, John E., to accompany Orson Hyde to, V4:109

JEWS (continued)

    repentance, called to, by Orson Hyde, V4:378.
    See also Hyde, Orson; Jerusalem.

Jimison, Charles, wounded at Haun's Mills by mob, V3:326, ftnt only.

Job, Andrew J., witness for state in Missouri trials of saints, V3:210.

Joel, Book of, Moroni quotes, V1:13
    prophecy by, fulfilled, V1:101
    prophecy of, dispensation of last days considered, IntroV1:XXXI.

Joes, Seba, covenanted to assist saints in removing from Missouri, V3:253.

John, Gospel of, Chapter 14:16-23, interpreted by Joseph, V3:380-1
    Chapter 17:1, retranslated, V6:476
    received D&C § 76 while translating, V1:245.

John the Apostle, difference of opinion of Joseph and Oliver respecting, settled, V1:35-6
    question about, V1:35
    ten tribes, among, V1:176, ftnt only.

John the Baptist, Aaron descendant of, V5:257
    Aaronic Priesthood, confers upon Joseph and Oliver, V1:39
    Aaronic Priesthood, had keys of, V5:258
    appearance of, V1:39
    authority, acting under, V1:40
    Christ, greater because, V5:258
    Joseph, on greatness and mission of, V5:260
    kingdom, only administrator of, V5:261
    Kingdom of God, had, V5:258
    Moses, from, to, IntroV1:XXVIII.

Johnson, Mr., mentioned, V6:559.

Johnson family, V1:260, ftnt only.

Johnson, Aaron, high council, sustained to Nauvoo, after death of Joseph, V7:296
    Joseph, affidavit on accusations against, V6:350
    Kirtland Camp, subscribed to constitution of, V3:93
    lies, affiant to public proclamations on mob, V6:495
    Missouri, covenanted to assist saints in removing from, V3:252
    Nauvoo, delegate to political convention in, V6:390
    Nauvoo Temple, appointed to officiate in, V7:548.

Johnson, Artemas, appointed elder, V4:13.

Johnson, Benjamin F., Kirtland Temple, blessing for work on, V2:206
    Missouri, covenanted to assist saints in removing from, V3:252
    Prophet, instructions from, V6:60

JOHNSON, BENJAMIN F. (continued)

Prophet, remarks of, to, V5:391

westward movement, captain of 16th company in, V7:482.

Johnson, Charles M., militia to fight Indians, V7:627.

Johnson, Colonel, mentioned, V6:226.

Johnson, David, death of, V1:441.

Johnson, Edward, in apostasy, V1:260.

Johnson, Eli, in apostasy, V1:260.

Johnson, Ezekiel, mentioned, V2:407.

Johnson, Garr, carries proposals to saints from mob, V1:398.

Johnson, General, mentioned, V7:622.

Johnson, Israel, grandfather to Luke, V1:260, ftnt only.

Johnson, J. H., appointed to preside over new Church district, V7:305.

Johnson, J. W., appointed to preside over new district of Church, V7:305.

Johnson, Jesse, mission and field of labor, V6:339.

Johnson, Joel H., Kirtland Camp, mentioned in, V3:102, 129, 139

Kirtland Camp, subscribed to constitution of, V3:92

Kirtland Temple, blessing for work on, V2:205.

Johnson, John, elder, ordained, V1:327

genealogy, V1:260

healed after mob encounter, V1:264 and ftnt

high council, blesses son Luke at organization of, V2:32

high council, rejected as member of Kirtland, V2:510

high priest, ordained, V1:353

Joseph, lives with, V1:260

Joseph, lives with in Hiram, V1:215

Kirtland Temple, blessing for work on, V2:206

mentioned, V1:219; V2:28

presidency, on high council to try, V2:484.

Johnson, John, Jr., in apostasy, V1:260.

Johnson, John, Mrs., healed, V1:215-6, ftnt only.

Johnson, Joseph, mentioned, V4:467.

Johnson, Joseph E., records items on Dr. Hurlburt, V1:355, ftnt only.

Johnson, Julia, subscribed to constitution of Kirtland Camp, V3:92.

Johnson, Luke S., apostasy of, V2:528

confesses and retains membership and apostleship, V2:512

council, in, at Kirtland, V1:389

disfellowshipped, rejected as apostle and, V2:509

elder, ordained, after apostasy, V7:622

JOHNSON, LUKE S. (continued)

    high council, receives blessing of father at organization of, V2:32

    Joseph, reports sentiment of country to, V2:81

    Twelve Apostles, blessing of, as member of, V2:190

    Twelve Apostles, chosen as one of the, V2:187

    Zions Camp member, V2:184.

Johnson, Lyman E., confesses and retains membership and apostleship, V2:512

    disfellowshipped, rejected as apostle and, V2:509

    excommunication of, V3:20

    genealogy, V1:322 and ftnt

    high council, charges preferred against by, at Far West, V3:20

    mission to Canada, V2:35

    Nauvoo, at, V4:389

    Twelve Apostles, blessing of, as member of, V2:188

    Twelve Apostles, chosen a member of the, V2:187

    Zions Camp member, V2:184.

Johnson, Noah, dies of cholera in Missouri, V2:120

    Zions Camp member, V2:184.

Johnson, Ole, ordained teacher, V6:400.

Johnson, Olmsted, son of John Johnson, prophecy about, V1:260.

Johnson, Orson, exonerates Joseph's actions in Zions Camp, V2:149

    high council, ordained to, in Kirtland, V2:151

    high council, testimony before, V2:274

    Kirtland Temple, blessing for work on, V2:206

    mentioned, V2:329, 346.

Johnson, Richard M., letter to, on feelings toward saints, V6:65.

Johnson, Robert, mob, carries proposals to saints from, V1:398

    mob, spies for, V1:427 and ftnt

    Pratt, Parley P., attacks, V1:427

    saints, committee to rid Missouri of, V1:395

    saints, reports committee declarations against, in Missouri, V1:396, et seq.

Johnson, Seth, funeral of, V2:204

    mentioned, V2:87, ftnt only

    Zions Camp member, V2:184.

Johnson, Susan, death and funeral of, V2:407.

Johnson, Thomas B., mentioned, V6:379, 418-23, 450-1, 494.

Johnson, Walker, mentioned, V4:215

    represents branch of Church at English conference, V4:148.

Johnston, Benjamin, appointed elder, V4:12.

Johnston, Edward, appointed elder, V4:12
  refuses to be Joseph's counsel, V6:553.

Johnston, Jesse W., affidavit concerning Missouri persecutions, V4:64.

Johnstone, George G., affidavit on militia to move to Nauvoo, V6:530.

Johnstone, Robert, letter on Nauvoo post office name, V4:121.

Jolley, H. B. M., Joseph, on relief expedition for, V5:482.

Jolly, Elizabeth, baptized, V1:81.

Jolly, Harriet, baptized, V1:86.

Jolly, John, baptized, V1:86.

Jolly, Julia Ann, baptized, V1:86.

Jolly, Vincent, baptized, V1:81.

Jolly, William, baptized, V1:81.

Jonas, A., Ford's messenger to Nauvoo, V7:149.

Jonas, Abraham, Grand Master Mason, on Nauvoo and the Mormons, V4:565, et seq.

Jones, Brother, mentioned, V3:319.

Jones, Mr., prayer to soften heart of, V2:24.

Jones, Mr., aged saints attacked by mob, V1:469.

Jones, Benjamin, elder, appointed, V4:12
  Joseph, on relief expedition for, V5:482
  Missouri, arraigned for treason, murder, burglary, arson, robbery and larceny at Richmond, V3:209.

Jones, Colonel, mentioned in mob action in Missouri, V3:156.

Jones, Colonel, mentioned, V7:111.

Jones, Dan, baptism recorded, V5:354
  British Mission, sails for, V7:324
  Joseph, on relief expedition for, V5:482
  mentioned, V6:603; V7:99, 261
  mission call to Wales, V5:386
  prison, with the Prophet in, V6:601
  prophecy by Joseph that he would not die in jail, V6:601
  Prophet, sent by, with message to Governor Ford, V6:602-4.

Jones, David, mission and field of labor, V6:339
  mission in Illinois to disabuse public mind over arrest of Joseph, V5:485
  Missouri, covenanted to assist saints in removing from, V3:252.

Jones, Edward, farmer, member of martyrdom mob, V7:144.

Jones, Henry, ordained priest, V4:138.

Jones, Isaac, Zions Camp member, V2:184.

Jones, John, mentioned, V4:127.

Jones, John, mission and field of labor, V6:339.

Jones, John, mission and field of labor, V6:337.

Jones, Levi, Zions Camp member, V2:184.

Jones, Luther A., mission call in Illinois to disabuse public mind over arrest of
      Joseph, V5:485.

Jones, R., delegate to political convention in Nauvoo, V6:390.

Jones, Samuel, churches, given charge of, at Keys-End Street, Wind Point,
      Colwell, Pale House, Malvern Hill, V4:139
   elder, appointed, V4:138.

Jones, Stephen, counselor of stake at Quincy, V4:233
   Missouri, covenanted to assist saints in removing from, V3:253.

Jones, Thomas, given care of Church at Pale House, V4:138.

Jones, William, volunteers for service in vineyard, V4:217.

Jordan, William H., mentioned, V7:158 ·
   mission and field of labor, V6:340.

Joseph, City of, Nauvoo, name changed to, V7:394
   organized, to be, V7:387.

Joseph, Hirsh, mentioned, V4:175.

Joshua the Jewish Minister, doctrines of, V2:305
   Joseph, visit to, V2:304
   Matthias of New York, V2:306-7.

journal, Joseph's daily, V1:416, ftnt only, 422-3, ftnt only.

"Jubilee Song," mentioned, V5:246, 252.

Judah, David, (also spelled Juda), mission and field of labor, V6:340
   mob, appointed to watch movements, V3:169.

Judd, Arza, Jr., witness for defense of saints in Missouri, intimidated, V3:211.

Judd, Joel, subscribed to constitution of Kirtland Camp, V3:91.

Judd, Nelson, attempted killing of, V6:179-80.

Judd, Rebecca, witness, suggested to appear before Congress on redress,
      V4:97
   witnessed Haun's Mills massacre, V3:185.

Jude, Enoch appeared to, V4:209.

judgment, evils of hasty, V3:27
   Joseph sees and signs of, V3:391

JUDGMENT (continued)

men not capable unless pure in heart, V2:25
priesthood, right of, rests in, V4:257
saints, will suffer and hardly escape, V4:11.

judgments of God, reason come upon people, V1:278.

Judiciary Committee, Senate report on saints vs. Missouri, V4:90, et seq.

Juliet Courier, letter in, on Joseph's trial at Monmouth, Illinois, V4:380.

Justice, article by Church on retributive, V6:460.

—K—

Kane, Thomas L., mentioned, V7:611-12, 622

Kanesville, general conference at, December 1847, Brigham Young sustained as President of the Church, all other authorities sustained at, V7:623-4.

Kavanaugh, Reverend, participated in Missouri mob, V1:372, ftnt only 392.

Kaw Township, first Missouri conference held in, V1:199
Zion founded in, V1:196.
See also Latter-day Saints, Church of Jesus Christ of; Zion.

Kay, John, witness in *Epositor* trial of Joseph, V6:457
mentioned, V7:372.

Kay, William, British Mission, mission in, V4:149, 176
Church, represents branches of, at English conference, V4:147; V5:101.
high priest, ordained, V4:333
immigrants, in charge of, from England, V6:244
ministry, devote all time to labors of, V4:148
Nauvoo, arrives with company at, V6:333.

Kazey, James, appointed by public to assist saints in removal from Zion, V2:455.

Kearns, Henry, mentioned, V5:67.

Kearns, Samuel, rescued from drowning, V5:390.

Kearny, Stephen W., raises Mormon Battalion, V7:611.

Keele, John, mission in Illinois to disabuse public mind over arrest of Joseph, V5:485.

Keele, Samuel, mission call in Illinois to disabuse public mind over arrest of Joseph, V5:485.

Keeler, Mr., settle differences or will excommunicate, V2:228.

Keeler, Elder, mentioned, V3:140.

Keeler, Joseph, asks forgiveness, V2:163.

Keeler, Rueben, mentioned, V2:227
  trial for oppressing a sister and executing on property, V2:317.

Keith, Mr., mentioned, V6:144.

Kelley, James, mentioned, V4:303.

Kellog, Brother, mentioned, V3:145.

Kellog, Phebe, covenanted to assist saints in removal from Missouri, V3:253.

Kellogg, Hiram, high priests, president of, at Kirtland, V4:362
  mob, leads in Kirtland against Church, V7:484.

Kelly, Mr., publishes *Missouri Enquirer,* V1:470.

Kelly, Charles, (also spelled Kelley), excommunicated for unchristianlike
    conduct, V2:443-4
  fellowship withdrawn from, V2:442
  seventies, named to first quorum of, V2:203
  Zions Camp member, V2:184.

Kelly, Jesse, witness for state in Missouri trials of saints, V3:210.

Kelly, John, mission and field of labor, V6:338.

Kelsey, S. A. P., covenanted to assist saints in removing from Missouri,
    V3:252.

Kelting, Joseph A., delegate to present truth to public, V6:483
  mission and field of labor, V6:338
  Nauvoo, publishes notice of goodness of, V7:360-1
  volunteers for exploring, V6:224
  witness in *Expositor* trial of Joseph, V6:457.

Kempton, Benjamin, mission and field of labor, V5:349.

Kendall, Amos, mentioned, V7:577.

Kendall, L. N., mission and field of labor, V6:339.

Kendrick, Benjamin, petitions Governor Boggs on mob violence in DeWitt,
    V3:82.

Kendrick, Jno., petitions Governor Boggs on mob violence in DeWitt,
    V3:83.

Kennedy, J. H., on conversion of S. Ryder by miracle, *Early Days of Mormon-
    ism,* V1:158, ftnt only.

Kent, Horatio N., covenanted to assist saints in removing from Missouri,
    V3:253.

Keokuk, Indian chief meets Joseph, V4:401.

Kerr, K., saints, agrees to expulsion of, V3:216.

Kerron, Isaac, covenanted to assist saints in removing from Missouri, V3:253.

Kershner, D. J., mission and field of labor, V6:340.

keys, Apostles, of mission call, V3:384
    exaltation, to, V5:403
    Relief Society, given to, V5:20
    temple, to be given in, V4:608.
    See also Apostles; doctrine; mysteries; priesthood; Smith, Joseph.

kidnapping, Allred, J., statement on, V4:156-7
    Avery, D., affidavit on, by Missourians, V6:145
    Avery, P., affidavit on, by Missourians, V6:122
    Boyce, Benjamin, of, V4:180
    Brown, Alanson, of, V4:154-6, 180
    Chapman, D., affidavit on, of D. Avery, V6:100
    Church, some of, and taken to Missouri, V4:155
    Elliott, John, arrested for, of D. Avery, V6:117.
    See also persecution.

Kilbourn, Mr., nuisance of, removal, becomes bitter enemy of Church, V4:444, ftnt only.

Kilbourn, D. W., justice of the peace in Iowa, V4:50
    militia, attempts to cause ill feeling at, review of, V4:416-7, 444, ftnt only
    mob, charged with designs of bringing to Nauvoo, V5:61
    stirs agitation, V4:416.

Kilbourn, Edward, charged with designs of bringing mob to Nauvoo, V5:61.

Killian, Captain, mentioned, V3:457.

Killien, John, mentioned, V6:548.

Killion, John, covenanted to assist saints in removing from Missouri, V3:254.

Kimball, Mr., mentioned, V6:599.

Kimball, Charles, brother to Heber C. Kimball, V1:296, ftnt only.

Kimball, George, arraigned for treason, murder, burglary, arson, robbery and larceny at Richmond, Missouri, V3:209.

Kimball, Heber Chase, America, departs for, V3:22
    America, sails for, V4:352
    baptizes after street meeting, V4:184
    Bennett, John C., letter on mission to confound, V5:161-2
    biography, V1:296, ftnt only
    British Mission, arrives at Nauvoo from, V4:381
    British Mission, called to preside over, V2:489-90 and ftnt
    British Mission, departs for, V2:493
    British Mission, letter on affairs of, V4:114, et seq

KIMBALL, HEBER C. (continued)

British Mission, letter reporting affairs of, October 12, 1840, V4:220, et seq

cholera, remarks on Sidney Gilbert's death by, V2:118 and ftnt

conference, discourse of, at October 1844, V7:299-300

dream at Cincinnati, V5:515-6

dream concerning receiving endowments, V7:561

dream on continuance and organization of Church, V7:228

dream on preaching gospel in London, V4:203

elders, discourse to, V6:324-5

endowments, receives, V5:409

endowments, receives, in Nauvoo Temple, V7:543

England, arrives in, V4:102

England, condition of, during trip and arrival, V4:104-5

England, farewell visit to churches in, V3:21

England, leaves for, sick and whole family sick, V4:9-10 and ftnt

England, reports of, from, V4:182, et seq

England, sails for, V4:94

English conference, represents branches of Church at, V4:147

evil spirits, attacked by, in England, V2:503

Far West, arrival of, at, V3:48

First Presidency, sustained counselor to, in Salt Lake City, V7:628

foreign tongue, speaks in, in temple, V7:558

heals child on board ship for England, V2:498

The Herald of Grace, designated as, V7:435

illness, almost kills on way to England, V4:15-6

Jefferson City, appointed to visit in the interest of the prisoners in Liberty and Richmond, V3:285, 288-9

Joseph, false writ against, for aiding, etc., V7:444

Joseph, gives bond for collection of funds for, V5:414

Joseph, one of two original Apostles that had not fought, V5:412

King, Judge, interview with, V3:306

Kirtland, arrives at, from England, V3:36

Kirtland, on conditions in, V2:2 and ftnt

Kirtland, visits Prophet in, V1:295-6

labors, of in New York and Vermont, V2:441

ministry, devote all time to labors of, V4:148

Missouri, covenanted to assist saints in removing from, V3:252

mob, attack of, on, V3:322

mob, secretes himself from, V3:319

morphine, given to, V4:15-6

Nauvoo, discourse on leaving and blessings of, V7:466-7

KIMBALL, HEBER C. (continued)

Nauvoo Temple, appointed to officiate in, V7:547

Pratt, Orson, on the ordination of, V2:194, ftnt only

prophecy of, concerning apostasy of Thomas Webster, V3:21

Prophet, efforts of, to free, V3:264-5

saints, discourse of, on blessings of, V7:424

saints, signs memorial of, in Missouri, V3:224

Salt Lake Valley, arrival in, V7:628

second communication on mission in Delaware with Lyman Wight, V7:157-8

second first presidency, chosen first counselor in, V7:621 and ftnt

Seventies Hall, report of discourse at dedication of, V7:335

Seventies Hall, second discourse at dedication, on following authorities, V7:339-40

sickness prophecy, testimony of, as to Joseph's, V2:107, ftnt only

Twelve, blessing as member of, V2:189

Twelve, on the ordination of the, V2:187-8 and ftnts

Twelve Apostles, chosen member of, V2:187

Twelve Apostles, letter of, to Joseph on affairs of, June 19, 1844, V7:136, et seq

Twelve Apostles, mission in Delaware with Lyman Wight, V7:129

Twelve Apostles, sustained member of, V2:509

Twelve Apostles, sustained member of, by Church after death of Joseph, V7:294

Winter Quarters, departs from, to mountains, V7:626

Winter Quarters, statistics of company of, leaving, V7:627

witness, suggested to appear before Congress on redress, V4:97

Word of Wisdom, remarks on, V5:428

Young People's Association, takes initiative in organizing, V5:320, et seq

Zelph, on, V2:80, ftnt only

Zions Camp member, V2:184

Zions Camp, on the outbreak of cholera in, V2:116, ftnt only

Zions Camp, on preaching in, V2:78, ftnt only.

See also Apostles; British Mission; letters.

Kimball, Hiram, cowardice, accuses Joseph of, V6:549

delegate to present truth to public, V6:483

Nauvoo, elected alderman of, V4:442

wickedness of revealed to Joseph, V5:12-3

witness for Joseph at Carthage martyrdom, V6:576.

Kimball, Horra, bishop's counselor, appointed, V4:233.

Kimball, Samuel, witness for state in Missouri trials for saints, V3:210.

Kimball, Vilate Murray, endowments, receives, in Nauvoo Temple, V7:543
    temple, commences ordinances administration in, V7:541
    wife to Heber C., V1:296, ftnt only.

Kimball, William H., in Indian trouble, V7:627
    MIA, aids in movement toward, V5:322.

Kinderhook plates, found and translated by Joseph, V5:372-8 and ftnt.
    See also plates; Smith, Joseph; translation.

King, Austin A., Allred, Captain, advises that prisoners be set free, V3:75
    Daviess County, agrees to try the Prophet and Lyman Wight in, V3:70
    Daviess County, orders militia forces of, disbanded, V3:75
    Far West, holds circuit court at, V3:48
    inflammatory communication, sends more to Boggs, V3:166
    Joseph, hears trial of while drunk, V3:209
    mentioned, V3:234, 248, 289
    Missouri, prisoners in, arraigned before, V3:209, et seq
    Prophet, tried before, V3:72-3
    saints, cohart of angels could not convince him of innocence of, V3:213.
    See also persecutions.

King, Elder, V7:260.

King, Eleazer, (also spelled Eleaser), Kirtland Camp, mentioned in, V3:142
    Kirtland Camp, subscribed to constitution of, V3:92
    Legion, martial band member of, V7:135.

King, Eleazer, Jr., subscribed to constitution of Kirtland Camp, V3:91.

King, Enoch M., Joseph, on relief expedition for, V5:482.

King, John M., Kirtland Camp, subscribed to constitution of, V3:92
    Legion, martial band member of, V7:135
    mission in Illinois to disabuse public mind over arrest of Joseph, V5:485.

King, Joseph, mission and field of labor, V6:337.

King, Thomas, sheriff of Adams County, V4:364.

kings, proclamation to, V4:483-4.

Kingdom of God, see God, Kingdom of.

kingdom of heaven, mustard seed parable explained, V3:389.
    See also parable.

kingdoms, heaven, more than one in, (D&C § 76), V1:245, et seq
    qualifications to reach, V1:283.
    See also Celestial Kingdom; God; Smith, Joseph.

Kingsbury, H., mentioned, V2:324.

Kingsbury, Horace, letter attesting to Joseph's integrity, V3:174.

Kingsbury, Joseph C., Church, appointed to preside over new district of, V7:305
    endowments, in Nauvoo Temple, V7:543
    high council, appointed to, V4:352
    high council, elected to at Kirtland, V2:366
    high council, rejected as member of Kirtland, V2:510
    Joseph, on relief expedition for, V5:482
    Kirtland Temple, blessing for work on, V2:206
    presidency, on high council to try, V2:484.

Kingsley, Samuel, Zions Camp member, V2:184.

Kingston, Thomas, mentioned, V6:196; V7:368.

Kington, Thomas, conversion of, V4:151
    high priest, ordained, V4:148
    mentioned, V4:134, 147, 323
    priesthood, explained to, V4:140
    volunteers for service in vineyard, V4:216.

Kinnamon, Richard H., mission labors of, reported, V6:274
    presides over Virginia conference, V7:260.

Kirlins, Mr., conference at home of, V2:24-5.

Kirtland, Ohio, apostasy at, V2:528-9
    building up, brethren disapprove, V4:443-4
    Church, false spirits in, at, V1:146
    conditions at, 1838, V3:1
    conditions in, V2:487-9 and ftnts
    disfellowship for any moving to, V4:39
    gathering, decision of Prophet toward, on, V4:476
    hostility at, V7:484
    Joseph and company arrive at from Missouri, V1:206
    Joseph and party leave, V1:188
    Joseph leaves Missouri to return to, V1:202
    Lamanite mission, arrival at, V1:120
    mob spirit at, V2:2 and ftnt
    presidency for, appointed, V7:326
    Rigdon, Sidney, converted at, V1:120
    solemn assembly of Church at, V2:475, et seq
    subscriptions for problems, V2:239.
    See also persecutions; temples.

Kirtland Bank, money, problems with, V3:113.

Kirtland Camp, arrest, leaders of, again threatened with, V3:113
    assaulted, V3:112-3

KIRTLAND CAMP (continued)

assistant council of three appointed for, V3:121-2

breaking up, question of, V3:137

brethren arrested, rejoin, V3:109

Chester, depart from, V3:101

Columbus, Ohio, pass through, V3:106

constitution of, V3:90-1

covenants, renewal of, by, V3:101

Dayton, move from, V3:132-3

Dayton, preparations to leave encampment near, V3:130, 131, 132

deserters, return of, to, V3:108

destroyer, afflicts camp with sickness, V3:124

destroyer in camp, V3:101

disband, proposition to, rejected, V3:144-5

disbanded, arrival of, at Adam-ondi-Ahman and, V3:147-8

disfellowshipped, Abram Bond, for murmuring, V3:117

disorders in family, Nathan Staker requested to leave for, V3:128

dissension in, V3:119

encampment, beauty of, V3:110

end of, V3:147-8

excluded, J. A. Clark, from Camp, V3:130

expelled, Josiah Miller, because nonmember son-in-law would not live laws of, V3:128

explanation concerning, V3:42, ftnt only

Far West, armies in, V3:85

Far West, arrival in, V3:147

Far West, trouble at, heard of, by, V3:143

gathering and commencement of, V3:98-9

God, instructed to keep families in strict subjection to laws of, V3:101

Grand River, Missouri, arrival at, V3:146

halted, threatened with being, at Huntsville, V3:144-5

halts by the way, V3:114

head of family, John Hammond excluded for not standing at, V3:130

house in order, G. W. Brooks expelled for failure to keep, V3:127-8

Illinois, enters state of, V3:136-7

Illinois, Springfield, pass through, V3:139

Indiana, enter state of, V3:133

Indiana, Terre Haute, pass through, V3:136

journal of, V3:87-148

Kirtland Safety Society, several brethren arrested for money of, V3:108

labor, reprimands for abstaining from, with no excuse, V3:122

leaders, reprimanded by, V3:114-5

KIRTLAND CAMP (continued)

    levee, part of take contract raising a, V3:119, 125, 129

    members, extreme poverty of, V3:98

    military salute of, V3:108

    national road, travels on the, V3:115

    number of families and members of, V3:100

    numbers, enumeration of, V3:100

    obstacles to, V3:98

    order, resolutions adopted for, V3:102-3

    order of the camp, Charles Thompson called to question for teachings concerning, V3:126

    organization and journey of, V3:87, et seq

    Page, John E., Canadian company of, overtakes near Dayton, V3:117

    prairie country, arrival in, V3:109

    Prophet, greeted by, and leading elders of Far West, V3:85-6

    reorganization of, V3:143

    Rulison, John, turned out of camp, V3:131

    sickness in, V3:138

    Sunday service in, V3:107, 112, 116-7, 123, 140

    tea and profane language, George W. Brooks called in question for wife's use of, V3:127

    unchristianlike conduct, Nathan K. Knight expelled from for, V3:128

    unchristianlike conduct, Abram Bond tried for murmuring and, V3:107, 110

    Voorhees, stage incident, V3:135 and ftnt

    Wood, Charles, expelled from, V3:132

    Word of Wisdom, Nickerson's tent placed in order for breaking, V3:131

    work, takes contract of, on Springfield-Dayton turnpike, V3:118, 120.

    See also destroyer; letters; seventies; Smith, Joseph.

Kirtland High School, mentioned, V2:200, 474-5.

Kirtland Mills, see Kirtland.

Kirtland Safety Society, articles of agreement, V2:470, et seq

    brethren arrested for money of, V3:108

    Joseph announces that bills are of no worth, V2:507-8

    Joseph resigns from, V2:497

    notes rejected, V2:487-8 and ftnt

    organization of, V2:467, 470, et seq

    Prophet, remarks of, on, V2:472-3

    reasons for disaster of, V2:487, ftnt only

    script, Joseph writes caution on receiving, V6:429.

Kirtland Temple, see Temple, Kirtland.

Kis-kish-kee, Indian chief, V6:401.

Kis-ku-kosh, Indian chief meets Joseph, V4:401-2.

Knight, Joseph, Sr., and wife, baptized, V1:88
    blesses son, Newel, V2:124

Knight, Joseph, Sr., genealogy, V1:47, ftnt only
    Joseph, comments as friend, V5:124-5
    Joseph, moves to Fayette, New York, V1:109
    Joseph, provides for, V1:47
    Joseph, retains counsel for, V1:89
    Joseph, visited by, V1:81
    Knight, Polly, wife of, V1:199, ftnt only
    mob at house of, V1:88
    mob surrounds house, V1:88
    Nauvoo, lot and house donated to, by high council at, V4:76
    new dispensation, desires to know his duty in connection with, V1:48
    priest, ordained, V4:311
    Prophet, early acquaintance with, V1:47, ftnt only
    Prophet, goes in search of assailants of, V1:47, ftnt only
    revelation to, V1:80
    Universalist faith, member of, V1:81.

Knight, Joseph, Jr., baptized, V1:88
    comments of Joseph on, as friend, V5:125.

Knight, Lenos M., appointed regent of University of Nauvoo, V4:293.

Knight, Lydia, confirmation of, V1:106, 108
    wife of Newel, dream of, V1:101.

Knight, Nathan K., corncutter, saw McBride cut down with, V3:187
    Kirtland Camp, expelled from for unchristianlike conduct, V3:128
    Kirtland Camp, subscribed to constitution of, V3:91
    Missouri, covenanted to assist saints in removing from, V3:253
    wounded at Haun's Mills by mob, V3:326, ftnt only.

Knight, Newell K., appointed branch president in Missouri, V1:409 ftnt only
    baptized, V1:84
    counselor to bishop, V1:363
    covenant breakers, intercedes for, V1:180
    devil, cast out of, V1:83
    devil, possessed of, V1:82
    devil, requests Joseph to cast out, V1:83
    devil, sees leave him, V1:83
    devil, testifies to Joseph casting out, at trial, V1:92
    dreams Joseph will visit, fulfilled, V1:101

KNIGHT, NEWELL, K. (continued)

endowments, called to go to Kirtland to receive, V2:113
exaltation, to gain, V1:85
Far West High Council, sustained member of, V2:523
heals Philo Dibble in midst of mob, V1:431, ftnt only
heavens opened to, V1:85
high council, sustained to Missouri, V2:124
Joseph on, as friend, V5:125
Joseph, pays money to, in hour of need, V2:327
Knight, Joseph, son of, V1:82
Lord, saw, V1:85
marriage of, to Lydia Goldthwaite, V2:320
meetings, attended regularly, V1:82
Missouri, appointed to go to, V1:181
Missouri, leads Thompson Branch to, V1:181, ftnt only
mob at house, V1:88
moved, refused to act when, by spirit, V1:82
Nauvoo High Council, appointed to, V4:12
Nauvoo High Council, sustained to, after death of Joseph, V7:296
perplexes attorney Seymour, V1:93
Prophet, labors with, V1:82
Spirit of Lord, caught up by, V1:83
wife confirmed, V1:108
Zion, appointed leader of Colesville Branch in moving to, V1:181, ftnt only.

Knight, Polly, baptized, V1:88
dies, wife of Joseph Knight, Sr., V1:199, ftnt only.

Knight, Vinson, bishop, appointed, of lower ward, Commerce, V4:12
bishop, counselor to, at Kirtland, V2:365
bishop, sustained counselor at Kirtland, V2:509
death of, V5:84
elder, to be, V2:354
high priest, ordained, V2:365
Joseph, accompanies in arrest, V4:366
Nauvoo, first elected councilor of, V4:287
Prophet, entertains at Perrysburg, New York, V2:45.

knowledge, light, compared with, all taken from he who rejects, V2:265
priesthood, all revealed through, V4:207
salvation, Joseph on, through, V5:387
saving power, V6:314.

Knowlen, George, mentioned, V6:162.

Knowles, Joseph, British Mission, mission in, V4:149

KNOWLES, JOSEPH (continued)

    devote all time to labors of ministry, V4:148

    volunteers for service in vineyard, V4:217.

Knowlton, Messr., attorney against Joseph, influences public mind in Illinois, V4:367.

Knowlton, Sidney A., utility committee member to aid Church removal, V7:474.

Knox, John, president of Warsaw anti-Mormon meeting, V6:462, 466.

Kohler, Kaufman, rabbi comments on Christ, V3:358, ftnt only.

Kreymer, Christian, bodyguard to Joseph's body on return to Nauvoo, V7:135.

Kreymeyer, C. M., in Nauvoo Legion, V4:296.

—L—

Ladd, A., letter to Joseph on wharf use matter, V6:472.

Laffity, Dr., mentioned, V3:306-7.

Lake, Brother, high council, under influence of evil spirit and license taken, V1:333

    revelations, claimed, V1:333.

Lake, Cyrus, blessing for work on Kirtland Temple, V2:206.

Lake, Dennis, in council at Kirtland, V1:389

    Zions Camp, member, V2:184.

Lake, Jabez, elder, appointed, V4:12

    Kirtland Camp, subscribed to constitution of, V3:93

    petitions Governor Boggs on mob violence in DeWitt, V3:83.

Lake, James, Kirtland, attends council at, V1:389

    Kirtland, commanded to remain in, V1:389

    Kirtland Temple, blessing for work on, V2:206.

Lake, Samuel, petitions Governor Boggs on mob violence in DeWitt, V3:83.

Lamanites, extent and importance of, V1:183, ftnt only, et seq

    gathering of, V2:357-8

    mission to, V1:118, 183, ftnt only

    mission commenced, V1:120 and ftnt.

    See also mission, Lamanite.

Lamb, Abel, Church, appointed to preside over new district of, V7:305

    mission and field of labor, V6:340

    Missouri, covenanted to assist saints in removing from, V3:252

    Mount Hope, appointed stake president at, V4:233

LAMB, ABEL (continued)

    presidency, issues complaint against, V2:484.

Lamb, Brother, store, not to patronize, V3:285.

Lamborn, Josiah, attorney general of Illinois, opinion stating Nauvoo Legion not state militia, V6:95

    Illinois Legislature, letter to Brigham Young as friend on attitude of, V7:370

    Joseph, attorney for prosecution of murderers of, V7:50

    Mormons, letter proposing to write history of, V7:568.

Lambson, Alfred B., mission and field of labor, V6:337; V7:260.

Lamech, next patriarch from Enoch, V4:210.

lamentation, of Alexander Neibaun on martyrdom, V7:191-2.

Lameraux, John, subscribed to constitution of Kirtland Camp, V3:93.

Lamereaux, Andrew, Kirtland Camp, subscribed to constitution of, V3:93

    Kirtland Camp, trouble with wagon in, V3:101, 128-9.

Lamoreaux, A. L., Church, appointed to preside over new district of, V7:306

    mission and field of labor, V6:339.

Land of Inheritance, Joseph leaves for, V1:188

    New Jerusalem is, V1:188.

    See also Missouri, Independence; Zion.

Landau, A. L., Jewish rabbi, letter to son concerning joining Church, V3:356-7 and ftnt.

Landon, Ezra, mentioned, V1:296, ftnt only.

Lane, Dorcus, mentioned, V7:436-7.

Lane, J. F., Joseph, on relief expedition for, V5:482.

Lane, Matham, mentioned, V7:436-7.

Lane, William F., Joseph, on relief expedition for, V5:483.

Lane, William W., counselor to deacons quorum in Nauvoo, V4:312.

Laney, Isaac, elder, ordained, V3:155

    Haun's Mills, wounded at, by mob, V3:186, 326, ftnt only

    witness suggested to appear before Congress on redress, V4:97.

Lang, George W., mob, reports movements of, V7:442.

Langley, George W., Joseph, on relief expedition for, V5:482

    mission and field of labor, V6:338

    mission in Illinois to disabuse public mind over arrest of Joseph, V5:485.

Langley, Thomas, mobber in Missouri, V4:72.

language, pure, given at time of gathering, V2:357.

    See also doctrine; gathering; Smith, Joseph.

Lansing, R. R., clerk of northern district of New York, V1:59.

larceny, expelled from Church for, V4:454.

Lathrop, Asahel A., affidavit concerning Missouri persecutions, V4:65-7
    child of, dies, due to mob, V4:66.

Latter-day Saints, Church of Jesus Christ of, Aaronic Priesthood, restored,
    V1:39
    abolition, stand on, V3:29
    advice, letter of, to President of United States and governors on
        persecution and request for, V7:402, et seq
    America, to be organized into Church districts, V7:251
    ancient, establishment of, IntroV1:XXVI
    anniversary of organization of, celebrated, V4:326-31
    anniversary, 13th of, V4:582
    Apostalic Interregnum, explanation of, V7:246
    apostate, beasts represent in scripture, V5:324
    apostates, purged of, IntroV2:XXXIII
    apostates, spreading falsehoods, V2:22
    Apostles, duty in regulating, V2:220
    Apostles, article to Churches on unity by, V7:347-8
    Apostles, William Smith accepts organization under, V7:406
    Apostles, subject to no other than the First Presidency, V2:374
    Apostles, westward movement, plan and common ownership, on, V7:442
    Arkansas, Governor Drew of, cannot protect in, suggest settle out
        West, V7:419 and ftnt
    Articles of Faith, Wentworth letter on, V4:535 and ftnt, et seq
    authorities, move to Zion, V2:429
    authorities, presentation of, V5:327, et seq
    Baptist excommunicated for joining, V5:166
    Baptist Church, differences from, V4:348-50
    Baptist Church, minister of, requests duty in, V1:143
    Baptist Church, participated in Missouri mob, V1:392
    Bennett, John C., elders sent forth to defend, against, V5:131-2
    Bennett, John C., sustained assistant president of, V4:341
    Bennett, John C., traitor to, IntroV5:XVII, et seq
    best people of age ever, V7:302
    "Beware of False Prophets," tract against, V1:373 and ftnt
    Bible, believes and other churches do not, V3:28
    birthday, first celebration of, V1:337
    blessings of, enumerated, V7:424
    Boston Bee, article on, in, V5:322
    calamitous events, review of, IntroV2:XXXII, et seq

LATTER-DAY SAINTS, CHURCH OF JESUS CHRIST OF (continued)

California, movement to, considered, V7:350

California and Oregon, delegation sent to investigate, for future movement, V6:222

camp journal, minutes from, V7:593, 594-5

Carroll, James, expelled from, V7:376

Carthage, illustration of false report against action at, V7:4

Catholic deputation visits Nauvoo on property sale, V7:539

Catholic, intention to sell Nauvoo to, V7:490

Catholic, interest in lands of, in Nauvoo, V7:537

Catholics, offers to sell Nauvoo property to, V7:508

Christ, ancient Church organized by, IntroV1:XXVI

Christ, Church of, organized by apostate groups, V2:528

Christian denominations, differs from, V2:379

Church, ancient, displaced by churches of men, IntroV1:LXXXVII, et seq

Church, ancient, established by Jesus Christ, IntroV1:XXVI

Church, instructions of Twelve to, on, V7:280, et seq

Church, letter of Orson Hyde on movement of, route, V6:373, et seq

Church, Rigdon's claimed vision after martyrdom on regulation of, V7:229-30

Church, rise of false teachings in ancient, IntroV1:XLVII, et seq

Church, speeches of Twelve on who is to lead, V7:231, et seq

Church, sustain Apostles as leaders of, V7:392

Church, Brigham Young's address on organization of, and authority of Twelve, V7:230

Church, Joseph Young appointed president of, at Nauvoo as Apostles leave, V7:584

Church districts, high priests selected to govern over, V7:305

Church historians, explanation of Vol. 7 divisions given by, IntroV7:XXI

Church historians, testimony of, V7:243

Church periodicals, John Taylor on subscriptions to, V7:328-9

commandments, if knew all would condemn one-half, V2:477

Commerce, Illinois, introduced to, V3:265, et seq

common consent, principle of, V5:522, ftnt only

Comprehensive History of the, referred to, V7:614-6

conference, first, V1:84 and ftnt, et seq

conference, first in Missouri, V1:199

conference of September 26, 1830, V1:115, et seq

conference of January 2, 1831, V1:140

conference of June 3, 1831, V1:175 and ftnt, et seq

conference of October 11, 1831, V1:219

LATTER-DAY SAINTS, CHURCH OF JESUS CHRIST OF (continued)

    conference of October 25, 1831, V1:219, ftnt only

    conference of November 1, 1831, V1:222 and ftnt

    conference of September 3, 1837, sustaining officials of, V2:509, et seq

    conference of April 7, 1838, at Far West, V3:14-5

    conference of May 4, 1839, at Quincy, Illinois, V3:344, et seq

    conference of October 1839, in Commerce, V4:12-4

    conference of April 6, 1840, general, V4:105, et seq

    conference of October 3, 1840, V4:204, et seq

    conference of October 3, 1840, report of presidency at, V4:212, et seq

    conference of October 6, 1840, general, in England, V4:214, et seq

    conference of February 14, 1841, in London, V4:298

    conference of April 7, 1841, general, V4:336, et seq

    conference of October 2, 1841, general in Nauvoo, V4:423, et seq

    conference of April 6, 1842, in Nauvoo, V4:583, et seq

    conference of August 29, 1842, special at Nauvoo to defend Church, V5:136, et seq

    conference of April 6, 1843, minutes of general, V5:327, et seq

    conference of October 6, 1843, trial of Sidney Rigdon, V6:47, et seq

    conference of April 1844, V6:287, et seq

    conference of October 1844, sustaining of authorities, V7:293, et seq

    conference of October 6, 1844, V7:284, et seq

    conference of April 6, 1845, attendance, V7:391, et seq

    conference of April 1848, general, V7:624-5

    conference of October 1848 in Salt Lake City, sustains new First Presidency, V7:628-9

    conferences, no individual cases to be brought before, V4:109

    confirmation, first members done, V1:78

    Congress, suggested that acquire a land grant from, and move, V7:367

    consecration, see consecration and stewardship, law of

    court, cases of members' unfair dealings before, V5:371-2

    court, council of high priests to try Church cases, V1:335-6

    court, procedure of same, (D&C § 102) V2:28, et seq

    covetousness, Joseph left, uninformed because of, V7:545

    Cowdery, Oliver, appointed recorder for, V2:273

    Cowdery, Oliver, Joseph to ordain an elder in, V1:60-1

    Cowdery, Oliver, ordained assistant president of, V2:176 and ftnt

    creed, has no, believes all truth, V5:215

    data, compilation of, by historians, V6:547, ftnt only

    death, first in, V1:199 and ftnt

    death unimportant to, V7:575

    debts of, expounded, V2:480

LATTER-DAY SAINTS, CHURCH OF JESUS CHRIST OF (continued)

debts, old of, dropped, V7:393

disconsolate state, August 1834, V2:146

divine manifestations at conference of January 22, 1833, V1:323

doctrinal development, IntroV5:XXVIII

documentary history of, closed, V7:630

duty of, V1:275-6

eastern papers, Brigham Young advises on publications of, V7:445

educational, first movement of, IntroV2:XXIV

enemies will never weary till overcome, V5:141

England, members in, enumerated, V4:147, et seq

England, pruning takes place in, of, V3:162

England, saints in, V4:224

England, street meeting held in, accused, V4:183

English immigrants, gives aid to, V5:412

English saints, first sail to America, V4:134

evils, little, do most injury to, V5:140

evils, should be separate from all, V4:570

example, should maintain faultless, V1:275-6

excommunicate anyone who follows Rigdon or Strang, V7:574

expelled for various reasons, V4:454

exterminate, proposed plans by government to, V7:544

false spirits and notions at Kirtland, V1:146

falsehoods, assailed by, V1:158

Far West High Council, held illegal body, V3:8

Federal Government, appeal to, IntroV4:XXVI, et seq

financial affairs, meeting on, 1844, V7:322

First Presidency of, everlasting, V1:258 and ftnt

First Presidency, reorganization of, V7:621 and ftnt

Ford, Governor, demands on, to expell from state, V7:28

Ford, Governor, had plan to rid state of, V7:14

Ford, Governor, political considerations of, V7:44, et seq

Ford, Governor, reorganization of, after Joseph's death, V7:37, et seq

Ford, Governor, on sermons of, V7:41

Ford, Governor, suggests western movement of, V7:398

Ford, Governor, on teachings and spread of, V7:398

foreign affairs, of, November 1845, V7:536, et seq

foreign ministry, organization of, IntroV2:XXIV, et seq

Fox Island, work of, on, V4:418-9

gather, at Nauvoo, V4:362

gathering, meeting of saints at Quincy, Illinois, discussion on, V3:260-1

gathering, several stakes for, V3:390

LATTER-DAY SAINTS, CHURCH OF JESUS CHRIST OF (continued)

general agent, Amos Fielding appointed, in England of, credentials, V6:263-4

general clerk, James Sloan elected, V4:424

general clerk, Robert B. Thompson appointed, V4:204

general recorder, Willard Richards appointed, V5:522

German meetings, provision for holding, V6:103

Germany, pamphlet on, published, V5:142

God, considered themselves favored of, IntroV3:XXXIII

government of, explained, V5:61, et seq

Great Salt Lake Valley, company to go to on prospective move of Church, V7:439

high priests, propose building for, V7:364

historian, Oliver Cowdery released as, V1:166 and ftnt

historical data, committee appointed to gather all, concerning, 1839, V3:346

historical sketch of, V6:9-10

history, anxiety of Joseph concerning, V6:66

history between 1842-1843 reviewed, IntroV5:XVII

history, divisions of Vol. 7 explained, IntroV7:XXI

history, general concerning, V6:66, 224; V7:242, 325, 426

history, induced to write, V1:1

history, J. Lamborn proposes to write, V7:568

history, Joseph begins writing, V3:25

history, to be kept by clerk, V1:298 and ftnt

history, time period covered by Volume 6, IntroV6:XXI

history, Vol. 1, reviewed, IntroV2:XXI

history, Vol. 2, reviewed, IntroV2:XXI

history, written, begun, V1:2 and ftnt

Holy Ghost, gifts of, manifest in, V1:84

Hulet Branch, errors of administration and doctrine in, V2:137, et seq

Hyde, Orson, preaches on continuation of, V7:197-8

Illinois, comments on conditions of, and acceptance of, into, Intro-V4:XIX, et seq

Illinois militia, proposal to move presented to, V7:449

Indians, communicated with, in Missouri, IntroV3:XXX

Indians in Missouri, IntroV3:XXIX, et seq

Indians, position on, in Missouri, IntroV3:XXXI

Indians, problem with, made possible expulsion from Missouri, Intro-V3:XXXII

Isle of Man, comes to, letter against, V4:234, et seq

Joseph, certificate of, as trustee, V4:287

LATTER-DAY SAINTS, CHURCH OF JESUS CHRIST OF (continued)

Joseph, comments by historians of, on period of, and compiled history of, V7:242-3

Joseph, Oliver Cowdery to ordain elder in, V1:61

Joseph, elected sole trustee of, V4:286

Joseph, ordained Hyrum to lead, V6:546, ftnt only

Joseph, proclamation in favor of, to people of Hancock after death of, V7:133-4

Joseph, words of consolation to, at death of, V7:152

Joseph's mother, provides for, V7:434

keys, restoring of, of gathering to, IntroV2:XXVI, et seq

Kirtland Camp, members of, in, V3:100

Kirtland Camp, poverty of members, V3:98

land purchases of members enumerated, V3:424

larceny, A. Brown expelled from, for, V4:454

law and government, position on, V2:7

leadership, reason given for haste in selecting new, V7:284-5

Lord, address of First Presidency to Church on building house of, V4:184, et seq

MIA, beginnings of, in, V5:320, ftnt only, et seq

Manuscript History of Brigham Young, discontinuance of daily quotations from, V7:604-5

Manuscript History of Brigham Young, Part V, V7:246

meeting, first of, V1:81

meetings, branches instructed on how to conduct, V1:219

members' duty, V1:275-6

members, fate of, if cut off from, V1:299

members, first confirmed, V1:78

members, how to treat, explained, V1:338-9

members in Kirtland, 2,000, V2:379

members left in hands of enemies in Missouri, IntroV3:XLI

members, mobbing, reaction to, V1:393

members numbered who were driven from Missouri, V3:431

members receive assistance from citizens of Quincy, V3:263

members, tried for fellowship if influence emigrants improperly, V4:404

mission of the Apostles to England, IntroV4:XXX

mission of governing districts of Church explained, V7:306-7

mission, history of British written, V4:313, et seq

mission of Orson Hyde to Palestine, IntroV4:XXXI, et seq

missions, assigned in, V4:429-30

missionary work among Scandinavians in Illinois, V5:395

missionary movement, commences great, V5:347

LATTER-DAY SAINTS, CHURCH OF JESUS CHRIST OF (continued)

Missouri, growth in, IntroV3:XLIII

Missouri persecutions of, causes, IntroV3:XVII, et seq

Missouri persecutions, the doctrinal petition of, to Federal Government on, V4:24, et seq

mob, Governor Boggs refuses aid to, against, V3:157

mob, makes proposition to, V7:441-2

mob, members requested to help evacuate Yelrome from, V7:441

morals, strict of, recited, V3:341-2

Mormon Battalion, requests raising of, V7:611

Morrish, W. J., warns flock against, V4:254

movement west, commencement of, V7:581

murderers of Joseph will not participate in trial of, V7:406

name, Church of the Latter-day Saints was first official, V2:62, ftnt only

name first used, V2:136

name official of, V3:24, ftnt only

name, still unsure, several used, V2:22

Nauvoo, actions in, after martyrdom, V7:198-9, 226-9

Nauvoo, founding of, IntroV4:XXII, et seq

Nauvoo, history of, for expulsion from, referenced but not included, V7:614 and ftnt

Nauvoo, Heber C. Kimball's discourse on leaving and blessings of, V7:466-7

Nauvoo, members of, defended in, V5:32-4

Nauvoo offers to sell property in, at 50 percent valuation, V7:538

Nauvoo, other places of settlement considered than, V6:260

Nauvoo, property of, exempt from tax, V6:110

Nauvoo Temple, call for all able men to help build, V7:357-8

Negro, position on, in Missouri, IntroV3:XXIV, et seq

New Orleans, branch of, organized in, V6:176

New Testament, organized according to, V1:79

obedience, comment on, in April 1845, V7:394

Ohio, commanded to go to, (D&C § 37) V1:139

oneness, Amasa Lyman's address on, and more of Saints, V7:468-9

organization, Apostles placed in proper place in, V4:403

organization, completed, V2:432

organization, day of revealed, (D&C § 20:1) V1:64

organization, first of, under Apostles, V7:248-9

organization, members baptized after, V1:79

organization, number baptized, before, V1:76, ftnt only

organization, vision on, of Apostles and seventy, V2:182, ftnt only

organized, V1:2, ftnt only, 75, et seq

LATTER-DAY SAINTS, CHURCH OF JESUS CHRIST OF (continued)

organized according to New Testament, V1:79

organized by vote, V1:77

paid, question over, V2:527

papers, to cease publication of all, at Nauvoo, V7:453-4

party politics, neutral as to other, V3:30-1 and ftnt

patriarch, Hyrum Smith of, V4:229 and ftnt

patriarch, John Smith voted, V7:622

patriarch, William Smith ordained, V7:418

pecuniary, in, embarrassment, V2:478

periodical, members to patronize, V6:63-4

persecuted, will be and destroyed if Zion not delivered, V2:53

persecution, marvel not at, V3:331

Philadelphia, branch organized at, V5:8

Pioneer Company, instructions to, on movement, V7:591-2

political issues, concerned little with, in Missouri, IntroV3:XXVII

political motto of, V3:9

political motto of, in Missouri, IntroV3:XXIX

political power, fear of, in Missouri as a cause of persecution, IntroV3:XXIX

politics, mob jealously in Missouri, IntroV3:XXVIII

politics, power of, concerned mob, IntroV3:XXVIII

politics, reason for union in, V5:232

politics, suggestions on, V7:252

politics, voted as unit, V7:2

presidency, proclamation of, on Church and Nauvoo, V4:267, et seq

presidency, report of April 7, 1841, V4:336, et seq

president of, William Smith declares himself, V7:433

priesthood, organization of belongs to, only and not to Council of Fifty, V7:213

priesthood, power of, manifest in first conference of, V1:85

priesthood quorums stand ready to fight mob, V7:443-4

principles, fundamental of, V3:30

property, committees appointed to sell, V7:473-4

property, disposition of, by bishop's court, V3:47-8

Prophet, admonished by, V4:5

public address, first in, V1:81

public meetings of members in Missouri, V3:249-50

public meetings in Missouri, decides against holding, V2:136

publications for and against enumerated, V4:253, et seq, 487, et seq; V6:154; V7:345-6, 558-9

purifying, necessity of, itself, V2:205

LATTER-DAY SAINTS, CHURCH OF JESUS CHRIST OF (continued)

raising of dead in, V5:121

Relief Society, organization of, V4:552

Relief Society, penny subscription of, demanded by, V7:322

resolutions by Missouri Senate on difficulties, V3:246

revelation, led by, V7:285

revelation, need, plus Book of Mormon and Zion, or will fall, V2:52

revelations, order of receiving explained, V1:338

rise and progress, V1:1

saints, letter of John C. Calhoun on policy towards, if elected, V6:155-6

Satan gives revelation concerning, V1:109-10

scatter, no authority to, V7:254-5

school books, to print for instruction, V7:474

sects, differs from others, V3:28

seventies, duty in, V2:221 and ftnt

seventies in, to be purged of all wickedness, V7:372

spirit of speculation enters and tries to destroy, V2:487 and ftnt

stake of Ramus, Illinois, abandoned, V4:468

stakes, new, appointed, V4:205

supplies, list made of, necessary for crossing plains, V7:454-5

sustaining of authorities, rejection of William Smith, V7:458, et seq

sustaining of authorities in various conferences, V2:509, 522-4; V7:629-30

sustaining of officers in April 1845, V7:392

swearing, drinking, etc., expelled members for, V3:341

Taylor's, John, Memoirs, Part III, V7:54

temporal kingdom, organization of falsely converted to, V3:211

testimony on capture and trial of leaders in Missouri, V3:446, et seq

tithing, to enforce law of, V7:251

transgression of members in Missouri enumerated, IntroV3:XL, et seq

trustee-in-trust, new appointed for, V7:247

unwisdom, a factor in Missouri persecutions, IntroV3:XLVII

unwisdom of, in Missouri, IntroV3:XXXII, et seq

unwisdom, Zion as part of, in Missouri problem, IntroV3:XXXIV, et seq

vote, cannot anymore than Negro, V3:57

ward of, proposes co-operative store in, V6:263

wards, Nauvoo divided into, V5:119

west, the prospective move to, IntroV5:XXVII

west, search out for location of, V7:379

westward camp, incidents in, of, V7:582

westward camp, instructions to, on deportment, V7:585-6

westward companies, organization of, V7:481-2

westward establishment, letter to, on, V7:499, et seq

LATTER-DAY SAINTS, CHURCH OF JESUS CHRIST OF (continued)

westward movement, number organized for, V7:532

westward movement, outfit for, for family of five proposed, V7:447

Wight, Lyman, disclaims letters and opinion of, to *Quincy Whig*, V3:354-5

Wight, Lyman, letter to R. B. Thompson and First Presidency complaining of, V3:351-2

Zion, driven from, reason for, IntroV3:XXXIX

Zion, stake of, organized, V3:38-9

Zions Camp, IntroV2:XXII, et seq

Zions Camp, failure of, reason for, IntroV3:XXXIX.

Latter-day Saints, Church of Jesus Christ of, historian and recorder, comments on, V7:242

Cowdery, Oliver, acts as, V1:166, ftnt only

Ford's History of Illinois, first compilation from, 1842-1846, et seq, Part I, V7:1-31

extended compilation, Part II, V7:33-51

second compilation of, Part IV, V7:127-243

testimony of, V7:243

Whitmer, John, appointed as, V1:166 and ftnt.

Laurence, John, mission and field of labor, V6:340.

Lavender, James, counselor on sailing from England, V4:297.

law, blessings predicated upon, V5:325

God, reason for, giving, V2:12

God's laws, man must observe all to gain His presence, V2:13

gospel, versus, IntroV1:XXVII

heaven, of explained, V2:8

man, God has given certain to, V2:12

official opinion of, V2:7

revelation on obedience to, V1:403-6

secular and religious influenced by God, V2:15

suits at, weaken love and spirituality, V4:504-5.

See also doctrine; Smith, Joseph.

Law, Jane, excommunicated for unchristianlike conduct, V6:341.

Law, Samuel, mobber in Missouri, V4:66.

Law, William, affidavit of, concerning character of John C. Bennett and Joseph, V5:75

affidavit on treachery of, V6:500

apostasy, impressions of John Taylor after, V7:57

apostates, appointed prophet of new church by, V6:347

character of, V7:57

LAW, WILLIAM (continued)

Church, traitor to, V6:170
endowments, receives, V5:409
excommunicated for unchristianlike conduct, V6:341
First Presidency, appointed to, by revelation, V4:284-6
First Presidency, to replace Hyrum in, (D&C § 124:90) V4:282
foul and malicious, publishes article that is, V6:210
genealogy, meets prophet and, V4:20 and ftnt
Joseph, counselor to, V7:56
Joseph, declares gratefulness for aid rendered while in seclusion, V5:108
Joseph, secretly goes to inform of movement of sheriff, V5:97
martyrdom, member of mob at, V7:146
mission, on, V5:146, 183
murderous intentions of, V7:227
Nauvoo, defends saints in, V5:32-4
Nauvoo, en route to, V4:20 and ftnt
persecution, publishes exhortation on, as trial, V5:144
police, difficulty with, V6:162-5
police, second trouble with, V6:166-70
Prophet, confidential friend to, V5:89-90
Prophet, hearing on putting away of, V6:162
Prophet, swears to stand by, V6:165.

Law, Wilson, apostasy, impressions of John Taylor of, after, V7:57
apostates, apostle of new church by, V6:347
apostates, appointed counselor of new church by, V6:347
court-martial of, V6:362
doggerel written by, V6:210
excommunicated for unchristianlike conduct, V6:341
Joseph declares gratefulness for aid rendered while in seclusion, V5:108
Joseph, letter to, advising him to hide in Nauvoo, V5:114
Joseph, letter to, advising retirement from Nauvoo until next governor elected, V5:110
Joseph, takes in custody for trial, V5:209
Legion, requests war provisions for, to aid marshal, V6:108
martyrdom, member of mob at, V7:146
Mormon Church, secedes from, V7:9
Nauvoo, first elected councilor of, V4:287
Nauvoo Legion, elected brigadier-general of first cohort of, V4:296
Nauvoo Legion, general of, V7:57
Nauvoo Legion, letter to Joseph expressing willingness to use, in his behalf, V5:96
Prophet, seeks to get warrant against, V6:568.

Lawless, Judge, Missouri persecutor, V2:462.

Lawrence, Edward, mentioned, V5:22.

Lawrence, Maria, mentioned, V6:427.

Lawson, Jesse B., dies of cholera in Missouri, V2:120
    Zions Camp member, V2:184.

Lawson, John, appointed to preside over new Church district, V7:305.

lawyers, general comments on, V6:238-41
    Young, Brigham, will not pay, V7:386
    Young, Brigham, willingly ridicules, V7:258.

laying on of hands, Melchizedek Priesthood holds power of, V1:60
    Works, Angeline, restored to senses by, V2:328.
    See also Holy Ghost, gift of.

Layne, Elder, mentioned, V4:22.

Leach, General, mentioned, V3:267.

Leach, George T., mentioned, V5:552.

Leach, James, charged with disorderly conduct, V6:155.

Leach, Matthew, appointed bishop, V4:233.

Leach, Samuel, (also spelled Leech), letter of, V3:349-50
    mentioned, V3:267; V4:267
    recommends Brother Green to collect for poor, V3:348.

Leach, William, ordained elder, V4:333.

Leal, Clark, mentioned, V5:11; V6:179.

Leather, E., mentioned, V4:215.

leaven, parable of, explained, V2:270.

Leavens, William F., covenanted to assist saints in removal from Missouri,
    V3:253.

Leavitt, Nathaniel, mission and field of labor, V6:338-40.

LeBaron, Alonzo, mission and field of labor, V6:337.

Lee, Brother, mentioned, V3:273.

Lee, Alfred, covenanted to assist saints in removing from Missouri, V3:253.

Lee, Ann, founder of Shaking Quakers, V1:167, ftnt only.

Lee, Eli, elder, appointed, V4:13
    Missouri, covenanted to assist saints in removing from, V3:253.

Lee, Francis, covenanted to assist saints in removing from Missouri, V3:253.

Lee, J., ordained priest, V5:419.

Lee, John, killed at Haun's Mills by mob, V3:326, ftnt only.

Lee, John D., genealogy of, and warned not to vote, V3:56
    mission and field of labor, V6:338
    Missouri, covenanted to assist saints in removing from, V3:253
    Nauvoo, policeman in, V6:149
    seventies, elected trustee of Library and Institute Association, V7:328
    seventies conference, clerk of, V7:345
    westward movement organization, in, V7:626.

Lee, Ralph, father of John, V3:56, ftnt only.

Lee County Democrat, account of martyrdom in, V7:178
    anonymous article on liberty and justice and martyrdom, V7:164.

Leech, Brother, mentioned, V5:406.

Leech, Samuel, letter of, V3:349-50.

Leffingwell, William, mentioned, V7:593.

Legare, Hugh L., false accusation against Joseph by, V5:363.

Leigh, John, mentioned, V4:216
    volunteers for service in vineyard, V4:217.

Leithead, James, Legion, martial band member of, V7:135
    Missouri, covenanted to assist saints in removing from, V3:253.

Leland, Benjamin, mission and field of labor, V5:349.

Lemon, John, chosen to Adam-ondi-Ahman High Council, V3:38.

Lemon, Washington, mission and field of labor, V6:339.

Lemons, Peter, mission and field of labor, V5:349.

Leonard, A., Missouri attorney for Church, V1:478-9.

Leonard, Abigail, affidavit on Missouri persecutions, V1:480.

Leonard, Lyman, whipped by mob, V2:140
    witness, suggested to appear before Congress on redress, V4:97.

Leonard, Moses, mentioned, V4:452.

Lethead, James, subscribed to constitution of Kirtland Camp, V3:93.

letters, accounting trial of Joseph at Monmouth, Illinois, V4:369-70
    Adam, C., to Joseph concerning cause of saints before Illinois legislature, V4:53
    Adams, James, to Joseph advising to appear before court, V5:206
    Anthon, Professor to E. D. Howe on Martin Harris' visit, V1:20, ftnt only
    Apostles to all the Churches, V4:517-8
    Apostles calling for assistance for Joseph, V5:279-80
    Apostles to Church from retirement, V7:412, et seq
    Apostles to Morley settlement requesting material help, V6:176-7

LETTERS (continued)

Apostles to President of the United States and governors of respective states, V7:402-4

Apostles to Ramus on assistance for Joseph, V5:293

Apostles to saints abroad on continuing on, V7:189-90

Apostles to saints abroad on disfellowship of John E. Page, V7:582-3

Apostles to saints on temple and proposed tabernacle, V7:427

Apostles to Lyman Wight pleading for union, V7:400-1

Apostles to Wilford Woodruff in England, V7:407-8

appointment of Stephen Markham, V3:367

Arthur, M., Esq. to the representatives from Clay County, V3:213-4

Atchison, General to Governor Boggs explaining Missouri uprising, V3:80-2

Atchison and Lucas to Governor Boggs, V3:176-7 and ftnt

Backenstos, J. B. to Apostles on Durfee's murder, V7:525

Backenstos, J. B. on members of mob at martyrdom, V7:142, et seq

Backenstos, J. B. on trial by mob, V7:483

Backenstos, J. B. to Brigham Young, V7:445

backwoodsman to the Church, V7:499-502

baptism of dead, instructions on, V5:142-4, 148-53

Barnes, Lorenzo D. reporting labors, V4:569-70

Barratt, William on mission to England, V4:161

Bennett, J. A. to J. G. Bennett, V5:170-2

Bennett, J. A. to Joseph on anti-Mormon book of John C. Bennett, V5:112-4, 162-4

Bennett, J. A. to Joseph indicating resignation from Legion, V6:71-3

Bennett, John C. announcing passage of Nauvoo Charter, V4:248-9

Bennett, John C. on attitude of, V4:544, et seq and ftnts

Bennett, John C. to Joseph announcing arrival soon, V4:179

Bennett, John C. to Joseph declaring intent to join Church, V4:168-9

Bennett, John C. to Joseph expressing anxiety to be with, V4:172

Bennett, John C. on Missouri, V4:547-8

Bennett, John C. on new attempts to arrest Joseph, V5:250-1

Bennett, John C. to Sidney Rigdon and Orson Pratt against Church, V5:250-2

Bennett, John C. on slavery and Missouri persecutions, V4:545-7

Bennett, John C. tendering services to Church, V4:169-70

Bent and Harris to Presidency reporting labors of collecting money, V4:199-200

Bernhisel, John M. to Governor Ford confirming Joseph's letter on *Expositor* affair, V6:467-8

Billium, Cornelius to *Enquirer*, V2:121

LETTERS (continued)

Boggs, Governor, to General Clark, V3:173-4, 204

Boggs, Governor, to General Lucas, V3:192

Boggs, Governor, to Wiley C. Williams, V3:262

Booth, Ezra, anti-Mormon, published, V1:241, 216-7 and ftnts

Bosworth, J. B., to, informing him of error, V2:163-4

Boynton, John F. to Joseph, V2:40-1

Brannan, Samuel S. on attempt to take Nauvoo property, V7:587-8

Brannan, Samuel S. on A. G. Benson and Company, attempt to take Nauvoo property, V7:587-91

Brannan, Samuel S. on report of company to go to California by ship, V7:588-9

brethren in Clay County, Missouri to Governor Dunklin, V2:49 and ftnt

brethren in Clay County, Missouri to Jackson mob, V2:107

British Mission, instructions to, after martyrdom, V7:171-5

Burnham, James on gospel in England and opposition, V4:297

Butterfield, Justin to Joseph assuring him success in being discharged from Missouri warrants if pursue court remedy, V5:206

Butterfield, Justin to Sidney Rigdon, opinion on requisition of Missouri for Joseph, V5:173, et seq

Calhoun, John C. to Joseph on policy towards saints if elected, V6:155-6

Carlin, Governor to Emma on Joseph's difficulties in Missouri, V5:130-1

Carlin, Governor to Emma on Nauvoo's powers, V5:153-5

Carlin, Governor to Joseph on Bennett affairs, V5:49-51

Carlin, Governor to Joseph on Bennett problems, V5:82-3

Church confirming actions of Elias Higbee in Washington and listing possible witnesses, V4:96-8

Church to M. Hewitt inquiring of interest in, V2:232 and ftnt

Church offering to sell Nauvoo property to Catholics, V7:508-9

Clark, General to Governor Boggs, V3:206-7

Clay, Henry to Joseph on position on persecution, V6:376

Clayton, William on condition in Nauvoo while Joseph in Carthage jail, V6:598-9

Clayton, William to saints of Nauvoo, V5:169

Clayton, William to *Times & Seasons* on Joseph's second trial in Illinois, V6:380, et seq

Cole, Joseph informing of election returns threatened, V7:227

commissioners to Nauvoo City Council, V7:150

committee of Church to President of the United States and governors on persecution and request for advice, V7:402-4

complaints against G. James, V2:170

Cordon, Alfred on affairs in England, V4:515-6

LETTERS (continued)

Corrill, John to *Evening & Morning Star*, V2:92-3, ftnts only

Corrill, John requests saints' arms from Colonel Pitcher and compromises, V2:135-6

council of high priests to bishop and saints in Zion, V1:317, et seq

council to Lyman Wight, a plea for union, V7:400-1

Cowdery, Oliver to Joseph Bosworth on errors, V2:163-4

Cowdery, Oliver to high council at Far West on excommunication trial, V3:17-8, ftnts only

Cowdery, Oliver to Joseph accusing of priestcraft, V1:104-5

Cowdery, Oliver offers aid in western movement, V7:482

Cowdery, Oliver on western Missouri Mission and gathering, V1:182-3

Cowdery, Warren A. on Kirtland Temple subscriptions, V2:239

Cowdery, Warren A. to *Messenger & Advocate*, V2:374-5, ftnts only

Deming, Miner R. on admissions to see Joseph in jail, V6:593

Deming, Miner R. on R. D. Foster, V7:169

Deming, Miner R. to saints to keep quiet concerning martyrdom, V6:625

Doniphan, A. W. to General Atchison, V3:78-9

Drew, Governor of Arkansas to the Twelve on protection, V7:419 and ftnt

Dunham, General to Ford for more militia to check mob, V7:159

Dunklin, Daniel to Clay County saints questioning their conduct, V2:461-2

Dunklin, Daniel from elders describing status of saints, June 26, 1834, V2:117-8

Dunklin, Daniel from S. Gilbert on restoring saints' possessions and Missouri persecutions, V1:472-4

Dunklin, Daniel to W. W. Phelps, et al, V2:178-9, ftnts only

Dunklin, Daniel to W. W. Phelps ordering army back, V2:89

Dunklin, Daniel to Colonel Pitcher ordering him to return the Mormons' arms, V2:89

Dunklin, Daniel replies to petitions of saints, V2:178, ftnt only

Dunklin, Daniel to saints stating only redress is courts, V2:383-4

Dunklin, Daniel to Colonel Thornton suggesting possible compromise proposals but refusing to assist in negotiation, V2:84-7

Dyer, Charles V. to Brother Bennett on slavery, V4:544-5

Dykes, G. P. on work among Illinois Scandinavians, V5:395

elders in Clay County to Messrs. Doniphan and Atchison, V2:92

Emma to Governor Carlin defending Joseph and arraigning Missouri, V5:132-4

Emma to Governor Carlin pleading cause of Joseph, V5:115-7

Emma to Joseph on movements and business, V5:110

LETTERS (continued)

Emmett, James and company, counseling them, V7:377-8

Ewing, L. D. on state payment for service in Nauvoo Legion, V6:95

extract from a letter to the *Juliet Courier*, V4:380-1

Far West saints reporting groundbreaking for house of the Lord, V2:496-7

Female Relief Society to Governor Carlin, V5:146-8

First Presidency to branch in Thompson, V1:324-5

First Presidency to brethren in Zion, V1:368-70

First Presidency to Eugene Branch disfellowshipping John Smith, V1:371

First Presidency to Orson Hyde concerning raising funds for Zion, V2:48-9

First Presidency to *Quincy Whig*, V3:354-5

First Presidency to saints consoling them and sending news, V1:474-6

First Presidency to saints, important doctrinal development on law, gospel, atonement, revelation and apostates, V2:4 and ftnt. et seq

First Presidency to John Smith at Eugene, V1:370

First Presidency to R. B. Thompson, V3:363-4

Ford, Governor, authorizing use of Legion to protect courts, V7:309-10

Ford, Governor to A. Babbitt, vacillation on trial of murderers, V7:409-11

Ford, Governor to Backenstos informing that U.S. Government after saints, V7:562-4

Ford, Governor to citizens of Hancock County, warning, V6:189-90

Ford, Governor to General Deming on defense of court in murder case, V7:409

Ford, Governor to General Deming on threatened outbreaks after martyrdom, V7:146

Ford, Governor, desiring brethren to come converse with him on martyrdom, V7:200

Ford, Governor to Joseph dispelling ideas of invasion by Missourians, V6:35

Ford, Governor to Joseph guaranteeing safety in Carthage, V6:533, et seq

Ford, Governor to Joseph on Missouri writs and kidnapping, V6:113-5

Ford, Governor to Joseph refusing to recind arrest order, V5:205-6

Ford, Governor to Joseph requesting he come to Carthage, V6:521

Ford, Governor to George Miller repudiating O. Spencer's letter accusing of guilt in martyrdom, V7:505-8

Ford, Governor to Nauvoo City Council, V7:150

Ford, Governor on organization of town government within Nauvoo, V7:396-8

Ford, Governor to people at Warsaw, V7:214-5

LETTERS (continued)

Ford, Governor to W. W. Phelps on official position and feelings toward saints, V7:203-8 and ftnt

Ford, Governor to Sheriff Reynolds, V5:492-3

Ford, Governor to O. Spencer repudiating former's letter, V7:505-8

Ford, Governor to Warsaw committee, V7:160-2

Ford, Governor to Brigham Young on organization of town governments within Nauvoo, V7:396-8

Foster, Robert D. to John Procter, instructions as to property, V6:520

Galland, Isaac to *Quincy Argus* on saints' reception in Iowa, V3:317

Galland, Isaac to D. W. Rogers concerning welfare of members, V3:265-7

Gilbert, A. S. to Governor Dunklin on restoring saints' possessions, V1:446-7

Gilbert, A. S. to A. Leonard, Esq., V1:478

government officials from Church on western movement of the saints, V7:547

Hall, J. on arrest and trial of Joseph, V5:538-9

Hancock, S. on Durfee's murder, V7:528

Hedlock, Reuben to Church on mission, V6:44-5

Hewitt, John, letter of introduction from council of pastors, V2:230, et seq

Heywood, Joseph L. to Joseph suggesting a memorializing of Congress on Missouri persecutions, V6:62-3

Hickok, L. W. on probability of indictment of Joseph at Springville, V6:450

Higbee, Elias, concerning affairs of saints in Washington, V4:94-5

Higbee, Elias to Joseph, fourth letter reporting cause before Senate committee, V4:88

Higbee, Elias to Joseph reporting cause before Senate committee, V4:81-3

Higbee, Elias to Joseph, second letter reporting cause before Senate committee, V4:83-5

Higbee, Elias to Joseph on sufferings, V3:319-20

Higbee, Elias to Joseph telling him papers before Congress have been withdrawn, V4:98-100

Higbee, Elias to Joseph, third letter reporting cause before Senate committee, V4:85-7

high council in Missouri to saints instructing them on Church standards, V2:138-9

high council to the saints abroad, V5:15-7

Hollister, D. S. to Joseph on election matters, V6:416-8

Hotchkiss, Horace R. concerning progress before Congress, V4:98

Hotchkiss, Horace R. to Joseph, V4:405-8

LETTERS (continued)

Hotchkiss, Horace R. to Joseph on anti-Mormon sentiment in Carthage, V6:55

Hotchkiss, Horace R. to Joseph on bankruptcy, V5:51

Hotchkiss, Horace R. to Joseph offering land for sale, V4:100-2

Hotchkiss, Horace R. to Joseph on property titles, V5:382-3

Hugins, H. T. to Joseph on probable indictment of Joseph at Springfield, V6:494

Hugins, H. T., warning Joseph of probable indictment, V6:451

Hyde, Orson in behalf of Twelve to Joseph, V2:209-10

Hyde, Orson to Rabbi Hirschell calling Judah to repentance, V4:374, et seq

Hyde, Orson to Joseph on complaints, V2:335-7

Hyde, Orson to Joseph detailing events en route to Jerusalem, July 17, 1841, V4:384, et seq

Hyde, Orson on labors in Washington and Joseph's memorial to Congress, V6:369, et seq

Hyde, Orson on mission to Holy Land, V4:496-9

Hyde, Orson on movement of the Church, route, V6:373, et seq

Hyde, Orson noting signs in heavens, V4:202-3

Hyde, Orson, on Palestine Mission, V4:128-9

Hyde, Orson, pleading for W. W. Phelps, V4:142-3

Hyde, Orson, prayer of dedication on Mount of Olives, V4:454, et seq

Hyde, Orson, recounting incidents on Jerusalem trip, V4:372-4

Hyde, Orson on remarkable sign of time, V4:439

Hyde, Orson, requesting to proceed to mission endeavors, V4:123-5

Hyde, Orson to saints, warning against land speculators, V7:348

Hyde, Orson to Major Warren reporting Durfee's murder, V7:525

Hyde, Orson and Hyrum Smith to Missouri on January 14, 1833, V1:317, et seq

Hyrum to Joseph and Judge Higbee concerning raising funds for him and state of affairs in Nauvoo, V4:50-2

Hyrum to Parley P. Pratt on printing of Book of Mormon in New York, V4:47

Hyrum to saints in Kirtland disapproving building up of, V4:443-4

Illinois Attorney General on difficulties of collecting evidence for trial of martyrdom murderers, V7:415-6

introducing Sidney Rigdon to President of the United States, et al, V3:349-50

Isle of Man, against work on, V4:234-6

Johnston, Ed, refusing counsel to Joseph, V6:553

Johnstone, Robert to Senator Young, V4:121

ETTERS (continued)

Joseph, adding to letter to Martin Van Buren on previous treatment, V6:65

Joseph, announcing intended visit to Quincy, V6:213-4

Joseph to Apostles to return home, V6:519

Joseph, appointing John Smith as patriarch, V6:110

Joseph to Ballantyne and Slater, advice on moving into Nauvoo, V6:515

Joseph to Mr. Bartlett, editor of *Quincy Whig*, V5:15

Joseph to J. A. Bennett, comments of position of religion and prophet and J. A. Bennett, V6:73, et seq

Joseph to J. A. Bennett on forthcoming book of John C. Bennett, V5:156, et seq

Joseph to John C. Bennett on slavery, V4:544

Joseph to John C. Bennett welcoming him to Nauvoo, V4:177-9

Joseph to Mark Bigler, V3:366

Joseph to brethren in Zion of April 21, 1833, counseling them to good works, V1:340-1

Joseph to brethren in Zion, instruction on the Book of Commandments, lost books of Bible and organization, V1:362, et seq

Joseph to brother on tithing, V4:518

Joseph to Mrs. Norman Bull, V3:285-6 and ftnt

Joseph to Josiah Butterfield on John C. Bennett's movements, V5:250

Joseph to John C. Calhoun and other candidates on feelings toward saints, V6:64-5

Joseph to John C. Calhoun showing contempt for latter's position on saints, very remarkable letter, V6:156-60

Joseph to Canadian saints, V1:441-3

Joseph to Governor Carlin, satisfied with attitude on Bennett affair, V5:83

Joseph to Brother Carter correcting doctrine and procedure, V1:338-40

Joseph to the Church, V2:508-9, 511; V3:226, et seq; V4:517

Joseph to citizens of Hancock County, V5:55-6

Joseph to Henry Clay, severely criticizes position on persecution, V6:376-7

Joseph to Judge Cleveland, V3:362-3

Joseph consenting to go to Carthage, accepting protection of Governor, V6:550

Joseph to counsel on excitement in Carthage, V6:595

Joseph to county recorder, V4:287

Joseph to Oliver Cowdery to see if he wants to repent, V5:368

Joseph on debts of Church, V4:441-2

Joseph to editor of *Neighbor*, V6:221

LETTERS (continued)

Joseph to elders on gathering and parables and first principles, V2:253, et seq

Joseph to elders on New Jerusalem and missionary work, V2:259, et seq

Joseph to Emma detailing prospective movements August 16, 1842, V5:103-5

Joseph to Emma on Ford's sending troops to protect Nauvoo, V6:56

Joseph to Emma on instructions as to how to receive Governor Ford V6:605

Joseph, encouraging movement to Nauvoo of volunteers, V6:425

Joseph engaging counsel, V6:551, 590-1

Joseph engaging further counsel, V6:613

Joseph to exiled saints in Missouri, sympathy and exhortation to stay in Zion, V1:453-6

Joseph to Governor Ford, account of *Expositor* affair, V7:125-6 and ftnt

Joseph to Governor Ford from Carthage jail requesting interview V6:575-6

Joseph to Governor Ford defending actions in *Expositor* affair, V6:538-4

Joseph to Governor Ford explaining *Expositor* affair, V6:466-7

Joseph to Governor Ford explaining return to Nauvoo, V6:556

Joseph to Governor Ford inviting to come to Nauvoo, V6:525-7

Joseph to Governor Ford inviting same to Nauvoo to keep peace. V6:48

Joseph to Governor Ford on kidnapping affidavits and mob action V6:153

Joseph to Governor Ford on kidnapping by Missourians, V6:100-

Joseph to Governor Ford submitting documents on mob action, V6:52

Joseph to Governor Ford supporting position on Avery kidnapping V6:109-10

Joseph to Isaac Galland on Nauvoo affairs, V4:8-9

Joseph to Isaac Galland on settlement of accounts, V4:499-500

Joseph to Oliver Granger on affairs at Kirtland, V4:164-7

Joseph to E. W. Harris, V3:362

Joseph and Elias Higbee concerning preliminary hearing of grievances in Washington to high council at Nauvoo, V4:43-4

Joseph to Horace Hotchkiss on bankruptcy, V5:52

Joseph to Horace Hotchkiss on land purchase contract, V5:195-6

Joseph to Horace Hotchkiss on lands, V4:469

Joseph to Horace Hotchkiss on Nauvoo land transactions, V4:406-8

Joseph to Horace Hotchkiss on purchase of lands, V4:170-2

Joseph to H. T. Hugins congratulating Jeremiah Smith on release V6:501-2

ETTERS (continued)

Joseph to Edward Hunter on business affairs in Nauvoo, V4:481-3

Joseph to Edward Hunter on business transactions, V4:548-9

Joseph to Edward Hunter reporting opening of new store, V4:491-2

Joseph to Hyrum reporting state of affairs in Washington, V4:39-42

Joseph to Illinois Governor on John C. Bennett affair, V5:42-4

Joseph, indicating elders to be sent to Arkansas, V6:459

Joseph to George James, complaints against, V2:170

Joseph to Vienna Jaques, personal counsel, V1:407-9

Joseph to Wilson Law indicating probable movements August 16, 1842, V5:105-6

Joseph to Wilson Law ordering out Nauvoo Legion, V6:120

Joseph to Wilson Law on proceedings of Legion if arrested, V5:93-5

Joseph to lawyers on payment of notes, V4:468-9

Joseph et al to John Lincoln et al, V2:121-2

Joseph to Missouri brethren on November 27, 1832, V1:297, et seq

Joseph to Missouri brethren on January 14, 1833, on olive leaf, V1:316-7

Joseph to Missouri brethren requesting information and exhorting to be faithful, V1:448, et seq

Joseph to Isaac Morley on instructions on resisting mob, V6:482-3

Joseph to Moses C. Nickerson in Canada, V1:441-3

Joseph to Oliver on personal history and temptation, V1:10, ftnt only

Joseph to Bishop Partridge, V1:448, et seq

Joseph to W. W. Phelps, V3:358-9 and ftnt

Joseph to W. W. Phelps welcoming back to fellowship, V4:162-4 and ftnts

Joseph on political views, V6:388

Joseph to Judge Pope introducing Jeremiah Smith, V6:422-3

Joseph, postscript to Emma from Carthage prison, V6:605

Joseph to the Presidency of the Church at Kirtland, V3:10-12

Joseph to presidential candidates on their feelings toward Mormons, V6:63, 64-5

Joseph on removing families to Nauvoo, V6:515

Joseph reproving John Smith, V1:370

Joseph to Jenetta Richards, V5:40-1

Joseph and Sidney Rigdon to George James, V2:170

Joseph to Sidney Rigdon on suspicions of conspiracy with John C. Bennett, V5:312-4

Joseph to L. D. Rupp thanking for book of religions in United States, V6:428

Joseph to saints in Clay County, V2:455-6

Joseph to saints in England, V6:69-70

LETTERS (continued)

Joseph to saints at Kirtland, reproving for failure to aid in Missouri persecutions, V4:225-6

Joseph to the saints scattered abroad, V2:229 and ftnt, et seq

Joseph to N. E. Seaton exhorting him to publish all of precious letter against sectarianism, V1:326

Joseph to N. E. Seaton for publication written by commandment, V1:312 and ftnt, et seq

Joseph to John Smith on instructions in case of mob violence, V6:485-

Joseph to William Smith, V2:340, et seq

Joseph to Jacob Stollings, V3:378-9

Joseph to Mr. Tewkesbury seeking to restore him to fellowship, V6:42

Joseph to Judge Thomas, V6:590-1

Joseph to John Thornton et al requesting mediation in Clay Count problems, V2:456, et seq

Joseph to *Times & Seasons*, V4:356-8

Joseph to Smith Tuttle on land troubles, V4:430-3

Joseph to President Tyler appealing for help, V6:508

Joseph to J. R. Wakefield soliciting as witness, V6:551

Joseph to the *Wasp* on participation in politics, V5:259

Joseph to John Wentworth, Articles of Faith, V4:535 and ftnt et se

Joseph to Harvey Whitlock, V2:314-6

Joseph to John Whitmer demanding notes on Church history, V3:15-

Joseph to Bishop Whitney asking him to settle at Commerce, V3:36

Joseph to Lyman Wight on R. B. Thompson complaint, V3:366-7

Joseph to Messrs. Woods and Reid, excitement at Carthage, V6:59

Joseph to Honorable R. M. Young in payment of loan and Nauvoo pos office matters, V5:266-7

Joseph to Zion's attorneys informing them of disbursement of Zion Camp, V2:114-5

Joseph to Zion on condition of Church in Kirtland and suggeste program for redemption of Zion in two years, V2:144-6

Kelting, Joseph A., deputy sheriff of Nauvoo, to the public, V7:360-1

Kimball, Heber C. on affairs of Apostles, June 19, 1844, V7:136, et se

Kimball, Heber C. et al to bishop at Nauvoo recommending Englis saints, V4:132

Kimball, Heber C. on mission to confound John C. Bennett, V5:161-

Kimball, Heber C. on movements of Apostles, V7:157-8

Kimball, Heber C. to saints on affairs of British Mission, V4:114, et se 220-4

Kimball, Heber C. et al to *Times & Seasons*, V4:234

King, Austin A. to keeper of the jail at Liberty, V3:214-5

ETTERS (continued)

Kingsbury and Hawden, attesting to character of Joseph, V3:174

Ladd, A. on wharfage matter, V6:472

Lamborn, Josiah, attorney general of Illinois, opinion stating Nauvoo Legion not state militia, V6:95-6

Lamborn, Josiah, proposing to write history of Mormons, V7:568

Lamborn, Josiah to Brigham Young on attitude in Illinois Legislature, V7:370-1

Law, William to *Times & Seasons,* V5:144

Law, Wilson to Joseph advising him to hide in Nauvoo, V5:114-5

Law, Wilson to Joseph advising retirement from Nauvoo until next governor, August 16, 1842, V5:110-2

Law, Wilson to Joseph expressing willingness to use Legion in his behalf, V5:96-7

Law, Wilson to Joseph on war provisions for Legion to aid marshal, V6:108

Legare, Hugh L. to Joseph, at Canard, V5:363

Lucas, General to Governor Boggs, V3:150

Lucas, General to Governor Boggs, V3:195-9

Lucas, Governor, governor of Iowa, to Isaac Galland, V3:317-8

Lucas, Governor to Sidney Rigdon, V3:333

Lucas, Governor to Wilson Shannon, Governor of Ohio, V3:334

Lucas, Governor to President VanBuren respecting the saints, V3:333-4

Maginn, E. P. on mission travels, V4:566-7

McDougall, J. N. to state auditor for refusing payment for services in Nauvoo Legion, V6:96

McRae, Alexander to *Deseret News,* V3:256, ftnt only, et seq

Miller, George to Governor Reynolds on character of John C. Bennett, V5:46-8

missions, excerpts from missionaries reporting, V1:387-8

Missouri Attorney General to saints' attorney, V1:444-5

Monmouth trial of Joseph by nonmember in *Juliet Courier,* V4:380-1

Morley, I. to Joseph on mob threats, V6:481-2

Mulholland, James to Isaac Russell, V4:5-6

Murdock, John on false tongues, V1:325-6

Nauvoo High Council to Church informing of westward movement, V7:570-2

Nauvoo High Council on excommunicated saints, V6:228-9

Nickerson, Moses C. to the Prophet on Canada Mission, V2:40

Owen, T. H., reporting threats against Nauvoo, V7:192-3

Owens, Samuel C. to Governor Ford on Missouri indictment of Joseph, V5:422

LETTERS (continued)

Page, John E. to presidency reporting progress of Palestine Mission, V4:201-2

Parks, H. G. to General Atchison, V3:149-50

Parks, H. G. to General Atchison, V3:155-6

Parks, H. G. to Governor Boggs, favorable to saints on peace in Missouri, V3:83-4

Parrish, Warren to Joseph on illness, V2:385

Parrish, Warren, relating mob abuses in Tennessee, V2:447-8

Partridge, Edward to Joseph, V3:272-3, 376-7

Phelps, W. W. on Avery charges and witnesses, V6:132-3

Phelps, W. W. to brethren in Kirtland, V2:61-2

Phelps, W. W., confessing errors in Missouri, V4:141-2

Phelps, W. W. to John P. Greene, V3:334

Phelps, W. W. to Reverend John Hewitt, V2:232

Phelps, W. W. to Joseph asking what to do, V1:457-8

Phelps, W. W. from Joseph requesting him to stay out of Church business, V3:358-9 and ftnt

Phelps, W. W. to Joseph on status of Missouri persecutors, V2:61-2

Phelps, W. W. to Kirtland brethren describing regions of Far West, V2:444-5

Phelps, W. W., requests aid from Missouri Senator, V1:487-8

Phelps, W. W. to Esquire Thompson on rights in Jackson County, V2:177-8

Phelps, W. W. and David Whitmer et al to the *Evening & Morning Star,* an appeal, V2:126 and ftnt, et seq

Pierce, Robert to Joseph, satisfaction of financial statement, V4:519

Pratt, Addison on Society Islands Mission, V7:271-3

Pratt, Orson, denying association with John C. Bennett, V5:167

Pratt, Orson to wife concerning movement of brethren in Eastern states, V4:54

Pratt, Orson to Brigham Young on purchasing arms and selling Nauvoo property, V7:509-10

Pratt, Parley P. on emigration and work in England, V4:441

Pratt, Parley P. to Joseph et al denouncing actions of Augustine Spencer, V6:354-5

Pratt, Parley P. to Joseph reporting progress of Church in East, V4:22

Pratt, Parley P. to Judge Austin A. King, V3:352-4

Pratt, Parley P. to Sidney Rigdon informing that all churches in England against saints, V4:266

Pratt, Parley P. to Twelve on conditions in New York, V7:425-6

presidential election matters by central committee, V6:404

LETTERS (continued)

Quincy committee requesting written declaration of intent to move, V7:449-50

Quincy committee, second letter of, V7:450-1

recommendation to Oliver Granger from First Presidency, V3:350

recommending John P. Greene from citizens of Quincy, V3:348

Reed, H. T. to Joseph on documents for defense in Carthage trials, V6:558-9

Reese, Amos to Governor Dunklin requesting guard for court and witnesses, V1:447-8

Reynolds, J. H. to Newell Whitney on imprisonment of O. P. Rockwell, V5:352-3

Rich, C. C. to Ford on additional militia, V7:275-6

Rich, C. C. to Alanson Ripley, V6:355-6

Richards, Levi on gospel in England, mob action, V4:296-7

Richards, Willard to J. A. Bennett on affairs in Nauvoo and westward movement, V6:516-8

Richards, Willard to J. A. Bennett on candidacy for vice president, V6:231-3

Richards, Willard to commissioners for Nauvoo City Council, V7:150-1

Richards, Willard, declaring that saints would take no part in trial of murderers, V7:193-4

Richards, Willard on double taxing of lots, V5:304

Richards, Willard to Ford on interview concerning martyrdom, V7:201

Richards, Willard informing General Deming that R. D. Foster was in Nauvoo, V7:169

Richards, Willard to Orson Hyde on western movement, V6:405-7

Richards, Willard to A. Jonas indicating all peace in Nauvoo, V7:175-6

Richards, Willard, reporting labors, V4:130

Richards, Willard et al to saints at Nauvoo, second message announcing martyrdom, V6:624-5

Richards, Willard and John Taylor to Nauvoo, V7:110

Richards, Willard to Twelve on news of martyrdom, V7:147-8

Richards, Willard to Brigham Young on recent events in Nauvoo, V5:511-3

Rigdon, Sidney to Mr. Bryant, V5:273

Rigdon, Sidney for First Presidency to brethren in Zion, exhorting them to be careful in gift of tongues and other instructions, V1:369-70

Rigdon, Sidney to Governor Ford on *Expositor* affair, V6:469-71

Rigdon, Sidney to Joseph, V4:102

LETTERS (continued)

Rigdon, Sidney to Joseph denying conspiracy with John C. Bennett, V5:314-6

Rigdon, Sidney to Joseph, plans for the impeachment of Missouri, V3:310-1

Rigdon, Sidney to Alfred Stokes correcting Nauvoo misrepresentations, V5:280-1

Ripley, Alanson to the Prophet, V3:311-3

Rockwell, O. P. on flight to avoid arrest, V5:198

Rogers, D. W. from Joseph cancelling power of attorney, V4:495

Rogers, Noah, of work in Society Islands, 1844, V7:313-4

Russell, Isaac from Church reproving pretended revelation, V4:5-6 and ftnt

Russell, Isaac to saints in England, V3:343-4

Ryland, John F. to saints' attorney, V1:445-6

Ryland, Judge E. M. to Rees and Williams, V3:172-3

Ryland, Judge, requesting peace conference with saints at Liberty, V2:89-90

saints in Missouri to Governor Dunklin requesting order for guard to return to Jackson County, V2:84

saints to mob answering proposal to buy lands, V2:98-9

saints' proposal to purchase lands of gentiles, V2:113-4

saints rejecting mob's offer to buy lands, V2:107

saints to Judge Ryland accepting peace offer and outlining proposals, V2:91-2

Shaw, Thomas to saints of the most high, introduces J. Hewitt, V2:230, et seq

Smith, Agnes M. to Hyrum and Joseph, V3:314

Smith, Asael, grandfather of Joseph, V1:285-7, ftnt only

Smith, Don Carlos to Hyrum Smith, V3:313-4

Smith, Don Carlos to Joseph and others in Liberty jail, V3:273-4

Smith, Don Carlos to Joseph on trip to Zion, V3:43

Smith, George A. on conference at Newark, Illinois, V6:399-401

Smith, George A. reporting labors, V4:343-4

Smith, Hyrum to Governor Ford consenting to go to Carthage, accepting protection of governor, V6:550

Smith, Hyrum to Brigham Young, calling home apostles, V6:486-7

Smith, John to Joseph, instructions on mob movements, V6:485

Smith, William to Joseph, V2:338-40

Smith, William to Joseph asking not to be censured, V2:296

Smith, William to Joseph and Hyrum, V3:274

Smith, William to Joseph on land transactions, V4:391-2

LETTERS (continued)

Spencer, Orson to Governor Ford, V7:489-90

Spencer, Orson to Governor Ford, very harsh towards, V7:502-5

Stollings, Jacob to the Prophet, V3:316-7

Taylor, John, affairs of British Mission, V4:96

Taylor, John to *Quincy Argus* warning against imposters, V3:341-2

Taylor, Leonora to Ford requesting protection for saints, V7:201-2

Thompson, J. T. V. to W. W. Phelps on Jackson case, V2:171

Thompson, R. B. to First Presidency complaining of Lyman Wight, V3:351-2

threatened invasion of Nauvoo, V6:426

Tippits, Alvah L. to Joseph, V2:172-4

Tucker, W. to Joseph requesting elders in Arkansas, V6:458-9

Wakefield, J. R. to Ford on *Expositor* affair, V6:469

Walker, G. to Brigham Young et al on affairs of British Mission, V4:505, et seq

Walker, Joel H. to Joseph proposing to join in westward volunteer movement, V6:424-5

Watt, George D., reporting arrival of emmigrants, V5:184-5

Weber, John B. to Joseph concerning supplementing effort to obtain redress, V4:55-6

Wentworth, John to Joseph requesting creed of Church, V4:535

Wesleyan, a staunch, to the *Manx-Liberal*, V4:234-6

westward camp to Governor of Iowa on planting crops, V7:601

Whitlock, Harvey to the Prophet, V2:313-4

Whitmer, David to John Murdock, V3:19, ftnt only

Whitney, Newel K. to Eugene Branch on fellowship of John Smith, V1:371

Whitney, Newel K. et al to the saints scattered abroad, V2:515, et seq

Wight, Lyman to First Presidency on preaching to Indians and migrating to Texas, V6:255-7

Wight, Lyman to Joseph on affairs of Apostles, June 18, 1844, V7:136, et seq

Wight, Lyman to Joseph suggesting southwest movement of Church, V6:257, et seq

Wight, Lyman on movements of Twelve, V7:157-8

Williams, F. G. to Missouri requesting information about mobs, V1:417-9

Wood, J. W. to Joseph on documents for defense, V6:558-9

Wood, Reese, Doniphan, Atchison to saints in Zion, V1:424-5

Woodruff, Wilford to the *Millennial Star*, reporting incidents of ministry, V4:150, et seq

LETTERS (continued)

Woodruff, Wilford to the *Millennial Star* reporting labors, August 5, 1840, V4:176

Woodruff, Wilford to D. C. Smith accounting mission, V4:122-3

Woodruff, Wilford to D. C. Smith of March 29, 1841, affairs in England, V4:323-4

Woodruff, Wilford to Brigham Young reporting Joseph's death, V7:194

Woods and Dixon to Governor Boggs, V3:168-9

Young, A. to Heber C. Kimball on mob in Iowa, V7:572

Young, Brigham, answer to J. B. Backenstos, V7:445

Young, Brigham to the Church in Philadelphia, V5:413

Young, Brigham on family prayer, V4:308-9

Young, Brigham to Governor Ford, invited to review the Nauvoo Legion, V7:277

Young, Brigham to S. Hancock advising movement of all but brethren to Nauvoo as result of mob at Yelrome, V7:440-1

Young, Brigham to Reuben Hedlock on instructions on immigration matters, V6:351, et seq

Young, Brigham to Joseph, V4:119-20

Young, Brigham to Joseph on British Mission, V4:125-7

Young, Brigham to Joseph on labors in England, December 30, 1840, V4:251-2

Young, Brigham on mission to confound John C. Bennett, V5:161-2

Young, Brigham to John Page appointing him to go to Washington, V6:81-3

Young, Brigham to Presidency on movements of British Mission, December 5, 1840, V4:237-8

Young, Brigham to Relief Society requesting their penny subscriptions, V7:322

Young, Brigham to Charles C. Rich, organized quorums to be used in all emergencies, V7:444

Young, Brigham to Willard Richards on proceedings of Apostles, V7:209-11

Young, Brigham to Wilford Woodruff, England, V7:373

Young, Brigham to Wilford Woodruff, progress and unity in Nauvoo, V7:430-2

Young, Brigham, word to the churches abroad, V7:347-8

Young, Richard to Elias Higbee, V4:111-2

Young, Senator to Judge Elias Higbee, V4:121-2

Zion to churches abroad, concerning situation in Zion and state of gathering, V1:379, et seq

Zion to Governor Dunklin again asking for return of arms, V2:75-6

LETTERS (continued)

Zion, to lawyers of, indicating mob would not accept saints' offer to purchase lands, V2:119.

See also affidavits; Apostles; epistles; Latter-day Saints, Church of Jesus Christ of; Smith, Joseph.

letter, Wentworth, Articles of Faith and brief history of Church, V4:535, et seq and ftnts.

Levans, William J., ordained priest, V2:525.

Levett, Phebe, reports mob firing on guard, V6:530.

Levy, Aaron, mentioned, V4:176.

Levy, Israel, mentioned, V4:176.

Lewell, Amos, mission call in Illinois to disabuse public mind over arrest of Joseph, V5:485.

Lewis, Benjamin, killed at Haun's Mills by mob, V3:326, ftnt only.

Lewis, Brother, mentioned, V2:41; V6:67, 133.

Lewis, Clark, mission and field of labor, V6:338.

Lewis, David, mission and field of labor, V5:348; V6:340
mission in Illinois to disabuse public mind over arrest of Joseph, V5:485.

Lewis, J., mentioned, V2:324.

Lewis, Job L., excommunicated for treating Church with contempt, V2:444
mentioned, V2:244.

Lewis, John, mentioned, V6:67.

Lewis, Joshua, Missouri conference at home of, V1:199
Ryland, Judge, sent as messenger from saints in Missouri to, V1:429

Lewis, L. B. , delegate to political convention in Nauvoo, V6:389.

Lewis, L. S., Zions Camp member, V2:184.

Lewis, Lloyd, conversation with Joseph on dislike of Church, V2:318.

Lewis, Lorenzo L., adultery, trial for, V2:285
Church, convicted and cut off from, V2:285
Prophet, conversation with, on dislike of Church, V2:318.

Lewis, Nathan, covenanted to assist saints in removing from Missouri, V3:253.

Lewis, Philip B., affiant to public proclamation on mob lies, V6:495
affidavit on kidnapping, V6:103
donates to Society Islands Mission, V6:52
mentioned, V6:492; V7:70.

Lewis, Tarlton, (also spelled Tarleton), bishop, appointed, V5:119

LEWIS, TARLTON (continued)

    bishop, sustained of a Nauvoo ward, V7:298

    Haun's Mills, wounded at, by mob, V3:326, ftnt only

    high priest, ordained, V5:136

    Joseph, leaves to rescue, V4:365

    Joseph, on relief expedition for, V5:482

    witness, suggested to appear before Congress on redress, V4:97.

Lewis, Timothy, witness for state in Missouri trials of saints, V3:210.

Leyland, Benjamin, martyrdom, escorts messenger of, to Nauvoo, V6:622.

liberty, *Lee County Democrat,* plea for, V7:164

    Nauvoo, religious in, V4:306.

Liberty, Missouri, occurrences of peace meeting at, V2:97

    saints, mob presents offer to buy out, V2:96.

licenses, marriage ceremony, for elders to perform, V2:408

    preach, new to be issued and regulations concerning, to, V2:403

    resolutions concerning, V2:403.

light, knowledge compared to, V2:265.

Lightfoot, Levi, ordained priest, V6:400.

lightmindedness, saints do away with, V6:52.

Lightner, Adam, offered life if leave Far West, V3:410.

Likens, Reverend, participated in Missouri mobs, V1:392 and ftnt; V1:372, ftnt only.

Lincoln, John, proposition of Mormons addressed to, V2:122.

Lindsay, Mr., mentioned, V3:263.

Linn, Mr., hears saints petition in Congressional Committee, V4:83, et seq

Linn, William A., questions authenticity of Kinderhook plates, V5:378 and ftnt.

Linvill, Thomas, mob member killed by saints, V1:430.

Lions, Father, testifies in Kirtland High Council, V2:33.

"Lions of the Press," parable by Joseph, V5:274, et seq.

liquor, Far West, influence to be used to stop selling of, at, V3:48

    grog shop of P. S. Cahoon removed, V4:442

    Joseph, by ordinance allowed to distribute, V6:111

    Joseph, views of, on, V2:406

    Kirtland High Council to try to stop selling and use of, V2:520

    Nauvoo, becoming stranger in, V4:331

    Nauvoo, licenses in, V4:383

    Nauvoo, ordinance against vending in, V7:315

    Nauvoo, ordinance on, in, V4:299

LIQUOR (continued)

Nauvoo, ordinance on sale of, in, V6:178

saints, commanded to put out of mind, V7:350

sale, members cannot participate in, V2:491

sale, men fined for offering, V5:57.

See also alcohol; drinking; intemperance; temperance; Word of Wisdom.

Lisle, B. M., Adjutant General Missouri militia, V3:65.

Literary Firm, agents appointed for, V2:273

sustained, V2:482.

literature, of Latter-day Saints, V4:487

pro et con, V4:487-9.

Little, Jesse C., California, proffers 1,000 settlers for, V7:611

Eastern States Mission, president of, at Washington, D. C., V7:611

Latter-day Saints, application for assistance for, V7:611

Mormon Battalion, requests raising of, V7:611

saints, assurance to sustain that assistance would be given, V7:611.

Little, Sidney A., lawyer for Joseph, V4:366.

Little, Sidney H., death of, V4:389.

Littlefield, Brother, proprietor of "Half Way House," north of Far West, V3:67.

Littlefield, Josiah, Zions Camp member, V2:184.

Littlefield, Lyman O., mission and field of labor, V5:347; V6:339

mission in Illinois to disabuse public mind over arrest of Joseph, V5:485

slander, action against, for, V4:514

Zions Camp member, V2:184.

Littlefield, Waldo, Zions Camp member, V2:184.

Littlewood, Martin, English conference, represents branches of Church at, V4:148, 215

volunteers for service in vineyard, V4:217.

Litz, A., charged for preaching against authorities, V4:501.

Litz, Stephen, mission call, V7:260.

Livesey, Richard, Methodist priest publishes anti-Mormon pamphlet in England, V3:22

publishes anti-Mormon literature, V4:255, 320.

Lloyd, George, mission and field of labor, V6:335.

Lockhart, John, witness for state in Missouri trials for saints, V3:210.

Lofthouse, Mr., represents branch of Church at English conference, V4:147.

Lofton, John G., affidavit of mob attempting to draft into service, V6:511.

Logan, Mr., Illinois legislator, V5:294.

Logan, Wm. H., reports on difficulties with Mormons, V3:151.

Long, James, ordained elder, V5:349.

Long, Jas. H., proposition of Mormons addressed to, V2:122.

Long, John V., statement as to original members of Church, V1:76, ftnt only.

Longnecker, W., testifies to finding Kinderhook plates, V5:377.

Longstroth, Stephen, Nauvoo Temple, appointed carpenter on, V7:326.

Loomis, Mr., Illinois mobber, V6:278, 280.

Lord, House of, cornerstones of, laid, V3:41
    Far West, discontinued, V2:521
    Far West, ground breaking for, at, V2:496
    Kirtland, cornerstone of, laid in, V1:400
    Nauvoo, to be built in, V4:205
    rules and regulations of, V2:368
    tithing, built on principle of, V4:205
    Zion, Houses of Lord in, V1:359, et seq.
    See also Latter-day Saints, Church of Jesus Christ of; temple; Temple, Kirtland; Temple, Nauvoo.

Lord, law of, book of, kept by Joseph, V5:124, 420 and ftnt
    mentioned, V4:339, 518, 563.

Lord, spirit of, descends upon Newel Knight, V1:83.
    See also Holy Ghost.

Loree, Albert, petitions Governor Boggs on mob violence in DeWitt, V3:83.

Loring, Frederick, Carthage Greys, member of, V7:142.

lost books, of Bible, V1:132 and ftnt.
    See also Bible; doctrine; Smith, Joseph.

Lot, Judge, mentioned, V7:276.

Lott, Cornelius P., mission call amidst mob action in Missouri, V3:154 and ftnt
    Nauvoo Temple, receives endowment in, V7:544.

Lott, P., falsely accused of threatening A. Black, V3:65.

Lott, Permelia, receives endowment in Nauvoo Temple, V7:543.

Louisa, emigrant ship, V4:594.

love, of Joseph for fellow men, V5:498.

Lovelace, John, mission and field of labor, V6:339.

Lovelady, Reverend, participated in Missouri mobs, V1:372 and ftnt; 392 and ftnt.

Loveland, Chester, mob actions toward, V6:504.

Loveland, Daniel, mission and field of labor, V6:335.

Loveless, John, utility committee member to aid Church removal, V7:474.

Lovell, Charles A., recommends California for movement, V7:510.

Loveridge, William, ordained teacher, V4:135.

Lowd, Mr., prayer to soften heart of, V2:24.

Lowell, Susan, marriage to John F. Boynton, V2:377.

Lower, Amos, trial for assault, V5:317.

Lowry, John, mission and field of labor, V6:340
    mission in Illinois to disabuse public mind over arrest of Joseph, V5:485
    Missouri, covenanted to assist saints in removing from, V3:252
    Missouri persecutions, affidavit concerning, V4:56.

Lucas, Robert, Governor of Iowa territory, how saints would be treated in, V3:317-8
    letter of, addressing United States President, V3:333
    mentioned, V3:266, 334; V4:108.

Lucas, Samuel D., Boggs, Governor, letter to, describing Mormons as base and degrading beings, V3:150
    Boggs, Governor, report of militia movements to, V3:195, et seq
    colonel and judge of the court, signed mob manifesto, V1:376
    extermination ordered by Governor Boggs to complete job of, V3:192
    falsely reports on conditions in upper Missouri, V3:150
    Joseph, opinion of, on, V3:151
    major general in Missouri militia, V3:65
    Missouri, mobbers in, V3:327
    mob, carries proposals to saints from, V1:398
    Mormons, requests Governor Boggs to come to seat of war with, V3:176 and ftnt
    prisoners, condemns to be shot, V3:190 and ftnt
    report, unfriendly of, V3:176, ftnt only
    saints, avowed enemy of, V1:435
    saints, ordered to restore arms of, V1:491
    secretary to anti-Mormon meeting in Missouri, V1:395.
    See also letters; Missouri correspondence; persecutions, Missouri.

Luce, Brother, mentioned, V7:387.

Lucifer, see devil.

Lucy, Jonathan, given care of Church at Caldwell, V4:138.

Ludington, Elam, (also spelled Luddington), delegate to political convention in Nauvoo, V6:390
  delegate to present truth to public, V6:483.

Lundow, William P., petitions Governor Boggs on mob violence in DeWitt, V3:83.

Luse, Jason R., reports mob threats against Nauvoo, V6:452.

lying spirit, when abroad truth hard to understand, V2:512.

Lyman, Mr., prayer to soften heart of, V2:24.

Lyman, Amasa M., Apostleship, ordained to, V5:120
  endowment, receives in Nauvoo Temple, V7:543
  First Presidency, taken from Twelve into, V5:255
  genealogy, V1:332 and ftnt; V5:120
  gift of healing of, V7:271
  Joseph, accompanies in arrest, V4:365
  Joseph, declares gratefulness for aid rendered while in seclusion, V5:109
  Joseph, secretly goes to inform of movement of sheriff, V5:97
  Joseph, speech of, on successor to, V7:236-7 and ftnt
  martyrdom, arrives in Nauvoo after, V7:214
  mission, assigned to go on, V4:429
  mission and field of labor, V1:332; V6:339
  Missouri, arraigned for treason, murder, burglary, arson, robbery and larceny at Richmond, V3:209
  Missouri trials, discharges as innocent from, V3:211
  mob, enters camp of, at Missouri, V3:189, ftnt only
  mob, taken by, to Independence, V3:194
  Nauvoo Temple, appointed to officiate in, V7:548
  Quorum of Twelve, to stand as member of, V7:248
  Quorum of Twelve, sustained member of, V7:236, ftnt only
  Quorum of Twelve, sustained member of, at Salt Lake City, V7:628
  report of, on James Emmett's company, V7:377-8
  saints, address on oneness and move of, V7:468-9
  seventies, named to first quorum of, V2:204
  Seventies Hall, dedication, discourse at on unity of saints, V7:338-9
  Seventies Library and Institute Association, elected trustee of, V7:328
  shot, sentenced to be, in public square at Far West, V3:190
  sustained to "stand in his lot," V7:295 and ftnt
  University of Nauvoo, elected regent of, V5:120

LYMAN, AMASA M. (continued)

Zions Camp member, V2:184

Zions Camp, recruiting officer in, V2:72.

Lyman, Asa, blessing for work on Kirtland Temple, V2:205

exonerates Joseph's actions in Zions Camp, V2:149.

Lyman, Boswell, father of Amasa M., V1:332, ftnt only.

Lyman, Mariah Louisa, receives endowment in Nauvoo Temple, V7:543.

Lyman, Martha Mason, mother of Amasa M., V1:332, ftnt only.

Lyman, William D., mission and field of labor, V6:337.

Lynch, J., mentioned, V3:317.

Lynch, Patrich, witness for state in Missouri trials of saints, V3:210.

Lyne, Thomas A., a tragedian, V6:349

witness for Joseph at Carthage martyrdom, V6:576.

Lyon, Mr., babe of dies, V5:207.

Lyon, Mr., martial band member of Legion, V7:135.

Lyon, Aaron E., (also C.), Kirtland Temple, blessing for work on, V2:205

trial of, for claiming revelation that another married woman should be his wife, convicted and priesthood taken, V3:26.

Lyon, Carlos W., affidavit on arms to mob, V6:507.

Lyon, James H., witness for Joseph at Carthage martyrdom, V6:576.

Lyon, William, mentioned, V2:290.

Lyons, Mr., pursues Joseph as mob, V3:2-3.

Lyons, David, covenanted to assist saints in removing from Missouri, V3:252.

Lyons, Father, (also spelled Lyon), mentioned, V2:27, 446.

Lyons, Windsor P., mentioned, V5:184; V7:274.

Lytle, Andrew, covenanted to assist saints in removing from Missouri, V3:252

Expositor, arrest for destruction of, trial, V6:487, et seq; V7:484-5

mentioned, V6:285

policeman in Nauvoo, V6:150.

Lytle, John, *Expositor,* arrest for destruction of, trial, V6:487, et seq; V7:484-5

Joseph, on relief expedition for, V5:482

mentioned, V6:179

Missouri, covenanted to assist saints in removing from, V3:253

Nauvoo, policeman in, V6:150.

—M—

Maba, John, Missouri, covenanted to assist saints in removing from, V3:252.

Maccauslin, Y., Nauvoo, delegate to political convention at, V6:390.

Mace, Brother, mentioned, V3:275.

Mace, Hiram, Nauvoo Temple, appointed carpenter on, V7:326.

Mace, Wandel, (also spelled Wandell, Wandall), Church, appointed to preside over new district of, V7:305
mission call and field of labor, V5:347
Nauvoo Temple, appointed carpenter on, V7:326.

Mack, family genealogy, V1:2 and ftnt.

Mack, Chilion, mission appointment published and field of labor, V6:335.

Mack, Ebenezer, grandfather to Lucy Mack Smith, V1:2 and ftnt.

Mack, Lucy, ancestry of, V1:2 and ftnt.

Mack, Lydia, grandmother to Joseph, V4:189.

Mack, Solomon, father of Lucy Mack Smith, V1:2
grandfather of Joseph, V4:189.

Mack, Temperance, visits the Prophet, V5:119.

Mackey, John, mission appointment published and field of labor, V6:339.

Mackley, Elizabeth, covenanted to assist saints in removing from Missouri, V3:252.

Mackley, Jeremiah, asks assistance from Church, V3:261.

Mackley, Sarah, covenanted to assist saints in removing from Missouri, V3:252.

Maclin, Peter, ordained teacher, V6:400.

Maddison, Mr., anti-Mormon committee member of Warsaw meeting, V6:464.

Madison, Mades, ordained priest, V6:400.

Madison, R. T., at anti-Mormon meeting, V5:537.

Magan, Elder, mentioned, V4:332.

Maginess, Benjamin, mentioned, V5:525.

Maginn, Eli P., mentioned, V5:435
missions of, V4:566-7, V5:322.

Maginn, Ezekiel, mission travels, letter on, V4:566
Missouri persecutions, affidavit concerning, V4:64.

Mahon, James, volunteers for service in vineyard, V4:217.

"Maid of Iowa," Joseph, expedition to relieve, on second arrest, V5:482-4
Nauvoo, arrives at, with English passengers, V6:333
purchase of, V5:386, 417-8
sale of, V7:395.

mail, mob prevents delivery of, V3:166
Nauvoo, uncertainty of, in, V7:65.

Maith, John W., Carthage Greys, member of, V7:143.

Major, William W., martyrdom, exhibits painting of, V7:390
westward movement, counselor in, V7:626.

Majors, Benjamin, anti-Mormon committee member, V1:399.

Malachi, Joseph retranslates, V6:183-4
Moroni quotes, V1:12.

Males, Mr., stabbed, V2:98.

Mallory, Lemuel, called on mission and field of labor, V5:348.

man, commandments, must strictly observe all God's, V2:13
fall, no change in constitution of, since, V2:17
God, relationship to, V6:312-3
gospel, position of, in, V2:8
judging, capable of, only when pure in heart, V2:25
must be careful or will fall short, V1:299
salvation, when prevents another from hearing gospel then responsible
for his, V7:546
sin, men of revealed, V1:175 and ftnt
spirit, can be excited by own, and have neither spirit of God nor devil,
V2:279
wickedness, cannot be compelled to do, V4:358.
See also doctrine; gospel.

Man, Isle of, Mormonism comes to, letter against, V4:234, et seq.

"Man, To," article in first *Star* declaring status, V1:273, et seq.

Manchester, Asa, petitions Governor Boggs on mob violence in DeWitt,
V3:83.

Manchester, New York, Hill Cumorah near, V1:15
Joseph leaves, V1:19
Joseph moves to, V1:2.

Manhard, David, gives to assist Joseph, V5:299
mentioned, V5:368, V6:424.

manifestations, spiritual, in Kirtland Temple, V2:410, et seq.
See also God; Holy Ghost; Jesus Christ.

manifesto, of Missouri mob, V1:374 and ftnt
  Missouri mob accusation concerning Negroes, V1:376 and ftnt
  Missouri mob, signatures thereto, V1:376
  Pratt, Parley P., answers to, V1:376, ftnt only, et seq
  saints, caused by religious beliefs of, IntroV3:XLVIII.
  See also Missouri persecutions; mob.

Mann, William, Haun's Mills massacre, member of mob at, V3:325
  mob gathers at home of, V3:184
  mobber in Missouri, V4:68.

manna, shower of, V4:383.

Manning, Egbert S., solicits Joseph's views on politics and issues, V6:387-8.

Manship, Esq., justice of peace in Missouri, witnesses beating of member, V2:46.

Manx-Liberal, anti-Mormon letter published on labors in Isle of Man, V4:234, et seq.

Mar, Mr., mentioned, V7:75-6.

March, Enoch C., mentioned, V6:587-8.

Marcy, William S., mentioned, V7:547.

Margetts, Thomas, British conference, represents branches at, V5:419, V6:329.

Markham, Stephen, affidavit that Nauvoo to be attacked, V6:492
  alderman, resigns as, V5:288
  arrest for destruction of *Expositor,* trial on, V6:487, et seq
  Carthage, forced out of, V6:614
  Carthage, with Joseph at, V7:101
  Carthage prison, with Joseph in, V6:592
  conspiracy, reveals existence of, V5:451-2
  Dixon, attends court at, V6:350
  Far West, arrival at, V3:263
  Joseph, arms, V5:443
  Joseph, meeting with, V5:439
  Joseph, messenger to warn of impending arrest, V5:436, 438, et seq
  Legion, elected colonel in, V5:165
  life, attempt upon, V3:314-5
  messenger to Governor Ford, V5:484
  mission appointment published and field of labor, V6:340
  mission call and field of labor, V5:348
  Missouri, on committee for removal from, V3:255
  Missouri, covenanted to assist saints in removing from, V3:253

MARKHAM, STEPHEN (continued)

    mob, chased by, V3:332-3

    mob, escape from, V3:316

    Nauvoo, appointed market master of, V4:308

    priests quorum, counselor to in Nauvoo, V4:312

    prophecy, present in Missouri at Apostles' departure to fulfill, V3:339

    Springfield, report on movements at, V5:500

    vision, told to escape by, of Joseph, V3:316

    witness, suggested to appear before Congress on redress, V4:97

    witness at trial of Joseph then arrested by mob and threatened in
        front of judge and jury, V3:314.

Marks, Ephraim, funeral of, V4:586-7.

Marks, Sophia, dream of on visit to two dead brothers, V5:250.

Marks, William, Church, traitor to, V6:170

    financial settlement of Joseph with, V4:582

    genealogy of, V2:486, ftnt only

    Kirtland, elected agent to bishop at, V2:513

    Kirtland Camp, blesses, V3:100

    Kirtland High Council, ordained to, V2:511

    Kirtland High Council, sustained to, V2:510

    life, fears for, V6:166, et seq

    Messenger & Advocate, transferred to, V2:486 and ftnt

    Missouri warrants, accompanies Joseph for trial on, V5:210

    Nauvoo, bodyguard to Joseph's body on return to, V7:135

    Nauvoo, first elected alderman of, V4:287

    Nauvoo, leaves, V7:387

    Nauvoo Mansion, landlord of and party in, V7:280

    Nauvoo stake, appointed president of, V4:12

    Nauvoo stake, president of, V4:323

    Nauvoo stake president, rejected as, V7:296

    vision, Joseph has concerning status of, V3:12

    witness for Joseph at Carthage martyrdom, V6:576.

Marr, S. M., member of mob at martyrdom, V7:146.

Marr, William H. J., member of mob at martyrdom, V7:146

    mentioned, V6:281.

marriage, certificate form used, V2:377

    Church, if outside, considered weak in faith, V2:247

    eternal life, necessity of, for, V5:391

    Garden of Eden, instituted in, V2:320

    monogamy, article on, August 17, 1835, advocating, V2:246 and ftnt

    obedience to God's laws bring happiness in, V5:134-6.

MARRIAGE (continued)

    plural, V6:46

    polygamy, rejects, V2:247

    proposed ceremony for, in Church, V2:247

    revelation on, V5:501-7.

    See also doctrine; Latter-day Saints, Church of Jesus Christ of; Smith, Joseph.

Marsh, Mr., mentioned, V6:598.

Marsh, Elder, mentioned, V5:378, ftnt only.

Marsh, Eliphas, covenanted to assist saints in removing from Missouri, V3:253.

Marsh, I., appointed by public to assist saints in removing from Zion, V2:455.

Marsh, James G., death of, son of Thomas B. Marsh, V3:28.

Marsh, Thomas Baldwin, apostasy of and joins mob, affidavit against saints, V3:166-7 and ftnt

    apostatizes and fights Church, V3:172

    Apostles, chosen one of the, V2:187

    Apostles, blessing of as member of, V2:194 and ftnt

    Apostles, recognized as president of the, V2:219-20 and ftnts

    Apostles, sustained as one of, to Church, V2:509

    biography, V1:117, ftnt only

    buffetings of Satan, turned over to and condemned as openly sinning against Jesus, V3:232

    endowments, chosen to receive, V2:113

    excommunication from Church, V3:284

    general assembly, moderator in of Church at Missouri, V3:3-6

    high council, presides in, V3:7-8

    high council, sustained to Missouri, V2:124

    Lord, inquires of, V1:186

    mission, inquires of Joseph for, V1:186

    Missouri, appointed branch president in, V1:409, ftnt only

    Missouri, appointed to go to with Ezra Thayre, V1:178

    revelation to, V1:116, 186; V2:499

    son dies, V3:28

    Zion, elected president pro tempore in, V3:6.

Marshall, Sam, killed by Sheriff M. R. Deming, V7:428.

martial law, in Nauvoo, V7:6, 70.

Martin, Edward, mentioned, V4:296.

Martin, John S., covenanted to assist saints in removing from Missouri, V3:253.

Martin, Moses, court-martialed, V2:67
    sentry, asleep on duty, V2:66
    seventies, named to first quorum of, V2:204
    Zions Camp, member of, V2:184.

Martin, Sheriff, kind to prisoners, V3:365-6.

Martin, Thomas, delegate to political convention in Nauvoo, V6:389.

Martin, Thomas J., accuses saints of murder and burning, V3:165.

Martin, William, kidnaps members and takes to Missouri, V4:155.

Martin, William, mission call in Illinois to disabuse public mind over Joseph's arrest, V5:485.

Martindale, William, heavens, records seeing of 1860 in, V6:121
    mission appointment published and field of labor, V6:339.

martyr, Barber, Andrew, first killed by mob, V1:431 and ftnt
    Joseph and Hyrum honored in Liverpool, V7:226.
    See also Illinois persecutions; martyrdom; Smith, Hyrum; Smith, Joseph.

martyrdom, account of, V6:616, et seq
    account in Doctrine & Covenants of, V6:629, et seq
    anti-Mormons, activities of after, V7:42
    conditions preceding event, V7:56
    Joseph and Hyrum in poetry, V7:154, et seq
    lamentations of, V7:191
    mob, false rumors by, Mormon reaction to, V7:25
    mob, members of enumerated, V7:142, et seq
    murderers, acquitted at trial, V7:420
    murderers, minutes of trial of, V7:421, et seq
    newspaper, various accounts of, V7:164, 177, et seq
    painting of exhibited, V7:390
    review of published in *Times & Seasons*, V7:186
    Taylor's memoirs of, V7:55, et seq.
    See also Carthage, Illinois; Carthage Greys; Carthage jail; Ford, Thomas; Latter-day Saints, Church of Jesus Christ of; martyrs; persecutions; Smith, Hyrum; Smith, Joseph.

Marvin, Edward W., mission appointment to East, V2:35
    Zions Camp member, V2:184.

Mason, Mr., mentioned, V5:473.

Mason, Arnold, tannery purchased by Church, V1:336.

Mason, Carnot, member of Hiram mob, V1:264, ftnt only.

Mason, Perez, grandfather of Amasa M. Lyman, V1:332, ftnt only

Mason, Perley, son of Perez Mason, V1:332, ftnt only.

Mason, Robert, foretells need of "true church," V3:337, ftnt only.

masons, Bennett, John C., expelled, V5:22, 32
  Grand Master dies and Joseph's comments, V5:370
  Joseph receives first degree of, V4:551
  Joseph rises in, V4:552
  Montrose, organized in, V5:85
  Nauvoo and Joseph, evaluation by, V4:565
  temple, cornerstone of laid in Nauvoo, V5:446
  temple, dedication of in Nauvoo, V6:287.
  See also Masonic Temple; Nauvoo; Smith, Joseph.

Masquerier, Lewis, solicits Joseph's views on politics and issues, V6:387-8.

Massachusetts, memorial to on Missouri persecutions, V6:236.

Massachusetts conference, of Twelve Apostles, V2:241.

massacre, Haun's Mills, Daniel Ashby admits being in, V3:212
  counsel, lives lost because would not heed, V5:137
  injured still suffering from, V4:389
  killed and wounded, list of, at, V3:186, 326, ftnt only
  mob, names of enumerated, V3:325
  narrative of Amanda Smith concerning, V3:323, et seq
  narrative of by Joseph Young, V3:183, et seq
  witnessed by Jacob K. Potts and Levi Stilly, V4:95.

Masters, Mr., mob messenger, V4:72.

Matlock, W. E., issues prospectus of *Hancock Eagle,* V7:596.

matter, eternal duration of, treatise by Parley P. Pratt on, V4:54, ftnt only.
  See also doctrine; Smith, Joseph.

Matthew, Book of, Joseph retranslates chapter 24:2, V6:184.

Matthews, Mr., mentioned, V3:378.

Matthews, Anson, accused before Church courts for unfair dealings,
  V5:371-2.

Matthews, Brother, mentioned, V2:42.

Matthews, Clarissa, mentioned, V2:317.

Matthews, D. W., merchant, member of martyrdom mob, V7:144.

Matthews, David, restored to fellowship after suspension for unchristianlike conduct, V2:227.

Matthews, J. B., merchant, member of martyrdom mob, V7:144.

Matthews, John, mentioned in Kirtland Camp, V3:124.

Matthews, Timothy R., baptized, agrees to be but fails to show up, V2:506
  baptizes self and attacks elders, V2:507
  mentioned, V4:489
  minister in England invites missionaries to use his chapel, V2:504
  work, trifles with, V2:506-7.

Matthias, Apostle, Robert Matthias claims spirit of, resurrected in him, V2:307.

Matthias, Robert, Christ, claimed possessed soul of, V2:307
  Joshua the Jewish minister, evil doer visits Joseph as, V2:306
  Matthias, Apostle, claimed that spirit of was resurrected in him, V2:307.

Maughan, Peter, elder, ordained, V4:296
  genealogy of, V4:493 and ftnt.

Maupin, Jesse P., Hauns Mills, blew brains out of boy at, V3:187
  Joseph, thirty dollar messenger sent to, V3:315.

Maxwell, James, solicits Joseph's views on politics and issues, V6:387-8.

Mayberry, John, gives cow to Joseph, V5:264.

Maynard, Jonathan, excommunicated from Church, V3:336.

Maynard, Nelson, excommunicated from Church, V3:336.

Maynard, Silas, Missouri, arraigned for treason, murder, burglary, arson, robbery, and larceny at Richmond, V3:209
  Missouri trials, discharged as innocent from, V3:211.

McAnley, James, presides over British Mission conference, V4:333.

McArthur, D., asks assistance from Church, V3:261.

McArthur, Daniel, covenanted to assist saints in removing from Missouri, V3:252.

McArthur, Duncan, Church, appointed to preside over new district of, V7:306
  Kirtland Camp, mentioned in, V3:116
  Kirtland Camp, subscribed to constitution of, V3:91
  mission appointment published and field of labor, V6:340
  Missouri, covenanted to assist saints in removing from, V3:252
  stake presidency, appointed counselor in, V4:233.

McAuley, Captain, mentioned, V6:529.

McAuley, John, represents area in British conference, V5:10.

McAuley, John, member of martyrdom mob, one of worst men in Hancock, V7:144.

McBradney, Brother, mentioned, V7:145.

McBride, Mr., Joseph stays at home of, V2:41.

McBride, Judge, mentioned, V6:38.

McBride, Rueben, bishop, counselor to at Kirtland, V4:362
Kirtland, appointed president at, V7:326
Zions Camp member, V2:184.

McBride, Robert, British conference, represents branch of Church in, V4:148
British Mission, mission in, V4:150
Church, appointed to preside over new district of, V7:305
ministry, devote all time to labors of, V4:148.

McBride, Thomas, Haun's Mills, further report of death at, V3:220 and ftnt
Haun's Mills, killed at, by mob, V3:186, 326, ftnt only.

McCanley, John, anti-Mormon committee chairman, V6:8.

McCanse, James A., mentioned, V6:418.

McCartney, John, Missouri mobber, V4:396.

McCarty, Mr., mobber in Missouri, V3:438.

McCarty, Richard, false arrest, gets warrant against Sidney Gilbert for, V1:431
Gilbert & Whitney, breaks into store of, V1:428, ftnt only
saints, caught by, but released by courts, V1:428.

McCaseland, Joseph, subscribed to constitution of Kirtland Camp, V3:91

McClary, Brother, mentioned, V5:302.

McClary, William, mentioned, V3:43.

McClaughny, Matthews, farmer, member of martyrdom mob, V7:144.

McClellan, Abraham, signs proposition to buy land of saints, V2:96-7.

McClentic, Mr., mobber of Joseph, V1:264.

McComsay, J. D., testifies on Joseph's second arrest in Illinois, V6:67.

McConnel, Murray, mentioned, V7:274.

McCord, Dr., resigns from Church and gives up license, V3:31.

McCord, Robert, Missouri, dies of cholera in, V2:120
Zions Camp member, V2:184.

McCown, Marcellus, mob, makes conciliation offer to, V7:441-2.

McCoy, Isaac, Church, opposes, V1:372, 392 and ftnts
Missouri mob, prominence in, noted, V1:372, ftnt only
Missouri mob, participated in, V1:392
mob, heads one of the companies of, V1:436.

McCoy, Joseph C., kidnapper of saints, V6:122
kidnaps Daniel Avery, V6:146.

McCue, Peter, British conference, represents, V5:419
elder, ordained, V5:419.

McCustian, Anthony, to lead mob in Missouri, V4:64.

McDonald, Michael, subscribed to constitution of Kirtland Camp, V3:93.

McDonald, Zuba, covenanted to assist saints in removing from Missouri, V3:253.

McDougal, J. A., member Quincy committee on saints' removal, V7:450.

McDougall, Mr., mentioned, V7:507.

McDougall, J. N., letter refusing payment for services in Nauvoo Legion, V6:96.

McDowell, James, mentioned, V7:326.

McDowell, Professor, reviews Kinderhook plates, V5:378-9, ftnt only.

McDwellin, John W., judge in Missouri, V6:148.

McEwan, Henry, represents British conference, V5:419.

McEwan, John P., witness in *Expositor* trial of Joseph, V6:457.

McFall, Hugh, delegate to present truth to public, V6:483
military order, denies signing, V5:164
Nauvoo, replaced as council member at, V5:13.

McFate, James, mission call in Illinois to disabuse public mind over arrest of Joseph, V5:485.

McGee, Joseph, H., witness for state in Missouri trials of saints, V3:210.

McGirk, Matthias, supreme court justice in Missouri, V3:289.

McGown, Mr., mentioned, V2:42.

McGregor, Malcolm, postmaster of Carthage, Illinois, V4:121.

McGuffie, Mr., accompanies mission to Ireland, V4:170 and ftnt.

McGuin, James, petitions Governor Boggs on mob violence in DeWitt, V3:83.

McHenry, Mr., persecutes saints, V3:243.

McHoney, William L., arrested for supplying mob and trial, V3:75-6.

McIlvaine, G., appointed by public to assist saints in removing from Zion, V2:455.

McIlwaine's Bend, destroyer seen upon waters at, V1:203.
See also devil.

McIlwick, John, (also spelled McIllwrick), delegate to present truth to public, V6:483

McILWICK, JOHN (continued)

elder, ordained, V4:333.

McIntosh, J. A., mission appointment published and field of labor, V6:338.

McIntyre, Jesse, elder, appointed, V4:12.

McIntyre, William P., mission appointment published and field of labor, V6:337.

McKay, Mr., mentioned, V6:283, ftnt only.

McKay, John, mobber, V6:524.

McKee, Brother, mentioned, V7:600.

McKenzie, Thomas, mentioned, V7:274.

McKennie, Mr., mentioned, V5:441.

McKeown, Marcellus, mission appointment published and field of labor, V6:336.

McKinney, A., mentioned, V7:130.

McKinney, Wilson, oath that saints have acted as mob, V3:61.

McLeary, William, Joseph's brother-in-law, V6:514.

McMahon, Mr., anti-Mormon, V5:390.

McMaster, Cyrus, Presbyterian persecutor named, V1:97.

McMillan, James, covenanted to assist saints in removing from Missouri, V3:251.

McMinn, Sister, mentioned, V7:157.

McNeil, Mr., mentioned, V6:240.

McOlney, Davies, policeman in Nauvoo, V6:150.

McPherson, Mr., mentioned, V6:421.

McQueen, Mr., mentioned, V5:292.

McRae, Alexander, grand jury brings in bill against for treason, murder, etc., V3:315
    Liberty, Clay County, sent to stand trial for murder and treason at, V3:212
    Liberty imprisonment, letters concerning facts of, V3:256, ftnt only; 258, ftnt only
    mission appointment published and field of labor, V6:337
    Missouri, arraigned for treason, murder, burglary, arson, robbery, and larceny at Richmond, V3:209
    Missouri, writ against to take to, V5:448
    Nauvoo Temple, appointed to officiate in, V7:548.

McRae, Daniel, ordained elder, V5:349.

McTaggart, Thomas, mission appointment published and field of labor, V6:336.

McWhithy, E. A., marriage of to E. Webb, V2:331.

McWithy, Isaac, (also spelled McWethy, McWithey), Church, charges to high council for failure to give to, V2:445

elder, ordained, V1:327

high council, appointed to Zion, V2:367

Kirtland, appointed to raise funds for relief of, V2:44

Kirtland High Council, before, V2:446

Prophet, entertains, V2:45.

McWithy, Joel, blessing for work on Kirtland Temple, V2:205.

Meacham, Elam, prepares harvest feast in Nauvoo, V7:437.

Mecham, Joseph, counselor to bishop, V4:399.

Medagh, Mr., mentioned, V6:38.

Medfo, Rachel, covenanted to assist saints in removing from Missouri, V3:254.

Medford, immigrant ship, V5:165, 185.

medicine, Joseph, on use of, V4:414.

meekness and lowliness of Christ explained, V5:218.

Meeks, James, clerk of British conference, V4:140.

Meeks, John, given care of Church at Old Starridge, V4:139.

Meeks, Priddy, mission call in Illinois to disabuse public mind over arrest of Joseph, V5:485.

Meeks, Sister, mentioned, V3:319, 376.

Meeks, William, Joseph, on relief expedition for, V5:482

mission call in Illinois to disabuse public mind over arrest of Joseph, V5:485.

meetings, ancient order of, elders instructed in, V1:219

Bennett, John C., at Nauvoo, Prophet denounces, V5:34-5

Church, conducting in, taught, V1:219

Clay County, citizens of, V2:96

Clay County, second of citizens of, V2:454

disturbance in, V2:98

false reports, public at Nauvoo, to correct, V6:48?

Joseph on leaving at close of, V5:363

Kirtland Temple, of classes in, V2:474

Kirtland Temple, minutes of, V2:512

local affairs at Nauvoo, appeal to government on, V6:107

Missouri, aggressions of, V6:111-3

Nauvoo, public at, V6:101

MEETINGS (continued)

    political at Nauvoo, addressed by Prophet, V5:19

    saints, of, in Clay County, minutes of, V2:452, et seq

    saints, general of, in Missouri, V2:524

    Spirit, public to be conducted by, V1:163, ftnt only

    Twelve Apostles, at which are chosen, V2:181, et seq

    Warsaw, mass at, V6:462-6.

meetings, street, held in England, Church accosted, V4:182-4.

Meetze, Mr., mentioned, V7:175.

Meginness, Benjamin, V5:525.

Mellen, J. D., merchant, member of martyrdom mob, V7:144.

Melling, John, ordained priest, V4:148.

Melling, Peter, British Church assignment, V4:149

    British conference, represents branch of Church at, V4:116, 48

    Church, appointed to preside over branches of, V4:149

    high priest, ordained, V5:136

    Nauvoo, reports to the Prophet at, V4:543

    patriarch, ordained and genealogy, V4:120 and ftnt.

memorial, action of meeting on, V6:88

    answer to Joseph and high council at Nauvoo, V4:138, 141 and ftnt, 144-5

    Congress, Joseph's, V6:275

    House of Representatives, before, V6:282 and ftnt

    Joseph to President John Tyler, V6:281-2

    Joseph to high council at Nauvoo, V4:136-7

    Kirtland, bishopric's, V2:513, 515, et seq

    Missouri persecutions, of John Frierson to Congress on, V6:84, et seq

    Nauvoo City Council, petitioning Congress for redress and protection, V6:125, et seq

    officially signed by mayor and city council, V6:116

    origin of Joseph's westward memorial, V6:270

    saints to Senate and House of Representatives, V4:24, et seq.

Mendenhall, Solomon, witnesses celestial phenomenon, V6:121.

Mercantile and Mechanical Association, proposed formation of in Nauvoo, V7:369.

mercantile stores, establishment of common among brethren, V1:270 and ftnt.

mercy, Relief Society exhorted to exercise, V5:23-5.

Meriam, Dr., mentioned, V1:287, ftnt only.

meridian of time, of the, IntroV1:XXIX

MERIDIAN OF TIME (continued)

    fulness of time, as to, considered, IntroV1:XXX.

    See also dispensation.

Merkley, Christopher, mentioned, V4:488.

Merriam, Edwin P., child of dies, V3:134

    Kirtland Camp, leaves, V3:140

    Kirtland Camp, mentioned in, V3:106

    Kirtland Camp, subscribed to constitution of, V3:93

    stake president, appointed, V4:236.

Merriam, Elijah, subscribed to constitution of Kirtland Camp, V3:92.

Merrick, Charles, killed at Haun's Mills by mob, age nine, V3:326, ftnt only.

Merrick, Lemuel, covenanted to assist saints in removing from Missouri, V3:253.

Merrick, Levi N., killed by mob at Haun's Mills, V3:326, ftnt only.

Merrill, Philemon C., Joseph, mission to rescue, V5:451

    mentioned, V7:622

    militia to fight Indians, V7:627.

Merrimam, Colonel, anti-Mormon troops of, V7:46-7.

Merryweather, F., delegate to political convention in Nauvoo, V6:389

    mentioned, V6:386.

mesmerism, objected to in Nauvoo, V5:383.

messenger, John the Baptist appears, V1:39

    Joseph instructed to return to plates every four years, V1:16

    plates, calls for, V1:18

    plates, delivers and charge, V1:18

    plates, forbids taking, V1:16

    plates, still has, V1:18-9

    sacrament, reveals instructions on, V1:106

    Urim and Thummim, returns to Joseph, V1:21.

    See also John the Baptist; Moroni.

Messenger and Advocate, Latter-day Saints, Church doctrine, first number of prints basic, V2:167 and ftnt

    Cowdery, Oliver, editor of, V1:409

    Marks, William, transferred to, V2:486

    published, to be, at Kirtland, V1:409

    Star, commenced to replace the, V2:167, ftnt only

    Whitmer, John, to conduct, V2:227.

    See also Latter-day Saints, Church of Jesus Christ of; newspapers.

Messenger, Mr., Universalist minister, hears truth but will not accept, V2:311.

Messiah, spirit of comes after that of Elijah, V6:254.

Methodist priest, Booth, Ezra, was, before baptism, V1:215
  publishes anti-Mormon pamphlet in England, V3:22.

Methodists, baptized in England so fast becoming scarce, V4:96
  contending for, V1:3
  excitement commenced with, V1:2
  excommunicated from, for hearing missionaries, V2:312
  joining, uncertainty at, V1:3
  Joseph partial to, V1:3
  martyrdom, mistake of lady member of, at, V7:112
  ministers, forty, converted in England, V4:117
  ministers of, join Church in England, V4:123
  Missouri mobs, participated in, V1:392
  mob, minister at head of, V3:158
  opinion on oath of priest of, V2:448
  others try to disapprove, V1:4
  persecution commences, V1:108
  preacher hears vision story, V1:6
  Presbyterians against, V1:4
  right or wrong cannot conclude, V1:4
  spirit of righteousness, destitute of the, V2:319
  Squires, A. J., confesses error of joining, V2:319
  vision, rejects, V1:6
  writer of against Church on Isle of Man, V4:234.

Metoka, sailing of with saints, V6:4.

Meyers, Mr., delegate to political convention in Nauvoo, V6:389.

Michael the Archangel, is Adam, V3:386.
  See also Adam.

Middah, George, mission call in Illinois to disabuse public mind over arrest of Joseph, V5:485.

Middleton, Reuben, covenanted to assist saints in removing from Missouri, V3:253.

Middleton, William, kidnapper of saints, V6:123
  kidnaps Daniel Avery, V6:146.

Middow, George, called on mission and field of labor, V5:348.

Mifflin, Mr., baptism of, V5:311.

Mikesell, Garret W., mission appointment published and field of labor, V6:338.

Mikesell, Hiram W., elder, appointed, V4:13
    mission appointment published and field of labor, V6:338.

Mikesell, J. A., delegate to political convention in Nauvoo, V6:390.

Milam, William, covenanted to assist saints in removing from Missouri, V3:252.

Miles, Daniel S., approved for ordination, V2:400
    seventies, sustained president of, V2:510, V7:297.

Miles, Ira S., Joseph, accompanies in arrest, V4:366
    volunteers for exploring expedition, V6:225.

Miles, Joel S., Joseph, accompanies in arrest, V4:366
    witness at *Expositor* trial, V6:491.

Miles, William H., mentioned, V6:286.

militia, arms, requisitions saints, V1:434
    Atchison, General, report of, to Governor Boggs concerning, V3:80-1
    disarmed, V3:192
    mob, called out by Lieutenant Governor Boggs, composed of, V1:433
    mob as, report of movements of, by General Lucas, V3:195, et seq
    movements of, V3:78
    prisoners, contends among self for, V3:200 and ftnt.
    See also mob; persecutions, Missouri.

"Millennial Harbinger," anti-Church pamphlet, V2:268.

Millennial Star, editor, Parley P. Pratt resumes as, V4:224
    emigration, article on to Nauvoo and opposition to same, V4:510, et seq
    England, monthly periodical to be published in, V4:119
    first issuance of, first foreign Church paper, V4:133 and ftnt
    numbers published enumerated, V4:253
    prospectus of, V4:122, 133, ftnt only
    publications to cease, V5:194.

millennium, Christ, reign described, V5:212
    saints, ancient to reign with Christ during, V2:53
    wickedness to be on earth during, V5:212.
    See also doctrine; Jesus Christ.

Miller, Mr., aged saint attacked by mob, V1:469.

Miller, Allen, arrested for supplying mob and trial, V3:75-6.

Miller, Bethuel, mission appointment published and field of labor, V6:335.

Miller, Charles, represents area in British conference, V5:9, 419; V6:2, 327.

Miller, Daniel, bishop, appointed, V4:233
    elder, appointed, V4:13.

Miller, Eleazer, (also spelled Eleazur), baptized, V4:110, ftnt only
    mission to Canada, V1:296, ftnt only
    seventies, ordained president of, V7:314
    utility committee member to aid Church removal, V7:474
    westward movement, in, V7:626
    Zions Camp, brings reinforcements to, V2:76
    Zions Camp member, V2:184
    Zions Camp, speaks in, V2:78, ftnt only.

Miller, George, arrested at Carthage for treason, defiance of court, V7:442-3
    bishop, appointed by revelation to, V4:286
    Church, appointed trustee-in-trust for, V7:247
    Church, sustained second bishop of, V7:297
    endowment, receives in Nauvoo Temple, V7:543
    excommunicated from Church, V3:336
    fellowship withdrawn from, V7:618
    high priest quorum, to preside over at Nauvoo, V4:424
    high priest quorum, sustained president of after death of Joseph, V7:296
    interview with Governor Ford, V7:492-3
    Joseph, accompanies in arrest, V4:366
    Joseph declares gratefulness for aid rendered while in seclusion, V5:108
    Joseph, secretly goes to inform of movement of sheriff, V5:97
    Legion, general in, V5:165
    letter to Missouri governor on John C. Bennett character, V5:46, et seq
    masons, publishes expulsion of John C. Bennett from, V5:32
    messenger, sent as, to Governor Ford, V7:490
    Michigan, letter to recommending petitioning Congress for grant of land in, V7:367
    mission, returns from, V6:61
    Nauvoo, delegate to political convention at, V6:390
    Nauvoo Temple, appointed to officiate in, V7:547
    remarks of at conference, V7:293.

Miller, Henry W., Church, appointed to preside over new district of, V7:306

MILLER, HENRY W. (continued)

    elder, appointed, V4:13

    mentioned, V7:541

    revelation, requests on duties, V4:311

    stake president, appointed at Freedom, V4:233.

Miller, John, mission call in Illinois to disabuse public mind over Joseph's arrest, V5:485

    Missouri, covenanted to assist saints in removing from, V3:252

    Zions Camp member, V2:184.

Miller, Josiah, Kirtland Camp, expelled from for sins of son-in-law, V3:128-9

    Kirtland Camp, subscribed to constitution of, V3:92.

Miller, Joshua, mentioned, V6:452.

Miller, Mary Catharine, receives endowment in Nauvoo Temple, V7:543.

Miller, Reuben, bishop, ordained, V7:312

    Melchizedek Priesthood, records testimony of restoration of, V1:41, ftnt only

    poor, aid solicited by, V7:293.

Miller, Sarah, testifies of C. L. Higbee's adulterous actions, V6:407.

Miller, Thomas, charged with disorderly conduct, V6:155.

Miller, William, Millerism, founder of, teachings of, V5:272 and ftnt

    second coming, false prediction of noted, V5:326 and ftnt.

Miller, William, Bogus Brigham incident, arrested as Brigham Young, V7:549

    elder, ordained, V4:333

    Nauvoo, delegate to political convention in, V6:389.

Millerism, exposed as false, V5:272 and ftnt.

Millet, Artemus, Kirtland Temple, blessing on for work on, V2:205

    Presidency, issues complaint against, V2:484.

Milliken, Mrs., mentioned, V7:176.

Milliken, Nathaniel, appointed doorkeeper to House of Lord, V2:367.

Millikin, Arthur, Joseph declares gratefulness for aid rendered while in seclusion, V5:109

    Smith, Lucy, husband to, V5:109.

Millport, mob, burn their own houses at, V3:164 and ftnt

    mob troubles at, V3:163.

Mills, Alexander, mentioned, V5:42

    policeman in Nauvoo, V6:149.

Mills, Ira, witness suggested to appear before Congress on redress, V4:97.

Milner, Albert, elder, ordained, V4:13.

Miner, Albert, Kirtland Temple, blessing for work on, V2:206
  Missouri, covenanted to assist saints in removing from, V3:253.

Minger, Jeremiah, mentioned, V2:454.

ministers, sectarian, mobbing, connection with in Jackson County, V1:392 and ftnt
  opposition of, V1:372 and ftnt

Minor, James L., mentioned, V5:464.

Minor, Private, mobbed, V6:525.

miracle, Church, first done in, V1:82-3
  devil cast out considered, V1:83
  gospel not to be established by, V2:317
  healing of dead child, V6:187
  Hiram, in, V1:215 and ftnt
  Joseph, seen but not recognized, V1:109.
  See also healing; Holy Ghost; Smith, Joseph.

mission, Apostles, first commenced, V2:222
  Australian opened, V4:343
  Canadian Provinces, report of J. W. Crosby on, V7:317
  China, earthquake in blamed on Church, V1:158 and ftnt
  Church policy in respect of, V3:154 and ftnt
  Eastern states, call to, V5:413
  Flanigan, James H., report of labors of, V7:522
  foreign ministry, review of organization of, IntroV2:XXIV
  Fox Island, V2:507 and ftnt
  France, V6:356
  Germany, V5:368
  great movement commenced on, V5:347, et seq
  East India, V4:168
  Ireland, introduction to, V4:170 and ftnt
  Isle of Man, V4:234, et seq
  members get assigned to, V4:429-30
  Nova Scotia, call to, V5:413
  Pacific Island, report of success in, V7:618
  Palestine, mission to, V4:106, IntroV4:XXXI, et seq
  Russia, V5:417, V6:41
  Snow, J. C., report on, V7:527
  Society Islands, letter of Addison Pratt on, V7:271
  Society Islands, report of work in 1844, V7:313

MISSION (continued)

South, report of B. L. Clapp to, V7:316
South America, opened, V4:413
South Wales, opened in, V5:281-2
Southern states, progress of, V7:253
volunteers called to go on, V3:153-4.
See also Latter-day Saints, Church of Jesus Christ of.

Mission, Australian, opened, V4:343; V4:154
report of work in, V4:343-4.

Mission, Lamanite, Catteraugus tribe, visit to, V1:210, ftnt only
departure of, V1:120
Independence, arrives at, V1:182
Kirtland, arrives in, V1:120
report of, V1:182-5 and ftnts.
See also Lamanites.

Mission, Nova Scotia, opened, V5:413.

Mission, Pacific Isles, opened, V5:385, 404-5.
See also mission.

Mission, Palestine, Hyde, Orson, credentials of, to, V4:112
Hyde, Orson, letter of July 17, 1841, detailing events en route to Jerusalem, V4:384, et seq
Hyde, Orson, reproved for delaying, V4:274
Hyde, Orson, returns from, V5:200
Page, Elder, rejects chance to proceed on, V4:372
viewed, IntroV4:XXXI, et seq.
See also Orson Hyde, John E. Page.

Mission, Society Islands, missionaries' arrival at, V7:252-3
opened to, V5:404
Pratt, Addison, letter on, V7:271
work, report of, V7:313.
See also mission, Pacific Isles.

Mission, South America, opened, V4:413.

Mission of Elijah, preparing for second coming, V3:390.
See also Elijah.

missionaries, children, preach first to parents before, V2:262
cry repentance and first principles only, V5:344
England, arrival of some in, V4:104
families, leave provided for, V5:350
gospel, endeavors in establishing, V2:40
instructions to, as leave to labors, V5:350, et seq
instructions to in *Evening & Morning Star*, V1:280

MISSIONARIES (continued)

   liberty statement published in *Times & Seasons*, V4:234
   not boys unless accompanied by adult, V1:468
   requirements, V5:350
   special list of, V5:485
   teach in plainness, should not go forth unless qualified to, V2:136
   two by two, need not go, V2:431.

missionary movement, called and commenced amidst mob action in
        Missouri, V3:154 and ftnt.
   See also missions.

missionary work, Lamanites, starts to, V1:181
   be seventy if desired to do, V7:308
   parable of fisher's net compared to, V2:272
   tribe of Joseph, voted to open door to remnants of, V2:222.
   See also missions.

Mississippi River, commercial dam proposed in, V7:377
   floods of, 1846, V7:8
   Montrose, frozen over at, V7:598
   Nauvoo, dam to be erected on, at, V6:106
   westward camp, members cross on ice, V7:600.

Missouri, apostrophe to, by E. R. Snow, V6:192
   curse to remain on until redress to saints, V5:211
   "Friendly hint," to, V6:245-7
   internal civil regulation explained, V3:455-6
   Legislature, action of on Mormon difficulties, V4:299 and ftnt
   peace proposals to, V6:218-20
   saints petition to governor of, V1:410, et seq.
   See also Boggs, Lilburn W.; Missouri correspondence; persecutions,
        Missouri.

Missouri, Caldwell County, See Caldwell County, Missouri.

Missouri, Independence, Jackson County, *Evening & Morning Star*,
        to be published at, V1:217
   Joseph arrives at, V1:188
   Joseph's impression of, V1:189
   Joseph leaves for Kirtland from, V1:202
   mob, first regular in, V1:342
   temple spot west of, V1:199.
   See also Missouri; mob; persecutions; Zion.

Missouri correspondence, arms, letter to Colonel Lucas requesting return
        of, V1:492 and ftnt

MISSOURI CORRESPONDENCE (continued)

Dunklin, Governor, letter to brethren in Missouri, reasoning because no general emergency "of a public nature" cannot give constant protection, V1:476-8 and ftnt

Dunklin, Governor, letter to, informing him of damages and that arms had been given to mob, V1:491-2

Dunklin, Governor, letter to informing him that members would be arriving from the East to give aid and assistance, V1:489-91

Dunklin, Governor, letter to saints informing that their arms were wrongfully taken and an order had been issued to return them, V1:491

First Presidency, letter to scattered saints consoling them and sending news of events in Kirtland, V1:474-6

Gilbert, Sidney, letter of, concerning civil trial problems for damages, V1:478-9

Gilbert, Sidney, letter to Governor Dunklin expressing difficulty in Mormons' testifying because of mob in Jackson County, V1:472-4

mob, affidavit of Abigail Leonard concerning beating given to her husband by, V1:480

Phelps, W. W., letter to brethren in Kirtland detailing attempt at legal redress and the effort of the officers of Missouri to enforce the law, V1:481-3 and ftnt

Phelps, W. W., letter to Judge Woodward requesting a copy of the trial of Colonel Pitcher, V1:479-80

president, Governor Dunklin's letter to the saints refusing to write the, in their behalf, V1:488-9

president, W. W. Phelps' letter to Senator Benton of Missouri on the subject of the petition to, V1:487-8

president, letter of brethren to Governor Dunklin requesting that he write the, in their behalf, V1:487

president, letter to saints refusing to give assistance, V1:493

saints, order to Colonel Lucas to restore arms to, V1:491

United States, Sidney Gilbert's letter to president of, accompanying petition, V1:485-7

United States, petition to the president of, for aid and assistance and protection, V1:483-5

witnesses, letter to Judge Ryland from brethren requesting guard for, V1:479.

See also affidavit; Boggs, Lilburn W.; Latter-day Saints, Church of Jesus Christ of; letters; Missouri trials; mob; persecutions; saints; Smith, Joseph.

Missouri Enquirer, Evening & Morning Star, started from ruins of, V1:470
    Zions Camp, publishes communication between Joseph and Sheriff Gilliam while in, V2:121.
    See also newspapers.

Missouri Legislature, appropriation to mob, V4:74, ftnt only
    investigation, character of, before, V3:240
    mob, member of heads, V3:158
    Mormons, hears report on, is in total uproar, V3:238
    saints, appropriation of, to, and use of, V3:243 and ftnts
    saints, case of, before, V3:217, et seq, 234, et seq
    saints' petition, action of, on, V3:242-3 and ftnts.

Missouri Republican, account of martyrdom in, V7:180.

Missouri Senate, resolutions by, on Mormon difficulties, V3:246.

Missouri trials, arraignment hearing, conclusion of, V3:212
    Avard, Sampson, first witness against saints at, V3:209
    brethren, some discharged, V3:211
    Church leaders arraigned, V3:209
    mittimus of transferring prisoners to jail, V3:214
    prophecy of Daniel included in, V3:212 and ftnt
    witnesses called and sworn at bayonet point at, V3:209
    witnesses for saints jailed or threatened, V3:210-11
    witness for state enumerated, V3:210
    witnesses, some called for defense, V3:211.
    See also Missouri persecutions

Mitchell, Samuel L., Book of Mormon characters shown to, V1:20 and ftnt
    Harris, Martin, calls upon, V1:20 and ftnt.

Mitchell, William, mentioned, V4:215.

Mitchelson, Mr., represents branches of Church at English conference, V6:327.

Mitchelson, George, raises child from death, V6:186-7.

Mitchelson, Mary Jane, raised from death, V6:186-7.

mittimus, Carthage, false that imprisoned Joseph and Hyrum at, V6:569-70
    Carthage, second of, remanding Joseph and Hyrum to prison at, V6:597
    Liberty, of court transferring prisoners to jail, V3:214-5.

M'Lellin, William E., apostasy of, V3:215 and ftnt
    challenge, accepts Campbellite preacher's , V2:218

M'LELLIN, WILLIAM E. (continued)

    commandment, attempts to write, V1:226
    excommunication of, V3:31, ftnt only
    fellowship withdrawn for insulting School of the Prophets, V2:240
    genealogy of, V1:220 and ftnt
    high council, sustained to Missouri, V2:124
    revelation to, V1:220-1
    saints, plunders and robs houses of, V3:215 and ftnt
    stealing and looting, accused of from Joseph's house, V3:287
    transgression of, failure to pray, V3:31 and ftnt
    Twelve Apostles, blessing on as member of, V2:190
    Twelve Apostles, chosen as one of, V2:187
    Twelve Apostles, sustained as one of to Church, V2:509.

mob, actions of November 1, 1833, V1:427-8 and ftnts
    actions of November 2, 1833, beating of David Bennett, V1:429
    actions of November 4, 1833, battle of Big Blue River, first encounter
        between two armed groups, V1:429-32
    actions of November 5 and 6, 1833, ravaging of saints, V1:436
    actions of December 24, 1833, on aged saints, V1:469
    Adam-ondi-Ahman, action of toward, V3:162-3
    agreement between, in Jackson County and saints, V1:394-5
    Allen, C., Missouri, tars and feathers, V1:391 and ftnt
    attacks saints at Big Blue October 31, 1833, V1:426
    attacks settlement outside Independence, V1:427
    baptism, breaks dam for, V1:86
    baptism, collects at, V1:88
    Boggs, Lilburn, leader of,V1:437
    British Mission, violence in, V4:361
    burning and murder, leaders of, accuse saints of, V3:165
    Caldwell, attacks and plunders, V3:192
    Caldwell County, action of towards saints in, V3:74
    Call, Anson, beaten by, V3:245
    citizens and saints covenant to defend against, V3:60
    Colesville, threatens branch at, V1:109
    composed of Campbellites, Methodists, Baptists, V1:265
    constitution, secret, of slavery question, IntroV3:XXIV
    converts, attempts to disuade, V1:87
    Cowan, Horace, Missouri, jailed for debt, V3:289
    Crooked River, battles saints at, V3:170-1
    Daviess County, commences in, V3:57, et seq
    description of July 23, 1833, V1:394-5 and ftnts
    DeWitt, drives saints from, V3:159

MOB (continued)

DeWitt, warns saints of, to leave, V3:77

DeWitt, General Wilson endorses actions of, at, V3:157

expulsion, Missouri, committee of, agrees to terms of, of saints, V3:216

extermination order, Missouri, march of, under, V3:182

Far West, actions and depravations of, at, V3:202

Far West, commences action near, V3:165-6

Far West, plunders and pillages, V3:191

Far West, plunders saints' property at, V3:322-3

Gilliam, Cornelius, raises more, V3:161

Haun's Mills, composed of, V3:186

Jackson County, action of in, V1:426, et seq

Jackson County, activities of to prevent saints' return to, V2:92-3 and ftnts

Joseph advises to "mow a hole through them," V6:99

Joseph, attacks, March 24, 1832, V1:261, et seq and ftnt

Joseph, follows to Newel Knight's home, V1:88

Joseph, Missouri, George M. Hinkle makes secret arrangements with to turn over, V3:188

Joseph, Missouri, swears not to eat nor drink until kill, V3:306

Joseph and Oliver, pursues, V1:97

Kirtland, forces Joseph and Sidney to flee, V3:1

Kirtland, pursues Joseph after leaving, V3:3

Kirtland Temple, guarded against, V2:2

Knight, Joseph, again convenes at, V1:97

Knight, Joseph, surrounds home of, V1:88

lion, member of, reported brethren fought like, V3:59

mail, prevents, to saints, V3:166, V6:450

manifesto of, V1:374, et seq

meeting, attends, V1:86

members of described, V1:372-3 and ftnts

members, fate of, V1:264-5

member of shoots cow to get strip of hide to tie up horse, V3:323

militia composed of, V1:433

Missouri, again begins in, V1:372

Missouri, character of, IntroV3:XIX

Missouri collects and demands, July 20, 1833, V1:390 and ftnt

Missouri, composition of, IntroV3:XVIII

Missouri, composition of, names, sects, station, V1:392 and ftnt

Missouri, enlightened, IntroV3:XVII, et seq

Missouri, tars and feathers and does violence to brethren in, V1:390-1 and ftnts

MOB (continued)

Missouri persecutions, political fears of, in, IntroV3:XXVII, et seq

mob, leaders of swear oath that saints are, V3:61

Mormons, all not opposed to, May 1, 1834, V2:62

Mormons, burns own houses and accuses, V3:164 and ftnt

Patten, David W., kills, V3:171

Pinkham, raids house of and takes prisoners, V3:169

political issues concerned saints very little, IntroV3:XXVII

political jealousy, prompted by, IntroV3:XXVIII

political power, fears of, concerning saints, IntroV3:XXVIII

politics, a real cause of, in Missouri, IntroV3:XXIX

prisoners, takes, V3:182

prophecy, Missouri, Joseph gives, against, V3:227

prophecy, threat of one, and self destroying, V2:99-100

religious life, comments on, of saints, IntroV3:XLVIII, et seq

Root, Henry, affidavit of, concerning, in DeWitt, V3:149

saints, answering proposal to buy land, V2:98-9

saints, assures, of losses, V1:400

saints, complaints of, to Governor Boggs against, V3:77

saints, declare independence from, V3:41

saints, expelled from Van Buren County, Missouri, V1:456-7

saints, fires cannon to alarm, V2:2

saints, forced to leave homes in rain, V3:58

saints, none to escape, V1:469

saints, offer to buy lands of, rejected, V2:107

saints, presents offer to buy out, V2:96-7

settlement terms of, V3:196-7

storm, prevented by, V2:103-4 and ftnt

threats, first of, V1:44

treaty between, and saints, V1:394-5

Turley, Brother, Missouri, action of, against, V3:322

women and children, authorities expounded upon driving of, blood path across wilderness, V1:438 and ftnt

Zion, declarations of, as parting to, V1:398

Zion, first regular in, V1:342

Zions Camp, invades and threatens destruction, V2:103.

See also affidavit; Latter-day Saints, Church of Jesus Christ of; letters; Missouri correspondence; persecutions, Missouri; persecutions; saints; stories.

mob, **Carthage,** affairs in resisting officers, V6:171, et seq

complaints before Nauvoo City Council, V6:173-4.

See also Illinois persecutions.

Mobley, Myres, lends firelock shop to Zions Camp, V2:88, ftnt only.

Modisett, Doctor, British missionaries, aids, V4:15
    Kimball, Heber C., gives morphine to, V4:15.

Modisett, James, mission, assists Elders Young and Kimball on, V4:17.

Moeser, Frederick H., to go on mission to Germany, V5:368.

Moeser, Frederick J., mentioned, V5:541.

Moesseur, O. F., witness at *Expositor* trial, V6:489.

Moffit, Levi, accompanies Joseph for trial on Missouri warrants, V5:210.

Moffitt, Armstead, (also spelled Moffet), mission appointment published
        and field of labor, V6:338
    Nauvoo, policeman in, V6:150.

molest, of Mormon women by Missouri mob, V3:422
    of Mormon women in Missouri, V3:428, 464.

money, members responsible for Church and poor, V3:29.
    See also bishop, poor.

money-digger, accusation, source of, V1:17
    Joseph accused of being, V1:93
    Joseph as a, V3:29.
    See also Smith, Joseph.

Monjar, William, mentioned, V3:319.

monogamy, article accepting, V2:246-7.
    See also Latter-day Saints, Church of Jesus Christ of; doctrine;
        marriage.

"Monroe," Cowdery, Oliver, discussion on steamer, V2:168-9.

Monroe, Henry, Kirtland Camp, dissents against, V3:138.

Monroe, James M., (also spelled Munroe), MIA, aids in movement
        toward, V5:322
    mission call and field of labor, V5:347
    Seventies Library and Institute Association, elected trustee of, V7:328.

Montague, John, no business, member of martyrdom mob, V7:144.

Montgomery, Mr., mentioned, V5:449, 458, 526.

moon, reason called by feminine name, V5:211.

Moon, Francis, England, on first sailing of saints from, V4:134
    English conference, represents branch of Church at, V4:117.

Moon, Henry, on first sailing of saints from England, V4:134.

Moon, Hugh, on first sailing of saints from England, V4:134.

Moon, John, England, on first sailing of saints from, V4:134
    English conference, represents branch of Church at, V4:116

MOON, JOHN (continued)

gather, arrival in New York from England, first to, V4:162
mission appointment published and field of labor, V6:335.

Moon, William, elder, ordained, V4:333.

Moore, Mr., mentioned, V5:540.

Moore, Andrew, anti-Mormon committee chairman, V6:8.

Moore, David, elder, ordained, V5:349.

Moore, Ethan A., Kirtland Camp, leaves, V3:138
Kirtland Camp, subscribed to constitution of, V3:93.

Moore, Harvey J., covenanted to assist saints in removing from Missouri, V3:253.

Moore, Henry, elder, ordained, V5:349
England, on first sailing of saints from, V4:134.

Moore, James, mentioned, V6:161.

Moore, John, mentioned, V4:479, 480.

Moore, Lorenzo, mission appointment and field of labor, V6:338.

Moore, Robert C., Joseph, on relief expedition for, V5:482.

Moore, Samuel, mentioned, V4:484.

Moore, Thomas, Joseph blesses, V5:264
mentioned, V5:386.

Moppin, Perry, seeks Mormon life, V4:63.

More, Andrew, covenanted to assist saints in removing from Missouri, V3:252.

Morehead, C. R., mentioned, V3:172
sends more inflammatory communication to Boggs, V3:166.

Morehead, George R., proposition of Mormons addressed to, V2:122.

Morey, Captain, mentioned, V3:409.

Morey, Elder, manliness of, V2:401.

Morey, George, apostates, plundered and robbed by, V3:215
Far West, elected to high council at, V2:504
high constable, sworn as, V4:308
Joseph, pays money in hour of need, V2:327
Missouri, arrival from, V2:321.

Morey, Sister, mentioned, V5:209.

Morgan, Arthur, anti-Mormon committee chairman, V6:8.

Morgan, Captain, mentioned, V7:274, 494.

Morgan, Elizabeth, death of in England, V4:551.

Morgan, James, British Mission, mission in, V4:150
devote all time to labors of ministry, V4:148.

Morgan, James D., mentioned, V3:267, 271.

Morgan, John, ordained priest, V4:138
  president English branch, V4:140.

Morgan, Samuel G., mentioned, V2:350, ftnt only.

Morgan, Thomas, mentioned, V5:282.

Morgan, William, mentioned, V3:321, ftnt only
  sheriff for Daviess County, mob leader accuses saints of false actions,
      V3:165.

Morin, Joseph, Joseph, notifies of writ for him, V3:63
  saints, warns people to vote against, V3:56
  State Senator, elected, V3:60.

Morley, Harley, mission appointment published and field of labor, V6:335.

Morley, Isaac, affidavit of mob attempting to draft into service, V6:510
  bishop, to be, in Zion, V1:363
  endowments, called to go to Kirtland to receive, V2:112
  endowments, receives in Nauvoo Temple, V7:543
  Far West, opposes local presidency at, V3:5
  Far West, sustained counselor to bishop at, V2:524
  Joseph, letter to, on mob threats, V6:481
  Lima, president at, V5:427
  mission, appointed to Missouri, V1:178
  Missouri, arraigned for treason, murder, burglary, arson, robbery,
      and larceny at Richmond, V3:209
  Missouri trials, discharged as innocent at, V3:211
  patriarch, sustained at Far West, V2:524
  ransom, offers himself for saints in Jackson County, V1:394, ftnt only
  revelation, stating Lord was pleased with, V2:302
  saints, signs memorial of, in Missouri, V3:224
  stake president, appointed at Lima, V4:233, V5:427
  westward movement, captain of fourth company in, V7:481
  westward movement, president in, V7:626
  Zion, arrives in, V1:191.

Morley, Lucy, receives endowment in Nauvoo Temple, V7:543.

Morley settlement, burnings at, V7:440.

Mormon, Book of, ancient ruins evidence of, V6:53
  Anthon, Professor, translation taken to, V1:20
  apostles preach on, V6:24
  copyright arranged, V1:71
  copyright of, V1:58-9 and ftnt

MORMON, BOOK OF (continued)

corrections of, V4:494

counted as strange thing, V1:84

Cowdery, Oliver, assists translation, V1:32, 33

England, first edition in, V4:274, 286

Grandin, Egbert B., published, V1:71

Harding, Stephen, statement of respecting translation of, V1:75, ftnt only

Harris, Martin, sister-in-law to see translation of, V1:21

Hebrew writing in, in general, V1:71

index finished to in England, V4:286

Isaiah, fulfills prophecy of, V1:84

Joseph arrested for preaching, V1:88

Joseph author and proprietor, V1:58, ftnt only

Joseph, preface of, to, V1:56-7

Joseph states is most correct and keystone of religion, V4:461

Joseph, stick of, V1:84

language, copies of ancient, V1:19

language, written in, V1:20

manuscript, Martin Harris loses, V1:21

manuscript, two copies of, made, V1:75, ftnt only

mustard seed, likened to parable of, V2:268

Nauvoo edition, proofs of read by Prophet, V4:494, 500-1

New Testament translation, proposed to be published with, V1:341

obtained, how, V3:28

plates, A. Beaman helps conceal, V2:43, ftnt only

plates, first seen by Joseph, V1:16

poem on, V6:181-3

printing, first arranged, V1:71

printing, difficulties and care in, V1:75-6, ftnt only

printing house, guard on, V1:75, ftnt only

Prophet, delivered to the, V1:18

publish, attempt to, in periodical, V1:76, ftnt only

published, V1:84

Rigdon, Sidney, presented to, V1:122-3, ftnt only

salvation, Almon W. Babbitt tried for teaching not essential for, reproved, V2:252

testimony of, in obituary of Samuel Smith, V7:216, et seq

three witnesses, provides for, V1:52 and ftnt

title page, literal translation, V1:71

translation began, V1:20

translation commences, V1:32

MORMON, BOOK OF (continued)

  translation drawing to close, V1:71
  Victoria, Queen, presented to, V6:181
  vision where located, V1:13
  witnesses, several of , assist in, V1:49.
  See also angel; doctrine; Egyptian; Harris, Martin; Moroni; Smith,
    Joseph; stories; Urim and Thummim.

Mormon, Book of, lost pages of, taken from Martin Harris, V1:21.

Mormonism, *Boston Weekly Bee* on, V5:322, et seq
  publications pro and con for, 1843, V6:154
  Western Monitor on, V1:395, et seq
  See also Latter-day Saints, Church of Jesus Christ of; Smith, Joseph.

"Mormonism, Early Days of," article by J. H. Kennedy, V1:158, ftnt only.

"Mormonism Unveiled," anti-Mormon article by E. D. Howe, V1:217,
    ftnt only.

Mormon Battalion, Church requests raising of, for U. S. Army, V7:611
  misapprehensions concerning, V7:613
  raising of, V7:612
  raising, time element in, V7:613
  Salt Lake Valley, invalided companies reach, V7:616.

"Mormon Beef," human flesh fed to Joseph and prisoners in Missouri,
    V3:420.
  See also flesh; persecutions, Missouri.

Mormon Spring, spring discovered by Zions Camp, V2:73.

Mormon War, The, militia action in Missouri called, V3:429.

Mormonism in China, earthquake blamed on Church, V1:158 and ftnt.

Mormons, Bennett, J. A., article by, defending, V5:170, et seq
  damned, everyone but, V3:28
  definition of, V5:399
  improvements by, V6:195-6
  Nauvoo and the, V4:565, et seq
  obliterated, must be from the face of the earth, V7:544
  obliteration, prayer against, V7:544
  Jackson County, propositions to citizens of, V2:121-2
  Jackson County, proposition of people to, V2:96-7
  reproach, name used as, V2:254
  sectarian ministers in Missouri, action against, V2:3
  Taylor, apprehensions of, V7:62
  uprising of, false reports, V7:4.
  See also Latter-day Saints, Church of Jesus Christ of; Mormonism;
    Smith, Joseph.

Mormons, History of the, by Smucker, records M. Harris's visit to Professor Mitchell, V1:20, ftnt only.

Moroni, Acts, Book of, quotes from, V1:13
   appearance, first of, V1:11 and ftnt
   Brewster, C., claims to have seen, V2:520
   description of, V1:11
   heaven, ascension into of, V1:13
   Nephi, erroneously called, V1:11, ftnt only
   reappearance, first, V1:13
   reappearance, second, V1:14
   reappearance by fence, V1:15
   Whitmer, David, speaks to, V1:54
   witnesses, appears to, V1:54-5.
   See also angel; messenger.

Morrill, Franklin J., mobber in Illinois, V5:528.

Morris, Mr., mentioned, V3:270-1, 351.

Morris, I. N., recommends Brother Green to collect for poor, V3:348.

Morris, J. N., mentioned, V4:267.

Morris, Jacob, mission appointment published and field of labor, V6:339.

Morris, Laban, subscribed to constitution of Kirtland Camp, V3:93.

Morrish, W. J., warns flock against Mormons, V4:254.

Morrison, Mr., mentioned, V7:66.

Morrison, A., mentioned, V7:158.

Morrison, Arthur, mentioned, V6:426.

Morrison, Doctor, mentioned, V7:172.

Morrison, Thomas, anti-Mormon meeting, messenger to Governor Ford from, V6:466
   martyrdom mob, member of, lawyer, V7:144
   Nauvoo City Council, affidavit against, V7:66-7.

Morse, John, justice of the peace in Missouri, V3:152.

Morse, Justin, Zions Camp member, V2:184.

Morse, Justus A., mentioned, V5:302
   mission appointment published and field of labor, V6:337.

Morton, William B., V3:149.

Moses, John the Baptist, gospel from, to, IntroV1:XXVIII
   Law of, added to gospel because of transgression, V2:17

MOSES (continued)

Pearl of Great Price, word of God revealed to, in, V1:98, et seq
priesthood, gave keys of to Peter, James, and John on Mount, V3:387.
See also gospel.

Moses, Brother, child of buried, V3:376.

Moses, Law of, added to gospel because of transgression, V2:17.

Moss, Mr., family of refuses drink to Joseph and is attacked by cholera, V2:115.

Moss or Morse, Mr., one of the Durfee murderers, member of martyrdom mob, V7:145.

Moss, David, volunteers for service in vineyard, V4:216.

Moss, I., mentioned, V2:456.

Moss, J., mentioned, V2:449.

Moss, Thomas, on first sailing of saints from England, V4:134.

Moss, W. J., committee member to talk to saints on removal, V2:452
drafts resolutions of public meeting in Missouri, V2:449.

Moss, William, heads English saints sailing to America, V4:310.

Mott, Hiram, mission appointment published and field of labor, V6:340.

motto, political, of Church, V3:9
of saints and *Nauvoo Neighbor,* V5:305.

Mouer, Henry, mission appointment published and field of labor, V6:337.

Mount, Hiram B., affidavit of mob attempting to draft into service, V6:508-9.

Mount, Joseph, mission appointment published and field of labor, V6:338
mission call and field of labor, V5:349.

Mount Ensign, engraved on cover of Volume VII and comments on, IntroV7:III.

Mount Ephraim, stake appointed at, V4:205.

Mount of Olives, prayer of dedication on, V4:454, et seq.
See also Orson Hyde; Jews; mission; Palestine.

Mount Pisgah, Mormon Battalion, Captain Allen at, to raise, V7:612
Pratt, Parley P., named by, V7:607.

Mower, E. H., mentioned, V5:300.

Mulholland, James, death of, V4:88-9 and ftnt
Prophet, clerk to, V3:375
Prophet, clerk to, appointed clerk of land contracts, V4:16
salary of, V4:17
witness to apostate vandalizing of saints' homes, V3:288.

mulatto, law concerning in Missouri, IntroV3:XXIV.

Mullholland, Sister, mentioned, V5:371, 384.

Mulliner, Samuel, England, appointed to go with Twelve to, V3:347
  England, arrives in, V4:45
  Kirtland Camp, subscribed to constitution of, V3:93
  mission appointment published and field of labor, V6:340
  Scotland, mission to, V4:48.

Mullone, James, lie concerning Joseph recorded, V5:218.

mummies, Abraham, Book of, found with, V2:236
  Egyptian, rumors over, V2:348
  Egyptian, exhibited in Kirtland, V2:235
  Joseph gives history and description of, V2:348, et seq
  saints, purchased by, V2:236.
  See also Book of Abraham; Egyptian; Smith, Joseph.

Munroe, Henry, subscribed to constitution of Kirtland Camp, V3:93.

Munroe, James M., mentioned, V7:337, 365
  mission call in Illinois to disabuse public mind over arrest of Joseph, V5:485.

murder, Backenstos, J. B., acquitted for, V7:541
  baptized, cannot be, if have committed, V6:253
  Durfee, Edmund, case of, V7:523, et seq
  eternal life, cannot have if commit, V4:359
  perdition, son of, can be classified if commit, V6:253.
  See also doctrine; martyrdom; murderers.

murderers, Church, will take no part in prosecuting Joseph's, V7:193
  defense attorneys for martyrdom, V7:50
  martyrdom, fix own terms of surrender, V7:47
  mob, counter-movements for, V7:312
  perdition, son of, possible to be classified as, V6:253
  trial of martyrdom, V7:49-50
  witnesses from Nauvoo against martyrdom, V7:311.
  See also murder.

Murdock, John, bishop, appointed, V5:119
  bishop, sustained of a Nauvoo ward, V7:298
  Church, appointed to preside over new district of, V7:305
  DeWitt, petitions Governor Boggs on mob violence in, V3:83
  false tongues, letter to Thompson Branch on, V1:325
  Far West High Council, sustained member of, V2:523
  general assemblies, moderator of, in sundry places in Caldwell County, V3:5-6

MURDOCK, JOHN (continued)

general assembly, in, of the Church at Far West, V3:3

high council, appointed to at Far West, V3:225

high council, elected to, at Zion, V2:367

high council, sustained to Missouri, V2:124

Joseph, on relief expedition for, V5:482

mission appointment, V4:403

mission call in Illinois to disabuse public mind over Joseph's arrest, V5:485

Pratt, Orson, accompanies to Kirtland, V2:44

presidency, speaks against local, V3:4

saints, signs memorial of, in Missouri, V3:224

Salt Lake High Council, sustained member of, V7:629

stake, appointed counselor at Lima, V4:233

Zions Camp member, V2:184.

Murdock, Joseph S., birth of, V1:260, ftnt only
death of, V1:265, ftnt only.

Murdock, Joseph, Sen., mentioned, V5:165.

Murdock, Julia, birth of, V1:260, ftnt only.

Murie, Sister, mentioned, V3:261.

Murray, Mr., father to Sister Kimball, V4:11, 20.

Murray, Roswell, blessing for work on Kirtland Temple, V2:206.

Murray, Vilate, wife of Heber C. Kimball, V1:296, ftnt only.

Musgrove, Samuel, sheriff of Clark County, Missouri, V6:148.

Musick, Samuel, appointed elder, V4:12.

Musselman, Mary, wife of D. Whitmer, Sen., V1:48, ftnt only.

mustard seed, parable explained, V2:268.
See also parables.

Mutual Improvement Association, beginning of, V5:320 and ftnt.

Myers, Father, mentioned, V3:376-7.

Myers, George, wounded at Haun's Mills by mob, V3:326, ftnt only.

Myers, Jacob, (also spelled Myres), elder, ordained, V2:228
Haun's Mills, wounded at by mob, V3:326, ftnt only
Kirtland Camp, mentioned in, V3:147
prayer to gain influence over, V2:54.

Myers, Jeremiah, witness for state in Missouri trials of saints, V3:210.

Myers, John, killed at Haun's Mills by mob, V3:326, ftnt only.

mysteries, apostasy, high road to explained as key to, V3:385
Apostles preach on, V6:18

MYSTERIES (continued)

grand key to unlock, V5:389
missionaries, not to be taught by, V5:344
Rigdon, Sidney, known to but not revealed, V6:290-1
saints, to be taught among, V4:426.
See also doctrine; gospel; keys; Smith, Joseph.

—N—

Napier, Mr., mentioned, V1:419.

Napier, Charles, mentioned, V5:415.

Napier, William, killed at Haun's Mills by mob, V3:326, ftnt only.

Nash, Anna, wife of Alpheus Gifford, V4:109, 484, ftnt only.

Nash, N., appointed by public to assist saints in removing from Zion, V2:455.

Nashville, city of, meetings at, V4:182, ftnt only.

nations, status in world, July 1837, V2:497.

Nauvoo, Agricultural and Manufacturing Association, incorporation of, V4:303-5

apostate conspirators in, IntroV6:XXXVI
apostate newspaper prospectus issued in, V6:363
arsenal of dedicated to Lord, V7:271
astronomical calculations of,V7:554
attack, preparation of marshal and Legion for, V6:493
attacked, affidavit that was to be, V6:492
Bennett, John C., first mayor of, V4:287-92
Bennett, John C., mayor of, V7:56
Bennett affair, city council petitions Governor Carlin on, V5:67-8
bogus money, makers of, in, V7:574
brothels, action of city council against, V7:248 and ftnt
burying ground for, V4:353, 414
Carthage, complaints of citizens of before city council, V6:173-4
charter, attempt to repeal, V5:294
charter, debated before legislative committee, V7:363
charter, devised by Joseph, V4:249
charter, part of repealed, V5:295
charter, problems with, affect industry in, V5:436-8
charter, Prophet speaks at, on his second arrest and writs under, V5:465, et seq
charter repealed, V7:365

NAUVOO (continued)

    charter, to be repealed, V7:325
    charter, resolution introduced for repeal of, V5:201
    charter, speech defending before legislature, V5:201, et seq
    Church, public center of, V7:395
    Church, words of consolation by council of, to, V7:152-3
    city council, replacements in, V6:347
    City of Joseph, name changed to, V7:394
    city officials, named by council, V4:292, et seq
    civil authorities rebuked for lack of energy in discharge of their duties,
        V7:350
    comments on by visitor, May 1844, V6:367-8
    Commerce, to incorporate city plat of, into, V4:307
    Commerce, merged into, V4:322
    Commerce, name changed from, V4:21
    Commerce, post office name changed from, V4:121
    concentration at, V4:362
    conditions in November 1845, V7:536
    Congress, ordinance proposed to be adopted by for protection of
        saints, V6:130-2
    conspiracies in, V6:272
    constitutional authority, position of, in, V5:289-90
    convention, presidential held at, V6:386-97
    cooperative store by Church planned in, V6:263
    coroner, Dimick B. Huntington elected, V5:18
    council, George A. Smith elected to, V5:13
    council, William Smith, elected to, V5:13
    currency, ordinance on, V5:297
    Danites, none in, V5:68
    debates held regularly in, V4:514
    debating society established in, V6:80
    debt, members at, not to leave in, V7:475
    definition of, V4:121
    drinking, limited in, V5:34
    economic policy of, expounded, V7:303-4
    education in, IntroV6:XXIV
    education in, outlined, V4:290
    election, first of officers by, V4:287
    elections of, V5:264-5
    elections, municipal of January 1845, V7:370
    Episcopal minister preaches at, V5:427
    Federal Government, to petition to be placed under, and Nauvoo

NAUVOO (continued)

    Legion to be U.S. troops, V6:107

food, supplying, for, V7:158

Ford, Thomas, advice of, on status sought, V7:389

Ford, Thomas, infamous speech of, V6:623

Ford, Thomas, instructions of, V7:150

Ford, Thomas, letter of on organization of town government within, V7:396-8

founding of, in Illinois by Church, IntroV4:XXII, et seq

Fourth of July celebration in, report of, V5:488, et seq, 491

Fourth of July celebration planned in, V5:453-4

Free Masonry in, V4:551

gather, saints commanded to, at, V7:267

gathering, appointed stake in Zion and place for, V4:12

gathering, continued place of, V7:250

goodness, notice of, published, V7:360-1

government, enlargement of, V5:263

grain, report of two-year supply, V7:445

habeas corpus, city court of, issues writ of, for Joseph, V5:463-5

habeas corpus, city court right to hear challenged, V6:418-20

habeas corpus, ordinance on, V5:57

habeas corpus, ordinance on proceedings on writs of, V5:185, et seq

habeas corpus, ordinance on return of, V5:161

Hancock Eagle prospectus published in, V7:596

Hardin, General, threat against by, V7:481

Higbee, Chauncey, vexatious actions of, against authorities of, V6:286

on horse thieves, V6:38

Illinois militia, search of, by, V7:447-8

incorporated, small portion of, as town of, V7:399-400

incorporation act of, V4:239, et seq

incorporation, resolution passed thanking parties in, V4:292-3

inhabitants of October 1840, V4:229

jealousy of promising greatness of, IntroV6:XXV

Joseph, arrival in under arrest for trial, V5:458, et seq

Joseph, conditions of, while in Carthage jail, V6:598-9

Joseph, expresses thanks to citizens of Dixon for aid to, V5:474-6

Joseph, mass meeting at, affirms character of against Bennett, V5:70

Joseph, only one allowed to fight in, V5:283

Joseph, proclamation of, to keep peace and quiet, V6:449

Joseph, special ordinance on future arrests of, V6:105-6

Joseph, testimony of, against dissenters at, V6:408, et seq

Joseph, trial of, to be at, V5:456

NAUVOO (continued)

jury and witness fees, ordinance on, V6:179

kidnapping, action of citizens to, V4:157, et seq

kidnapping, order to marshal of to secure from further, V6:103-4

Latter-day Saints, committee of to write of treatment received by from the United States, V7:454 and ftnt

law, comment on, in, V7:394

Law, William, city council hears case of putting away of, V6:162, et seq

lecture on by J. B. Newhall, V5:432-3

Legion of, organized, V4:293-4

legislative powers of, V4:245, et seq

libels, ordinance on and other purposes, V6:433-4

liberty and justice, plea for, published, V7:164, et seq

liquor, becoming stranger in, V4:331

liquor, council of prohibits vending of spirits, V7:315

liquor, ordinance allowing Joseph to distribute, V6:111

liquor, ordinance on sale of, V6:178-9

Mansion, opening of, V6:33

manufacturing center, viewed as, IntroV6:XXIII and ftnt

Marks, William, city council hears fears concerning life, V6:166, et seq

martial law, proclaimed under, V6:497

martyrdom, first message of, V6:621-2 and ftnt

martyrdom, letter sent to, on, V7:110

martyrdom, second message concerning, V6:624-5

martyrs' bodies, arrival of, V6:626

Masonic Temple, cornerstones of, laid, V5:446

Masonic Temple, dedication of, V6:287

Masons, evaluation of, by, V4:565-7

mayor, John C. Bennett resigns as, V5:12

mayor, Hyrum elected vice, V5:12

mayor, Joseph elected, V4:501, V5:12

mayor, Joseph re-elected, V5:264

mayor's court in, V5:365, et seq

memorial of petitioning Congress for redress and protection, V6:125, et seq

memorial to Governor Carlin on, V4:159-60

Mercantile and Mechanical Association, formation of, V7:369

military duty, all citizens between 18-45 subject to, V4:300

military organization of, V5:489-90

Mississippi, ordinance to erect dam on, V6:106

NAUVOO (continued)

Missouri as factor in affairs, IntroV6:XXXV, et seq

Missouri, public meeting on aggressions of, V6:111-3

Missourians, public meeting at, on extradition and kidnapping by, V6:101-2

mob, defense of, against, V7:68

mob, in danger from, V6:119

moral principles extolled, V5:34

municipal seal of, V5:194-5

murderers, voice from, on witnesses at trial of, V7:406

museum started in, V5:406

New Haven Herald, comments on, V6:32-3

new order of things, V7:596

notary public, James Sloan elected, V5:165

Nauvoo Expositor, destruction of apostate newspaper by Joseph, V6:432-3

Nauvoo Expositor, synopsis of city council proceedings on destruction of, V6:434, et seq

Nauvoo Expositor, trials on destruction of, V6:487, et seq, 554, et seq

Nauvoo house, incorporation of, V4:301-2

Nauvoo Legion, arsenal to be built in, by, V5:430

Nauvoo Legion, order of mayor to assist marshal, V6:104

Nauvoo Legion, request of marshal for assistance from, V6:103-4

office, oath of, type of, V4:295, ftnt only

officers elected of, V5:270-1

officers, ordinance creating new city, V4:307

order, public meeting on, V5:34-5

ordinance on hawkers, peddlers, etc., V4:461

ordinances, repeal of certain, V6:212

organized, inaugural address of mayor elect, V4:288, et seq

peace council at, V7:148-9

people, certificate on retention of, V6:553

persons, notable, visit, V4:356-8

police, deacons watch over as, V7:399

police offered double bribe for reporting same, V6:153

police force, address of Joseph to, V6:150-2

police force named, V6:149

police force, ordinance enlarging, V6:110

political and religious parties at, V7:58

politics, public meeting on, V6:211

population of, V5:232

postmaster position problems, V5:273

NAUVOO (continued)

post office changed to, V4:121
powers of, Governor Ford speaks against, V5:200
powers of, questioned by Governor Carlin, V5:153-5
Pratt, Orson, credentials of, as agent for, V6:262
press, opposition, arrives at, V6:357
prices, council should control, V5:271
priesthood government to replace civil of, V7:443
property, attempt to take by devious contract, V7:589-91
property of, to be in hands of trustees after Twelve leave, V7:573
prophecy that no judge would set aside laws of, V4:516-
prosperity of, V6:9-10
public meeting at, on appeal to general government and local affairs,
    V6:107-8
public meeting at, on mob actions and false accusations, V6:483
public meetings, ordinance on, V4:306-7
public proclamation on mob lies, V6:495
public records, buried, V7:129
registrar, Joseph selected of, V4:543
religious liberty, ordinance on, V4:306
resolutions of by council of, after Joseph's death, V7:150-1
saints, case of before Senate Judiciary Committee, V4:157-9
saints, at Philadelphia instructed to move to, V5:413
salaries, items of, of employees, V6:331-2
sickness spreads and healings at, V4:3 and ftnt
state convention held at, V6:386
state militia, arrival of, to keep peace, V7:130-1
status of affairs in May 1844, V6:377-8
status of in March 1844 published, V6:265-7
stealing, proclamation against, V5:310-1
stock in house of, certificate receipt, V5:414
strangers, ordinance in, concerning, V5:457-8
tax, ordinance exempting Church property from, V6:110
tax collector, Mr. Bagley unjust, V6:4
temperance, ordinance on, V4:299
temple, general meeting concerning ordinances of, V6:236, et seq
University, all schools under authority of, V4:301
University organized, V4:293
vagrants, ordinance on, V4:447
wards, division of, into, V4:305; V5:119-20 and ftnt, 199-200
water power company of, and vision of, IntroV6:XXIII and ftnt
wharfage problems, meeting of city council on, V6:234-6

NAUVOO (continued)

wickedness, meeting of citizens of, and proclamation against, V7:354-6

wickedness, proclamation of city council against, V7:352. et seq

wind, destructive at, V6:267

Young, Brigham, leaves for West, V7:585

See also bogus money; Danites; discourse; Douglas, Stephen A.; Ford, Thomas; gathering; habeas corpus; persecutions, Illinois; mob; Nauvoo charter; Temple, Nauvoo; Smith, Joseph; stories; Apostles, Twelve.

Nauvoo, University of, Bennett, John C., discharged as chancellor of, V5:120

incorporation, act of, V4:239-43

Lyman, Amasa, elected regent of, V5:120

in operation, V4:400

organized, V4:293

schools, all under authority of, V4:301

Spencer, Orson, elected chancellor of, V5:120.

Nauvoo Agriculture and Manufacturing Association, incorporation of, V4:303, et seq.

Nauvoo charter, Joseph, devised by, V4:249

Joseph, speaks on and writs under, V5:465, et seq

legislative committee, debated before, V7:363

legislature, speech defending, before, V5:201, et seq

Nauvoo, problems with, affect industry in, V5:436, et seq

perpetual, article on, secession, V5:306

powers of, questioned, V5:153, et seq

repeal, attempt to, V5:294

repeal, call for, V5:201

repeal, resolution introduced for, V5:201

repealed, to be, V7:325

repealed, V7:365

repealed, part of, V5:295.

See also Nauvoo; Smith, Joseph.

Nauvoo City Council, affairs, adjustment of, V7:247-8

financial affairs, minutes of, V7:322

habeas corpus, relieved by, from David Bettisworth's court, V7:67

ordinances, drastic, by, V7:248 and ftnt

riot, writ issued against for, V7:66-7

voice of Nauvoo, V7:352-4.

See also Nauvoo.

Nauvoo Expositor, arrests and trial on, V6:487, et seq
Bernhisel, J. M., letter to Ford confirming Joseph's on, affair, V6:467-8
city council proceedings against, V6:434, et seq
destroyed, declared a nuisance and, V6:448
destruction, acquittal of leading Mormons for, V7:50-1
destruction, affidavit concerning, V7:130
destruction by Nauvoo Council as nuisance, V6:432
destruction, Francis M. Higbee on, V6:451-2
first number of, published, V6:430
Joseph's account of the affair, V7:125-6 and ftnt
Nauvoo Municipal Court, V6:454-8
Neighbor, comment on, V6:460
nuisance, bill for removal as, V7:63
prospectus of, V6:443
prospectus of issued, V6:363
Taylor, John, comments on, V7:121
Taylor, John, impressions of, V7:61, et seq
trial for, acquitted, V7:484-5
Warsaw mob meeting on, V7:122, et seq.
See also Nauvoo; Smith, Joseph.

Nauvoo House Association, commenced construction of, V7:436
incorporation of, V4:301
revealed to be built, (D&C § 124:59) V4:279.

Nauvoo Legion, affairs of, V4:362-3
affairs of explained, V4:354-6
arms, surrenders, V6:557
assembly, first of, V4:326
Bennett, John C., cashiered from, V5:49
Bennett, John C., elected major-general of, V4:296
character of, V4:269
citizens, resolution on military duty of, V4:300
companies, organization of, V4:353
courts, authorized to use for protection of, V7:309-10
disbanded, V6:557
drilling of, V7:69
equipment of, after giving up state arms, V7:12
Ewing, W. L. D., on state payment for service in, V6:95
federal troops, petition to make, of, V6:107
Ford, Governor, state arms of, demanded by, V6:555
Foster, R. D., court-martial on, called, V6:355-6

NAUVOO LEGION (continued)

    fourth regiment of second cohort of, V4:582

    general orders, V4:354, 400-1, 502, 601-2

    grog shop, removes, V4:442

    history of, V5:3

    incorporation, act of, V4:239, et seq

    Joseph, actions and movements of, to relieve, V5:454-6

    Joseph, commission of lieutenant-general by governor, V4:309-10

    Joseph, defended by, V4:355-6

    Joseph elected lieutenant-general of, V4:296

    Joseph, last speech of, to, V6:498, et seq

    kidnappers, used to aid arrest of, V6:119

    marshal, request of, for war provisions to aid, V6:108

    martial band, members of, V7:135

    minutes of, V4:382, 415

    minutes of on election of officers, V4:382

    minutes of, extract from, V4:549-50

    muster of, V6:34

    Nauvoo, arsenal to be built by, in, V5:430

    Nauvoo marshal, ordered to assist, V6:103-4

    Nauvoo marshal, orders to be placed under command of, V6:493

    officer's drill of, V5:369

    officers of, V4:296

    organization meeting of, V4:295-6

    organized, V4:293-4

    parade of, V5:383-4

    prophecy, fulfills of maintaining law and order, V7:313

    public arms, to receive, V6:31

    religion, services in, non-compensated for state because of, V6:95-6

    religious ceremonies, marched to at temple site, V4:326-7

    "Repast Militaire" of, V4:601-2

    script, issues, V5:518

    self, requested to protect, V7:445

    trial and sham battle of, V5:4-5

    Young, Brigham, elected lieutenant-general of, V7:265.

    See also Nauvoo; Smith, Joseph.

Nauvoo mansion, first social party of, V6:42-3

    opening of in Nauvoo, V6:33.

Nauvoo Municipal Court, city council, members of, before, V6:460-1

    Expositor case, hearing before, V6:456-8

    Expositor case, petition of Prophet before, V6:454-6

    Smith, Jeremiah, case before, V6:379, 418-20

NAUVOO MUNICIPAL COURT (continued)

Smith, Jeremiah, minutes of case, V6:420-3
Smith, Joseph, petitioned for trial by, V6:357, et seq.
See also Nauvoo; Smith, Joseph.

Nauvoo Neighbor, closed, V7:473
Durfee murder and house burning, extra on, V7:528
Expositor, destruction of, V6:460
first edition, V5:380
grand jury, prints addendum on, in Illinois, V7:493
martyrdom, account in, V7:176-7
motto of, V5:305
name was *Wasp,* V5:305
publication to cease, V7:453
prospectus of, V5:305.

Nauvoo Temple, see Temple, Nauvoo

Navajo Indians, mission to, V1:182 and ftnt.
See also Indians; Lamanites; mission.

Neal, Nancy O., mother of Charles Rich, V2:507, ftnt only.

Needham, John, British conference, represents area in, V5:10
British Mission, mission in, V4:149
devote all time to work of ministry, V4:148
volunteers for service in vineyard, V4:217.

Negro, Cain, son of, V4:501
Church, Missouri mob's accusation against concerning, V1:376 and
ftnt
Church position and membership of, in 1839, V1:377, ftnt only
Church position on in Missouri, IntroV3:XXV
free, do not believe in setting, V3:29
"Free People of Color," article by Church, V1:377, et seq and ftnt
Ham, descendants of, V1:191
Joseph expounds on, V5:217-8
Joseph's views on, IntroV3:XXVI
Missouri law concerning, IntroV3:XXIV
Missouri vs. retribution, fought against, IntroV3:LXX
Nauvoo, fined in, for attempting to marry white women, V6:210
saints cannot vote any more than, V3:57
slaves, came into world, V5:217
Star, extra in concerning, problem, V1:378 and ftnt
Texas, would send to, after annexation and then to Mexico, V6:244
whipping, case of one Chism, V6:281, 284.

Neibaur, Alexander, lamentation of on martyrdom, V7:191-2 and ftnt mentioned, V6:271.

Nelson, Abraham, (also spelled Abram), Black, A., falsely accused of threatening, V3:65
mob, attacked by, at voting incident, V3:57.

Nelson, Elder, mentioned, V3:126.

Nelson, George, excommunicated from Church, V3:336.

Nelson, Hyrum, (also spelled Hiram), Black, A., falsely accused of threatening, V3:64
mob, attacked by, at voting incident, V3:57.

Nelson, James, mission appointment published and field of labor, V6:340.

Nelson, Joseph, excommunicated from Church, also wife and mother, V3:336.

Nelson, William, mission appointment published and field of labor, V6:338
mission call in Illinois to disabuse public mind over arrest of Joseph, V5:485.

Nephi, mistakenly called for Moroni, V1:11, ftnt only.

Nephite, relics of, discovered, V5:44
Tower Hill named for tower or altar of, V3:35.

Nephite Record, see Book of Mormon.

Nesbit, William, mentioned, V6:531-2.

Netherton, John, oath of that saints have acted as mob, V3:61.

New Jerusalem, built, two to be, V2:262
Joseph, expounds on, V2:260
Missouri, city of, to be in, V1:188.
See also doctrine; Smith, Joseph.

New Orleans, branch organized in, V6:176.

New Testament, Church, organized according to, V1:79
Mormon, Book of, translation to be published with new translation of, V1:341
translation of completed, V1:324 and ftnt.

New York Daily Advertiser, publishes anti-Church article, V2:351.
See also newspapers.

New York Evening Star, publishes anti-Church article, V2:351.
See also newspapers.

New York Herald, publishes Book of Abraham fac-simile, V5:11.
See also newspapers.

New York Messenger, The, Church paper, V7:444-5.
   See also newspapers.

New York Sun, accounts shower of flesh and blood, etc., V4:414.
   See also newspapers.

New York Tribune, Missouri persecutions, article on, V4:551
   Nauvoo, comment on troubles at, V7:170.
   See also newspapers.

New York Weekly Herald, Bennett, J. G., editor of, course of approved,
      V4:477-8.
   See also newspapers.

Newberry, James, elder, ordained, V3:315
   mission appointment published and field of labor, V6:339
   Missouri, on committee for removal from, V3:255
   Missouri trials, discharged as innocent from, V3:211.

Newcomb, Samuel, mission of, V4:408.

Newell, G. T., clerk of New York conference, V7:520.

Newhall, J. B., lecture delivered on Joseph and Nauvoo, V5:432-3

Newland, William, mission appointment published and field of labor,
      V6:336.

Newlight Church, see Campbellites.

Newman, Elijah, mission appointment published and field of labor,
      V6:339
   Missouri, arraigned for treason, murder, burglary, arson, robbery,
      and larceny at Richmond, V3:209.

news, of foreign activities, V1:281.

News, The, weekly paper to be published in Nauvoo, never materialized,
      V4:112 and ftnt.

newspapers, account of martyrdom in, V7:176, et seq
   Boston Daily Ledger, publishes fac-simile of Book of Abraham in,
      V5:11
   Courier des Estes Unis, publishes proposed statement of Pilate con-
      demning Jesus, V4:420-1
   Dogberry Paper, attempt to publish Book of Mormon in, V1:76,
      ftnt only
   Dollar Week Bostonian, publishes Book of Abraham fac-simile,
      V5:11
   Elder's Journal, saints' paper in Ohio, V2:505
   Evening & Morning Star, to be commenced, V1:217
   Hancock Eagle, prospectus published in Nauvoo, V7:596

NEWSPAPERS (continued)

Hawk Eye, article on Mormon improvements, V6:195

Illinois Springfield Register, publishes article on Joseph's candidacy for President, V6:268

Illinois State Register, political trick to arrest Joseph, V5:513-5

imposters, *Quincy Argus*, publishes Church warning against, V3:341-2

Iowa Democrat, publishes article on Joseph's candidacy for President, V6:268-70

Joseph, *Boston Bee* publishes articles on, character sketch of, V5:406-8

Joseph, publishes every falsehood about, V4:383

Latter-Day Saints Messenger & Advocate, established, V1:409

Lee County Democrat, article concerning martyrdom in, V7:164, et seq

Manx-Liberal, publishes anti-Mormon letter on Isle of Man, V4:234, et seq

martyrdom, John Taylor's impressions of, in area prior to, V7:60, et seq

Millennial Star, first foreign, of Church, V4:133 and ftnt

Missouri Enquirer, started from ruins of *Star*, V1:470

Missouri Republican, account of martyrdom in, V7:180

Mormonism, *Boston Bee* on, V5:322, 518-20

Nauvoo Expositor, prospectus of, V6:443-4

Nauvoo Neighbor, prospectus of, V5:305

New Haven Herald, comments on Nauvoo in, V6:32

New York Herald, publishes fac-simile of Book of Abraham in, V5:11

New York Messenger, published by Church, V7:444-5

New York Sun, accounts shower of flesh and blood, V4:414

New York Tribune, article on Illinois persecutions in, V7:170-1

New York Tribune, article on Missouri persecutions in, V4:551-2

New York Tribune, Nauvoo, comment on troubles at, V7:170

New York Weekly Herald, Bennett, James G., editor of, V4:477-8

News, The, weekly to be published in Nauvoo, V4:112 and ftnt

North Staffordshire Mercury, publishes differences between Baptists and Mormons, V4:348, et seq

North Star, The, publishes article on Church papers, V2:40

Northern Times, weekly of the Church, V2:227, 434 and ftnt

Ohio Star, publishes anti-Mormon letters, V1:241

Prophet, The, Church, commenced in New York, V7:177

Quincy Herald, account of martyrdom in, V7:178-9

Quincy Whig, editor of, member of martyrdom mob, V7:144

St. Louis Evening Gazette, account of martyrdom in, V7:177

saints, teeming with lies about, V4:380

Salem Advertiser & Argus, article on Nauvoo and Joseph, V5:432-3

Sangamon Journal, martyrdom account in, V7:179-80

NEWSPAPERS (continued)

　　Times & Seasons, published by Church at Commerce, V4:23

　　Tompkins Democrat, account of martyrdom in, V7:182

　　Upper Missouri Advertiser, weekly in connection with *Evening & Morning Star,* V1:281

　　Warsaw Signal, editor of anti-Mormon, V4:487, ftnt only

　　Wasp, The, weekly of Church, V4:600

　　Weekly Dispatch, refuses reply to anti-Mormon article, V4:236

　　West Messenger, article in on meteor, V4:588-9

　　Western Monitor, Missouri paper, V1:395.

　　See also editorials; press.

Newton, Elder, mentioned, V5:326.

Newton, Henry, mentioned, V6:8.

Newton, J. H., delegate to political convention in Nauvoo, V6:389.

Nicholas, Joseph, Zions Camp member, V2:184.

Nichols, Jesse B., Joseph, on relief expedition for, V5:486.

Nichols, John, mission appointment published and field of labor, V6:339.

Nicholson, James B., counselor to bishop of Philadelphia branch, V4:331, V5:8.

Nickerson, A. C., mission appointment published and field of labor, V6:340.

Nickerson, Amos, subscribed to constitution of Kirtland Camp, V3:92.

Nickerson, Charles, mentioned, V1:442.

Nickerson, Eleazer, father of Freeman, V1:416, ftnt only.

Nickerson, Freeman, Canada, accompanies Prophet to, V1:416, et seq
　　genealogy, V1:416, ftnt only
　　Kirtland, appointed to raise funds for relief of, V2:44
　　Kirtland Camp, subscribed to constitution of, V3:91
　　Kirtland Camp, tent of placed in order for breaking Word of Wisdom, V3:131
　　mission appointment published and field of labor, V6:340
　　Prophet, entertains, V2:41
　　Westfield, New York, accompanies Prophet to, V2:45
　　Zions Camp member, V2:184.

Nickerson, Freeman A., baptized, V1:422
　　Canada, Joseph stays at, in, V1:421
　　elder, ordained, V1:422
　　gospel, accepts, V1:422
　　Nickerson, Freeman, son of, receives Prophet and Sidney Rigdon, V1:421.

Nickerson, Huldah Chapman, wife of Freeman, V1:416, ftnt only.

Nickerson, Lydia, mentioned, V1:442.

Nickerson, Levi S., mission appointment published and field of labor, V6:340

 Missouri, covenanted to assist saints in removing from, V3:253

 Zions Camp member, V2:184.

Nickerson, Moses Chapman, Iowa, counselor to stake in, V4:352, 399

 Joseph, letter to on Canada mission, V2:40.

Nickerson, Ransom, mentioned, V1:442.

Nickerson, Thankful Chase, mother of Freeman, V1:416, ftnt only.

Nickerson, Thomas, child of dies, V3:136

 Kirtland Camp, subscribed to constitution of, V3:91.

Nickerson, Uriah C., (also spelled Uriel), Joseph, leaves to rescue, V4:365

 mission call in Illinois to disabuse public mind over arrest of Joseph, V5:485

 Zions Camp member, V2:184.

Nightingale, J., ordained priest, V5:419.

Niles Register, Mormon political views published in, V6:195.

Niswanger, William, Nauvoo Legion, elected officer in, V4:382.

Nixon, Stephen, ordained elder, V4:311.

Noah, Adam, held same keys as, V4:210

 Adam, next to, V3:386

 flood and, V1:283

 Gabriel is, held keys of gospel, V3:386.

Noah, M. M., accusations towards Joseph, V2:351.

Noble, Esquire, mentioned, V6:347.

Noble, Joseph Bates, bishop, counselor to, V4:399

 Church, appointed to preside over new district of, V7:305

 England, appointed to go to with Twelve, V3:347

 Joseph commands to be healed, V4:4

 Joseph declares gratefulness for aid while in seclusion, V5:109

 Kirtland Camp, subscribed to constitution of, V3:92

 mission appointment published and field of labor, V6:336

 Prophet, healed by, V4:4, ftnt only

 seventies, named to first quorum of, V2:203

 Zions Camp member, V2:184.

Noland, Mr., mob member in Missouri, V1:480.

Noland, S. V., signs proposition to buy lands of saints, V2:96-7.

Noland, Smallwood, signs petition to buy lands of saints, V2:96-7.

Nordau, Max, Rabbi opinion on Christ, V3:358, ftnt only.

Norris, Eliza, disfellowshipped for following false revelations, V2:525.

Norris, Moses R., disfellowshipped for following false revelations, V2:525.

Norris, Patrick, mission appointment published and field of labor, V6:337.

North Staffordshire Mercury, publishes difference between Baptists and Mormons, V4:348, et seq.
    See also newspapers.

North Star, The, publishes article on Church papers, V2:40.
    See also newspapers.

North, Ur., Zions Camp member, V2:184.

Northern Times, weekly paper of the Church, commenced February 1835, V2:227, 434 and ftnt.
    See also newspapers.

Norton, Mr., charges treason to Smiths, V7:85.

Norton, Eli, mentioned, V6:163-4.

Norton, Henry O., *Expositor* trial, witness at, V6:489
    martyrdom, member of mob at, V7:146.

Norton Township, Medina County, Ohio, council held at, on legality of ordinations,V1:343.

Nourn, E. B., mentioned, V5:22.

Nowlin, Smallwood, mobber in Illinois, V6:137.

nuisance, owner of refused compensation for removal of, V4:444 and ftnt.
    See also *Nauvoo Expositor.*

Nuptire, Daniel L., subscribed to constitution of Kirtland Camp, V3:93.

Nye, G. M, grandmaster of Masons dies, Joseph's comments, V5:370.

Nyman, Hyrum, mission appointment published and field of labor, V6:337.

Nyman, Margaret J., testifies of C. L. Higbee's adulterous actions, V6:407.

Nyman, Matilda J., testifies of C. L. Higbee's adulterous actions, V6:407.

—O—

Oakley, Ezra, mentioned, V5:399.

Oakley, John, mentioned, V5:272.

Oakley, Thomas, given care of Church at Gadfield Elm, V4:135

O'Banion, Patrick, Crooked River battle, death of at, V3:170
  Missouri, killed by mob in, V4:61, 65.

obedience, Apostles on, V6:12
  man must have absolute in all things to be saved, V6:223.

O'Brien, Thomas, mobber who prevents group from traveling to Missouri, V3:323.

Odle, Nehemiah, witness for state in Missouri trials of saints, V3:210.

Odle, Thomas M., witness for state in Missouri trials of saints, V3:210.

Oglesby, William, justice of the peace, V4:62.

Ohio, Kirtland, see Kirtland, Ohio.

Ohio Star, Ravenna, Ohio, newspaper published Ezra Booth's anti-Mormon letters, V1:241 and ftnt.

oil, anointing with, in Kirtland Temple, V2:379.

Oldham, Leonidas, anti-Mormon committee member, V1:399.

Olive, James, affidavit on mob movements on Carthage road, V6:529.

Olive Leaf, The, paper to be published in Kirtland, disapproved, V4:443-4.

Olived, John W., minister seeks Prophet, astonished at doctrine, V2:378-9.

Oliver, Alexander, anti-Mormon committee chairman, V6:8.

Oliver, Brother, mentioned, V7:413.

Olmstead, H., mission appointment published and field of labor, V6:340.

Olmstead, Harvey, (also spelled Olumstead), Church, appointed to preside over new district of, V7:306
  high council, chosen to, at Adam-ondi-Ahman, V3:38.

Olmstead, N. K., anti-Mormon committee member, V1:399
  medical doctor, signed mob manifesto, V1:376.

Olney, John F., mentioned, V4:303.

Olney, Oliver, Adam, claimed to see, V5:269
  DeWitt, petitions Governor Boggs on mob violence in, V3:83
  disfellowshipped for setting self up as prophet, V4:552
  Kirtland Camp, subscribed to constitution of, V3:92
  stealing, trial for, V5:269
  teachers, presides over, V2:371
  witness suggested to appear before Congress on redress, V4:97.

Olson, Severt, ordained priest, V6:400.

Olvord, T., affidavit concerning Missouri persecutions, V4:57.

Onandagus, prophet of Book of Mormon time, V2:79.

One Hundred Forty-Four Thousand, selection of already commenced, V6:196.

O'Neal, George, W., mobber, beats Brother Call, V3:245.

Ongee, (Indian), mentioned, V7:496-7.

orders, arms, Joseph to General Dunham surrender of state, V6:556
  court, to bring prisoners into, V6:596
  guard to A. P. Rockwood to notify, V6:494
  Nauvoo Legion, to, V6:119
  Nauvoo Legion, general to, V6:532
  Nauvoo Legion, to major-general of, V6:493
  Nauvoo Legion, mayor's to, V6:104
  Nauvoo Legion to Wilson Law calling out, V6:120
  marshal, to city, V6:103-4.
  See also Nauvoo Legion; mob; persecutions.

ordinances, Carthage citizens complaint of against, V6:173-4
  habeas corpus, on writs of, V5:57, 87-8
  hawkers, peddlers, etc., on, in Nauvoo, V4:461
  kept, must be, exactly, V4:209
  libels, concerning, and other purposes, V6:433-4
  liquor, on sale of, V6:111, 178-9
  Mississippi, for erection of a dam in, V6:106
  Nauvoo, creating new city officers, V4:307
  Nauvoo, on vagrants and disorderly persons, V4:447
  on currency, V5:297
  police force, enlarging, V6:110-1
  proceedings, regulating, V5:185-92
  Prophet, special on, V6:105-6
  public meetings, V4:306
  religious liberty in Nauvoo, V4:306
  saints, proposed to be adopted by Congress for protection of, V6:130, et seq
  soul, for each, V6:319
  strangers, concerning, in city, V5:457-8
  United States citizens, for protection of, asking Congress to pass, V6:275-7
  unlawful arrests, to prevent by foreign process, V6:124
  witnesses and jurors' fees, on, V6:179
  writs, on returns of, V5:161.
  See also Nauvoo.

ordination, Aaronic Priesthood, to, V1:39

ORDINATION (continued)

Apostles, of, V2:187, et seq and ftnts
Apostles, order of considered, V2:187, ftnt only
Apostles, resolutions concerning, amended by, V2:305, 395
Boynton, John F., of, V2:191
Church, of first elders of, V1:77-8
elder, to be deferred, V1:61
England, to be only at direction of Twelve in, V4:216
First Presidency accepts, V2:398
high council, accepted by, in Zion, V2:397
high council, adopted by in Kirtland, V2:396-7
Hyde, Orson, of, V2:189-90
instruction on, as to haste, V1:468
Johnson, Luke S., of, V2:190
Johnson, Lyman E., of, V2:188
Kimball, Heber C., of, V2:189
licenses, new, to be issued, V2:404
Marsh, Thomas B., of, V2:194
Melchizedek Priesthood, to, V1:40, ftnt only, et seq
M'Lellin, William E., of, V2:190
Patten, David W., of, V2:190
Pratt, Orson, of, V2:194 and ftnt
Pratt, Parley P., of, V2:192, et seq
presentation for, some accepted and rejected, V2:400
priesthood, to different offices of, V1:79
problems of and resolutions concerning vote of Church conferences on, V2:394-5
propriety of, V2:400
quorum, cannot without voice of, V2:388
rejection of some placed for, V2:407
resolutions, final concerning adopted, V2:403, et seq
seventies, of, V2:203, et seq
seventies and others, V2:207
spirit, receive and give as directed by, V1:79
Young, Brigham, of, V2:188
Zion, regulated in by Council of Priesthood, V1:407 and ftnt.
See also Latter-day Saints, Church of Jesus Christ of; Smith, Joseph.

Oregon, exploring expedition organized for, and California, V6:224.

Orme, Mr., mentioned, V6:264.

Ormsby, Gideon, blessing for work on Kirtland Temple, V2:206.

Ormsby, John, blessing for work on Kirtland Temple, V2:206.

Orton, Amos R., elder, ordained, and mission to Lamanites, V2:207
Kirtland Temple, blessing for work on, V2:206.

Orton, David, bishop's counselor, appointed, V4:236
Kirtland Camp, mentioned in, V3:140.

Orton, Roger, chastised for allowing horses to break loose, V2:90
excommunicated for showing contempt for authorities of Church, V2:527
Kirtland, appointed to raise funds for relief of, V2:44
seventies, named to first quorum of, V2:203
seventies, dropped as one of presidents of, V7:461-2
vision, sees heavenly, V2:386
Zions Camp, member, V2:184.

Orton, William R., covenanted to assist saints in removing from Missouri, V3:252.

Orum, Benjamin, mentioned, V5:484.

Osborn, David, mentioned, V4:68.

Osgood, Levi, Kirtland Camp, subscribed to constitution of, V3:92
Kirtland Temple, blessing for work on, V2:206.

Ospray, Ship, captain of calls on Joseph Smith, V6:451
election on board for President of U.S., V6:384-5.

Otis, Brother, mission appointment, V7:434.

Ott, Frederick, mission appointment published and field of labor, V6:339.

Outhouse, John, mission call in Illinois to disabuse public mind over Joseph's arrest, V5:485
Missouri, covenanted to assist saints in removing from, V3:253.

Outhouse, Joseph, called on mission and field of labor, V5:349.

Overton, Aaron, anti-Mormon committee member, V1:399.

Overton, Mahala, mentioned, V5:23.

Owen, Abel, mentioned, V5:287.

Owen, Ephraim, confession of accepted, V4:12
mentioned, V3:275.

Owen, Jedediah, (also spelled Owens), Missouri, covenanted to assist saints in removing from, V3:253
Missouri persecutions, affidavit concerning, V4:56
Missouri trials, discharged as innocent from, V3:211.

Owen, Joseph, case of in mayor's court, V6:4.

Owen, Reverend, mentioned, V7:507.

Owen, Robert, ancestor of E. Hunter, V4:416, ftnt only.

Owen, Stephen, anti-Mormon committee chairman, V6:8
anti-Mormon meeting, at, V5:537.

Owen, Thomas B., mentioned, V5:294.

Owen, Thomas H., communist in U.S., V7:537 and ftnt
Nauvoo, letter of reporting threats against, V7:192-3.

Owen, W., appointed by public to assist saints in removing from Zion,
V2:455.

Owens, Ephraim, falsely accused of threatening A. Black, V3:64.

Owens, Horace B., mission appointment published and field of labor,
V6:338.

Owens, James C., witness for state in Missouri trials of saints, V3:210.

Owens, Judge, mentioned, V7:617.

Owens, Samuel C., adventure, ludicrous, of, V2:99-100
anti-Mormon committee member, V1:399
Joseph, letter to Governor Ford on Missouri indictment of, V5:422
mentioned, V2:113, 119, 135
mob manifesto, county clerk, signed, V1:376
saints, bitterness against, V2:99
saints, helps, V1:432
saints, speaks against, V2:97
saints, signs proposition to buy land of, V2:96-7.

Owens, Zedekiah, arraigned for treason, murder, burglary, arson, robbery,
and larceny at Richmond, Missouri, V3:209.

Owings, James F., mentioned, V5:238.

Owsley, John H., kidnaps some members and takes to Missouri, V4:155.

—P—

Pace, James, mission call and field of labor, V5:349
policeman in Nauvoo, V6:150.

Pace, William, policeman in Nauvoo, V6:149.

Pacific Isles, development of work in, V7:252
mission opened, V5:386.
See also missions.

Pack, John, Joseph, on relief expedition for, V5:486
mentioned, V7:383
mission appointment published and field of labor, V6:337

PACK, JOHN (continued)

Missouri, covenanted to assist saints in removing from, V3:253.

Packard, Elder, assists Joseph, V2:326.

Packard, Noah, Church, appointed to preside over new district of, V7:306

high priest, rejected as, V4:341

Kirtland, elected to high council at, V2:366

Kirtland, ordained to high council at, V2:511

Kirtland, sustained to high council at, V2:510

Kirtland Camp, subscribed to constitution of, V3:92

Kirtland Temple, blessing for work on, V2:205, 207

Missouri persecutions, sends memorial to Massachusetts on, V6:236

money, gives to temple committee, V2:281

presidency, on high council to try, V2:484.

paganization, of early Christianity's doctrine of God, IntroVl:LXXXII.

Page, Ebenezer, father of John, V3:240, ftnt only

Missouri, arraigned for treason, murder, burglary, arson, robbery, and larceny at Richmond, V3:209.

Page, Ebenezer, Jun., ordained John Page, V3:240, ftnt only

Page, Hiram, baptized, Vl:81

mobbed in Jackson County, V4:394-5

Satan, received revelations from, Vl:109-10

Satan, renounces stone of, Vl:115

testimony as one of eight witnesses, Vl:57-8

Zion, messenger from saints in, to Judge Ryland, Vl:429

Zion, worthy of inheritance in, Vl:236, ftnt only.

Page, Hyrum, Jerusalem mission, actions of, heard on, V4:583

Joseph, carries message for, V2:120

Page, James B. T., expelled from Church for larceny, V4:454.

Page, John E., Apostle, ordained and genealogy, V3:240-1 and ftnt

Apostle, rejected as, V4:341

Apostle, sustained as, by Church after death of Joseph, V7:295

Apostle, to be, (D&C § 118:6) V3:47

Canadian Company, arrives at DeWitt with, V3:85

endowments, receives, in Nauvoo Temple, V7:543

excommunication of, V7:582

genealogy of, ordained elder, V2:253, ftnt only

Israel, preaches on gathering of, V3:125-6, ftnt only

Jews, to accompany Orson Hyde on mission to, V4:109

Kirtland Camp, exhorts the, V3:120

Kirtland Camp, preaches in, V3:119

PAGE, JOHN E. (continued)

labors, gives account of, V7:343

mission fruits of Canada recorded, V2:491

Missouri, covenanted to assist saints in removing from, V3:254

Mormon, Book of, address on, V4:1-2

New York conference, presides at, V4:462-3

Palestine, reproved for delaying mission to, V4:274

Palestine Mission, letter to Presidency reporting progress of, V4:201

Palestine Mission, rejects charge to proceed on, V4:372

sects, acts unwisely in preaching against, V5:521

Sundial, designated as, V7:435

Washington, commanded to go to, to labor, V6:81

writ, false, against for aiding Joseph, and etc., V7:444.

Page, Katharine, baptized, V1:81.

Page, Mary, receives endowments in Nauvoo Temple, V7:543.

Page, Rachel, Missouri, covenanted to assist saints in removing from, V3:254.

mother of John, V3:240, ftnt only.

paid ministry, anti-scriptural, cannot because, V2:528

Far West, had in, V2:527.

Painter, A., ordained teacher, V4:298.

Palestine, see Mission, Palestine.

Palmer, Mr., delegate to political convention in Nauvoo, V6:390.

Palmer, Mr., reports conference proceedings, V2:25.

Palmer, Elder, mentioned, V2:408.

Palmer, Abraham, (also spelled Abram), bishop, appointed, V4:236

Church, appointed to preside over new district of, V7:306

mission appointment published and field of labor, V6:339

mission, assigned to go on, V4:430

Nauvoo, policeman in, V6:150.

Palmer, Ambrose, Church, speaks at conference of, V2:53

council meeting, presides at, V2:317

high council, presents case to, V2:162.

Palmer, H. P., Joseph, on relief expedition for, V5:482.

Palmer, Horace, meteor falls on, V4:588-9.

Palmer, James, Church, given care of, at Kilcott, V4:135

teacher, ordained, V4:135.

Palmer, Jonathan, appointed bishop's counselor, V4:236.

Palmer, Seth, volunteers for exploring, V6:224.

Palmyra, Wayne County, New York, Harris, Martin, resident of, V1:19
 Joseph moved to, V1:2
 Mormon, Book of, copyright secured at, V1:71.

Pancoast, J., mentioned, V2:350, ftnt only.

panic of 1837, conditions in, V2:487-9 and ftnts only, 497.

parables, fisher's net, V2:272
 Joseph on "Lions of the Press," V5:274, et seq
 kingdom of heaven, mustard seed as, V3:389
 leaven, V2:270
 leaven in three measures of meal explained, V5:207
 mustard seed, V2:268
 pearl of great price, V2:272
 potters clay, Jeremiah's explained, V4:478
 prodigal son interpreted, V5:261
 sower, expounded upon, V2:265, et seq
 talents, applied to last dispensation, V2:24
 treasure, V2:271-2
 wheat and tares, (D&C § 86), V1:300, V2:267.

parents, children, censured for letting, prowl at night, V7:350
 children should stay with and obey, V2:247
 children, taught gospel after, V2:262
 children, unruly reported to, V2:520
 children, if not properly instructed brings charges before high council,
    V2:242
 Joseph expounds on and praises, V2:289.

Park, James, mission appointment published and field of labor, V6:337,
    V7:260

Parker, Elias, mentioned, V6:135-6.

Parker, John, represents British conference, V5:419.

Parker, John D., Joseph, arrests, V6:355-60
 Joseph, goes secretly to inform of movements of sheriff, V5:97
 Joseph declares gratefulness for aid rendered while in seclusion,
    V5:109
 Joseph, guard to in seclusion, V5:160
 Kirtland Camp, subscribed to constitution of, V3:91
 Kirtland Camp, joins near Dayton, Ohio, V3:116
 mission, assigned to go on, V4:430
 seventies, named to first quorum of, V2:203
 westward movement, captain of tenth company in, V7:482
 Zions Camp member, V2:184.

Parker, Lucius, mentioned, V2:470, ftnt only.

Parker, Mary, subscribed to constitution of Kirtland Camp, V3:92.

Parker, Robert, represents British conference, V5:419.

Parker, Samuel, Kirtland Camp, mentioned in, V3:111
    Kirtland Camp, subscribed to constitution of, V3:93
    mission appointment published and field of labor, V6:339
    mission call and field of labor, V5:349.

Parker, Samuel, subscribed to constitution of Kirtland Camp, V3:92.

Parker, Samuel, mentioned, V7:170.

Parker, Selah, mentioned, V4:395.

Parkhurst, Reuben, mission call in Illinois to disabuse public mind over arrest of Joseph, V5:485.

Parkinson, John, British Mission, mission in, V4:150
    elder, ordained, and devote all time to ministry, V4:148
    volunteers for service in vineyard, V4:216.

Parks, H. G., DeWitt, calls out militia to settle troubles at, V3:149-50
    DeWitt, letter to General Atchison concerning situation in, V3:155-6
    mob, orders dispersement of, V3:163
    saints, letter to Governor Boggs favorable to, V3:83-4.

Parks, William, appointed to preside over new Church district, V7:306.

Parr, Prudence, to receive Church aid in emigrating from England, V5:412.

Parr, William, British Mission, mission in, V4:150
    ministry, devote all time to labors of, V4:148
    volunteers for service in vineyard, V4:217.

Parrish, Betsy, dies of cholera in Missouri, V2:120
    Zions Camp member, V2:185.

Parrish, Warren, apostasy of, V2:528, 484-6
    clerk, V2:243, 250, 252, 285
    hands, relieved through laying on of, V2:321
    Joseph, attacks character of, V2:489, ftnt only
    letter to Joseph on illness, V2:385
    Prophet, becomes scribe to, V2:293
    Raymond, Martha H., marriage to, V2:324
    revelation to, forgiving sins and giving blessings, V2:311
    scribe, resumes duties as, V2:393
    seventies, named to first quorum of, V2:203
    seventy, ordained, V2:244
    Tennessee, letter relating mob abuses in, V2:447-8

PARRISH, WARREN (continued)

Zions Camp member, V2:184.

Parry, John, given care of Church at Stanley Hill, V4:138.

Parshall, William H., mission appointment published and field of labor, V6:336.

Parsons, James, to leave for British Mission, V7:171.

Parsons, Joseph, mentioned, V7:326.

Parsons, Thoret, mob, threatened by, V3:169
witness for defense of saints in Missouri, intimidated, V3:211
witness suggested to appear before Congress on redress, V4:97.

Partial, Mr., mentioned in Kirtland Camp, V3:112.

Partington, Rebecca, to receive Church aid in emigrating from England, V5:412.

Partridge, Edward, bishop, appointed of upper ward in Commerce, V4:12
bishop, sustained at Far West, V2:524
Clay County, at conference in, V2:1
council, report of, V2:527
death of, V4:132
endowment, chosen to go to Kirtland to receive, V2:112
Far West, defends local presidency of the Church at, V3:4
Far West, presides at public meeting at, V3:62
genealogy, V1:128-9, ftnt only
general government, appointed on committee to write petition to, V3:241
Joseph, inquires of duty, V1:128
Kirtland, starts for, V1:145
Liberty jail, letter to Joseph in concerning saints, V3:272-3
Lord, revelation stating pleased with, V2:302
mission, leaves Kirtland for, V1:188
Missouri, appointed to purchase lands in, V2:112
Missouri, arraigned for murder, treason, burglary, arson, robbery, and larceny at Richmond, V3:209
Missouri governor, signs petition to, V1:415
mob, his own narrative of treatment by, V1:390-1
mob, tars and feathers, V1:390
poor, on helping the, V3:247
ransom, offers himself as for saints in Jackson County, V1:394 and ftnt
revelation to, V1:131
saints, signs memorial of, in Missouri, V3:224
united order, bishop administrating, (D&C § 51:13-14) V1:174
West, instructs saints on removal, V4:39

PARTRIDGE, EDWARD (continued)

   witness, suggested to appear before Congress on redress, V4:97
   Zion, accompanies Prophet to, V1:188
   Zion, acknowledged head of Church in, V1:409
   Zions Camp, arrives in from Clay County, V2:95
   Zion Temple, at dedication of, V1:199.

Partridge, Eliza, mentioned, V5:391.

Partridge, Harriet Pamela, death of, V4:132.

Partridge, Jemima, mother of Edward, V1:128, ftnt only.

Partridge, Lydia, mentioned, V5:391.

Partridge, William, father of Edward, V1:128, ftnt only.

patriarch, Albertson, John, ordained second, in England, V4:333 and ftnt
   Church, Hyrum Smith appointed of, V4:229 and ftnt
   Draper, William Sen., called to be, V7:624
   evangelist, is, V3:381
   Far West, to receive pay for services, V2:527
   Kirtland High Council, provides remuneration for, V2:273
   Lamech next from Enoch, V4:210
   Melling, Peter, ordained, V4:120 and ftnt
   Morley, Isaac, sustained, V2:524
   office, notes on, V7:301
   office, right to, V7:300, et seq
   ordination, form of, V7:302
   Smith, Asael, ordained, V7:302-3
   Smith, John, ordained, V6:173
   Smith, John, voted of Church, V7:622
   Smith, William, ordained to Church, V7:418.

patriarchal order, comment on, V2:234, ftnt only.

patriarchal blessings, Albertson, John, of, V4:334
   meeting giving, V2:346-7
   paid, recorder of, to be, V2:528
   pay, to receive for, V2:273
   pay, Frederick G. Williams to receive for scribing same, V2:273
   record book of, causes problems, V2:275.

Patrick, Mr., mentioned, V1:422, ftnt only; V5:538; V6:347.

Patrick, Hugh, to receive Church aid in emigrating from England, V5:412.

Patrick, Shepherd G., Joseph, affidavit on conduct of arrest and trial of, V5:476, et seq
   Joseph, testifies of second arrest of, in Illinois, V6:67.

Patrick Henry, emigrant ship, V4:94.

Patten, Archibald, appointed to preside over new Church district, V7:305.

Patten, Charles, mentioned, V7:158.

Patten, David W., Apostle, blessing as member of, V2:190
    Apostle, chosen one of, V2:187
    Apostle, sustained to Church, V2:509
    Apostles, does not recommend certain of, to conference at Far West, V3:14
    Crooked River, leads charge in battle of, V3:170
    dispensations, epistle on, V3:49-54
    Far West, presides in high council at, V3:7, 8
    Far West, speaks in favor of the Prophet in general assembly at, V3:4, 5
    funeral of, V3:175
    killed by mob in battle of Crooked River, V3:171
    mob, dispatched by order to retake prisoners and disperse, V3:170
    mob, incident with, V2:447-8
    tongues, interprets speaking in, V2:428
    Zion, elected president pro tempore in, V3:6
    Zions Camp member, V2:184.

Patten, James, excommunicated for improper conduct, V2:241.

Patten, John, baptisms for dead, appointed recorder of in Iowa, V4:382
    Iowa Territory, appointed to high council at, V4:12
    Missouri, covenanted to assist saints in removing from, V3:254
    tried for failure to keep contracts, V2:482.

Patten, Phebe Ann, house of plundered and robbed by apostates, V3:215.

Patterson, Mr., mob member in Missouri, V1:480.

Patterson, Captain, mentioned, V6:244.

Paul, Brother, enters complaint, V1:355.

Paul, the Apostle, Abel appeared to, V4:208
    Enoch appeared to, V4:209.

Pea, Sarah D., wife of Charles Rich, V2:507, ftnt only.

peace, Joseph not to cry after seeing signs of second coming, V3:391.

Peacock, George, petitions Governor Boggs on mob violence in DeWitt, V3:83.

pearl of great price, parable of explained, V2:272.
    See also parables.

Peart, Jacob, mentioned, V7:395.

Peck, Hezekiah, baptized, and wife, V1:88
bishop, appointed, V5:119
bishop, sustained, of a Nauvoo ward, V7:298
counselor to bishop and high priest, V1:363
priests quorum, counselor to, in Nauvoo, V4:312
prophecy, present in Missouri at Apostles' departure to fulfill, V3:339.

Peck, John, policeman in Nauvoo, V6:149.

Peck, Martha, prophecy, present in Missouri at Apostles' departure to fulfill, V3:339.

Peck, Martin H., Church, appointed to preside over new district of, V7:306
Kirtland Camp, joins at Petersburgh, V3:100
Kirtland Camp, mentioned in, V3:108
Kirtland Camp, subscribed to consitution of, V3:92
son run over and healed, V3:113.

Peck, Mary Ann, prophecy, present in Missouri at Apostles' departure to fulfill, V3:339.

Peck, Polly, wife of Joseph Knight, Sen., V1:47, ftnt only.

Peck, Reed, buffetings of Satan, turned over to and condemned as openly sinning against Jesus, V3:232
excommunicated from Church, V3:284
Missouri trials, witness for state in, V3:210.

Peck, Washington, witness, V6:435.

Pemberton, Collins, mentioned, V5:509.

Penn, G., mission appointment published and field of labor, V6:338.

Penniston, William P., (also spelled Peniston), burning and murder, accuses saints of, V3:165
mob, headed in Clay County and incites people against Mormons on election day, V3:56-7
mob, oath of that saints have acted as, V3:61
saints, agrees to expulsion of, V3:216.

penny subscription, temple glass and nails bought by, V6:236.
See also Relief Society.

Penrose, Charles B., mentioned, V6:418.

pentecostal, times of experienced in Kirtland, V2:379-83.

people, receive judgments of God when, V1:278.

perdition, son of, fate of not revealed, V7:413-4
many going to be, V5:19
murderers possible to be classified as such, V6:253.

periodical, *Dogberry Paper*, attempt to publish Book of Mormon in, V1:76, ftnt only.

Perkins, Mr., appointed states attorney at trial of saints, V2:448.

Perkins, Andrew H., bishop's counselor, ordained, V7:375
　　Church, appointed to preside over new district of, V7:306
　　delegate to present truth to public, V6:483
　　mission appointment published and field of labor, V6:340
　　utility committee member to aid Church removal, V7:474
　　westward movement, captain of seventeenth company in, V7:482.

Perkins, Brother, mentioned, V3:378; V6:485; V7:388, 442, 564.

Perkins, Ute, mentioned, V4:477.

Perkins, William G., bishop, ordained, V7:375
　　Church, appointed to preside over new district of, V7:305
　　utility committee member to aid Church removal, V7:474
　　westward movement, in organization of, V7:626.

Perkins, William J., mentioned, V4:477.

Permain, H., Joseph, on relief expedition for, V5:482.

permit, to David Holman to live in Caldwell County or leave state, V3:206
　　to Mormon committee to go through Daviess County during winter, V3:210.

Perry, Asael, excommunicated for unchristianlike conduct, V2:444
　　fellowship reinstated, V4:14.

Perry, Brother, mentioned, V5:307, 390, 531.

Perry, Gustavus A., gives money for lands in Zion, V2:174.

Perry, Isaac, chosen to Adam-ondi-Ahman High Council, V3:38.

Perry, Josiah H., mission appointment published and field of labor, V6:336.

Perry, Luther, mobber, makes threats, V6:481
　　mobber, requests members to join mob, V6:511.

Perry, S. A., delegate to political convention in Nauvoo, V6:389.

Perry, Stephen C., MIA, aids in movement toward, V5:321
　　mission call and field of labor, V5:349
　　priesthood, ordains many to, V4:109
　　trial on *Expositor* affair, V6:453, 460, 448-9, 554, 568; V7:67.

Perry, William, Kirtland Camp, mentioned, V3:107
　　Kirtland Camp, subscribed to constitution of, V3:92
　　marriage of, V2:292

PERRY, WILLIAM (continued)

    temple, blessing for work on, V2:205.

persecution, apostates, receive severest from, V2:23

    baptism, spirit of, after, V1:43-4

    blasphemy, elder imprisoned for, V4:380

    Christianity, becomes persecuting religion, IntroV1:XLI, et seq

    Christianity, of heretics by early, IntroV1:LXV

    dissertation on, V5:98, et seq

    England, of saints in, noted, V4:296-7

    Joseph after his first vision, V1:6-7

    Joseph, all sects united to persecute, V1:7

    Joseph, almost in infancy, V1:7

    Joseph, extends to family of, V1:19

    Joseph, from first vision to Moroni, V1:9

    Joseph, reflections on, V1:97-8

    life, if ye live godly, ye shall suffer, V5:98

    Manchester, in, V1:19

    Methodists, commences again by, V1:108

    Missouri persecutions, blame placed upon mobbers and state, V1:471

    Missouri persecutions, was from enlightened people, IntroV3:XVII

    Mormon, Book of, increases after published, V1:84

    plates, increasing with, V1:18

    religion, as a result of, V1:97

    spirit of at Harmony, V1:44.

    See also affidavits; Latter-day Saints, Church of Jesus Christ of; letters; mob; persecutions, Illinois; persecutions, Iowa; persecutions, Missouri; persecutions, Ohio; Smith, Joseph.

persecutions, Illinois, affidavits on, V6:528, et seq

    anti-Mormon, river disaster by, V7:582

    Apostles, appeal of, to Governor Ford concerning mob, V7:489-90

    Appanoose, mob action at, V7:407

    Avery, D., proceedings of kidnapping of, V6:109

    Backenstos, J. B., acquittal of on murder charge, V7:541

    Badham, R., mob attacks and robs and stabs, V6:110

    Carlin, Governor, opinion and designs of, V5:118-9

    Carthage, anti-Mormons meet in, preamble and resolutions of mob, V6:4, et seq

    Carthage, letter of Governor Ford requesting Joseph come to, V6:521

    Carthage, mob action at, concerning aid from Governor Ford, V6:502

    Carthage, mob rumors around, V5:541

    Carthage, movements of mob, V6:520

PERSECUTIONS, ILLINOIS (continued)

Carthage, John Taylor's account of interview with Governor Ford at, V6:543, et seq

Carthage jail, mob action, attack on, V7:30-1

Carthage mob, affairs of, V6:171-3

character of people in western Illinois, IntroV6:XXVI, et seq

Church, why, welcome in Illinois, IntroV6:XXVIII

Deming, General, actions by mob bring death of, V7:439

Durfee murder, *Neighbor* extra on, and house burning, V7:528-30

Durfee murder trial farce, V7:527

Durfee murder trial farce ended, V7:532

editorial on, V5:98, et seq

educational status of people in western Illinois, IntroV6:XXVIII

election, increase at close of the 1843, V5:528

Expositor affair, Joseph and others arrested and trial of, on, V6:487, et seq

expulsion, anti-Mormon meeting on, from Illinois, V6:221

exterminate, proposed plan by government to, V7:544

extradition, legal opinion given on, V5:173, et seq

Hancock, interview with Governor Ford on militia and mob in, V7:492-3

Hancock, meeting on anti-Mormons at, V5:537-8

horse thieves, anti-Mormonism article on, V6:43-4

Illinois, notice that either saints or others must leave, V7:195

Illinois militia, search of Nauvoo by, V7:447-8

Joseph, account of second trial of, in Illinois by William Clayton, V6:380, et seq

Joseph, accusations and indictments for adultery against, V6:403

Joseph, actions against witness in murder of, V7:384

Joseph, answer of Ford to mob, review of murder of, V7:160, et seq

Joseph, arrest of, on second writ, V5:439, et seq

Joseph, attempted arrest of, by Missourians September 3, 1842, V5:145-6

Joseph, attorneys' affidavits concerning second trial of, in Illinois, V5:476-8

Joseph, Governor Carlin attempts to trap, V5:168

Joseph, Governor Carlin offers reward for capture of, V5:167

Joseph forced to move into seclusion on false warrants, V5:89, et seq

Joseph, Governor Ford receives Missouri indictment for, V5:422

Joseph, Governor Ford threatens writ against, V5:433

Joseph, letter of Governor Carlin to Emma on difficulties of, V5:130-1

PERSECUTIONS, ILLINOIS (continued)

Joseph, letter of Governor Ford to, refusing to recind arrest orders, V5:205-6

Joseph, letter to President of the U. S. for aid, V6:508

Joseph, probability of indictment of, at Springville, V6:450

Joseph, purported order of arrest of, by U. S. President, V5:363

Joseph, recording Governor Ford's reception of information of, V6:542

Joseph remarks on possible traitor in own quorum, V6:170

Joseph, report of search for, on Missouri warrant, V5:92

Joseph suggests to fight future mobs, V6:94

Joseph, testimony of, against dissenters at Nauvoo, V6:408, et seq

Joseph, writs against brethren for aid to, V7:444

Joseph, writs against, returned, V5:461, et seq

Judd, Nelson, attempted killing of, V6:179-80

larceny, false arrests on, V7:373

legislature, anti-Mormons expression in Illinois, V7:368

legislature, attitude of, V7:370-1

martyrdom, false rumors spread by mob of Mormon reaction to, V7:25

martyrdom, Warsaw mob actions after, V7:159

martyrdom mob, leaders and members of, enumerated, V7:143, et seq

memorial of Nauvoo City Council petitioning Congress for redress and protection, V6:125, et seq

mob, accusations by, dispel Joseph and Mormons, V6:451

mob, actions toward C. Loveland, V6:504-5

mob, affidavit of Orson Hyde on threats to drive out saints by, V6:145

mob, affidavit on movements of, V6:480-1

mob, arms supplied to, V6:507

mob, brethren on feelings toward future action by, V6:94-5 and ftnt

mob burnings, V7:444

mob burns home of David Holman, V6:133

mob chases sheriff, one killed by Rockwell, V7:446

mob, control of and action of grand jury, V7:493-4

mob controls grand jury, V7:486

nob, false writs issued by, V7:380

mob, fever of, October 1845 very high, V7:481

mob, letter on threats of, V6:481-2

mob militia raised, V7:445

mob, other actions by, V7:439-40

mob, petition of Relief Society to Governor Carlin for protection against, V5:146-8

mob, plan of attack by, V7:388

PERSECUTIONS, ILLINOIS (continued)

mob poisons Joshua Smith, V7:514

mob, rumors of "wolf hunt" by, V7:270

mob shoots and poisons member, V7:523-4

mob threats against Sheriff Backenstos, V7:390

mobocrat suggests westward movement by Church, V7:499, et seq

Mormons, proposal to take state arms from, V5:201

Mormons, Major Warren reportedly turned friendly to, V7:530-1

murderers, mob activities at Carthage at trial of martyrdom, V7:312

murderers, mob attempts to elect officers to screen martyrdom, V7:223

murder trial, inflammatory speeches against Church by defense counsel at martyrdom, V7:420

Nauvoo, defense of prepared for, V6:479

Nauvoo, mail to cut off, V6:450

Nauvoo, plans of mob to drive all saints to, V7:442

Nauvoo, previous attempt on attack of, disclosed, V6:575

Nauvoo, public meeting at, on mob actions and false accusations, V6:483

Nauvoo, some arrests in, 1845, V7:428

Nauvoo charter, powers of questioned, V5:153-5

Nauvoo charter, resolution proposed to repeal, V5:201

Nauvoo Expositor, episode, V6:432, et seq

Nauvoo Legion, auditor refuses state payment for service in, V6:95

Nauvoo Neighbor, article to public on mob affair, V6:496

Nauvoo Temple, writs for Twelve cause search of, V7:553-4

New York Tribune, article on feared repeat of Missouri in, V7:170-1

persecution, letter of Thomas Ford on U. S. Government involvement in, V7:562-4

press, opposition, arrives in Nauvoo, V6:357

prophecy by Joseph on mob, V6:532

retributive justice, article by Church on, V6:460

Redden, J., mob attempts capture of, V7:486-7

saints, Esquire Goodwin petitions Governor to not persecute, nonmember, V6:101

saints, letter of John C. Calhoun on policy towards if elected, V6:155-6

saints removal, people of Illinois acquiesce to, V7:450-1

saints removal, resolutions of citizens of Quincy accepting, V7:451-3

Spencer, O., interview with Governor Ford, V7:423-4

Times & Seasons, article on, to October 1845, V7:510-2

Warsaw, mass meeting at, preamble and resolutions of mob, V6:462, et seq

Warsaw mob action arises in, threatens Nauvoo, V6:119-20

PERSECUTIONS, ILLINOIS (continued)

westward camp, because of, incomplete and unprepared, V7:605

"wolf hunt," for Mormons called for, V6:222

writs out for several brethren, V5:448

Yelrome, mobs burning houses of brethren at, V7:439

Yelrome, mob forces members from, V7:440

Yelrome, proposition to mob at, V7:441-2

Young, Brigham, reflections of, on exodus of saints from Nauvoo, V7:602-3

Young, Brigham, writs on, issued, V7:396.

See also affidavits; Carthage Greys; Carthage, Illinois; Carthage jail; Latter-day Saints, Church of Jesus Christ of; Ford, Thomas; letters; martyrdom; mob; Smith, Joseph; stories; Apostles, Twelve.

persecutions, Iowa, mob actions in, V7:572

See also affidavits; letters; mob.

persecutions, Missouri, affidavits on, V5:495-7

Alvord, T., affidavit of, concerning, V4:57

assassin, article on O. P. Rockwell as, V6:35-6

Avery, Daniel, affidavit of, concerning, V4:60-1

Avery, Daniel, affidavit of, on his treatment in Missouri, V6:145, et seq

Avery, Daniel, release of, from imprisonment, V6:142

Baptist Church, part of, V1:392

barbarities, examples of, by mob, V3:411

Beebe, George, beating of, recorded, V3:437

Belknap, G., affidavit of on threats of invasion from Missouri, V6:502

Bernhisel, J. M., affidavit of on threats of invasion from Missouri, V6:511

Black, Adam, major role against saints in, V3:59-60, 64-5, 166, 205

blood, trail of indicates path of expelled saints, V3:439

bloody footmarks, trace outcasts by, V4:369-70

Bogart, Samuel, major role against saints in, V3:158, 165, 169, 210-1

Boggs, Governor, extermination order of, V3:175, 426

Boggs, Governor, part of, in, expounded, V3:328

Boggs, Governor, sends orders to expel saints and punish leaders, report to, V3:204-7

Burk, John M., affidavit concerning, V4:56

Cahoon, William F., affidavit of, concerning, V4:52-3

Canfield, Cyrus, affidavit of on threats of invasion from, V6:502-3

Carter, Simeon, affidavit of on sufferings of, V4:49-50

Casper, Thomas D., affidavit of, concerning, V4:63-4

cause, religion was, IntroV3:L

cause, religious life was chief, IntroV3:XLVII

PERSECUTIONS, MISSOURI (continued)

causes of, considered, IntroV3:XVII, et seq

character, difference of, one of causes of, IntroV3:XXII

Christian persecution compared, IntroV3:LIV, et seq

Civil War, Missourians killed as result of, IntroV3:LXXII, et seq

Clark, Joseph, affidavit of, concerning, V4:63

Clark, Timothy B., affidavit of, concerning, V4:58

Clay, Henry, receives history of, V6:94

Clay County, petition of citizens of to Mormons to move out, V2:448, accepted, V2:454

Cole, Owen, affidavit of, concerning, V4:64

Congress, letter suggesting memorializing of, V6:62-3

Curtis, Simons P., affidavit of, concerning, V4:67-8

Dryden, William, affidavit of stating law and order cannot be had in Caldwell County, V3:77

enlightened age, came from people of, IntroV3:XVIII

enlightenment, responsibility increases with, IntroV3:XVIII

extermination order of Governor Boggs, V3:426

extradition, legal opinion given on, V5:173, et seq

extradition presented to Governor Ford for repeal, V5:205-6

extradition and kidnapping, public meeting at Nauvoo on, by Missourians, V6:101-2

false certificate on conduct of General Clark in, V3:359, ftnt only

federal government, petition of saints to, concerning, V4:24, et seq

Foutz, Jacob, affidavit of, concerning, V4:68-9

"Friendly Hint to Missouri," article on, V6:245-7

Gates, Gibson, affidavit of, concerning, V4:71

God, John B. Clark invokes unknown to aid liberalization of gospel practices, IntroV3:XLIX

gospel, efforts to live strictly was major factor, IntroV3:XLVII

Green, Addison, affidavit of, concerning, V4:65

Greene, John P., affidavit of, concerning, V4:65

Groves, Elisha H., affidavit of, concerning, V4:68

Haun's Mills massacre, narrative of, V3:183, et seq

Hawk, William, affidavit of, concerning, V4:58

Humphrey, Smith, affidavit of, concerning, V4:62

Hyrum's statement of sufferings in, V3:373-4

Illinois, continue into, V4:365, et seq

Indians, Church communicated with, IntroV3:XXX

Indians, Church position on, in Missouri, IntroV3:XXXI

Indians, mob militia painted as, V3:411

PERSECUTIONS, MISSOURI (continued)

Indians, one problem that made possible the expulsion of saints, IntroV3:XXXII

Indians, word against Missourians, IntroV3:LXXI

Indians, the saints and, IntroV3:XXIX, et seq

indictments, new, of old charges, V5:307

Jayhawkers formed from, IntroV3:LXX

Johnston, Jesse W., affidavit of, concerning, V4:64

Joseph, affidavit of, to Governor Ford on, V5:493, et seq

Joseph, arrest of, on extradition warrants, V5:209

Joseph, arrest of, on second writ, V5:439, et seq

Joseph, attempted arrest of, by Missourians, September 3, 1842, V5:145-6

Joseph, continue to indict in, V5:422

Joseph, gives impressions on, V3:327, et seq

Joseph, governor of Missouri offers reward for capture of, V5:167

Joseph, incident of acquiring accommodations by, V5:211

Joseph, narration of experiences in Missouri, V3:368, et seq

Joseph, presents amounts concerning losses to Congress, V4:74

Joseph, Moses Wilson tries to take to Missouri, V5:500

kidnapping, affidavits of Philander Avery on Illinois, V6:122

kidnapping, affidavit of D. Chapman on Daniel Avery, V6:100

kidnapping of Daniel Avery, V6:99 and ftnt

Kirtland saints, letter of Joseph to reproving for failure to aid in, V4:225, et seq

land purchases lost by members enumerated, V3:424

lands, lost in value, IntroV3:XVII

Lathrop, Asahel A., affidavit of, concerning, V4:65-7

legislature gives mob appropriation, V4:74, ftnt only

legislature, petition concerning, tabled by, V3:242 and ftnt

Liberty Jail, persecutions at, V3:258, 420, 448

Lowry, John, affidavits concerning, V4:56

Lucifer as a factor in, IntroV3:LIX

Lucifer, bitterness and work of, as sole cause, IntroV3:LXI

Maginn, Ezekiel, affidavit of, concerning, V4:64-5

Maine, petition of Benjamin Andrews to, for aid in redress of, V6:178

martyr, first, killed in, November 4, 1833, V1:431 and ftnt

Massachusetts, appeal of Phinehas Richards to, on redress for, V6:193

Massachusetts, memorial of Noah Packard sent to, for aid in redress, V6:236

PERSECUTIONS, MISSOURI (continued)

memorial of Nauvoo City Council, petitioning Congress for redress and protection, V6:125, et seq

memorial for redress of, to Congress by John Frierson, V6:83 and ftnt, et seq

memorial of saints to state legislature concerning, V3:217, et seq

minutes of committee on removal, V3:254-5, 274-5, 284-5

Missouri, accounts of actions of generals of, V4:394, et seq

Missouri, affidavit of Canfield and Belknap concerning threats of invasion from, V6:502-3

Missouri, apostrophe to by E. R. Snow, V6:192-3

Missouri, General Sterling Price's raids on, IntroV3:LXV

Missouri, jayhawkers' destruction in, IntroV3:LXVI

Missouri, Joseph relates treatment of witnesses in, V6:108

Missouri, public meeting in Nauvoo on aggressions of, V6:111-3

Missouri, sends "Whitewash" to Congress on, V4:299

Missouri, type of people in, character, descendants from, social existence, IntroV3:XIX, et seq

"Missouri Rapped," article on enlargement of Mormonism, V5:518-20

Missourians' loss of property enumerated, IntroV3:LXXIII

Missourians, slaves fought, IntroV3:LXX

mob, burns own houses that had been purchased by saints and blamed Church, V3:409

mob, comments on gospel life, IntroV3:XLVII, et seq

mob, composition during, IntroV3:XVIII

mob, feeds Joseph and others poison and human flesh while imprisoned, V3:420, 448

mob, from Missouri to go to Illinois, V6:481

mob, slavery part of secret constitution of, IntroV3:XXIV

mob, memorandum of between, and saints, V1:394

mob manifesto, religious beliefs of saints caused, IntroV3:XLVIII

mob manifesto, quoted on religious differences, IntroV3:XLVII

molesting, perpetrated on Mormon women by mob, V3:420, 428

Negro, Church position on, in Missouri, IntroV3:XXV

Negro, Joseph's views on, 1844, IntroV3:XXVI

Negro or mulatto, law concerning in Missouri, IntroV3:XXIV

New York Tribune, article on, in, V4:551-2

Owen, Jedediah, affidavit concerning, V4:56-7

Pennsylvania, Sidney Rigdon's peroration to, on redress for, V6:191-2

Pettigrew, David, affidavit of, concerning, V4:71-3

Phelps, W. W., confesses errors against Church in, V4:141-2

PERSECUTIONS, MISSOURI(continued)

Pitkin, George W., testimony of, concerning, V3:432-3

political fear a real cause of, IntroV3:XXIX

political fears of, IntroV3:XXVII, et seq

political issues concerned saints very little, IntroV3:XXVII

political jealousy prompted part of, IntroV3:XXVIII

political motto of Church in Missouri, IntroV3:XXIX

political power, mob fears concerning, of saints, IntroV3:XXVIII

Powell, James, affidavit of, concerning, V4:61

Pratt, Parley P., account of escape of, and others, V3:399, et seq

Pratt, Parley P., letter of, concerning wrongs and his imprisonment, V3:352-4

Pratt, Parley P., testimony of, concerning, V3:424, et seq

prophecy of Joseph concerning extradition trial, V5:219-20

prophecy of Joseph concerning wrath of God as a result of, Intro-V3:LXVIII

prophecy of Joseph he would not go to Missouri, V5:216

public feeling, state of, expressed, V3:172

redress, letter of Sidney Rigdon to Joseph indicating none possible, V4:102

religious freedom, Missouri constitution on, IntroV3:LX

removal, committee on, in Missouri, V3:251, 254-6, 274

removal, committee on, sends families away, V3:319

removal, visit of mob to committee on, in Missouri, V3:306-7

resolutions by Missouri Senate, on, V3:246

retribution for, IntroV3:XLII, et seq

retribution summarized, IntroV3:LXXIV

Richards, Levi, affidavit of, concerning, V4:70-7

Rigdon, Sidney, discourse of, commented on, IntroV3:XLIV

Rigdon, Sidney, Joseph's comments on discourse of, IntroV3:XLV

Rigdon, Sidney, testimony of, concerning, V3:449, et seq

Riggs, Burr, affidavit of, concerning, V4:67

Rockwell, O. P., statement of, concerning imprisonment, V6:135, et seq

Root, Henry, affidavit of, concerning, V4:62-3

saints, agreement between Jackson County mob and, V1:394-5

saints, all hardships of, returned more abundantly, IntroV3:LXIII

saints, character, area, and type of descendants from, IntroV3:XX, et seq

saints, considered themselves favored of God, IntroV3:XXXIII

saints driven from state enumerated, V3:431

saints, fifty killed as result of, IntroV3:XVII

PERSECUTIONS, MISSOURI (continued)

saints, growth in Missouri enumerated, IntroV3:XLIII and ftnt

saints, left in hands of enemies, reasons for, IntroV3:XLI

saints, number of, driven from state, IntroV3:XVII

saints, position compared with statements of decline and fall of Roman Empire, IntroV3:LI, et seq

saints, reaction to, explained, IntroV3:XLIV

saints, required to eat bark of trees to survive, V3:405

saints, sins of, in Missouri enumerated, IntroV3:XL

Senate Judiciary Committee, case before and report of, V4:81, et seq

Shumaker, David, affidavit of, concerning, V4:69-70

slavery, question of, IntroV3:XXII, et seq

slavery, reason why became issue in, IntroV3:XXVII

Sloan, James, affidavit of, concerning, V4:69

Smith, Hyrum, testimony of, concerning, V3:404, et seq

Smith, John, affidavit of, concerning, V4:59-60

Smith, John, affidavit of, concerning, V4:62

Smith, Samuel, affidavit of, concerning, V4:60

Stewart, Urban V., affidavit of, concerning, V4:58-9

Tennessee, appeal of Alphonzo Young to, on redress for, V6:226

transgressions of saints not violations of law, IntroV3:XL

treason, belief in Daniel prophecy condemned as, IntroV3:L

unwisdom a definite factor in, IntroV3:XLVII

unwisdom, the facts of, IntroV3:XXXIII

unwisdom, of the saints in, IntroV3:XXXII, et seq

unwisdom, Zion as part of, IntroV3:XXXIV

unwise statements set forth, IntroV3:XLVI

VanBuren, President, investigation asked for, of, V3:333-4

Vermont, appeal of Joseph to native state, to aid, V6:88, et seq

Wight, Lyman, testimony of, concerning, V3:437, et seq

Williams, Frederick G., affidavit of, concerning, V4:69

Young, Brigham, testimony of, concerning, V3:433, et seq

Zion, fears of Missourians exaggerated as to possession of, IntroV3:XLII

Zion, saints driven from, reason for, IntroV3:XXXIX

Zions Camp, failure of, IntroV3:XXXIX.

See also affidavit; Boggs, Lilburn W.; Latter-day Saints, Church of Jesus Christ of; Doniphan, Alexander W.; Dunklin, Daniel; Far West; King, Austin A.; letters; Lucas, Samuel D.; militia; Missouri correspondence; Missouri trials; mob; persecution; saints; Smith, Joseph; stories.

persecutions, Ohio, mob takes over temple, V7:484.

PERSECUTIONS, OHIO (continued)

See also affidavits; letters; mob; persecution.

persecutions, United States, Church, proposed plans by government to exterminate, V7:544

Joseph, purported arrest order for, from President, V5:363

Nauvoo Temple, writs for Apostles cause search of, V7:553.

pestilence, God rules, dissertation in *Star*, V1:282.

Peter, James and John, Elias gave keys of priesthood to on Mount, V3:387

John the Baptist under the direction of, V1:40

Presidency, held keys of First, V1:258, ftnt only.

Peterson, Canute, ordained priest, V6:400.

Peterson, Richard B., baptized, V1:81.

Peterson, Ziba, buffetings of Satan, turned over to, V1:367

Lamanites, mission to, V1:118-9

Lamanites mission, dropped from, V1:195

revelation to, V1:118.

petition, Boggs, Governor, saints in DeWitt to, V3:82

Carlin, Governor, Nauvoo City Council, to, V5:68-70

Congress, Elias Higbee and Robert B. Thompson to, V4:237

Dunklin, Governor, of December 6, 1833, to, V1:451-2

Dunklin, Governor, presented to, V1:423

Dunklin, Governor, of saints to, V1:410, et seq

habeas corpus, Joseph Smith for writ of, V5:461-5

House of Representatives, presented to, V4:250-1

legislature, of saints tabled by, V3:242

Lord, Joseph asks for six specific blessings both personal and for Church, V2:2-3

Missouri persecutions, of saints to federal government on, V4:24, et seq

Missouri saints, in behalf of, V2:329

President of the United States, for redress and assistance in Missouri problem, V1:483, et seq

Prophet, to hear speak, V6:533.

See also affidavits; Latter-day Saints, Church of Jesus Christ of; letters; Missouri correspondence;persecutions; Smith, Joseph.

Pettibone, Rosetta L., mother of Lorenzo Snow, V4:162, ftnt only

Pettigrew, David, Indiana conference, president of, V7:315

Iowa Territory High Council, appointed to, V4:12

mission appointment published and field of labor, V6:336

PETTIGREW, DAVID (continued)

Missouri, arraigned for treason, murder, burglary, arson, robbery, and larceny at Richmond, V3:209

Missouri persecutions, affidavit concerning, V4:71-3

stake, counselor to, in Iowa, V4:352, 399.

Pettigrew, Elizabeth, covenanted to assist saints in removing from Missouri, V3:254.

Pettigrew, Hiram, death of, V3:376.

Pettigrew, Louise P., child of dies, V3:376.

Pettingill, Alanson, subscribed to constitution of Kirtland Camp, V3:92.

Petty, Albert, justice of the peace, Far West, prisoners tried before, V3:75

Pew, George, mission appointment published and field of labor, V6:338.

Phelps, J. R. G., mission appointment published and field of labor, V6:336.

Phelps, Laura, death of caused by Missouri persecutions, V4:510, 513

husband arrives at jail to see, V3:382, 399, ftnt only.

Phelps, Morris, Church, appointed to preside over new district of, V7:306

Columbia prison, escape from, V3:399-402, ftnt only

high priest, ordained, V2:244

Joseph, accompanies in arrest, V4:366

mission appointment published and field of labor, V6:339

Missouri trials, witness for state in, V3:210

Richmond jail, placed in to stand trial for murder and treason, V3:212

wife of, leaves in prison, V3:335.

Phelps, Sally, marriage of to W. W., V1:186, ftnt only

receives endowment in Nauvoo Temple, V7:543.

Phelps, Waterman, son of W. W., V2:227.

Phelps, William Wine, affiant to public proclamation on mob lies, V6:495

Avery charges, letter of, on, and witnesses, V6:132-3

Benton, Senator, letter to, requesting aid, V1:487-8

buffetings of Satan, turned over to, and condemned as openly sinning against Jesus, V3:232

case of, concerning his return to Kirtland taken before high council, V2:125

Church business, letter of Prophet requesting he stay out of, V3:358-9 and ftnt

consolation, word of, V7:152-3

delegate to, political convention in Nauvoo, V6:389

destroyer, sees, in open vision riding upon waters, V1:203

endowments, called to go to Kirtland to receive, V2:112

PHELPS, WILLIAM WINE (continued)

endowments, receives, in Nauvoo Temple, V7:543

Evening & Morning Star, to commence publishing, V1:217

excommunicated from Church, V3:284

excommunication of, for mortgaging Church, V3:8

Expositor, arrest for destruction of and trial on, V6:487, et seq

Far West, accepted as counselor to president at, V2:523

Far West, charges preferred against in high council at, V3:6-8

Far West, letter of, describing regions of, V2:444-5

Far West, resigns as postmaster at, V3:56

fellowship, letter accepting back into, V4:162-4 and ftnts

Ford, Governor, mission to, V6:61

genealogy, V1:186, ftnt only

hymns, arranged printing of, V2:273

Joseph, letter to, asking what to do, V1:457-8

Joseph, letter to, concerning status of Missouri persecutors May 1, 1834, V2:61-2 and ftnt

Joseph's letter to, V4:162-4 and ftnt

Joseph, speech of, on succession to, V7:237-8

Joseph, writes Vade Mecum to, V5:253-4 and ftnt

Kirtland, appointed to assist printing establishment in, V2:112

Kirtland, arrival in, V1:184-5, V2:227

Kirtland Temple, subscribed to and pays within one hour, V2:234

Lord, requests to do will of, V1:185

Missouri, arrives in Kirtland from, V1:206

Missouri, leaves Kirtland for, V1:188

Missouri, letter to Joseph confessing errors in, V4:141-2 and ftnt

Missouri, preaches first Sabbath in, V1:190

Missouri, tried for selling lands in, V3:3, et seq

Missouri trials, witness for state in, V3:210

mob destroys house and works in Missouri, V1:390 and ftnt

Nauvoo, elected mayor's clerk and fire warden, V5:270

Nauvoo, letter of informing General Deming that R. D. Foster was in, V7:169

Nauvoo, reads Prophet's views at, V6:210-1

Nauvoo Temple, appointed to officiate in, V7:548

petition, carries to Missouri governor for saints, V1:410

Prophet, makes his home with, V2:227

ransom, offers himself as, for saints in Jackson County, V1:394, ftnt only

revelations, to review and prepare for printing, V1:270

Rigdon, Sidney, no support for, V7:237-8

PHELPS, WILLIAM WINE (continued)

schoolbooks, selected to write, V7:475

Seventies Hall, composes hymn for dedication of, V7:331-2

signs attempted whitewash of General Clark's activity, V3:360, ftnt only

sin, revelation states he is in, V2:511

sin, under condemnation for, repents, V2:304

tongues, sings hymn of Nephites in, V1:409

trial for improper actions and improper use of Church funds, V2:483-4, ftnts only

Zion, rejected as president of, V3:5

Zion, sustained assistant president in, to David Whitmer, V2:126

Zion Temple, at dedication of, V1:199.

See also Latter-day Saints, Church of Jesus Christ of; letters; Missouri correspondence.

Phelps and Company, destruction of by Missouri mob, V1:411-2.

phenomena, strange reported, V6:121.

Philadelphia Saturday Courier, publishes anti-Church article, V2:351. See also newspapers.

Philips, E. I., mentioned, V4:111.

Philips, Mark, mentioned, V4:508.

Philips, Robert, mentioned, V4:508.

Phillips, David, Baptist pastor, V1:121, ftnt only.

Phillips, Edward, given care of Church at Ashfield and Crowcut, V4:139.

Phillott, Henry Wright, mentioned, V4:422, ftnt only.

Phippin, James W., mission appointment published and field of labor, V6:336.

phrenology, Apostles, some of receive, V6:37

chart of Joseph's head by, V5:52, et seq

chart of Willard Richards, V5:58, et seq.

Pierce, Isaac W., subscribed to constitution of Kirtland Camp, V3:93.

Pierce, John, called on mission and field of labor, V5:347.

Pierce, Joseph W., covenanted to assist saints in removing from Missouri, V3:253.

Pierce, Robert, acknowledges satisfaction of financial settlement, V4:519.

Pierce, T. P., child of, dies, V3:140.

Pierson, Edwin D., mentioned, V4:76.

Pierson, William, mentioned, V4:76.

Piexotto, Dr., teacher of Hebrew, V2:355.

Pike, John, reports mob movements, V6:519.

Pilate, Pontius, statement of, condemning Christ found, V4:420-1 and ftnt.

Pine, Delia F., witness for defense of saints in Missouri, intimidated, V3:211.

Pine, Joseph, subscribed to constitution of Kirtland Camp, V3:92.

pinery, expedition to, started, V5:57
  temple, lumber from for, V5:45-6.

Pinkham, Nathan, raid on home of, taken prisoner, V3:169, 177, ftnt only

Pioneer Company, Church, instructions to, concerning, V7:570
  instructions to, V7:591-2
  projected, V7:591
  west, organized to proceed and plant seed, V7:557
  Young, Brigham, report of upon reaching Salt Lake City, V7:616.

pioneers, see westward movement.

Pitcher, Colonel, court-martial, arrested for driving Mormons out, to be tried at, V1:469
  Missouri militia, leads, V1:433
  mob, takes saints' arms and agrees to disarm, does not, V1:435 and ftnt
  saints, against, V1:436, 491; V2:89, 135-6
  saints, avowed enemy of, V1:435.

Pitcher, Thomas, deputy constable, signed mob manifesto, V1:376.

Pitkin, George W., England, appointed to go to, with Twelve, V3:347
  mission call in Illinois to disabuse public mind over Joseph's arrest, V5:485
  Missouri, aids Joseph to, V1:266
  Missouri persecutions, testimony concerning, V3:432-3.

Pitman, James M., anti-Mormon sheriff in Missouri, V5:134, 212, 237.

Pitt, William, musician performs, V7:561
  priest, ordained, V4:135.

Pixley, Reverend, Church, writes tract against, V1:373 and ftnt
  Missouri mob, participated in, V1:392
  Missouri mob, prominence in, explained, V1:372 and ftnt

Pixton, Elizabeth, to receive Church aid in emigrating from England, V5:412.

planets, travel between believed possible by Hyrum, V6:300.

Plasket, Captain, mentioned, V6:52.

plates, angel, final return to, V1:2, ftnt only

PLATES (continued)

    angel, taken again by, V1:23

    baptism, translation raises question of, V1:39

    Cowdery, Oliver, asks for testimony of, V1:35

    Cowdery, Oliver, hears of, V1:32 and ftnt

    deposited, V1:12

    Joseph, beheld by, V1:16

    obtained, when to be, V1:16

    Kinderhook, Joseph receives and translates, V5:372

    received, V1:18

    received, cannot show when, V1:13

    returned the second time, V1:23

    stone box, in, V1:15

    strategy to get, V1:18

    translation, commencement of, V1:19

    three witnesses to see, V1:52

    vision where located, V1:13

    witnesses and Joseph pray to view, V1:54.

Player, William W., to receive Church aid in emigrating from England, V5:412

    temple, capstone of Nauvoo, laid by, V7:388, 417.

Pluck, Colonel, mentioned, V7:48.

poem, of Eliza R. Snow to John Taylor, V7:211.

Pogue, John, guard for prisoners in Missouri, V3:309.

poison, Joseph receives, V1:271

    Mormon prisoners given in Missouri, V3:420.

    See also Latter-day Saints, Church of Jesus Christ of; saints; Smith, Joseph.

police, Law, William, difficulty with, V6:162-5

    special, names of, V6:149-50.

    See also Nauvoo.

political motto, of Church, V3:9

    saints in Missouri, of, IntroV3:XXIX.

politics, Calhoun, John C., letter on policy towards saints if elected, V6:155

    Calhoun, John C., letter of Joseph to showing contempt for latter's position on saints, very remarkable letter, V6:156, et seq

    Church, balance of power factor of, IntroV6:XXII

    Church, suggestions on, V7:252

    Church history, the Illinois phase of, in, IntroV6:XXVIII

    convention, resolutions of, V6:390, et seq

POLITICS (continued)

    counsel, false in, IntroV6:XXIX
    Ford, Governor, comments on saints' voting habits, V7:2
    Joseph advises saints in Illinois on, V5:55
    Joseph, attitude of, V5:526
    Joseph, attitude of in Illinois, V4:479, et seq and ftnts
    Joseph, candidacy of for President, IntroV6:XXXIV
    Joseph, killed to keep out of presidency, V6:606
    Joseph on, V5:489
    Mormons union in, V5:232
    Nauvoo, state convention at, V6:386
    subserviency in, IntroV6:XXXI.

Polk, James K., mentioned, V6:431, V7:402-4, 482, 563, 611.

Pollard, Captain, mentioned, V7:75, 262, 433.

Pollitt, Thomas, volunteers for service in vineyard, V4:217.

polygamy, article rejecting, V2:246-7
    authorship, phraseology evidence of Joseph's, IntroV5:XXXVIII
    authorship, style as evidence of, IntroV5:XLIV
    devil projects sinful prototype in Nauvoo, V5:36-7
    devil reveals prototype of, V3:26
    Emma's rejection of, IntroV5:XXXII
    false type of practiced in Nauvoo, V5:79 and ftnt
    Joseph, not practiced yet, only holds keys of, V6:46
    Mormons, do not believe in, V3:28
    Prophet, reproves, in, IntroV5:XXXVI
    revelation, authorship of, IntroV5:XXXIV, et seq
    revelation, date of explained, IntroV5:XXIX
    revelation, given in answer to inquiry, IntroV5:XXXIV
    revelation on, explained, IntroV5:XXIX, et seq
    revelation, recurrence of principles as in other, IntroV5:XLII
    revelation, section recorded, V5:501, et seq.

poor, bishop, responsibility of, toward, V1:365
    Church members to support, V3:29
    help, means solicited to, V3:254
    Kirtland, not to be sent to but cared for in local branches, V2:468
    Nauvoo, to have labor in, V5:25
    neglect, do not, V1:381-3
    Partridge, Bishop, refuses to help, V3:247
    repentance, brought to by administering to wants of, V5:24-5
    rich cursed if not impart to, V5:35
    rich not to cast out, V1:339
    rich must give to, V4:608.

"Poor Wayfaring Man of Grief," hymn, V7:101
   Carthage Jail, sung in, V6:614-5.

Poorman, John, baptized, V1:86
   Prophet, defends against mob, V1:263.

Pope, Nathanial, Joseph, decision on trial of at Springfield, V5:223, et seq
   opinion, modifications of his, V5:244-5.

Porter, Mr., Joseph stays at public house of, V1:271.

Porter, Mr., mentioned, V5:508.

Porter, Dr., attends Brother Whitney, V1:271.

Porter, Francis, inquires for land in Kirtland, V2:295.

Porter, Jared, Kirtland Camp, mentioned in, V3:111
   Kirtland Camp, subscribed to constitution of, V3:93
   mission appointment published and field of labor, V6:339.

Porter, Malinda, witness for defense of saints in Missouri, intimidated
   V3:211.

Porter, Nathan T., mission appointment published and field of labor
   V6:339.

Porter, Sandford, Joseph, gives to assist, V5:300
   mission call and field of labor, V5:349.

Possons, William, given care of Church at Moor-End-Cross, V4:138

Post, Stephen, mission appointment and field of labor, V6:337.

Pottawatamie, Joseph, chiefs of interview, V5:479, et seq
   saints, depredations against, V7:627.

Potter, R., Brigham Young visits, V4:21.

potters clay, parable of from Jeremiah explained, V4:478.

Potts, Jacob, wounded at Haun's Mills by mob, V3:326, ftnt only

Potts, Jacob K., witnesses Haun's Mills massacre, V4:95.

poverty, extreme in Kirtland Camp, V3:88, 98.

Powell, Baden, quoted, V6:309, ftnt only.

Powell, Brother, beaten by mob, V3:411.

Powell, James, affidavit of Missouri persecutions, V4:61.

Powell, John, given care of Church at Lugwardine, V4:139.

Powers, Mr., lawyer in the service of the Prophet, V5:89, 91, 95.

Powers, Mr., mentioned, V6:414.

Powers, J. M., mission appointment published and field of labor, V6:339

Pratt, Addison, Hanks, Elder, on death of, V6:64
   mission call to Pacific Isles, V5:386

PRATT, ADDISON (continued)

 mission call and field of labor, V5:349
 mission, letter on Society Islands, V7:271, et seq
 mission, set apart to Society Islands, V5:404-5, 406.
Pratt, Anson, mentioned, V7:313.
Pratt, Charity, mother of Parley P., V1:119, ftnt only.
Pratt, Christopher, great-grandfather of Parley P., V1:119, ftnt only.
Pratt, Elizabeth, great-great-great-great-grandmother of Parley P., V1:119, ftnt only.
Pratt, Hannah, great-great-grandmother of Parley P., V1:119, ftnt only.
Pratt, Jared, father of Parley P., V1:119, ftnt only.
Pratt, Jemima, grandmother of Parley P., V1:119, ftnt only.
Pratt, Joseph, great-great-great-grandfather of Parley P., V1:119, ftnt only.
Pratt, Mary Ann, mentioned, V5:354.
Pratt, Nathan, mentioned, V6:99.
Pratt, Obediah, grandfather of Parley P., V1:119, ftnt only.
Pratt, Orson, Adam's sin, discourse on, V7:344-5
 America, fate of, V5:552 and ftnt
 America, sails for, V4:352
 astronomical observations, makes from Nauvoo Temple, V7:554
 Apostle, rebaptized and ordained, V5:256
 Apostle, restored to, V5:255
 Apostle, sustained as, to Church, V2:509
 Apostle, sustained as, by Church after death of Joseph, V7:295
 Apostles, blessing of, as member of, V2:194, ftnt only
 Apostles, chosen one of the, V2:187
 Apostles, one of, addresses saints at Nauvoo, V4:4
 Apostles, sustained member of at Salt Lake City, October 1848, V7:628
 Avon, New York, at conference in, V2:44
 baptized, V1:127
 Bennett, John C., letter denying association with, V5:167
 confidence, restored to, V5:252
 Eastern states, letter to wife concerning movement of brethren in, V4:54
 Edinburgh, opens mission in, V4:120
 Edinburgh, success in, V4:251
 endowments, receives in Nauvoo Temple, V7:544
 England, arrives in, V4:102
 England, condition of, during trip and arrival in, V4:104
 England, sails for, V4:94

PRATT, ORSON (continued)

England, starts on mission to, V4:7

Gauge of Philosophy, designated as, V7:435

genealogy, V1:127, ftnt only

Higbee, affidavit against, V6:177, 178

high council, sustained by Missouri, V2:124

Joseph, denounced by, V5:139

Joseph, gives bond for collection of funds for, V5:414

Joseph, turns letter of John C. Bennett over to, V5:252

Kirtland, appointed to return to, preaching by way, V2:44

Lord, inquires concerning his duty, V1:127-8

missing from Nauvoo, V5:60-1

mission appointment to travel, V2:35

Missouri, appointed with others to visit scattered saints in, V2:136

Nauvoo, credentials of as agent for City of, V6:262

Nauvoo property, letter on purchasing arms and selling, V7:509-10

Nauvoo Temple, appointed to officiate in, V7:548

Nauvoo University, elected Professor of Mathematics at, V4:414

prison, assists brother Parley to escape from, V3:399, ftnt only

"Remarkable Visions," publishes, V4:224-5

saints, farewell message to, of the eastern and middle states, V7:515, et seq

westward camp, takes astronomical position of, V7:598

Zions Camp member, V2:184

See also Apostles, Twelve; Latter-day Saints, Church of Jesus Christ of; letters.

Pratt, Parley Parker, America, returns to, for family, V4:177

apostate feelings, entertains, V2:488, ftnt only

Apostle, blessing of as member, V2:191-2

Apostle, chosen one of, V2:187

Apostle, sustained to Church, V2:509

Apostle, sustained by Church after death of Joseph, V7:294

Apostle, sustained one of, at Salt Lake City, October 1848, V7:628

apostolic charge, given to by Oliver Cowdery, V2:192-4 and ftnt

Archer of Paradise, designated as, V7:435

Boone County, removal of, with fellow prisoners to, V3:360-1, 363, 364-6, 368

Boston, attends conference at, V6:11

branch president, appointed in Missouri, V1:409, ftnt only

Church, to take presidency of all Eastern branches of, V7:317

Columbia, arrives prisoner at, V3:364-6

PRATT, PARLEY PARKER (continued)

at conference in Avon, New York, appointed to visit Churches in Black River, V2:44

confesses sin in Missouri, left them alive, V6:93

constitution and democracy, sentenced to be shot for believing in, V3:191 and ftnt

discourse of at October 1844 conference, V7:298-9

drunkards and thieves, preaches that all leave Nauvoo, V7:279

Dunklin, Governor, sent with message to, V2:88

endowments, called to go to Kirtland to receive, V2:113

endowments, receives, V6:98

England, arrives in, V4:102

England, condition of during trip to, V4:104

England, letter of informing that all churches in, against saints, V4:266

England, letter of on emigration and work in, V4:441

England, returns from, V4:224

England, sails for, V4:94

eternal duration of matter, treaties on, V4:54-5, ftnt only

eulogy of Lorenzo D. Barnes written by, V5:319-20

extradition of demanded by Governor Boggs, V4:198

Far West, arrives at, V3:27

Far West, records scene in, as he was taken prisoner, V3:193, ftnt only

genealogy, V1:118-9, ftnt only

Green Mountain Boys, enthusiastic on appeal to, V6:93-4

high council, sustained to Missouri, V2:124

jail, letter to Judge Austin A. King from, asking for trial or banishment , V3:352-4

Joseph, embittered against, V2:488 and ftnt

Joseph, speech on succession to, V7:238-9

letter from Hyrum to, on printing of Book of Mormon in New York, V4:47-8

letter of denouncing actions of Augustine Spencer, V6:354-5

letter to Joseph reporting progress of Church in East, V4:22

letter to Twelve on conditions in New York, V7:425-6

Millennial Star, editor of, V4:133

Millennial Star, resumes as editor of, V4:224

mission, accompanies Prophet on, to New York. V2:41

mission, called on, to Quakers, (D&C § 49) V1:167-9 and ftnt

mission, on for his church when converted, V1:121

mission, report of in Eastern states, V7:437

mission report of to Lamanites, V1:181, 183, ftnt only, et seq

mission, returns from, V1:181

PRATT, PARLEY PARKER (continued)

mission, starts on, to England, V4:7

mission to Lamanites, (D&C § 32) V1:118-20

Missouri, account of escape from, V3:399 and ftnt, et seq

Missouri, arraigned for treason, murder, burglary, arson, robbery, and larceny at Richmond, V3:209

Missouri, demands trial or banishment from, V3:352-4

Missouri, reports to Kirtland High Council conditions in, V2:39

Missouri, writ against to take to, V5:448

Missouri persecutions, testimony of, V3:424, et seq

mob, attacked by spies of, V1:427 and ftnt

mob enters camp of, in Missouri, V3:189 and ftnt

mob manifesto, answers Negro accusation in, V1:377, ftnt only

mob manifesto, response to, V1:376-7, ftnts only

Mount Pisgah, names, V7:607

murder and treason, placed in Richmond jail to stand trial for, V3:212

Nauvoo, one of the Twelve, preaches at, V4:4,6

Nauvoo, return to, V5:354

Prophet, description of associations with, V2:43, ftnt only

Prophet, sent as messenger to, V2:1

Rigdon, Sidney, had been preacher in church of, V1:121

Rigdon, Sidney, preaches at chapel of, V1:124

Rigdon, Sidney, presents Book of Mormon to, V1:122 and ftnt

Richmond, before grand jury at, V3:334-5

Richmond prison, reports story of Joseph rebuking guards at, V3:208, ftnt only

sacrifice, discourse on purpose of, V7:463-4

"Voice of Warning," first doctrinal work of the Church, V2:518 and ftnt

witness, suggested to appear before Congress on redress, V4:97

westward move, proposes outfit for family of five for, V7:447

writings, errors in, V4:7

Zion, ministry in, V1:400-1, ftnt only

Zions Camp member, V2:184

Zions Camp, recruiting officer in, V2:73, ftnt only.

See also Apostles, Twelve; British Mission; Latter-day Saints, Church of Jesus Christ of; letters.

Pratt, Sarah, great-grandmother of Parley P., V1:119, ftnt only.

Pratt, Sarah Marinda, endowments, receives in Nauvoo Temple, V7:544 rebaptism of, V5:256.

Pratt, T., ordained elder, V5:419.

Pratt, William, great-great-grandfather of Parley P., V1:119, ftnt only.

Pratt, William, great-great-great-great-grandfather of Parley P., V1:119, ftnt only.

Pratt, William D., (also B.), Church, appointed to preside over new district of, V7:306

Kirtland Camp, subscribed to constitution of, V3:92

mission appointment published and field of labor, V6:336

seventies, named to first quorum of, V2:204

Zions Camp member, V2:184.

prayer, Coltrin, Zebedee, special in behalf of mission of, V2:54

dedication accepted, V2:427

Evening & Morning Star, for success of the, V2:24

high priests required to state whether have family, V5:84

Kirtland Temple, dedicatory of, V2:420, et seq

Melchizedek Priesthood, sought by, V1:60

necessity of urged, V2:31

Prophet for deliverance of Zion, V2:50

Prophet et al for deliverance from debt and triumph over Hurlburt, V2:47-8

Prophet et al, special of, for means to go up to Zion, V2:291

Prophet et al for special blessings, V2:2-3

Prophet and Oliver Cowdery for continuance of blessings, V2:175

Prophet, Oliver Cowdery, F. G. Williams for deliverance from Dr. Hurlburt, V2:24

results if do not when moved to, V1:82

special to assist Church and blessings, V2:50-2

wicked man can do good by, V5:208

wicked, to be preserved by, V2:175

Young, Brigham, letter on family, V4:308-9.

predestination, election, doctrine of, and, explained, V4:360

election, in doctrine of, V4:258.

Preece, John, given care of Church at Ledbury, V4:138-9.

Prentice, Mr., mobber in Illinois, V5:528.

Prentice, Mr., mentioned, V5:213, 217, 223.

Prentice, Lyman, mentioned, V4:477.

Prentiss, Lyman, messenger to Governor from anti-Mormon meeting, V6:466

no business, member of martyrdom mob, V7:144.

Prentiss, William, mentioned, V5:239.

Presbyterian, Baptists, against, V1:4

PRESBYTERIAN (continued)

Canada mission episode, refused entry, V1:421
Coburn, Emily, divine of attempts to prevent conversion, V1:87
contending for, V1:3
Joseph preaches and exposes abominations of, V2:347
Joseph's family proselyted to, by, V1:3
Joseph's family, joined by four of, V1:3
Missouri mobs, participated in, V1:392
mob, clergyman of heads, V3:158
not true, V1:6
persecutors belong to, V1:97
Seymour, Lawyer, member of, V1:92.

Presidency, First, Adam had keys to, V3:385
anointing of oil, V2:379
Apostles, reconciliation between, and, V2:372, et seq and ftnt
Church proclamation to, scattered abroad, V4:267, et seq
Church would fall without, V7:629
Cowdery, Oliver, meeting with, V2:176 and ftnt
debts of, V2:480
embarrassments of, V2:479
everlasting in prior times also, V1:258, ftnt only
House of Lord, address to Church on building, V4:184, et seq
pay, Far West, to receive for services, V2:527
report of at general conference, V4:212, et seq
resolutions on ordinations, V2:398
Rigdon, Sidney, and F. G. Williams ordained to, V1:334
seven members in, V2:509
sustained as prophets at temple dedication, V2:417
trial of some before high council causes confusion, V2:485-6
washing body, ordinance of, V2:379
write to brethren scattered abroad, V2:4
Zion, removal to contemplated, V2:407.
See also Apostles, Twelve.

press, attitude of generally, V1:273
Church, purchase for, V1:217
Kirtland, established in and reprints all of the *Star* issues, V1:465 and ftnt
Kirtland, resolutions to establish at, V1:409
parable by Joseph on "Lions of the Press," V5:274, et seq
prayer for safety, printing of, V2:3
Star taken by mob, V1:390 and ftnt.
See also newspapers.

Price, Mr., mentioned, V7:157.

Price, Addison, witness for state in Missouri trials of saints, V3:210.

Price, Charles, Churches, given care of at Ledbury, Moorend Cross, Ridgway Cross, V4:139
    elder, ordained, V4:138
    ministry, devote all time to labors of, V4:148.

Price, E., appointed by public to assist saints in removing from Zion, V2:455.

Price, Jesse, affidavit on murderous intentions of William Law, V7:227.

Price, John W., reports on difficulties with Mormons, V3:151.

Price, Sterling, Missouri, named one of chief mobbers in, V3:205, 208, ftnt only, 327, 372
    Prophet, is sent to bring from Independence to Richmond, V3:205
    retribution, raids of, on Missouri as, IntroV3:LXV.

pride, Joseph rebukes among saints, V3:299.

priest, calling of, high nature of, V2:478
    contentions among, V1:3
    duties of, in Zion expounded, V2:229, ftnt only
    good feelings pretended among, V1:3
    Jackson County, of all denominations unite to prevent saints from returning to, V2:3
    learned confounded, V1:59
    ordinations, none without conference of high priests, V1:407
    priesthood, few worthy to be, under law of, V2:478.
    See also priesthood, Aaronic; priesthood.

priestcraft, Cowdery, Oliver, accuses Joseph of, V1:105.

priesthood, Adam first to hold, V4:207
    Adam had, V3:385
    article on given at conference of Church, V4:207, et seq
    blessings of, are all possible, V7:546
    Christ ordained to, V4:257
    Church publications, proceeds of, devoted to, V7:273
    council of, at Kirtland, May 2, 1835, V2:219 and ftnt
    dispensation, nature of, as to, V4:209
    earth, prior to, V4:207
    Elijah last to hold keys prior to Christ, V4:211
    everlasting and without days, V3:386
    gambling, taken for, V2:241
    gospel, always where ordinances of, are, V3:387
    home, taken for failure to rule, V2:241

PRIESTHOOD (continued)

judgment, right of rests in, V4:257
key signs and words, V4:555
keys of given to Peter, James, and John on Mount, V3:387
keys to be restored in temple, V4:608
knowledge of will bring salvation, V5:403
knowledge and doctrine, all, revealed through, V4:207
lesser organized in Nauvoo March 21, 1841, V4:312
lesser officers of, importance of, V2:478
Melchizedek and Aaronic explained, (D&C § 20) V1:67-8
Meridian of Times, identity of, as to fulness of time considered,
    IntroV1:XXX, et seq
Moses to John the Baptist, from, IntroV1:XXVIII, et seq
ordained according to Spirit, V1:79
order of, instructions concerning, V2:477-8
order of assembly meetings in, V2:391
ordinances, all of all dispensations shall be in last, V4:211
ordination, none without conference of high priests, V1:407
organization of at Kirtland Temple dedication, V2:411
priest, under requirements of, few even worthy to be, V2:478
sealing power of, discoursed, V6:183-5
spirits, governs, V4:575
taken for contrary teachings and illegal ordinations, V2:137-8
taken for failure to have discretion and understanding to act wisely,
    V2:141
translation, doctrine of, belongs to, V4:209
two in scripture, V4:207
voting, rule of, in, V4:340
1836, licenses received by, during second quarter, V2:446
1836, licenses issued in third quarter, V2:466
1836, licenses issued in fourth quarter, V2:468
1837, licenses issued in first quarter, V2:475
1837, licenses issued in second quarter, V2:490.
See also Priesthood, Aaronic; Adam; Latter-day Saints, Church of
    Jesus Christ of; deacon; doctrine; elder; high priest; Priesthood,
    Melchizedek; priest; seventy; Smith, Joseph; teacher; Apostles,
    ·Twelve.
Priesthood, Aaronic, conferred, had been, V1:60
Cowdery, Oliver, Joseph ordains to, V1:39
Holy Ghost, cannot give, V1:39
inheritance, none if cut off, V1:299
Joseph, Oliver Cowdery ordains to, V1:40

PRIESTHOOD, AARONIC (continued)

members, fate if names not found in, V1:299

Nauvoo, organized in, V4:312

order established, V7:351

powers of, V1:39

restored, V1:39

teachers quorum, vote to exclude membership to those who could not settle own difficulties, V3:25.

See also deacon; John the Baptist; priest; priesthood; teacher.

Priesthood, Melchizedek, angel, promised by, V1:60

confirmed, to be, V1:40

high priest, calling of conferred, V1:176 and ftnt

Holy Ghost, gift of under, V1:60

inheritance, none if cut off, V1:299

Joseph, anxious to receive, V1:60

keys, held by, V1:40

laying on of hands, power of, V1:60

manifestation, manner of, V1:175, ftnt only

members, fate of whose names not found, V1:299

power of manifested, V1:175-6

prayer, sought by, V1:60

priesthoods, all others part of, V4:207

restoration, evidence of, V1:40, ftnt only

restoration of explained, V1:60 and ftnt.

See also Apostles; elders; high priests; priesthood; seventies.

Primm, Mr., mentioned, V3:255.

Prince, Jesse, counselor to bishop at Philadelphia branch, V4:331.

Principles, First, of gospel enumerated, V2:255.

See also doctrine; Latter-day Saints, Church of Jesus Christ of.

Prior, Samuel A., Methodist minister in Nauvoo, V6:154.

prison, life sentence to anyone arresting Joseph on Missouri difficulties, V6:105.

See also Carthage jail; persecutions; Smith, Joseph.

Pritchard, Elder, mentioned, V5:420.

proclamation, Church and Nauvoo, of Church Presidency on, V4:267, et seq

Joseph, against false charges, V6:484-5

Joseph, to Nauvoo marshal, V6:493

kings, instructions to write to, V6:80

Mormons, to people of Hancock County, Illinois, to leave alone, V7:133

PROCLAMATION (continued)

  Nauvoo, Joseph to keep order in, V6:449

  stealing, against in Nauvoo, V5:310-1.

Proctor, John, petitions Governor Boggs on mob violence in DeWitt, V3:83.

Prodigal Son, parable of explained, V5:261.

  See also parables.

Progenitors, Joseph Smith and His, book by Lucy Smith mentioned, V1:2, ftnt only.

prophecy, Adam first by, V4:207

  China, earthquake in, V1:158 and ftnt

  Church, of Joseph that would be out of power of old enemies, V6:225

  Church, privilege of to receive, V1:278

  Civil War, V1:301

  commandments, of Brigham Young that all will be carried away if live, V7:465

  Cowdery, Oliver, after baptism, V1:42

  Douglas, Stephen A., of Joseph on head of and fulfillment, V5:393, 395, ftnt only, et seq

  Enoch, of, V1:133

  Expositor affair, of Joseph on, fulfilled, V7:485

  Foster, James, to be healed, V2:88, ftnt only

  God, reject and gain judgments of, V1:278

  jail, of Joseph that companions in would not die in, V6:601

  Johnson, Olmstead, on head of, V1:260

  Joseph concerning debt, V2:175

  Joseph exhorts to exercise, V2:428

  Joseph that he would triumph over enemies, V2:26

  July 8, 1838, fulfilled, V3:339

  Kimball, Heber C., of apostasy of Thomas Webster, V3:21

  Legion, fulfilled of maintaining law and order, V7:313

  massacred, that would be if fell into hands of mob again, V6:546

  Missouri, against, V3:227

  mob, of Joseph on, V6:532

  mobber on Joseph, seals own fate, V2:99-100

  Nauvoo, of Joseph that saints of would not fire a single shot, V6:520

  Nauvoo, no law of would be set aside by judges, V4:516

  Nauvoo, of Brigham Young that would be a winter of peace in, V7:443

  Richards, Willard, that all would move and want for nothing, V7:453

  Rocky Mountain, statement of, V5:85-6

PROPHECY (continued)

saints, of Joseph that government in power would fall if would not aid, V6:116 and ftnt

sickness by Joseph, V2:107 and ftnt

spirit of, instructions by, V1:64

thirst for blood, of Joseph on curious at Carthage that will be fulfilled, V6:566

word, more sure of, V5:388.

See also Apostles, Twelve; doctrine; Doctrine & Covenants; revelation; Smith, Joseph.

prophecy, spirit of, testimony of Jesus is, V3:28, 389.

prophet, acting as, is only when, V5:265

Apostles on heeding, V6:23

explained, what constitutes, V5:215

fallen, when one is considered, V4:478

Holy Ghost, is witness of, V6:13

man, of righteousness, denied as being not a, V5:278

Olney, O., disfellowshipped for setting self up as, V4:552

pagan, remarks of on temple, V5:283-4

what is, V5:231-2.

Prophet, The, Church, newspaper publication commenced in New York by, V7:177

false doctrines, warning against, V7:199.

prophets, false, article on, V1:373 and ftnt.

Prophets, School of the, closes, V2:218

commence, preparation to, V2:169

established by revelation, V1:310-1

Joseph in, V1:322

lectures on faith, begins with, V2:176 and ftnt

meeting of, V1:322

organization of, V1:334

Zion, V1:400, ftnt only.

prospectus, see newspapers.

proverb, Joseph on great men, V5:298, 300

recorded, V5:300.

Pryer, George M., reports mob depredations, V3:214.

Psalm 87, read at Zion Temple dedication, V1:199.

publications, pro and con concerning Church in 1843, V6:154.

See also Latter-day Saints, Church of Jesus Christ of; newspapers.

Pugmire, Jonathan, Jr., relates drowning at baptism, V6:160.

Pugmire, Jonathan, Sr., accident at baptism where person drowned, V6:160.

Pugmire, Tom, Mrs., mentioned, V6:161.

Pullen, Joseph, mentioned, V4:140.

Pulsipher, Daniel, Kirtland Camp, leaves, V3:140
   Kirtland Camp, subscribed to constitution of, V3:92.

Pulsipher, Elias, Kirtland Camp, leaves, V3:140
   Kirtland Camp, subscribed to constitution of, V3:92.

Pulsipher, John, subscribed to constitution of Kirtland Camp, V3:92.

Pulsipher, Sarah, daughter of Zera Pulsipher, Zions Camp member, V2:185.

Pulsipher, Zera, (also spelled Zerah), Kirtland Camp, member of First
   Council of Seventy, one of the presidents of, V3:93
   Kirtland Camp, subscribed to constitution of, V3:91
   seventies, sustained as one of the presidents of, V7:297
   seventies, sustained president of at Salt Lake City, V7:629.

Purcell, John B., Nauvoo, inquires to buy lands of, V7:537
   Roman Catholic bishop of Cincinnatti, V7:537 and ftnt

Purple, Norman H., mentioned, V7:476, 483-4, 487-9, 541.

Purtelow, Luther, mentioned, V6:2.

Purtle, Mr., discovers J. Campbell's corpse, V2:100.

Putnam, James, blessing for work on Kirtland Temple, V2:205.

Putnam, Jonas, Kirtland Camp, leaves with family by consent and
   blessing, near Dayton, Ohio, V3:127, 140
   Kirtland Camp, subscribed to constitution of, V3:92
   Zions Camp, exonerates Joseph's actions in, V2:149.

Putton, D. J., delegate to political convention at Nauvoo, V6:390.

—Q—

Quakers, Rigdon, Sidney, called on mission to, V1:167-8, 169, ftnt only
   sect of, V1:167, ftnt only.

Quarters, Mr., Catholic bishop of Chicago, V7:537.

Quigley, Robert, blessing for work on Kirtland Temple, V2:206.

Quimby, Betsy, wife of S. Roundy, V2:298, ftnt only.

Quincy, Adams County, Illinois, Church conference held at, V3:260,
   283, 344-8
   Church council, meeting at, V3:335
   Democratic association at, V3:263, 267-1, 275

QUINCY, ADAMS COUNTY, ILLINOIS (continued)

Nauvoo, arrival of mayor in, V7:142

Nauvoo, committee of, at, V7:449

public meeting and false rumors at, V7:25

saints, citizens accept removal of, by resolution, V7:451-3

stake organized at, V4:233.

See also persecutions, Illinois.

Quincy Argus, newspaper at Quincy, Illinois, publishes Church warning against imposters, V3:341-2.

Quincy committee, move, letter from requesting written declaration of intention to, V7:449

saints, write acquiescence of people to remove, V7:450.

See also persecutions, Illinois.

Quincy, Democratic Association of, denunciation of state of Missouri by, V3:271

saints, formal welcome and resolution to aid and assist, V3:267, et seq

saints, meeting of, concerning, V3:263

saints, minutes of, concerning settlement of, V3:275.

See also persecutions, Illinois.

Quincy Herald, account of martyrdom in, V7:178-9.

Quincy, Josiah, writes article on Joseph, V6:3, ftnt only.

Quincy Whig, Bartlett, S. M., editor of, member of martyrdom mob, V7:144

Boggs, account of assault on Governor, V5:14-5

First Presidency, letter of, to disclaim letter of Lyman Wight, V3:354

Kinderhook plates, report of, in, V5:377.

quorums, order of their meetings in solemn assembly, V2:391.

—R—

race, riot between in Philadelphia, V5:84.

Raglin, John, Joseph tried at house of, V3:72-3

witness for state in Missouri trials of saints, V3:210.

railroad, Albany and Schenectady, note on, V2:463, ftnt only.

rainbow, when withdrawn then tribulations and second coming, V6:254.

See also doctrine; Smith, Joseph.

Rainey, D. P., (also spelled Raney), clerk of Tennessee conference, V6:408

mission appointment published and field of labor, V6:338.

Raleigh, Alonzo H., lays first brick on Nauvoo House, V7:436.

Ralph, Mr., killed by lightning in Nauvoo, V7:436.

Ralston, James H., lawyer for Joseph, V4:367
  mentioned, V5:242, V7:572
  Taylor, John, visits at Carthage after martyrdom, V7:111.

Ralston, Judge, attorney for the Prophet, V5:89, 91.

Ralston, L. V., recommends Brother Green to collect for poor, V3:348.

Ramus, Illinois, Church, town plat assigned to, V4:491
  conferences at, V4:467
  meeting, minutes of, at, V4:453
  Prophet, deeds to certain lands of, transferred to, V4:477.

Rancliff, Thomas, complains of swindle, failed to hear counsel, V5:409.

Rand, Ebenezer, Carthage Greys, member of, V7:143.

Randall, Alfred, affidavit on threats on Joseph's life while in Carthage jail, V6:586-7
  Joseph, accompanies in arrest, V4:365.

Randall, Dr., member of Haun's Mills mob, V3:186.

Randall, James, blessing for work on Kirtland Temple, V2:205.

Randall, Miles, covenanted to assist saints in removing from Missouri, V3:253.

Raney, Jewel, leads mob in Kirtland against Church, V7:484.

Rapids, Des Moines, canal around, V6:80 and ftnt.

Rapley, Tunis, (also spelled Rappellee, Rappleyee), blessing for work on Kirtland Temple, V2:206
  elder, ordained, V4:13
  marriage to Louisa Cutler, V2:376.

Rathbone, Robert, arrival from Missouri, V2:321

Rathbun, Allen, witness for state in Missouri trials of saints, V3:210.

rattlesnakes, camp, do not destroy but carry out of, V2:71
  Humphreys, S., protected by, V2:73.

Rawlins, James, utility committee member to aid Church removal, V7:474.

Rawson, Horace, high council, named to, at Lima, V5:428.
  high priests quorum, selected president of, at Yelrome, V6:346
  mob, makes conciliation offer to, V7:441-2
  utility committee member to aid Church removal, V7:474.

Ray County, committee formed to confer with saints, V3:62.

Raymond, Martha H., marriage to Warren Parrish, V2:324.

Razer, Aaron, mission appointment published and field of labor, V6:337.

Reads, George, mentioned, V5:372.

Reckard, Michael, farmer, member of martyrdom mob, V7:144.

Reckard, Noah M., Carthage Greys, member of, V7:143.

records, ancient, Kinderhook plates found, V5:372.

Redden, Jackson, mob attempts capture of, V7:486-7.

Redding, Hyrum, claims to having seen sign of Son of Man, V5:290.

Redding, John, mentioned, V7:446, 596.

Redfield, David Harvey, Black, A., falsely accused of threatening, V3:65
Church, appointed to preside over new district of, V7:305
Expositor, arrest for destruction of, trial, V6:487, et seq
Kirtland Camp, views on, V3:96
mission appointment published and field of labor, V6:336
Missouri, arrival from, V2:320
petitions state and interviews Governor Boggs, V3:234-5
proceedings of approved, V3:242 and ftnt
witness, suggested to appear before Congress on redress, V4:97.

Redfield, Harlow, Church, suspended from office in until trial, V4:12
fellowship restored to, V4:16
Joseph, stealing and looting from home of, V3:287 and ftnt
Kirtland High Council, ordained to, V2:511
Kirtland High Council, sustained to, V2:510
presidency, issues complaint against, V2:484
vindicated, V3:287, ftnt only

Redfield, William, elder, ordained, V2:207
Kirtland Temple, blessing for work on, V2:206.

Redman, Mr., member of Missouri Legislature, favors investigation of Mormon troubles, V3:239.

Reece, E., delegate to political convention in Nauvoo, V6:389.

Reed, Calvin, Joseph, on relief expedition for, V5:482
mission appointment published and field of labor, V6:335.

Reed, Elijah, mission appointment published and field of labor, V6:336
mission call in Illinois to disabuse public mind over arrest of Joseph, V5:485.

Reed, Jesse N., covenanted to assist saints in removing from Missouri, V3:252.

Reed, John, Kirtland Temple, blessing for work on, V2:206
Missouri, covenanted to assist saints in removing from, V3:252
Missouri, permit to travel in, V3:210.

Rees, Mrs., mentioned, V3:172.

Reese, Amos, (also spelled Rees), guard, letter of, to Governor Dunklin requesting, for court and witnesses, V1:447-8
    letters, V1:445-6; V2:119; V3:212
    mentioned, V3:172
    Missouri saints, attorney for, V1:425.

Reeves, General, mentioned, V4:53.

Reid, H. T., (also spelled Reed), Joseph, counsel for, at Carthage affair, V7:85
    Joseph, defends at trial at Carthage, V6:567, et seq
    Joseph, letter to, on documents for defense, V6:558-9
    opinion on the false mittimus, V6:574
    opinion on part of Carthage trial, V7:97.

Reid, John S., (also H.), Joseph, counsel for at Colesville, New York, V1:93
    Joseph, counsel for at South Bainbridge, V1:89
    Joseph, synopsis of early history and persecutions of, V6:392, et seq
    mission appointment published and field of labor, V6:338
    Nauvoo, delegate to political convention in, V6:389
    Prophet, account of early persecution of, V1:94, ftnt only, et seq
    Prophet, lawyer for in early experience, V6:377.

Relief Society, Female, admission to by petition only, signed by members, V5:23
    admittance to, Joseph counsels on, V5:23
    Church, penny subscription demanded by, V7:322
    gifts of spirit, Prophet's remarks on, V4:602-7
    Joseph, remarks before, V5:139-41
    Joseph remarks on composition of, V4:570
    mob, petition to Governor Carlin for protection against, V5:146
    organization of, V4:552
    purposes of outlined, V4:567
    tongue, evils of, teaches on, V5:19-21, 23-5
    voice of innocence from, V6:248.

religion, excitement, unusual in, V1:2
    manifesto of mob, of saints caused, IntroV3:XLVIII
    Missouri persecutions, cause of, IntroV3:L
    Missouri persecutions, of Church was cause of, IntroV3:XLVII
    mob and saints, differences between, IntroV3:XLVII
    saints, General Clark asks unknown God to change, IntroV3:XLIX
    sects, excitement among all, V1:2.

religion, professors of, corrupt, all, V1:6
    godliness, form of, V1:6

RELIGION, PROFESSORS OF (continued)

    Joseph, prejudiced against, V1:7
    Joseph, persecutors of, V1:97.

religious confusion, religious sects, among, V1:3
    vision, prior to first, V1:3.

religious creeds, abominations in sight of God, V1:6.

religious freedom, see freedom, religious.

religious sects, all wrong, V1:6
    join, forbidden to, V1:9
    right, which one, V1:4.
    See also religion; religious confusion.

Remmick, J. G., attempt to swindle Joseph, V5:162, 266, 335.

Renfrow, John, mobber wounded at Haun's Mills massacre, V3:326, ftnt only.

repentance, Christ, crucified expressly for, V2:256, et seq
    Jews, of, V6:253
    membership, must have to remain in, V2:22
    pleasing, cannot trifle with, daily is not, V3:379
    preach, duty to, to all mankind, V2:255.
    See also doctrine; Smith, Joseph.

reprobation, doctrine of expounded upon, V4:256, et seq.

reproofs, authorities have right to, after baptism, V6:238
    necessity of, V2:478.

Repsher, Daniel M., mentioned, V6:546; V7:158
    Nauvoo, policeman in, V6:149.

Repsher, Roxanna, disfellowship for following false revelation, V2:525.

resolutions, action on ordinances and licenses, V2:402
    Congress, Church's feelings on actions of, V4:107
    First Presidency, action on, V2:398
    Kirtland High Council, action on, V2:396
    licenses, on, V2:403-4
    Nauvoo, mass meeting passes, V5:70
    ordinations, concerning, V2:388
    ordinations, Prophet's draft to govern, V2:394
    Prophet, vindicating, V2:147, et seq
    Twelve, action on, V2:395
    Zion, action of high council on, V2:397.

responsibility, our greatest, V6:313.

restitution, law of expounded, V4:557, ftnt only.

resurrection, bodies, how come forth in, V4:555

RESURRECTION (continued)

    children, V4:556 and ftnt

    children, in general and of, V4:553, et seq and ftnt

    Christ, attested to, V2:18

    disappointment in, V6:51

    gospel, relation to law of, V2:18

    gospel, necessary to, V3:379

    Joseph preaches on life and, V5:529

    Joseph's remarks on, V5:360

    Kimball, Heber C., on, V7:299-300

    man to attain with Christ through righteousness, V2:19

    restitution, connection with, V4:557, ftnt only.

    See also doctrine; Smith, Joseph.

retribution, Missouri for persecutions, of, IntroV3:LXII, et seq

    summarized, IntroV3:LXXIV.

Reuben, David, mentioned, V4:175.

revelation, Aaronic Priesthood restored, (D&C § 13) V1:39

    Adam-ondi-Ahman found, (D&C § 116) V3:35 and ftnt

    admonish, privilege of priesthood to reprove, rebuke, and, V2:477

    almost all comes as a result of inquiry, V2:210 and ftnt

    Apocrypha, on, (D&C § 91) V1:331-2

    appendix, called, (D&C § 133) V1:229, et seq

    atonement and eternal punishment, first doctrinal development of, (D&C § 19) V1:72 and ftnt, et seq

    baptism for dead, on house of Lord at Nauvoo and, (D&C § 124) V4:274, et seq

    Bible, authorizes modern, V3:30

    bishop, can be condemned, Zion, debt, (D&C § 64) V1:211, et seq

    bishop, duty of outlined, (D&C § 72) V1:239, et seq

    bishop established in Missouri, storehouse, man to do good of self, (D&C § 58) V1:191, et seq

    bishop, office defined, scripture defined, (D&C § 68) V1:227, et seq

    bishops storehouse, order of, to certain members, (D&C § 83) V1:269-70

    blessings predicated upon law, (D&C § 130) V5:325

    Book of Revelation, explaining some of, (D&C § 77) V1:253, et seq

    Brewester, J. C., false, V5:214 and ftnt

    Burnett, Stephen and Eden Smith, call of, (D&C § 80) V1:257

    Cahoon, Reynolds, chastisement of, by Lord, V2:299

    calling, to officer for his, V2:477

    Canadian Mission, comfort and direction to Joseph and Sidney Rigdon while on, (D&C § 100) V1:420-1

    Carter, Jared, call of, (D&C § 79) V1:257

REVELATION (continued)

Church, appointing elders to travel two by two to Missouri, (D&C § 52:10) V1:177, et seq

Church, comes to Presidency, V2:477

Church, common consent in, (D&C § 26) V1:104

Church, government of, (D&C § 20) V1:64, et seq

Church, Joseph as head of, (D&C § 28) V1:110-1

Church led by, V7:285

Church, to William Marks and others on debts of, (D&C § 117) V3:45-6

Church named officially and the will of Lord at Far West, (D&C § 115) V3:23-5 and ftnts

Church at Kirtland, instructions to leading elders at, (D&C § 41) V1:147

common lands, division of, (D&C § 96) V1:352-3

consecration, law of, (D&C § 85) V1:298-9 and ftnt

consecration and stewardship, withdrawal of, (D&C § 54) V1:181 and ftnt

I Corinthians 7:14, explanation of, (D&C § 74) V1:242

Covill, James, call of, (D&C § 39) V1:143-5

Covill, James, why rejected call, (D&C § 40) V1:145

Cowdery, Oliver, companion to Missouri, (D&C § 69) V1:234-5 and ftnt

Cowdery, Oliver, to be Joseph's scribe, (D&C § 6) V1:33-5

Cowdery, Oliver, on manner of translation, (D&C § 9) V1:37-8

Cowdery, Oliver, power to translate taken from, (D&C § 9) V1:37-8

Cowdery, Oliver, to review and prepare for printing, V1:270

Cowdery, Oliver, told to translate, (D&C § 8) V1:36-7

Cowdery, Warren A., call of, (D&C § 106) V2:170-1

doctrinal instruction, (D&C § 130) V5:323-4

doctrinal instruction, (D&C § 131) V5:392-3 and ftnts

elders, call of, (D&C § 60) V1:201-2

elders, to Joseph on duties of, (D&C § 73) V1:241-2

elders, in presence of six, (D&C § 29) V1:111, et seq

Elijah, mission of foretold, (D&C § 2) V1:12

Enoch, prophecy of, V1:133 and ftnt, et seq

Gilbert, Algernon Sidney, call of, (D&C § 53) V1:179-80

God, privilege of, to obtain on mind and will of, V2:477

God, total purposes of, to rely on, V2:17

gospel, commanded to proclaim, (D&C § 71) V1:238-9

gospel, on those who have died without receiving, V2:380

REVELATION (continued)

government, declaration of belief of, and laws in general, (D&C § 134) V2:247, et seq

Harris, Martin, new covenant for, (D&C § 5) V1:28, et seq

heart, judged by desires of, V2:380

heaven, grand keys of, (D&C § 129) V5;267

Holy Ghost, gifts of, explained, (D&C § 46) V1;163-5 and ftnts

Hyde, Nancy, given to on circumstances, V4:467

individuals on duties, V4:311

intelligence, information concerning Christ, knowledge and, (D&C § 93) V1:343, et seq

Iowa, of saints in, (D&C § 125) V4:311

John the Revelator remaining in the flesh, (D&C § 7) V1:36

Joseph, call of, (D&C § 21) V1:78-9

Joseph, epistle to Church from Liberty prison, (D&C § 121, 122, 123) V3:289 and ftnt, et seq

Joseph, exhortation to, (D&C § 90) V1:329, et seq

Joseph, how given through, V1:173, ftnt only

Joseph, missionary call to father, (D&C § 4) V1:28

Joseph starts to compile, V1:104

Joseph to go to Missouri, (D&C § 52) V1:177-9

Joseph and Oliver Cowdery, call of, (D&C § 24) V1:101, et seq

Joseph, Oliver Cowdery and John Whitmer, how time to be spent, (D&C § 26) V1:104

Kimball, Hiram, revealing wickedness, V5:12

kingdom, prayer to go forth, (D&C § 65) V1:218

kingdoms of glory, (D&C § 76) V1:245, et seq

Kirtland High Council, organization of, (D&C § 102) V2:28, et seq

Kirtland Temple, chastisement for slowness in building, (D&C § 95) V1:350-2

Kirtland Temple, dedicatory prayer of, (D&C § 109) V2:420, et seq

Kirtland Temple designed, (D&C § 94) V1:346-7

Kirtland Temple, on size of, V1:352

Knight, Joseph, Sen., for, (D&C § 12) V1:48

Knight, Newel, directing him to move to Missouri, (D&C § 54) V1:181 and ftnt

Lamanites, mission to, (D&C § 32) V1:118-20

lands, purchasing of, (D&C § 48) V1:166-7

Lord, how proceeds in, V7:372

Lord, on last days and coming of, (D&C § 133) V1:229, et seq

Lyon, Aaron, false to, concerning type of polygamy, V3:26

man will not be called by, who does not believe in, V4:257

REVELATION (continued)

manuscript, Book of Mormon altered, therefore do not translate over, (D&C § 10) V1:23 and ftnt

manuscript, concerning lost of Book of Mormon, (D&C § 3) V1:22-3

Marsh, Thomas B., call of, (D&C § 31) V1:116-7

Marsh, Thomas B., concerning Apostles, (D&C § 112) V2:499, et seq

Marsh, Thomas B., received at request of, (D&C § 56) V1:186-7

martyrdom, (D&C § 135) V6:612, et seq

members, duties of individual expounded, (D&C § 23) V1:80

mission to Massachusetts, (D&C § 111) V2:465-6

missionaries, conference call for, (D&C § 44) V1:157

missionary work outlined, (D&C § 75) V1:243, et seq

M'Lellin, William E., call of, (D&C § 66) V1:220-1

Morley, Isaac, and Edward Partridge, Lord well pleased with, V2:302

Moses, Pearl of Great Price, V1:98, et seq

Ohio, commanded to go to, (D&C § 37) V1:139

Ohio, Prophet to go to, (D&C § 38) V1:140, et seq

Olive leaf, the, (D&C § 88) V1:302 and ftnt, et seq

Order of Enoch, Church in Zion on, (D&C § 82) V1:267, et seq

Order of Enoch, to Joseph on, (D&C § 78) V1:255-7

Page, John E., to Joseph to send to Washington to labor, V6:82

Parrish, Warren, forgiving sins and giving blessings, V2:311

Partridge, Edward, call of, (D&C § 36) V1:131

Partridge, Edward, giving directions to settle New York saints at Kirtland, (D&C § 51) V1:173-4

Patten, David W., for mission, (D&C § 114) V3:23

Phelps and Whitmer, Presidents, to Joseph condemning, V2:304

Phelps, William W., call of, (D&C § 55) V1:185

Phelps, William W., not before published, V3:46, ftnt only

Phelps, William W., and John Whitmer, reveals that, are in sin, V2:511

poor, establishing the, (D&C § 78) V1:255-7

Pratt, Orson, call of, (D&C § 34) V1:128

preaching and translating, continue, (D&C § 73) V1:241-2

preface to Doctrine and Covenants, (D&C § 1) V1:222-4 and ftnt

priesthood, on, (D&C § 84) V1:287, et seq

priesthood, Church organized and duties of outlined, (D&C § 20) V1:67-8

priesthood, great revelation on, (D&C § 107) V2:210 and ftnt, et seq

Quakers, missionaries to, (D&C § 49) V1:167, et seq

rebaptism of previously baptized members, (D&C § 22) V1:79-80

received but cannot be located, V3:44, ftnt only

REVELATION (continued)

receives, who, for whom, V1:338

repent, admonition to, (D&C § 82) V1:267, et seq

repentance and forgiveness, law of, (D&C § 98) V1:403, et seq

revelation, Joseph to receive all for Church, (D&C § 43) V1:154

revelations, on, and language, (D&C § 67) V1:225

Rigdon, Sidney, call of, (D&C § 35) V1:129, et seq

rock of, to build Church on, V5:258

sabbath outlined, (D&C § 59) V1:200-1

sacrament, messengers on, (D&C § 27) V1:106-10

saints, defining duties of respecting laws of the land, (D&C § 98) V1:403, et seq

saints in Zion commanding them to return East, (D&C § 60) V1:201-2

salvation, cannot have, without, V3:389

Satan, given by, V1:109

scripture, answers to questions on, (D&C § 113) V3:9-10

second coming, signs of, (D&C § 45) V1:159, et seq

second coming and spiritual laws, (D&C § 29) V1:111, et seq

self, for, V7:286

Sherman, Lyman, duty and calling of, (D&C § 108) V2:345

Smith, Emma, call of, (D&C § 25) V1:103-4

Smith, Hyrum, call of, (D&C § 11) V1:45-6

Snyder, John and Amos Fuller, V4:483

spirit of expounded, V3:381

spirits, discernment of and teaching by, (D&C § 50) V1:170, et seq and ftnts

stewardship, law of, missionary work, repentance and teaching, (D&C § 42) V1:148, et seq

stewardship, temporal expounded, (D&C § 70) V1:236-7 and ftnt

three witnesses called, (D&C § 17) V1:53

Thayre, Ezra, and Northrop Sweet called, (D&C § 33) V1:126-7

tithing, (D&C § 119) V3:44

tithing property, disposition of, (D&C § 120) V3:44

Twelve Apostles, call of, and building up of Church, (D&C § 18) V1:62-4

Twelve Apostles, condemnation of, for sins of covetousness and lack of humility, V2:300

Twelve Apostles, instructions to, (D&C § 118) V3:46-7 and ftnt

Twelve Apostles, taking over *Times & Seasons* editorials, V4:503

unbelief, sin of, explained, V2:415

United Order, dissolving, (D&C § 104) V2:54, et seq

United Order established, (D&C § 51) V1:173-4

REVELATION (continued)

United Order given, (D&C § 92) V1:333

Urim and Thummim, first, given through, (D&C § 3) V1:22-3

visions and keys restored, (D&C § 110) V2:435-6

war, prophecy on, (D&C § 87) V1:301-2

waters, commanded to stay off, (D&C § 61) V1:203-4

wheat and tares, explanation of, (D&C § 86) V1:300

Whitlock, Harvey, to, forgiving and directing, V2:315-6

Whitmer, David, call of, (D&C § 14) V1:49-50

Whitmer, John, call of, (D&C § 15) V1:50-1

Whitmer, John, call of to be historian, (D&C § 47) V1:166

Whitmer, Peter, call of, (D&C § 16) V1:51

Whitmer, calls of David, Peter, and John, (D&C § 30) V1:116

Williams, Frederick G., call of to First Presidency, (D&C § 81) V1:257-8 and ftnt

Williams, Frederick G., directing to go teach relatives, V2:300

Williams, Frederick G., and W. W. Phelps, duty of, V3:46, ftnt only

wives, plurality of, (D&C § 132) V5:501 and ftnt, et seq

woman pretends to, V1:154 and ftnt

Word of Wisdom, (D&C § 89) V1:327, et seq

Young, Brigham, to, (D&C § 126) V4:382

Young, Brigham, commanded to stay home and provide for family, V3:23

Zion, defining the *pure in heart*, (D&C 97) V1:402

Zion, elders to go to, (D&C § 62) V1:206

Zion, information concerning, (D&C § 63) V1:207, et seq

Zion revealed, (D&C § 57) V1:189-90

Zion, tribulations of, and School of the Prophets, (D&C § 97) V1:400-2 and ftnts

Zion, why saints driven from (D&C § 101) V1:458

Zion would not be redeemed at the present time, (D&C § 105) V2:108, et seq

Zions Camp, on Fishing River, disbanding, (D&C § 105) V2:108, et seq

Zions Camp, organization of and redemption of Zion, (D&C § 103) V2:36, et seq

See also doctrine; Doctrine & Covenants; Latter-day Saints, Church of Jesus Christ of; prophecy; Smith, Joseph.

Revelation, Book of, beasts in expounded on, V5:324, 339, et seq

beasts, John saw actual, V5:343

Joseph explains some of, V1:253

Joseph on, 144,000 priests spoken of in, V5:326.

reverends, named as mob participators, V1:392 and ftnt.

Reynolds, Dr., lectures in Nauvoo, V6:281.

Reynolds, Joseph H., Joseph, of Jackson County, Missouri, arrests, V5:439, et seq

 Joseph, returns writ on, V5:464

 letter on imprisonment of O. P. Rockwell, V5:352-3

 Nauvoo, refuses to submit to habeas corpus proceedings at, V5:465.

Reynolds, Judge, Missouri prisoners to be tried by, V3:368.

Reynolds, Thomas, governor of Missouri, warrant of, against Joseph, V3:403, 421; V5:464

 Spencer, Orson, reported interview with, V7:423-4.

Rhett, B., mentioned, V6:62, 83, ftnt only.

Rhodes, Eric, mentioned, V5:184, 394; V6:53.

Rhodes, Franklin, martyrdom, guard on jail at, V7:142.

Rhodes, Hugh, mentioned, V4:582.

Rice, Asaph, called on mission and field of labor, V5:348.

Rice, Brother, house burned, V7:522, 525, 527.

Rice, James, anti-Mormon committee member of Warsaw meeting, V6:464.

Rice, William, mentioned, V7:530.

Rich, Charles C., brigadier general, elected, V4:414

 genealogy, ordained president of high priests quorum in Missouri and, V2:507 and ftnt

 Joseph, accompanies in arrest, V4:365

 Joseph, on relief expedition for, V5:483, 486-8

 militia, letter to Ford on additional, V7:275-6

 mission appointment published and field of labor, V6:339

 mission call in Illinois to disabuse public mind over arrest of Joseph, V5:485

 mission call and field of labor, V5:348

 Nauvoo, first elected councilor of, V4:287

 Nauvoo, policeman in, V6:149

 Nauvoo, sworn in a councilor of, V4:295

 Nauvoo High Council, appointed to, V4:12

 Nauvoo stake, counselor of, V4:323

 Nauvoo Temple, to administer in, V7:555

 Nauvoo Temple, appointed to officiate in, V7:548

 Salt Lake stake, president of, V7:629

 westward movement, captain of thirteenth company in, V7:482

RICH, CHARLES C. (continued)

witness, suggested to appear before Congress on redress, V4:97
Zions Camp member, V2:184.

Rich, Joseph, father of Charles, V2:507, ftnt only

Rich, Leonard, blessing of Prophet on, V2:329
Church, leads mob in Kirtland against, V7:484
Doctrine and Covenants, bears testimony to, V2:245
high council, testifies before, V2:137
Joseph, proposed to supply with wood, V2:329
seventies, named president of, V2:203
word of wisdom, tried before council for breaking, V2:27
Zions Camp member, V2:184.

Rich, Thomas, appointed elder, V4:13.

Richards, Ellen, mother of Jennetta, V2:504, ftnt only.

Richards, Franklin D., Church, appointed to preside over new district
of, V7:306
high priest, ordained, V6:397
mission appointment published and field of labor, V6:339
Nauvoo Temple, appointed to officiate in, V7:548
Nauvoo Temple, to administer in, V7:555.

Richards, George S., killed at Haun's Mills by mob, V3:326, ftnt only.

Richards, Heber John, death of, V4:48.

Richards, Jennetta, bickerings in British Mission over marriage and clothing of, V3:276-7
coffin of opened, V7:580
death of, V7:433
genealogy, baptized in England, first confirmation and, V2:504 and
ftnt; V4:316.

Richards, John, father of Jennetta, V2:504, ftnt only
Kimball, Heber C., invites to preach from his pulpit, V2:506.

Richards, Joseph, father to Willard, V2:469, ftnt only.

Richards, Joseph, martial band member of Legion, V7:135.

Richards, Levi, affiant to public proclamation on mob lies, V6:495
British Mission, report on labors in, V5:6
Griffiths, Sara, marriage to, V6:134
England, letter on gospel and mob action in, V4:296
Expositor, trial, arrest for destruction of, V6:487, et seq
made high priest, V3:68
mission call in Illinois to disabuse public mind over arrest of Joseph,
V5:485

RICHARDS, LEVI (continued)

  Missouri, covenanted to assist in removing saints from, V3:253
  Missouri persecutions, affidavit concerning, V4:70-1
  Nauvoo, delegate to political convention at, V6:390
  Nauvoo, return of, to, V5:354.

Richards, Phinehas, (also spelled Phineas), affiant to public proclamation
        on mob lies, V6:495
  Kirtland High Council, ordained to, V2:511
  Kirtland High Council, sustained to, V2:510
  Missouri persecutions, writes appeal to Massachusetts on, V6:193
  Nauvoo, on city council in, V6:347, 357; V7:370
  Nauvoo, prepares harvest feast in, V7:437.

Richards, Rhoda, mentioned, V4:76
  mother to Willard, V2:469, ftnt only.

Richards, Rhoda Ann, birth of, V6:34.

Richards, Samuel W., exploring, volunteers for, V6:224
  mission appointment published and field of labor, V6:339
  priesthood, received signed testimony of restoration of, V1:42, ftnt
        only.

Richards, Willard, affidavit of, V6:119-20
  America, sails for, V4:352
  Apostle, sustained as, by Church after death of Joseph, V7:295
  Apostle, to be, (D&C § 118:6) V3:47
  Apostleship, ordained to, V4:114
  apostolate, is given revelation of his call to, V3:277
  Book of Mormon, assists in indexing, V4:274, 286
  British Mission, departs for, V2:493
  British Mission, secures funds to continue on, V2:494
  British Mission, set apart for, V2:492
  British Mission, writes history of, V4:313-21
  camp journal of, records discomfort of the camps, V7:592-5
  Carthage jail, pass of, to enter, V6:612
  Carthage prison, movements of in, V7:105
  Carthage trials, subpoenaed as witness to, V7:313
  devil seeks to destroy in England, V3:276-7
  double taxing, letter of, on, V5:304
  elder, ordained, V2:492
  election and reprobation, on, V4:256-66
  endowment, receives, V5:409
  endowment, receives in Nauvoo Temple, V7:543
  England, arraigned for murder because member died in, V3:149

RICHARDS, WILLARD (continued)

England, arrives in Nauvoo from, V4:402

England, counselor to president in, V3:20

English conference, represents branch of Church at, V4:117, 148, 495

First Presidency, sustained counselor to in Salt Lake, V7:628

genealogy and baptism, V2:469-70 and ftnts

Joseph, accompanies for trial on Missouri warrants, V5:210

Joseph expresses faith in, V5:41

Joseph, expresses willingness to be with and love for, V6:616

Joseph, false writ against for aiding, et al, V7:444

journal, excerpts from, of miscellaneous events between June 22 and June 29, 1844, V7:129, et seq

Keeper of the Rolls, designated as, V7:435

labors, letter of, reporting, V4:130

martyrdom, account of, V6:619-21

martyrdom, announces, of Patriarch and Prophet, V6:621-2 and ftnt

martyrdom, letter to British Mission, instructions on, V7:171, et seq

martyrdom, letter to Twelve on news of, V7:147-8

martyrdom, report of, to Nauvoo, V7:110

martyrdom, unscathed at, and fulfillment of prophecy, V6:619-21

Millennial Star, to be editor of, V4:218

ministry, devote all time to labors of, V4:148

mob, lists members of, V7:146

murderers, letter of declaring that saints would take no part in trial of, V7:193-4

Nauvoo, addresses people at, V6:626

Nauvoo, conveys bodies of martyrs to, V6:626

Nauvoo, delegate to political convention at, V6:390

Nauvoo, elected to council of, V4:442

Nauvoo, letter informing General Deming that R. D. Foster was in, V7:169

Nauvoo, letter to A. Jonas indicating all peace in, V7:175-6

Nauvoo, letter to Brigham Young on recent events in, V5:511-3

phrenological chart of, V5:58-60

recorder, appointed general Church, V5:522

saints, letter of Leonora Taylor to Ford requesting protection for, V7:201

second First Presidency, chosen second counselor in, V7:621 and ftnt

son of dies in England, V4:48

temple recorder, appointed private secretary to the Prophet and, V4:470

Times and Seasons, to take over, V4:463

RICHARDS, WILLARD (continued)

Twelve, one of the, visits Staffordshire, V:7

vice president, letter to J. A. Bennett on candidacy for, V6:231-3

west, leaves Nauvoo for, V7:585

westward movement, letter on, V6:405-7

westward movement, letter to J. A. Bennett on affairs in Nauvoo and, V6:516-8

witness in *Expositor* trial, V6:490

Young, Brigham, chief counselor in Nauvoo until arrival of, V7:228.

See also Apostles, Twelve; British Mission; letters.

Richards, William P., Congress, suggests saints acquire land grant from, V7:367

judge introduced to Joseph, V6:343.

Richardson, Mr., repents of part in Avery case, V6:133.

Richardson, Colonel, mentioned, V7:148-9.

Richardson, Darwin, seventies, named to first quorum of, V2:204

Zions Camp member, V2:184.

Richardson, Ebenezer, elder, ordained, V4:13

kindapper of saints, V6:122

kidnapping, repents of Missouri, V6:133.

Richardson, Stephen, subscribed to constitution of Kirtland Camp, V3:92.

Richardson, Thomas, British conference, represents branch of Church at, V4:117

British Mission, mission in, V4:149

high priest, ordained, V4:333

ministry, devote all time to labors of, V4:148

volunteers for service in vineyard, V4:217.

Richardson, W., delegate to political convention in Nauvoo, V6:390.

Richardson, William A., attorney for defense of murderers of Joseph, V7:50.

Richerson, Nancy, subscribed to constitution of Kirtland Camp, V3:91.

Richey, Mrs., mentioned, V4:95.

Richmond, Missouri, county seat of Ray County, mob gathered at, V3:182

Mormon prisoners, trial of, at, V3:208-12 and ftnts

Richmond, Missouri, jail, Joseph rebukes guards at, V3:208, ftnt only.

Ricketts, B., appointed by public to assist saints in removal from Zion, V2:455.

Rickman, Robert, signs proposition to buy land of saints, V2:96-7.

Ricks, Thomas E., wounded by Indians at Heber C. Kimball's camp, V7:627.

Rider, Alonzo, excommunicated for repeated sins and failure to repent, V1:469.

Rider, Brother, mentioned, V2:46.

Rider, Ezekiel, chastened for speaking against bishop, repented and confessed, forgiven, V1:470.

Ridge, H., ordained elder, V4:322.

Ridge, W., ordained elder, V4:322.

Riding, Christopher, ordained priest, V5:419.

Riding, Hugh, Nauvoo Temple, appointed carpenter on, V7:326.

Ridgon, Ann Lucy, grandmother to Sidney, V1:120, ftnt only.

Rigdon, Athalia, daughter of Sidney, V1:122, ftnt only.

Rigdon, Eliza, raises from dead and occurrences, V5:121-2.

Rigdon, John, Campbellite preacher, refuses elders to preach, V5:409

Rigdon, John W., son of Sidney, writes biography of father, V1:122, ftnt only, et seq.

Rigdon, Nancy, mother of Sidney, V1:120, ftnt only.

Rigdon, Nancy, witness for defense of saints in Missouri persecutions, V3:211.

Rigdon, Phebe Brook, gift of healing, exercised in behalf of, V2:400 wife to Sidney, V1:121, ftnt only.

Rigdon, Sarah, daughter of Sidney, V5:121.

Rigdon, Sidney, affliction of rebuked, V2:367
    apoplectic fits, experiences slight, V3:445
    apostates, house of plundered and robbed by, V3:215
    Avon, New York, attends conference at, V2:44
    baptized and converted, V1:120 and ftnt, et seq
    baptized, wife is, V1:125
    Bennett, John C., letter to Joseph denying conspiracy with, V5:314-6
    Bible, scribe with translating, V1:238
    Bible translation, scribe for Joseph in, V1:219
    Book of Mormon presented to, V1:122
    Book of Mormon, revelations of, to authorship of, V1:122-3 and ftnts
    Canada, accompanies Prophet on mission to, V1:416

RIGDON, SIDNEY (continued)

Church, claimed vision of, after martyrdom on regulation of, V7:229 and ftnt

Church, Joseph comments that he would lead to destruction, V6:592-3

Columbus, Ohio, sickness of, left at, V4:21

common ownership, opposes, V3:342

congregation had all things in common, V1:124

Congress, letter of Horace Hotchkiss to concerning progress before, V4:98

conversion of, V1:125

disfellowshipped, V5:532

escape of from Missouri recounted, V3:465-6

extradition of demanded by Governor Boggs, V4:198

excommunication and trial of, V7:268-9 and ftnts

Expositor affair, letter to Governor Ford confirming Joseph's letter on, V6:469-71

false reports, alarmed by, V5:369

family of, to receive support from Church for service, V3:32

Far West, arrival of, at, V3:13

Far West, counselor to president of Church of, V2:522

Far West, delivers political address at, V3:30, 31 and ftnt

Far West, recommended for postmaster at, V3:56

First Presidency, ordained to, V1:334

First Presidency, sustained as counselor in, V2:509

gathering, dedicates Zion for, V1:196 and ftnt

genealogy, V1:120-1, ftnt only

Grand River, accompanies Prophet to locate lands on, V3:34-7

Harris, Martin, brings before council, V2:26

Hill, Isaac, instructs Church incorrectly on case of, V2:303

history of Church, address at April 1844 conference on, V6:288, et seq

Independence, preaches at, V1:270-1

Independence, taken by mob to, V3:194-5

Joseph, accompanies on second visit to Missouri, V1:266

Joseph, addresses saints at Nauvoo on successor for, V7:229-30 and ftnt

Joseph, assists in public ministry in Kirtland and vicinity, V1:239, 241

Joseph, blessed by, V2:51

Joseph, denies betraying, V5:556

Jospeh, denounced by, V5:139

RIGDON, SIDNEY (continued)

Joseph, inquires of, as to his duty, V1:128

Joseph, leaves Kirtland for mission with, V1:188

Joseph, on status of, V5:553-4, 556

Joseph, opinion of, unsatisfied with, V1:443

Joseph, restored good feelings with, V5:270

Joseph, with, in Geneseo, preaches, V2:44

Kirtland, accompanies Prophet from New York to, V2:44

Kirtland Temple, appointed to bless those who had labored on, V2:205

Kirtland Temple, blessing for work on, V2:205

Kirtland Temple, discourse of, at the dedication of, V2:413, et seq

law, commences the study of, V3:69

Liberty, Clay County, sent to stand trial for murder and treason at, V3:212

Liberty prison, released from and escapes mob, V3:264

martyrdom, agitates situation in Nauvoo after, V7:226

martyrdom, arrives in Nauvoo after, V7:223

means to be provided for, V1:219

Medina County, Ohio, presides at a council at, V1:343

misrepresentations, letter of, correcting, V5:280-1

mission appointment to Strongville, V2:35

mission, fulfills, V1:169, ftnt only

missionaries, allows to preach at chapel, V1:124

Missouri, arraigned for treason, murder, burglary, arson, robbery, and larceny at Richmond, V3:209

Missouri, arrives in, V1:191

Missouri, arrives in Kirtland from, V1:206

Missouri, writes to Joseph on plans to impeach, V3:310-1

Missouri persecutions, discourse in Missouri explained as related to, IntroV3:XLIV

Missouri persecutions, letter to Joseph indicating no redress possible, V4:102

Missouri persecutions, peroration of, to Pennsylvania on redress for, V6:191-2

Missouri persecutions, testimony of, concerning troubles in, V3:449, et seq

mob, attacked by, March 24, 1832, V1:262

mob, betrayed to at Far West, V3:188-9 and ftnt

mob enters camp of in Missouri, V3:189 and ftnt

mob, forced to flee Kirtland by, V3:1

Mormonism, investigates, V1:124

RIGDON, SIDNEY (continued)

Nauvoo, elected city attorney in, V5:271

Nauvoo, first elected councilor of, V4:287

Nauvoo, petition on postmaster of, V5:273

Nauvoo scandals, Prophet's interview with, on, V5:8, 46

Nauvoo Temple, speech of, at laying cornerstone of, V4:327-9

New Portage, question of his removal from Kirtland to, V2:25

note on trial of, V7:269, ftnt only

Ohio, moves to, V1:265 and ftnt

oration at cornerstone ceremony at Far West Temple, V3:41-2 and ftnt

ordination, holds council on legality of, V1:343

parents, baptized in behalf of, V4:486

Partridge, Bishop, reconciled to, V1:267 and ftnt

Philadelphia, in, V4:76

preacher, was, V1:120-1 and ftnts

president, actions of, in Nauvoo, attempt to select new, V7:224

President of United States, letter of introduction to, V3:349

Prophet, reconcilation with, V5:270

Prophet, Seer, Revelator, ordained, V4:364

Quakers, called on mission to, (D&C § 49) V1:167-9 and ftnt

raising of his dead daughter, testifies to and occurrences, V5:121-2

remuneration of for services, V3:31, 32

revelation to, (D&C § 35) V1:129-31

shot, sentenced to be, in public square at Far West, V3:190 and ftnt

temple, speaks two hours at dedication of, V2:414

tongues and instructions, letter of to Zion on, V1:369

trial of before Church, Joseph does not want sustained, V6:47

Twelve, address of, to, V4:2-3

Twelve, refuses to be counseled by, V7:267

Vice President of United States, nominated for, V6:356

Washington, appointed to accompany Prophet to, V4:13

Washington, appointed to present the case of the saints before general Government at, V3:346

Washington, in, V4:48

Washington, leaves Nauvoo for, V4:19

witness, suggested to appear before Congress on redress, V4:97

Zion, writes description of, V1:197

Zions Camp, confirmed to head Church while Joseph with, V2:51

Zions Camp, remains in Kirtland during, V2:64

Zion Temple, at dedication of, V1:199

See also affidavits; Latter-day Saints, Church of Jesus Christ of; letters; Smith, Joseph.

Rigdon, Sidney, Life of, book on, V1:123, ftnt only.

Rigdon, Thomas Baker, grandfather to Sidney, V1:120, ftnt only.

Rigdon, Thomas Baker, great-grandfather to Sidney, V1:120, ftnt only.

Rigdon, William, father of Sidney, V1:120, ftnt only.

Rigg, Levi, ordained elder, V5:419.

Riggs, Burr, Joseph, accused of stealing and looting from home of, V3:287 and ftnt
  excommunicated from Church, V3:284
  excommunicated for neglect of duty and disgracing high priesthood, V1:327
  Missouri persecutions, affidavit concerning, V4:67
  Missouri trials, witness for state in, V3:210
  neglect of duty, proceedings before high council for, etc., V1:327
  plunders and robs houses of saints, V3:215
  seventies, named to first quorum of, V2:203
  Zelph, keeps arrow found with, V2:79
  Zions Camp member, V2:184.

Riggs, Harpin, elder, ordained, V1:327
  seventies, named to first quorum of, V2:203
  Zions Camp member, V2:184.

Riggs, Nathaniel, Zions Camp member, V2:184.

righteous, to dwell in burnings, V6:306, et seq
  See also doctrine.

rights, taken from one can take from another, V2:132.

Riley, B., appointed by public to assist saints in removing from Zion, V2:455.

Riley, James, British conference, represents area in, V5:9
  high priest, ordained, V4:333.

Riley, John, mentioned, V4:296.

Riley, Milcher, Zions Camp member, V2:184.

Riley, Reverend, Baptist speaks against saints in Clay County, V2:97; V3:421.

Riley, W. W., mission appointment published and field of labor, V6:338.

Ripley, Mr., Zions Camp member, V2:185.

Ripley, Alanson, affiant to public proclamation on mob lies, V6:495
  bishop, appointed to ward in Ohio Territory stake, V4:12
  bishop, ordained, V4:42
  bishop, rejected as, V4:341

RIPLEY, ALANSON (continued)

Black, A., falsely accused of threatening, V3:64

Joseph, petitions for release of, V3:264-5

Joseph, on relief expedition for, V5:483, 486

Missouri, appointed to dispose of real estate in, V3:261-2

Missouri, arraigned for treason, murder, burglary, arson, robbery, and larceny at Richmond, V3:209

Missouri, covenanted to assist saints in removing from, V3:252

Missouri, letter to Joseph, very harsh against, V3:311 and ftnt, et seq

Nauvoo, appointed city surveyor of, V4:308

Nauvoo, elected surveyor of, V5:270

vote, rejected by, V4:342

witness, suggested to appear before Congress on redress, V4:97

Zions Camp member, V2:184.

Ripsher, Roxanna, prayed for, V5:141.

Riser, G. C., mission appointment published and field of labor, V6:338.

Riser, J. J., mission appointment published and field of labor, V6:338.

Rivinus, E. F., mentioned, V2:350, ftnt only.

Robbins, Lewis, mentioned, V7:554.

mission call and field of labor, V5:348

Nauvoo Temple, to administer in, V7:555

seventies, named to first quorum of, V2:203

Zions Camp member, V2:185.

Roberts, J., testify to finding Kinderhook plates, V5:377.

Roberts, John W., mission and field of labor, V6:339.

Roberts, Sidney, excommunication for false revelation, V4:237

Joseph, on relief expedition for, V5:483.

Roberts, U. S. Marshal, V7:553.

Robertson, Mr., mentioned, V7:168.

Robertson, Andrew, committee member to talk to saints on removal, V2:452

drafts resolution of public meeting in Missouri, V2:449.

Robinson, Mr., mentioned, V4:95.

Robinson, Athalia Rigdon, daughter of Sidney Rigdon, V1:122, ftnt only.

Robinson, Brother, mentioned, V4:99.

Robinson, Chauncey, messenger to Governor from anti-Mormon meeting, V6:466

sheriff's movements, reports, against Joseph, V5:97.

Robinson, Dr., delegate to present truth to public, V6:483.

Robinson, E., mission call in Illinois to disabuse public mind over Joseph's arrest, V5:485.

Robinson, Ebenezer, baptized, V2:290

    Far West, clerk of conference at, V3:155

    Far West High Council, clerk of, V3:8

    genealogy, V2:290, ftnt only

    marriage to Angeline Works, V2:331

    mission call and field of labor, V5:348

    Missouri, arraigned for treason, murder, burglary, arson, robbery, and larceny at Richmond, V3:209

    Nauvoo, delegate to political convention in, V6:389

    Nauvoo Mansion, rents, V6:185

    Smith, Don Carlos, co-partnership with dissolved, V4:239

    Times & Seasons, becomes editor of, V4:402

    Times & Seasons, publisher of, V4:23.

Robinson, Edward, affidavit on threats against Nauvoo, V6:528-9

Robinson, George, ordained priest, V5:419.

Robinson, George W., anti-Mormon committee member of Warsaw meeting, V6:464

    Church recorder, elected general, V2:513

    Far West, clerk of public meeting at, V3:62

    Far West, secretary of meeting at, V3:56

    Gallatin, in command of company going to assist the brethren at, V3:58

    Independence, taken by mob to, V3:194

    Joseph, denounced by, V5:139

    Missouri, arraigned for treason, murder, burglary, arson, robbery, and larceny at Richmond, V3:209

    Missouri, enters camp of the mob in, V3:189 and ftnt.

Robinson, Isaac, testifies on Joseph's second arrest in Illinois, V6:67.

Robinson, J. L., appointed to preside over new Church district, V7:305.

Robinson, James, death of, V4:352

    Nauvoo, appointed assessor of, V4:308

    Nauvoo, elected assessor of, V4:292.

Robinson, Lewis, delegate to present truth to public, V6:483.

Robinson, Mary, mother to Ebenezer, V2:290, ftnt only.

Robinson, Nathan, father to Ebenezer, V2:290, ftnt only.

Robinson, Zebediah, witness suggested to appear before Congress on redress, V4:97.

Robinson and Smith, Publishers, *Times & Seasons,* publishers of, V4:23.

Robison, Eliza, wife of D. H. Wells, V4:155, ftnt only.

Robison, Lewis, Nauvoo, elected constable and coroner of, V5:270.

Rochester, steamboat, V2:464.

Rockwell, Caroline, baptized, V1:86.

Rockwell, Electa, baptized, V1:86.

Rockwell, George, anti-Mormon member of Warsaw meeting, V6:464
  druggist, member of martyrdom mob, V7:143.

Rockwell, Lorenzo, mentioned, V6:412.

Rockwell, Orrin Porter, arrest, letter on flight to avoid, V5:198
  article on as persecuted by Missourians, V6:35-6
  Backenstos, J. B., defends, V7:446
  baptized, V1:79
  Boggs, ex-Governor, affidavit implicating in assassination attempt of,
    V5:67
  Boggs, ex-Governor, arrested for assassination of, V5:86
  capture, reward offered for, V5:167
  drunk, arrival in Nauvoo mistaken for, V6:134-5
  Expositor, arrest for destruction of, trial on, V6:487, et seq
  Expositor, witness in trial of Joseph, V6:457
  imprisonment, letter concerning, V5:352-3
  Joseph, accuses F. M. Higbee of seeking life of, V7:130
  Joseph, blessing of, on, V5:125
  Joseph, comments as friend, V5:125
  Joseph prophesies that will get away honorably, V5:305
  kills Frank Worrell in mob action, V7:446
  Missouri, arrested in, V5:298
  Missouri, covenanted to assist saints in removing from, V3:254
  Missouri, statement of on, V6:135, et seq
  Nauvoo, affidavit on Governor Ford in, V6:588-9
  Nauvoo, arrested in, V7:428
  Nauvoo, warned of Prophet to stay at, V6:565
  Neighbor, editorial in on return of, V6:144
  Washington, leaves Nauvoo for, V4:19
  West, accompanies Prophet in his start for the, V6:548, et seq
  witness suggested to appear before Congress on redress, V4:97.

Rockwell, Peter, baptized, V1:86.

Rockwood, Albert P., assessor and collector for Nauvoo First Ward,
  V6:71

ROCKWOOD, ALBERT P. (continued)
> genealogy and baptism, V2:501 and ftnt
> mentioned, V4:294-6; V5:4, 297; V6:363, 493-4
> Mormonism, investigates, V2:501-2 and ftnt
> Prophet, assists in retirement, V5:90
> relief expedition, his account of second, V5:454-6
> seventies, ordained president of, V7:538
> seventies, sustained president of at Salt Lake City, V7:629
> temple quarry, in charge of, V7:381
> witness for Joseph at Carthage martyrdom, V6:576.

Rocky Mountains, prophecy by Joseph that saints would go to, V5:85 and ftnt.

Rogers, Mr., member of mob at Haun's Mills massacre, V3:325.

Rogers, Amos P., mission appointment and field of labor, V5:349.

Rogers, Brother, mentioned, V3:260, 272, 275; V3:315; V5:153, 164-5.

Rogers, Chandler, mentioned, V3:226.

Rogers, Charles, mentioned, V1:287, ftnt only.

Rogers, D. H., mission appointment published and field of labor, V6:338.

Rogers, Daniel W., mentioned, V3:284.

Rogers, David W., hymn book by, discarded, V4:14
> Jackson County lands, reports sales of, V3:315
> poor, donates money to remove from Missouri, V3:323
> trial of for various sins, forgiven, V4:106.

Rogers, Elijah T., petitions Governor Boggs on mob violence in DeWitt, V3:83.

Rogers, Hiram, recommends Brother Green to collect for poor, V3:348.

Rogers, Isaac, Kirtland Camp, subscribed to constitution of, V3:93
> presidency, issues complaint against, V2:484.

Rogers, Jack, mobber at Haun's Mills, V3:239.

Rogers, John, English brother preaches at place where burnt at stake, V4:182 and ftnt.

Rogers, Noah, blessing for missionary work, V5:405
> heals Sister Webster of inability to walk, V5:518
> kidnapped by Missourians, V4:156-7
> mission call to Pacific Isles, V5:386
> mission call and field of labor, V5:349
> Missouri, covenanted to assist saints in removing from, V3:253
> Society Islands, letter on work in, V7:313-4
> Society Islands, returns from mission, V7:556
> Tahiti, work in, V7:253.

Rogers, Peter, committee member to talk to saints on removal, V2:452
  drafts resolutions of public meeting in Missouri, V2:449
  Zion, appointed by public to assist saints in removal from, V2:455.

Rogers, Samuel H., called on mission and field of labor, V5:348.

Rolf, T. J., mentioned, V6:537.

Rolf, Tallman, threatens against Nauvoo, V6:452.

Rolfe, Benjamin, Joseph, on relief expedition for, V5:482
  Nauvoo Temple, appointed carpenter on, V7:326.

Rolfe, Gilbert, mentioned, V5:454.

Rolfe, Ianthus, mentioned, V6:274.

Rolfe, P. T., *Expositor,* witness at trial, V6:489
  martyrdom mob, aided and abetted, V7:146.

Rolfe, Samuel, (also spelled Rolph, Rolf), exploring, volunteers for, V6:224
  Joseph, pays money in hour of need, V2:327
  Kirtland Temple, blessing for work on, V2:206
  mission of to Indians, V2:208
  Missouri, covenanted to assist saints in removing from, V3:252
  Nauvoo Temple, appointed carpenter on, V7:326
  priests, president of quorum in Nauvoo, V4:312.

Rollason, William H., no business, one of martyrdom mob, V7:144, 146.

Rollasson, Mr., store robbed, V6:281.

Rollins, Mr., V3:243.

Rollins, L., appointed by public to assist saints in removing from Zion, V2:455.

Rollinson, William H., anti-Joseph, V6:414.

Rollo, J. B., mentioned, V4:488.

Roman Empire, saints' position compared with decline and fall of, Intro-V3:LI, et seq.

Romney, Edward, mentioned, V6:405.

Romney, Miles, Nauvoo Temple, carpenter on, V7:326.

Roosevelt, Mr., mentioned, V6:464, V7:123

Root, Colonel, mentioned, V6:8.

Root, Henry, DeWitt, affidavit concerning mob in, V3:149
  DeWitt, encourages saints to settle in, V3:450
  DeWitt, petitions Governor Boggs on mob violence in, V3:83
  DeWitt, requests saints to leave, V3:159
  Missouri persecutions, affidavit concerning, V4:62-3.

Rose, Mr., mentioned, V5:277.

Rose, Andrew, covenanted to assist saints in removing from Missouri, V3:253.

Rose, Joseph, mission appointment published and field of labor, V6:339
  Missouri, covenanted to assist saints in removing from, V3:253.
  teachings of questioned and repentance, V2:223.

Rosecran, George W., Joseph, on relief expedition for, V5:482.

Ross, Captain, mentioned, V7:158.

Ross, Colonel, proposes work for Zions Camp, V2:80.

Ross, John, mentioned, V6:375.

Roundy, Brother, mentioned, V1:417.

Roundy, Shadrach, Church, appointed to preside over new district of, V7:305
  Ford, Governor, messenger to, V5:509
  genealogy of, V2:298 and ftnt
  Joseph, accompanies in arrest, V4:365
  Joseph, accompanies for trial on Missouri warrants, V5:210
  Joseph, entertains, V2:40, 298, ftnt only
  Kirtland Temple, blessing for work on, V2:205
  Missouri, covenanted to assist saints in removing from, V3:252
  Nauvoo, bodyguard to Joseph's body on return to, V7:135
  Nauvoo, policeman in, V6:149
  Nauvoo Legion, officer in, V4:296
  prophecy, present in Missouri at Apostles' departure to fulfill, V3:339
  Salt Lake High Council, sustained member of, V7:629
  westward movement, captain of fifth company in, V7:481-2

Rowe, Oliver, subscribed to constitution of Kirtland Camp, V3:93.

Rowe, Stephen, subscribed to constitution of Kirtland Camp, V3:93.

Rowland, Samuel, elder, ordained, V5:349
  mission call and field of labor, V5:349.

Royce, John, called on mission and field of labor, V5:349.

Roylance, William, volunteers for service in vineyard, V4:217.

Royle, Cooper, represents British conference, V5:419.

Royle, Henry, British conference, represents branch of Church in, V4:148
  British Mission, mission in, V4:150
  devote all time to labors of ministry, V4:148
  volunteers for service in vineyard, V4:217.

Rudd, Brother, meeting at house of, V1:416.

Rudd, Elder, mentioned, V5:420.

Rudd, Erastus, cholera, dies of in Missouri, V2:115
    Kirtland Temple, blessing for work on, V2:206
    Zions Camp member, V2:185.

Rudd, John, Joseph, pays money in hour of need, V2:327
    Zions Camp, exonerates Joseph's actions in, V2:149.

Rule, William G., mission appointment published and field of labor, V6:340.

Rulison, John, Kirtland Camp, subscribed to constitution of, V3:93
    Kirtland Camp, turned out of, V3:131.

Rupp, I. Daniel, (also L.), letter to, V6:428
    mentioned, V6:9, ftnt only.

Rushton, Edwin, ordained teacher, V4:311.

Rushton, Frederick, ordained teacher, V4:311.

Rushton, Lettice, serenades Joseph at Christmas, V6:134.

Rushton, Richard, mentioned, V5:299.

Russell, Mr., states attorney for Portage County, treatment of Prophet, V2:47.

Russell, A. C., hears false story of Joseph, V2:26.

Russell, Daniel, mentioned, V5:330
    utility committee member to aid Church removal, V7:474.

Russell, Isaac, apostate, turns and claims Lord appointed him in Joseph's stead, V3:226
    apostasy of in England, V3:342
    England, establishes Alston branch in, V2:508
    evil spirits, attacked by in England, V2:503
    excommunicated from Church, V3:336
    false doctrine, letter to saints in England, V3:343-4
    genealogy, joins English Mission at New York and, V2:494 and ftnt
    mission of, V2:490, ftnt only
    revelations, letter from Church reproving his pretended, V4:5-6 and ftnt
    Twelve Apostles, prophecy astonishes, V3:339-40.

Russell, Mary, excommunicated from Church, V3:336.

Russell, Samuel, mentioned, V5:330
    mission call in Illinois to disabuse public mind over arrest of Joseph, V5:485.

Russell, William, father of Isaac, V2:494, ftnt only.

Russia, Adams, George J., appointed to mission to, V5:417
    Hyde, Orson, appointed on mission to, V5:488
    mission appointment to, V6:41
    mission to planned, V5:417.
    See also mission.

Rust, William W., called on mission and field of labor, V5:348.

Ruther, T., Kirtland Camp, mentioned in, V3:135.

Ryan, Charles, elder, ordained, V5:349
    mission call and field of labor, V5:349.

Ryder, Simonds, apostasy of, V1:260 and ftnt
    China earthquake, converted by, V1:158 and ftnt
    mob, member of, V1:264 and ftnt

Ryland, E. M., Liberty, letter to saints requesting peace conference at, V2:89-90
    mob, saints petition but refuse to issue process agianst, V1:429, ftnt only
    public feeling, letter showing in Missouri, V3:172-3.

Ryland, John F., letter to saints' attorney, V1:445-6
    peace and justice urged by in Missouri, V1:429, ftnt only; V1:479; V2:89-90, 96; V2:91-2; V3:353.

—S—

Sabin, E. J., Joseph, on relief expedition for, V5:482.

Sabine, Brother, mentioned, V5:208.

Saco, Maine, conference of Twelve at, V2:252.

sacrament, Apostles, administered by, V2:283
    Apostles, officiated by, passed by presidency, V2:435
    Church, first performed in, V1:78
    consecration, prayer of, V1:69
    Emma rebuked for leaving meeting before, V2:304
    false doctrine, some banned for teaching, V1:366
    instructions given by messenger, V1:106
    Kirtland Temple, administration in, manner of, V2:431
    Lord will withdraw Spirit and priesthood will be forbidden to pass, V2:204
    partake, commanded to, V1:61
    Rigdon, President, speaks during, V2:393
    Spirit, outpouring of, at, V2:408

SACRAMENT (continued)

    water, first recorded use of, V2:480 and ftnt

    wine, commanded not to purchase for, (D&C § 27:3) V1:106

    wine, prepares own for, V1:106

    word of wisdom, cannot administer if breaking, V2:34.

sacrifice, Abel, of, accepted by faith, V4:208

    Abel's accepted and explained, V2:16

    atonement must be by shedding of blood or no faith, V2:15

    blood, reason for, by, V2:17

    Cain cursed for offering in unrighteousness, V4:209

    Cain's contrary to law, V2:15

    priesthood, always part of, V4:211

    purpose, discourse on, V7:463

    sons of Levi, will be restored when, purified, V4:211.

Saddis, Nathan, mentioned, V4:175.

Sadler, James C., anti-Mormon committee member, V1:399.

Sagers, Harrison, Adam-ondi-Ahman, chosen to high council of, V3:38

    charged with teaching spiritual wife doctrine and neglecting family, V6:333

    elder, ordained, V2:526

    mission appointment to travel, V2:35

    mission, assigned to go on, V4:429

    mission, to go on to West Indies, V4:413

    mob, appointed to raise funds to purchase lands of, V3:84

    trial of, on charge of seduction, V6:81.

Sagers, William Henry, Zions Camp member, V2:185.

saints, abominations, commanded to put out of mind, V7:350

    accused of burning mob's houses, V3:164 and ftnt

    activity, renewed of, V1:424

    Adam-ondi-Ahman, ordered to leave, V3:207

    Adams, C., letter to Joseph concerning cause of, before Illinois Legislature, V4:53

    Agriculture Companies, organization of, V3:64

    ancient to reign with Christ 1,000 years, V2:53

    appeal of, to world concerning freedom and rights, V2:126 and ftnt, et seq

    armory, in Missouri to build, V2:69

    arms, of Caldwell give up, V3:192

    arrest of, V3:209

    Baptist Church, differs from former day, V4:350-1

    base and degraded beings, described as by General Lucas, V3:150

SAINTS (continued)

Big Blue, attacked on, V1:426

blood, trail of, indicates path of expelled members, V3:439

Caldwell, attacked and plundered at, V3:192

character, difference of, cause of persecution, IntroV3:XXII

character of at June 3, 1831 conference, V1:176-7

character of, in Missouri, IntroV3:XX

charges, false against refuted, V1:376-7, ftnt only

Clay County, requested to evacuate, V2:448-9, et seq

Clay, Henry, receives history of persecution of, V6:94

condition of, V2:39

condition of May 1, 1834, V2:62

covenant of to assist each other, V3:251, et seq

Daviess County, agree to purchase mob's lands in, V3:84

DeWitt, expelled from, V3:159-60

Diahman, their agreement with mob, V3:216

endowments, to receive, V5:2 and ftnt

English, condition of, at Nauvoo, V5:25

expelled from Diahman, V3:207

Far West, found, V2:468, 482, 483, ftnt only, 491

Far West High Council, authorizes petition to general government in
behalf of, V3:241

First Presidency, address to, by, V4:184, et seq

Gallatin, trial at, V3:84

gathering, Missouri dedicated for, V1:196

gathering to cities, V3:166

God, considered themselves favored of, IntroV3:XXXIII

God, General Clark asks unknown to help, IntroV3:XLIX

growth of, in Missouri, IntroV3:XLIII

hardship of, in Missouri returned back to people, IntroV3:LXIII

healing of the, V4:3-5, ftnt only

horns, thought to have, V5:214

Independence, attack on, V1:427-8

Indians, and the, in Missouri, IntroV3:XXIX, et seq

Indians, charged with communication with in Missouri, IntroV3:XXX

Indians, problem with, made possible expulsion from Missouri, Intro-
V3:XXXII

Jackson County, preparations of to return to, V2:24

Kirtland, counseled by Nauvoo High Council not to return to, V4:45
and ftnt

Kirtland, depression of, at, V3:98

Kirtland, from New York come to, V1:173

SAINTS (continued)

Kirtland Camp, list of who signed constitution of, V3:91-3

Kirtland Camp, organized into, V3:87, et seq

memorial of, to Missouri Legislature concerning grievances and occurrences, V3:217, et seq

Missouri, case of before Senate Judiciary Committee, V4:81, et seq

Missouri, number accounted driven from, IntroV3:XVII

Missouri, position in, IntroV3:XXXI

Missouri, unwise statements of, in, IntroV3:XLVI

Missouri, value of lands lost in, IntroV3:XVII

Missouri persecutions, compared with early Christians, IntroV3:LIV, et seq

Missouri persecutions, fifty killed in, IntroV3:XVII

Missouri persecutions, petition to Federal Government on, V4:24, et seq

Missouri persecutions, reaction to, explained, IntroV3:XLIV

Missouri persecutions, religious life chief cause of, IntroV3:XLVIII

Missouri persecutions, unorganized in, V1:434 and ftnt

Missouri persecutions, unwisdom a factor in, IntroV3:XLVII

Missouri persecutions, unwisdom of, in, IntroV3:XXXII, et seq

mob, agreement between and Jackson County, V1:394-5

mob, falsely accused by, V3:76-7

mob manifesto, beliefs of caused, in Missouri, IntroV3:XLVIII

mysteries, to be taught, V4:426

Nauvoo, defend in, by William Law, V5:32-4

Nauvoo, resolutions of, before Senate Judiciary Committee, V4:157-9

Nauvoo, Quincy Committee requests removal from, acquiescence, V7:449-51

Nauvoo, sickness among at, V4:3

newspapers teeming with lies about, V4:380

Ohio, commanded to assemble in, revelation, (D&C § 37) V1:139

order, admonished to set houses in, V4:4, 5

parable, compared to, of treasure hidden in field, V2:271-2

people, should be separate from all evils, V4:570

petition of, at DeWitt to the governor, V3:82-3

petition of, to governor of Missouri, V1:410, et seq

political fear, a cause of Missouri persecutions, IntroV3:XXIX

political jealousy of mobs in Missouri of, IntroV3:XXVIII

political motto of, in Missouri, IntroV3:XXIX

political power, mobs feared, in Missouri, IntroV3:XXVIII

politics, concerned little over, in Missouri, IntroV3:XXVII

prairie, attacked on, V1:427

SAINTS (continued)

Ray County, asked to confer with committee from, V3:62

religious life, mobs comment on, IntroV3:XLVIII, et seq

Richmond, treatment of, before court at, V3:210, 211

Roman empire, position of, in Missouri compared to decline and fall of, IntroV3:LI, et seq

sectarian, enjoined to live in rigid style of, wrong, V4:445

settling of, revelation, (D&C § 51) V1:173-4 and ftnt

Shoal Creek, gather at, V2:467, 468

sin, left in lands of enemies because of, IntroV3:XLI

sins of, enumerated, IntroV3:XL

slow in understanding, V6:184-5

temporal matters, must act for themselves without testimony of Spirit in, V3:94

tied to trees and required to eat bark to sustain life, V3:405

treason, belief of, in Daniel prophecy condemned as, IntroV3:L

unite, to, means for work and business, V5:45

Zion, driven from, reasons for, IntroV3:XXXIX

Zion, feelings toward, unwise, IntroV3:XXXIV

Zions Camp, failure of, IntroV3:XXXIX.

See also epistles; Latter-day Saints, Church of Jesus Christ of; letters.

Sale, Robert, mentioned, V4:516.

Salem Advertiser and Argus, article on Nauvoo and the Prophet, V5:432-3.

Salisbury, Catherine, Joseph's sister in poor times, V5:247.

Salisbury, Wilkins Jenkins, charges against and dismissed, V1:470

excommunicated for unchristianlike conduct, V2:442

mission call, V1:332

ordained, V1:333

Prophet, entertains, V2:4

seventies, named to first quorum of, V2:204

unwisdom of, V2:442

Zions Camp member, V2:185.

Salmons, Abraham S., mentioned, V4:175.

Salt, William W., mentioned, V7:562.

Salt Lake Valley, considered as a place of settlement, V7:439.

Salt River Branch, Zions Camp stays at and encounters at, V2:87 and ftnt.

salvation, children, salvation and resurrection of, V4:553, et seq

Enoch, ministers to heirs of, V4:209

Knight, N., discussions with concerning, V1:82

knowledge, gained through, V5:387, et seq

SALVATION (continued)

   plan of revealed through priesthood, V4:207
   responsibility, when one prevents another from hearing gospel he has, of his, V7:546
   revelation, cannot have, without, V3:389
   Taylor, John, on, V7:289.
   See also dead; doctrine; Holy Ghost; knowledge; resurrection

Sanborn, Enoch S., subscribed to constitution of Kirtland Camp, V3:92.

Sanders, Ariel, mobber in Missouri, V4:61.

Sanders, Ellis M., Church, donates money for, V7:405
   mentioned, V6:368
   Nauvoo, delegate to political convention in, V6:390.

Sanders, John, elder, ordained, V4:148
   English conference, represents branches of Church at, V4:148
   high priest, ordained, V4:333
   volunteers for service in vineyard, V4:217.

Sanders, Moses M., policeman in Nauvoo, V6:150.

Sanderson, James, mission appointment published and field of labor, V6:337.

Sands, John, ordained elder, V4:333.

Sangamon Journal, martyrdom, account in, V7:179
   Whig newspaper, announced governor in alliance with the Mormons, V7:29.

Sanger, Lucien P., mentioned, V5:442, V7:514
   testifies on Joseph's second arrest in Illinois, V6:67.

Sasnett, J. J., mission appointment published and field of labor, V6:338.

satan, see devil.

Saunders, Brother, mentioned, V7:138.

Saunders, John, mentioned, V6:424.

Savage, David, mission appointment published and field of labor, V6:339.

Savage, Gehiel, clerk of Michigan conference, V6:175
   mentioned, V4:342.

Savage, William, mission appointment published and field of labor, V6:339.

Savary, Richard, mentioned, V5:515.

saved, cannot be, without temple ordinances, V6:184
   children who die before age of accountability are, V2:381.
   See also salvation.

Saville, Joseph, baptized, V4:317.

Sayers, Edward, Joseph moves to house of to avoid arrest, V5:90.

Sayers, Ruth, mentioned, V7:209.

Scandinavian, missionary work to, in Illinois, V5:395.

Schoby, Almira, mentioned, V2:324.

Schofield, Joseph S., Nauvoo Temple, appointed carpenter on, V7:326.

school, books to be printed for, V7:474
    common to be established, V1:276-7 and ftnt
    elders, house for to be built by, V1:342
    Kirtland, report of general, V2:200
    Kirtland Temple, organized in, V2:474.
    See also education; Elders, School of the.

Sconce, Colonel, enters Zions Camp as enemy and leaves as friend, V2:105-6.

Sconce, John, proposition of Mormons addressed to, V2:122.

Scott, Mr., mentioned, V7:415.

Scott, Ann, excommunicated from Church, V3:336.

Scott, Dr., mentioned, V3:150.

Scott, Isaac, excommunicated from Church, V3:336.

Scott, Jacob Jun., excommunicated from Church, V3:336.

Scott, Jacob Sen., and wife, excommunicated from Church, V3:336.

Scott, John, counselor in apostate church, V6:354
    England, appointed to go to with Twelve, V3:347
    mentioned, V5:371, V7:129, 593
    Nauvoo Temple, appointed to officiate in, V7:547.

Scott, Robert, warns Joseph of threat on life, V6:280, ftnt only.

Scott, Walter, Campbellites, Joseph interviews founder of, V1:188
    and ftnt
    Joseph opposes, V1:188
    reformed Baptist, relations with Sidney Rigdon, V1:121, ftnt only.

Scovil, Abner, witness for state in Missouri trials of saints, V3:210.

Scovil, Lucius N., Joseph, on relief expedition for, V5:482
    Kirtland Camp, mentioned in, V3:135
    Kirtland Camp, subscribed to constitution of, V3:93
    mentioned, V7:158
    mission call to England, V5:386
    Nauvoo, delegate to political convention at, V6:390
    Nauvoo Temple, appointed to officiate in, V7:547.

scripture, ancient, Joseph translates, V1:170

SCRIPTURE (continued)

God, admitting of, binds us to obey, V2:11
interpretation of, V5:261, et seq
Joseph answers questions on, (D&C § 113) V3:9-10
Joseph on, V5:339, et seq
lost books of, V1:132 and ftnt
Moroni, passages of ancient, quoted by, V1:12
New Testament, translation of, completed, V1:324, ftnt only, 341, 369
Prophet, understanding of, opened respecting, V1:43
translation, commenced, V1:132.
See also Bible.

Seabury, William, mission appointment published and field of labor, V6:336.

sealing, power of just men made perfect, V6:51
powers of, V6:183-4.
See also doctrine.

Seaman, Murray, mentioned, V5:370.

Searles, Samuel, witness for Joseph at Carthage martyrdom, V6:576.

Seaton, N. E., genealogy, V1:312 and ftnt
newspaper publisher, V1:312.

Sebolo, Antonio, first found Egyptian mummies, V2:348.

second comforter, Jesus Christ is, V3:381
Joseph delivers second message on, V4:10 and ftnt.

second coming, false prediction of exposed, V5:326 and ftnt
false prediction of made, V5:272, ftnt only
Joseph indicates would be in fifty-six years, V2:182
Joseph on, V5:336-7
prophecy that will not be within 40 years, V6:254
rainbow, when withdrawn is close, V6:254
signs of commenced, V3:390.

second death, lecture on, V6:317.

Secret Constitution, The, see manifesto of Missouri mob.

sectarian baptism, see baptism, sectarian.

sectarian churches, all wrong, V1:6.

sectarian priests, instigated mob to destroy baptismal dam, V1:86.

sects, debate, do not challenge for, V6:82
mob, named as participators in, V1:392
priests of all prevent saints from returning to lands in Missouri, V2:3
unbelief, exercise sin of, V2:415.

seeing, gift of, of the devil, V2:141.

Seely, William, taken prisoner by mob, V3:169.

Seer, Joseph evidenced as one, V1:272, ftnt only
    what constitutes, V1:12.

"Seer, The," hymn sung at Seventies Hall dedication, V7:333.

Seichrist, William, excommunication from Baptists for joining Mormon
    Church, V5:166.

Seixas, Joshua, Abraham, attests to authenticity of record of, V2:388
    family, sends for, V2:406
    Hebrew, engaged to teach, V2:368
    Kirtland, arrival of, in, V2:385
    Kirtland, lectures in, V2:390
    misunderstanding with, V2:402
    Prophet's regard for, V2:397.

self-righteousness, doctrine of devil, V5:24
    reproof of, V5:401.

Semple, James, mentioned, V6:369.

Semple, Judge, mentioned, V7:138.

Sene, J., delegate to political convention in Nauvoo, V6:389.

Seneca County, first missionary work in, V1:51.

serenade, on Christmas morning, V6:134.

Sessions, David, covenanted to assist saints in removing from Missouri,
    V3:253.

Sessions, Perrigrine, (also spelled Perrygrine, Perigrine), death of, V7:365
    mission call and field of labor, V5:348
    Missouri, covenanted to assist saints in removing from, V3:253.

seventh day, designated as Saturday, V7:418.
    See also doctrine.

seventies, Apostles, declares them, to the nations, V7:308
    Apostles, forbidden to ordain new, V4:162
    Apostles, serve directly under, V2:202 and ftnt
    Apostles, sustained as, and special witnesses, V2:418
    apostleship, call considered as an, V2:346
    call of, explained, not to preside but preach, V2:431
    "Come to Me," W. W. Phelps sang at conference of, V7:331
    conference, five days of, V7:330-45
    conference, to receive mission charge, V2:218
    council, minutes of, V7:365-7
    councilors pro-tem chosen in, V3:89-90
    devil attacks and causes disunity, V2:352

SEVENTIES (continued)

duty in Church, V2:221 and ftnt
elders, all, under 35 to be ordained to, V7:305
endowments, first presidency of, with wives, receive, V7:544
English grammar to be taught, V7:365
faith of, V2:395
God, blessing of, upon efforts of, V3:97-8
guard duty, relieved from, V3:111
Hall, dedication of, at Nauvoo, V7:330, et seq
Hall, dedicatory prayer at, V7:332-3
Hall, instructions to, on construction of, for, V6:271
high priests, not, but elders, V4:105
high priests, not to be, V2:477
high priests, presidents that were, moved out and new chosen, V2:476 and ftnt
high priests, wrong to be also, V2:476
instructions of, to overseers of tents, V3:109
Joseph, spoken of by, V2:181, ftnt only, 182, ftnt only
Kirtland Camp, exhortation to, V3:135
Kirtland Camp, organize, V3:87-93
Kirtland Camp, take practical steps for organizing, V3:95-6
Kirtland Temple, anointed in, V2:388
Library and Institute Association organized, V7:325
members and presidents named, V2:203 and ftnt
ministry and Church to support, V2:221
missionary, if desire, be, V7:308
Mormonism, mission to undeceive local people on, V7:351-2
number of, to be chosen, V2:221 and ftnt
organization of, V2:201-2 and ftnts
poverty, extreme of in Kirtland, V3:98
preached, those who have not yet, forbidden to, V3:347
presidency organized, V7:260 and ftnt
presidents, all sustained but one, V2:510
presidents, entire first quorum ordained, V7:279
presidents, Roger Orton dropped as one of, V7:461-2
presidents, sustained at Far West, V2:524
presidents, to be chosen from among, V2:476 and ftnt
presidents quorum chosen, V7:274
quorum, second of, V2:391
quorum, 11th organized, V7:307
quorum, 15th and 16th organized, V7:352
quorum, 16th and 17th organized, V7:362

SEVENTIES (continued)

quorum, 27th organized, V7:424

quorum, 28th organized, V7:432

quorum, 31st organized, V7:481

quorum, 32nd organized, V7:549

"Seer, The," John Taylor's, sung for the first time at conference of, V7:333-5

sinners, minutes of meeting of presidents of on forbearance with, V7:365-7

Spirit, attested by, to move as quorum, V3:89

vacancies to be filled from elders, V2:222

wickedness, to be purged of all, V7:372

Young, Brigham, instructions of to, V7:307-8

Zion, should move to, as a quorum seen in vision, V3:88.

See also priesthood.

Seventies Hall, dedicatory prayer at, V7:332-3

Nauvoo, dedication at, V7:330, et seq

Young, Joseph, second dedicatory prayer, V7:342.

Seventies Library and Institute Association, organization of, V7:325

stockholders and trustees of, V7:328.

sex, Joseph repudiates sins of, V6:81.

Seyley, William, witness suggested to appear before Congress on redress, V4:97.

Seymour, John S., attests to honesty of saints in Kirtland, V3:165.

Seymour, Lawyer, Knight, Newel, answer of to, V1:92-3

Presbyterian prosecutor at Joseph's trial, V1:92.

Shafer, Abraham, mentioned, V2:454, V3:281.

Shaking Quakers, Copley, Leman, member of, V1:167

gospel, reject, V1:169, ftnt only

mission to, (D&C § 49) V1:167

origin, V1:167, ftnt only.

Shamp, J., deaf daughter of, healed, V4:361.

Shamp, Margaret, healed of deafness, V4:361.

Shannon, Wilson, Governor of Ohio, V3:334.

Sharon, Vermont, Joseph born at, V1:2.

Sharp, J. R., testify to finding Kinderhook plates, V5:377, 378, ftnt only.

Sharp, Thomas C., anti-Mormon committee chairman, V6:8

editor *Warsaw Signal,* anti-Mormon, the Prophet on, V4:487 and ftnt

Joseph, acquitted of murder of, V7:420

Joseph, indicted for murder of, V7:314

SHARP, THOMAS C. (continued)

    martyrdom mob, member of, V7:143

    mentioned, V4:489.

Shaw, Osmond, British conference, represents, V5:420

    elder, ordained, V4:322.

Shaw, Thomas, letter of to Joseph introducing John Hewitt, V2:230, et seq.

Shearer, Daniel, mission appointment published and field of labor, V6:336

    Missouri, arraigned for treason, murder, burglary, arson, robbery, and larceny at Richmond, V3:209

    Missouri, covenanted to assist saints in removing from, V3:252

    prophecy, present in Missouri at Apostles' departure to fulfill, V3:339

    revelation, goes with Apostles to fulfill, V3:335.

Shearer, Norman B., mission call and field of labor, V5:348

    Missouri, arraigned for treason, murder, burglary, arson, robbery, and larceny at Richmond, V3:209

    prophecy, present in Missouri at Apostles' departure to fulfill, V3:339

    Richmond jail, placed in to stand trial for murder and treason, V3:212

    Richmond jail, charges against dismissed, V3:335

    seventy, ordained, V3:338.

Shearer, Reverend, Coburn, Emily, tries to prevent conversion of, V1:87

    Presbyterian minister, V1:87.

Sheets, Elijah F., mission, reports, V5:436

    Nauvoo, delegate to political convention in, V6:390.

Sheffield, emigrant ship, V4:296.

Sheffield, John, ordained priest, V4:298.

Shelton, S. C., mission appointment published and field of labor, V6:337.

Shem, descendants of represented at meeting in Missouri, V1:191

    Indians, descendants of, V1:191.

Shenask, Mr., delegate to political convention at Nauvoo, V6:390.

Shepherd, Ranson, mentioned, V7:584.

Shepherd, Samuel, utility committee member to aid Church removal, V7:474.

sheriff, forced to do duty by fines, V4:368.

Sherman, Mr., mentioned, V6:173.

Sherman, Alman, exonerates Joseph's actions in Zions Camp, V2:149.

Sherman, Almon, blessing for work on Kirtland Temple, V2:206.

Sherman, Henry, Zions Camp member, V2:185.

Sherman, Jason H., lawyer, member of martyrdom mob, V7:144

SHERMAN, JASON H. (continued)

    messenger to Governor from anti-Mormon meeting, V6:466.

Sherman, Lyman, Far West, appointed to high council at, V3:225
    Lord, seeks word of, V2:345
    Kirtland High Council, elected to, V2:518
    revelation to on status, V2:345
    seventies, named president of, V2:203
    Zions Camp member, V2:185.

Sherman, Sister, mentioned, V3:376.

Sherry, James, covenanted to assist saints in removing from Missouri, V3:254.

Sherwood, Brother, mentioned, V1:340.

Sherwood, Dial, mentioned, V5:300.

Sherwood, Henry G., assessor and collector for Nauvoo First Ward, V6:71
    Clay County, appointed to sell lands in, V3:308
    DeWitt, petitions Governor Boggs on mob violence in, V3:82
    England, appointed to go to with Twelve, V3:347
    Expositor, witness in trial of Joseph, V6:457
    healed by the Prophet, V4:4, ftnt only
    Joseph, accompanies in arrest, V4:366
    Joseph, accompanies for trial on Missouri warrants, V5:210
    Joseph declares gratefulness for aid rendered while in seclusion, V5:109
    Kirtland High Council, ordained to, V2:511
    Kirtland High Council, sustained to, V2:510
    Kirtland Temple, blessing for work on, V2:206
    mission appointment, V4:403
    Nauvoo, delegate to political convention in, V6:389
    Nauvoo, elected marshal of, V4:292
    Nauvoo, elected marshal and market master of, V5:270
    Nauvoo High Council, appointed to, V4:12
    Nauvoo High Council, sustained to after death of Joseph, V7:296
    Nauvoo Legion, requests assistance from, V6:104
    Salt Lake High Council, sustained member of, V7:629
    witness, suggested to appear before Congress on redress, V4:97.

Shibley, Henry, seventies, named to first quorum of, V2:204
    Zions Camp member, V2:185.

Shirts, Peter, elder, ordained, V2:207
    Kirtland Temple, blessing for work on, V2:206.

Shumaker, David, see Jacob Shumaker.

Shumaker, Jacob, (also spelled Shoemaker), affidavit concerning Missouri persecution, V4:69-70
  mission appointment published and field of labor, V6:337.

Shuman, William, subscribed to constitution of Kirtland Camp, V3:92.

Shumway, Charles, exploring, volunteers for, V6:224
  mission, sent on to Lamanites, V7:401
  westward movement, captain of twelfth company in, V7:482.

Shumway, Otis, child of dies, V3:133, 136
  Kirtland Camp, subscribed to constitution of, V3:92.

Shumway, Stephen, Kirtland Camp, joins, at Petersburgh, V3:100
  Kirtland Camp, leaves, V3:140
  Kirtland Camp, subscribed to constitution of, V3:92.

Shurtliff, Luman A., mentioned, V5:525
  mission, call amidst mob action in Missouri, V3:154.

Shurtliff, V., mentioned, V7:508.

sickness, teaching that all is of devil rebuked, V2:147.

Sidney, emigrant ship, V5:164.

sign, baptism ordained of God as, V4:554.

signs of the times, bloody war, seen by Joseph of forthcoming, V5:301
  cholera, epidemics of, as, V1:347-8
  flesh and blood, shower of, V4:383
  God, word spelled out, V5:309
  Hyde, Orson, seen in heavens by, V4:202-3
  Joseph, enumerated by, V4:252-3
  reported, V1:301; V5:433
  reported April 1833, V1:337
  reported May 1833, V1:347-8
  reported July 1833, *Star,* V1:388
  reported July 1841, V4:383
  stars, shower of, V1:439-40 and ftnt
  sword and arm in heaven seen, V4:439
  sword and ring seen, V5:304
  swords, two appear, V5:310
  year 1860 seen in heavens, V6:121.

Silcock, Nicholas T., Nauvoo Temple, appointed carpenter on, V7:326.

Silvers, Esq., refuses to issue process against mob, V1:429.

Simmons, A. A., mission appointment published and field of labor, V6:338.

Simmons, John, publishes anti-Mormon literature, V4:254.

Simmons, William B., appointed elder, V4:13.

Simpson, Mr., mentioned, V6:333, 403, 409.

Simpson, Alexander, mentioned, V6:594.

Simpson, George, anti-Mormon committee member, V1:399.

Simpson, George, English conference, represents branches at, V6:328
> high priest, ordained, V4:333.

Simpson, Richard, anti-Mormon meeting, heads in Missouri, V1:395
> mob, carries proposals to saints from, V1:398.

sin, Christ committed no, V2:23
> Church, preventing one from joining is, V2:247
> confession of in open meeting, V2:385
> enemies, saints left in hands of, for, IntroV3:XLI
> faith, without is, V2:16
> forgiveness of, V6:314, et seq
> men of revealed, V1:175 and ftnt
> Missouri, of saints in enumerated, IntroV3:XL
> remission of expounded on, V2:256
> spirits, if oppose will have all corrupt against, V5:141
> unpardonable, Joseph on, V6:313-4
> wickedness, man cannot be compelled to do, V4:358, et seq

sin, unpardonable, Joseph on, V6:313-4.
> See also doctrine; sin.

Singer, Isadore, rabbi comments on Jesus, V3:358.

Singleton, Captain, militia, in command of from Brown County, V7:12
> Nauvoo, ordered to keep peace at, V7:131.

sinners, forbearance with, V7:366.

Sirrine, Mephiboseth, Church, appointed to preside over new district of,
> V7:305
> president of Michigan conference, V6;175
> westward movement, captain of twenty-third company in, V7:482.

Sitgraves, William, on first sailing of saints from England, V4:134.

Skinn, James, ordained teacher, V4:138.

Skinn, Joseph, ordained priest, V4:138.

Skinner, Onias C., Joseph, attorney for defense of murderers of, V7:50
> martyrdom mob, lawyer, member of, V7:144
> mentioned, V5:317.

Slade, Benjamin, witness for state in Missouri trials of saints, V3:210.

Slade, Roxa, testifites before high council, V2:137.

Slater, Brother, mentioned, V6:515.

Slater, George, called on mission and field of labor, V5:348.

Slater, Peter, delegate to present truth to public, V6:483.

Slater, Richard, mentioned, V5:372.

slavery, Church stand on, V3:29
    Missouri, law concerning in, IntroV3:XXIV
    Missouri persecutions, question of, in, IntroV3:XXII, et seq
    Missouri persecutions, reason why issue in, IntroV3:XXVII
    mob, part of secret constitution of, IntroV3:XXIV
    petition to eliminate, V5:283 and ftnt

slaves, fought against Missouri vs. retribution, IntroV3:LXX.

Slinger, Joseph, ordained priest, V4:148.

Sliter, Brother, mentioned, V3:146.

Sloan, Mr., English conference, represents branches at, V6:328.

Sloan, Albert, elder, ordained, V3:155
    Missouri, covenanted to assist saints in removing from, V3:253.

Sloan, James, Church clerk, elected general, V4:424
    mission, call to Ireland, V5:386
    missionary call to Ireland, V5:413
    Missouri persecutions, statement of, concerning, V4:69
    Nauvoo, elected recorder of, V4:292
    Nauvoo, elected recorder and notary public in, V5:270
    Nauvoo, elected notary public in, V5:165.

Small, Mr., excommunicated for believing in Sidney Rigdon, V7:299.

Smalley, Ellis, solicits Joseph's views on politics and issues, V6:387-8.

Smalling, Cyrus, mentioned, V6:66
    seventies, named to first quorum of, V2:203
    Zions Camp member, V2:185.

Smallwood, Noland, signs proposition to buy land of saints, V2:96-7.

Smith, Aaron, ordination illegal and rejected, V1:343.

Smith, Agnes C., daughter of Don Carlos, V4:399.

Smith, Agnes M., endowment, receives in Nauvoo Temple, V7:543
    mob, flees to avoid, V3:163
    prison, letter to Joseph and Hyrum in, V3:314
    wife of Don Carlos Smith, home of burned, V3:163.

Smith, Alexander Hale, son of Joseph, born, V3:37 and ftnt.

Smith, Alma, witness suggested to appear before Congress on redress, V4:97

SMITH, ALMA (continued)

wounded at Haun's Mills by mob, age seven, V3:326, ftnt only.

Smith, Alvin, Celestial Kingdom, seen by Joseph in, V2:380
description of, V5:247
dies, V1:16-7
Joseph, brother to, V1:2
Joseph, comments on as friend, V5:126.

Smith, Amanda, narrative of, of Haun's Mills massacre, V3:323, et seq
witness suggested to appear before Congress on redress, V4:97.

Smith, Arthur, cuts timber on Joseph's land illegally, V6:80

Smith, Asael, patriarch, ordained, V7:302
patriarch, sustained as, V7:301 and ftnt.

Smith, Asael, death of, V2:443
Joseph, grandfather of, V1:2
letter concerning character of ancestors, V1:285, ftnt only
prophesied a prophet would be in his family, V2:443.

Smith, Asahel, Iowa Territory High Council, appointed to, V4:12
Kirtland High Council, ordained to, V2:511
Kirtland High Council, sustained to, V2:510.

Smith, Avery, Zions Camp member, V2:185.

Smith, Bathsheba W., receives endowments in Nauvoo Temple, V7:543.
See also Bigler, Bathsheba W.

Smith, Caroline Grant, death of, V7:417.

Smith, Catherine, sister to Joseph, V1:2.

Smith, Charles H., receives patriarchal blessing, V2:387.

Smith, Clarissa, endowment, receives in Nauvoo Temple, V7:543
mother of George Albert Smith, V3:338, ftnt only.

Smith, David B., ordained elder, V4:13.

Smith, Don Carlos, baptized, V1:86
biography of, V4:393, et seq
children of, V4:399
death of, V4:393
description of, V4:399
healings, account of, V4:398
high council, appointed by to raise means, V3:84
high priest, ordained and chosen to be president of, V2:370
high priests, president of at Commerce, V4:12
Hyrum, letter to informing that family was well, V3:313-4
Joseph, brother to, V1:2
Joseph, comments as friend, V5:127

SMITH, DON CARLOS (continued)

    Kirtland Temple, blessing for work on, V2:205

    letter of, on trip to Zion, V3:43

    Liberty jail, letter to Joseph while in, V3:273-4

    McDonough County, Illinois, settles in, V3:377

    mission, return from in Tennessee and Kentucky, V3:241

    Missouri, covenanted to assist saints in removing from, V3:252

    Missouri, journal on mission while in, V4:394, et seq

    mob, carries petition to, V3:261

    Nauvoo, first elected councilor of, V4:287

    Nauvoo, sworn in as councilor of city of, V4:295

    Nauvoo Legion, elected brigadier-general of second cohort of, V4:296

    Robinson, dissolves partnership with, V4:239

    Times & Seasons, publisher of, V4:23.

Smith, Don Carlos, infant son of Joseph dies, V4:402.

Smith, Eden, mission call and field of labor, V5:349

    prayer to soften heart of, V2:24

    president of branch at Eugene, Ohio, V1:369 and ftnt

    withdrawal of fellowship, V1:370-1.

Smith, Elias, bishop, appointed in Iowa, V4:154

    bishop, ordained, V4:161

    bishop, sustained as, V4:399

    England, appointed to go with Twelve, V3:347

    judge, kept record of Kirtland Camp, V3:87, ftnt only

    Kirtland Camp, historian for, V3:42, ftnt only

    Kirtland Camp, subscribed to constitution of, V3:91

    Missouri, on committee for removal from, V3:255

    Missouri, covenanted to assist saints in removal from, V3:252

    Nauvoo, alderman of, V6:357

    Ohio Territory High Council, appointed to, V4:12

    prophecy, present in Missouri at Apostles' departure to fulfill, V3:339

    seventy, chosen member pro tem in first council of, V3:90

    witness, suggested to appear before Congress on redress, V4:97.

Smith, Elijah, saints to purchase farm of, V1:335.

Smith, Elisha, covenanted to assist saints in removing from Missouri, V3:253.

Smith, Elizabeth, petitions Governor Boggs on mob violence in De Witt, V3:83.

Smith, Elizabeth Ann, marries Newel K. Whitney, V1:146, ftnt only.

Smith, Emma, adopts Murdock twins, V1:260 and ftnt

    baptized, V1:88

SMITH, EMMA (continued)

Bible translation, called on for and will not give up, V7:260
birth, time and place, V1:17 and ftnt
child, gives birth to stillborn, V5:209
confirmed, V1:108
genealogy, V1:17, ftnt only
hymns, proceeds to select, V2:273 and ftnt
hymns, to select, V4:17
Joseph, entreats to return and give up, V6:549
Joseph, induces to return to his death, V6:552
Joseph, letter to Governor Carlin to defend, arraigning Missouri, V5:132, et seq
Joseph, letter to Governor Carlin pleading cause of, V5:115, et seq
Joseph, letter to on movements and business, V5:110
Joseph, marries, V1:17
Joseph, meets in seclusion, V5:89, 92, 95
Joseph rebukes for leaving meeting before sacrament, V2:304
Joseph, seeks letters of administration for, V7:194
Joseph's sentiments towards, V5:107
kindness of to husband, V6:165-6
labors, assists husband in, V4:510
Relief Society, president of, V4:552
revelations to, V1:103
sick, baptized in river for, V5:167-8.
See also Hale, Emma.

Smith, Ephraim, brother to Joseph, V4:189.

Smith, Frederick G. W., son of Joseph, V6:342
tells dream of Missourians, V5:45.

Smith, George Albert, Adam-ondi-Ahman High Council, chosen to, V3:38
America, sails for, V4:352
Apostle, ordained an, V3:337
Apostle, sustained by Church after death of Joseph, V7:295
Apostles, acknowledged member of, V3:345
Apostles, sustained member of at Salt Lake City, V7:628
baptized, V1:285
Bigler, Bathsheba W., marries, V4:389
Black, A., falsely accused of threatening, V3:64
British Mission, leaves Nauvoo for, sick, V4:10
British Mission, returns from, V4:383
city council, elected member of, V5:13
conference, letter on, at Newark, Illinois, V6:399-401

SMITH, GEORGE ALBERT (continued)

    consecration, discourse of at general conference, October 6, 1845, V7:464

    endowment, receives, V6:98

    endowment, receives in Nauvoo Temple, V7:543

    England, arrives in, V4:102

    England, begins outdoor preaching in, V4:182, et seq

    England, condition of during trip and arrival, V4:104 and ftnt

    England, sails for, V4:94

    Entablature of Truth, designated as, V7:435

    genealogy, V1:285 and ftnt, 348 and ftnt

    healed of rheumatic infection, V2:354

    health, injures, V4:236

    Joseph, armor bearer for, V2:88

    Joseph, false writ against for aiding, V7:444

    Joseph, gives bond for collection of funds for, V5:414

    Joseph, love of, V5:390

    Joseph, testimony of as Church historian to period of, V7:243

    Kirtland, arrives in, V1:348 and ftnt

    labors, letter reporting, V4:343

    ministry, devote all time to labors of, V4:148

    mission, return of, from in Tennessee and Kentucky, V3:241

    Missouri, covenanted to assist saints in removing from, V3:252

    mob's lands, appointed to raise funds to purchase, V3:84

    murderers, letter of attorney general of Illinois on difficulties of collecting evidence of trial of martyrdom, V7:415-6

    Nauvoo Temple, appointed to officiate in, V7:547

    preaches at Richmond, New York, V4:75

    seventies, named to first quorum of, V2:204

    Seventies Library and Institute Association, elected trustee of, V7:328

    spring, discovers, V2:73

    statement as to original members of Church, V1:76, ftnt only

    temple, labors on, V1:353

    union, report of discourse on admonition on, V7:335

    West, leaves Nauvoo for, V7:585

    witness, suggested to appear before Congress on redress, V4:97

    writ issued against, V3:77

    Zions Camp member, V2:67, ftnt only, 185.

Smith, Gibson, mentioned, V2:241.

Smith, Harvey, blessing for work on Kirtland Temple, V2:206.

Smith, Hiram, arrives from England with immigrants, V6:346.

Smith, Howard S., excommunicated for unchristianlike conduct, V6:341

MITH, HOWARD S. (continued)

stake presidency, appointed counselor to, V4:236.

mith, Hyrum, address of at April 1844 conference, V6:298, et seq

Apostles, letter of, calling home, V6:486-7

arrest of for treason, V6:562

bankruptcy of, V5:200

bankruptcy, discharged in, V5:205

baptized, V1:51

begins work, V6:61

Bennett, John C., affidavit of concerning character of and Joseph, V5:71, et seq

body of viewed, V6:627

Book of Mormon, letter to Parley P. Pratt on printing of, in New York, V4:47-8

Carthage, advised not to go to, V6:558

Carthage, illegal imprisonment at, V6:569-70

Carthage, letter consenting to go to, accepting protection of Governor, V6:550

Carthage jail, preaches to guards in, V6:592

Carthage jail, receives pistol in, V6:607-8

Church, sustained counselor to president of at Far West, to replace Frederick G. Williams, V2:522

elders, discourse to, V6:322-4

endowments, receives, V5:409

epistle to saints, testimony of Book of Mormon, V4:46 and ftnt

Expositor, arrest for destruction of and trial, V6:487, et seq

Far West, made prisoner at, V3:190

First Presidency, sustained assistant counselor to, V2:509

funeral, mock and secret burial, V6:628-9

genealogy, V1:45 and ftnt

grand jury brings in bill against, for treason, murder, etc., V3:315

high council, ordained to, to replace Sylvester Smith, V2:165

human flesh, subjected to eat while in Liberty prison, V3:420

Joseph, brother to, V1:2

Joseph, captain of life guards of, V2:88

Joseph, secretly goes to inform of movement of sheriff August 1842, V5:97

Joseph suggests that he leave, won't, V6:520

Joseph's regard for, V5:107-8

Kirtland Camp, assists in organizing, V3:89-95

Kirtland Camp, gives advice to, V3:94-5

Kirtland Temple, blessing for work on, V2:205

SMITH, HYRUM (continued)

Kirtland Temple, breaks ground for, V2:352

knee joint, injures, V6:98

letter from Don Carlos Smith to, informing that families were well V3:313-4

letter to Kirtland disapproving building up of, V4:443-4

letter to Missouri January 14, 1833, V1:317, et seq

Liberty, Clay County, sent to stand trial for murder and treason at V3:212

Liberty jail, letter of William Smith to, while at, V3:274

life, receives threat on, V6:367

life record and characterization of, IntroV6:XLIII

martyrdom of, V6:617

martyrdom, official account of, V6:629-31

Masonic Temple, lays cornerstone of, V5:446

meeting conducting committee, V1:219

meeting house, appointed to collect money to pay rent of, V1:342-3

Missouri, arraigned for treason, murder, burglary, arson, robbery, and larceny at Richmond, V3:209

Missouri persecutions, testimony concerning, V3:404, et seq

Missouri sufferings, statement of, V3:373-4

Missouri warrants, accompanies Joseph for trial on, V5:209-10

mob enters camp of in Missouri, V3:189 and ftnt

mob, taken by to Independence, V3:194

Nauvoo, appointed on committee to establish, V4:39

Nauvoo, arrival of body at, V6:626

Nauvoo, elected vice mayor of, V5:12

Nauvoo, first elected councilor of, V4:287

Nauvoo, letter to Joseph concerning raising funds for him and state of affairs in, V4:50-2

Nauvoo, sworn in as councilor of City of, V4:295 and ftnt

patriarch of the Church, V4:229 and ftnt

poisoned while at Liberty jail, V3:390

Presbyterian Church, joins, V1:3

Prophet, presented and sustained as to the 19th century, V7:392

Prophet, refuses to leave, V6:546 and ftnt

Prophet, seeks to comfort, V6:592, 600

Prophet, visits at Harmony and inquires respecting work, (D&C § 11) V1:45

remonstrance of with Prophet, V6:403

revelation, appointed by, a prophet and revelator, V4:286

revelation, asks for, (D&C § 23) V1:80

SMITH, HYRUM (continued)

Rocky Mountains, notes the warning to flee to the, V6:547
settlement, assists in locating lands for, V3:37
slander of, by O. F. Botswick, V6:225
son dies, V4:418
Temple committee, appointed to, V6:53
theft, affidavit denouncing, V4:460
thieves, remarks on, V5:332-4
Washington, letter of Joseph to reporting state of affairs in, V4:39-41
Warsaw Signal, denial of threats against and editor, V6:495, 500
witness, suggested to appear before Congress on redress, V4:97
Zions Camp, joins at Salt River with recruits from Michigan, V2:87
    and ftnt
Zions Camp member, V2:185.
See also Latter-day Saints, Church of Jesus Christ of; letters; Smith,
    Joseph.

Smith, Hyrum, son of Hyrum dies, V4:418.

Smith, J. M., mentioned, V5:391.

Smith, Jackson, mission appointment published and field of labor, V6:338
Zions Camp member, V2:185.

Smith, Jazeniah B., mentioned, V2:72, 252
named to first quorum of seventies, V2:204.

Smith, Jeremiah, case of, V6:420, et seq, 501-2
kidnap, threats to, V6:412
Municipal Court, before, V6:418-25
Nauvoo, issues out writ of habeas corpus at, V6:343.

Smith, Jerusha Barden, baptized, V1:86
dies, Hyrum's wife, V2:519.

Smith, Jesse, mentioned, V2:441.

Smith, Jesse J., attacked by cholera while burying one of its victims,
    V2:115
dies of cholera, V2:120
mission appointment to East, V2:35.

Smith, John, Church, given care of at Lime Street, V4:135.

Smith, John, Carthage jail, visit of to Joseph in, V6:597-8
Church, chosen one of the presidents of the, V2:510
council, in, at Kirtland, V1:389
disfellowshipped, V1:370-1
endowments, receives in Nauvoo Temple, V7:543
father of George Albert Smith, V3:338, ftnt only
First Presidency, reproved sharply by letter from, V1:370

SMITH, JOHN (continued)

    First Presidency, sustained assistant counselor to, V2:509

    heroism of, V6:515

    high priest, ordained, V4:217

    Iowa, president of stake at, V4:399

    Joseph, reproved by, and confesses, V2:303

    Joseph's uncle arrives at Kirtland, V1:348 and ftnt

    Keokuk, called to move to, to build city, V5:164

    Kirtland Temple, blessing for work on, V2:206

    mission of to Eastern states, V2:446

    Missouri, covenanted to assist saints in removing from, V3:251

    Missouri persecutions, affidavit concerning, V4:59-60, 62

    mob movement, letter of requesting instructions on, V6:485

    murderers, letter to Illinois attorney general on difficulties of col-
        lecting evidence for trial of martyrdom, V7:415-6

    Nauvoo Temple, appointed to officiate in, V7:548

    partriarch, appointed, V6:110

    patriarch, ordained, V6:173

    patriarch, sustained to Church at Salt Lake City, V7:628

    patriarch to the Church, V7:247 and ftnt

    patriarch, voted to the Church, V7:622

    Smith, Joseph, Sen., visit of, V1:285, ftnt only

    stake president, appointed counselor to, V4:233

    stake president, appointed of Iowa Territory, V4:12

    stake president, sustained as Nauvoo, V7:296

    Zion, chosen president of stake of, V3:38 and ftnt.

    See also letters.

Smith, John, ordained priest, V4:148.

Smith, John, signed mob manifesto, justice of the peace, V1:376

Smith, John G., mission appointment published and field of labor, V6:339

Smith, Joseph, Aaronic priesthood given to, V1:40

    Aaronic priesthood, Oliver Cowdery ordains to, V1:40

    abolition, views on, V2:436, et seq

    Abraham, rebukes lady for disbelief of ancient writings of, V2:229-3

    Abraham, relates story of acquiring writings of, V2:348-50 and ftn

    Abraham, Book of, arranged alphabet for the, V2:238

    Abraham, Book of, publishes, V4:520, et seq

    Abraham, Book of, works on translation of, V2:238, 286, 289, 320

    accusation against, sample of public mind, V2:351

    accusers, ridicules, V2:269-70

    Adam, saw, V3:388

    Adam-ondi-Ahman, changes name of Spring Hill to, V3:35 and ftn

SMITH, JOSEPH (continued)

Adams, James, discourse on life and death on demise of, V6:50-2
adultery, on, V6:81
adversary, aware of call of, V1:6
Albany and Boston, visits, V1:295
aloof from early revivals, V1:3
ancient councils, order of, V2:25
angels, accused of having destroying, V5:364
angels, ministered unto by, V2:381
anti-Mormon articles, admonishes restraint on, V6:221
Apocrypha, not to translate, (D&C § 91) V1:331-2
apostate conspirators at Nauvoo, IntroV6:XXXVI
apostates, condemns to sin of murder, V3:228
apostates, enumerates who helped imprison and persecute saints, V3:228
apostates, suggestions of, concerning, V2:493
apostates, turns over to buffetings of Satan, V3:232
apostasy, Church members begin against, V2:488 and ftnt
arrest, account of in *Chicago Democrat*, V5:448-9
arrest, anxiety of, in Carthage, depression, V6:592
arrest, anyone doing so on Missouri difficulties sentenced to life imprisonment, V6:105
arrest as political trick, V5:513-5
arrest, attempted of, by Missourians on September 3, 1842, V5:145-6
arrest, corrections in public statements concerning second, V6:67-9
arrest, discharge of from, V5:244
arrest, editorial on second, V5:507-8
arrest for destruction of *Expositor*, trial on, V6:487, et seq
arrest in Illinois on second writ, V5:440, et seq
arrest, in seclusion from possible, V5:89, et seq
arrest, moves to Edward Sayers' to avoid, V5:90
arrest on Missouri extradition, V5:209
arrest, purported order of by United States President, V5:363
arrest, records expedition of "Maid of Iowa" to relieve him on, V5:482-4
arrest, released on second, V5:474
arrest, report of relief expedition of Charles C. Rich on, V5:486-8
arrest, report of search for, on Missouri warrant, V5:92
arrest, speech of, on second, V5:465-73
arrest, writ issued for, in Far West, V3:63 and ftnt
arrest and hearing, on *Expositor* affair, V6:453-8
arrested by constable at confirmation meeting, V1:88

SMITH, JOSEPH (continued)

arrested, to be sent to Missouri, V4:365

arrests, special ordinance on future of, in Nauvoo, V6:105

Articles of Faith, writes Wentworth letter containing, V4:535, et seq and ftnt

assistance, receives from Ramus saints, V5:294

astronomy, learns ancient principles of, V2:286

Atchison, General, confers with on Daviess County troubles, V3:69

attracted by religious excitement, V1:2-3

Avon, Livingston County, New York, attends conference at, V2:44

Babbitt, Almon W., prefers charges against and withdraws them V4:187-8

Babbitt, Almon W., prefers charges against for traducing his character, V2:346

Bagby, Mr., assault of, on, V5:524

Bagby, Mr., settlement of taxes with, V4:542

Bainbridge, New York, married at, V1:17

Bainbridge, New York, arraingment in court at, V1:89

bankruptcy of, V4:594

bankruptcy, letter on, V5:6-7

baptism, on, V6:316-7

baptism, Church does not, in name of, V3:29

baptism, comment on, of other churches, V3:29

baptism, premonition of, V2:294

baptism for dead, on, V6:365

baptism for dead, consents to in Iowa, 1841, V4:383

baptism for dead, discourse on, V4:568-9

baptism for dead, expounds on, V4:595, et seq

Barnes, Lorenzo D., remarks of, on death of, V5:360-3

Bennett, John C., denounces, V5:35-8, 156-7

Bennett, John C., extols sins of, V5:35

Bennett, John C., receives whisperings concerning, V5:4-5

Bible, cannot settle religious questions from, V1:4

Bible, completes translation of New Testament of, V1:324 and ftnt

Bible, new translation of cannot be obtained from Emma, Intro V7:XXVII

Bible, on the, V6:57

Bible, translating of, V1:132, 170, 211, 215 and ftnt, 219, 324 and ftnt 369

bishops, to expose iniquity, V5:18

Black, Adam, affidavit concerning voting and incident, V3:70-2

Black, Adam, gives opinion on, V3:65

SMITH, JOSEPH (continued)

Black, Adam, interview with, V3:59

blessing on father, mother, Hyrum, Samuel, and William, V1:465-7

blessing, seeks special for himself and brethren, V2:281

blessings, petitions the Lord for six specific, both personal and for Church, V2:2-3

blood, none in quickened tabernacle, V6:366

blood atonement, on, before city council, V5:296

body, search for, V7:448

body viewed, V6:627

bodyguard, names of recorded, V7:135

Boggs, ex-Governor, arrested for assassination of, V5:86-7

Boggs, Governor, comments on attitude of, V3:178

Boggs, Governor, denial of association with assassination attempt of, V5:15

Boggs, Governor, extradition of demanded by, V4:198

Book of Commandments, see Commandments, Book of, infra

Book of Mormon, see Mormon, Book of, infra

Book of Revelation, see Revelation, Book of, infra

born, V1:2

Bowman, William, swears not to eat nor drink until kill, V3:306

breastplates, beheld by, V1:16

brethren, receives money and goods from, blessings of, V2:326-7

bribery, offers to pay double the price for attempted, of police, V6:153

Burdick, Thomas, rebukes affliction of, V2:301-2

burial, mock funeral and secret of, V6:628-9

Calhoun, John C., comments on, V4:80

calling, duty of to rebuke and admonish, V2:478

calling and election, made sure, V5:402-3

California and Oregon, delegation sent to investigate for future movement, V6:222

California and Oregon, organizes exploring expedition to, V6:224

Canada, leaves for, October 5, 1833, V1:416, et seq

Canada, returns from to Kirtland, V2:508

Canada, views on annexation of, V6:244

canal, suggests building around Des Moines rapids, V6:80, ftnt only

capture, reward offered for, V5:167

Carlin, Governor, acknowledges proceedings against as illegal, V5:91

Carlin, Governor, letter of, on Bennett affair, V5:49-51, 82-3

Carlin, Governor, orders arrest of, V4:198-9

Carlin, Governor, proclamation of, in Springfield trial, V5:236-7

SMITH, JOSEPH (continued)

Carthage, enumeration of those who persuaded to return to, V6:552

Carthage, final departure for, V6:558

Carthage, illegal imprisonment at, V6:569-70

Carthage, paraded before military at, V6:563-4, V7:83-4 and ftnt

Carthage, proceeds to, to face indictments by grand jury, V6:412-5

Carthage, reception upon arrival in, V6:559

Carthage, returns to Nauvoo, prepares to go to, V7:81-2

Carthage, starts for, V6:554-8

Carthage jail, assault on, V6:617-9

Carthage jail, committed to, for greater security, V7:12

Carthage jail, interview with Governor Ford at, V6:577-9

Carthage jail, interview with Governor Ford at, John Taylor's account of, V6:579-85

Carthage jail, last night of, in, V6:600

Carthage jail, leading brethren of Nauvoo visit in, V7:99

Carthage jail, preaches to guards at, V6:592

Carthage jail, receives pistol in, V6:607, V7:100

Carthage jail, requests Brother Taylor to sing in, V6:614-5

Carthage jail, requests Willard Richards to go into cell with him at, V6:616

Carthage jail, visit of John Smith to, in, V6:597-8

Celestial Kingdom, Alvin seen in, V2:380

Celestial Kingdom, presidency seen in, V2:382

Celestial Kingdom, revelation as to those in, V2:380

Celestial Kingdom, sees, V2:380

character, development in, IntroV5:XXVIII

character of early youth, V1:9-10

character sketch of, in *Boston Bee*, V5:406-8

character, testifies of John C. Bennett's, V5:13

characterizes himself, V5:401

children, birth of son, V1:295

children born to, V1:295, ftnt only

children, deaths of, V6:316

children, takes Murdock twins to raise, V1:260 and ftnt

cholera, stays the, V2:120

cholera, rejected at house and disease attacks and kills, V2:115

Christ, imitates crucifiers of, V1:91

Christ, retranslates words of, to thief on cross, V5:424-5

Christ, second coming of, V5:336-7

Christ, on sign of, V5:290-1

Christendom, reflection on divided, V1:3

SMITH, JOSEPH (continued)

Christianity's hope in salvation based on devil, V5:218

Christmas, holds party at Mansion, V6:134

Christmas, receives serenade at, V6:134

Church, answers questions on, V3:28-30

Church, anxiety of concerning history of, V6:66

Church, organized with a view to independence, V1:269

Church history, begins writing, V3:25, 26

Church publications, editorial to support *Times & Seasons* and other, V6:69-70

churches, all wrong, V1:6

churches, decides not to join any, V1:8

churches, indicates in disconsolate state, V2:146

churches, questions all, V1:4

city council in Nauvoo, submit to law, V7:11

city council, introduces several bills in, V4:293

city ordinance, recommends repeal of "extra," V6:212

Clark, General, seeks to try, by martial law, V3:206

Clay, Cassius M., sketches reply to, V6:227

Clay County, visits with brethren in, V2:120

Clayton, William, becomes clerk to, V5:49

Colesville, dream of Sister Knight of visit, V1:101

Colesville, ministry at, V1:86-8

Colesville, returns to after trial for confirmation, V1:97

Colesville, trial at, V1:89-91, 92-5 and ftnts

Colesville, visits, V1:81

Colesville branch, visits, V1:269 and ftnt

collecting funds, on, V5:329, et seq

collection, taken to help relieve persecution expenses, V5:491

Comforter, receives Second, (D&C § 88:3-4) V1:302

Commandments, Book of, appoints steward of, and dedicates, V1:234-6 and ftnts

Commerce, takes up residence at, V3:349

Commerce, description of, V3:375

committee, consults with, from Chariton County, V3:73-4

conference, address of at April 1844, V6:287-8

conference, attends New Portage, V2:50

conference, attends Norton, Ohio, V2:52-4

conference, elders pronounced clean at January 23, 1833, V1:323

conference, general at Commerce, V4:12-4

conference on Gallatin troubles, V3:58-9

conference, preaches at special at Nauvoo from hiding, V5:137

SMITH, JOSEPH (continued)

Congress, presents amount to, as claims for losses, V4:74

Conover, P. W., on relief expedition for, and reveals plot against, V5:450-3

consecrates all to Lord, V1:219, ftnt only, et seq

conspiracy, affidavit of, on, against his life, V6:523

conspiracy, affidavit of L. H. Calkins on, against, in Nauvoo, V6:531

conspiracy, affidavit of M. G. Eaton on, against, V6:279

conspiracy, affidavit of A. B. Williams on, against, V6:278

constable, first and second arrests by, aids, V1:88-9, 95-6

constable, surrender of, to, V6:561

constitution, on the, V6:56-7

constitutional powers, on, V5:289

converts, energy to friend by eloquence of the spoken word, V2:105-6 and ftnt

coroner's jury on death of, V7:108

Corrill, John, reproved for unwise conduct, V3:65-6

counsel, advises to use aged men in, V5:389-90

counsel, saints refuse to obey, V3:166

courage and calmness of, while in seclusion, V5:97-8

court, attends at Chardon, V2:46

covenants with God to be relieved from debt, V2:175

covetousness, left people uninformed because of, V7:545

cowardice, accused of, for leaving, V6:549

Cowdery, Oliver, Aaronic Priesthood given to, V1:39

Cowdery, Oliver, accuses of priestcraft, V1:104-5

Cowdery, Oliver, baptized, V1:39

Cowdery, Oliver, blesses and chastens, V1:465

Cowdery, Oliver, ordained assistant president of the Church, V2:176 and ftnt

Cowdery, Oliver, ordained elder, V1:77

Cowdery, Oliver, rebukes, V1:105

Cowdery, Oliver, reconverts with Whitmers, V1:105

Cowdery, Oliver, scribe for, V1:32-3

Cowdery, Oliver, takes tithing covenant with, V2:175

create, meaning of, V6:308-9 and ftnt

crimes, accused of, in Missouri, V3:206-7

Cumorah, first visit to, V1:15-6

currency, question of before city council, V5:296-7

Danites, named, V3:180

Danites, remarks on, V3:179-82

Davis, Matthew S., description of person and sermon by, V4:78, et seq

SMITH, JOSEPH (continued)

dead, voice of warning on too little time to save, V6:184

death of, V6:618, V7:105

death, hears reported and comments, V2:168-9 and ftnt

death, indication of foreseeing of, V2:396

death, prophesied of forthcoming, V7:212

debate, Alexander Campbell challenged to public by, V2:269, ftnt only

debate, opinion of, in Church, V2:317-8

debates, purpose of in Nauvoo, V4:514

Derby, Erastus H., blesses for rendering aid, V5:106-7

destroying angels, J. C. Bennett accuses of having, V5:364

devil, cast out by, V1:215, ftnt only

devil, Christianity's hope in salvation based on, V5:218

devil, discourse on, V4:358

devil, tempts with riches of plates, V1:14

devil, tries to kill, V5:22-3

DeWitt, goes to assist saints at, V3:152-3

Diahman, meeting with Mill Port citizens at, V3:60

die, now can, V4:587

dispensation, place of, in new, extolled, IntroV7:XXVII

dispensation, stands at head of this, V7:250

doctrine, corrects Cowdery and Whitmer as to, V1:104-5

doctrine, corrects Orson Hyde on, V5:323-4

doctrine, instructions to Twelve Apostles on faith, repentance, baptism, Holy Ghost, tongues, resurrection, judgment, election, V3:379-81

doctrine, teaches stronger in public than private, V6:474

doctrines, newly discovered letter of, on various, V7:412-4

Doniphan's report and comments on, V3:78-9

Douglas, Stephen A., prophecy on head of, by, V5:393 and ftnt, et seq

dream, being beaten by representatives, V5:254-5

dream, concerning enemies at Nauvoo, V6:461-2

dream, counsels Brigham Young by, V7:435

dream, saw pattern of Nauvoo Temple in, V6:197

dream, troubled waters overcome, V6:194-5

dream while in Carthage prison, V6:609-10

dream of death of, by James A. Bennett, V7:261

dreams, interprets, V4:501

Dunklin, Governor, received word that refuses to reinstate saints upon lands, V2:94 and ftnt

earth, describes in sanctified state, V5:279 and ftnt

Editor's Journal, edits, V3:49

Egyptian alphabet, studies, V2:286

SMITH, JOSEPH (continued)

Egyptian language, arranges grammar for, V2:238

Egyptian mummies given to that contained scrolls of Abraham, V2:235, 349

elder, ordained by Oliver Cowdery, V1:78

elder, to be ordained an, V1:61

elders, instructions to in Zion, V2:228-9 and ftnt

elder, ordained by Oliver Cowdery, V1:78

elder, to be ordained an, V1:61

elders instructions to in Zion, V2:228-9 and ftnt

election day troubles, explains on, V5:531-2

election troubles, starts for Gallatin on hearing of, V3:58

elements, eternal existence of, V6:308-9 and ftnt

Emma, entreated by to return and give up, V6:549

Emma seeks letters of administration of estate, V7:194

endowment, introduces ceremonies of, V5:2 and ftnt

endowments, gives first, V5:409

endowments, selects by revelation those who will go to Kirtland to receive, V2:112-3

enemies, actions of, toward work of, V6:314-5

enemies, escaped en route from Kirtland to New Portage, V2:50

epistle, to Church from Liberty prison, (D&C § 121, 122, 123) V3:289 and ftnt, et seq

error, labors with those in, V2:303-4

escape from intoxicated guard and Missouri, V3:320-1 and ftnt

evangelical order, preaches on, V2:234 and ftnt

Evening & Morning Star, receives first copy of, V1:273

evil, exhorts Relief Society not to expose for time, V5:20

evil spirit, accused of possessing, V2:274

exaltation, of spirit of, V5:108-9

exaltation, three grand keys to, V5:403

excommunication, assents and acknowledges of W. W. Phelps and John Whitmer, V3:11

exhibited, with his friends to state troops, V7:83-4 and ftnts

Expositor, writ against for destruction of, V7:66-7

Expositor affair, account of, on, V7:125-6 and ftnt

Expositor affair, mental attitude of, in, V7:63

Expositor affair, the, IntroV6:XXXVII, et seq

extradition, first Missouri attempt, IntroV5:XXII, et seq

extradition, second Missouri attempt, IntroV5:XXIV, et seq

extradition attempts, legal opinion on, V5:173, et seq

faith, expounds on, and fruits of, V5:218

SMITH, JOSEPH (continued)

false accusations, proclamation of, on, V6:484-5

family, V1:2

family, reunion of grandparents and uncle, V2:442-3

family, visits, V1:21

Far West, arrives at, November 1837, V2:521

Far West, departure from, V3:193-4 and ftnts

father, heals, V2:289

father, promised would live, V2:289

father, receives blessing from, V1:323

father and mother, baptized, V1:79

Fayette, Seneca County, New York, removes to, V1:49

feast, attends after order of the Son of God, V2:362

fellowship, discusses possible return of R. D. Foster, V6:430

fight, handsome of, V6:617-8

flattery, admonition against, rebuke to do good, V3:295

flesh and blood, reports shower of, V4:383

Follet, King, delivers sermon on doctrine, V6:302 and ftnt, et seq

Ford, Governor, account of messengers to, on surrender, V6:552

Ford, Governor, admits pledging safety of, V7:49

Ford, Governor, article on Pacific Inuendo by, answering, V6:218-20

Ford, Governor, attitude of, at death of, V7:24

Ford, Governor, comments of John Taylor on responsibility of, for murder of, V7:113, et seq

Ford, Governor, comments on reactions to saints' pleas, V6:115

Ford, Governor, description and opinion of, V7:35, et seq

Ford, Governor, interview of, with, V7:88, et seq

Ford, Governor, opinion of actions of, at Carthage, on mob, 6:542

Ford, Governor, order commanding obedience to order of, V6:556

Ford, Governor, petition of, to quash Carlin's writ, V5:201, 204-5

Ford, Governor, refused escort for safety to Carthage by, V6:552

Ford, Governor, threatens writ against, V5:433

Freedom, New York, preaches at, V2:42-3

friends, expresses joy for, V5:107, et seq

friendship, on, V5:517

friendship, weakened by oaths, V3:303

funds, on collecting of, V5:329-32

funds, takes bond of brethren collecting, V5:414

garments, shakes against Robert D. Foster, V6:345

gathering, calls for, at Nauvoo, V4:362

gathering, instructs British Mission to not preach, V2:492

gathering of Christ, V2:259

SMITH, JOSEPH (continued)

gathering, purpose of, V5:423-7
gathering, to organize other stakes of Zion for, V2:514, et seq
Genesis 2:7, corrects, V5:392-3 and ftnt
German, studies, V5:264, 272, 292
gift of healing at Commerce, Nauvoo, V4:3-5 and ftnts, V4:7
gift of healing, on use of medicine and, V4:414
gift of Holy Ghost, editorial on, V5:26-32
gift of Spirit, elaborates on, V5:219
gift of tongues, views on, V4:485-6
God, character of, V6:303-4
God, decides to seek, V1:4
God, an exalted man, V6:305
God, eternal life to know, and Jesus, V6:305-6
God, rebuked before, (D&C § 93:47) V1:346
God, relation of, to man, V6:312-3
God's judgment, attempts to heal cholera but is stricken himself to
       know that he cannot stay, V2:114
God's promises, reproves brethren for trifling with, V2:95-6 and ftnt
Gods, discourse on Christian godhead and plurality of, V6:473, et seq
Gods, men must learn how to be, V6:306
Gog and Magog, on battle of, V5:298
gospel, answers questions on, V3:28-30
gospel, comments on question why men cannot see, V6:3
gospel principles, learn after passing through veil, V6:307
government, sends views on, to national officials, V6:225-6
grand jury, brings in bill against, V3:315
Grand River, locates lands for settlement of saints on, V3:34-8
Grand River, meeting concerning Canadian saints at forks of, V3:55
gratitude to friends and family that have helped him, V5:124, et seq
Great Basin, to proceed to, V6:548
Green Mountain Boys, dictates appeal to, V6:80
guards, chooses life, V2:88
guards, rebukes at Richmond prison, V3:208 and ftnt
gun, drawn on, by Charles Foster, V6:344
habeas corpus, petition for, against F. M. Higbee, V6:357
habeas corpus, petition for, to court at Nauvoo, V6:454-5
Hale, Isaac, purchases farm of, V1:28
happiness, essay on, V5:134 and ftnt, et seq
Harris, Martin, receives $50.00 from, V1:19
healing, lectures on, V2:95-6 and ftnt
healing, sees in vision, V2:381

SMITH, JOSEPH (continued)

heals E. Fordham, V4:4, ftnt only

heals Mrs. J. Johnson and converts E. Booth, V1:215 and ftnt (see also gift of healing, infra)

Hebrew, begins translation from, V2:396

height of, V5:210

hide, retreats to, at Carlos Granger's, V5:118

hides at home of James Taylor to elude enemies, V5:169

hiding, goes into at home of Edward Hunter, V5:160

hiding, returns from, V5:129

hiding, returns home from, against Missouri warrants, V5:119

Higbee, Francis M., talks to, on exposing, V5:49

high council, blesses individuals on first, V2:32

high council, charged before at Kirtland for criminal conduct, V2:142, et seq

high council, charges against Reynolds Cahoon before for failure to correct and properly instruct children, V2:242

high council, organized at Kirtland, V2:31-2

high council, organizes in Missouri, V2:122-4

high council, prefers charges against Robert D. Foster before, V6:333

high council, receives blessing of father at organization of, V2:32

high council, reviews and corrects minutes of, V2:31

high priests, indicated mission of 144,000, V5:326

high priests, states that selection of 144,000 already commenced, V6:196

Hinkle, George M., betrays to mob, V3:188-9 and ftnt

Hinkle, George M., sues for robbing house, V4:423

Hiram, moves to, V1:215

history of Church, reason for writing, V1:1

history, testimony of by Church historians, V7:243

history and persecution, synopsis of early given, V6:392, et seq

honest, delight to be, V2:281

house, to have built for, (D&C § 41:7) V1:147

House of Representatives, opinion on visit to, V4:41

human flesh, subjected to eating while in Liberty prison, V3:420

Hurlburt, Dr., attempts by to discredit, V1:475

Hurlburt, Dr., prays to be delivered from in lawsuit, V2:24

Hurlburt, Dr., triumph over, V2:49 and ftnt

hymn book, commences selections for, V4:3

Illinois, ministry in, V3:377-8

Illinois, opposing counsel inflamed against, V4:367

Illinois, Quincy, arrives in from Missouri prison, V3:327

illness, accused of sins because of, V2:493

SMITH, JOSEPH (continued)

Independence, preaches at, V3:202

Independence, removed from, to Richmond, V3:205-6

Indians, meets chiefs of, V4:401-2

Indians, speech on waste of, V5:358-9

indicted, for false swearing and polygamy, V6:405

indictments, new against, in old Missouri charges, V5:307

injury, escapes in carriage wreck, V5:182

insolvency, cause of, V4:600

inspiration, doctrine on, V5:406, et seq

inspiration, receives to go West to remove from mob, V6:545, 546, ftnt only

insulted by Josiah Butterfield and results, V5:316

intelligence, the immortal, V6:310-2 and ftnts

intemperance, reflections on, V2:406

Iowa, conditions in, April 1843, V5:334-6

Jackson County, arrival in, V3:200 and ftnt

Jackson County, preaches at, fulfills prophecy, V3:201

jail, in, as testimony for Jesus, V3:226

James, instructed by, V1:4

Jesus, explains meekness and lowliness of, V5:218

John, Book of, Chapter 14:16-23 interpreted by, V3:381

John the Apostle, questions about, (D&C § 7) V1:35-6

John the Baptist, on mission of, V5:260-1

Joshua the Jewish minister, meets, V2:304, et seq

journal, difficulties of keeping daily, V4:470

judgment, on evils of hasty, V3:27

judgment, responsibility of those who sit in, V2:26

judgment, sees signs preceding, V3:391

judgments, preaches on, V4:11

keys of kingdom never taken from, (D&C § 90:3-4) V1:329

keys of leadership not taken from at death, V7:287

kidnappers, receives one of, shows repentance, V6:133

kill, apostates swore to, V6:566

kill, mobber swears not to eat nor drink until, V3:306

kill, plot to kidnap and, V5:451-3

Kinderhook plates, receives and starts to translate, V5:372

King, Judge, trial of, before, V3:72-3

kingdom of God, has whole plan and only one who has, V5:139

kingdom of God, teaches of, V5:256, et seq

kingdoms, arguments for many, of glory, V1:252

Kirtland, arrival at, V1:272, V2:139, 528

SMITH, JOSEPH (continued)

Kirtland, arrival at from Missouri, V1:206

Kirtland, concerning business affairs in, V3:164-5

Kirtland, leaves for Missouri, V1:188

Kirtland, persuades saints at, to give up common stock concern, V1:146-7 and ftnt

Kirtland, return from Michigan to, V2:253

Kirtland, return to, V2:54

Kirtland, return to from Canadian Mission, V1:422

Kirtland, settles difficulty in between brethren, V1:219

Kirtland, starts for, V1:145

Kirtland, to move from, to Hiram, V1:211

Kirtland bank note, accosted for, pays, V4:368

Kirtland Safety Society, caution to public on receiving script of, V6:429

Kirtland Safety Society, resigns from, V2:497

Kirtland Temple, blessing for work on, V2:205

Kirtland Temple, dedicates pulpits of, V2:410, et seq

Kirtland Temple, filled with angels, V2:428

Kirtland Temple, foreman in quarry for, V2:161

Kirtland Temple, instructions given to ministry in, V2:431-2

Kirtland Temple, subscribes to and pays within one hour, V2:234

Knight, Joseph, Sen., assisted by, V1:47

Knight, Joseph, visits after Church conference, V1:86

Knight, Joseph, visits April 1830, V1:81

knowledge as saving power, V6:314

knowledge, sermon on salvation through, V5:387-9

knowledge, to receive all from God, V3:296

labors, temporal of, V2:50

law, adaptness of expressed, V5:280

law, commences the study of, V3:69

law, method of studying, V5:307

Law, William, swears to stand by till death, V6:165

lawsuits, detained at Painesville by, V2:502

lawsuits, enumerates against since start, V5:518

lawsuits, on vexatious, V6:99

lawyers, employed to defend, V7:85

lawyers, pays Missouri about $50,000, V3:327

lawyers, remarks on, V6:238-9

laying on hands in behalf of, V2:321

laying on hands, scribe relieved by, V2:321

laying on hands, Angeline Works gains senses by, V2:328

SMITH, JOSEPH (continued)

legislature, petition of, to Missouri, V3:247-9

letter of C. Adams to, concerning cause of saints before Illinois Legislature, V4:53

letter announcing intended visit to Quincy, V6:213

letter to J. A. Bennett, comments of position of religion and Prophet and J. H. Bennett, V6:73, et seq

letter of John C. Bennett to, announcing arrival soon, V4:179

letter of John C. Bennett to, declaring intent to join Church, V4:168

letter of John C. Bennett to, expressing anxiety to be with, V4:172

letter on John C. Bennett's movements, V5:250

letter to John C. Bennett on slavery, V4:544

letter of John C Bennett to, tendering services to Church, V4:169-70

letter to John C. Bennett welcoming him to Nauvoo, V4:177-8

letter to brethren in Missouri requesting information and exhorting to faithfulness, December 5, 1833, V1:448-51

letter to brethren in Zion counseling them to good, April 21, 1833, V1:340-1

letter to brethren in Zion on instructions, June 25, 1833, V1:362, et seq

letter to brother on tithing, V4:518

letter to Mrs. Norman Bull, concern for saints shown, V3:285-6 and ftnt

letter to John C. Calhoun and other candidates on feelings toward saints, V6:64-5

letter to John C. Calhoun showing contempt for latter's position on saints' very remarkable letter, V6:156, et seq

letter to Canadian saints, V1:441-3

letter to Governor Carlin, satisfied with attitude on Bennett affair, V5:83

letter to Brother Carter on instructions, V1:338-9

letter from Carthage jail, postscript to Emma, V6:610-1

letter from Carthage jail requesting interview with Governor Ford, V6:575-6

letter to Henry Clay, severely criticizes position on persecution, V6:376-7

letter consenting to go to Carthage accepting protection of Governor Ford, V6:550

letter to counsel on excitement in Carthage, V6:595

letter to Oliver Cowdery to see if he wants to repent, V5:368

letter to elders abroad reviewing actions and motives of settling Church in Missouri, V2:253 and ftnt, et seq

letter to Emma detailing prospective movements, August 16, 1842, V5:103-5

SMITH, JOSEPH (continued)

letter to Emma on Ford's sending troops to protect Nauvoo, V6:565

letter to Emma on instructions as to how to receive Governor Ford, V6:605

letter encouraging movement to Nauvoo of volunteers, V6:425

letter engaging counsel, V6:551, 590-1

letter engaging further counsel, V6:613.

letter to Eugene Branch on disfellowship of John Smith, V1:371

letter exhorting publishing of letter against sectarianism to N. E. Seaton, V1:326

letter to exiled saints in Missouri, sympathy and exhortation to stay in Zion, V1:453-6 and ftnt

letter on forthcoming book of John C. Bennett, V5:156-9

letter to Governor Ford defending actions in *Expositor* affair, V6:538-41

letter to Governor Ford explaining *Expositor* affair, V6:466-7

letter to Governor Ford explaining return to Nauvoo, V6:556

letter to Governor Ford inviting to come to Nauvoo, V6:525-7

letter to Governor Ford inviting to come to Nauvoo to keep peace, V6:480

letter to Governor Ford on kidnapping affidavits and mob action, V6:153

letter to Governor Ford on kidnapping by Missourians, V6:100-1

letter to Governor Ford submitting documents on mob action, V6:522, et seq

letter to Governor Ford supporting position on Avery kidnapping, V6:109-10

letter to Isaac Galland on settlement of account, V4:499-500

letter to Oliver Granger on affairs at Kirtland, V4:164-7

letter of Elias Higbee concerning affairs of saints in Washington, V4:94-5

letter of Elias Higbee exhorting in suffering, V3:319-20

letter of Elias Higbee reporting cause of saints before Senate committee, V4:81-3

letter of Elias Higbee, second, reporting cause of saints before Senate Committee, V4:83-5

letter of elias Higbee, third, reporting cause of saints before Senate Committee, V4:85-7

letter of Elias Higbee, fourth, reporting cause of saints before Senate Committee, V4:88

letter of Elias Higbee telling papers before Congress had been withdrawn, V4:98-100

SMITH, JOSEPH (continued)

letter to high council at Nauvoo concerning preliminary hearing of grievances in Washington, V4:43-4

letter of Horace Hotchkiss concerning progress before Congress, V4:98

letter of Horace R. Hotchkiss offering land for sale, V4:100-2

letter of Horace Hotchkiss on land purchase contract, V4:195-6

letter to Horace Hotchkiss on bankruptcy, V5:52

letter to Horace Hotchkiss on Carthage anti-Mormons, V6:55-6

letter to Horace R. Hotchkiss on lands, V4:469

letter to Horace R. Hotchkiss on Nauvoo land transactions; V4:406-7

letter to Horace R. Hotchkiss on purchase of lands, V4:170-2

letter to Edward Hunter on business affairs in Nauvoo, V4:481-3

letter to Edward Hunter on business transactions, V4:548-9

letter to Edward Hunter reporting opening of new store, V4:491-2

letter to Orson Hyde on Palestine Mission, V4:128-9

letter of Hyrum concerning raising funds for him and state of affairs in Nauvoo, V4:50-2

letter to Hyrum reporting state of affairs in Washington, V4:39-42

letter to Illinois governor on John C. Bennett affairs, V5:42-4

letter indicating elders to be sent to Arkansas, V6:459

letter, instructions on baptism for dead, V5:142-4, 148, et seq

letter, instructions on resisting mob, V6:482-3

letter to Vienna Jaques, personal counsel, V1:407-9

letter to General Law ordering out Nauvoo Legion, V6:120

letter to Wilson Law indicating probable movements August 16, 1842, V5:105-6

letter to Wilson Law on proceedings of Legion if arrested, V5:93-5

letter to lawyers on payment of notes, V4:468-9

letter to Reuben McBride on debts of Church, V4:441-2

letter on Missouri indictments, concerning, V5:422

letter to Missouri of November 27, 1832, V1:297, et seq

letter on olive leaf to Missouri of January 14, 1833, V1:316-7

letter, parables discussed to Church, V2:264, et seq

letter of Edward Partridge to, while at Liberty jail, V3:272-3

letter on payment of loans and Nauvoo Postmaster problem, V5:266-7

letter on personal character, V1:10, ftnt only

letter to W. W. Phelps accepting confession and offering fellowship, V4:162-4 and ftnts

letter to W. W. Phelps requesting he stay out of Church business, V3:358-9 and ftnt

letter on political views, V6:388

SMITH, JOSEPH (continued)

letter to Judge Pope introducing Jeremiah Smith, V6:422-3

letter of Parley P. Pratt reporting progress of Church in East, V4:22

letter to presidential candidates on their feelings toward Mormons, V6:63, 64-5

letter received refusing counsel, V6:553

letter removing families to Nauvoo, V6:515

letter reproving John Smith, V1:370

letter requesting payment of postage, V2:325

letter to Jenetta Richards, V5:40-1

letter of Sidney Rigdon airing plans to impeach Missouri, V3:310-1

letter of Sidney Rigdon indicating no redress for Missouri persecutions possible, V4:102

letter to Sidney Rigdon on suspicions of conspiracy with John C. Bennett, V5:312-4

letter of Alanson Ripley to, harsh against Missouri, V3:311-3

letter to L. D. Rupp thanking for book on religious sects in United States, V6:428

letter to saints in Clay County, V2:455-6

letter to saints in Kirtland, V3:10-2

letter to saints in Kirtland reproving for failure to aid in Missouri persecutions, V4:225-6

letter to saints from Liberty jail, V3:226, et seq

letter to N. E. Seaton on state of Christian world, V1:312 and ftnt, et seq

letter of Don Carlos Smith while at Liberty jail, V3:273-4

letter to Jeremiah Smith on release, V6:501-2

letter to John Smith on instructions in case of mob violence, V6:485-6

letter to William Smith forgiving, V2:340, et seq

letter of William Smith while at Liberty jail, V3:274

letter on taking out bankruptcy, V5:6-7

letter to Mr. Tewkesbury seeking to restore to fellowship, V6:427

letter to John Thornton et al requesting mediation in Clay County, to problems, V2:456, et seq

letter to Smith Tuttle on land troubles, V4:430-3

letter to President Tyler appealing for help, V6:508

letter to Martin Van Buren on previous treatment, addendum to, V6:65

letter to J. R. Wakefield soliciting as witness, V6:551

letter of John B. Weber to, concerning supplementing effort to obtain redress, V4:55-6

letter to John Whitmer demanding notes on Church history, V3:15-6

SMITH, JOSEPH (continued)

letter to Lyman Wight suggesting he take care of grievances, V3:366-7

letter of Brigham Young on British Mission, V4:119-20

letter to Zion's attorneys informing of disbursements of Zions Camp, V2:114-5

letter to Zion on condition of Church in Kirtland and suggested program for redemption of Zion in two years, V2:144-6

letters concerning his integrity in Kirtland business, V3:174

liberty, gives specimen of Missouri, living permit, V3:206

Liberty prison, taken from, to jail in Daviess County, V3:308-9

lie, concerning, recorded, V5:218

life and death, the resurrection and salvation of little children, sermon on, V4:553, et seq

"life is no value to friends," V6:549

life record and characterization of, IntroV6:XLIII, et seq

liquor, ordinance allowing to distribute, V6:111

literary methods of, V4:1

loneliness of in passing ancient battle field, V2:66

Lord, anxiety to obtain word of, on every subject, V1:207

"Lord whom Mormons worshipped," viewed as, V3:200-1

Lucas, General, opinion on, V3:151

Macedonia, visits, V6:59

Madison, interview of with gentlemen from, V6:479

man, discourse on his love for fellow, V5:498-500

Manchester, leaves, V1:19

manuscript, design of enemies in relation to revealed, (D&C § 10) V1:23, et seq

Marks, Ephraim, remarks at funeral of, V4:587

marriage, on eternal, V5:391-2

marriage, joins John F. Boynton and Susan Lowell in,, V2:377

marriage, joins William F. Cahoon and Maranda Gibbs in, V2:376

marriage, joins Thomas Carrico and Elizabeth Baker in, V2:369

marriage, joins Newel Knight and Lydia Goldthwaite in, V2:320

marrigae, joins Warren Parrish and Martha H. Raymond in, V2:324

marriage, joins Tunis Rapley and Louisa Cutler in, V2:376

marriage, joins Ebenezer Robinson and Angeline Works in, V2:331

marriage, joins Harvey Stanley and Larona Cahoon in, V2:376

marriage, joins E. Webb and E. A. McWhithy in, V2:331

marriage, joins John Webb and Catherine Wilcox in, V2:369

marriage certificate, form of, V2:377

marriage covenants, address of, at Nauvoo on, V5:510

married at South Bainbridge, New York, V1:17

SMITH, JOSEPH (continued)

married at Squire Tarvill's, V1:17

marries Emma Hale, V1:17

Marsh, Thomas B., comments on, V3:171-2

martyrdom of, V6:618-21

martyrdom, account of, by John Taylor, V7:102, et seq

martyrdom, Governor Ford's account of, V7:30

martyrdom, official account of, V6:629-31

martyrdom, John Taylor's memoirs on affairs leading to, V7:55, et seq

martyrdom, John Taylor reports of imprisonment and occurrences of before, V7:97, et seq

masonic, rides in procession, V5:41

masons, becomes sublime degree in, V4:552

masons, comments on Grand Master of, V5:370

masons, evaluation of, by, V4:565-6

masons, receives first degree of, in Nauvoo, V4:551

masons, grand chaplain of Nauvoo free, V4:550

means to be provided, V1:219

meeting, declares principle of leaving before close of, V5:338-9

members, reproved for accusing each other, V4:445

memorial, high council reconsiders and approves, V4:144-5

memorial, report of before Congress by Orson Hyde, V6:369, et seq

memorial, requesting to be relieved of all secular responsibilities and to be provided for by Church, V4:136-7

memorial, vetoed vote of high council on, V4:141 and ftnt

mesmerism, opinion of on, V6:56

Methodist, becomes partial to, V1:3

militia, comments on bravery and silence of, V3:198 and ftnt

millennial reign, described and conditions, V5:212

Millerism, exposes, V5:272 and ftnt

ministry, burden of, V5:516-8

ministry, remarks on, V2:394

minutes, instructs to take in all meetings, V2:199

miracle, seen but not recognized, V1:109

mischief, from false legal and political counsel, IntroV6:XXIX, et seq

mission, signs of his divine, V3:29

mission, elders to defend against John C. Bennett, V5:131-2

mission, starts on to Canada, V2:502

mission to Michigan, V2:168-9

mission with others to Salem, Massachusetts, V2:463, et seq

missionaries, sends out special to proclaim facts of his arrest, V5:485

missionary work, instructs to just get Holy Ghost, V4:13

SMITH, JOSEPH (continued)

Mississippi River, crosses for West, V6:548

Mississippi River, John Taylor's report of crossing for West, V7:78-9

Missouri, arraigned for treason, murder, burglary, arson, robbery, and larceny at Richmond, V3:209, et seq

Missouri, arrives at Independence, V1:188

Missouri, bill of damages against and experiences in, V3:368-73

Missouri, calls for volunteers to go to, V2:39

Missouri, comment on affidavits concerning, V4:73-4 and ftnt

Missouri, curse to remain in until redress to saints, V5:211

Missouri, dedicates temple spot in Zion in, V1:199

Missouri, departs from for Kirtland, V2:525

Missouri, describes people of, V1:180

Missouri, excommunication of presidency at approved, V3:11

Missouri, incident of acquiring accommodations while in, V5:211

Missouri, leaves for, April 1832, V1:265

Missouri, leaves for Kirtland, V1:202

Missouri leaves for Kirtland, July 1834, V2:135

Missouri, journey to, April 1832, V1:265

Missouri, rejected by household in and cholera attacks and kills them, V2:115

Missouri, relates treatment of his witnesses in, V6:108

Missouri persecutions, affidavit of to Governor Ford, V5:493-5

Missouri persecutions, appeal of, to native state, Vermont, to aid in redress for, V6:88, et seq

Missouri persecutions, article on "Friendly Hint" to, V6:245-7

Missouri persecutions, blame on mobbers and state, V1:471

Missouri persecutions, comments on, IntroV3:XLV

Missouri persecutions, gives impressions of, V3:327-33

Missouri persecutions, treachery of Lilburn Boggs, V1:434-5 and ftnts

Missouri procedure, reflections of, on, V5:87

mob, abused by constable after arrest and first trial, V1:91

mob, appeal to spirit of, IntroV6:XXXIX

mob, attacked by, March 25, 1832, and tarred, V1:261, et seq

mob, betrayed to, at Far West, V3:188, et seq and ftnts

mob, chased by, V3:63

mob, contends with and escapes from, V1:88-9

mob, forceably taken to courthouse by, V6:595

mob, forced to flee Kirtland by, V3:1

mob, opinion of, on offer to purchase lands, V2:99

mob, pursues after leaving Kirtland, V3:3

mob, reflections on in Missouri, July 1833, V1:393

SMITH, JOSEPH (continued)

mob, reflections of on scenes about Diahman, V3:162-3

mob, reviews saints' position with regard to action of, V3:67-8

mob, swears not to eat nor drink until kill, V3:306

mob, taken prisoner by from family to Independence, V3:193-5 and ftnts

mobs, address to Nauvoo police force on impending, V6:150-2

mobs, suggests to fight future, V6:94

mobbers, enumerates chief, V3:327

money, Eastern saints loan to, V2:172-3

money-digger, V1:17

money-digger, as a, V3:29

Mormon, defines word, V5:399-400

Mormon, Book of, author and proprietor of, V1:58, ftnt only

Mormon, Book of, efforts of enemies to get plates of, V1:18

Mormon, Book of, manuscript of entrusted to Martin Harris, V1:21

Mormon, Book of, most correct book on earth, V4:461

Mormon, Book of, plates of obtained, V1:18

Mormon, Book of, testifies of to guards, V6:610

Mormons, uses term as describing Church, V2:3

Moroni, first visit of, V1:11

Moroni, message and instruction from, V1:11-2

Moroni, returns Urim and Thummim, V1:21

Moroni, visitation to three witnesses of, V1:54-5 and ftnt

Moses, revealed word of God to, V1:98

moved to Palmyra, V1:2

murder, acquitted of, of M. Aldrich, V7:420

murder, indicted for, of M. Aldrich, V7:314

murderers, discourse on, V4:358-9

name to be known for good and evil, V1:11

narrative, end of personal, V6:546, ftnt only

nations, reports status of, in July 1837, V2:497

Nauvoo, address of to police, V6:150-2

Nauvoo, appointed to several committees in, V4:295

Nauvoo, arrival of back in prior to martyrdom, V6:552

Nauvoo, arrival of body at, V6:626, V7:134

Nauvoo, attends debates in, V4:514

Nauvoo, calls special meeting on settling saints elsewhere than, V6:260-1

Nauvoo, denounces enemies that he has in, among saints, V5:510

Nauvoo, devised charter of, V4:249

Nauvoo, discourse on conspiracies at, V6:272-4

SMITH, JOSEPH (continued)

Nauvoo, elected mayor of, V4:501, V5:12, 264
Nauvoo, first elected councilor of, V4:287
Nauvoo, for moral reform in, V5:8
Nauvoo, instructions for order in, V6:124
Nauvoo, holds mayor's court in, V5:365
Nauvoo, instructions to new arrivals in, do not expect perfection, V5:181
Nauvoo, issues proclamation against stealing in, V5:310-1
Nauvoo, leaves for Washington, V4:19
Nauvoo, marshal and Legion to prepare for attack on, V6:494
Nauvoo, meets John Taylor on return to prior to martyrdom, V7:81
Nauvoo, only one allowed to fight in, V5:283
Nauvoo, petition of, to court for habeas corpus, V5:461-3
Nauvoo, politics and military organization of, V5:489-90
Nauvoo, proclamation to keep peace and quiet of, V6:449
Nauvoo, remarks of to new emigrants in, April 1843, V5:354, et seq
Nauvoo, returns to, V4:88-9, V6:557
Nauvoo, returns to after arrest, V5:246-8
Nauvoo, selected registrar of, V4:543
Nauvoo, suggests petition to make, Unites States territory, V6:107
Nauvoo, sworn in as councilor of, V4:295
Nauvoo, on temporal economics of, V6:58-9
Nauvoo, under martial law, V6:497
Nauvoo charter, on writs under, V5:465-73
Nauvoo charter, views on privileges of, V4:516
Nauvoo Expositor, destruction of apostate newspaper, V6:432
Nauvoo Legion, appointment as Lieutenant-General of, V4:309-10
Nauvoo Legion, counter-signs order for state arms of, V6:556
Nauvoo Legion, elected Lieutenant-General of, V4:296
Nauvoo Legion, inspects, V6:34
Nauvoo Legion, last speech of, to, V6:498-500
Nauvoo Legion, order of as mayor to command to assist marshal, V6:104
Nauvoo Legion, on reason for demand of arms, V6:555
Nauvoo Legion, reviews, V5:56-7
Nauvoo Legion, seeks public arms for, V6:31
Nauvoo Legion, takes command of, V6:500
Nauvoo Legion, views on standing of, V6:97
Nauvoo Mansion, rents, V6:185
Nauvoo Temple, announcement on work on, V4:517
Nauvoo Temple, assists in laying cornerstone of, V4:329-31

SMITH, JOSEPH (continued)

Nauvoo Temple, dedication of baptismal font in, V4:446

Nauvoo Temple, remarks respecting signs and key words received in, V4:608

Nauvoo Temple, remarks to workmen, V5:284-7

Negro, expounds on race of, V5:217-8

Negro, views on, IntroV3:XXII, et seq

New Haven Herald, comments on, in, V6:32-3

New Jersey, in, V4:49

New Jerusalem, expounds on, V2:260-2

New York, journey from to Kirtland, V2:44-5

New York Sun, article on, in, V6:3 and ftnt

Newhall, J. B., lecture on, by, V5:432

newspaper, recommends establishment of weekly at Far West, V3:56

newspapers, publish every falsehood about, V4:383

Nickerson, Father, holds meetings at, V2:42

Ohio, commanded to go to, (D&C § 37) V1:139, (D&C § 38:32) V1:142

Ohio, Norton, Medina County, arrives in, V3:2

opinion of followers of, V7:36-7

opinion on treacherous and selfish ways of fellow man, V1:443

Other Comforter, preaches on, V4:10 and ftnt

Palmersville, preaches at, V2:42

parable of leaven in three measures of meal explained, V5:207

parable of lions of the press, V5:274, et seq

parables of Jesus explained, V5:261-2

parents, praises, V2:289

parents, visited by, V1:28

patriarch, appoints John Smith, V6:110

Patten, David W., comments of, on, V3:171-2

Paul, compares self to, before Agrippa, V1:7

pay, little received for public office, V6:332

pay, to receive, for patriarchal blessings, V2:273

payment, further of Missouri lawyers, V3:327

Pennsylvania, arrives in Susquehanna, V1:19

persecution, forces to move to Fayette, New York, V1:109

persecutors, sorrow over of, V1:7

Phelps, W. W., *vade mecum* to, by, V5:253-4 and ftnt

phrenology chart of head of, V5:52-5

physical challenge and success of, V5:302

Philadelphia, preaches at, V4:47

Pierce, Robert, settlement with, V4:519

SMITH, JOSEPH (continued)

plates, charges concerning, V1:18
plates, commences translation of, V1:19
plates, forbidden to take, V1:16
plates, gives back to angel, V1:18
plates, loses, V1:23
plates, returned to after loss of, V1:23
plates, to return to hill to see yearly, V1:16
plates, views with witnesses, V1:54-5
poisoned while at Liberty jail, V3:390
poisoned and healed, V1:271
poisoning, suspected of, and reaction, V6:65
police, comments on Marks' and Laws' fears of, V6:166-70
political attitude of the saints proclaimed, V4:479-80 and ftnt
political motto of the Church, V3:9
politics, attitude of, on, V5:526
politics, gives reasons for Mormon union in, V5:232
politics, in Illinois by saints, V5:55-6
politics, on participation in, V5:259
policy, views on civic, V5:270-1
polygamy, only holds keys of, V6:46
polygamy, Sarah Whitney wife of, IntroV5:XXXIV
poor, discusses ways to furnish with labor, V5:25
poor, sends $100.00 from prison to, V3:254
portrait, painted of, V5:164
postage, comments on receiving without prepaid, V2:325
postage, publishes that, refuses to receive any letter without paid, V2:475
Potawattamie chiefs, interview of, with, V5:479-81
Potawattamie chiefs, receives visit from, for advice, V5:365
Pratt, Orson, denounces, V5:139
Pratt, Orson, instruction to, V6:212
Pratt, Orson, restores confidence in, V5:252
prayer, first vocal of, V1:5
prayer, for welfare of saints, V2:41
prayer of wicked man accepted and comments, V5:208
prayer, with Bishop Whitney et al, V2:47
prayer, urges necessity of, V2:31
predestination, discourse on, V4:358-60
prejudice, first against, V1:7
Presbyterian, proselyted to, V1:3
Presbyterian, exposes abominations of, V2:347

SMITH, JOSEPH (continued)

presidency, candidacy for, IntroV6:XXXIV

presidency, comments by non-Mormons on will raise devil if elected to, V6:248

presidency, steamboat election on, V6:384-5

presidency, to be killed to keep out of, V6:606

president, article on, for, V6:226-7

president, article on, in *Times & Seasons*, V6:214-7

president, article on success as candidate for, V6:361

president, articles on candidacy for, V6:268-70

president, feelings toward being, V6:243

president, nomination for, of United States, reasons, V6:188

president, receives letters from Cass and Calhoun, candidates for, V6:144

president, resolves to go to Washington and lay matter before, V6:545, ftnt only

president, views of, on his candidacy for, of United States, V6:210-1

President of Church, sustained first, V2:126

President of Church, sustained as, V2:509

President of Church, sustained as, at Far West, V2:522

president of United States, Brigham Young would rather have clothes of, full of straw for, V7:256

presidential, on his campaign, V6:188

presidential election on steamboat, results, V6:423

priesthood, acknowledge as president of in Missouri, V1:267

priesthood, discourse on, V6:183-5

priesthood, on, V3:385, et seq, V5:554-5

priesthood, sustained as president of, V1:243, ftnt only

prison, life in, V3:256-9, ftnts only

private office, activities of sacred nature in, V5:1

profile, sits for drawing of, for lithograph, V5:44

prophecy against C. R. Hurlburt, V2:46

prophecy against mob, V3:227

prophecy, Church would be out of power of old enemies, V6:225

prophecy concerning Olmsted Johnson, obey gospel or suffer, V1:260

prophecy concerning trial on extradition warrants, V5:219-20

prophecy concerning Twelve leaving from Missouri, temple site revealed by mob, V3:306-7

prophecy, curious at Carthage that thirst for blood will be fulfilled, V6:566

prophecy, defines more sure word of, V5:392

SMITH, JOSEPH (continued)

    prophecy, government in power would fall if not aid saints, V6:116 and ftnt

    prophecy, healing of James Foster, V2:88, ftnt only

    prophecy, Mississippi will freeze over, V5:183

    prophecy, Missouri to receive wrath of God, IntroV3:LXVIII

    prophecy, murdered in cold blood, "lamb to slaughter," V6:555

    prophecy on mob, V6:532

    prophecy, none of the prisoners in Missouri would lose lives, V3:200, ftnt only

    prophecy on head of Stephen A. Douglas and explanation of fulfillment of, V5:393-5, ftnt only

    prophecy on O. P. Rockwell, V5:305

    prophecy, saints of Nauvoo would not fire a single shot, V6:520

    prophecy, of sickness, V2:107

    prophecy that he would triumph over enemies, V2:26

    prophecy that saints would go to Rocky Mountains, V5:85 and ftnt

    prophecy that those who defend him will prosper, V5:139

    prophecy to companion in jail that he would not die in jail, V6:601

    prophecy, trip from Greenville, Ohio, to Kirtland, June 1832, V1:271-2 and ftnt

    prophecy, would be massacred if fell into hands of mob again, V6:546

    prophecy, would not go to Missouri, V5:216

    prophecy fulfilled, *Expositor* affair, V7:485

    prophecy fulfilled, Mississippi freezing, V5:194

    prophecy fulfilled by preaching sermon to spectators and guards in Jackson County, V3:200-2 and ftnt

    prophesies after baptism, V1:42

    prophesies triumph over enemies, V2:26

    prophesies will be relieved from debt, V2:175

    prophesies that pure in heart will see vision fulfilled, V1:334

    prophesying, forbears from, concerning Mr. Seixas, V2:397

    prophet, accused as fallen by Laws, V6:347

    Prophet, appointed seer, translator, and, to the Church, (D&C § 21) V1:78

    prophet, if deny being, not a man of righteousness, V5:278

    Prophet, presented and sustained as, to the 19th century, V7:391-2

    prophet, what constitutes, V5:215

    Prophet-teacher, always the, IntroV6:XLI

    prophets, remarks concerning, V2:302

    prophetic calling, on defense of, V6:363, et seq

    proverb, on great men, V5:298

SMITH JOSEPH (continued)

race question, debates, V4:501

Ramus, instructions of, at, V5:323-7

Ramus, preaches at, V5:302

Ray County, addresses committee from, V2:106 and ftnt

rebuking, on, V5:300

reflections of John Taylor on death of, V7:106

reflections on new year, V2:352-3

reflections on opening year, 1842, V4:492-3

relatives, uncle first to obey gospel of, V1:348

relics, views on, on antiquity, V4:420-1 and ftnt

Relief Society, counsels on admittance to, V5:23

Relief Society, exhorts on evils of tongue, V5:19-20

Relief Society, organized, V4:552

Relief Society, remarks before, August 31, 1842, V5:139-41

Relief Society, remarks to on organization of, composition of, V4:570

religions, all wrong, V1:6

religious freedom, V6:304-5

religious intolerance, reflections on, in New England, V2:464-5

repentance, relationship between, and chastisement, V4:479

reproves a young lady, V2:329-30

reproves men because he loves them, V6:240

reproves people for standing in aisle, V5:400

responsibility, our greatest, V6:313

resurrection of dead, V6:363, et seq

resurrection, on the, V5:360, et seq

resurrection, preaches on death of Elias Higbee, life and, V5:529-31

retranslates Genesis 6:6, V6:57

retranslates Hebrew 6:1, V6:58

retranslates "house" as "kingdom," in my Father's, V6:184

retranslates John 14, V6:365

retranslates Malachi 4:5, V6:183-4

Revelation, Book of, on beasts in, V5:324, 339, et seq

revelation, call of pertaining to, (D&C § 43) V1:154

revelation concerning lost manuscript, (D&C § 3) V1:22-3

revelation for Nancy Hyde, V4:467

revelation, gives reasons for not receiving further, V4:478-9

revelation, how given through, V1:173, ftnt only

revelation, instructions concerning forthcoming, V2:429

revelation, President Phelps and Whitmer under condemnation, V2:304

SMITH, JOSEPH (continued)

revelation, promise that three special witnesses shall see the plates, (D&C § 5) V1:28, et seq

revelation, received according to promise, (D&C § 42) V1:148 and ftnt, et seq

revelation, sister-in-law would be spared, V2:293

revelation, spirit of, V3:381

revelation, to send John E. Page to Washington to labor, V6:81-3

revelations of J. C. Brewster false, V5:214 and ftnt

revelations, copies and arranges, V1:104

revelations, receives number of, V1:147-70

reveiws state of world, close of 1832, V1:301

revival, attended meetings, V1:3

reward for capture of, V5:92

Richmond, Missouri, taken from Independence to, V3:204-5

Richmond prison, rebuked the guards in, V3:208, ftnt only

Rigdon, Sidney, blesses, V2:51

Rigdon, Sidney, comments that would lead Church to destruction, V6:592

Rigdon, Sidney, denounces, V5:139

Rigdon, Sidney, does not want for counselor, sustained anyway, V6:47-9

Rigdon, Sidney, public ministry at Shalersville and Ravenna with, V1:241

Rigdon, Sidney, restores feelings with, V5:270

Rigdon, Sidney, sins of expounded and dissatisfaction with and prophecy concerning, V1:443

Rigdon, Sidney, status of, V5:553-4

righteous to dwell in everlasting burnings, V6:306-8

riot, taken before justice on, V6:567-8

Robinson, George W., denounces, V5:139

rock, interprets, "upon this," V5:258

rule, "when Lord commands, do it," V2:170

rumors, false spread of, V1:19

Rush Creek, Clay County, leaves, V2:115

Russia, appoints mission to, V6:41

sacrament, blesses, V2:378

sacrament, instruction on, V2:204

sacrament, receives instructions on, (D&C § 27:2-5) V1:106-7

sanctimoniousness, reproves, V4:445

saints, preaches will suffer and hardly escape, V4:11

saints, remarks on trials awaiting, V6:554

SMITH, JOSEPH (continued)

Salisbury, Wilkins Jenkins, visits, V2:4

salvation, defined, V5:392

saves the coach, receives praise until known, V4:23-4

Scott, Reverend Walter, meeting with at Cincinnatti, V1:188

scripture, answers questions on, V3:9-10

scripture, corrects, V5:264

scripture, received that cannot be recorded, V1:13

scripture, recommences translation of, V1:273

scriptures, expounds, V5:339, et seq

scriptures, on interpretation of, V5:261-2

second coming, signs of, commenced, V3:390

second death, on the, V6:317

secret meetings, receives instructions on, against, V6:280 and ftnt

seer, evidence of power of, V1:272 and ftnt

self-righteousness, reproves, V5:401

Seneca County, hearty reception by people of, V1:51

settling, comments on while in Liberty jail, V3:295

seventy, instructs the, V2:220, et seq and ftnts

sheriff, expresses rejoicings on secret meeting eluding, V5:107, et seq

shot, General Wilson wants, for believing in Constitution and democracy, V3:191

shot, sentenced to be in public square at Far West, V3:190-1 and ftnts

shower of blood, records detail on, V4:415

sick, prayers for, V6:31

signs of times, notes, V4:252-3

sin, announces to Church certain members of presidency are in, V2:511

sin, the unpardonable, V6:313-4

sins, asks for open confession of, V2:385

sins, the forgiveness of, V6:314, et seq

sign, in heaven of forthcoming bloody war, V5:301, 304

sign of the Son of Man, on the, V5:290-1

signs, reacts to cry for, V5:268

slander, accused of, by Francis Higbee, V6:174

slander, forgives Francis Higbee of, and accepts back into friendship, V6:178

Smith, George A., chosen armor bearer, V2:88

Smith, George A., love of for, V5:390-1

Smith, Hyrum, attempt to get, out so could avenge death, V6:520

Smith, Hyrum, asks for guidance on whether to return to Carthage, V6:549

SMITH, JOSEPH (continued)

Smith, Hyrum, had ordained to take his place, V7:288
Smith, Hyrum, made a Prophet, V5:510
Smith, Hyrum, in council with, V6:2
Smith, Hyrum, thoughts on, V5:107-8
Smith, Joseph, Sen., becomes, V3:404 and ftnt
Smith, William, argument with and resigns priesthood, V2:297
Smith, William, difficulty with, V2:334-5
Smith, William, feelings concerning, V2:343
Smith, William, reconciled to, V2:353
snake eggs, episode of eating, V2:82, ftnt only
snakes, poisonous, lecture on, V2:95-6 and ftnt
socialism, does not believe in, V6:33
son born, V3:37 and ftnt
son, death of, V4:402
spirit, all is matter, V5:393
states' rights, says doctrines of are a stink to heaven and encourage
    mobs, V6:95
steward, appointed over commandments, (D&C § 70) V1:236-7 and
    ftnt
Stoal, Josiah, witness at first trial of, V1:89-90
Stollings, Jacob, answer to, V3:378-9
Stollings, Jacob, requests return books to him for general release from
    debt, V3:316-7
Stowel, Josiah, works for, V1:17
sufferings, reflections on, of DeWitt saints, V3:158-60
summons, issued against, on old Higbee case, V6:399 and ftnt
sun and moon, explains why named, V5:211
support, family to receive from Church, paid for service, V3:32
Supreme Court of Missouri, petition of, to, V3:277-81
sustained in all actions, V5:124
Taylor, John, feelings of at death of, V7:106
temperance societies, on, V5:404
temptations, early, and sins of, V1:9-10 and ftnt
Ten Tribes, prophesies of, and John the Revelator, V1:176, ftnt only
testimony, adulterous actions of apostates, V6:407
testimony against dissenters at Nauvoo, V6:408, et seq
testimony of Book of Mormon, while in Carthage jail, V6:610
testimony, saints hated purely for, of Jesus, V3:229
Texas, views on annexation of, V6:243-4
thieves, denunciation of, V4:461-2
Times & Seasons, announces editorship of, V4:551

SMITH, JOSEPH (continued)

Times & Seasons, editor of, V4:542

Times & Seasons, resigns as editor of, V5:193

tongue of, bound, V1:5

tongues, gift of revealed by, V1:297 and ftnt

traitor, remarks on possible, in own quorum, V6:170

treason, arrest for, V6:561-2

treason, charge of, against, V7:11, 85

trial, acquitted at Coleville, V1:91

trial, acquitted at second at Coleville, V1:96

trial, argument and, of murderers that, was not murdered, V7:423

trial, arrival of, in Nauvoo under arrest for, V5:458, et seq

trial at Richmond, V3:209, et seq

trial at Springfield on extradition warrants, V5:212, et seq

trail before drunken judge and jury, V3:309-10, 314-5

trial, bound over for, in Daviess County, V3:73

trial, change of venue acquired and moved to Boone County, V3:319

trial, decision at Springfield on, V5:223, et seq

trial, extradition, on, V4:365, et seq

trial expenses at Monmouth, V4:419-20

trial, first of, V1:89-91

trial, freed on extradition attempt, V4:370

trial, leaves for Springfield, Illinois, on Missouri extradition, V5:209, et seq

trial, murderers, of, V7:49, et seq

trial, nobility of, in hour of, IntroV6:XL

trial, official papers of, in Springfield, on extradition warrants, V5:233, et seq

trial, order of release of, in Springfield, V5:244

trial, receives second warrant at close of first, V1:91

trial, sent to stand, for murder and treason at Liberty, Clay County, V3:212

trial, submits to, in Daviess County, V3:70

trial, to be taken to Nauvoo for, V5:456

trial, transporting for, to Quincy, Illinois, V5:447, et seq

trial, witness accounted and threatened by mob in front of jury and judge, V3:314-5

trial, writ, on *Expositor* affair before municipal court at Nauvoo, V6:453, et seq

tribulation, glories in, V3:227

trustee, elected sole of Church, V4:286

trustee-in-trust, responsible to the state as, V5:197

SMITH, JSOEPH (continued)

truth is Mormonism, states that, V3:297

"Try the Spirits," editorial on, V4:571, et seq

Twelve Apostles, calls meeting for choosing the, V2:180

Twelve Apostles, comforts and instructs, V2:287

Twelve Apostles, confirms ordination of, V2:186-8, ftnts only

Twelve Apostles, declares that only two of original had not fought him, V5:412

Twelve Apostles, epistle on sundry instructions, V4:226, et seq

Twelve Apostles, gives credentials to, form of, V5:416-7

Twelve Apostles, gives instructions to on mission, V5:366-7

Twelve Apostles, instructs the, V2:198-200, 219, et seq and ftnts, V3:383, et seq

Twelve Apostles, proclamation by, to raise funds for Joseph, V5:248-9

Twelve Apostles, recounts mission of, to England, V4:390-1

Twelve Apostles, writes to, to return home, V6:519

Unitarian, minister of, confounded, V2:364

united order, prays for brethren in, V2:24

United States, guilty of Missouri crimes because would not help, V4:145

United States, states will receive judgments of God, V1:315

United States, views on powers and policy of the government of, V6:197, et seq

United States Constitution, upholds, V3:304

Urim and Thummim, earth, of the, becoming, V5:279 and ftnt

Urim and Thummim, inquires through, V1:33

Urim and Thummim, loses, V1:21, 23

Urim and Thummim, returned to, V1:21, 23

Van Buren, President, interview with and comments on, V4:80

Van Buren, President, meets, V4:39, et seq

Van Buren, President, places wish of non-election on, V4:89 and ftnt

verbiage, attacked in and gives prayer of rebuke, V2:323-4

vice president, nominates James A. Bennett for, V6:230

virtue, explains Luke 8th chapter where Christ loses, V5:303

virtue, interview with Sister Foster concerning accusations on Joseph's, V6:271

virtue, is spirit of life, V5:303

virtue, leaves after blessings, V5:303

vision, Church organization, of, V2:182 and ftnt

vision, concerning William Marks, V3:12

vision, confident would receive, V1:11

vision, first of, V1:5-6

SMITH, JOSEPH (continued)

vision, instructs British Mission not to teach, V2:492

vision, receives of escape, V3:316

vision, receives of three glories, (D&C § 76) V1:245, et seq

vision, relates to sectarian priest, V1:6-7

visions, tells father of, V1:15

visitor, comments on, by, May 1844, V6:367-8

warrants, Iowa governor will not recall, against, V5:385

washing of feet, of elders, V1:323

washing of feet, instructions on, V2:430

washing of feet, Frederick G. Williams, by, V1:323

Washington, arrives in, V4:24

Washington, leaves on return to Nauvoo, V4:47

Washington, returns to, V4:77

Washington, voted to go to as delegate for Church, V4:16

waters, witnesses dangers upon, V1:203

western country, memorial of, on protection for, before Congress, V6:282 and ftnt

western country, report of exploration, V5:542, et seq

western country, sends elders on excursion to, V5:509

western United States, memorial of, to Congress on organizing protection for, V6:275-7

Westfield, preaches at, V2:41

Whitmer family, becomes acquainted with, V1:48

Whitney, Bishop, blessing of, upon, V2:288-9

Whitney, N. K., meets parents of, V2:294

Whitney, Newel K., prays, to home, V1:146, ftnt only

Whitney, Newel K., thoughts on faithfulness of, V5:108

wickedness, general reproof of, V4:587-8

wickedness, on restraining to expose, V6:608

wife, statement that had married second, IntroV5:XXXIV

Wilkie, John, blessing of, on, V6:264-5

Williams, F. G., expresses full confidence and trust in, V1:444

Willis, Ira J., comments concerning beating of, in Zion, V2:46

wine, takes at Carthage jail, V7:101

witness for Father Johnson at Chardon, V2:47

women, zeal of dangerous in religious capacity, V5:19

wood supplied to, V2:328

Word of Wisdom, states that should be observed, V3:15

words, last of, V7:103

world, accused of being meanest man in, V6:451

Young, Brigham, protected by angel with sword, V2:381

SMITH, JOSEPH (continued)

Young, Brigham, provided money in time of need by, V3:2

Young, Brigham, receives visit from, and Heber C. Kimball, V1:295, 296

Zelph the Lamanite, gives history of, by inspiration, V2:79-80 and ftnt

Zion, again enters "goodly land," V2:120

Zion, arrival in, March 1838, V3:8

Zion, arrives second time in, V1:266

Zion, contributions requested for, V2:50

Zion, course of travel of, when seeking volunteers for, V2:40, et seq

Zion, declares intention of going to, V2:39

Zion, gives directions concerning literary affairs and stores in, V1:270 and ftnt

Zion, leaves for Kirtland, V1:271

Zion, meets elders heading for, V1:205

Zion, nominated commander-in-chief of armies of Israel for redemption of, V2:39-40

Zion, receives money for deliverance of, V2:61

Zion, resolves to move to, March 1836, V2:407

Zion, sees redemption of, V2:381

Zion, whole of America, V6:318-21

Zion, takes leave of brethren bound for, V2:281

Zions Camp, accepts a rejected supper in, V2:81

Zions Camp, authorizes discharge of members of, V2:123 and ftnt

Zions Camp, charged for criminal conduct in, V2:142-4, 147-9

Zions Camp, commander-in-chief of, V2:88, ftnt only

Zions Camp, disperses, V2:114-5

Zions Camp, first time disclosed identity in, V2:108

Zions Camp, instructs relative to animals, V2:71-2

Zions Camp member, V2:185

Zions Camp, prophesies a scourge on, V2:80 and ftnt

Zions Camp, reproves cook of for partiality, V2:75

Zions Camp, sickness of, in, V2:101

Zions Camp, starts with, for Missouri, V2:63

Zions Camp, writes from, to brethren in Missouri, V2:75-6.

See also doctrine; letters; and each heading infra.

Smith, Joseph, ordained priest, V5:419.

Smith, Joseph, Sen., baptized, V1:79

benediction of on Hyrum Smith, V4:229, ftnt only

biography of, V4:189, et seq

born, V1:2

death of, V4:189

SMITH, JOSEPH, SEN. (continued)

Eastern Mission, return to Kirtland from, V2:467
First Presidency, sustained assistant counselor to, V2:509
funeral services of, V4:191-7
healed, V2:289
illness of, V2:288, 289
Johnson, John, blesses, V2:32
Joseph, blesses, V1:323
Joseph, comments on as friend, V5:126
Joseph's father, V1:2
Joseph and William, reconciles, V2:353
Joseph, visits at Harmony, V1:28
Kirtland Temple, blessing for work on, V2:205
mission of to Eastern States, V2:446
Moroni, encourages Joseph to follow instruction of, V1:15
Palmyra, New York, moved to, V1:2
patriarch, blessed as, V2:379-80
patriarchal blessings, gives, V2:347
revelation to, V1:80
Samuel H., blesses, V2:32
sorrow of, over his son William's errors, V2:338
Vermont, leaves, V1:2.

Smith, **Joseph the Third**, born 1832, V1:295.

Smith, **Joseph F.,** mentioned, V1:56, ftnt only; 75, ftnt only.

Smith, **Josephine D.,** daughter of Don Carlos, V4:399.

Smith, **Joshua,** bibliography, death and, V7:514.
elders quorum, sustained counselor in, V7:297
mob, poisoned by, V7:514.

Smith, **Katherine,** baptized, V1:86.

Smith, **Levira A. C.,** daughter of Samuel Smith, V7:222.

Smith, **Louisa C.,** daughter of Samuel Smith, V7:222.

Smith, **Lucy,** Joseph, sister to, V1:2
Presbyterian Church, joins, V1:3.

Smith, **Lucy B.,** daughter of Samuel, V7:221.

Smith, **Lucy J. C.,** daughter of Samuel Smith, V7:222.

Smith, **Lucy Mack,** address of, to conference on her position and family, V7:470-3
Apostles, satisfied with, and course of Church, V7:433
baptized, V1:79

SMITH, LUCY MACK (continued)

 burial, at general conference, October 1845, if she went West, desired
  to be returned to Nauvoo for, V7:470-3

 Church, desirous of purchasing copyright of history of, V7:519 and ftnt

 Church, her family in founding, V7:375

 Church provides for, V7:434

 city lot, bequest of, V7:434

 eight witnesses, record view of, V1:57 and ftnt

 endowments, present at dedication of east room for, V7:542

 endowments, receives, in Nauvoo Temple, V7:544

 Joseph blesses, V1:466

 Joseph, comments on as friend, V5:126

 Joseph's mother, V1:2

 Joseph, recounts joy of, at having three witnesses, V1:55, ftnt only
  public dinner given to and family, V7:433.

Smith, Lyman, seventies, named to first quorum of, V2:204
 Zions Camp member, V2:185.

Smith, Mary, great-great-great-grandmother to Joseph, V4:189.

Smith, Mary, Joseph, grandmother to and death of, V2:443
 Kirtland, arrives in, V2:442.

Smith, Mary, mentioned, V3:273; V5:252, 525; V6:46, 143, 627
 wife of Hyrum, receives endowments in Nauvoo Temple, V7:543

Smith, Mary B., daughter of Samuel, V7:221.

Smith, Mary Jane, wife of George W. Gee, V4:500, ftnt only.

Smith, Miriam, mother of Joshua, V7:514.

Smith, Moses, volunteers for exploring expedition, V6:227.

Smith, Priscilla, great-grandmother to Joseph, V4:189.

Smith, Rebecca, great-great-grandmother to Joseph, V4:189.

Smith, Robert, Joseph's great-great-great-grandfather, V1:2.

Smith, Robert F., anti-Mormon meeting at Carthage, at, V6:4
 appointment to guard Carthage jail, pros and cons of, V7:18-9
 Carthage Greys, member of, V7:142
 Carthage Greys, ordered to guard Carthage jail, V7:17
 mayor, aldermen, councilors of Nauvoo arraigned before, V7:84
 writs, issues illegal, against Joseph, V7:85.

Smith, Samuel, Joseph's great-great-grandfather, V1:2.

Smith, Samuel, great-grandfather of Joseph, V1:2.

Smith, Samuel, uncle to Joseph, V2:443.

Smith, Samuel Harrison, baptized and converted, V1:44

SMITH, SAMUEL HARRISON (continued)

  bishop, appointed, V5:119
  brother to Joseph, V1:2
  character of, *Times & Seasons*, V7:222
  death of, V7:213-4
  Foster, R. D., prefers charges against, V5:14
  genealogy, V1:44, ftnt only
  high council, receives blessing of father at organization of, V2:32
  Joseph, declares gratefulness for aid rendered while in seclusion, V5:109
  Kirtland High Council, ordained to, V2:511
  Kirtland High Council, president of, V2:518
  Kirtland High Council, sustained as member of, V2:510
  Kirtland Temple, blessing for work on, V2:206
  Literary Firm of the Church, appointed to, V2:273
  martyrdom, death of as a result of, V7:111
  military duty, charged with neglecting, V2:292
  Missouri persecutions, affidavit concerning, V4:60
  mob, escapes from, V7:111
  Nauvoo, bodyguard to Joseph's body on return to, V7:135
  Nauvoo, first elected alderman of, V4:287
  obituary, biographical note from, V7:216, et seq
  Presbyterian Church, joins, V1:3
  presidency, on high council to try, V2:484
  revelation to, V1:80
  wife healed by knowledge of God, V2:292-3.

Smith, Samuel Harrison Bailey, son of Samuel, V7:221.

Smith, Sarah, aunt to Joseph, V2:443.

Smith, Sardius, killed at Haun's Mills by mob, age 10, V3:326, ftnt only

Smith, Sidney, mentioned, V7:210.

Smith, Silas, uncle to Joseph, V2:441, 443.

Smith, Sophronia, Joseph, sister to, V1:2
  Presbyterian Church, joins, V1:3.

Smith, Sophronia C., daughter of Don Carlos, V4:399.

Smith, Stephen, father of Joshua, V7:514
  uncle to Joseph, V2:443.

Smith, Susannah B., daughter of Samuel, V7:221.

Smith, Sylvester, confession, decision and, V2:159 and ftnt
  high council, released from, V2:165
  Joseph prefers charges against, V2:150

SMITH, SYLVESTER (continued)

Joseph, refuses to accept decision of high council on charges against, rebuked, V2:149

Joseph, reproved by, V2:68

Joseph, trial of for slandering, V2:142, et seq

Joseph, vindicates, in a signed statement, V2:160, ftnt only

seventies, named president of, V2:203

seventy, sees pillar of fire on, V2:386

trial before Kirtland High Council, V2:151, et seq

Zions Camp, creates division in, V2:100

Zions Camp, member of, V2:65, 185

Zions Camp, rebellion in, V2:83 and ftnt.

Smith, Thomas, affiant to public proclamation on mob lies, V6:495

America, heads English saints sailing to, V4:310

British Church assignment, V4:149

Church, appointed to preside over branches of, V4:149

Church, assistant care of at Deerhurst, V4:135

English conference, represents branches of Church at, V4:117, V6:328

high priest, ordained, V4:148

volunteers for service in vineyard, V4:216.

Smith, Vinson, mobber in Missouri, V4:68.

Smith, W., delegate to political convention in Nauvoo, V6:389.

Smith, Warren, killed at Haun's Mills by mob, V3:326, ftnt only

Kirtland Camp, joins near Dayton, Ohio, V3:117

Kirtland Camp, subscribed to constitution of, V3:92

Kirtland Temple, blessing for work on, V2:206.

Smith, Warren A., Kirtland Camp, leaves, V3:140

Kirtland Camp, subscribed to constitution of, V3:92

mission appointment published and field of labor, V6:338

Missouri, moves to, V3:323

Nauvoo, policeman in, V6:150.

Smith, Willard, martial band member of Legion, V7:135.

Smith, William, Apostle, allowed to retain standing as, V4:12

Apostle, blessing of as member of, V2:191

Apostle, chosen as one of, V2:187

Apostle, difficulty with Nauvoo police and, V7:428-9

Apostle, expresses satisfaction with organization of Church under, V7:406

Apostle, letter to Joseph asking forgiveness and resigning as, V2:338-40

Apostle, rejected as, V7:458-9

SMITH, WILLIAM (continued)

Apostle, restored to, V3:364 and ftnt

Apostle, suspended as, and asked to account, V3:345

Apostle, sustained as, by Church after death of Joseph, V7:294

Apostle, sustained as, to Church, V2:509

Apostles, trying to ride down the, V7:420

baptized, V1:86

brother to Joseph, V1:2

charges, formal, against, V2:346

Church, declares himself president of the, V7:433

Church, prayer that Lord will aid, against, V7:420

devil attacks, V2:352

excommunication of, V7:483

forgiveness, confesses to Joseph and asks, V2:353

genealogy of, V1:322, ftnt only

high council, disorderly conduct of, in, V2:295

Illinois Legislature, withdraws as candidate for, V6:378-9

improper course of discussed, V7:417

Joseph, assaults, V2:334-5

Joseph, difficulty with, and Hyrum, V2:296-7

Joseph, entertains, V3:377

Joseph, false writ against for aiding, etc., V7:444

Joseph, letter from, forgiving, V2:340, et seq

Joseph, letter to, asking that he not be censured, V2:296

Joseph, severe argument between, V2:295

land transactions, letter to Joseph on, V4:391-2

Liberty jail, letter to Joseph while at, V3:274

mission appointment published and field of labor, V6:337

Nauvoo, arrival at, with company of saints, V6:342

Nauvoo, elected council member at, V5:13

Nauvoo Charter, speech of, on, V5:201-4

patriarch, ordained, to Church, V7:418

patriarch, office of, to Church his by descent, V7:301 and ftnt

patriarch, rejected as, of the Church, V7:460

Patriarchal Jacob's Staff, designated as, V7:435

priesthood, confronts Joseph before Hyrum and severs connection with, V2:297

tongues, speaks in, at Kirtland, V1:323

trial before council, confesses and forgiven, V2:354

vision, sees heavenly, V2:387

vision, sees, of Twelve and seven in England, V2:392

Wasp, editor of, resigns as, V5:204

SMITH, WILLIAM (continued)

  Zions Camp member, V2:185.
  See also Apostles, Twelve; letters.

Smith, William, ordained priest, V4:298.

Smith, William, Bible dictionary of quoted, V6:309, ftnt only.

Smith, William S., petitions Governor Boggs on mob violence in DeWitt, V3:83.

Smith, Zechariah B., Zions Camp member, V2:185.

Smithies, James, musician performs, V7:561
  represents branch of Church at English conference, V4:117.

Smoot, Abraham O., Church, appointed to preside over new district of, V7:305
  England, appointed to go to, with Twelve, V3:347
  Iowa Territory High Council, appointed to, V4:12
  mission appointment, V4:403
  mission appointment published and field of labor, V6:338
  Nauvoo, policeman in, V6:150
  Nauvoo Temple, appointed to officiate in, V7:548
  Nauvoo Temple, to administer in, V7:555
  Salt Lake High Council, sustained member of, V7:629
  Tennessee, presides in, V7:129.

Smucker, Samuel M., quoted from, V1:437, ftnt only.

Snailam, William, (also spelled Snalam), British conference, represents branch of Church at, V5:419, V6:328
  volunteers for service in vineyard, V4:217.

snakes, episode of eating eggs of, V2:82, ftnt only
  provoke to bite and no claim upon healing power, V2:95 and ftnt.

Snider, John, in Nauvoo Legion, V4:296.

Snively, Henry, judge in Missouri, V6:148.

Snively, Sister, mentioned, V7:314.

Snodgrass, Robert, witness for state in Missouri trials, V3:210.

Snow, Charles, mission appointment published and field of labor, V6:336.

Snow, Eliza R., apostrophe to Missouri by, V6:192, et seq
  martyrdom, in poetry by, V7:154, et seq
  Relief Society, secretary of, V4:567
  Taylor, John, poem to, V7:211-2
  Victoria, Queen, poem to, V6:181-3.

Snow, Erastus, counselor in Salt Lake stake, V7:629
  Far West, preaches in, V3:55

SNOW, ERASTUS (continued)

    genealogy, of, V3:55, ftnt only
    Iowa Territory High Council, appointed to, V4:12
    libelous reports, appointed to gather, V3:346
    mission appointment, V4:403
    mission appointment published and field of labor, V6:336
    Nauvoo Temple, appointed to officiate in, V7:547
    Nauvoo Temple, to administer in, V7:555
    Salem, labors of, V4:433
    Salt Lake Stake presidency member, V7:629
    westward movement, captain of 15th company in, V7:482
    witness, suggested to appear before Congress on redress, V4:97.

Snow, Gardner, (also spelled Gardiner), affiant to mob threats, V6:481-2
    bishop, appointed, V4:233
    bishop, appointed at Lima, V5:427
    Kirtland Camp, child of born in, V3:130
    Kirtland Camp, subscribed to constitution of, V3:93
    mob, affidavit of attempting to draft into service, V6:510.

Snow, George, subscribed to constitution of Kirtland Camp, V3:93.

Snow, Gordon, mentioned in Kirtland Camp, V3:122.

Snow, James C., bishop's clerk, V4:233
    clerk at Lima, V5:428
    high council, named to at Lima, V5:427
    high priests quorum, selected clerk of at Yelrome, V6:346
    Kirtland Camp, joins, V3:141
    mission appointment published and field of labor, V6:336
    mission, report of to Church, V7:527.

Snow, Levi, father of Erastus, V3:55, ftnt only.

Snow, Lorenzo, Church, appointed to preside over new district of, V7:305
    England, arrives in, V4:233
    England, presents Book of Mormon to Queen of, V6:181
    genealogy of, V4:161 and ftnt
    gift of healing, exercised on board ship, V5:309 and ftnt
    mission appointment and field of labor, V6:338; V7:129
    Nauvoo, return to, V5:353
    Nauvoo Temple, to administer in, V7:555
    Pioneer Company, captain of, V7:626
    public discussion with Mr. Barker, V4:234
    saints, arrives in New Orleans with company of, V5:252.

Snow, Lucina, mother of Erastus, V3:55, ftnt only.

Snow, Oliver, father of Lorenzo, V4:162, ftnt only

SNOW, OLIVER (continued)

Missouri, permit to travel in, V3:210.

Snow, W., mission appointment published and field of labor, V6:335.

Snow, Warren, mission appointment published and field of labor, V6:337
  petitions to hear Joseph speak, V6:533.

Snow, Warren, mission appointment published and field of labor, V6:336.

Snow, Willard, Church, appointed to preside over new district of, V7:306
  England, appointed to go to, withTwelve, V3:347
  Iowa Territory High Council, appointed to, V4:12
  mission, appointed president of, V7:405
  Nauvoo Temple, to administer in, V7:555
  Salt Lake High Council, sustained member of, V7:629
  seventies, named to first quorum of, V2:203
  Zions Camp member, V2:185.

Snow, William, Church, appointed to preside over new district of, V7:306
  England, appointed to go to with Twelve, V3:347
  mission appointment published and field of labor, V6:339
  Nauvoo Temple, to administer in, V7:555.

Snow, Zerubbabel, mission, appointed on, V1:332
  mission, sent on to Canada, V2:139
  seventies, named to first quorum of, V2:204
  Zions Camp, chosen commissary general of, V2:64
  Zions Camp member, V2:185.

Snowden, Samuel, seeks Mormon life, V4:63.

Snyder, Adam W., biography of, V4:479 and ftnt

Snyder, John, England, appointed to go to with Twelve, V3:347
  England, leaves for, V4:568
  genealogy, joins English Mission at New York and, V2:494 and ftnt
  mission call to or damned, V4:503-4
  mission, reaction to call, V4:504
  Nauvoo, bodyguard to Joseph's body on return to, V7:135
  revelation to, V4:483
  set apart and instructed, V4:568.

Soby, Leonard, disfellowshipped for following Sidney Rigdon, V7:268
  high council, sustained to, V4:341
  mission call and field of labor, V5:348
  witness for *Expositor* trial of Joseph, V6:457.

socialism, Joseph does not believe in, V6:33.

Society, Young Gentlemen's and Ladies' Relief, beginnings of MIA, V5:320-2.

solemn assembly, see assembly, solemn.

Sollars, Mr., mentioned, V5:218.

Son of God, feast after order of, V2:362.
    See also Christ, Jesus.

Son of Man, sign of, appear, how will, V5:337
    devil does not know, V4:608
    Joseph on, V5:290-1.
    See also Christ, Jesus.

sons of perdition, fate of not revealed, V1:366.
    See also devil; doctrine.

sorcerer, Alexander Campbell accused of being wicked, V2:268-9.

soul, eternal nature of, V6:310-1
    Hyrum indicates Mormons have large, V6:300
    transmigration of, devil, doctrine of, V2:307
    resurrection, spirit passing from father to son as in, V2:307.

South, James, mentioned, V5:308.

South America, mission opened to, V4:413.

South Australia, mission opened in, V4:154.

South Bainbridge, New York, Joseph, constable takes to, V1:89
    Joseph, married at, V1:17.

South Carolina, cessation of recorded, V1:301.

South Wales, mission work increases, branch organized, opposition, V5:312
    mission work opened in, V5:281-2.

Southcott, Johanna, (also spelled South Cote), false prophetess, V1:397, V4:577.

Southwick, Dr., mob, report on movement, V6:507
    Prophet, reports officers' meetings to, V6:605-6.

Southwick, Edward, affidavit on conduct of arrest and trial of Joseph, V5:476, et seq
    mentioned, V5:439
    testifies on Joseph's second arrest in Illinois, V6:67.

sower, parable of, explained, V2:266-7.

Sparks, Quartus S., mentioned, V5:509
    mission appointment published and field of labor, V6:336.

Speakman, William, English conference, represents branches at, V5:420; V6:328
  volunteers for service in vineyard, V4:217.

Spencer, Augustine, brother, assaults his, V6:344
  martyrdom mob, member of, V7:146
  slander, writes, V6:354.

Spencer, Catharine C., receives endowment in Nauvoo Temple, V7:543.

Spencer, Charles E., missionary call to Wisconsin, V5:413.

Spencer, Claudius V., MIA, aids in movement toward, V5:321.

Spencer, Daniel, Emmett's Camp, accompanies Elder Lyman to, V7:377
  exploring, volunteers for, V6:224
  mission appointment and field of labor, V6:335
  mission call and field of labor, V5:348; V7:170, 210
  Nauvoo, mayor and alderman of, V6:132; V7:248, 354-6, 370, 377
  Salt Lake High Council, sustained member of, V7:629
  western country, to go to investigate for settlement, V6:223
  westward movement, captain of seventh company in, V7:482
  witness for Joseph at Carthage martyrdom, V6:576.

Spencer, Earl, mentioned, V5:438.

Spencer, J., represents branches of Church at English conference, V4:147.

Spencer, John, represents branch of Church at English conference, V4:147.

Spencer, Orson, affiant to public proclamation on mob lies, V6:495
  British mission of, V7:624
  conspiracies, discourse on at Nauvoo, V6:272
  endowments, receives, V6:98
  endowments, receives in Nauvoo Temple, V7:543
  Ford, Governor, appeal to, V7:489-90
  Ford, Governor, interview with and Governor Reynolds, V7:423-4
  Ford, Governor, letter to very harsh towards, V7:502, et seq
  Ford, Governor, president pro tem city council appeal to for Nauvoo, V7:158
  mission call and field of labor, V5:348
  Nauvoo, elected mayor of, V7:370
  Nauvoo Temple, to administer in, December 27, 1845, V7:555
  University of Nauvoo, elected chancellor of, V5:120
  witness for Joseph at Carthage martyrdom, V6:576.

Spencer, William W., appointed bishop, V5:120.

Spires, John, given care of Church at Leigh, V4:135.

spirit, aspiring, beware of, V4:345
    branches, phenomena of, in, V1:170 and ftnt
    composition of, V4:575-6
    discernment of, V1:172
    discerning of, Apostles on, V6:29
    eternal and existed throughout all eternity, V3:387
    eternal duration of, V4:54 and ftnt
    evil, assail elders in England, V2:503
    priesthood, governed by, V4:575
    revealed only by flaming fire and glory, V6:51
    try the, V4:571-81
    understanding of, V1:170
    wicked have bounds, V4:576.
    See also doctrine; Smith, Joseph.

spirit, gifts of the, Christianity, lost in early, IntroV1:LXXVI
    elaborated upon, V5:219
    exhibited in conference of January 22, 1833, V1:322
    faith, none without, V5:218
    healing gift, no claim on when provoke snake bite, V2:95 and ftnt
    Joseph's remarks to Relief Society on, V4:602, et seq
    prison, in, V5:424-5.
    See also gift of being healed; Holy Ghost.

spirit, ministering, difference from angel explained, V4:425.

spirits, false, in Church at Kirtland Branch, V1:146.

spiritual wife doctrine, false teaching of, V6:279-80.

Splawn, William, witness for state in Missouri trials of saints, V3:210.

Sprague, Brother, member of Nauvoo Legion band, V7:135.

Sprague, R. C., mission appointment published and field of labor, V6:339.

Sprague, Richard D., policeman in Nauvoo, V6:149.

Spurgin, Jesse, utility committee member to aid Church removal, V7:474.

Spring Hill, Adam-ondi-Ahman, place of, V3:35 and ftnt.

Springfield, Illinois, courts at modified toward saints, V7:545
    stake organized at, V4:236.

Spry, Charles, mission appointment published and field of labor, V6:338.

Squire, Charles, covenanted to assist saints in removing from Missouri, V3:254.

Squires, Andrew Jackson, confesses to error of joining Methodists, restored to fellowship, V2:319

SQUIRES, ANDREW JACKSON (continued)

Kirtland Camp, mentioned in, V3:130.

St. Clair, D. L., publishes anti-Mormon literature, V4:255.

St. John, Stephen N., covenanted to assist saints in removing from Missouri, V3:253.

St. Louis Evening Gazette, account of martyrdom in, V7:177.

Stafford, Augustus, witness in *Expositor* trial of Joseph, V6:457.

stake, Adam-ondi-Ahman organized, V3:38
Crooked Creek established, V4:145
discontinued, all except two areas, V4:476
Geneva, Illinois, organizes at, V4:236
Lima, new appointed, V4:233
Mount Hope, Illinois, V4:233
Payson, Illinois, at, V4:233
Quincy, Illinois, appointed, V4:233
Ramus, Illinois, abandoned, V4:468
Salt Lake City, High Council of, sustained, V7:629
Springfield, at, V4:236
Zarahemla, discontinued at, V4:493.

Staker, Nathan, Kirtland Camp, requested to leave, V3:128-9
Kirtland Camp, subscribed to constitution of, V3:93.

Standley, Ann, wife of E. Hunter, V4:416, ftnt only.

Standley, Hyrum, commands mob that attacks saints, V3:157; V4:62.

Standley, Jacob, father of A. Standley, V4:416, ftnt only.

Standley, Martha, mother of A. Standley, V4:416, ftnt only.

Stanley, Mr., mentioned, V3:185.

Stanley, Harvey, Cahoon, Larona, marriage to, V2:376
Joseph, pays money in hour of need, V2:327
seventies, named to first quorum of, V2:204
Zions Camp member, V2:185.

Stanton, Daniel, Adam-ondi-Ahman High Council, chosen to, V3:38
bishop, counselor to, V1:363
branch president, appointed, in Missouri, V1:409, ftnt only
Church, appointed to preside over new district of, V7:305
high council, named to at Lima, V5:427
Missouri, permit to travel in, V3:210
stake president, appointed at Quincy, V4:233.

Staples, Abner F., carries proposals to saints from mob, V1:398
mob manifesto, captain signed, V1:376
mobber in militia appointed to receive arms of the saints, V1:434.

Stapp, General, mentioned, V7:141.

Stark, General, mentioned, V6:92.

Starks, Mr., mentioned, V2:45.

Starks, Stephen, Kirtland Camp, leaves, V3:140
Kirtland Camp, subscribed to constitution of, V3:91
unchristianlike conduct, tried for, V3:115.

stars, fall from heaven, V1:439-40 and ftnt.

states, indebtedness of, V5:306.

states' rights, doctrines of are stink to heaven and encourage mobs, V6:95.

stealing, Nauvoo, proclamation against in, V5:310-1
saints commanded to put out of mind, V7:350.

Stedwell, Mary, wounded at Haun's Mills massacre, V3:326, ftnt only.

Steel, Samuel, anti-Mormon committee chairman, V6:8.

Steele, Richard, volunteers for service in vineyard, V4:217.

Steffey, William C., ordained elder, V6:62.

Steghall, George W., jailor in Carthage, V7:99.

Stenhouse, T. B. H., mentioned, V5:378, ftnt only.

Stephens, Mr., records celestial phenomena, V1:440, ftnt only.

Stephens, Daniel, seventies, named to first quorum of, V2:204
Zions Camp member, V2:185.

Stephens, Henry, lawyer, member of martyrdom mob, V7:143.

Stephens, Henry, appointed bishop's counselor, V4:236.

Stephens, Messr., mentioned, V5:44, V6:506.

Stephens, Roswell, covenanted to assist saints in removing from Missouri, V3:252.

"Sterling," song sung at temple dedication, V2:412-3 and ftnt.

Sterrett, William G., affidavit on conduct of Governor Ford and posse while in Nauvoo, V6:589-90
reporter, V6:497.

Stevens, Arnold, (also spelled Stephens), Church, appointed to preside over new district of, V7:305
Kirtland Camp, subscribed to constitution of, V3:93
stake presidency, appointed counselor to, V4:236.

Stevens, Charles C., mentioned, V6:8.

Stevens, Henry, at anti-Mormon meeting at Carthage, V6:4.

Stevens, Henry, subscribed to constitution of Kirtland Camp, V3:92.

Stevens, Jonathan, ordained elder, V2:253.

Stevens, Lyman, elder, ordained, V2:253
    Missouri, covenanted to assist saints in removing from, V3:254.

Stevens, Uzziel, ordained elder, V2:253.

Stevenson, Lewis C., Carthage Greys, member of, V7:143.

Steward, Mr., mentioned, V4:100.

stewardship, law of, given, (D&C § 42) V1:148
    Satan establishes similar law, V1:146.
    See also consecration; doctrine.

Stewart, Mr., mentioned, V6:614.

Stewart, Benjamin, mentioned, V7:596.

Stewart, George W., clerk of conference in Alabama, V6:210.

Stewart, Levi, Joseph, on relief expediton for, V5:482
    mission appointment published and field of labor, V6:340
    mission call and field of labor, V5:349
    mission call in Illinois to disabuse public mind over arrest of Joseph,
        V5:485
    warned not to vote, V3:56.

Stewart, Riley, Black, A., falsely accused of threatening, V3:65
    strikes mob member and is attacked, V3:57.

Stewart, Urban V., Joseph, on relief expedition for, V5:482
    mission appointment published and field of labor, V6:339
    mission call to Illinois to disabuse public mind over arrest of Joseph,
        V5:485
    Missouri persecutions, affidavit concerning, V4:58-9.

Stewart, William J., covenanted to assist saints in removing from Missouri, V3:252.

Stigall, George W., jailor at Carthage, receives Prophet et al, V6:574
    reports intention to attack Nauvoo, V6:575.

Stiles, George P., affiant to public proclamation on mob lies, V6:495
    councilor in Nauvoo, V6:212
    lawyer in case of Jeremiah Smith, V6:419
    witness for Joseph at Carthage martyrdom, V6:576.

Stiles, John, Nauvoo Temple, appointed carpenter on, V7:326.

Stillman, Dexter, blessing for work on Kirtland Temple, V2:206.

Stilly, Levi, witnessed Haun's Mills massacre, V4:95

Stoddard, Calvin W., devil attacks, V2:352
    Kirtland Temple, blessing for work on, V2:206.

Stoddard, Lyman, Church, appointed to preside over new district of, V7:305

mentioned, V7:315, ftnt only

mission appointment published and field of labor, V6:337

mission, assigned to go on, V4:429.

Stoddard, Sylvester B., bishop, appointed counselor to, V4:233

Church, appointed to preside over new district of, V7:305

Church, leads mob in Kirtland against, V7:484

evil, reproved for giving appearance of, V6:229

Joseph, on relief expedition for, V5:482

mission appointment published and field of labor, V6:335.

Stoker, John, mentioned, V7:625.

Stokes, Gershom, covenanted to assist saints in removing from Missouri, V3:254.

Stollings, Jacob, (also spelled Stollins), accused of stealing from Joseph's home, V3:288

requests Joseph to return books for release of all Church from debt, V3:316-7

returns to mob scene, V3:461.

stone, renounced by Hiram Page and Church, V1:115

Satan gives revelations through, V1:109.

Stone, Captain, mentioned, V4:77.

Stone, James, accuses saints of burning and murder, V3:165.

stone box, plates in, V1:15.

Storey, Isaac, exonerates Joseph's actions in Zions Camp, V2:149

mentioned, V2:33

trial and forgiven, V1:470.

Stories, Apostles departure for British Mission with themselves and families sick and very poor, V4:9-10 and ftnts.

baptism in England where person wanted to be drowned if was such a fool to join Church, upon baptism was drowned, V6:160, et seq

"Bogus Brigham incident," writ to arrest Brigham Young but arrested Brother Miller instead, V7:549-51

Book of Abraham, acquisition of, and Egyptian mummies, V2:235-6, 348, et seq

Book of Mormon, of lost pages of manuscript of, V1:21, et seq

Carthage, illegal jailing of Joseph and Hyrum prior to the martyrdom, V6:569, et seq

cholera attack on household that rejects Joseph, V2:115

STORIES (continued)

Coburn, Emily, efforts to prevent baptism of, into Church, V1:86-8

commandment, attempts at writing by other than Prophet, V1:226

Cowdery, Oliver, of meeting with Joseph and conversion, V1:32, et seq

Crooked River, the battle of, first open battle between saints and mob in Missouri, V3:170-1

devil, of, in British Mission causing dissension over clothing of Sister Richards, V3:276-7

DeWitt, of, in Missouri of mob siege and forcing saints to leave and hardships concerning, V3:156, et seq, 450, et seq

expulsion of saints from Jackson County, V1:426, et seq

hitchhiker, spirit directing to leave, turns out to be a mobber, V2:50

jail, escort to, V6:573-4

Joseph, arrest of, and episode with constable, V1:88, et seq

Joseph, arrival in Nauvoo under arrest for trial, V5:458, et seq

Joseph, becoming angry and striking tax collector, V5:524

Joseph, Christmas serenade to, in early morning, V6:134

Joseph, description of and followers, by Governor Ford, V7:35, et seq

Joseph, dream of concerning enemies at Nauvoo, V6:461-2

Joseph, has fire commanded from heaven by visitor to consume him, laughs, V5:267-8

Joseph, leaving for West and asked to return by Emma, V6:547, et seq

Joseph, letter to John C. Calhoun showing contempt for latter's position on saints, very remarkable letter, V6:156, et seq

Joseph, man claiming to be prophet calls on, V6:342

Joseph, mob member prophesies of destruction of, and seals own fate, V2:99-100

Joseph, reception of information and delegation to Governor Ford at Carthage, return of and decision to leave Nauvoo for the West to avoid death, V6:542, et seq

Joseph, saving stagecoach and comments after finding out he was Mormon Prophet, V4:23-4

Joseph, second arrest and treatment, refused lawyer, threatened to shoot, pretended to be elders, V5:440, et seq

Joseph, treatment at Carthage answering charges of grand jury, V6:412, et seq

martyrdom, by Governor Ford, V7:30-1

martyrdom, lamentation of, V7:191-2

martyrdom, of, V6:616, et seq

martyrdom, poetry, in, V7:154, et seq

martyrdom, responsibility of Governor Ford in, V7:113, et seq

martyrdom, review of, by Governor Ford, V7:160-2

STORIES (continued)

Methodist lady mistakenly thinks Sister Taylor was asking for repentance after death of Joseph, V7:112

Missouri, imprisonment and poisoning and feeding of human flesh, V3:420

Missouri trials, of drunken grand jury brawl in, V3:422-3

mob action against C. Loveland for refusing to go up to arrest Joseph, V6:504-5

mob attempts to kill Sheriff Backenstos and his solicitation of aid from O. P. Rockwell, V7:446

mob, list of the members of, that martyred Joseph and Hyrum, also professions of each mobber which tells a story in itself, V7:143-6

mobber killing member's cow to cut strip of hide to tie up his horse, V3:322-3

molesting of Mormon women in Missouri, V3:422, 428, 464

murderers, witnesses going to Carthage for trial of martyrdom, V7:311

Nauvoo, search of, for bodies of Joseph and Hyrum, V7:447-8

Nauvoo Expositor, destruction of apostate newspaper, V6:432-3

Nauvoo Legion, part of, which went to defend Joseph under promise that no harm would come, expenses of, V6:514-5

Nauvoo Temple, devotion of Brigham Young and brethren when commenced endowments in, tireless officiating and service, V7:543, et seq

Phelps, Morris, escape of, from Missouri by cursing as good as the rest of them, V3:401, ftnt only

poisoning of Joseph and others, V1:271

polygamy, story of revelation on, taken to Emma by Hyrum and Hyrum receiving tongue lashing over it, IntroV5:XXXII-XXXIII

Pratt, Parley P., assistance to crossing of stream while prisoner in Missouri, V3:360-1

prayer, of results of refusal to, V1:82, et seq

prophecy, by Joseph on curious at Carthage that their thirst for blood would be satisfied, V6:566

rattlesnakes, of carrying out of camp and killing squirrel for purpose of need, V2:71-2

Rigdon, E., returning from death, V5:121-3

successor, claims of Sidney Rigdon and Twelve as to, in authority from Joseph, V7:224-7, 229, et seq

tar and feathering, first of Joseph, details the occurrences and then preaches in Church as usual, V1:261, et seq

tar and feathering in Missouri of Bishop Partridge, V1:390-1

STORIES (continued)

taverns, refusal of, to keep Mormons en route to Missouri and results, V5:211

three witnesses, call of and vision, V1:52, et seq

treatment of Joseph's witnesses in Missouri, V6:108

trial before grand jury in Missouri where Brother Markham as witness for Joseph and others was accosted and threatened by mob before judge and jury with no results, V3:314-5

trial of G. W. Brooks for non-member wife breaking Word of Wisdom, V3:127-8

voting incident where mob attempts to prevent members from voting in Missouri, V3:56, et seq

Whitmer, John, of mob revealing prophecy yet unfulfilled and Turley's questioning of the testimony of, V3:306-8

Young, Brigham, talking to oxen to go to pull wagon out of mud, V7:224

Young, Brigham, telling that will convert world faster if persecuted, V7:308

Young, Brigham, transformation of, to the likeness and speech of Joseph, V7:236, ftnt only

Zions Camp, sudden storm prevents mob from attacking, V2:103-4 and ftnts.

See also Apostles, Twelve; British Mission; Latter-day Saints, Church of Jesus Christ of; mob; persecutions; persecutions, Illinois; persecutions, Missouri; Smith, Joseph; Zions Camp.

Story, Mr., chastened for speaking against bishop, repents and forgiven, V1:470

mentioned, V3:33.

Stout, Allen J., elder, appointed, V4:13

Joseph, on relief expedition for, V5:482

Missouri, arraigned for treason, murder, burglary, arson, robbery, and larceny at Richmond, V3:209

Missouri trials, discharged as innocent from, V3:211.

Stout, Hosea, elder, appointed, V4:13

exploring expedition, volunteers for, V6:226

Joseph, leaves to rescue, V4:365

Joseph, on relief expedition for, V5:486

Nauvoo, delegate to political convention at, V6:390

Nauvoo, policeman in, V6:149

Nauvoo Legion, serves in, V4:415; V5:443, 486-7; V6:362, 497

Nauvoo Temple, appointed to officiate in, V7:547

westward movement, captain of 24th company in, V7:481

STOUT, HOSEA (continued)

    westward movement, guard in, V7:626.

Stow, Nahum Milton, excommunicated for false prophecy, V2:163
    mentioned, V4:15
    mission appointment published and field of labor, V6:339.

Stowel, Josiah, (also spelled Stoal), Joseph, daughter's testimony at trial
    of, V1:90
    Joseph works for, V1:17
    Joseph, witness at first trial of, V1:89
    New York, lived at, V1:17.
    silver mine, seeks, V1:17.

Stowell, W. R. R., mission appointment published and field of labor,
    V6:336.

Strang, J. J., excommunicate those who follow, V7:574.

Strange, Mr., mentioned, V4:85.

Stratton, Hyrum, (also spelled Hiram), camp, carries rattlesnakes out of
    the, V2:101
    seventies, named to first quorum of, V2:204
    Zions Camp member, V2:185
    Zions Camp, repairs firelocks of, V2:88, ftnt only.

Stratton, Joseph A., high priest, ordained, V6:397
    mission, reports, V5:436
    mentioned, V7:573.

Street, Joseph, volunteers for service in vineyard, V4:217.

Street, Levi, martyrdom, guard on jail at, V7:142.

Streeter, Mr., member of mob, V1:264.

Stringham, George, elder, ordained, V3:123
    Kirtland Camp, mentioned in, V3:122
    Kirtland Camp, subscribed to constitution of, V3:92.

Stringham, Julia, baptized, V1:88.

Stringham, Lucy, mentioned, V5:216.

Stringham, William, and wife baptized, V1:88.

Strong, Elial, cholera, dies of, in Missouri, V2:120
    gospel, brings to Brigham Young, V1:296, ftnt only.

Strong, Elias, Zions Camp member, V2:185.

Strong, Ezra, high priest, ordained, V5:136
    Kirtland Temple, blessing for work on, V2:205
    mission appointment published and field of labor, V6:339.

Strong, Harvey, covenanted to assist saints in removing from Missouri, V3:252.

Strong, Levi Elial, baptized, V4:110, ftnt only.

Strong, Reuben W., mission appointment published and field of labor, V6:339.

Strop, James, subscribed to constitution of Kirtland Camp, V3:93.

Struthers, Mr., represents area in British conference, V5:9.

Stuart, John J., mentioned, V4:480, ftnt only.

Styles, George P., appointed city attorney, V6:331-2.

Sublet, Littlebury, committee member to talk to saints on removal, V2:452.

Sumner, Josiah, mob, severely beaten by, V1:483
mob, whipped by, V2:140.

sun, reason called by masculine name, V5:211.

Sunday Morning News, publishes anti-Church article, V2:351.

sustain, First Presidency, of, V4:340
Joseph, people to, in all actions, V5:124
order, true of, V4:340-1
performed by rising, V2:417-8
rejection, example of, at conference, V4:341
Smith, William, conference refuses to, V7:458-9
voting, rule of, in, V4:340
Williams, Frederick G., not unanimous, V2:509.

Sutton, William, on first sailing of saints from England, V4:134.

Swakhammer, Elijah R., delegate to political convention in Nauvoo, V6:389
delegate to present truth to public, V6:483.

Swanton, emigrant ship, V5:252.

Swarner, Samuel, called on mission and field of labor, V5:349.

Swartout, Mr., mentioned, V5:537.

Swazey, Ezekial W., mentioned, V4:416.

Swazey, General H., offers to assist Nauvoo, V7:140.

swearing, members expelled from membership for, V3:341
saints commanded to put out of mind, V7:350.

Sweat, John, subscribed to constitution of Kirtland Camp, V3:92.

Swinder, Captain, mentioned, V7:274.

Swindlehurst, John, ordained priest, V4:148.

Swiss, J. S., delegate to political convention at Nauvoo, V6:390.

Swope, G. M., at anti-Mormon meeting, V5:537.

Swymler, Joseph, affidavit of on Durfee murder, V7:530.

Sympson, Alexander, land shark, member of martyrdom mob, V7:144, 146.

Syphret, Jacob, bishop of Philadelphia branch, V4:331.

—T—

tabernacle, canvas, proposed, V7:427
  canvas received for, V7:483
  Salt Lake, plan and architect of, V6:1, ftnt only.

Taggart, George W., martial band member of Legion, V7:135.

Tahiti, mission report on, V7:252-3.

Tait, Light T., kidnaps members and takes to Missouri, V4:155.

tale-bearing, Benjamin Winchester reproved for, V4:443.

talents, parable of, applied to last dispensation, V2:24.

Talley, Allen, covenanted to assist saints in removing from Missouri, V3:252.

Taney, Roger B., chief justice, V5:238.

Tanner, Elder, mentioned, V2:180.

Tanner, Francis, grandfather of John, V1:410, ftnt only.

Tanner, John, killed at Haun's Mills, V3:222, 411.

Tanner, John, gathering, requests instructions on, V1:410
  genealogy, V1:410, ftnt only
  Kirtland Temple, blessing for work on, V2:206
  Lord, sends sons to Kirtland to learn will of, V1:410
  mission appointment published and field of labor, V6:336.

Tanner, John Joshua, Missouri, arraigned for treason, murder, burglary, arson, robbery, and larceny at Richmond, V3:209
  Missouri trials, discharged as innocent at, V3:211
  Zions Camp member, V2:120, 185.

Tanner, Joshua, father of John, V1:410, ftnt only.

Tanner, Martin H., mission appointment published and field of labor, V6:336.

Tanner, Nathan, great-uncle to John, V1:410, ftnt only.

Tanner, Nathan, mission appointment published and field of labor, V6:339

TANNER, NATHAN (continued)

    Zions Camp member, V2:185.

Tanner, Sidney, blessing for work on Kirtland Temple, V2:206.

Tanner, Thankful Tefft, mother of John, V1:410, ftnt only.

Tanner, William, great-uncle to John, V1:410, ftnt only.

tar and feathering, Allen C., by Missouri mob, V1:391 and ftnt
    Joseph, of, V1:263, et seq
    Partridge, E., by Missouri mob, V1:390-1.

Tarbill, Squire, Joseph married in his home, V1:17.

Tate, Dr., accompanies Joseph for trial on Missouri warrants, V5:210.

Tate, Harvey, labors of, V5:409
    mission call and field of labor, V5:348.

Taylor, Agnes, mother of John, V3:154, ftnt only.

Taylor, Allen, in westward movement organization, V7:626.

Taylor, Christopher, great-grandfather to John, V3:154, ftnt only.

Taylor, E. D., mentioned, V7:44-5.

Taylor, Elizabeth, visits Brother Taylor in Carthage after martyrdom,
    V7:116.

Taylor, J., ordained elder, V4:322.

Taylor, James, father of John, V3:154, ftnt only
    Joseph, in seclusion at home of, V5:169, 180.

Taylor, Jeremiah, to receive Church aid in emigrating from England,
    V5:412.

Taylor, John, affiant to public proclamation on mob lies, V6:495
    America, sails for, V4:352
    anti-Mormons, on the, V7:60, et seq
    apostates, impressions of the, V7:56, et seq
    Apostle, sustained as, Apostle, to be, (D&C § 118:6) V3:47
    Apostle, sustained to at Salt Lake City, October 1848, V7:628
    baptism for dead, on, V7:292
    Book of Mormon, testimony of, V4:2
    British Mission, arrives in Nauvoo from, V4:381
    British Mission, letter on affairs of, V4:96
    Carthage, account of Governor Ford's interview with Joseph at,
      V6:579-85, V7:88, et seq
    Carthage, account of interview with Governor Ford at, V6:543-5,
      V7:75-7
    Carthage, appointed delegate to governor at, V6:522
    Carthage, arrival, on, in, V7:83

TAYLOR, JOHN (continued)

Carthage, brought to Nauvoo from, V7:117-9

Carthage, comments on reaction of citizenry at, V7:107, et seq

Carthage jail, wounded at, V7:104-5

Champion of Right, designated as, V7:435

Church periodicals, on subscriptions to, V7:328

comments on affidavits of Marsh and Hyde against saints, V3:167-8, ftnts only

coroner's jury, V7:108

delegate to political convention in Nauvoo, V6:389

discourse of at October 1844 conference, V7:288, et seq

economic policy, on, in Nauvoo at October 1844 conference, V7:303-4

endowment, receives, in Nauvoo Temple, V7:543

enemies, classification of, into parties, V7:58

England, arrives in, V4:76

England, sails from New York for, V4:46

English conference, represents branch of Church at, V4:117, 147

Expositor, arrest for destruction of and trial, V6:487, et seq

Expositor, bill for removing, V7:63

Expositor, on the, V7:61-4

Expositor affair, comments on, and Governor Ford's suggested dealing with it, V7:121

Expositor affair, records Joseph's account of, V7:125

Expositor affair, Warsaw mob meeting preamble and resolutions on, V7:122-5

Expositor affair, writ issued against Joseph et al for, V7:66-7

Ford, Governor, comments on whether or not, was responsible for the martyrdom murder, V7:113, et seq

Ford, Governor, remonstrance of, to, V6:571-3, V7:86

Ford, Governor, sent as committee to, occurrences, V7:71, et seq

Ford, Governor, signal for the murder heard by, V7:110

Ford, Governor, states he will not interfere with expulsion from state, V7:94, et seq

Ford, Governor, quotes pledge of, for safety, V7:77

genealogy, accepts call to Apostleship and, V3:154-5 and ftnts

genealogy, ordained Apostle and, V3:240 and ftnt

general government, appointed on committee to write petition to the, V3:241

God, preserved by act of, V7:119-20

God, second discourse at Seventies Hall dedication, relationship of Church to, V7:340-2

Hays, Reverend Robert, defense against attacks of, V4:238

TAYLOR, JOHN (continued)

Hyrum, feelings and comments on character of, V7:107

illegal arrests, serves notice he will not submit to, V7:396

imposters, letter of, warning citizens of Quincy, Illinois, against, V3:341-2

Ireland, introduces gospel to, V4:170 and ftnt

Isle of Man, preaches and debates on, V4:235, ftnt only

Joseph, accompanies for trial on Missouri warrants, V5:210

Jsoeph, feelings of knowledge of death of, V7:106

Joseph, fires the gun, results, V7:102-3

Joseph, gun given to, V7:100

Joseph, last words of, V7:103

Joseph, informs Governor Ford of illegal arrest of, for treason, V7:85

Joseph, meeting with, on return to Nauvoo, V7:81

Joseph, on relief expedition for, V5:482

Joseph, reply of, on Missouri letter on arrest and trial of, V5:539-40

Joseph, reports crossing river of, to go West, V7:78

Joseph, sustains through speculative times, V2:488-9, ftnts only

Joseph and Hyrum, testimony of against murderers of, V7:264

Kirtland, preaches at, V4:21

martyrdom, account of, V7:102, et seq

martyrdom, article on, in Nauvoo Neighbor, on tragedy of, V7:176-7

martyrdom, imprisonment of Joseph and occurrences before, V7:97, et seq

martyrdom, injury of, at, V6:618

martyrdom, letter of, to British Mission, instructions on, V7:171, et seq

martyrdom, letter sent to Nauvoo notifying of, V7:110

martyrdom, newspapers in the area prior to the, V7:60-1

martyrdom, Samuel H. Smith dies indirectly from mob at, V7:111

memoirs of, on affairs in Nauvoo leading to martyrdom of Joseph and Governor Ford's responsibility in, V7:53-5, et seq

Methodist lady, mistake of at martyrdom scene, V7:112

ministry, devote all time to labors of, V4:148

Missouri, covenanted to assist saints in removing from, V3:252

Missouri trials, witness for state in, V3:210

Nauvoo, defense of, V7:68-9

Nauvoo, removal of from Carthage to, V7:117-9

Nauvoo, sale of printing establishment at, to, V6:185

Nauvoo Temple, on building of, V7:292

newspaper, to control rather than travel to preach, V5:367

newspapers, discourse on, V7:473

notes of, V7:120-6

TAYLOR, JOHN (continued)

persecution of the Church in Illinois, *Times & Seasons,* V7:5i0-2
"Poor Wayfaring Man of Grief," sings, in Carthage jail, V6:614-5
President of United States, sent memorial to for protection of western
    country, V6:282 and ftnt
prison, reflections of, in, V7:106
Prophet, his proposition to free the, V7:100
saints, signs memorial of, in Missouri, V3:224
salvation, on, V7:289-90
Seventies Hall, composes hymn for dedication of, V7:333-5
shot strikes watch of, V7:119-20
Snow, Eliza R., poem to, by, V7:211
socialism, on, V6:33
surgery, rough, upon, V7:107
Times & Seasons, appointed editor of, V4:513, V5:193
Times & Seasons, leases *Nauvoo neighbor* and, V7:248
Warren, Major, conference of, with, V7:487-8
Wasp, new editor of, V5:204
West, crosses river for, V7:79
wine taken in Carthage jail, V7:101.
See also British Mission; Latter-day Saints, Church of Jesus Christ of;
    letters; Apostles, Twelve.

Taylor, John, grandfather to John, V3:154, ftnt only.

Taylor, John, elder, ordained, V4:296.

Taylor, Jonathan, Joseph stays at home of in Norton, Ohio, V2:50.

Taylor, Leonora, Carthage, goes to care for husband, V7:111
endowment, receives in Nauvoo Temple, V7:543
prays for husband, V7:112
saints, letter to Ford requesting protection for, V7:201.

Taylor, Levi, mentioned, V4:68.

Taylor, Robert, boy tried for stealing and sentenced to jail in Nauvoo,
    V5:282.

Taylor, Sarah, to receive Church aid in emigrating from England, V5:412.

Taylor, Thomas, writes anti-Mormon pamphlet, V4:255.

Taylor, William, covenanted to assist saints in removing from Missouri,
    V3:252.

Taysum, Charles, represents British conference, V5:419.

teachers, duties of in Zion expounded, V2:230, ftnt only
quorum votes to exclude membership to those who could not settle
    own difficulties, V3:25.

TEACHERS (continued)

See also Priesthood, Aaronic; priesthood.

teachers, false, rise of in early Church, IntroV1:XLVII.

teachers of religion, lack of understanding among, V1:4.

telestial kingdom, salvation in without baptism, V1:283.

temperance, ordinance on in Nauvoo, V4:299.

temperance societies, Joseph on, V5:404.

temple, Christ directs what people shall build, V4:328
cornerstones, proper method of laying of, V7:545
"Holiness to the Lord," written underneath must be, V1:359
sacrifice, to be restored with all things in, V4:211.

Temple, Kirtland, angel sits in, on service, V2:427
building, blessing of, who assisted in, V2:205, et seq
building, names of those who assisted in, V2:205-6
building, progress in, V2:363
Church, sustaining authorities of, at, V2:417, et seq
circular on, V1:349
commenced, V1:349
commenced foundations dug, V1:353
contributions to, V2:411
cornerstones laid July 23, 1833, V1:400
dedication of, V2:410, et seq
dedication, rushing wind sound at, V2:428
dedicated a second time for others, V2:433
dedicatory prayer accepted by congregation, V2:427
Joseph and brethren subscribe to at special meeting and pay within one hour, V2:234
Lord manifests acceptance of, V2:428
mob, taken over by, V7:484
New York Evening Star, on, V2:351
organizations of meetings and school in, V2:474
preparations to build, V1:349
priesthood meeting in, minutes of, V2:370
rules to be observed, V2:368
size of received by revelation, V1:352
subscriptions sent out, V1:349
subscriptions to, V2:234
veils, arrangement of, V2:399
washing and anointings, V2:379.

Temple, Masonic, dedicated, V6:287.

Temple, Nauvoo, accounting committee of, satisfactory, V5:169

TEMPLE, NAUVOO (continued)

Apostles, epistle of, to saints on, V4:590, et seq
Apostles, on building of, V6:13
Apostles, word of on, V4:517
arsoned by Joseph Agnew, V7:617-8, ftnts only
attic story dedicated, V7:534
baptism in font of, V4:557-8
baptismal font of dedicated, V4:446
baptisms for dead, no more until performed in, V4:426
capital, placing of last, on, V7:323-4
carpenters selected for steady employment at, V7:326
Catholic Church, inspected by, V7:539
Church, not to have conference until can meet in, V4:426
committee, complaints against and trial of, V5:337-9
committee meets on emphasizing completion of, V6:230
construction, general meeting concerning, V6:236, et seq
cornerstone, bishop laid, V4:330
cornerstone, high council laid, V4:330
cornerstone, high priesthood laid, V4:330
cornerstone, order of laying, V4:331
cornerstone, presidency laid, V4:329
cornerstones, proper order of laying, Brigham Young, V7:545
dancing ceased in, V7:566
dancing in, V7:557
destruction of, V7:617-8, ftnts only
dream, Joseph saw pattern of in, V6:196-7
editorial on progress of, V4:608, et seq
endowments, anxiety to receive and work hours of Brigham Young, V7:567
endowments, completed and ready for, V7:541
endowments, clothes washed at night to receive further, V7:548
endowments, first general in, V7:542-3
endowments, high priests numbered, V7:552
endowments, members waiting for, V7:565
endowments, 1,000 had received, V7:556
endowments, performed day and night, V7:570
endowments, preparation for, V7:538
endowments, reopened by Brigham Young because of desires of saints for, V7:579
fire in, V7:581
floor settled in, creates confusion, V7:594
general conference in, minutes, V7:457, et seq

TEMPLE, NAUVOO (continued)

gift of tongues in song, V7:557

"Holiness to the Lord," special inscription in west end, V7:457

importance of building, V7:298-9

interior finishings progress, V7:532

Joseph, announcement on work on, V4:517

Joseph's remarks to workmen on, V5:284, et seq

Lord, placed in hands of, V7:617

meeting, first in, October 5, 1845, V7:456-7

members board laborers of, V4:434

New York Sun, article on, V7:434-5

officers appointed for attic rooms, V7:535

ordinances, administering of, commenced in, V7:541

ordinances, announcement that no further, for present, V7:552-3

ordinances, anxiety for continuance of, in, V7:547

ordinance work in, and prayer, V7:560

overseer appointed, V5:353

prayer for, upon leaving, V7:580

procedure in, President Young, V7:552-3

rooms of, assigned, V7:535

rooms and assignments, division of, V7:542

sacrament administered in, V7:538

saints, first duty of, V7:292

saints, instructions on, to, by temple committee, V7:318, et seq

saints to meet in, V5:180

sealing alter erected, V7:566

stone, last, laid, V7:417-8

tithes, agents for collections of donations and, given, V7:369

tithing, time required as donation to build, V4:473

trial of committee of, acquitted, V5:196-7

United States deputy marshal, et al visit, V7:553-4

west, conversation on building a, in the, V7:622

women's subscriptions, plan for, V6:142-3

workers, additional names of, V7:555

workers in appointed, list of, V7:547-8.

See also Latter-day Saints, Church of Jesus Christ of; Nauvoo; Relief Society; Smith, Joseph

Temple, Salt Lake, building of proposed, V7:622.

Temple, Zion's, dedication of site of, V1:199

description of first to be built in, V1:359, et seq

Far West High Council, resolves to build, V2:481

must build prior to redemption of, V2:239

TEMPLE, ZION'S (continued)

    names of, V1:359

    site of, in revelation, V1:189.

temple, veil of, constructed for Kirtland Temple, V2:399 and ftnt.

temple work, importance of, V6:184.

temptations, Joseph's early, V1:9-10 and ftnt.

Tenney, William, appointed counselor in stake presidency, V4:233.

Tenny, William, death of, V3:131.

terrestial kingdom, salvation in without baptism, V1:283.

    See also translation.

Terrill, E. G., mission appointment and field of labor, V5:349.

Terry, Err, mission call and field of labor, V5:349.

Terry, Jacob E., elder, ordained, V5:349

    mission call and field of labor, V5:349.

Terry, Joel E., Joseph, on relief expedition for, V5:486.

testimony, Benbow, J., receives, of gospel, V4:150

    doctrines, as to truth of, V1:86

    eight witnesses, of, V1:57 and ftnt

    three witnesses, of, V1:56 and ftnt.

    See also Latter-day Saints, Church of Jesus Christ of; Mormon, Book of; Smith, Joseph.

Tewkesbury, Mr., letter to on fellowship, V6:427.

Texas, Joseph's views on annexation of, V6:243-4

    Wight, Lyman, proposes migration of Church to, V6:255-7.

Thatcher, George W., county clerk, member of martyrdom mob, V7:144.

Thatcher, George W., Joseph, on relief expedition for, V5:482

    mission call in Illinois to disabuse public mind over arrest of Joseph, V5:485.

Thayer, Franklin N., petitions Governor Boggs on mob violence in DeWitt, V3:83.

Thayer, Perry, petitions Governor Boggs on mob violence in DeWitt, V3:83

Thayre, Ezra, (also spelled Thayer), Adam-ondi-Ahman High Council, chosen to, V3:39

    cholera, seized with, V2:106

    consecration and stewardship, breaks law of, V1:180, ftnt only

    high council, presents first case before, V2:33

    Kirtland, appointed to purchase tannery in, V1:335

    mission appointment to Missouri, V1:178

THAYRE, EZRA (continued)

    revelation to, V1:186

    suspended from Church until bishop's court could hear complaint, V2:221

    Zion, ordained to purchase land for stake of, V1:335

    Zions Camp member, V2:185.

theology, Doctrine and Covenants, to be published in, V2:180

    lectures on, V2:176, ftnt only.

    See also doctrine; Smith, Joseph.

thief, Joseph retranslates words of Christ to, on cross, V5:424.

thieves, Apostles' warning against, V4:463, et seq and ftnts

    horse thieves, article on, V6:38

    Joseph denounces officially, V4:461

    theft, affidavit of Hyrum Smith denouncing, V4:460

    warning and condemnation of, V5:332-3.

Thomas, Colonel, mentioned, V3:150.

Thomas, D., non-Mormon, petitions Governor Boggs on mob violence in DeWitt, V3:83.

Thomas, Daniel S., Missouri, arraigned for treason, murder, burglary, arson, robbery, and larceny at Richmond, V3:209

    Missouri trials, discharged as innocent from, V3:211.

Thomas, David, mentioned, V3:450

    requests saints to leave DeWitt, V3:159.

Thomas, Dudley, petitions Governor Boggs on mob violence in DeWitt, V3:82.

Thomas, Jesse B., Carthage, holds court at, V6:398

    city council, advises hearing of, before Esq. D. H. Wells, V7:92

    Expositor affair, advice of, to Prophet, V6:479

    Prophet, courtesy of, to, V6:413.

Thomas, Tinney, Zions Camp member, V2:184.

Thompkins, George, supreme court justice of Missouri, V3:289.

Thompson, Albert, Carthage Greys, member of, V7:143.

Thompson, Beulah, mother of Wilford Woodruff, V3:337, ftnt only.

Thompson, Colonel, mentioned, V3:199.

Thompson, Charles, Church, appointed to preside over new district of, V7:306

    Kirtland Camp, subscribed to constitution of, V3:92

    Kirtland Camp, tried for questioning order of, V3:126

    mentioned, V4:488

    mission appointment published and field of labor, V6:336

THOMPSON, CHARLES (continued)

Missouri, covenanted to assist saints in removing from, V3:254.

Thompson, E., delegate to political convention in Nauvoo, V6:389.

Thompson, General, mentioned, V1:491.

Thompson, Ira O., Kirtland Camp, mentioned in, V3:145.

Thompson, Isaac, missionary call to Wisconsin, V5:413.

Thompson, James L., Zions Camp member, V2:185.

Thompson, James T. V., committee member to talk to saints on removal, V2:121, 452
Missouri, drafts resolutions of public meeting in, V2:449.
Senate, informs of injustice of mob, V2:177-8.

Thompson, Jonathan, testifies at Joseph's trial, V1:90.

Thompson, Mary Jane, daughter of Robert, V4:411.

Thompson, Mercy R., receives endowment in Nauvoo Temple, V7:544.

Thompson, Robert Blashel, biography of, V4:411-2
Church clerk, appointed general, V4:204
Church committee, on, V4:107
Congress, writes petition to, V4:237
death of, V4:411
editor, appointed associate of *Times & Seasons*, V4:353
Joseph, accompanies in arrest, V4:366
Joseph, letter of, reporting trial of, at Monmouth, Illinois, V4:369
Joseph, Sen., discourse of, at death of, V4:191, et seq
letter to First Presidency complaining of Lyman Wight, V3:351-2
letter to E. Higbee, V4:96-8
libelous reports, appointed to gather, V3:346
Nauvoo, elected treasurer of, V4:292
Nauvoo High Council, clerk of, V4:144-5.

Thompson, Robert T., mentioned, V3:273.

Thompson, Samuel, Kirtland Temple, blessing for work on, V2:206
Zions Camp member, V2:184.

Thompson, William, covenanted to assist saints in removing from Missouri, V3:254.

Thompson, William P., mobber in Missouri, V4:66.

Thompson Branch, Colesville Branch, settled here, V1:180, ftnt only
consecration and stewardship, lived law of, (D&C § 51) V1:180, ftnt only
covenant, broke, V1:180
difficulties in, V1:180, 181, ftnt only
Missouri, commanded to move to, (D&C § 54) V1:181.

Thor, Andrew, falsely accused of threatening A. Black, V3:65.

Thornton, Colonel J., letter appointing mediator in Jackson Co., V2:84-7.

Thornton, Ira P., child of dies, V3:139
Kirtland Camp, leaves with consent of council, V3:135, 140
Kirtland Camp, subscribed to constitution of, V3:93.

Thornton, John, appointed to assist saints in removing from Zion, V2:454
Missouri, drafts resolutions of public meeting in, V2:449.

Thornton, Stratton, called on mission and field of labor, V5:349.

Thornton, William, sends more inflammatory communications to Boggs, V3:166.

Thorp, John, DeWitt, petitions Governor Boggs on mob violence in, V3:83
Kirtland Camp, subscribed to constitution of, V3:93
Missouri, covenanted to assist saints in removing from, V3:253.

Tidwell, Absolom, covenanted to assist saints in removing from Missouri, V3:254.

Tidwell, John, mentioned, V5:282.

Tiffin, Clayton, baptism of, V7:592.

Tillery, Samuel, jailor in Missouri, V3:215, 308.

Tillford, John, petitions Governor Boggs on mob violence in DeWitt, V3:82.

Timely Warnings, writings of Orson Hyde deposited for sectarian priests in New York, V2:495.

Times and Seasons, Abraham, Book of, cuts prepared for, V4:519, et seq
Abraham, Book of, facsimile of published in, V5:11
Bennett, John C., article in, on character of and extolling innocence of Joseph, V5:71, ftnt only, 78
calamities, recorded up to June of 1843, V5:433
Commerce, Church paper published at, V4:23
editorial on temple progress, V4:608, et seq
editorials to be taken over by Apostles, V4:503
financial settlement with Robert Pierce acknowledged satisfactory, V4:519
God, government of, disertation on, in, V5:61, et seq
Joseph announces himself as editor of, V4:551
Joseph, article on for president, V6:214, et seq
Joseph editor of, V4:542
Joseph's parable on Lions of the Press, V5:274, et seq
Joseph retires as editor of, John Taylor appointed to, V5:193
liberty, statement of, of the missionaries published in, V4:234

TIMES AND SEASONS (continued)

martyrdom, review of, V7:186, et seq
numbers published enumerated, V4:253
persecutions, article on to October 1845 in Illinois, V7:510-2
persecution, exhortation on, as trial, V5:144
publication, to be continued until volume is closed, V7:473
publication to cease, V7:454
Richards, Willard, to take over, V4:463
Robinson, Ebenezer, becomes editor of, V4:402
temple committee, accounting of, satisfactory, V5:169
Thompson, Robert B., appointed associate editor of, V4:353.
See also Latter-day Saints, Church of Jesus Christ of; newspapers.

Tindale, S., sent on mission to Lamanites, V7:401.

Tippets, Alvah L., (also spelled Tippits), Church, appointed to preside
over new district of, V7:306
letter on gathering of money, V2:172-3
Missouri trials, discharged as innocent from, V3:211
violence, affidavit of J. Williams upon, V6:514
Zion, gives money for lands in, V2:174.

Tippets, Alvin G., Missouri, arraigned for treason, murder, burglary,
arson, robbery, and larceny at Richmond, V3:209.

Tippett, Alna L., petitions to hear Joseph speak, V6:533.

Tippetts, William P., Zions Camp member, V2:184.

Tippits, Caroline, Church, loans money to, V2:172
Zion, gives money for lands in, V2:174.

Tippits, J. W., to purchase lands for Church, V2:253.

Tippits, John H., Church, report of branch of, V2:172
Zion, gives money for lands in, V2:174.

Tippits, Joseph H., Church to purchase lands for, V2:253
Kirtland Temple, blessing for work on, V2:206
Zion, gives money for lands in, V2:174.

Tippits, William, starts for Missouri, V2:281.

tippling shops, members disfellowshipped for keeping, V4:80.

tithing, covenant of, taken by Joseph and Oliver Cowdery, V2:175
enforced, to be, V7:251
law of given in answer to question, (D&C § 119) V3:44
Nauvoo, for temple at, V4:493
one-tenth of income due, V7:358
record of, V4:518
rich man on, V7:320

TITHING (continued)

    saints must live, is little thing, V7:292-3
    Young, Brigham, on, V7:301.

title page, of Book of Mormon, V1:71-2.

Titus, Martin, mission appointment published and field of labor, V6:336.

Todd, William, appointed by public to assist saints in removing from Zion, V2:455.

Tomlin, John L., mob member writes lies concerning DeWitt, V3:156.

Tomlinson, Amos B., mission appointment and field of labor, V5:349.

Tomlinson, Brother, sells farm under counsel and provides for Joseph, V3:2.

Tomkins, Judge, petition of Joseph to, V3:277-81.

Tomkins, Samuel, blessing of, V2:207.

Tomkins Democrat, account of martyrdom in, V7:177.

tongues, gift of, Cottrin, Zebedee, speaks in, V1:323
    devil uses to deceive saints, V2:140-1
    exercised, V4:110, ftnt only
    exercised by priesthood in solemn assemblies, V2:392
    exercised in Kirtland, V2:383
    exercised in meeting for instruction, V2:292
    exercised in Nauvoo Temple in song, V7:557
    experienced as a mighty wind, V2:376
    first exercised, V1:297 and ftnt
    first time in Church, V1:296 and ftnt
    gift exercised in Canada, V1:422
    given for teaching language not understood, V3:379
    Hulet Branch tried for improper use of, V2:139
    hymn sung in and interpreted, V1:409
    Joseph explains use to teach gospel, not to govern Church, V2:162
    manifested at January 22, 1833 conference, V1:323
    necessary in Church and reason for, V4:485
    prophecy by should not be made public, V1:419
    purpose of, to speak to foreigners, V5:31
    using and hearing, exhorted in Zion to take care in, V1:369
    Young, Brigham, speaks in, V1:297, ftnt only
    Young, Brigham, speaks in, at temple dedication, V2:428.

Topham, John, mentioned, V5:371.

Toronto, Joseph, consecration of gold to Church, V7:433.

Tower Hill, named for old Nephite tower or alter, V3:35.

Town, David, rebukes the Prophet's captors, V5:445.

Town, Jacob, letter to, V1:286, ftnt only.

Townsend, Mr., mentioned, V6:285.

Township, Kaw, conference held in, V1:199
Jackson County, Missouri, Colesville Branch settled in, V1:196.

Tracy, J.M., Campbellite preacher that challenged in open debate the Book of Mormon, V2:218.

Tracy, Moses, called on mission and field of labor, V5:349.

transgression, rebuked for not punishing, V1:371.

translated beings, Enoch, was to be terrestial, V4:209
purpose of, V4:425.

translating, Abraham, Book of, alphabet for, V2:238
Abraham, Book of, published, V4:520, et seq
baptism, question about while, V1:39
close, drawing to, V1:71
completed at Whitmer home, V1:49
continues, V1:35
Cowdery, Oliver, power taken from, V1:37
delay in, V1:28
helped by Joseph's father-in-law, V1:44
Kinderhook plates, found and, V5:372, et seq and ftnts
Mormon, Book of, commenced, V1:32
witness of, God testifies to, V1:55.

translation, doctrine of, explained, V4:210
Enoch, of to be terrestial, V4:209
priesthood, doctrine of, belongs to, V4:209
resurrection, compared to, V4:210
righteousness, of man possible through, V2:8
terrestrial order, beings to, V4:210

treason, Joseph arrested for, V6:561-2.

treasure, parable of, explained, V2:271-2.

treaty, between mob and Zion, July 23, 1833, V1:394, ftnt only.
See also persecutions, Missouri.

Tremont, emigrant ship, V4:393, 516.

trial, child, reproved for improper training of, V2:295
Elliot, David, for whipping daughter unreasonably, V2:293
first proceedings of before the high council, V2:33-4
Gould, Dean, for speaking unadvisedly against Sidney Rigdon, V2:286
Gould, John, for injurious expressions and dissatisfaction of teachings of Presidency, V2:286

TRIAL (continued)

    Joseph, arguments presented in Springfield, V5:220

    Joseph, at Springfield on extradition warrants, V5:212, et seq

    Joseph, attorneys' affidavits concerning second of, in Illinois, V5:476, et seq

    Joseph, official papers of, in Springfield on extradition warrants, V5:233, et seq

    Joseph, transcript of, second of, sent to Governor Ford, V5:478

    Joseph, transporting of, for, to Quincy on second writ, V5:447, et seq. See also persecutions; Smith, Joseph.

Tribbs, Nelson, Zions Camp member, V2:184.

Tribes, Ten, John the Revelator with, V1:176, ftnt only.

Tribes, Twelve, honored at establishment of Zion, V1:196.

Tripp, Thomas, excommunicated for imprudent conduct, V2:54.

Truly, Ekells, mission appointment published and field of labor, V6:337.

truth, honorable men, call to heed, V1:282-4

    obtain, best way to, V4:425

    same in all churches, V5:517.

Truthiana, a series of tracts, V5:318.

Tubbs, Amos, falsely accused of threatening A. Black, V3:65.

Tubbs, Nelson, repairs firelocks of Zions Camp, V2:88, ftnt only.

Tucker, Father Hamilton, Nauvoo property, Roman Catholic Church, attempts purchase of, V7:539-40

    Nauvoo property, reports inability of Catholic Church to purchase, V7:565.

Tucker, Washington, letter of requesting elders in Arkansas, V6:458-9.

Tufts, Elbridge, Joseph, on relief expedition for, V5:482

    mission appointment published and field of labor, V6:335

    Nauvoo, policeman in, V6:150

    Nauvoo, testifies at trial in, V6:344.

Tulley, Allen, mission appointment published and field of labor, V6:339.

Tullidge, Edward, writes biographical sketch of Orson Hyde, V1:217, ftnt only.

Turley, Theodore, British Mission, leaves Nauvoo sick for, V4:10

    Commerce, builds first house by saints in, V3:375

    England, appointed to go to with Twelve, V3:347

    England, arrives in, V4:76

    England, sails from New York for, V4:46

    English conference, represents branch of Church in, V4:148

    imprisonment of, V4:127

TURLEY, THEODORE (continued)

jail, released from in England, V4:127

Joseph, accompanies for trial on Missouri warrants, V5:210

mentioned, V3:322, 383; V7:532

ministry, devote all time to labors of, V4:148

Missouri, covenanted to assist saints in removing from, V3:252

Nauvoo, appointed weigher and sealer of, V4:308

Nauvoo, elected weigher and sealer in, V5:271

poor, superintends removing of the, V3:261

prophecy, present in Missouri at Apostles' departure to fulfill, V3:339

Richmond, appointed to visit Jefferson City in the interest of prisoners in Liberty and, V3:285-9

saints, signs memorial of in Missouri, V3:224

testimony, questions John Whitmer on, V3:307-8

witness in *Expositor* trial of Joseph, V6:456.

Turner, Mr., bill of passes Senate, V3:254

bill of tabled in House, never heard, V3:256, ftnt only

Mormon problem, introduces bill to investigate, V3:246, ftnt only

Mormons, report of to Missouri Legislature, V3:235, et seq

Turner, Charles, ordained priest, V5:419.

Turner, Dr., mentioned, V6:56.

Turner, James B., witness for state in Missouri trials of saints, V3:210.

Turner, Nelson, kidnap, proposed of, V6:100.

Turner, Sidney, Missouri, arraigned for treason, murder, burglary, arson, robbery, and larceny at Richmond, V3:209.

Turnham, Mr., moderator in Clay County meeting, speaks in defense of the saints, V2:97.

Turnham, Joel, appointed by public to assist saints in removal from Zion, V2:454.

Turnham, Judge, mentioned, V3:264, 372, 421.

Turpin, John, covenanted to assist saints in removing from Missouri, V3:252.

Tuttle, Smith, letter to on land troubles, V4:430.

Tweddle, Thomas, British Mission, represents branch of Church at conference, V4:215

service, volunteers for in vineyard, V4:217.

Twelve Apostles, see Apostles, Twelve.

Twiss, John S., mission appointment published and field of labor, V6:335.

Twist, James, mission call in Illinois to disabuse public mind over arrest of Joseph, V5:485.

Tyler, Mr., restored to fellowship, V2:50.

Tyler, Daniel, mission appointment published and field of labor, V6:338
mission call and field of labor, V5:349
Missouri, covenanted to assist saints in removing from, V3:253
mob, makes conciliation offer to, V7:441-2.

Tyler, John, appeal to as President of United States, V6:508.

Tyler, Samuel D., Kirtland Camp, keeps journal of, V3:125, ftnt only
Missouri, covenanted to assist saints in removing from, V3:252.

Tyler, Stephen H., anti-Mormon committee chairman, V6:8
anti-Mormon meeting, at, V5:538
messenger to governor from anti-Mormon meeting, V6:466.

Tyler, T. D., asks assistance from Church, V3:261.

Tyler, William, mentioned, V5:359.

Tyrean, emigrant ship, V4:417, 441, 460.

—U—

unbelief, lack of understanding result of, V2:267.

unbelievers, disrupt meeting with outrageousness, V2:42.

unchristianlike conduct, examples of, for trial purposes, V2:442, ftnt only
failure to attend meetings, possessing spirit of dissenters are examples of, V3:18
unlawful marriage and deceiving examples of, V2:511.
See also disfellowship; excommunication.

understanding, cannot have if have unbelief, V2:267.

Unitarian, Joseph confounds minister of, V2:364.

United Brethren, minister of church of, baptized by Wilford Woodruff, V4:123.

united order, deed forms used, V1:365-7, ftnt only
devil, establishes similar, V1:146
established at Thompson, Ohio, (D&C § 51) V1:173
Kirtland, dissolved in, V2:49
Kirtland saints, given to, (D&C § 92) V1:333
prayer for lives of those living, V2:2.
See also consecration; doctrine; Latter-day Saints, Church of Jesus Christ of; Smith, Joseph.

United States, article on, concern as to next president of, V6:39
bloodshed, to be scene of and receive judgments of God, V1:315

UNITED STATES (continued)

Church, appeal to government by, IntroV4:XXVI, et seq

Church, division of, into districts for, V7:249, 251-2

gathering to, argued as anti-scriptural, V4:250

government, foundation of on justice and virtuous principles, V2:10

government and laws in general, V2:247

Harrison, William Henry, inaugurated president of, V4:308

Joseph, memorial of, to Congress on organizing protection for western
    states, V6:275

Joseph, purported arrest order by President of, V5:363

Joseph sees end of, if refused petitions of virtuous citizens, V4:89

Joseph's views on powers and policies of, V6:197, et seq

letter from government of, refusing assistance, V1:493

Missouri, guilty of crimes of, because would not help, V4:145

President, interview of Joseph with, V4:80

president, rather have Joseph's clothes full of straw than present
    candidates, V7:256

prophecy that government in power would fall if not aid saints,
    V6:116 and ftnt.

See also Constitution; persecutions; Smith, Joseph.

United States House of Representatives, Joseph's opinion on visit to, V4:41.

United States President, Joseph, if elected will raise devil, V6:248

mentioned, V4:42; V6:188, 361

"Who Shall Be Our Next," V6:39, et seq

United States Senate, report of judiciary committee of on saints vs. Mis-
    souri, V4:90, et seq.

Universalist, Knight, Joseph, and family members of, V1:81.

Upper Missouri Advertiser, published weekly in connection with the
    Evening & Morning Star, V1:281.

Urim and Thummim, gold plates, with, V1:12

Joseph, beheld by, V1:16

Joseph, returned to, V1:21

Joseph, used by, V1:33

receive, cannot show when, V1:13

received, V1:18

returned the second time, V1:23

Smith, Hyrum, inquired through for, V1:45

taken again, (D&C § 3) V1:23

three witnesses, used to determine, V1:53

translation used in, V1:19

Whitmers, duties of, requested through, V1:49.

URIM AND THUMMIM (continued)

See also Mormon, Book of; plates; Smith, Joseph; translation.

Utley, Brother, mentioned, V2:447.

—V—

Vade Mecum, to Joseph, V5:253.

vagrants, ordinance on in Nauvoo, V4:447.

Valance, James, petitions Governor Boggs on mob violence in DeWitt, V3:83.

Van Allen, Isaac, attorney general of Iowa territory, V3:266.

Van Buren, Cheney G., mission call in Illinois to disabuse public mind over arrest of Joseph, V5:485.

Van Buren, Martin, Joseph's interview with, "I can do nothing for you," V4:40, 80
  Joseph, addendum to letter to, by, on previous treatment, V6:65
  Joseph places wish of non-election on, V4:89
  letter to on feelings toward saints, V6:65
  Missouri persecutions, asked to investigate, V3:333
  United States, president of, V4:40.
  See also Smith, Joseph; United States.

Van Buren County, Missouri, mob violence spreads to, V1:456.

Van Orden, Mr., mentioned, V6:424.

Vanausdell, W., delegate to political convention in Nauvoo, V6:389

Vance, Mr., mentioned, V6:283

Vance, Brother, mentioned, V3:378.

Vance, John, mission appointment published and field of labor, V6:340
  Salt Lake High Council, sustained member of, V7:629.

Vance, Joseph, mentioned in Kirtland Camp, V3:114.

Vance, W. P., mission appointment published and field of labor, V6:338.

Vanleuven, Cornelius, Kirtland Camp, dissents against, V3:138
  Kirtland Camp, subscribed to constitution of, V3:92.

VanLeuven, Frederick M., Canada branch, appointed elder of Luborough, V2:235
  Kirtland Camp, child of born in, V3:130
  Kirtland Camp, subscribed to constitution of, V3:92.

Vanleuven, John Jr., daughter of nearly killed, V3:107
  Kirtland Camp, subscribed to constitution of, V3:93.

VanLeuven, Ransom, blessing for work on Kirtland Temple, V2:206.

VanNatta, J. H., mission appointment published and field of labor, V6:336
   mission call in Illinois to disabuse public mind over arrest of Joseph,
   V5:485.

Vanvelver, Mr., priest, V4:22.

Vaughn, Joel, Zions Camp member, V2:184.

Venable, Samuel, Dr., accuses saints of burning and murder, V3:165.

Vermont, Joseph appeals to as native state for aid in redress for Missouri
   persecutions, V6:88.

Vermont conference, of Twelve Apostles, exhortation to move to Zion,
   V2:238.

Vernon, John, given care of Church at Apperley, V4:135.

vice, instructions of Twelve to Church on, V7:282.

Vicker, Mr., mentioned, V5:384.

Victoria, Queen, crowned Queen of England, V3:40
   Mormon, Book of, presented to, V6:181.

Vincent, Ezra, mission appointment published and field of labor, V6:339.

virtue, Christ, on leaving explained, V5:303
   spirit of life, is, V5:303.

vision, Celestial Kingdom, Prophet's of, V2:380
   destroyer, seen riding on waters, V1:203
   England, of William Smith of Twelve and seven in, V2:392
   English Mission, first, not to be taught in, V2:492
   kingdoms of glory, of, V1:245
   Kirtland Temple, in, V2:435
   Lord's host, of Zebedee Coltrin of, V2:392
   Marks, William, Joseph receives on status of, V3:12
   Mormon, Book of, where was, V1:13
   Orton, Roger, sees heavenly, V2:386
   persons, of other, V2:382, 386, 387, 392
   pure in heart, seen by, according to prophecy, V1:334
   Saviour seen by many, V1:335
   temple, seen in, V2:432
   Twelve, of the, V2:381.
   See also doctrine; Smith, Joseph.

"Voice of Warning," published by Parley P. Pratt, first doctrinal work of
   Church, V2:518.

Voorhees, Washington, Carthage martyrdom, wounded at, V7:162

VOORHEES, WASHINGTON (continued)

Missouri, arraigned for treason, murder, burglary, arson, robbery, and larceny at Richmond, V3:209.

Vose, Sister, mentioned, V7:195.

vote, Church organized by, V1:77
election, saints in Missouri instructed not to, at, V2:137
Joseph and Oliver accepted by, V1:77
ordination, to accept proceedings of, V1:61.
See also Latter-day Saints, Church of Jesus Christ of; Smith, Joseph; sustain.

—W—

Wade, Moses, called on mission and field of labor, V5:348.

Waggoner, George C., Carthage Greys, member of, V7:143.

Wait, Allen T., Kirtland Camp, leaves, V3:140
mission appointment published and field of labor, V6:336
mob, affidavit on attempt to draft into service of, V6:509.

Wait, John, prepares harvest feast in Nauvoo, V7:437.

Waite, Truman, (also spelled Wait), Kirtland Temple, blessing for work on, V2:205
mission call, V1:332
mission call and field of labor, V5:348
testifies at trial of Brother Hodges, V2:33.

Wakefield, Joseph R., affidavit concerning destruction of *Nauvoo Expositor,* V7:130
letter to Governor Ford confirming Joseph's letter on *Expositor* affair, V6:469
witness for Joseph at Carthage martyrdom, V6:576
witness in *Expositor* trial of Joseph, V6:456, 490.

Wakefield, John, mission call in Illinois to disabuse public mind over arrest of Joseph, V5:485.

Wakefield, Joseph H., baptizes George A. Smith, V1:285.

Walker, Brother, mentioned, V3:146.

Walker, Cyrus, Joseph, affidavit on conduct of arrest and trial, of, V5:476
Nauvoo, political speech at, V5:521
Nauvoo, visits, V4:356
Prophet, becomes counsel for the, V5:500
Prophet, lawyer for, at Monmouth trial, V4:367, et seq.

INDEX—HISTORY OF THE CHURCH

Walker, Esquire, Joseph stays at home of in Palmersville, V2:42.

Walker, George, baptisms for dead, recorder for, V5:522
letter on affairs of British Mission, V4:505
priest, ordained, V4:148.

Walker, J. B., mission appointment published and field of labor, V6:338.

Walker, Joel Hamilton, letter proposing to join in western volunteer movement, V6:424.

Walker, John, wounded at Haun's Mills by mob, V3:326, ftnt only.

Walker, Joseph, ordained elder, V5:419.

Walker, Lorin, accompanies Joseph for trial on Missouri warrants, V5:210
MIA, aids in movement toward, V5:322
mentioned, V5:379.

Walker, Lydia, death of, V5:532.

Walker, Oliver, charges against derogatory statements against heads, V4:219-20.

Walker, William, MIA, aids in movement toward, V5:322
misleads Prophet's enemies, V5:91.

Wall, Mr., hears saints' petition in Congressional Committee, V4:83, et seq.

Wall, William, Carthage jail, refused entry to see Joseph in, V6:590
Joseph wrestles with and wins, V5:302.

Wallace, Captain, mentioned, V2:67, ftnt only.

Wallace, George B., mentioned, V6:81, V7:567.

Wallace, H. M., petitions Governor Boggs on mob violence in DeWitt, V3:83.

Wallace, James, house built for to compensate for wood used, V7:602.

Waller, Zachariah, anti-Mormon committee member, V1:399.

Wallock, Major-General, in Missouri militia, V3:175.

Walmsley, Thomas, mentioned, V4:296.

Walsh, John C., mentioned, V5:207.

Walter, George, signs attempted whitewash of General Clark's activity, V3:360, ftnt only.

Walton, George, witness for state in Missouri trials of saints, V3:210.

Walton, Mary, mother of Isaac Russell, V2:494, ftnt only.

Walton, Richard, covenanted to assist saints in removing from Missouri, V3:253.

Walton, Robert, excommunicated from Church, V3:336.

Walton, Sister, excommunicated from Church, V3:336.

Wandell, C. W., mission appointment published and field of labor, V6:336 presides at New York conference, V7:168.

Wanless, Ann, excommunicated from Church, V3:336.

war, article on British-Chinese, V5:277.

war, Canadian, saints escape from, V3:117 and ftnt.

Ward, G. W. F., testify to finding Kinderhook plates, V5:377.

Ward, Sarah, wife of Elias Higbee, V5:420, ftnt only.

Ward, Thomas, represents area in British conference, V5:9, 419.
Star, editor of, V7:346.

Warden, Hezekiah, mobber in Missouri, V4:72.

Warder, Mr., mentioned in mob action in Missouri, V3:156.

wards, Nauvoo divided into, V4:305-6, V5:199.

Ware, W. G., delegate to political convention in Nauvoo, V6:389 witness at *Expositor* trial, V6:491.

Warner, Mr., mentioned, V5:446.

Warner, Charles, delegate to present truth to public, V6:483
elected auctioneer in Nauvoo, V6:124
mission appointment published and field of labor, V6:337.

Warner, Salmon, mission appointment published and field of labor, V6:339
mission call in Illinois to disabuse public mind over arrest of Joseph, V5:485
seventies, named to first quorum of, V2:203
speaks at conference of Church, V2:53
Zions Camp member, V2:184.

Warning, Voice of, published, V2:518 and ftnt.

Warnock, William, excommunicated from Church, and wife, V3:336.

Warren, city of, to be built up, V4:405
consultation respecting, V4:486.

Warren, Calvin A., Joseph, attorney for defense of murderers of, V7:50
Joseph, lawyer for, V4:486-7, 513; V5:49, 155, 162, 164, 173, 184, 266
martyrdom mob, lawyer, member of, V7:144
mentioned, V4:470-1
murdered, argument that Joseph was not, V7:423
murderers, makes inflammatory speech against Church at defense trial of, V7:420.

Warren, Catherine, testifies of C. L. Higbee's adulterous actions, V6:407.

Warren, Charles A., lawyer for Joseph, V4:367
mentioned, V4:365.

Warren, Edward, recommends California for movement, V7:510.

Warren, Major, reportedly turned friendly to Mormons, V7:530.

Warren, Samuel, given care of Church at Keysend Street, V4:139.

Warren, W. B., martyrdom mob, damned villain, member of, V7:144
Quincy committee, on saints removal, V7:450.

Warrington, Benjamin, delegate to present truth to public, V6:483
witness at *Expositor* trial, V6:489.

Warsaw, Carthage, departure of posse from to, June 27, V7:30
expulsion, committee of, demanded of the people, V7:28
mass meeting, V6:462
movements in Illinois reported from, V7:195
Smiths, committe of, reported a party of Mormons had attempted to
rescue, V7:25.

Warsaw Signal, anti-Mormon paper, inflammatory articles in, V7:64.

washing of feet, conference, performed at of January 22, 1833, (D&C
§ 88:139-40) V1:312, 323
Joseph receives instructions on, at temple, V2:430
Kirtland, at conference in, V2:475-6
ordinance of expounded upon and necessary, V2:308
ordinance performed, V2:431.

Wasp, The, Nauvoo Neighbor, name changed to, V5:304
weekly newspaper published by William Smith, V4:600.

Wasson, Mr., mentioned, V5:440; V6:399; V7:98, 194.

Wasson, Mrs., mentioned, V5:431.

Wasson, Clara M., marriage to William Backenstos, V6:43.

Wasson, Harmon, affidavit on conduct of arrest and trial of Joseph, V5:476.

Wasson, Lorenzo D., Joseph, accuses of cowardice for leaving, V6:549
Smith, Emma, nephew of, V4:557; V5:83
witness for Joseph at Carthage martyrdom, V6:576.

Waste, Mr., aids in tarring Joseph, V1:262 and ftnt.

water, used in sacrament, V2:480
testimony of curse on, V5:56.
See also devil.

Waterman, John O., baptism of, V2:398.

Waterman, Sally, wife of W. W. Phelps, V1:186, ftnt only.

Waterman, Samuel, mentioned, V6:56.

Watkins, James, ordained teacher, V4:138.

Watkins, William, mission appointment published and field of labor, V6:338.

Watt, George, mission appointment published and field of labor, V6:337.

Watt, George D., baptism, first English, V2:504
British conference, represents area in, V5:10
Church, appointed to preside over new district of, V7:305
emigrants, letter reporting arrival of, V5:184
high priests ordained, V4:333
mission appointment published and field of labor, V6:337
murderers, records minutes of trial of, V7:421, et seq
Professor of Phonography, reports conference speeches, V7:394
volunteers for service in vineyard, V4:216
western country, to go investigate for settlement, V6:223.

Waugh, George P., English conference, represents branches at, V6:328.

Wayne, Mr., mentioned, V2:71.

Weatherford, William, anti-Mormon troop leader, V7:46-7.

Weaver, Russel, Unitarian minister confounded by Joseph, V2:364.

Webb, C. M., mentioned, V7:325.

Webb, E., marriage to E. A. McWhithy, V2:331.

Webb, E. M., Bennett, John C., reports movements of, V5:364
mentioned, V7:426
mission call in Illinois to disabuse public mind over arrest of Joseph,
V5:485
mission report, V5:364.

Webb, Edwin W., missionary call to Galena, V5:413.

Webb, John, marriage to Catherine Wilcox, V2:369.

Webb, Pardon, mission call in Illinois to disabuse public mind over arrest
of Joseph, V5:485.

Weber, Mr., mentioned, V4:53; V6:282, ftnt only.

Weber, John B., letter to Joseph on supplementing aid to obtain redress,
V4:55.

Webster, Daniel, mentioned, V6:116, ftnt only, 226.

Webster, Sister, healed by Noah Rogers, V5:518.

Webster, Thomas, elder, ordained, V3:20
prophecy concerning apostasy of, V3:21.

Weden, William, Zions Camp member, V2:184.

Weekly Dispatch, London paper refuses to print reply to anti-Mormon
article, V4:236.

Weeks, William, Nauvoo Temple, appointed overseer of, V5:353
    Nauvoo Temple, architect of, difference with Prophet, V6:196-7.

Weir, Captain, mentioned, V7:143.

Weld, John F., mentioned, V4:303.

Weldin, James, (also spelled Welden), mob commander, V4:61
    mobber in Missouri, V4:66.

Welding, Richard, attacks Samuel Brown while voting, V3:57.

Wells, Mr., mentioned, V1:481.

Wells, Benjamin, blessing for work on Kirtland Temple, V2:206.

Wells, Daniel, father of D. H., V4:154, ftnt only.

Wells, Daniel H., aide-de-camp to President Young, V7:626
    Carthage, call of Prophet upon, en route for, V6:554
    defender of Nauvoo, last phase, V7:614, ftnt only
    Expositor affair, trial of mayor and city council before, V6:487-91
    genealogy of, V4:154-5, ftnt only
    Joseph, affidavit of, concerning character of John C. Bennett and, V5:80-2
    Joseph examined before and acquitted, V7:92
    kidnapping, affidavit concerning, by Missourians, V4:154
    law, on Prophet's intuitive knowledge of, V2:4, ftnt only
    mentioned, V4:293; V5:369
    Nauvoo, first elected alderman of, V4:287
    temple, issues writ of ejectment from lands east of, V6:356-7
    witness for Joseph at Carthage martyrdom, V6:576.

Wells, Elias, Zions Camp member, V2:185.

Wells, John Patrick, wounded at Carthage martyrdom, V7:162.

Wells, R. W., Attorney General of Missouri, letter to saints' attorney, V1:444-5.

Wells, Samuel, ordained priest, V5:419.

Wells, Thomas, grandfather of D. H., V4:155, ftnt only.

Welton, Baldwin, ordination illegal and rejected, V1:343.

Welton, M., appointed by public to assist saints in removing from Zion, V2:455.

Welton, M. B., mission appointment published and field of labor, V6:338.

Wentworth, Mr., mentioned, V6:370.

Wentworth, John, letter of Prophet to, V4:535, et seq
    mentioned, V7:547.

Wesleyan Methodist, opposes Joseph on Canadian Mission, V1:421.

West, Benjamin, painting of exhibited, V6:471.

West, Nathan A., Brown, Samuel, prefers charges against, V2:137
  Hulet Branch, against, V2:139
  mission appointment published and field of labor, V6:340.

West, Samuel, mentioned, V4:396.

West Indies, mission opened in, V4:413.

West Messenger, article on meteor falling, V4:588.

Western Missouri, letter concerning, V1:182-3
  mission and gathering to, V1:182.

Western Monitor, Birch, Weston F., editor of, V1:395
  Missouri paper, article on Mormonism after mob treaty, V1:395, et seq.

western movement, captains named for companies, V7:481
  Church, circular to, informing of, V7:570, et seq
  Dunham, Jonathan, explores and reports on the West, V5:509, 541,
      542, et seq, V6:223
  exploration proposed for, V6:222, 224
  preparation for, V7:535
  west, reading on the explorations in the, V7:558.
  See also westward camp.

Western Reserve, History of the Disciples on the, Campbellite book,
  V1:158, ftnt only.

Weston, Joel, at anti-Mormon meeting, V5:538.

Weston, Samuel, anti-Mormon committee member, V1:399
  mob manifesto, justice of the peace, signed, V1:376
  mobber, releases, V1:428.

westward camp, Camp of Israel, given name of, V7:606
  Council Bluffs, reaches, V7:607
  encampment, prominent places of, V7:606
  Hemmic, J. M., discharged from for dueling, V7:609
  some of return to Nauvoo for families, V7:610
  incidents in, V7:592
  instructions by Brigham Young on work in, V7:597
  instructions to Pioneer Camp, V7:591
  minutes from journal of, V7:594
  Mississippi River, members of cross on ice, V7:600
  Mormon Battalion, raising of, from, V7:612
  Mount Pisgah, names, V7:607
  Pratt, O., takes astronomical position of, V7:598
  preparations, incomplete, of, V7:605

WESTWARD CAMP (continued)

son born to J. Redding in, V7:596

Sugar Creek, breaking up of, at, V7:604

travel, developments of methods of, V7:605

Young, Brigham, instructions to, on conditions and actions of, V7:608.

See also Latter-day Saints, Church of Jesus Christ of; Young, Brigham.

Wetherby, Oliver, blessing for work on Kirtland Temple, V2:206.

"Weymouth," song sung at temple dedication, V2:413 and ftnt.

Wharnot, William, counselor of Philadelphia branch, V4:331.

Wharton, William, called on mission and field of labor, V5:348.

Wheat, Almeron, mentioned, V5:242.

wheat and tares, parable of explained, (D&C § 86) V1:300, V2:267.

See also parables.

Wheatly, Henry, mentioned, V6:181.

Wheeler, Helen, mentioned, V3:337, ftnt only.

Wheeler, John, blessing for work on Kirtland Temple, V2:206.

Wheeler, Judge, mentioned in Kirtland Camp, V3:112.

Wheeler, Lucy, covenanted to assist saints in removing from Missouri, V3:252.

Wheeler, Nathan, raised Orson Hyde, V1:217, ftnt only.

Wheelock, Cyrus H., Carthage, leaves pistol with those in, V6:607-8, V7:100

Carthage, visits Prophet at, V7:100

Ford, Governor, warning of, to, V6:607

Joseph, hears threat on life of, V6:560

mission call and field of labor, V5:348

mission appointment published and field of labor, V6:336

Nauvoo, arranges to leave with John Taylor, V7:80

pass, receives, from Governor Ford to see Joseph, V6:604.

Whipple, Edson, Church, appointed to preside over new district of, V7:305

counselor of Philadelphia branch, V4:331

mission appointment published and field of labor, V6:337

Salt Lake High Council, sustained member of, V7:629.

whispering, not allowed in councils and assemblies, V2:367.

Whitaker, Mr., mobber in Missouri, V3:322.

Whitaker, James, falsely accused of threatening A. Black, V3:65.

Whitcher, Mary, sore grievances of, V2:304.

White, Mr., mentioned, V4:64.

White, Captain, mentioned, V6:188.

White, Evandor, stealing, hard labor for, V6:153.

White, Halsay, kidnaps some members and takes to Missouri, V4:155.

White, Hugh, mentioned, V3:342.

White, J., sheriff of Clark County, Missouri, V6:108.

White, Joseph, volunteers for service in vineyard, V4:217.

White, Robert, member of mob at Haun's Mills massacre, V3:325
    mobber in Missouri, V4:68.

White, Roswell, stealing, hard labor for, V6:153.

White, Samuel, mission appointment published and field of labor, V6:336.

White, William, anti-Mormon committee chairman, V6:8
    property of purchased by Church, V4:7.

Whitehead, James, high priest, ordained, V4:333
    high priest quorum, in, at Nauvoo, V5:136.

Whitehead, Judge, mentioned, V6:160, 162.

Whiteman, William, clerk of Crooked Creek Branch, V4:144.

Whitesides, Alexander, seventies, named to first quorum of, V2:203
    Zions Camp member, V2:185.

Whitesides, Isaiah, Joseph, on relief expedition for, V5:486.

Whitesides, Morris, death of, V7:375.

Whiting, Edwin, counselor to president at Lima, V5:427
    Missouri, covenanted to assist saints in removing from, V3:253.

Whitlock, Andrew W., Missouri, arraigned for treason, murder, burglary,
        arson, robbery and larceny at Richmond, V3:209
    Missouri trials, discharged as innocent from, V3:211
    Zions Camp member, V2:185.

Whitlock, Harvey H., devil binds, V1:175, ftnt only
    Joseph, letter to asking forgiveness, V2:314
    rebaptized, to be, V2:388
    revelation, Joseph answers with, forgiving and directing to come to
        Kirtland, V2:315.

Whitman, Erastus B., approved for ordination, V2:407.

Whitmer, Anne, baptized, V1:81.

Whitmer, Christian, baptized, V1:81.
    counselor to bishop and high priest, V1:363
    death of, V2:357
    endowments, called to go to Kirtland to receive, V2:113
    high council, sustained to Missouri, V2:124
    high priest, ordained, V1:407

WHITMER, CHRISTIAN (continued)

scriptures, accepts Joseph's version of, V1:105.

Whitmer, David, angels, sees, at temple dedication, V2:427

Apostle, called to be, (D&C § 18:9) V1:62

baptized, V1:51

branch president, appointed, in Missouri, V1:409, ftnt only

buffetings of Satan, turned over to and condemned as openly sinning against Jesus, V3:232

case of concerning his going East presented before high council, V2:125

duty, desire to know, V1:49

endowment, called to go to Kirtland to receive, V2:113

excommunication for various charges, V3:18-9 and ftnt

Far West, refuses to be tried by high council of, V3:7

Far West Branch, accepted as president of, V2:523

genealogy, V1:32, ftnt only, 48, ftnt only

high council, instructs, V2:136-7

Joseph, goes to Harmony to take, to father's house, V1:49

Knight, Newel, baptizes, V1:84

letter of, to high council concerning charges, V3:19, ftnt only

Literary Firm of the Church, appointed to, V2:273

meetings, appointed to instruct on how to conduct, V1:219

Missouri elections, instructs saints not to vote in, V2:137

mob, leads first company against, V1:430

Moroni speaks to, V1:54

plates, prays for witness of, V1:54

president, made, of high council and Church in Missouri, V2:124, 125

revelation to, (D&C § 14) V1:49-50

son of Peter Whitmer, Sen., meets Joseph, V1:48-9

tried before high council for use of tea, coffee, and tobacco, V3:4

tried for selling lands in Missouri, V3:3-5 and ftnt

witness, commanded to be of Book of Mormon, V1:55

witness, requests to be to Book of Mormon, V1:53

Zion, rejected as president in, V3:5

Zion, sustained president in, in Joseph's absence, V2:126.

See also three witnesses.

Whitmer, Elizabeth, baptized, V1:81.

Whitmer, Elizabeth Anne, (also spelled Ann), baptized, V1:81

married Oliver Cowdery, V1:32, ftnt only.

Whitmer, Jacob, baptized, V1:81

eight witnesses, testimony of as one of, V1:57-8

Zion, worthy of inheritance in, V1:236, ftnt only.

Whitmer, John, buffetings of Satan, turned over to and condemned as openly sinning against Jesus, V3:232

Church Historian, called to be, (D&C § 47) V1:166 and ftnt

Church history, Joseph's letter demanding notes on, V3:15

duty, desire to know, V1:49

endowments, called to go to Kirtland to receive, V2:113

excommunication for mortgaging Church, V3:8

Far West, in transgression at and trial of, V3:3-5 and ftnt

Far West, refuses to be tried by high council at, V3:7

Far West Branch, accepted as counselor to president of, V2:523

genealogy, V1:49, ftnt only

Joseph, assists in compiling revelation, V1:104

Kirtland Temple, subscribing to, and pays within one hour, V2:234

Messenger & Advocate, to replace Oliver Cowdery in conducting, V2:227

Missouri trials, witness for state in, V3:210

Mormon, Book of, testifies to seeing plates of, but denies knowing translation true, V3:307

ransom, offers himself as, for saints in Jackson County, V1:394 and ftnt

revelations, to review and prepare for printing, V1:270

revelation to, (D&C § 15) V1:50

sin, revelation states he is in, V2:511

sins, under condemnation for, repents, V2:304

son of Peter Whitmer, Sen., assists Joseph in writing Book of Mormon, V1:49

trial of, for improper use of Church funds, V2:483-4, ftnts only

Turley, Theodore, interview with, V3:307-8

Zion, appointed to accompany Oliver Cowdery to, V1:234, ftnt only, 235

Zion, rejected as president in, V3:5

Zion, sustained assistant president in, V2:126.

See also eight witnesses.

Whitmer, Mary, baptized, V1:81.

Whitmer, Peter, Jun., baptized, V1:51

duty, desire to know, V1:49

endowments, called to go to Kirtland to receive, V2:113

revelation to, V1:51

son of Peter Whitmer, Sen., friend of Joseph, V1:49, ftnt only

work, interest in, V1:49

Zion High Council, appointed to, V2:357.

Whitmer, Peter, Sen., baptized, V1:81

WHITMER, PETER, SEN. (continued)

blesses his sons, V2:124
Church organized at home of, V1:76, et seq
first public meeting held at home of, V1:81
genealogy, V1:48, ftnt only
Joseph, invites to live with, V1:109
Joseph, meets, V1:48
Lord appears to Joseph in home of, V1:60.

Whitney, Mr., member of Haun's Mills mob, V3:186.

Whitney, A. W., mission appointment published and field of labor, V6:337.

Whitney, Alonzo W. N., death of, V7:371
mission call and field of labor, V5:347.

Whitney, C. L., appointed to preside over new Church district, V7:306.

Whitney, Edson, anti-Mormon committee chairman, V6:8
anti-Mormon meeting at Carthage, at, V6:4.

Whitney, Elizabeth Ann Smith, endowment, received in Nauvoo Temple, V7:543
Relief Society, counselor in, V4:552
temple, commences ordinance administration in, V7:541
wife of Newel, V1:146, ftnt only.

Whitney, Horace K., mentioned, V5:385.

Whitney, J. W., mentioned, V3:263.

Whitney, Lyman, called on mission and field of labor, V5:349.

Whitney, Newel Kimball, bishop, appointed, V5:119
bishop, appointed, of middle ward in Nauvoo stake, V4:12
bishop, blessing of as, of Church, V2:288
bishop, sends greetings to Church, V2:515
bishop, sustained at Kirtland, V2:509
bishop, sustained first of Church, V7:297
bishop, sustained presiding, of Church at Salt Lake City, October 1848, V7:629
Church, appointed trustee-in-trust for, V7:247
council, in, at Kirtland, V1:389
endowments, receives, in Nauvoo Temple, V7:543
genealogy, V1:145, 146, ftnt only
Joseph, accompanies on second visit to Zion, V1:265
Joseph, accompanies to Albany, New York and Boston, V1:295
Joseph, blessing of, upon, V2:288
Joseph, friendship of, for, V5:108
Joseph, prayed to his place, V1:146, ftnt only

WHITNEY, NEWELL KIMBALL (continued)

    Joseph, receives, at Kirtland, V1:145

    Joseph, returns to Kirtland with, V1:271

    Joseph, secretly goes to inform of sheriff's movements August 1842, V5:97

    Kirtland, accident by the way to, V1:271

    Kirtland, renewal of journey to, V1:272

    Kirtland Temple, blessing for work on, V2:205

    letter to Eugene Branch on fellowship of John Smith, V1:371

    mission to New York, V2:288

    Nauvoo, first elected alderman of, V4:287

    Son of God, has feast after order of the, V2:362.

Whitney, Orson F., mentioned, V5:120, ftnt only.

Whitney, Samuel, father of Newel K., baptized with wife and daughter V2:298.

Whitney, Sarah Ann, polygamous wife of Joseph, IntroV5:XXXIV.

Whittington, Mrs., grandmother to John Taylor, V3:154, ftnt only.

Whittington, Richard, mentioned, V3:154, ftnt only.

Whittington, William, mentioned, V3:154, ftnt only.

Whittle, Alba, Kirtland Camp, mentioned in, V3:139

    Kirtland Camp, subscribed to consitution of, V3:92.

wicked, destroyed at end of world, V2:271.

wickedness, Joseph comments on restraining, V6:608

    reproof of, V4:588.

Wight, Lyman, Apostles, sustained member of at Salt Lake City October 1848, V7:628

    Apostleship, sustained to, V4:341

    Avon, New York, at conference at, V2:44

    best at his, V7:139 and ftnt

    branch president, appointed, in Missouri, V1:409, ftnt only

    conference, addresses, V4:13

    Corrill, J., prefers charges against, V2:147

    Daviess County, submits to trial in, V3:70

    Diahman, ordered to suppress mobs about, V3:163

    doctrine, accused of teaching false, V2:147

    doctrine, trial of, for teaching erroneous, V2:481

    endowments, called to go to Kirtland to receive, V2:113

    extradition of demanded by Governor Boggs, V4:198

    Far West High Council, sustained member of, V2:524

    Gould, Dean, baptizes, V2:95

    grand jury, brings in bill against for treason, murder, etc., V3:31?

WIGHT, LYMAN (continued)

Grand River, settles on, V3:35
high council, sustained to Missouri, V2:124
human flesh, ate in Missouri prison, V3:420
Independence, taken by mob to, V3:194
Indians, asks Prophet's advice on preaching to, V6:222
Jackson County, opposes sale of lands in, V3:4
Joseph, messenger to at Kirtland, V2:1
Joseph, refuses to obey counsel of, V2:100-1
Joseph, tells of prophecy by, on pending death, V7:212
letter, second on movements ot Twelve, V7:151
letter, preaching to Indians and migrating to Texas, V6:255-7
letter to Joseph on affairs of Apostles, June 19, 1844, V7:136-9
letter to Joseph suggesting southwest movement of Church, V6:257-60
Liberty, Clay County, sent to stand trial for murder and treason at, V3:212
Missouri, arraigned for treason, murder, burglary, arson, robbery, and larceny at Richmond, V3:209
Missouri, reports to Kirtland High Council conditions in, V2:39
Missouri, writ against to take to, V5:448
Missouri persecutions, testimony concerning, V3:437, et seq
mob enters camp of, V3:189, ftnt only
mob, leads company of saints against, V1:433
Nauvoo, delegate to political convention in, V6:389
Patten, D. W., sustained to fill the office of, V7:295
political address at Bunker Hill, V7:159
records capture and trial of Church leaders in Missouri, V3:446, et seq
sickness, teaches that all, of devil, rebuked for, V2:147
shot, sentenced to be in public square at Far West, V3:190
sustaining of, carried over until future time, V7:459-60
Texas, to go to, V7:249
tongues, interprets hymn sung in, V1:409
views of, considered in council, V6:260-1
Wild Ram of the Mountains, designated as, V7:435
witness, suggested to appear before Congress on redress, V4:97
Zion, second counselor of stake of, V3:38
Zions Camp, elected general of, V2:88 and ftnt
Zions Camp, joins at Salt River, V2:87 and ftnt
Zions Camp, makes division in, V2:100.
See also Apostles, Twelve; letters.

Wight, Sister, mentioned, V3:272.

Wightman, Charles, approved for ordination, V2:400.

Wightman, Major, death of, V5:165.

Wightman, William, approved for ordination, V2:400.

Wilber, Brother, mentioned, V4:11, 19
son dies, V3:104.

Wilber, M., delegate to political convention at Nauvoo, V6:390.

Wilber, Stephen, martial band member of Legion, V7:135.

Wilbur, Benjamin S., (also spelled Wilber), Kirtland Camp, rejoins
V3:135
Kirtland Camp, with 20 others from, takes contract to work at Dayton,
V3:127
Missouri, permit to travel in, V3:210
seventies, meeting, chosen clerk at, V3:89
seventy, chosen member pro tem in first council of, V3:90.

Wilbur, Melvin, mission appointment published and field of labor
V6:336
mission call in Illinois to disabuse public mind over arrest of Joseph,
V5:485.

Wilbur, W. S., subscribed to constitution of Kirtland Camp, V3:91.

Wilcox, Brother, Joseph preaches at home of, V3:378.

Wilcox, Catherine, marriage to John Webb, V2:369.

Wilcox, Eber, dies of cholera in Missouri, V2:116
Zions Camp member, V2:185.

Wilcox, Henry, blessing for work on Kirtland Temple, V2:206.

Wilcox, Samuel, blessing for work on Kirtland Temple, V2:206.

Wilder, Levi B., subscribed to constitution of Kirtland Camp, V3:92.

Wilding, David, British Mission, mission in, V4:149
counselor on sailing from England, V4:297
ministry, devotes all time to, V4:148
represents branch at English conference, V4:117, 148.

Wiley, Jacob, mission call in Illinois to disabuse public mind over
arrest of Joseph, V5:485.

Wiley, Robert, discovers Kinderhook plates, V5:372.

Wilkie, Mr., mentioned, V4:589.

Wilkie, David, represents area in British conference, V5:10.

Wilkie, John, blessing of Joseph upon, V6:264.

Wilkins, John, covenanted to assist saints in removing from Missouri
V3:254.

Wilkinson, Jemimah, false prophetess, V4:577.

Wilkinson, Stephen, Joseph, on relief expedition for, V5:486
  trial of, V6:181.

Wilkinson, Sylvester B., Zions Camp member, V2:185.

Willard, S. D., mission appointment published and field of labor,
  V6:339.

Willey, Bathsheba, death of, V3:135.

Willey, Jeremiah, subscribed to constitution of Kirtland Camp, V3:91.

Willey, Josiah, Kirtland Camp, mentioned, in, V3:138.

Williams, Abiathar B., Joseph, affidavit on conspiracy against, V6:278
  Joseph, witness for, at Carthage martyrdom, V6:576.

Williams, Abraham, delegate to political convention at Nauvoo,
  V6:390.

Williams, Alexander, mentioned, V7:117.

Williams, Archibald, lawyer for Joseph, V4:367.

Williams, Benjamin, given care of Church at Shucknell Hill, V4:139.

Williams, Edwin, called on mission and field of labor, V5:349.

Williams, Eli H., Carthage Greys, member of, V7:143.

Williams, Ezra, witness for state in Missouri trials of saints, V3:210.

Williams, Frederick Granger, angel, sees attend temple dedication,
  V2:427
  baptized at Kirtland, V1:125
  chastised for allowing horses to break loose, V2:90
  excommunicated from Church, V3:284
  fellowship, asks forgiveness and received into, V4:110
  First Presidency, call to, (D&C § 81) V1:257
  First Presidency, ordained to, V1:334
  First Presidency, sustained as counselor in, but not by unanimous
    vote, V2:509
  genealogy of, V1:125, ftnt only
  Joseph expresses full confidence and trust in, V1:444
  Joseph, washes feet of, V1:323
  Kirtland High Council, accused before, V2:485
  Kirtland Temple, blessing for work on, V2:205
  Kirtland Temple, subscribes to and pays within one hour, V2:234
  mission, joins Lamanite, V1:125
  Missouri, letter to saints in, requesting information, V1:417, et seq
  Missouri persecutions, affidavit of, concerning, V4:69

WILLIAMS, FREDERICK GRANGER (continued)

    Northern Times, to edit, V2:227

    patriarch of the Church, appointed scribe to, V2:273

    patriarchal blessings, to receive pay for scribing, V2:273

    President of Church, rejected as counselor to at Far West, V2:522

    rebaptized and confirmed, V3:55

    revelation directing to teach relatives, V2:300

    sickness, sent to Cleveland saints to administer to them for, V2:146

    Zions Camp, made paymaster of, V2:64

    Zions Camp member, V2:185.

Williams, John, ordained elder, V5:419.

Williams, John, kidnapper of saints, V6:123.

Williams, Levi, anti-Mormon committee chairman, V6:8

    anti-Mormon committee member of Warsaw meeting, V6:464

    Joseph, acquitted of murder of, V7:420

    Joseph, indicted for murder of, V7:314

    kidnapper of saints, V6:123

    martyrdom mob, farmer, member of, V7:143

    mob, heads at Yelrome in burning houses, V7:441

    Smiths, calls for volunteers to murder, V7:21 and ftnt.

Williams, Matthew, Methodist priest who leads mob against members in Tennessee, V2:447.

Williams, Robert, elder, ordained, V4:298

    priest, ordained, V4:148

    volunteers for service in vineyard, V4:217.

Williams, S. O., Carthage Greys, member of, V7:142.

Williams, Samuel, elder, ordained, V4:13

    elders quorum, sustained president of, V7:297

    Missouri, covenanted to assist saints in removing from, V3:252.

Williams, Samuel, anti-Mormon committee member of Warsaw meeting, V6:464.

Williams, Swain, funeral of, son of Frederick G., V3:33.

Williams, W. W., mentioned, V2:50.

Williams, Wiley C., mentioned, V3:172.

Williams, Wiley E., mobber in Missouri, V4:68.

Williams, William, mentioned, V4:140.

Willis, Mr., mentioned, V1:287, ftnt only.

Willis, Eleazar, called on mission and field of labor, V5:348.

Willis, Ira J., whipped and beaten by mob, in Zion, V2:46.

Willock, David, major-general in Missouri militia, V3:65.

Willsey, Ira, affiant to mob threats, V6:481-2.

Wilsey, A. M., mentioned, V6:400.

Wilson, Mr., mentioned, V4:63; V5:303-4.

Wilson, Bushrod W., Joseph, on relief expedition for, V5:482
mission appointment published and field of labor, V6:338
mission call and field of labor, V5:349.

Wilson, Bradley, death of, V5:193.

Wilson, Clabourn, martyrdom, guard on jail at, V7:142.

Wilson, Crocket, Carthage Greys, member of, V7:143.

Wilson, F. D., mission call and field of labor, V5:348.

Wilson, H. H., mission appointment published and field of labor, V6:338.

Wilson, Harmon T., Carthage, at anti-Mormon meeting at, V6:4, et seq
Carthage Greys, member of, V7:143
Joseph, arrests, V5:349, et seq
messenger to governor from anti-Mormon meeting, V6:466
mobber in Illinois, V5:528.

Wilson, James, witnesses celestial phenomenon, V6:121.

Wilson, John, at anti-Mormon meeting, V5:537.
mobber in Illinois, V5:528
tavernkeeper, member of martyrdom mob, V7:144.

Wilson, Lewis Dunbar, Joseph, on relief expedition for, V5:482
Nauvoo, bodyguard to Joseph's body on return to, V7:135
Nauvoo High Council, appointed to, V4:12
Nauvoo High Council, sustained to after death of Joseph, V7:296.

Wilson, Moses G., butchery, accounts acts of, in Missouri against Mormons, V4:394
carries proposals to saints from mob, V1:398
Missouri, lying in wait for Prophet to carry to, V5:500
mob manifesto, merchant, signed, V1:376
Willis, Ira J., whips and beats, V2:46.

Wilson, Reuben, Joseph lodges at in China, New York, V2:45.

Wilson, Robert, Adam-ondi-Ahman, ordered to arrest prisoners at, V3:204-5
Constitution and democracy, wants Joseph shot for believing in, V3:191
Diahman, orders the saints to leave, V3:207

WILSON, ROBERT (continued)

Independence, in charge of the Prophet and fellow prisoners en route for, V3:200, ftnt only
Missouri, named as one of chief mobbers in, V3:327.

Wilson, Thomas G., carries proposals to saints from mob, V1:398
mob, affidavit of, on movements of, V6:480
mob manifesto, merchant, signed, V1:376
sheriff, strikes Sidney Gilbert while in custody of, V1:432.

Wilson, Valentine, at anti-Mormon meeting, V5:537
farmer, member of martyrdom mob, V7:144.

Wilson, Whitford G., Joseph, on relief expedition for, V5:482.

Wilson, William, subscribed to constitution of Kirtland Camp, V3:93.

Wilson, Z., Missouri, permit to travel in, V3:210.

Wilson, Z. D., petitions to hear Joseph speak, V6:533.

Wilson's Store, gathering of mob at, V1:430.

Wimmer, Ellen, attests to mob depredations, V4:62.

Wimmer, Peter, attests to mob depredations, V4:62.

Wimmer, Susan, attests to mob depredations, V4:62.

Winchester, Alonzo, Zions Camp member, V2:185.

Winchester, Benjamin, Apostles, silenced by for not following counsel, V5:8-9, 403
Church, suspended from, for disobedience, V4:494
disfellowshipped, V5:409
excommunicated, V7:275
investigation of, V5:409
mission appointment, V4:54, 403
mission appointment published and field of labor, V6:337
president of Philadelphia branch, V4:331
tale bearing, reproved for, V4:443
trial of, V5:410
Warsaw, sent to preach at, V6:190
Zions Camp member, V2:185.

Winchester, Joseph, appointed to seventies, V2:208.

Winchester, Lupton, Zions Camp member, V2:185.

Winchester, Stephen, mission appointment published and field of labor, V6:337
mob, taken prisoner by, V3:182
seventies, named to first quorum of, V2:203
volunteers relief service, V3:190.

Windt, John, solicits Joseph's views on politics and issues, V6:387-8.

wine, Carthage jail, obtained for inmates in, V7:101
  sacrament, to be of own making, V1:106.

Winegar, Miss, daughter of Alvin Winegar, Zions Camp member, V2:185.

Winegar, Alvin, Missouri, covenanted to assist saints in removing from, V3:254
  Zions Camp member, V2:185.

Winegar, Samuel T., Missouri, covenanted to assist saints in removing from, V3:254
  Zions Camp member, V2:185.

Wingott, Edward, witness at *Expositor* trial, V6:490.

wings, angels never have, V3:392.

Winston, Wm., petitions Governor Boggs on mob violence in DeWitt, V3:83.

Winter, Arthur, mentioned, V4:556, ftnt only.

Winter, Hiram, Zions Camp member, V2:185.

Winter Quarters, Council of Twelve, meeting at, V7:617
  desolation of after departure of President Young, et al, V7:627-8
  founding of, V7:614
  pioneers return to, V7:615-6.

Winters, David, covenanted to assist saints in removing from Missouri, V3:253.

Winters, Hiram, bishop, counselor to at Kirtland, V4:362
  seventies, named to first quorum of, V2:203.

Wires, Captain, mentioned, V7:163.

wisdom, best way to obtain, V4:425.

Wisdom, Word of, break, Holy Ghost will not dwell in those who, V5:428
  breaking, disfellowshipped if, V2:482
  breaking, excommunicated for, V2:218, 228
  breaking, Holy Ghost, lack enjoyment of if, V2:223
  breaking, sacrament cannot be administered if, V2:34
  breaking, tried for, V2:27, 252, V3:127-8
  breaking, David Whitmer tried for, V3:4
  Doctrine and Covenants § 89, V1:327, et seq
  England, first taught in, V2:529
  high priests required to state whether they lived, V5:84

WISDOM, WORD OF (continued)

Joseph states should be observed, V3:15

Kirtland Camp, Hyrum advises not to be too particular in regard to, V3:95

Kirtland Camp, problems in, V3:131

Kirtland Camp Constitution, part of, V3:90

living, teachings on, V5:428

Missouri saints instructed in, V2:138

selling items against, saints not to support if, V2:524.

Wissmiller, Henry, Zions Camp member, V2:185.

Withers, Mr., mentioned, V6:413.

Withers, G., appointed by public to assist saints in removal from Zion, V2:455.

Withers, William, trial for assault, V6:211.

Withnal, Elder, represents branch of Church at English conference, V4:116.

Withnall, H., appointed charge of branch in England, V4:217.

Withnall, Richard, British Church assignment, V4:149

English conference, represents branch of Church in, V4:148.

Witnesses, Eight, testimony of, V1:57-8

time and place of receiving testimony, V1:57 and ftnt.

See also Mormon, Book of.

Witnesses, Three, angel appears to, V1:54

Book of Mormon, testifies of, (D&C § 5) V1:29, 52-3 and ftnts

parable of the leaven compared to, V2:270

promised revelation, V1:28, et seq

testimony of, V1:56-7

testimony, details connected with, V1:55, ftnt only

Twelve Apostles, to choose, (D&C § 43:37) V2:186 and ftnt

Twelve Apostles, propriety of choosing the, V2:187, ftnt only.

See also Apostles; Mormon, Book of.

Witnesses, Twelve, see Apostles, Twelve.

Witter, Daniel S., course of respecting settlement at Warren, V4:470-1

Joseph, solicits views of, on politics and issues, V6:387-8.

wives, to receive gospel only after consent of husband, V2:263.

Wixom, Sarah, covenanted to assist saints in removing from Missouri, V3:254.

"wolf hunt," dispersed, V7:47

nature of, V7:45-6.

See also persecutions.

women, character of Mormon, V4:568
  priesthood shared by, V4:604
  zeal of dangerous in religious capacity, V5:19.

Wood, Mr., attorney for Missouri saints, V1:425.

Wood, Abraham, subscribed to constitution of Kirtland Camp, V3:92.

Wood, Charles, Kirtland Camp, expelled from, V3:132
  Kirtland Camp, joins at Petersburgh, V3:100.

Wood, Daniel, false doctrine, silenced for preaching, V4:501
  restored to standing, V4:514.

Wood, David, counselor to deacons quorum in Nauvoo, V4:312.

Wood, Henry, case reheard but cut off, V2:235.

Wood, Jacob, case reheard but cut off, V2:235
  Kirtland, in council at, V1:389.

Wood, James H., blacksmith, member of martyrdom mob, V7:144.

Wood, James W., letter to Joseph on documents for defense, V6:558.

Wood, John, falsely accused of threatening A. Black, V3:65
  mentioned, V4:267.

Wood, Joseph, on Church committee, V4:107.

Wood, Mayor, of Quincy, V7:142, 148.

Wood, William T., committee member to talk to saints on removal, V2:452
  Missouri, at public meeting in, V2:488, et seq
  Missouri, drafts resolutions of public meeting in, V2:449.

Woodbury, Joseph J., mission appointment published and field of labor, V6:335.

Woodbury, W. H., mission appointment published and field of labor, V6:335.

Woodland, James H., affidavit on Durfee murder, V7:529-30.

Woodland, William, Lima High Council, named to, V5:427
  Missouri, covenanted to assist saints in removing from, V3:253.

Woodruff, Aphek, father of Wilford, V3:337, ftnt only.

Woodruff, Azmon, brother to Wilford, V3:337, ftnt only.

Woodruff, Beulah Thompson, mother to Wilford, V3:337, ftnt only.

Woodruff, Eldad, grandfather of Wilford, V3:337, ftnt only.

Woodruff, Eunice, sister of Wilford, V3:338, ftnt only.

Woodruff, Josiah, great-grandfather of Wilford, V3:337, ftnt only.

Woodruff, Ozem, ordained high priest, V7:283.

Woodruff, Phebe, wife of Wilford, V7:568.

Woodruff, Wilford, America, sails for, V4:352

Apostle, sustained as, by Church after death of Joseph, V7:295

Apostle, to be, (D&C § 118:6) V3:47

Apostles, sustained member of at Salt Lake City, October 1848, V7:628

Banner of the Gospel, designated as, V7:435

British Mission, appointed to preside over, and continent, V7:249

British Mission, arrival of, in, V7:349

British Mission, sails for, V7:324

Church, discourse of, on following, V7:262-3

conference, presides at, in Scarborough, Maine, V7:170

endowments, receives, V6:98

England, accounts labors in, and baptisms, V4:122-3

England, arrives in, V4:76

England, labors of, in, V4:182, et seq

England, sails from New York for, V4:46

English conference, represents branch of Church at, V4:117

Fox Island, mission to, V2:507 and ftnt

Fox Island, records work on, V4:418-9

Franklin Hall, Boston, preached at, V7:185

genealogy, ordained Apostle and, V3:337 and ftnt, et seq

heal the sick, sent by Prophet to, V4:5, ftnt only

healings, his account of, at Commerce by the Prophet, V4:3-5, ftnts only

high priest, ordains father to, V7:202

Joseph, feelings of, toward death of, V7:195

Joseph, furnishes powder to expedition going to relief of, V5:447

Joseph, gives bond for collection of funds to, V5:414

Joseph, testimony of as Church historian to period of, V7:243

journal, excerpts from on Apostles in Boston, V7:149

journal, excerpts from on miscellaneous events between June 22 and June 29, 1844, V7:129, et seq

journal, excerpts from, President Young in tears, V7:195

journal, excerpt from, the Twelve returning to Nauvoo, V7:228

journal, outline of Brigham Young's discourse, V7:254, et seq

journal, President Young urges him to keep up, V7:212

letter of March 29, 1841, affairs in England, V4:323-4

letter reporting labors, August 5, 1840, V4:176

letter to Brigham Young reporting Joseph's death, V7:194

ministry, devote all time to labors of, V4:148

WOODRUFF, WILFORD (continued)

ministry, reports details incident to his, V4:150, et seq

Mormon, Book of, obtains copyright for, and Doctrine and Covenants, Stationers Hall, London, V7:426

Nauvoo, elected to council of, V4:442

order, records public meeting in Nauvoo on, V5:34-5

railway wreck, in, V6:32

Zions Camp member, V2:185

Zions Camp, reports sudden severe storm incident of, V2:104, ftnt only.

See also Apostles, Twelve; British Mission; letters.

Woods, A. C., misrepresents the saints, V3:157.

Woods, C. M., recommends Brother Green to collect for poor, V3:348.

Woods, James W., fair to Church, V7:165-6.

Woods, Larkin H., mob member writes lies concerning DeWitt, V3:156.

Woods, Sashiel, (also spelled Wood), mob, leader of, V4:61

mob, solicits for Daviess County, assures that Mormons will not receive state aid, V3:161

Mormons, reports massacred citizens, V3:168-9

Presbyterian clergyman heads mob, V3:158, 407.

Woods, Sidney S., mob member writes lies concerning DeWitt, V3:156.

Woodson, Doctor, drafts resolutions of public meeting in Missouri, V2:449.

Woodstock, Willard, Presidency, on high council to try, V2:484.

Woodward, George, judge in Missouri, V1:479-80.

Woodworth, Lucien, architect of Nauvoo House, V5:283-4

endowment, receives in Nauvoo Temple, V7:543

Joseph, accompanies in arrest, V4:366

mission appointment to Texas, V6:356

mission, leaves for Texas on, V6:264.

Woodworth, Phebe, receives endowment in Nauvoo Temple, V7:543.

Woodyard, H. M., kidnaps some members and takes to Missouri, V4:155.

Woolley, Edwin D., Church, appointed to preside over new district of, V7:305

mission report, V5:309

Nauvoo, delegate to political convention in, V6:389.

Woolsey, Thomas, Joseph, on relief expedition for, V5:486.

Workman, Abraham S., ordained elder, V5:349.

Workman, John, mission call in Illinois to disabuse public mind over arrest of Joseph, V5:485.

Works, Angeline, laying on of hands, restored to senses by, V2:328
Robinson, Ebenezer, marriage to, V2:331.

Works, Asa, father-in-law to Brigham, V1:296, ftnt only.

Works, Asa, Sen., death of, biography, V7:374.

Works, Jerusha, mother-in-law to Brigham Young, V1:296, ftnt only.

Works, Miriam, wife of B. Young, V1:296, ftnt only.

world, commotions in, V4:125, 189, 383, 401, 415
Prophet's letter on, V1:312, et seq
spiritual and heavenly bounds of irrevocably fixed, V6:51
state of, V1:281, 301
state of in April, 1833, V1:337
state of reported in July 1833 *Star*, V1:388.

Worrell, Elisha, anti-Mormon committee member of Warsaw meeting, V6:464.

Worrell, Franklin A., (also spelled Worrel), at anti-Mormon meeting at Carthage, V6:4, et seq
Carthage Greys, commands company of, V6:595
Carthage Greys, member of, V7:142
Carthage jail, in command of guard at, V7:30
killed by Rockwell in mob action, V7:446
martyrdom, guard on jail at, V7:142.

Worsley, James, ordained elder, V4:148.

Worthen, Joseph, mentioned, V7:369.

Worthens, (family), mentioned, V7:143.

Worthington, George W., witness for state in Missouri trials for saints, V3:210.

Worthington, James, Joseph, on relief expedition for, V5:482.

Wrathey, Autherston, mobber in Missouri, V4:61.

Wren, Nicholas, recommends Brother Green to collect for poor, V3:348.

Wright, Mr., mentioned, V3:255.

Wright, Alexander, England, Preston, arrives at, V4:45
Kirtland Camp, subscribed to constitution of, V3:92
Missouri, covenanted to assist saints in removing from, V3:252
Scotland mission opened by, V4:48, 123.

Wright, Asa, Kirtland Camp, mentioned in, V3:119, 139
Kirtland Camp, subscribed to constitution of, V3:93.

Wright, John, mentioned in Kirtland Camp, V3:138.

Wright, Jonathan C., baptism and ordained elder, V5:415
  Carthage jail, affidavit on conspiracy against Joseph while in, V6:587
  mission call in Illinois to disabuse public mind over arrest of Joseph,
    V5:485
  Nauvoo, delegate to political convention in, V6:389.

Wright, Joseph, covenanted to assist saints in removing from Missouri,
  V3:253.

Wright, Nickerson, farmer, member of martyrdom mob, V7:144.

Wright, Orrin, Jun., mentioned, V5:208.

Wright, Silas, mentioned, V6:431.

Wych, John, (also spelled Wyche), British Mission, mission in, V4:149
  ministry, devote all time to labors of, V4:148
  volunteers for service in vineyard, V4:217.

Wyers, Captain, commands anti-Mormon company, V6:512.

—Y—

Yager, Uriah H., mentioned, V6:515
  petitions to hear Joseph speak, V6:533.

Yale, Gad, blessing for work on Kirtland Temple, V2:206, 208.

Yale, Porter, witness for state in Missouri trials of saints, V3:210.

Yates, Mr., mentioned, V6:549.

Yates, Aldelaide, mentioned, V5:358.

Yates, Brother, child of dies, V5:184.

Yates, Captain, Carthage, returns to, Ford's account of, V7:82
  Nauvoo, accompanies posse to, V7:82.

Yates, Sarah, mentioned, V5:358.

Yearsley, Brother, mentioned, V5:22.

Yearsley, David D., mentioned, V6:188
  mission appointment published and field of labor, V6:337
  western country, to go to investigate for settlement, V6:223.

Yelrome, house burnings at, V7:439-42
  meetings at, V5:387-90.

Yocum, Mr., mob member in Missouri, V1:480.

Yokum, William S., (also spelled Yocum), Haun's Mills, leg amputated
    injury from, V3:412, V4:389
  Haun's Mills, wounded at, by mob, V3:326, ftnt only

YOKUM, WILLIAM S. (continued)

Joseph, on relief expedition for, V5:482.

York, Aaron M., Kirtland Camp, mentioned in, V3:109
Kirtland Camp, subscribed to constitution of, V3:93
mission call, V5:429
mission call and field of labor, V5:348
Missouri, covenanted to assist saints in removing from, V3:252.

York, John, killed at Haun's Mills by mob, V3:326, ftnt only.

Yorkshire, emigrant ship, V5:299.

Young, Mr., bitter against Mormons, V3:239.

Young, A., Joseph, on relief expedition for, V5:482.

Young, A. D., mission appointment published and field of labor, V6:338.

Young, Alphonzo, mission appointment published and field of labor, V6:338
Missouri persecutions, appeals to Tennessee on, V6:226
mob, letter of, on, in Iowa, V7:572
western country, to go to investigate for settlement, V6:223.

Young, Brigham, America, sails for, V4:352
Angel and Booth, cares for families of, V2:64
Apostle, ordained as, for Church, V2:509
Apostle, sustained as, and President of Church, after death of Joseph, V7:294
Apostles, address of on organization of Church and authority of, V7:230
Apostles, blessing of as member of, V2:188-9
Apostles, chosen member of, V2:187 and ftnt
Apostles, chosen president of, V4:115 and ftnt
Apostles, directed by Prophet to call meeting for choosing the, V2:180-1 and ftnt
Apostles, in retirement with associate, V7:414
Apostles, one of two original that had not fought with Joseph, V5:412
Apostles, president of, V3:261 and ftnt
Apostles, president of the, meeting with fellow, at Salem, Massachusetts, V7:170
Apostles, proceeding of, on, V7:209-11
arrest, attempted of, arrest of Miller by mistake, V7:549-51
Bennett, James Arlington, baptizes and confirms, V5:556
Bennett, John C., letter on mission to confound, V5:161-2
bogus money, settles, V7:609 and ftnt
bond executed by, V5:414
Boston, in conference, V6:11, et seq
British Mission, arrives at Nauvoo from, V4:381

YOUNG, BRIGHAM (continued)

British Mission, letter to Joseph of May 7, 1840 on affairs of, V4:125-7

British Mission, letter on labors in, December 30, 1840, V4:251-2

British Mission, letter on movements of, December 4, 1840, V4:237-8

British Mission, letter to Prophet on, V4:119-20

camp deportment, instructions on in westward movement, V7:585-6

Camp of Israel, his high praise of, V7:608-9

Canada, returns to Kirtland from mission to, V1:388

Church, appoints trustee-in-trust for, V7:247

Church, chosen to be second president of, V7:621 and ftnt

Church, comment on Governor Ford's speculations on arrest of leaders of by United States troops, V7:564

Church, cut off from, if not live law, V7:259-60

Church, on scattering of the, V7:254-6

Church, remarks of, on claim of the Twelve to lead the, when there is no First Presidency, V7:231, et seq

Church, revelation has not ceased in, V7:256

Church, sustained as president of, in Salt Lake City, V7:628

Church, sustained as president of, at general conference in Kanesville, December 27, 1847, V7:623 and ftnt

Church, sustained president of in Great Britain and Pacific Islands, V7:629-30

Church, to receive support for living from, V7:257

Colorado, conversation on settling on the headwaters of the, V7:387

council, in, at Kirtland, V1:389

Deming, Miner R., comments of, on death of, V7:439-40

discourse of at October 1844 conference, V7:284, et seq

doctors, not to employ, V7:259

dream of, on use of Thomas Ford to knock down mob, V7:439

dream of seeing Joseph and counsel of, V7:435

Dublin, Indiana, at, V3:2

dumb animals kindness to, V7:569

East, leaves for visitation to, V7:310

elders, discourse to, V6:321-2

elders, instructions to, V6:325-6

election and reprobation, on, V4:256, et seq

Emmett's Company, remarks on, V7:385-6

endowment, receives in Nauvoo Temple, V7:543

endowments, receives, V5:409

England, arrives in, V4:102

England, condition of, on mission to, V4:111

England, leaves for sick and whole family sick, V4:9 and ftnt

YOUNG, BRIGHAM (continued)

England, sails for, V4:94

evil, premonition of, V7:376

family prayer, letter on, V4:308-9

Far West, forced to flee because of persecutions, V3:261

Far West, presides at quarterly conference of, V3:152-5

First Presidency, conversations of, on organizing second, V7:621 and ftnt

genealogy and conversion of, V1:296-7, ftnts only

immigration matters, instructions on, V6:351, et seq

Joseph commands to be healed, V4:4

Joseph, declares that clothes of, full of straw better president than candidates, V7:256

Joseph, feelings of, toward death of, V7:195

Joseph, gives a bond for collection of funds to, V5:414

Joseph, has sealed his testimony, V7:198

Joseph, provides money for, by spirit, V3:2 and ftnt

Joseph, revising history of, V7:389

Joseph, second speech of, on succession to, V7:239, et seq

Joseph, sees, protected by angel with sword, V2:381

Joseph, transformation of, to the voice and figure of, V7:236, ftnt only

Kirtland, flees, because would not stop testifying of truth, V2:529

laws, opinion of, on, of nation, V7:573

Lion of the Lord, designated, V7:435

Lucifer, episode with, V4:75

Manuscript History of, Part V of Vol. VII of *Documentary History of the Church,* taken from, V7:245-630

martyrdom, reports on message of Thomas Ford to legislature on, V7:328

ministry, devote all time to labors of, V4:148

mission, opens, to remnants of Joseph among Gentiles, V2:209

Missouri, covenanted to assist saints in removing from, V3:252

Missouri persecutions, testimony of, concerning, V3:433-7

mob, advising movement of all but brethren to Nauvoo as result of, at Yelrome, V7:440-1

mob, orders priesthood quorum to stand ready to fight, V7:443-4

Mormon, Book of, assists in indexing, V4:274, 286

Nauvoo, appoints trustees to Church property at, V7:573, 576

Nauvoo, interview with commanding general and resulting search of, V7:447-8

Nauvoo, leaves, for West, V7:585

YOUNG, BRIGHAM (continued)

Nauvoo, letter to Brother Woodruff on conditions in, and instructions, V7:373

Nauvoo, letter on progress and unity in, V7:430-2

Nauvoo, reflections of, on exodus of saints from, V7:602-3

Nauvoo, remarks of, at, V4:2

Nauvoo, returns to, V7:592

Nauvoo, returns to, after Eastern trip, V7:314

Nauvoo Council, elected to, V4:414

Nauvoo Legion, elected Lieutenant-General of, V7:265

New York, arrival in, V4:77

Ohio, Cleveland, arrival of, at, V4:19-20

oxen, talks to, V7:224

patriarch, presents a, V7:300-1 and ftnt

persecution, states that will convert world with or without, V7:308

Pioneer Company, reports on success of, by, upon reaching Salt Lake Valley, V7:616

poor, preaches at Nauvoo on providing labor for the, V5:44

presidency, views on, V5:521-2 and ftnt

proclamation of to saints, V5:248-9

prophecy of, that all will be carried away if live commandments, V7:465

prophecy of, that would be a winter of peace in Nauvoo, V7:443

Prophet, visits, V1:295-7

proposition, note discussing, V7:234-5, ftnts only

reception of, V7:617

Relief Society, letter to, requesting their penny subscriptions, V7:322

revelation, on doctrine of, V7:372

revelation to stay at home, V4:382

saints, exhortations to, V7:574

saints, farewell of the, to, V4:103

saints, signs memorial of, in Missouri, V3:224

Salt Lake Valley, organizes companies for moving to, V7:625

Saturday, designates seventh day as, V7:418

saving selves and others, on, V7:546

Seventies Hall, dedication prayer of, V7:332-3 and ftnt

seventies organized, V7:260 and ftnt

sickness, attacked by, anointed, V5:196

sickness, Joseph reports of, V5:253

Smith, Mother, pledges made to, V7:472

snake, tells others not to hurt but carry away, V2:102

temple, on, V7:385-6

temple, reopens, because of desires of saints for endowments, V7:579

YOUNG, BRIGHAM (continued)

    temple, setting the last trumpet stone on the capitals of the, V7:388

    temple, speaks in foreign tongue in, V7:558

    tongues, first to speak in, V1:297 and ftnt

    ungodly, deal not with, V7:258

    Westward Camp, instructions to, on conditions and actions of, V7:608

    wickedness, discourse against, V7:350

    wind and sea, calms the, V4:23

    Winter Quarters, arrival in Salt Lake City with company from, V7:628

    Winter Quarters, departs for Salt Lake City, V7:625

    Winter Quarters, returns to, V7:616

    Winter Quarters, statistics of company of, leaving, V7:627

    writ, false, against for aiding Joseph, etc., V7:444

    writs, interview with Major Warren on false, V7:492

    Zion, North and South America is, V6:321-2

    Zion, whole of, to be built up, V7:258

    Zions Camp, member of, V2:63, 185.

    See also Apostles, Twelve; "Bogus Brigham" incident; British Mission; doctrine; epistles; Latter-day Saints, Church of Jesus Christ of; letters.

Young, Henry J., Joseph, on relief expedition for, V5:482.

Young, John, mob member in Missouri, V1:480.

Young, John, Sen., death of, father of Brigham, V4:14

    father of Joseph Young, V1:295, ftnt only

    Kirtland Temple, blessing for work on, V2:205

    mentioned, V2:244; V6:255-60.

Young, John, Salt Lake Stake, counselor of, V7:629.

Young, Joseph, Church, appointed president of at Nauvoo as Twelve leave, V7:584

    endowment, receives in Nauvoo Temple, V7:543

    genealogy, V1:295 and ftnt

    Haun's Mills massacre, narrative of, V3:183, et seq

    Kirtland Camp, leaves, V3:141

    Kirtland Camp, member of First Council of Seventy, one of presidents of, V3:93

    Kirtland Camp, preaches at, V3:101, 123

    Kirtland Camp, subscribed to constitution of, V3:91

    Nauvoo Temple, appointed to officiate in, V7:547

    Nauvoo Temple, to administer in, V7:555

    ordination of, V2:201-4 and ftnts

    Prophet, visits, V1:295

YOUNG, JOSEPH (continued)

  seventies, made president of, V2:181 and ftnt
  seventies, named president of, V2:203
  seventies, president of, grants licenses, V4:501
  seventies, Prophet predicts that he would be president of, V2:181, ftnt
    only
  seventies, sustained president of first quorum of, V7:297
  seventies, sustained president of the, V2:510
  seventies, sustained president of, to Church at Salt Lake City, V7:629
  seventies conference, speech on, stand aganist wickedness, V7:372
  Seventies Hall, gives second prayer of dedication of, V7:342
  Seventies Library and Institute Association, elected trustee of, V7:328
  Tenney, William, attends funeral of, V3:131
  Zions Camp member, V2:63, 185.

Young, Joseph, grandfather of Joseph, V1:295, ftnt only.

Young, Joseph A., son of Brigham, V7:547.

Young, Judge, mentioned, V4:81, 94, 99; V5:449.

Young, Lorenzo D., England, appointed to go to with Twelve, V3:347
    England, assists Young and Kimball enroute for, V4:11
    Kirtland Temple, blessing for work on, V2:206
    mission appointment published and field of labor, V2:208; V6:339
    Zions Camp, exonerates Joseph's actions in, V2:149.

Young, Mary Ann, daughter of Brigham dies, V5:541.

Young, Mary Ann, endowments, receives in Nauvoo Temple, V7:543
    temple, commences ordinance administration in, V7:541.

Young, Miriam Works, wife to Brigham, V1:296, ftnt only.

Young, Nabby Howe, mother of Joseph Young, V1:295, ftnt only.

Young, Phineas H., high priest, ordained, V4:430
    Kirtland Temple, blessing for work on, V2:206
    mission appointment published and field of labor, V6:339
    mission, assigned to go on, V4:430
    mission to Canada, V1:296, ftnt only, V2:35
    mission to Lamanites, sent on, V2:208; V7:401
    Nauvoo Temple, appointed to officiate in, V7:547
    western country, to go to investigate for settlement, V2:223.

Young, Richard M., Illinois, senator from, V4:308
    letter to Elias Higbee, V4:111, 121-2
    poor, recommends Brother Green to collect for, V3:348.

Younger, Harvey H., member of mob committee, V1:412.

Younger, Henry, anti-Mormon committee member, V1:399.

Younger, Joseph W., Joseph, accompanies in arrest, V4:366
    mission appointment published and field of labor, V6:338
        Missouri, arraigned for treason, murder, burglary, arson, robbery, and
            larceny at Richmond, V3:209.

—Z—

Zarahemla, stake of discontinued, V4:493
    town site for selected, V3:382.

Zelph, a Lamanite, skeleton of, V2:79 and ftnt, 80.
    See also Lamanite; Nephite.

Zion, America, whole of, is, V6:318, et seq
    branches organized and presided over, V1:409 and ftnt
    celestial law, can only be built on the principles of, (D&C § 105:5)
        V2:108
    Church authority and organization of, established in, V1:335-6
    Church, first conference in, V1:199
    city of, revealed, (D&C § 57:2-3) V1:189
    city of, to be laid out, V3:67
    city and temples, plat of, set forth, V1:357, et seq
    contributions requested for, V2:50
    covenant to avenge enemies if driven from, V2:432
    death, first in, V1:199 and ftnt
    delivered, must be, or Church will be persecuted and destroyed, V2:53
    description of, V1:197-8
    elders, acts of, in are null and void, V2:228-9 and ftnt
    extension, reports concerning, V1:419
    foundation of laid, V1:196
    gathering, dedication for, V1:196 and ftnt
    gathering preparation explained, V1:339
    gentiles, proposal by saints to purchase lands of, V2:113-4
    God, designated exactly by, V2:254
    growth of, IntroV3:XLIII and ftnts
    high council, unorganized and elders or groups could not conduct
        affairs of, but only, V2:228
    house, first, V1:196
    inheritance purchased as parable of hidden treasure, V2:271-2
    innocence of members in, as to offensive conduct, V1:392 and ftnt
    Joseph appointed to receive money for, V2:434
    Joseph exhorts Church never to give up struggle for, V2:222

ZION (continued)

Joseph inquires of Lord concerning, V1:207

Joseph leaves consecrated horn in, V2:146

Joseph nominated commander-in-chief of armies of Israel to redeem Zion, V2:39

Joseph says to be redeemed two years from September 11, 1834, if saints repent, V2:145

Kirtland Temple, cannot be redeemed until built, V2:239

Missouri persecutions, unwisdom of saints toward brought, Intro V3:XXXIV

Missourians, fears of, toward, IntroV3:XLII

mob, first regular in, V1:342

mob, letter to, requesting information about, V1:417-9

mob, opinion of saints as compared with Negroes by, V1:396

mob, treaty of with, V1:394 and ftnt

Nauvoo appointed stake of, V4:12

New Testament, translation sent to for publication, V1:324 and ftnt

olive leaf, revelation, council at accepts, V1:327

pearl of great price, compared to purchase of, V2:272

prayer for deliverance of, V2:2-3

presidency to remove to, V2:407

presidency, trial of, at, V3:3-5

priesthood, action of, at Kirtland concerning deliverance of, V2:222

redeem or die, covenanted to, V2:282

redemption, Joseph sees, V2:381

Sabbath, first in, V1:190

saints, letter demanding confession of, V1:316-7

saints, preparation for return of, to, V2:24

saints, present rights and grievances to Missouri legislature, V2:177-8 and ftnt

saints procure lawyers, V1:424

saints, reason driven from, IntroV3:XXXIX

saints reply to Clay County, accepts request to move, V2:452-3

saints requested to move from Clay County, V2:448, et seq

Satan gives revelation concerning, V1:109

sons of blessed, V2:242

stake established on Ohio side of Missouri River near Montrose, V4:12

stakes, other than Kirtland to be appointed, V2:514

state of, in letter from elders in, V1:379, et seq

temple spot dedicated in, V1:199

temples, names of, set forth, V1:359

Twelve Tribes, honored at establishment of, V1:196.

ZION (continued)

  See also doctrine; Latter-day Saints, Church of Jesus Christ of, letters;
     Missouri; mob; persecution; Smith, Joseph; stories; Zions Camp.

Zion, stake of, committee formed to purchase land for, V1:335
  gathering, others to be organized for, V2:514
  organized in Geneva, in Springfield, V4:236
  Freedom, V4:233
  Lima, V4:233
  Mount Hope, V4:233
  Quincy, V4:233.
  See also Latter-day Saints, Church of Jesus Christ of; Zion.

Zions Camp, attack, false alarm as to, V2:82 and ftnt
  Baptist minister attempts to get legal help to stop, fails, V2:81-2
  battle, perform sham, V2:74-5
  bones, mound of found, V2:66
  camp, angels were companions and seen by, V2:73 and ftnt
  camp, curiosity concerning, by inhabitants, V2:67 and ftnt
  camp, drunken spy attempts to divert the, V2:77
  camp, Sylvester Smith rebels against, first to do so, V2:83 and ftnt
  camp, spies attempt to get into, V2:68
  Church, used to prune leaders for, V2:182, ftnt only
  company consisted of on June 8, 1834, V2:87
  consisted of, V2:64
  dispersed, V2:114
  discharged, members of, V2:123 and ftnt
  discord, and the horse foundering episode, V2:68
  Enquirer publishes Sheriff Gillium's and Joseph's correspondence while
     in, V2:121-2
  failure of, reason for, IntroV3:XXXIX
  first group 100 men, V2:64
  general of, Lyman Wight, V2:88 and ftnt
  horses taken sick, cure devised and recipe given, V2:76
  Indianapolis, pass through unnoticed, V2:70
  Joseph, commander-in-chief of, V2:88, ftnt only
  Joseph, discloses identity for first time while in, V2:108
  Joseph, kills squirrel to teach lesson of need, V2:72
  Joseph, leaves Kirtland with, V2:63
  land, receives word that Governor Dunklin refuses to reinstate saints
     upon, V2:94 and ftnt
  Martin, Moses, court martial of, V2:67
  Mississippi River, camp crosses, V2:82 and ftnt
  Missouri, first brethren depart for, V2:61

ZIONS CAMP (continued)

    mob, false alarm, V2:72

    mob, invaded and threatened with destruction by, V2:103

    mob, sudden severe storm incident with, V2:103-4 and ftnts

    money, receives from stranger, V2:77

    names, full list of, who participated, V2:183, et seq

    organization of, V2:64

    prayer, held morning and evening, V2:64-5

    preaching to inhabitants all day, V2:78 and ftnt

    prophecy, the milk sickness, V2:66

    prophecy, that sickness would come upon because of rebellion from His words, V2:106-7

    Prophet, Zebedee Cottrin reproved for favoring with sweet bread, V2:75

    rattlesnakes, carry out of camp episode and lesson attached, V2:71

    review of, IntroV2:XXII, et seq

    sickness, Joseph predicts of, because of unruly spirits, V2:80 and ftnt

    Smith, Sylvester, refuses to humble himself and horses die, V2:69

    spies very active, V2:76

    Twelve Apostles, special meeting called of all those who had participated, to choose, V2:180-1 and ftnt, et seq

    Zelph, Lamanite chieftain, Joseph discovers Lamanite mound and bones of, V2:79-80 and ftnt.

    See also destroyer; Latter-day Saints, Church of Jesus Christ of; Smith, Joseph; stories; Zion.

Zions Temple, see Temple, Zion.

Zobriski, Henry, (also spelled Zobriskie), Missouri, arraigned for murder, treason, burglary, arson, robbery,, and larceny at Richmond, V3:209

    Missouri, covenanted to assist saints in removing from, V3:254

    Missouri trials, discharged as innocent from, V3:211.

Zobriski, Lewis, Missouri, covenanted to assist saints in removing from, V3:254

    Zions Camp, injured in mock battle in, V2:75.

Zundall, Jacob, mission appointment published and field of labor, V6:337

    mission call to Germany, V5:368.

Zundall, John, called on mission and field of labor, V5:348.